lonely planet

Nepal

Joe Bindloss

Trent Holden, Bradley Mayhew

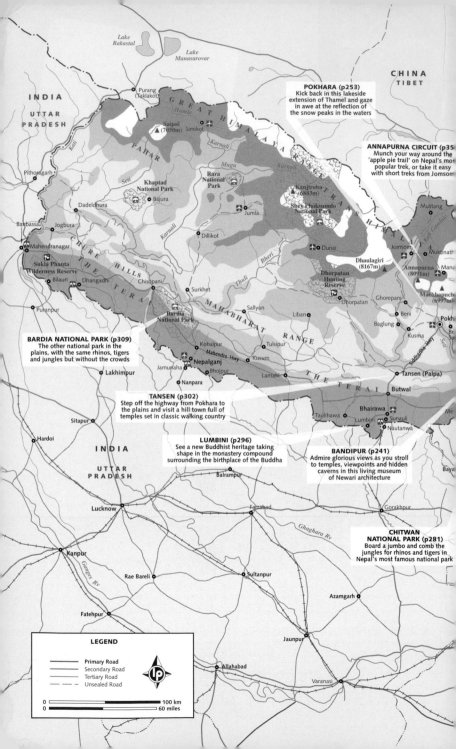

POKHARA (p253)
Kick back in this lakeside extension of Thamel and gaze in awe at the reflection of the snow peaks in the waters

ANNAPURNA CIRCUIT (p35)
Munch your way around the 'apple pie trail' on Nepal's mos popular trek, or take it easy with short treks from Jomsom

BARDIA NATIONAL PARK (p309)
The other national park in the plains, with the same rhinos, tigers and jungles but without the crowds

TANSEN (p302)
Step off the highway from Pokhara to the plains and visit a hill town full of temples set in classic walking country

LUMBINI (p296)
See a new Buddhist heritage taking shape in the monastery compound surrounding the birthplace of the Buddha

BANDIPUR (p241)
Admire glorious views as you stroll to temples, viewpoints and hidden caverns in this living museum of Newari architecture

CHITWAN NATIONAL PARK (p281)
Board a jumbo and comb the jungles for rhinos and tigers in Nepal's most famous national park

LEGEND

Primary Road
Secondary Road
Tertiary Road
Unsealed Road

0   100 km
0   60 miles

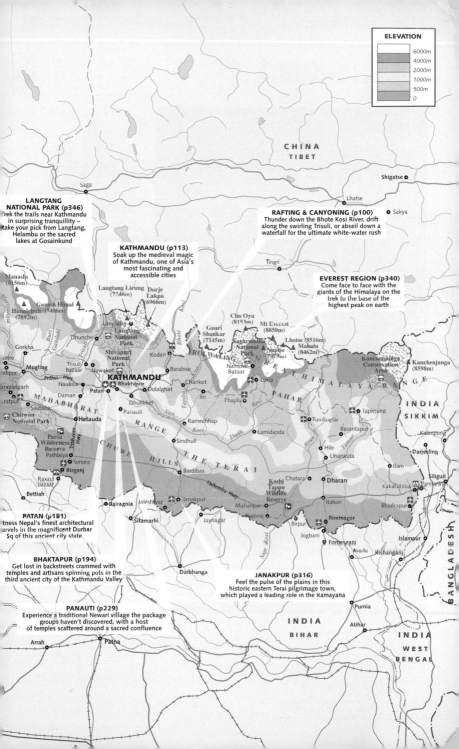

ELEVATION

6000m
4000m
2000m
1000m
500m
0

CHINA
TIBET

Shigatse

Saga

Lhatse

Sakya

**LANGTANG
NATIONAL PARK (p346)**
Trek the trails near Kathmandu
in surprising tranquillity –
take your pick from Langtang,
Helambu or the sacred
lakes at Gosainkund

RAFTING & CANYONING (p100)
Thunder down the Bhote Kosi River, drift
along the swirling Trisuli, or abseil down a
waterfall for the ultimate white-water rush

Tingri

KATHMANDU (p113)
Soak up the medieval magic
of Kathmandu, one of Asia's
most fascinating and
accessible cities

EVEREST REGION (p340)
Come face to face with the
giants of the Himalaya on the
trek to the base of the
highest peak on earth

Manaslu
(8156m)

Langtang Lirung
(7246m)

Dorje
Lakpa
(6966m)

Cho Oyu
(8153m)

Mt Everest
(8850m)

Ganesh Himal
(7892m)

Himalchuli
(7406m)

Gauri
Shankar
(7145m)

Sagarmatha
National
Park

Lhotse (8516m)
Nuptse
(7879m)

Makalu
(8462m)

Kanchenjunga
Conservation
Area

Kanchenjunga
(8598m)

Gorkha

Dhunche

Langtang
National
Park

Shivapuri
National
Park

Kodari

ROLWALING

Namche
Bazaar

Lukla

Mugling

Trisuli
Bazaar

Nuwakot

KATHMANDU

Barabise

HIMALAYA RANGE

INDIA
SIKKIM

Prithvi Hwy

Naubise

Patan

Bhaktapur

Dolalghat

Charikot

Jiri

Phaplu

PAHAR

Taplejung

Kalimpong

MAHABHARAT

Daman

Dhulikhel

Panauti

Ramechhap

Lamidanda

Hile

Basantapur

Darjeeling

Hetauda

RANGE

CHURE

Sindhuli

Dudh

Dhankuta

Ilam

Siliguri

Chitwan
National
Park

Parsa
Wilderness
Reserve

Pathlaiya

Bardibas

THE TERAI

Chatara

Dharan

Bhadrapur

Simara

Koshi
Tappu
Wildlife
Reserve

Itahari

Raxaul
Bazaar

Birganj

Bairagnia

Janakpur

Dharan

Biratnagar

Jogbani

Forbesganj

Islampur

PATAN (p181)
Witness Nepal's finest architectural
marvels in the magnificent Durbar
Sq of this ancient city state

Jaleshwar

Sitamarhi

Jaynagar

Rajbiraj

Birpur

Araria

Kishanganj

BHAKTAPUR (p194)
Get lost in backstreets crammed with
temples and artisans spinning pots in the
third ancient city of the Kathmandu Valley

Darbhanga

JANAKPUR (p316)
Feel the pulse of the plains in this
historic eastern Terai pilgrimage town,
which played a leading role in the Ramayana

Purnia

INDIA
BIHAR

Atihar

INDIA
WEST
BENGAL

PANAUTI (p229)
Experience a traditional Newari village the package
groups haven't discovered, with a host
of temples scattered around a sacred confluence

Arrah

Patna

On the Road

TRENT HOLDEN Here's me in Bardia National Park, accompanied by my crack team of safari guides. The day's wildlife-spotting yielded one-horned rhino, wild elephant, crocodile, monkey, deer and wart hog.

BRADLEY MAYHEW The views up here looking over Gokyo glacier are easily some of the best on the Everest trek. This is what it's all about for me: a hard climb to find a quiet spot overlooking some of the greatest views on earth.

JOE BINDLOSS Coordinating Author
I think the expression on my face says it all. When people talk about the mountains being 'close enough to touch', this is what they mean. That mass of rock and snow behind me is Cholatse (6440m) – you can see why people worship some of these mountains as gods.

For full author biographies see p408.

Nepal Highlights

Nepal means many things to many different people. It's a realm where the great outdoors, age-old cultures, adventure and spirituality create a distinctive whole. We spoke to travellers and asked them to recommend their favourite activities and places, impressions and experiences of this country at the top of the world.

RICHARD I'ANSON

1 JOYFUL BEGINNER'S TREK – SARANGKOT

An easy day trek up to Sarangkot (p272), in the middle of Pokhara, is the perfect way to test your legs for the style of trekking the Pokhara area has on offer. Enjoy the sunset and sunrise from the lovely little guest house at the top.

kez101, Traveller

2 RED TIKAS & SCATTERED ORANGE MARIGOLDS

Kathmandu (p113) is vibrant with the colours that Hinduism and Buddhism bring to a city. The 13th century defiantly lives on in architecture and culture, while the 21st century intrudes.

onesmallbag, Traveller

3 TREKKING TO EVEREST BASE CAMP

It's a trip you will never forget – thrilling, difficult, breathtaking. The mountains are higher than the clouds on the Everest trek (p340); experience a culture without cars and Western luxuries. You'll be pushed to the limit, create lifelong friends and help the local economy.

Emma Lindsay, Traveller, Australia

ELEPHANT SAFARI, CHITWAN NATIONAL PARK

At dawn climb aboard an elephant safari (p287) through Chitwan National Park to see myopic rhinos, then help to bathe the elephants in the river afterwards.

Sarah Devereaux, Traveller, UK

4

RICHARD I'ANSON

BARTERING AT MARKETS

Except for food and essentials, you haggle, whether buying or selling (in Namche they'll buy your shoes!). There is a local price and a tourist price, but no tax. Bargains galore here! Offer a third to half less than the price demanded – be prepared to be firm.

Emma Lindsay, Traveller, Australia

RICHARD I'ANSON

5

TOM COCKREM

6

SHERPA PEOPLE

The Sherpa people (p48) are some of the most wonderful, friendly, incredible people you will ever encounter. Their strength is a never-ending source of wonder, and their amazing spirit and hospitality are unforgettable.

sarabee, Traveller

8

RAINFOREST TREKKING

7

Trekking through a heavenly rainforest, glistening with dew, the air is so thick that my glasses keep fogging up. The rocks are mossy and slippery, but a Sherpa's hand is always there to prevent me from plunging to my death. A shaft of light appears.

Rachel Goodman, Traveller, Australia

9 TREKKING TO THE HEART – ANNAPURNA BASE CAMP

The Annapurna Sanctuary trek (p358) takes you to the very heart of the Annapurna region, weaving through the deep valley and arriving at the base camp of the highest peaks. Stunningly beautiful views.

kez101, Traveller

MOMOS

No, not the clothing option for the overweight. Delicate steamed dumplings dipped in a mouth-watering spicy tomato relish. These contrasting tastes are the epitome of Nepali flavours – chilli, garlic, ginger, tomato and onion. Totally addictive!

Rachel Goodman, Traveller, Australia

10

RICHARD I'ANSON

HOLI – FESTIVAL OF COLOUR, KATHMANDU

Holi (p23) is the ultimate in colour festivals. The highlight? Throwing coloured water and paint on everyone else! Warning: no one comes out without a full body of paint and firm abs from laughing.

cherry_blossom11, Traveller

11

RICHARD I'ANSON

12 TO EVEREST FROM JIRI

For a sample of rural Nepal you should trek to the Everest region from Jiri (p341), as opposed to flying to Lukla and trekking from there. It's hard work but the scenery in this area is beautiful, the lodges quiet and people friendly. You will get a taste of the 'real' Nepal – this was the most enjoyable part of the Everest trek for me.

bascule, Traveller

CHANG & TONGBA AT LUKLA

Celebrate the end of your Everest trek in Lukla with these 'beers' (p67). *Chang* (pictured) is a milky beer made with fermented barley, rice or millet. *Tongba* is made from fermented millet and drunk through a straw stuck into a huge tube, into which hot water is poured to top up the drink.

Lesley Dimmock, Traveller, Australia

13

RICHARD I'ANSON

MONKEY BUSINESS IN SWAYAMBHUNATH

Swayambhunath (p163), or the Monkey Temple, is one of the holiest Buddhist sites in Kathmandu. The troops of resident monkeys must have a taste for the high life; the climb to the top of the stairs leads to the stupa and prayer wheels, and affords magnificent views of the city and valley below.

Lisa Sinclair, Traveller, New Zealand

14

YELLOW STREET PHOTOS

JANE S

15 GET SNAPPED AT BY A COBRA

Walking the streets in Kathmandu you may be greeted by traditional snake charmers at work. These snakes are not well trained and snap at passers-by! Be warned – if you take a photo and don't hand over Rs 500 you will be cursed.

Lauren Baird, Traveller, Australia

Contents

Regional Map Contents

Pokhara p254

The Terai & Mahabarat Range p280, pp308-9, pp314-15

Kathmandu to Pokhara pp236-7

Kathmandu pp114-15

Around the Kathmandu Valley p168

15
15

Destination Nepal

For many travellers, Nepal is paradise on earth, or at the very least Shangri La. Wedged between the mountain wall of the Himalaya and the steamy jungles of the Indian plains, this is a land of yaks and yetis, monasteries and mantras, snow peaks and Sherpas, temples and tigers, magic and mystery. Ever since Nepal first opened it borders to outsiders in the 1950s, this tiny mountain nation has had an almost mystical allure for travellers. Explorers and mountaineers came to conquer the highest peaks, trekkers came to test themselves against some of the most challenging trails on earth and hippies came to wander in a stoned daze through the temple-filled towns at the end of the overland trail.

You'll still see a few of the original 'freaks' meandering through the backstreets of Kathmandu, but they have been joined by legions of trekkers, clad in the latest technical gear and drawn by the rugged trails that climb to such famous destinations as Everest Base Camp and the Annapurna Sanctuary. Other travellers are drawn here by the rush of rafting down a roaring Nepali river or bungee jumping into a bottomless Himalayan gorge. Adventure addicts can get their adrenaline flowing by canyoning, climbing, kayaking, paragliding and mountain-biking through some of the world's most dramatic landscapes.

Other travellers prefer to see Nepal at a more gentle pace, gazing towards the peaks from Himalayan viewpoints, strolling through the temple-lined medieval city squares of Kathmandu, Patan and Bhaktapur, and joining Buddhist pilgrims on a *parikrama* (ceremonial circuit) around the giant stupas scattered across the Kathmandu Valley. In Nepal's wild and wonderful national parks, nature buffs scan the treetops for exotic bird species and comb the jungles for rhinos and tigers from the backs of lumbering Indian elephants.

But big changes are afoot in Nepal. For one thing, Nepal is no longer a kingdom. A decade of Maoist uprising and civil war came to an end with the election of the Communist Party of Nepal and the declaration of the Federal Republic of Nepal on 28 May 2008. Since then the last Nepali king, Gyanendra Bir Bikram Shah Dev, has vacated the Royal Palace in Kathmandu and moved to a modest house in Nagarjun, and the word 'Royal' has been snipped from the signboards for Royal Nepal Airlines and Royal Chitwan National Park. After years of conflict, peace has returned to the mountains, and an air of optimism pervades the nation.

For travellers, this means Nepal is once again open for business. Trekkers are free to walk the mountain trails without fear of being stung for 'donations' or 'taxes' by Maoist cadres, and travellers can roam the countryside without having to endure the endless army roadblocks and searches that once turned bus travel into a draining ordeal. For the first time in years, the planes touching down on the tarmac at Tribhuvan Airport are packed full of GoreTex-clad trekkers and Nepal's trekking lodges, hotels and restaurants are often crammed to capacity. This is only the start of a long process of recovery, but locals are already breathing a sigh of relief.

There have been other less-obvious benefits to the end of hostilities. Soldiers have been pulled back from active duty to patrol the boundaries of Nepal's national parks – good news for wildlife, bad news for the poachers who reduced Nepal's rhino population by more than 30% during the uprising. The government has also turned its attention to improving living conditions for Nepal's workers, something that was rarely a priority under the autocratic rule of the Shah kings. One side effect of this is that guides

FAST FACTS

Population: 29.5 million

Surface area: 147,181 sq km (just larger than Greece)

UN Human Development Index: 142, out of 177 countries

Life expectancy: 62 years

Literacy rate: 48.6%

Gross national income: US$240 per capita

Doctors per 100,000 people: 5 (550 in Italy)

Number of seats in parliament held by women: 12 (out of 205)

Nepalis who live on less than US$2 per day: 82%

Average age: 20 years

and porters are charging higher fees for their services – you'll have to dig deeper into your pockets to go trekking than in years past.

However, there is definitely still work to do. Nepal's infrastructure was severely neglected during the conflict, and load shedding – a polite term for turning off the power to save the grid from meltdown – is a daily fact of life in the Kathmandu Valley. Fuel shortages are another problem: petrol stations run dry with monotonous regularity and prices for cooking kerosene are soaring, driving many locals to use firewood hacked from Nepal's dwindling forests. Hydroelectricity has been put forward as the panacea for all Nepal's power problems, but most of the hydro projects approved so far aim to channel electricity across Nepal's borders to India and China.

Getting around is also harder than it used to be, despite the easing of blockades. After decades of under-investment, the national airline has only four working aircraft for domestic flights, and some routes have been abandoned entirely. Private airlines have taken up some of the slack, but most of Nepal's rural airstrips can only receive flights in clear weather, so delays and cancellations are the rule rather than the exception. The dangers of flying in cloud were tragically illustrated in October 2008 when a plane carrying European trekkers crashed beside the runway at Lukla, killing 18 people.

It's easy to focus on the negatives. For most Nepalis, the election of a stable government and the end of armed conflict has been a massive cause for celebration. The rebels never targeted tourists during the uprising, and the new communist government is now wooing foreign travellers like never before. Visa conditions have been eased, so visitors can obtain a visa lasting up to six months on arrival, and there are plans to waive visa fees entirely in 2011 for Visit Nepal Year.

The biggest problem faced by visitors to Nepal is how to fit everything in. Many people have spent a lifetime exploring the mountain trails of the Himalaya and atmospheric temple towns of the Kathmandu Valley and the Middle Hills, and they still keep coming back for more. Our advice is to pick a handful of essential experiences and save the rest for trip two, and three, and four, and...

'Many people have spent a lifetime exploring the mountain trails and atmospheric temple towns'

Getting Started

There are few countries in the world that are as well set up for independent tourism as Nepal. You can rock up to the border or Kathmandu airport, obtain a visa on arrival, organise a TIMS permit for trekking (see p335) and be up in the Himalaya in a matter of days. However, there is so much to see and do that it pays to do a bit of preparation before you arrive, not least because delays, cancellations and other unexpected obstacles to travel are part of daily life in Nepal. After a decade of civil war things are finally getting back to normal in Nepal and tourism is bouncing back with gusto. Last time we updated this book many lodges were struggling to find guests. Today, in many areas, travellers are struggling to find beds.

WHEN TO GO

The climate of Nepal can be broadly divided into two seasons. The dry season runs from October to May and the wet (monsoon) season runs from June to September. Autumn (September to November) and spring (March to May) offer warm daytime temperatures, clear skies for mountain views and perfect weather for trekking, rafting or just roaming around the Kathmandu Valley. For more information on the trekking season see p329.

See Climate Charts (p363) for more information.

The peak season for tourism runs from October to November: the landscape is green and lush from the recent monsoon rains, the air is crisp and clean, and the views of the Himalaya are crystal clear. However, competition for seats on international and domestic flights can be fierce, and lodges and hotels fill up quickly – very frustrating if you have left your bag at a particular hotel while trekking. Always book ahead at this time of year. You should also consider the disruption caused by the annual Dasain festival in October (see p25).

By early December winter is starting to creep in and most trekkers retreat from the high-altitude trekking routes. Heading for Everest Base Camp at this

---

DON'T LEAVE HOME WITHOUT...

- A face mask against Kathmandu's air pollution, especially if you plan to rent a motorcycle or bike
- Earplugs for travel on noisy turboprop planes and local buses, and for those occasions when your hotel room faces onto a disco...
- Lip balm with sunscreen – when trekking the mountain winds and unfiltered sunlight will chap your lips in minutes
- Hiking boots or shoes – buying footwear in Nepal is a short cut to blisters
- A waterproof jacket or a solidly-built umbrella for monsoon squalls or sudden showers
- A good padlock – for closing hotel room doors and lockers at temples and museums, and locking your bag to bus baggage racks
- An LED torch for powercuts and night-time toilet trips while trekking
- Insect repellent for the Terai (plus anti-leech oil for monsoon travel)
- Swimming costume for rafting, kayaking, canyoning, elephant washing (yes, elephant washing, see p287) and, well, swimming!
- A reusable water bottle and iodine tablets – purify your own water, save money and protect the environment

time of year can be a real feat of endurance, and the Annapurna Circuit is often closed by snow on the Thorung La. Even the Kathmandu Valley can feel chilly after dark, and the morning mist can play havoc with flight schedules. Tourists start to leave Kathmandu in December like flocks of migratory birds, headed for the warmer climes of India or Thailand. However, this is a great time to enjoy the national parks of the Terai without the crowds.

Spring, from March to May, is the second-best time to visit. The weather gets steadily warmer in the run-up to the monsoon and the trekking routes are less crowded than in autumn, though cloud is more likely to roll in and obscure the views. This is also the time to observe Nepal's wonderful rhododendrons in technicolor bloom.

The pre-monsoon period in May and early June is a poor time to visit Nepal. The Terai and Kathmandu Valley become as hot and humid as a sauna, with temperatures soaring above 30°C, and the coming monsoon seems to hang over the country like a threat. Because of its lower altitude Pokhara is warmer and more pleasant than Kathmandu during winter, but hotter before the monsoon and wetter during it.

The monsoon rains lash Nepal from mid-June to September, driving all but the most dedicated tourists away. Rafting rivers become dangerously swollen, trails in the foothills turn into rivers of mud, roads are blocked by floods and landslides, national parks close, mountain views vanish behind rain clouds, and leeches come out of hiding to feast on fresh blood. If it's mountain scenery you are after, consider a trip to Tibet or Ladakh in India instead. On the other hand, there are fewer travellers around to spoil the peace and quiet, and there are plenty of colourful festivals in August and September (p24).

'It pays to monitor the political situation as you travel around Nepal.'

IS IT SAFE?

Since the end of Nepal's 10-year People's War in 2008, the simple answer to that question is yes. The Maoist rebels are now the elected government of the Federal Republic of Nepal, and the deposed former king lives as a civilian in a modest two-bedroom house in Nagarjun. Political violence still flares up occasionally – usually as a result of squabbles between the youth wing of the Maoists and the youth wing of the opposition – but travellers are rarely affected, except when there is a bandh (general strike) in Kathmandu.

In the event of a strike the best thing to do is to hole up in your hotel or a Thamel cafe with a good book. Huge crowds of protesters gather in the streets and things sometimes get out of hand. The mob may express its anger by smashing the windows of cars and shops – most locals pull down their shutters and wait till the storm blows over. During a strike all roads out of Kathmandu are blocked, buses stop running and taxi drivers refuse to travel; if you need to catch a flight try to travel first thing in the morning, before the crowds gather.

It pays to monitor the political situation as you travel around Nepal. The *Himalayan Times* (www.thehimalayantimes.com) and other newspapers contain advance warnings of upcoming demonstrations, and your hotel will probably warn you if there is likely to be trouble. If you have a rented motorcycle, keep it inside at your hotel until the strike is over. Do not try and run the blockades – travellers are as good a target as anyone else if the crowd feels like breaking something. See p366 for more advice on dealing with strikes and demonstrations.

During the uprising trekkers were often asked to pay unofficial 'trekking taxes' to help fund the Maoist cause. We have not heard of any such requests for money since the Communist Party of Nepal won the national elections in April 2008. However, there are still many armed people in the countryside and there is always the chance that travellers may be asked for these sorts of 'donations' again. As elsewhere, it makes sense to check the security situation before travelling off the beaten track.

In general, crime has declined markedly as the threat of violence from Maoists and the Nepali army has subsided. However, there is still massive inequality in Nepal so it pays to heed local warnings about areas where crime is a problem. The risk is probably highest in former Maoist strongholds such as Dolpo, the area between the Kathmandu Valley and the Arniko Hwy to Tibet, and the far east and west of the country.

A more serious risk to safety in Nepal comes from public transport. Bus accidents are depressingly common, and few years pass without some kind of plane or helicopter disaster in the mountains. The best way to stay safe is to avoid travelling by road at night, when drivers speed dangerously and overtake with reckless abandon. Air travel in Nepal is as safe as it can be considering the landscape and the limited technology at Nepal's domestic airports – and flying is still safer than travelling by road. However, you can reach many trailheads by road or on foot if you prefer not to fly.

To stay abreast of the political situation in Nepal, consider the following tips:

- Follow the local news through Nepali website such as www.kan tipuronline.com, www.thehimalayantimes.com, www.nepalnews.com, www.nepalitimes.com.np and www.nepalnews.net.
- Check out the latest postings on the Asia-Indian Subcontinent page of Lonely Planet's Thorn Tree (www.lonelyplanet.com/thorntree) or view the postings at www.trekinfo.com and http://blog.com.np.
- Always check the your government's travel advice before travelling (see boxed text Government Travel Advice, p362).
- Most travel warnings focus on administrative districts, which aren't shown on many maps; for an administrative map of Nepal go to www .ncthakur.itgo.com/map04.htm.

COSTS & MONEY

By Western standards Nepal is an amazingly cheap place to travel, though prices are creeping up as the Nepali economy recovers from the hard years of the People's War. Travelling by bus is a bargain and you can find budget accommodation almost everywhere, often for less than the price of a cup of coffee back home. Meals are also refreshingly inexpensive, except in Kathmandu where restaurants aimed at foreigners are increasingly charging Western prices.

If you go trekking food will be your biggest expense. Few lodges charge more than Rs 200 for a bed, but the bill for dinner and breakfast can easily top Rs 1000, particularly if you order alcoholic drinks. Guides and porters have also increased their rates, partly as a result of campaigns by the Maoists to ensure that rural people are properly rewarded for their labours. On one level this is righting a historical injustice, but you will have to dig deeper into your pockets than in previous years.

As a general guide you can live in Nepal for US$5 to US$10 a day if you stay in budget accommodation and adopt the Nepali diet of daal bhaat twice daily. However, this will not leave much left over to pay the admission fees to Nepal's national parks or historic sites. While trekking you can get by on US$7 to US$12 per day if you travel without porters and guides and stay in local teahouses, but budget for US$15 per day if you want a beer with supper. The budget for organised treks will depend on the number of staff, the destination and the level of luxury that you require; bank on at least US$25 per day.

HOW MUCH?

Budget hotel US$5-15

Room in a trekking lodge (per person) Rs 50-200

Admission to a museum or historic square Rs 100-200

Trekking porter per day US$8-12

Internet in Kathmandu per hour Rs 20-40

LONELY PLANET INDEX

Litre of petrol/gas Rs 90-100

Litre of bottled water Rs 12-15

Bottle of Tuborg Beer (in a restaurant) Rs 150-200

Plate of momos (steamed dumplings) Rs 20-40

Souvenir T-shirt Rs 400

If you eat at traveller-oriented restaurants, stay in more comfortable budget hotels, visit museums and historic sites, and take taxis from time to time, your living costs will be around US$15 to US$20 a day. If you move to a midrange hotel, travel by tourist bus or chartered taxi and get involved in organised activities such as rafting, group trekking or skydiving, expect to pay US$40 to US$60.

The tourist centres of Kathmandu and Pokhara seem to suck money out of you by osmosis, partly because there are so many ways to spend it. Add 30% to your normal daily budget in either of these cities. Conversely, in the mountains, there are few places where you can spend your money – the costs of meals, a bed for the night and occasional cups of tea will be your only expenses.

> 'You can often negotiate a cheaper rate for a room if you agree to stay several days'

During the Maoist uprising many hotels offered huge discounts, but this is much less widespread today. You can often negotiate a cheaper rate for a room if you agree to stay several days, but there is much less incentive for hotels to offer big discounts now that flights into Kathmandu are full. Discounts are easier to arrange in the off-season, from December to January and June to September. While trekking in the mountains you may be able to negotiate a cheaper room if you promise to eat your meals at the lodge where you stay.

Most midrange and top-end hotels and restaurants charge 13% VAT and a 10% service charge on top of published prices. Because of this, tipping is much less widespread than it used to be.

TRAVEL LITERATURE

The Snow Leopard, by Peter Matthiessen, is partly an account of a trek to Dolpo in the west of Nepal in search of the elusive snow leopard. On another level, however, this moving book pursues the 'big questions' of spirituality, nature and Buddhism, with the Himalaya as a constant backdrop.

Chomolungma Sings the Blues: Travels Around Everest, by Ed Douglas, is a thought-provoking 'state-of-the-mountain' address detailing the side effects of Everest mountaineering – litter, pollution, exploitation – that are often airbrushed out of conventional mountaineering books.

To the Navel of the World, by Peter Somerville-Large, is a droll account of adventures and misadventures on a journey from Nepal to Tibet in the company of two yaks named Muster and Sod. His encounters with tourism in remote locations are very funny.

Travelers' Tales Nepal, edited by Rajendra Khadka, is an anthology of 37 interesting stories from a variety of writers including Peter Matthiessen, Jan Morris and ex-US president Jimmy Carter.

Video Night in Kathmandu, by Pico Iyer, gallivants all around Asia but the chapter on Nepal has some astute and amusing observations on the collision between Nepali tradition and Western culture.

Escape from Kathmandu, by Kim Stanley Robinson, is a collection of oddball short stories set in the Himalaya, including the engaging tale of a yeti rescued from scientific experimentation by two eccentric climbers.

The Soul of the Rhino by Hemanta Mishra, one of Nepal's leading conservationists, is a insightful introduction to the challenges facing Nepal's one-horned rhinos and the lives of the people who share their habitat.

Arresting God in Kathmandu, by Samrat Upadhyay, is a collection of nine short stories from the first Nepali writer to be published in English, offering interesting insights into how Kathmandu residents see their own city.

Beyond the Clouds: Journeys in Search of the Himalayan Kings, by Jonathan Gregson, is a portrait of the diverse royal families of the Himalaya, including the kings of Nepal and Mustang. *Blood Against*

TOP PICKS

NEPAL•Kathmandu

FESTIVALS

Immerse yourself in Nepali culture by attending one of the country's thrilling festivals:

- Magh Sankranti, Devghat (January; p23)
- Losar, all Tibetan areas (February; p23)
- Maha Shivaratri, Pashupatinath (February/March; p23)
- Bisket Jatra chariot festival, Bhaktapur (mid-April; p23)
- Rato Machhendranath Festival, Patan (April/May; p24)
- Indra Jatra chariot festival, Kathmandu (August/September; p25)
- Dasain, nationwide (September/October; p25)
- Tihar and Deepawali, nationwide (October/November; p25)
- Mani Rimdu, Tengboche (November; p26)

CLASSIC EXPERIENCES

Pack your sense of adventure and hunt down the quintessential Nepali travel moment:

- Beating a path through the crowded bazaars of old Kathmandu en route to Durbar Sq (p119)
- Lighting a butter lamp in honour of the Buddha at Bodhnath (p173)
- Getting a blessing from a Hindu priest at Pashupatinath (p170) or Budhanilkantha (p179)
- Watching the sun rise over the temples and palaces of Patan (p181) or Bhaktapur (p195)
- Riding a rented motorcycle across the Kathmandu Valley to historic Panauti (p229)
- Tracking rhinos on elephant-back at Chitwan National Park (p287)
- Viewing Everest in the morning from Kala Pattar on the Everest Base Camp trek (p340)
- Abseiling down waterfalls on a canyoning trip near the Tibetan border (p88)
- Rafting the wild white waters of the Sun Kosi (p110)
- Jumaring to the summit of Island Peak, Nepal's most accessible trekking peak (p111)
- Throwing yourself off Asia's highest bungee jump (p87) at Bhote Kosi

BOOKS

Great titles to read before setting off into the Himalaya:

- *Annapurna* by Maurice Herzog – a mountaineering classic from 1950
- *Into Thin Air* by Jon Krakauer – the emotionally gripping story of the 1996 Everest disaster
- *The Ascent of Rum Doodle* by WE Bowman – a highly enjoyable spoof of the serious mountaineering tomes
- *The Snow Leopard* by Peter Matthiessen – see opposite
- *Nepal Himalaya* by WH Tillman – delightful wit from the 1950s
- *Everest* by Walt Unsworth – the ultimate Everest reference
- *Touching My Father's Soul* by Jamling Tenzing Norgay – a moving mountaineering odyssey from the son of Tenzing Norgay
- *Fallen Giants* by M Isserman – a comprehensive guide to Himalayan mountaineering
- *Himalaya* by Michael Palin – tales of adventure on Annapurna and Everest by the charming ex-Python

the Snows by the same author focuses on the violent history of the Shah dynasty.

There are numerous coffee-table books about Nepal – look out for *East of Lo Manthang* by Peter Matthiessen and Thomas Laird, *Caravans of the Himalaya* by Eric Valli and *Nepal: The Kingdom in the Himalayas* by Toni Hagen, one of the first Europeans to visit this once-forbidden kingdom. Mustang is also covered by Michael Peissel's *Mustang: A Lost Tibetan Kingdom,* describing the author's ground-breaking trip in 1964.

You can find all the books listed in this chapter in Kathmandu.

INTERNET RESOURCES

Explore Nepal (www.explorenepal.com) Nepal portal with links grouped into useful categories. Also try www.nepalhomepage.com or www.nepaltourism.info.

Lonely Planet (www.lonelyplanet.com) Get advice from other travellers on the Thorn Tree, check out the Nepal web links and book accommodation online.

Ministry of Tourism (www.tourism.gov.np) A dry but useful official site with information on tourism, climbing and trekking regulations.

Nepal Mountaineering Association (www.nepalmountaineering.org) Everything you need to know about climbing and trekking to the top of Nepal's mountains.

Nepal Tourism Board (www.welcomenepal.com) The official government tourism site with news, a rundown of the country's sights and info on new areas being developed for trekking.

Trekinfo.com (www.trekinfo.com) You guessed it – all the trekking information that you'll need to get started, with a cracking forum board.

Visit Nepal (www.visitnepal.com) A comprehensive site with detailed information for travellers and links to loads of organisations within the country.

Yeti Zone (www.yetizone.com) An excellent day-by-day description of the big treks.

Events Calendar

Any visit to Nepal is almost certain to coincide with at least one of the country's spectacular festivals. Celebrations range from masked dances to epic bouts of tug of war, but the most impressive are the chariot processions, during which hundreds of enthusiastic devotees drag the 20m-tall chariots through the crowded city streets.

Exact festival dates change annually due to Nepal's lunar calendar (see boxed text Nepali Calendars, p369); the following list gives Nepal's major festivals in the months they usually occur, with the Nepali lunar months listed in brackets.

JANUARY–FEBRUARY (MAGH)

MAGH SANKRANTI
One of the few festivals not timed by the lunar calendar, this ritual bathing is dated by the movement north of the winter sun. Soon after, on the new-moon day, the Tribeni Mela (a *mela* is a fair) is held at various places including Devghat (p280) and Ridi Bazaar (p305). Devotees also bathe in the Bagmati River at Patan's Sankhamul ghat.

BASANTA PANCHAMI
The start of spring is celebrated in the middle of the lunar month by honouring Saraswati; since she is the goddess of learning this festival has special importance for students. The shrine to Saraswati just below the platform at the top of Swayambhunath is the most popular locale for the festivities, although Kathmandu is also popular. This is also a particularly auspicious time for weddings.

LOSAR
Tibetan New Year commences with the new moon in February and falls in either Magh or Falgun. In the Kathmandu Valley it is welcomed with particular fervour at the great stupa of Bodhnath (Boudha), as well as at Swayambhunath and in the Tibetan community at Jawalakhel, near Patan. Tibetan peoples from Dolpo in the west of Nepal to the Solu Khumbu region in the east all celebrate during this time.

FEBRUARY–MARCH (FALGUN)

MAHA SHIVARATRI
Shiva's birthday falls on the new-moon day of the Nepali month of Falgun. Festivities take place at all Shiva temples, but most particularly at Pashupatinath, and hundreds of sadhus flock here from all over Nepal and India. The crowds bathing in the Bagmati's holy waters at this time are a colourful and wonderful sight.

HOLI
This exciting festival (also known as Fagu) takes place on the full-moon day in the month of Falgun. Occurring late in the dry season, the water that is sprayed around is a reminder of the cooling monsoon days to come. Also known as the Festival of Colours, coloured powder and water are also dispensed. Foreigners get special attention, so if you venture out on Holi leave your camera behind (or keep it well protected) and wear old clothes.

MARCH–APRIL (CHAITRA)

CHAITRA DASAIN
Also known as Small Dasain, this festival takes place exactly six months prior to the more important Dasain celebration. Both Dasains are dedicated to Durga and, once again, goats and buffaloes are sacrificed early in the morning in Kot Sq in central Kathmandu. The Chaitra Dasain sacrifices also signal the start of the month long Seto (White) Machhendranath chariot festival in Kathmandu (see p136).

SETO MACHHENDRANATH
This chariot festival isn't as spectacular as the larger Rato Macchendranath festival in Patan (see p24) but it's still impressive. The festival starts with removing the image of Seto Machhendranath from the temple at Kel Tole in Kathmandu and placing it on a towering, tottering *rath* (chariot), which crowds drag through the narrow backstreets of the old town for the next four days.

APRIL–MAY (BAISAKH)

BISKET JATRA
Nepali New Year starts in mid-April, at the beginning of the month of Baisakh; the Bisket chariot festival in Bhaktapur is the most spectacular welcome for the New Year, and one of the most exciting annual events in the valley (see p206).

BALKUMARI JATRA
The small town of Thimi celebrates this exciting festival at this time (see p209). The New Year is also an important time in the valley for ritual bathing, and crowds of hill people visit the Buddhist stupas of Swayambhunath and Bodhnath.

GHORA JATRA
The Nepali army takes over the Tundikhel parade ground in Kathmandu on horse-racing day to display its equestrian (and motorcycle) skills. Legend has it that the horses are raced to trample devils who may rise from the ground to create havoc.

BALAJU JATRA
Thousands of pilgrims keep an all-night vigil at the Swayambhunath temple. The following day they trek to the 22 waterspouts at Balaju for a ritual bath.

RATO MACHHENDRANATH
Patan's biggest festival involves the month-long procession of a temple chariot, culminating in the showing of the sacred vest of the god Machhendranath (see p189). The festival begins on the full moon.

MAY–JUNE (JETH)
BUDDHA JAYANTI
A great fair is held at Lumbini (the birthplace of the Buddha) on the date of the Buddha's birth (which is the same day as his enlightenment and passing into nirvana), and there are full-moon celebrations in Swayambhunath, Bodhnath and Patan. The Swayambhunath stupa's collection of rare thangkas is displayed on the southern wall of the courtyard only on this day each year. There are also colourful monk dances.

JULY–AUGUST (SAAUN)
GHANTA KARNA
This festival is named after 'bell ears', a horrible demon who wore bell earrings to drown out the name of Vishnu, his sworn enemy. This festival, on the 14th day of the dark fortnight of Saaun, celebrates his destruction when a god, disguised as a frog, lured him into a deep well where the people stoned and clubbed him to death. Ghanta Karna is burnt in effigy on this night throughout Newari villages to cleanse evil from the land for another year.

NAGA PANCHAMI
On the fifth day after the new moon in the month of Saaun, nagas (serpent deities) are honoured all over the country. Nagas are considered to have magical powers over the monsoon rains. Protective pictures of the nagas are hung over doorways of houses and food is put out for snakes, including a bowl of rice. See p202 for more information.

JANAI PURNIMA
Around the full moon in the month of Saaun, all high-caste men (Chhetri and Brahmin) must change the janai (sacred thread), which they wear looped over their left shoulder. Janai Purnima also brings crowds of pilgrims to sacred Gosainkund lakes (p350), where they garland a statue of Shiva and throw coins at a sacred lingam, and the Kumbeshwar Temple in Patan (p188).

AUGUST–SEPTEMBER (BHADRA)
GAI JATRA
This 'Cow Festival' takes place immediately after Janai Purnima and is dedicated to those who died during the preceding year. Newars believe that, after death, cows will guide them to Yama, the god of the underworld. On this day cows are led through the streets of the valley's towns and small boys dress up as cows. The festival is celebrated with maximum energy on the streets of Bhaktapur.

KRISHNA JAYANTI (KRISHNA'S BIRTHDAY)
The seventh day after the full moon in the month of Bhadra is celebrated as Krishna's birthday (also known as Krishnasthami). An all-night vigil is kept at the Krishna Mandir in Patan on the night before his birthday: oil lamps light the temple and singing continues through the night.

TEEJ
The Festival of Women lasts from the second to the fifth day after the Bhadra new moon, and is particularly celebrated at Pashupatinath (p170). The festival starts on the first day with a sumptuous meal and party, until midnight when women commence a 24-hour fast. On the second day women dress in their red wedding saris and head to Shiva temples across the country to pray for a happy marriage. A ritual bathing ceremony brings the festival to a close.

GOKARNA AUNSI
The Nepali equivalent of Father's Day is celebrated by visiting fathers at their homes or honouring deceased fathers at the Shiva temple in Gokarna, in the Kathmandu Valley.

INDRA JATRA

This colourful festival at the end of the month combines homage to Indra with an annual appearance by Kathmandu's Kumari (a living goddess), paying respect to Bhairab and the commemoration of the conquest of the valley by Prithvi Narayan Shah. It also marks the end of the monsoon. The most spectacular celebrations are in Kathmandu (p138).

SEPTEMBER–OCTOBER (ASHWIN)

PACHALI BHAIRAB JATRA

The fearsome form of Bhairab, Pachali Bhairab, is honoured on the fourth day of the bright fortnight in September or early October. Bhairab's bloodthirsty nature means that there are numerous animal sacrifices.

DASAIN

Nepal's biggest annual festival, Dasain, lasts for 15 days. It celebrates the victory of the goddess Durga over the forces of evil (personified in the buffalo demon Mahisasura): across the country hundreds of thousands of animals are sacrificed in Durga's honour. In the countryside, swings and primitive hand-powered Ferris wheels are erected at the entrance to villages. For information on disruptions to services during the festival see p370.

FULPATI (PHULPATI)

Fulpati ('Sacred Flowers') is the first really important day of Dasain and is called the 'Seventh Day' although it may not actually fall on the seventh day. A jar containing flowers is carried from Gorkha to Kathmandu and presented to the president at the Tundikhel parade ground. The flowers symbolise Taleju, the goddess of the former royal family. From the parade ground the flowers are transported on a palanquin to Hanuman Dhoka (the old Royal Palace) in Durbar Sq.

MAHA ASTAMI

The 'Great Eighth Day' and Kala Ratri, the 'Black Night', follow Fulpati, and mark the start of the sacrifices and offerings to Durga. The hundreds of goats you see contentedly grazing in the Tundikhel parkland prior to Maha Astami are living on borrowed time. At midnight, in a temple courtyard near Durbar Sq, eight buffaloes and 108 goats are beheaded, each with a single stroke of a sword or knife.

NAVAMI

The sacrifices continue on Kot Sq the next day: visitors can witness the bloodshed but you'll need to arrive early to secure a place. Blood is sprinkled on the wheels of cars and other vehicles to ensure a safe year on the road. At the airport, each Nepal Airlines aircraft will have a goat sacrificed to it! The average Nepali does not eat much meat but, on this day, almost everybody in the country will find that goat is on the menu.

VIJAYA DASHAMI

The 10th day of the festival is a family affair: cards and greetings are exchanged, family visits are made and parents place a *tika* on their children's foreheads. The evening is marked by processions and masked dances across the Kathmandu Valley. The Kharga Jatra, or sword procession, features priests dressed up as the various gods and carrying wooden swords. This day also celebrates the victory of Lord Rama over the evil demon-king Ravana in the Ramayana.

KARTIKA PURNIMA

The full-moon day in September/October marks the end of Dasain. It is celebrated with gambling in many households: you will see even small children avidly putting a few coins down on various local games of chance.

OCTOBER–NOVEMBER (KARTIK)

TIHAR

Tihar (also called Diwali or Deepawali after the third day of celebrations) takes place in late October or early November. It is the most important Hindu festival in India; in Nepal it ranks second only to Dasain. The festival honours certain animals, starting with offerings of rice to the crows ('messengers of death' sent by the god Yama). Dogs (who guide departed souls across the river of the dead) are honoured on day two, with cows and bullocks following on days three and four.

DEEPAWALI (FESTIVAL OF LIGHTS)

The third day of Tihar is the most important, when Lakshmi, the goddess of wealth, comes to visit every home that has been suitably lit for her presence. No one likes to turn down a visit from the goddess of wealth and so homes throughout the country are brightly lit with candles and lamps. The effect is highlighted because Deepawali falls on the new-moon day.

NEWARI NEW YEAR

The fourth day of Tihar is also the start of the New Year for the Newari people of the Kathmandu Valley.

BHAI TIKA

On the fifth day of Tihar, brothers and sisters are supposed to meet and place *tika*s on each others' foreheads. Sisters offer small gifts of fruit and sweets to their brothers, while the brothers give their sisters money in return. The markets and bazaars are busy supplying the appropriate gifts.

HARIBODHINI EKADASHI

An *ekadashi* (the 11th day after each new and full moon) happens twice in every lunar month and is regarded as an auspicious day. The Haribodhini Ekadashi, in late October or early November (on the 11th day after the new moon), is the most important. On this day Vishnu awakens from his four-month monsoonal slumber. The best place to see the festivities is at the temple of the sleeping Vishnu in Budhanilkantha (p179).

MAHALAKSHMI PUJA

Lakshmi is the goddess of wealth, and to farmers wealth is rice. Therefore this harvest festival, immediately following Haribodhini Ekadashi, honours the goddess with sacrifices and colourful dances.

MANI RIMDU

This popular Sherpa festival takes place at the monastery of Tengboche in the Solu Khumbu region (p343) and features masked dances and dramas. The dates for the festivals are worked out according to the Tibetan lunar calendar (see www.tengboche.org for details). Another Mani Rimdu festival takes place six months later at Thame Gompa, a day's walk west of Namche Bazaar (p343).

NOVEMBER–DECEMBER (MANGSIR)

BALA CHATURDASHI

Like *ekadashi,* there are two *chaturdashi*s each month. Bala Chaturdashi falls on the new-moon day in late November or early December. Pilgrims flock to Pashupatinath, burning oil lamps at night, scattering grain for the dead and bathing in the holy Bagmati River (see p173).

SITA BIBAHA PANCHAMI

On the fifth day of the bright fortnight in late November or early December, tens of thousands of pilgrims from all over Nepal and India flock to Janakpur (the birthplace of Sita) to celebrate the marriage of Sita to Rama. The wedding is re-enacted with a procession carrying Rama's image to Sita's temple by elephant (see p319).

Itineraries
CLASSIC ROUTES

THE KATHMANDU VALLEY   One Week / Kathmandu to Kathmandu
A week will give you time to whistle around the cultural highlights of the Kathmandu Valley. Start off with the **walking tour** (p134) south from Thamel to the stunning temples and palaces of **Durbar Square** (p119).

On day two, walk to towering **Swayambhunath** (p163) and the quirky **National Museum** (p166). You can fill the afternoon with a trip to the famous **stupa** (p174) at glorious Bodhnath.

Make time for a full-day trip to Patan's spectacular **Durbar Square** (p181), combined with a slap-up **lunch** (p192). Complete the trilogy of former royal kingdoms with a full-day visit to medieval **Bhaktapur** (p194), ideally with an overnight stay.

Next get your Himalayan kick with dawn views at **Nagarkot** (p222) or **Dhulikhel** (p226) before returning to Kathmandu the next morning. Fill another day by mountain biking to the southern valley towns of **Kirtipur** (p215) and **Bungamati** (p219).

On your last day, take time for some serious **shopping** (p157) in Kathmandu or the **fair trade shops** (p193) of Patan.

Fans of culture and human creativity will find glorious palaces, sanctified stupas and towering temples scattered across the hillsides on the 40km trip exploring the Kathmandu Valley.

FROM BUDDHA TO BOUDHA   Two Weeks / Lumbini to Bodhnath

To catch some culture as you head north from the Indian border to Kathmandu, kick off at **Lumbini** (p296), the birthplace of the Buddha, 20km from the border crossing. Take your time exploring this world map of Buddhist temples, then spend the next day at the little-visited archaeological site of **Tilaurakot** (p300), where the Buddha once ruled as a pampered prince.

From Lumbini make a beeline for **Chitwan National Park** (p281), taking two or three days to get up close and personal with the wildlife. You can't get more up close and personal than helping out at **elephant bathtime** (p287).

From Chitwan take the day-long tourist bus to **Pokhara** (p253) for your first proper peek at the mountains. While in the Pokhara area, take a few days to hike up to the **World Peace Pagoda** (p258), to enjoy the views at lofty **Sarangkot** (p272) or plummet past the peaks on a **tandem paraglide** (p88).

Another long bus trip will take you to **Kathmandu** (p113), where you can fill a week with the pick of the Kathmandu Valley itinerary (p27). Make time to explore the backstreets of Bhaktapur on a **walking tour** (p198), gain a deeper understanding of Buddhist art at **Patan Museum** (p186) and enjoy the views over the city at dusk from **Swayambhunath** (p163).

There should just be time for an overnight sortie to experience wild adventure activities at the **Last Resort** (p232) or **Borderlands Resort** (p231), which are both a half-day drive from Kathmandu towards the Tibetan border.

On your last day, give thanks for a head-spinning trip at **Bodhnath** (p173) where you can hit the **shops** (p178) and pick up a statue, Buddha or bundle of prayer flags to take home.

Mixing contemplative temple tours, ancient pilgrimage sites and ruins with wilderness adventures, this 500km route is one part meditation with two parts adrenaline.

ROAMING HIGH & LOW   One Month / Kathmandu to Kathmandu

With a month to spare, you can explore the Kathmandu Valley and fit in a trek into the mighty Himalaya. To truly experience Nepal and its people you have to do it on foot, but you don't have to give up all creature comforts. There are lodges along the major trail routes offering simple bedrooms, solar-powered showers, hot tea, high-carb meals, sanity-restoring chocolate and heated *chang* (rice beer).

From Kathmandu, fly east to **Lukla** (book return flights from Lukla to Kathmandu before arriving in Nepal). From here you can embark on a trek through truly wild scenery to **Everest Base Camp** (p340). This is perhaps the definitive Himalayan trek, climbing among snow peaks to the base of the tallest mountain on earth, but the trek takes at least two weeks because of the gain in altitude.

With a month to play with, consider doing an Everest loop, returning from Base Camp via the spectacular **Gokyo Valley** (p345) for a total trek of around 21 days. Because of the changeable weather in Nepal, it's wise to leave yourself a buffer at the end of the trip in case flights are cancelled. Do your Kathmandu Valley sightseeing *after* the trek, not before.

After the thrills and chills of the mountains, go southwest from Kathmandu to warm your toes in steamy **Chitwan National Park** (p281) while you scan the jungle for rhinos and tigers. Finish off by exploring the highlights of the Kathmandu Valley itinerary (p27). Go **shopping** (p157) for a singing bowl in Kathmandu before you board the plane home.

Experience Nepal's 'peaks and troughs' on a trek to the highest peak on earth and a ramble around the fascinating Kathmandu Valley. Take your time and pause at teahouses en route.

ROADS LESS TRAVELLED

ONCE AROUND THE MIDDLE

Many of the most interesting attractions are scattered like pearls around the impenetrable hills in the middle of Nepal. Start with Kathmandu's **temples and stupas** (p119), then book a **rafting trip** (p106) east along the Trisuli. After a few days churning on the rapids enjoy a smoother ride on the **Manakamana cable car** (p237) to experience the strange atmosphere of a Tantric temple.

Next stop is **Bandipur** (p241), a little-visited gem of a village where you can stroll to eerie caverns and relax among some wondrous Newari architecture. From here, roll on to Pokhara for a **row-boat ride** (p260) around the lake and a quick jaunt across to **Begnas Tal** (p274).

Take the winding Siddhartha Hwy south to charming **Tansen** (p302), the base for some great day hikes. Continue south to peaceful **Lumbini** (p296) to amble around the Buddhist monasteries by bicycle.

Having come this far, it would be a shame to miss **Chitwan National Park** (p281). If budget allows, stay at one of the lodges deep inside the park. You might also consider an uphill tramp to the **Chepang hills** (p238) or a thoughtful stroll to the sacred village of **Devghat** (p280).

The logical return route would be to follow the snaking Tribhuvan Hwy north to **Daman** (p306), but you could also travel east to the new highway from Bardibas to **Dhulikhel** (p226), allowing time for a detour to the temple-town of **Janakpur** (p316).

Ditch the crowds on a 400km loop around Nepal's cultural heartland, picking the best from the hills and plains. Take an excellent day hike that won't require trekking boots or muscles of steel!

TAILORED TRIPS

UNESCO WORLD HERITAGE SITES

The entire Kathmandu Valley is a World Heritage area made up of seven individual sites. Most visitors to the country are floored by the architectural wonders of the **Durbar Squares** (Kathmandu, p119; Patan, p181; Bhaktapur, p201).

There is a hierarchy to these three medieval sites – Patan's Durbar Sq is the most impressive, while Kathmandu's is the busiest and Bhaktapur's is the most peaceful, especially if you arrive there at first light, before the tourist crowds descend.

Patan;
Swayambhunath;
Bodhnath;
Pashupatinath;
KATHMANDU
Lumbini   Sagarmatha
            National Park
Chitwan   Bhaktapur;
National Park Changu Narayan
               Temple

Swayambhunath's swooningly beautiful Buddhist **stupa** (p164) is matched by the impressive **Bodhnath stupa** (p174), and both are on the heritage list, as is the revered Hindu **Pashupatinath temple complex** (p170), set beside the dirty but divine Bagmati River.

The last two cultural heritage sites are the statue-filled **Changu Narayan Temple** (p210), an open-air museum of priceless stone sculpture, and the **birthplace of the Buddha** (p297) at Lumbini, which is building itself a new heritage in the form of gleaming temples constructed by every Buddhist nation.

Nepal also has two natural World Heritage sites: the breathless, mountain scenery of **Sagarmatha National Park** (p343), surrounding Mt Everest and accessible on the Everest Base Camp Trek, and the steamy, rhino-rumbling, tiger-striped jungles of **Chitwan National Park** (p281).

A SPIRITUAL ODYSSEY

There's soul in them thar hills, and this is where to find it. Start your quest for inner knowledge with a dawn ceremonial circuit around **Swayambhunath hill** (p163) and a sunset trip to **Bodhnath** (p173) – come during full moon when the stupa is lit up by thousands of flickering butter lamps. Contemplate the meaning of life and death on the **cremation ghats** (p171) of Pashupatinath or the **sacrificial altars** of Dakshinkali (p218) or Manakamana (p237).

For less gruesome rituals, head north across the valley to **Budhanilkantha** (p179), where devotees pile offerings onto a giant floating statue of Narayan, the creator of the universe. Nepal's spiritual side goes into overdrive for its vivid festivals – visit in April or May when devotees haul a sacred image of Rato Machhendranath around Patan in a towering, medieval chariot at the **Rato Machhendranath festival** (p189).

Swayambhunath;
Bodhnath;
Pashupatinath;
Patan;
Budhanilkantha; Gosainkund
KATHMANDU
Manakamana   Sankhu
                        Gokyo
Dakshinkali;   Panauti
Bungamati

Often the most spiritual places are away from the crowds. Find space for reflection on the uplifting trek to the sacred lake at **Gosainkund** (p350) or pay your respects at Tengboche Monastery before crossing the Cho La pass from the Khumbu Valley to the sacred lakes at **Gokyo** (p345).

Lastly, see how ordinary people blend spirituality into their daily lives at **Sankhu** (p214), **Bungamati** (p219) or temple-filled **Panauti** (p229).

History

The history of Nepal began in, and centres on, the Kathmandu Valley. Over the centuries Nepal's boundaries have extended to include huge tracts of neighbouring India, and contracted to little more than the Kathmandu Valley and a handful of nearby city states, but the valley remained the crucible of political power and cultural sophistication. Though it has ancient roots, the modern state of Nepal emerged only in the 18th century and is in many ways still forging itself as a modern nation state.

Squeezed between the Tibetan plateau and the plains of the subcontinent – the modern-day giants of China and India – Nepal has long prospered from its location as a resting place for traders, travellers and pilgrims. An ethnic melting pot, it has bridged cultures and absorbed elements of its neighbours, yet retained a unique character.

After travelling through India and Nepal for a while, many travellers notice both the similarities and differences. 'Same, same', they say, '…but different'.

Nepal is said to get its name from Nepa, the name given to the Newari kingdom of the Kathmandu Valley; the word Nepa is derived from the name of a mythological Hindu sage, Ne, who once lived in the valley.

THE KIRATIS & BUDDHIST BEGINNINGS

Nepal's recorded history emerges from the mist with the Hindu Kiratis. Arriving from the east around the 7th or 8th century BC, these Mongoloid people are the first known rulers of the Kathmandu Valley. King Yalambar (the first of their 29 kings) is mentioned in the Mahabharata, the Hindu epic, but little more is known about them.

In the 6th century BC, Prince Siddhartha Gautama was born into the Sakya royal family of Kapilavastu, near Lumbini, later embarking on a path of meditation and thought that led him to enlightenment as the Buddha. The religion that grew up around him continues to shape the face of Asia.

You can visit the archaeological site of Kapilavastu, where Siddhartha Gautama (the Buddha) lived for first 29 years of his life, at Tilaurakot (p300).

Around the 2nd century BC, the great Indian Buddhist emperor Ashoka visited Lumbini and erected a pillar at the birthplace of the Buddha. Popular legend recounts how he then visited the Kathmandu Valley and erected four stupas around Patan, but there is no evidence that he actually made it there in person. Either way, his Mauryan empire (321–184 BC) played a major role in popularising Buddhism in the region, a role continued by the north Indian Buddhist Kushan empire, which spanned the 1st to 3rd centuries AD.

Over the centuries a resurgent Hinduism came to eclipse Buddhism across the subcontinent and by the time the Chinese Buddhist pilgrims Fa Xian (Fa Hsien) and Xuan Zang (Hsuan Tsang) passed through the region in the 5th and 7th centuries the site of Lumbini was already in ruins.

TIMELINE

60 million BC	100,000 BC	c 563 BC
The Himalaya rise as the Indo-Australian tectonic plate crashes into the Eurasian plate. The Tethys Sea is pushed up, resulting in sea shells atop Mt Everest and fossilised ammonites (saligrams) in the Kali Gandaki Valley.	Kathmandu Valley is formed as a former lake bed dries. Legend relates how the Buddhist Bodhisattva Manjushri created the valley by cutting the Chobar Gorge and draining the lake's waters.	Siddhartha Gautama, the Buddha, is born in Lumbini into royalty and lives as both prince and ascetic in Nepal before coming up with his Middle Way and gaining enlightenment under a Bodhi tree (pipal tree) in India.

WARNING ABOUT FACTS & FIGURES

References for most things in Nepal are inconsistent. For example, we've seen several different figures for the amount of square kilometres Nepal occupies. When temples were built is also a matter of speculation: some sources give a date of construction for a certain temple and the period of reign for the king who built it, and the two only sometimes coincide.

Many temples in Nepal have alternative names. For example, Vishnu Temple in Patan's Durbar Sq is referred to as Jagannarayan or Charnarayan Temple. Where possible we have provided alternative names that are commonly used.

Further confusion results from different systems of transliteration from Sanskrit – the letter 'h', or the use of the double 'hh' appears inconsistently, so you may see Machhendranath and Machendranath (and no one really knows how to spell Machhapuchhare!). This difference only occurs during transliteration, of course – the Nepali script is always consistent. The letters 'b' and 'v' are also used interchangeably in different systems – Shiva's fearsome manifestation is Bhairab or Bhairav.

Finally, texts differ in their use of the words Nepali and Nepalese. In this book we use Nepali for the language and for other terms relating to the country and the people.

LICCHAVIS, THAKURIS, THEN DARKNESS

Buddhism faded and Hinduism reasserted itself with the arrival from northern India of the Licchavis. In AD 300 they overthrew the Kiratis, who resettled in the east to become the ancestors of today's Rai and Limbu people.

Between the 4th and 9th centuries the Licchavis ushered in a golden age of cultural brilliance. Their strategic position allowed them to prosper from trade between India and China. The chaityas (a particular style of stupas) and monuments of this era can still be seen at the Changu Narayan Temple (p210), north of Bhaktapur, and in the backstreets of Kathmandu's old town. It's believed that the original stupas at Chabahil, Bodhnath and Swayambhunath date from the Licchavi era.

Amsuvarman, the first Thakuri king, came to power in 602, succeeding his Licchavi father-in-law. He consolidated his power to the north and south by marrying his sister to an Indian prince and his daughter Bhrikuti to the great Tibetan king Songsten Gompo. Together with the Tibetan king's Chinese wife Wencheng, Bhrikuti managed to convert the king to Buddhism around 640, changing the face of both Tibet and, later, Nepal.

From the late 7th century until the 13th century Nepal slipped into its 'dark ages', of which little is known. Tibet invaded in 705 and Kashmir invaded in 782. The Kathmandu Valley's strategic location and fertile soil, however, ensured the kingdom's growth and survival. King Gunakamadeva is credited with founding Kantipur, today's Kathmandu, around the 10th century.

For an online history of Nepal visit www.infoclub .com.np/nepal/history.

c 250 BC	57 BC	AD 464
Mauryan Emperor Ashoka (r 268–231 BC) visits Lumbini, embraces Buddhism and builds four stupas on the outskirts of Patan. Much of India and Nepal adopts the new religion, ushering in a golden age for Buddhism.	Nepal's official Vikram (Bikram) Samwat calendar starts, in spring. Thus to Nepalis the year 2010 is 2067.	Nepal's earliest surviving inscription is carved into the beautiful Changu Narayan Temple in the Kathmandu Valley on the orders of King Manadeva.

THE GOLDEN AGE OF THE MALLAS

The first of the Malla kings came to power in the Kathmandu Valley around 1200. The Mallas (literally 'wrestlers' in Sanskrit) had been forced out of India and their name can be found in the Mahabharata and in Buddhist literature. This period was a golden one that stretched over 550 years, though it was peppered with fighting over the valuable trade routes to Tibet.

The first Malla rulers had to cope with several disasters. A huge earthquake in 1255 killed around one-third of Nepal's population. A devastating Muslim invasion by Sultan Shams-ud-din of Bengal less than a century later left plundered Hindu and Buddhist shrines in its wake, though the invasion did not leave a lasting cultural effect (unlike in the Kashmir Valley which remains Muslim to this day). In India the damage was more widespread and many Hindus were driven into the hills and mountains of Nepal, where they established small Rajput principalities.

Apart from this, the earlier Malla years (1220–1482) were largely stable, reaching a high point under the third Malla dynasty of Jayasthithi Malla (r 1382–1395), who united the valley and codified its laws, including the caste system.

After the death of Jayasthithi Malla's grandson Yaksha Malla in 1482, the Kathmandu Valley was divided up among his sons into the three kingdoms of Bhaktapur (Bhadgaon), Kathmandu (Kantipur) and Patan (Lalitpur). The rest of what we today call Nepal consisted of a fragmented patchwork of almost 50 independent states, stretching from Palpa and Jumla in the west to the semi-independent states of Banepa and Pharping, most of them minting their own coins and maintaining standing armies.

The rivalry between the three kingdoms of the Kathmandu Valley found its expression not only in warfare but also in the arts and culture, which flourished in the competitive climate. The outstanding collections of exquisite temples and buildings in each city's Durbar Sq are testament to the huge amounts of money spent by rulers desperate to outdo each other.

The building boom was financed by trade, in everything from musk and wool to salt, Chinese silk and even yak tails. The Kathmandu Valley stood at the departure point for two separate routes into Tibet, via Banepa to the northeast and via Rasuwa and the Kyirong Valley near Langtang to the northwest. Traders would cross the jungle-infested Terai during winter to avoid the virulent malaria and then wait in Kathmandu for the mountain passes to open later that summer. Kathmandu grew rich and its rulers converted their wealth into gilded pagodas and ornately carved royal palaces. In the mid-17th century Nepal gained the right to mint Tibet's coins using Tibetan silver, further enriching the kingdom's coffers.

In Kathmandu King Pratap Malla (1641–74) oversaw that city's cultural highpoint with the construction of the Hanuman Dhoka palace, the Rani Pokhari pond and the first of several subsequent pillars that featured a statue

The mid-13th century saw the de facto rule of Queen Devaladevi, the most powerful woman in Nepal's history.

Nepal's flag is like no other, consisting of two overlapping red triangles, bearing a white moon and a white 12-pointed sun (the first mythological kings of Nepal are said to be descendents of the sun and moon).

629	879	c 1260
The Chinese Buddhist pilgrim Xuan Zang (Hsuan Tsang) visits Lumbini and describes the Ashoka pillar marking the Buddha's birthplace. His text helps archaeologists relocate and excavate the lost site in 1895.	Newari lunar calendar, the Nepal Samvat, is introduced as the national calendar and used officially until the late 18th century. It is still used for Newari festivals in the Kathmandu Valley.	Nepali architect Arniko travels to Lhasa and Kublai Khan's capital Dadu (Beijing), bringing with him Nepal's most profound export – the design of the pagoda – thus changing the face of religious temples across Asia.

of the king facing the protective temple of Taleju, who the Mallas had by that point adopted as their protective deity. The mid-17th century also saw a highpoint of building in Patan.

The Malla era shaped the religious as well as artistic landscape, introducing the dramatic chariot festivals of Indra Jatra and Machhendranath. The Malla kings shored up their position by claiming to be reincarnations of the Hindu god Vishnu and establishing the cult of the Kumari, a living goddess whose role it was to bless the Malla's rule during an annual celebration.

The cosmopolitan Mallas also absorbed foreign influences. The Indian Mughal court influenced Malla dress and painting, presented the Nepalis with firearms and introduced the system of land grants for military service, a system which would have a profound effect in later years. In the early 18th century Capuchin missionaries passed through Nepal to Tibet, and when they returned home gave the West its first descriptions of exotic Kathmandu.

For more on the Kumari see the boxed text Kumari Devi, p123.

But change didn't only come from abroad. A storm was brewing inside Nepal, just 100km to the east of Kathmandu.

UNIFICATION UNDER THE SHAHS

In 1768 Prithvi Narayan Shah, ruler of the tiny hilltop kingdom of Gorkha (halfway between Pokhara and Kathmandu), stood poised on the edge of the Kathmandu Valley, ready to realise his dream of a unified Nepal. It had taken more than a quarter of a century of conquest and consolidation to get here but Shah was about to redraw the political landscape of the Himalaya.

Shah had taken the strategic hilltop fort of Nuwakot as early as 1744, blockading the valley after fighting off reinforcements from the British East India Company, but it took him until 1768 to take Kathmandu, sneaking in while everyone was drunk during the Indra Jatra festival. A year later he finally took Kirtipur, after three lengthy failed attempts. In terrible retribution his troops hacked 120lb of noses and lips off Kirtipur's residents; unsurprisingly, resistance throughout the valley quickly crumbled. In 1769 he advanced on the three cowering Malla kings and ended the Malla rule, thus unifying Nepal.

Shah moved his capital from Gorkha to Kathmandu, establishing the Shah dynasty, whose line continues to this day. Shah died just six years later in Nuwakot but is still revered as the founder of the nation.

Shah had built his empire on conquest and his insatiable army needed ever more booty and land to keep it satisfied. Within six years the Gurkhas had conquered eastern Nepal and Sikkim. The expansion then turned westwards into Kumaon and Garhwal, only halted on the borders of the Punjab by the armies of the powerful one-eyed ruler Ranjit Singh.

Nepal's founding father, Prithvi Narayan Shah, referred to Nepal as 'a yam between two boulders' – namely China and India – a metaphor that is as true geologically as it is historically

The expanding boundaries of 'Greater Nepal' by this time stretched from Kashmir to Sikkim, eventually putting it on a collision course with the world's most powerful empire, the British Raj. Despite early treaties with the British, disputes over the Terai led to the first Anglo-Nepali war, which the British

13th to 15th centuries	1349	1380
The Nepali-speaking Khasa empire of the western Mallas reaches its peak in the far western Karnali basin around Sinja, Dullu and Jumla. Its lasting contribution is Nepali – the national language spoken today.	Muslim armies of Sultan Shams-ud-Din plunder the Kathmandu Valley, destroying the stupa at Swayambhunath and carrying off cartloads of booty.	Ame Pal founds the kingdom of Lo (Mustang). The present king of Mustang, Jigme Palbar Bista, traces his family back 25 generations to this king. Mustang remains an independent kingdom until 1951.

won after a two-year fight. The British were so impressed by their enemy that they decided to incorporate Gurkha mercenaries into their own army, a practice that continues to this day (Gurkha troops served recently in Iraq and Afghanistan).

The 1816 Sugauli treaty called a screeching halt to Nepal's expansion and laid down its modern boundaries. Nepal lost Sikkim, Kumaon, Garhwal and much of the Terai, though some of this land was restored to Nepal in 1858 in return for support given to the British during the Indian Mutiny (Indian War of Independence). A British resident was sent to Kathmandu to keep an eye on things but the Raj knew that it would be too difficult to colonise the impossible hill terrain and were content to keep Nepal as a buffer state. Nepalis to this day are proud that their country was never colonised by the British, unlike the neighbouring hill states of India.

Following its humiliating defeat, Nepal cut itself off from all foreign contact from 1816 until 1951. The British residents in Kathmandu were the only Westerners to set eyes on Nepal for more than a century.

On the cultural front, temple construction continued apace, though perhaps of more import to ordinary people was the revolutionary introduction, via India, of chillies, potatoes, tobacco and other New World crops.

The Shah rulers, meanwhile, swung from ineffectual to seriously deranged. At one point the kingdom was governed by a 12-year-old female regent, in charge of a nine-year-old king! One particularly sadistic ruler, Crown Prince Surendra (r 1847–81), expanded the horizons of human suffering by ordering subjects to jump down wells or ride off cliffs, just to see whether they would survive.

THE RANOCRACY

The death of Prithvi Narayan Shah in 1775 set in motion a string of succession struggles, infighting, assassinations, backstabbing and intrigue that culminated in the Kot Massacre in 1846. This bloody night was engineered by the young Chhetri noble Jung Bahadur and it catapulted his family into power, just as it sidelined the Shah dynasty.

Ambitious and ruthless, Jung Bahadur organised (with the queen's consent) for his soldiers to massacre 55 of the most important noblemen in the kingdom while they were assembled in the Kot courtyard adjoining Kathmandu's Durbar Sq. He then exiled 6000 members of their families to prevent revenge attacks.

Jung Bahadur took the title of prime minister and changed his family name to the more prestigious 'Rana'. He later extended his title to maharajah (king) and decreed it hereditary. The Ranas became a parallel 'royal family' within the kingdom and held the reins of power – the Shah kings became listless figureheads, requiring permission even to leave their palace.

Visit the birthplace and launching pad of Nepal's unifier, Prithvi Narayan Shah, at Gorkha (p239).

A History of Nepal by John Whelpton is one of the few available titles on the subject. It concentrates on the last 250 years and explains not only political events but also changes in people's lives. It's cheaper to buy in Nepal than abroad.

1428–82	1531–34	1641–74
Rule of Yaksha Malla, the high point of Malla kings, ends in the fracture of the Kathmandu Valley into the three rival kingdoms of Kathmandu, Patan and Bhaktapur.	Sherpas (literally 'easterners') settle in the Solu-Khumbu region near Mt Everest. The Nangpa La pass remains the most important Sherpa trade route with Tibet.	Rule of Malla king Pratap Malla, a dancer, poet and great supporter of arts, who shapes the face of Kathmandu, building large parts of Hanuman Dhoka palace.

The family line of Rana prime ministers held power for more than a century, eventually intermarrying with the Shahs. Development in Nepal stagnated, although the country did manage to preserve its independence. Only on rare occasions were visitors allowed into Nepal.

Jung Bahadur Rana travelled to Europe in 1850, attending the opera and the races at Epsom, and brought back a taste for neoclassical architecture that can be seen in Kathmandu today. To the Ranas' credit, while they were in power *sati* (the Hindu practice of casting a widow on her husband's funeral pyre) was abolished, 60,000 slaves were released from bondage, and a school and college were established in the capital. But while the Ranas and their relatives lived lives of opulent luxury, the peasants in the hills were locked in a medieval existence.

Modernisation began to dawn on Kathmandu with the opening of the Bir Hospital, Nepal's first, in 1889, the first piped water system, limited electricity and the construction of the Singh Durbar. In 1923 Britain formally acknowledged Nepal's independence and in 1930 the kingdom of Gorkha was renamed the kingdom of Nepal, reflecting a growing sense of national consciousness.

The arrival of the Indian railway line at the Nepali border greatly aided the transportation of goods but sounded a death knell for the caravan trade that bartered Nepali grain and rice for Tibetan salt. The transborder trade suffered another setback when the British opened a second, more direct trade route with Tibet through Sikkim's Chumbi Valley (the real nail in the coffin came in the 1960s, when the Chinese closed the border to local trade).

Elsewhere in the region dramatic changes were taking place. The Nepalis supplied logistical help during Britain's invasion of Tibet in 1903, and over 300,000 Nepalis fought in WWI and WWII, garnering a total of 13 Victoria Crosses – Britain's highest military honour – for their efforts.

After WWII India gained its independence and the communist revolution took place in China. Tibetan refugees fled into Nepal in the first of several waves when the new People's Republic of China tightened its grip on Tibet, and Nepal became a buffer zone between the two rival Asian giants. At the same time King Tribhuvan, forgotten in his palace, was being primed to overthrow the Ranas.

RESTORATION OF THE SHAHS

In late 1950 King Tribhuvan was driving himself to a hunting trip at Nagarjun when he suddenly swerved James Bond–style into the expecting Indian embassy, claimed political immunity and was flown to Delhi in an Indian Air Force jet. Meanwhile, the recently formed Nepali Congress Party, led by BP Koirala, managed to take most of the Terai by force from the Ranas and established a provisional government that ruled from the border town of Birganj. India exerted its considerable influence and negotiated a solution to Nepal's turmoil, and King Tribhuvan returned in glory to Nepal in 1951 to set up a new government composed of demoted Ranas and members of the Nepali Congress Party.

Jung Bahadur Rana broke a religious taboo by becoming the first Nepali ruler to cross the *kalo pani* (black water, or ocean) and thus temporarily losing his caste, when he travelled to Europe in 1850.

For an overview of Kathmandu's crumbling Rana palaces see the boxed text Kathmandu's Royal Palaces, p129.

The first cars were transported to the Kathmandu Valley in parts, on the backs of porters, before there were even any roads or petrol in the kingdom.

1729	**1750**	**1768–69**
The three kingdoms of the Kathmandu Valley send presents to the Qing court in Beijing, which from then on views Nepal as a tributary state.	King Jaya Prakash Malla builds Kathmandu's Kumari Temple. Not long afterwards comes the Nyatapola Temple in Bhaktapur, the literal highpoint of stupa-style architecture in Nepal.	Nepal unified under Prithvi Narayan Shah (1723–75), known as the father of the Nepali nation, to form the Shah dynasty. Kathmandu becomes the capital.

HISTORY OF MOUNTAINEERING IN NEPAL

Mountaineering became a fashionable pursuit in Europe during the second half of the 19th century and after knocking off the main Alpine peaks, Europeans turned their gaze to the greater challenge of the Himalaya. Englishman WW Graham reached the top of a 6000m Nepali peak in 1883 and he was followed by another Englishman, Tom Longstaff, who climbed the Indian peak of Trisuli (7215m) in 1907. For the next 20 years this remained the highest summit reached in the world, until Bill Tilman's ascent of India's Nanda Devi in 1936.

The opening of Nepal to foreigners in the 1950s ushered in the golden decade of Himalayan mountaineering. Trekker-mountaineers like WH Tilman and Eric Shipton pioneered the southern approach routes to Everest, which had previously been tackled from the northern Tibetan side. The French were the first to claim an 8000m peak, summiting Annapurna in 1950. Three years later Hillary and Tenzing 'knocked the bastard off', conquering Everest just in time for the coronation of Queen Elizabeth II. The big peaks fell like dominoes: Cho Oyu in 1954 (Austrians), Kanchenjunga (British) and Makalu (French) in 1955, Lhotse (Swiss) and Manaslu (Japanese) in 1956 and, finally, Dhaulagiri in 1960 (Swiss).

The 1953 British expedition to Everest marked the trend towards larger and larger military-style expeditions. The few climbers who reached the summit did so with aid of a huge pyramid of supporters below them, including dozens of Sherpa guides and hundreds of local porters.

By the early 1970s the emphasis had shifted to smaller-scale, more technical climbs such as the south face of Annapurna and the southwest face of Everest, both of which were climbed

Although Nepal gradually reopened its long-closed doors and established relations with other nations, dreams of a new democratic system were not permanently realised. Tribhuvan died in 1955 and was succeeded by his cautious son Mahendra. A new constitution provided for a parliamentary system of government and in 1959 Nepal held its first general election. The Nepali Congress Party won a clear victory and BP Koirala became the new prime minister. In late 1960, however, the king decided the government wasn't to his taste after all, and he had the cabinet arrested and swapped his ceremonial role for real control (much as King Gyanendra would do 46 years later).

In 1962 Mahendra decided that a partyless, indirect *panchayat* (council) system of government was more appropriate to Nepal. The real power remained with the king, who chose 16 members of the 35-member National Panchayat, and appointed the prime minister and his cabinet. Political parties were banned.

Mahendra died in 1972 and was succeeded by his 27-year-old British-educated son Birendra. Nepal's hippy community was unceremoniously booted out of the country when visa laws were tightened in the run-up to Birendra's spectacular coronation in 1975. Simmering discontent with corruption, the slow rate of development and the rising cost of living erupted into violent riots in Kathmandu in 1979. King Birendra announced a

1790–92	1814–16	1846
Nepal invades Tibet and sacks Shigatse. Avenging Chinese troops advance down the Kyirong Valley as far as Nuwakot. As part of the ensuing treaty the Nepalis pay tribute to the Chinese emperor until 1912.	Anglo-Nepali War ends in victory for Britain. The ensuing Treaty of Sugauli establishes Nepal's modern boundaries and gives Britain the right to recruit Gurkha soldiers in Nepal and maintain a residency in Kathmandu.	The Kot Massacre ends in the killing of the cream of the court aristocracy, ushering in the Rana era (1846–1951) and sidelining the Shah kings to puppet status.

brilliantly by expeditions led by Chris Bonington. The great Italian climber Reinhold Messner pulled off several spectacular ascents, including the first ascent of Everest without oxygen in 1978 and the first solo ascent from the north side in 1980 (from base camp to the summit and back in 48 hours). Messner became the first person to summit all 14 of the world's 8000m peaks.

The effect on the environment was devastating, as forests fell to provide firewood for the expeditions and vast amounts of mountaineering equipment, oxygen canisters, garbage and even dead bodies were left behind on the high glaciers. Everest Base Camp quickly earned the dubious title of 'world's highest garbage dump'.

By the 1990s climbing in general and Everest in particular had become increasingly commercialised. The much-publicised 1996 'Into Thin Air' disaster highlighted the reality that many inexperienced climbers are now assisted to the summit on commercial climbs. Stories of human traffic jams at the Hillary Step, and of sick climbers left to die on the mountain by climbers desperate to reach the summit have tarnished the mountain's reputation. With an organised climb fee averaging US$65,000 per person, Everest has become a moneymaker – a rock star surrounded by groupies eager to share in its fame. While Everest has come to symbolise the high point of human achievement, it also represents the worst of modern climbing.

'I think the whole attitude towards climbing Everest has become rather horrifying,' was the opinion of Edmund Hillary in 2006. 'Human life is far more important than getting to the top of a mountain.'

referendum to choose between the *panchayat* system and one that would permit political parties to operate. The result was 55% to 45% in favour of the *panchayat* system; democracy had been outvoted.

Nepal's military and police apparatus were among the least publicly accountable in the world and strict censorship was enforced. Mass arrests, torture and beatings of suspected activists were well documented, and the leaders of the main opposition, the Nepali Congress, spent the years between 1960 and 1990 in and out of prison.

During this time there were impressive movements towards development, namely in education and road construction, with the number of schools increasing from 300 in 1950 to over 40,000 by 2000. But the relentless population growth (Nepal's population grew from 8.4 million in 1954 to 26 million in 2004) cancelled out many of these advances, turning Nepal from a food exporter to a net importer within a generation. It is also widely accepted that huge portions of foreign aid were creamed off into royal and ministerial accounts.

During this time over one million hill people moved to the Terai in search of land and several million crossed the border to seek work in India (Nepalis are able to cross the border and work freely in India), creating a major demographic shift in favour of the now malaria-free Terai.

When King Gyanendra was crowned in 2001 he may well have experienced a feeling of déjà vu – he had already been crowned once before, aged three, and ruled as king for three months, after his grandfather Tribhuvan fled to India in 1950.

1854	**1856**	**1911**
Legal code called the *Muluki Ain* formalises the pre-existing Nepali caste system, defining diet, legal and sexual codes and enshrining state discrimination against the lower castes. The law is revised only in 1963.	Peak XV is declared the world's highest peak. It is later renamed Everest after the head of Trigonometric Survey, George Everest (who actually pronounced his name *eve*-rest).	King George V visits the Terai on a hunting trip as a guest of the maharajah of Nepal, bagging 39 tigers, 18 rhinos and four bears, travelling on elephant back and with a small army of beaters.

PEOPLE POWER

In 1989, as communist states across Europe crumbled and pro-democracy demonstrations occupied China's Tiananmen Sq, Nepali opposition parties formed a coalition to fight for a multiparty democracy with the king as constitutional head; the upsurge of protest was called the Jana Andolan, or People's Movement.

In early 1990 the government responded to a nonviolent gathering of over 200,000 people with bullets, tear gas and thousands of arrests. After several months of intermittent rioting, curfews, a successful strike, and pressure from various foreign-aid donors, the government was forced to back down. The people's victory did not come cheaply; it is estimated that more than 300 people lost their lives.

On 9 April King Birendra announced he was lifting the ban on political parties and was ready to accept the role of constitutional monarch. Nepal was a democracy.

In May 1991, 20 parties contested a general election for a 205-seat parliament. The Nepali Congress won power, with the Communist Party of Nepal-Unified Marxist-Leninist (CPN-UML) the next largest party. In the years immediately following the election, the political atmosphere remained uneasy. In April 1992 a general strike degenerated into street violence between protesters and police, and resulted in a number of deaths.

In late 1994 the Nepali Congress government, led by GP Koirala (brother of BP Koirala), called a midterm election. No party won a clear mandate, and a coalition formed between the CPN-UML and the third major party, the Rastriya Prajatantra Party (RPP), the old *panchayats*, with the support of the Nepali Congress. This was one of the few times in the world that a communist government had come to power by popular vote.

Political stability did not last long, and the late 1990s were littered with dozens of broken coalitions, dissolved governments and sacked politicians. After a decade of democracy it seemed an increasing number of people, particularly young Nepalis and those living in the countryside, were utterly disillusioned.

THE PEOPLE'S WAR

In 1996 the Maoists, a communist party splinter group, fed up with government corruption, the failure of democracy to deliver improvements to the people, and the dissolution of the communist government, declared a 'people's war'. The Maoists presented the then prime minister with a 40-point charter of demands that ranged from preferential state policies towards backward communities to an assertive Nepali identity, an end to public schools and better governance.

The insurgency began in the Rolpa district of midwestern Nepal and gathered momentum, but was initially ignored by Kathmandu's politicians.

Confusingly, three Koirala brothers have all served as prime ministers of Nepal; BP Koirala in 1959, MP Koirala in 1951 and 1953 and GP Koirala, four times, the latest in 2006.

For background on the Maoist rebellion read *Himalayan People's War: Nepal's Maoist Rebellion*, edited by Michael Hutt.

1934	1951	1953
A massive earthquake with its epicentre just south of Mt Everest destroys much of the Kathmandu Valley, killing over 8000 people in under a minute, injuring 16,000 and destroying a quarter of all homes in Nepal.	King Tribhuvan and the Nepal Congress Party, with Indian support, overthrow the Rana regime and establish a new coalition government. Nepal opens its doors to the outside world, including mountaineers.	Everest is summited for the first time by New Zealander Edmund Hillary and Tibetan Sherpa Tenzing Norgay on 29 May, just in time for the coronation of Queen Elizabeth II.

The repercussions of this nonchalance finally came to a head in November 2001 when the Maoists broke their ceasefire and an army barracks was attacked west of Kathmandu. The initial Maoist forces were armed with little more than ancient muskets and khukuris (Ghurkha knives) but they quickly obtained guns looted from police stations, homemade explosives and automatic weapons, all bankrolled by robbery and extortion and aided by an open border with India.

Initial police heavy-handedness fuelled a cycle of violence and retribution that only succeeded in alienating the local people. Political disenfranchisement, rural poverty, resentment against the caste system, issues of land reform and a lack of faith in the squabbling and self-interested politicians of distant Kathmandu swelled the ranks of the Maoists, who at their peak numbered 15,000 fighters, with a further militia of 50,000. Attacks spread to almost every one of Nepal's 75 districts, including Kathmandu. At their peaks Maoists effectively controlled around 40% of the country, including two protected areas in the far west and several of Nepal's main trekking routes (for years trekkers in the Annapurna region were forced to hand over 'donations' to Maoist gangs).

The political temperature rose after the king brought in the army and armed militias loyal to the government in 2001. The USA labelled Nepal's Maoists a terrorist group and handed over millions of dollars to help fight Nepal's own 'war on terror'. Although self-declared Maoists, the group owed more to Peru's Sendero Luminoso (Shining Path) than to any Chinese connection.

The Maoist insurgency only worsened the plight of the rural poor by bombing bridges and telephone lines, halting road construction, diverting much-needed government funds away from development and causing aid programs to suspend activity due to security concerns. An entire generation of rural Nepali children missed out on their education in the decade long conflict.

Several Maoist truces, notably in 2003 and 2005, offered some respite, though these reflected as much a need to regroup and rearm as they did any move towards a lasting peace. By 2005 nearly 13,000 people, including many civilians, had been killed in the insurgency, more than half of them following the royal order to send in the army. Amnesty International accused both sides of horrific human-rights abuses, including summary executions, abductions, torture and child conscription. Dark days had come to Nepal.

ROYAL TROUBLES & POLITICAL CHANGE

On 1 June 2001 the Nepali psyche was dealt a huge blow when Crown Prince Dipendra gunned down almost every member of the royal family during a get-together in Kathmandu (see the boxed text, p42). A monarch who had steered the country through some extraordinarily difficult times

Even wildlife was affected by the civil war. Nepal's population of rhinos dropped from 612 in 2000 to 379 in 2005, mostly due to increased poaching as park check-posts were destroyed and troops transferred away from national parks.

Forget Kathmandu: An Elegy for Democracy, by Manjushree Thapa, starts with Nepal's royal massacre, moves to a political history of the last 200 years, then ends with a description of a trek through Maoist-held areas in 2003. Its insights into the recent political chaos attempt to answer the question: 'What the hell happened to Nepal?'

1954	1955–72	1959
Boris Lissanevitch establishes Nepal's first hotel, the Royal, in the Bahadur Bhawan palace. Its Yak and Yeti Bar becomes the expat hub for mountaineers and diplomats until its closure in 1971.	Rule of King Mahendra sees the introduction of elections, which are then voided as the king seizes direct power, introducing the *panchayat* system of government.	Nepal's first general elections. The Dalai Lama flees Tibet and China closes the Tibet–Nepal border, seriously affecting trade of salt for grain and creating great social change in some northern regions of Nepal.

THE ROYAL MASSACRE – FOR THE LOVE OF A WOMAN?

The night of 1 June 2001 has entered the annals of history as one of Nepal's greatest tragedies, a bloodbath that could have been lifted straight from the pages of a Shakespearean tragedy.

That night, in a hail of bullets, 10 members of Nepal's royal family including King Birendra and Queen Aishwarya were gunned down during a gathering at the Narayanhiti Palace by a deranged, drunken Crown Prince Dipendra, who eventually turned a weapon on himself. Dipendra did not die straight away and, ironically, despite being in a coma, was pronounced the king of Nepal. His rule ended two days later, when he too was declared dead. The real motive behind the massacre will never be known, but many believe Dipendra's murderous drug-fuelled rage was prompted by his parents' disapproval of the woman he wanted to marry.

In the days that followed the massacre, a tide of emotions washed over the Nepali people – shock, grief, horror, disbelief and denial. A 13-day period of mourning was declared and in Kathmandu impromptu shrines were set up for people to pray for their king and queen. About 400 shaven-headed men roamed the streets around the palace on motorbikes, carrying pictures of the monarch. Half a million stunned Nepalis lined the streets during the funeral procession. All over the city, barbers were shaving the heads of other men, a mark of grief in Hindu tradition.

The initial disbelief and shock gave way to suspicion and a host of conspiracy theories, many concerning the new king, Gyanendra (who was in Pokhara at the time of the massacre), and his son Paras (who emerged unscathed from the attack). None of this was helped by an official enquiry that initially suggested the automatic weapon had been discharged *by accident* (killing nine people!), or the fact that the victims were quickly cremated without full post mortems and the palace building then razed to the ground. Other theories included that old chestnut – a CIA or Indian secret-service plot.

A surreal royal exorcism followed on the 11th day of mourning, as a high-caste priest, dressed in the gold suit, shoes and black-rimmed glasses of King Birendra and donning a paper crown, climbed onto an elephant and slowly lumbered out of the valley, taking with him the ghost of the dead king. The same scapegoat ritual (known as a *katto* ceremony) was performed for Dipendra, except that a pregnant woman dashed underneath his elephant en route, believing this would ensure she give birth to a boy. She was trampled by the elephant and died, adding a further twist to the tragedy.

Doubtless the truth of what really happened that night will never be known. In the words of Nepali journalist Manjushree Thapa: 'We lost the truth; we lost our history. We are left to recount anecdotes and stories, to content ourselves with myth.'

---

was gone. When the shock of this loss subsided the uncertainty of what lay ahead hit home.

The beginning of the 21st century saw the political situation in the country turn from bad to worse. Prime ministers were sacked and replaced in 2000, 2001, 2002, 2003, 2004 and 2005, making a total of nine governments in 10 years. The fragile position of Nepali politicians is well illustrated by Sher Bahadur Deuba, who was appointed prime minister for the second time in

1960	1973	1975
Eradication of malaria opens the Terai to rapid population growth for the first time. Today the Terai contains up to half of Nepal's population, as well as most of its industry and flat agricultural land.	Army operation to dislodge bands of Tibetan Khampa fighters, who have been launching raids into Chinese-occupied Tibet from bases in Mustang. The Dalai Lama sends a message asking the rebels to disband.	Birendra is crowned king in Kathmandu's Hanuman Dhoka, three years after the death of his father Mahendra. At a time ordained by astrologers, the king wears the jewel-encrusted and feathered headdress of the Shah kings.

2001, before being dismissed in 2002, reinstated in 2004, sacked again in 2005, thrown in jail on corruption charges and then released! Against such a background, modern politics in Nepal is generally perceived as having more to do with personal enrichment than any kind of public service.

Nepal's disappointing experiment with democracy faced a major setback in February 2005 when King Gyanendra dissolved the government, amid a state of emergency, promising a return to democracy within three years. Freedom of the press was curtailed and telephone lines were cut periodically to prevent mass demonstrations. The unpopular king was not helped by his son and heir, Prince Paras, who was allegedly involved in several drunken hit-and-run car accidents, one of which killed a popular Nepali singer. Tourism levels slumped as a mood of pessimism descended over the country.

Everything changed in April 2006, when days of mass demonstrations, curfews and the deaths of 16 protestors forced the king to restore parliamentary democracy. The following month the newly restored parliament voted to reduce the king to a figurehead, ending powers that the royal Shah lineage had enjoyed for over 200 years. The removal of the king was the price required to bring the Maoists to the negotiating table and a peace accord was signed later that year, drawing a close to the bloody decade-long insurgency.

The pace of political change in Nepal was remarkable. The Maoists achieved a majority in the elections of 10 April 2008 and a month later parliament abolished the monarchy by a margin of 560 votes to four, ending 240 years of royal rule. Former Maoist 'terrorists' became cabinet ministers, members of the People's Liberation Army joined the national army and a new constitution was being written at the time of research, all as part of a process to bind the former guerrillas into the political mainstream. A renewed optimism in the political process was palpable throughout Nepal.

THE HARD WORK BEGINS

By 2008 a new government was formed, with former guerrilla leaders Pushpa Kamal Dahal (known by his *nom de guerre* Prachanda, which means 'the Fierce') as prime minister and Dr Baburam Bhattarai as finance minister. Ironically the 'People's' armed struggle was led by two high-caste intellectuals.

A key aim for the future has been to complete a new, more inclusive Nepali constitution. For decades government in Nepal was dominated by a narrow band of castes and ethnicities – Newars, Chhetris and Bahuns – with little regional representation. Ethnic minorities, lower castes and women's groups have been clamouring for their voices to be heard in the new political environment.

There has still been plenty of potential for political instability. In 2009 Prime Minister Pushpa Kamal Dahal resigned due to infighting, leaving the leadership in tatters. Calls for greater representation by groups such as

Massacre at the Palace: The Doomed Royal Dynasty of Nepal, by Jonathan Gregson, takes a wider look at Nepal's royal family and reveals that assassination and murder have been part of royal life for centuries; it also examines the recent massacre. Also published as *Blood Against the Snows.*

Following the 2008 abolition of the monarchy, the king's face was removed from the Rs 10 note, the prefix 'Royal' disappeared from the name of the national airline as well as national parks, and the king's birthday was dumped as a national holiday.

1990	1996–2005	11 May 1996
The mass demonstrations of the People's Movement force King Birendra to accept a new constitution, restoring democracy and relegating the king to the role of constitutional Hindu monarch under a multiparty democracy.	A decade-long Maoist insurgency brings the country to its knees and results in the death of 13,000 Nepalis. Development projects stall and tourism levels plummet.	Eight climbers die on single day during a fierce storm on Mt Everest, making this the single-worst year for Everest fatalities. An IMAX film and Jon Krakauer's book *Into Thin Air* chronicle the disaster.

the Madhesi of the Terai (who make up 35% of the population and live in the most productive and industrialised part of country) have resulted in a familiar pattern of economic blockades and political violence, and are only the beginning of many more possible claims. Political violence has continued to simmer in the Terai. The wounds of the People's War will take a long time to heal. Over 1000 Nepalis remain unaccounted for, victims of political 'disappearance' or simple murder and finding justice for these crimes may prove elusive.

Moreover, after 40 years and over US$4 billion in aid (60% of its development budget) Nepal has remained one of the world's poorest countries, with seven million Nepalis lacking adequate food or basic health care and education. Nepal has one of the lowest health spending levels and the third-highest infant mortality rate in the world.

The majority of Nepalis have continued stoically with their rural lives but until the government delivers on real social change and economic development in the countryside, the frustrations that fuelled Nepal's recent political violence will remain unresolved.

Tourism generates around US$260 million each year in foreign earnings for Nepal and it is estimated that the money spent by each tourist supports 10 or 11 Nepalis.

2001	2006	2008
Prince Dipendra bursts into the Narayanhiti Palace and massacres 10 members of the royal family, including his father, King Birendra, before shooting himself. The king's brother, Gyanendra, is crowned king of Nepal.	After weeks of protests, King Gyanendra reinstates parliament, which votes to curtail his emergency powers. Maoists and government officials sign a peace agreement and the Maoist rebels enter an interim government.	Nepal abolishes the monarchy and becomes a federal democratic republic, with former Maoist guerrilla leader Pushpa Kamal Dahal ('Prachanda') as the first prime minister. Prachanda resigns a year later.

The Culture

THE NATIONAL PSYCHE

Nepal's location between India and Tibet, the diversity of its 60 or more ethnic and caste groups, its isolating geography and myriad (up to 100) languages have resulted in a complex pattern of customs and beliefs that make it hard to generalise about a 'Nepali people'.

Perhaps the dominant Nepali cultural concepts are those of caste and status, both of which contribute to a strictly defined system of hierarchy and deference. Caste determines not only a person's status, but also their career and marriage partner, how that person interacts with other Nepalis and how others react back. This system of hierarchy extends even to the family, where everyone has a clearly defined rank. The Nepali language has half a dozen words for 'you', each of which conveys varying shades of respect.

When it comes to their religious beliefs, Nepalis are admirably flexible, pragmatic and, above all, tolerant – there is almost no religious or ethnic tension in Nepal. Nepalis are generally good humoured and patient, quick to smile and slow to anger, though they also have a reputation as fierce fighters (witness the famous Gurkha forces; p259).

The Nepali view of the world is dominated by prayer and ritual and a knowledge that the gods are not remote, abstract concepts but living, present beings, who can influence human affairs in very direct ways. Nepalis perceive the divine everywhere, from the greeting *namaste*, which literally means 'I greet the divine inside of you', to the spirits and gods present in trees, passes, sacred river confluences and mountain peaks.

The notions of karma and caste, when combined with a tangled bureaucracy and deep-rooted corruption, tend to create an endemic sense of fatalism in Nepal. Confronted with problems, many Nepalis will simply respond with a shrug of the shoulders and the phrase *khe garne?*, or 'what is there to do?', which Westerners often find frustrating, and oddly addictive.

TRADITIONAL LIFESTYLE

The cornerstones of Nepali life are the demands (and rewards) of one's family, ethnic group and caste. To break these time-honoured traditions is to risk being ostracised from family and community. While young Nepali people, especially in urban areas, are increasingly influenced by Western values and lifestyle, the vast majority of people live by traditional customs and principles. The biggest modernising influences are probably satellite TV, roads and tourism – in that order.

In most ethnic groups, joint and extended families live in the same house, even in Kathmandu. In some smaller villages extended clans make up the entire community. Traditional family life has been dislocated by the large number (over one million) of Nepali men forced to seek work away from home, whether in Kathmandu or the Terai, or abroad in India, Malaysia or the Gulf States.

Arranged marriages remain the norm in Nepali Hindu society and are generally between members of the same caste or ethnic group, although there are a growing number of 'love marriages'. Child marriages have been illegal since 1963 and today the average age of marriage for girls is just under 19 years old. The family connections generated by a marriage are as much a social contract as a personal affair, and most families consult matchmakers and astrologers when making such an important decision.

If you are heading off on a trek (or flying on Nepal Airlines), bear in mind that according to Nepali superstition it's bad luck to start a journey on Tuesday or return on a Saturday.

Up to half a million Nepali men seek seasonal work in Indian cities; in 2007 they sent home US$760 million to one-third of Nepali families, making this Nepal's largest single source of foreign currency.

Nepal ranks 142 out of 177 countries, according to the 2008 UN Human Development Index, below India, Pakistan and Bangladesh. Only three other Asian countries rank lower.

MOVING TIGERS

Nepal's national board game is bagh chal, which literally means 'move the tigers'. The game is played on a lined board with 25 intersecting points. One player has four tigers, the other has 20 goats, and the aim is for the tiger player to 'eat' five goats by jumping over them before the goat player can encircle the tigers and prevent them moving. You can buy attractive brass bagh chal sets in Kathmandu and Patan where they are made.

Nepal's other popular game is *carom*, which looks like finger snooker; players use discs which glide over a chalked-up board to pot other discs into the corner pockets.

HIV/AIDS has become a major problem in Nepal. There are an estimated 75,000 Nepalis infected with the virus, 40% of whom are migrant workers. Over 30,000 intravenous drug users in Nepal are at risk of contracting the virus.

The website www .mountainvoices .org/nepal.asp has an interesting collection of interviews with Nepali mountain folk on a wide variety of topics.

To decide not to have children is almost unheard of and Nepali women will often pity you if you are childless. Having a son is particularly important, especially for Hindu families, as some religious rites (such as lighting the funeral pyre to ensure a peaceful passage into the next life) can only be performed by the eldest son. Girls are regarded by many groups as a financial burden whose honour needs to be protected until she is married off.

Children stay at school for up to 12 years; 70% of children will begin school but only 7% will reach their 10th school year, when they sit their School Leaving Certificate (SLC) board examination. Many villages only have a primary school, which means children either have to walk long distances each day or board in a bigger town to attend secondary school. The ratio of boys to girls at both primary and secondary schools is almost 2:1 in favour of boys.

Despite what you may see in Kathmandu and Pokhara, Nepal is overwhelmingly rural and poor. Farming is still the main occupation and debt is a factor in most people's lives. Large areas of land are still owned by *zamindars* (absent landlords) and up to 50% of a landless farmer's production will go to the landowner as rent. The UN estimates that 68% of Nepalis get by on less than US$2 per day.

Most rural Nepali families are remarkably self-sufficient in their food supply, raising all of it themselves and selling any excess in the nearest town, where they'll stock up on things like sugar, soap, cigarettes, tea, salt, cloth and jewellery. Throughout Nepal this exchange of goods has created a dense network of trails trodden by everyone from traders and porters to mule caravans and trekking groups.

Rice is grown up to altitudes of 2000m; corn, wheat and millet up to 2800m; then barley, buckwheat and potatoes up to 4000m. Fields of yellow-flowering mustard are planted for making cooking oil, and soya beans, lentils, chilli peppers and sesame are grown on the berms that divide plots.

The rhythms of village life are determined by the seasons and marked by festivals – New Year, harvest and religious festivals being most important. Dasain remains the biggest event of the calendar in the Middle Hills and a time when most Nepali families get together.

Older people are respected members of the community and are cared for by their children. Old age is a time for relaxation, prayer and meditation. The dead are generally cremated and the deceased's sons will shave their heads and wear white for an entire year following the death.

For a guide to some cultural dos and don'ts when visiting Nepal, see p74.

POPULATION

Nepal currently has a population of around 30 million (2008 estimate), a number that is increasing at the rapid rate of 2.1% annually. Over 2.5 million people live in the Kathmandu Valley and perhaps one million in Kathmandu. Four million Nepalis reside in India. Nepal remains overwhelmingly rural; 85% of people live in the countryside. Around half of Nepal's population live in the flat fertile lands of the Terai, which also acts as the nation's industrial base, and the population here is increasing rapidly.

There are around 130,000 refugees, some Tibetan, but most expelled from Bhutan, kept in camps in the far east of the country.

PEOPLE

The human geography of Nepal is a remarkable cultural mosaic of peoples who have not so much assimilated as learned to coexist. The ethnic divisions are complex and numerous; you'll have to do your homework to be able to differentiate between a Limbu, Lepcha, Lhopa or Lhomi – and that's just the Ls! Kathmandu remains the best place to see a wide range of ethnic groups, including Rai, Newar, Sherpa, Tamang and Gurung.

Simplistically, Nepal is the meeting place of the Indo-Aryan people of India and the Mongoloid peoples of the Himalaya. There are three main cultural zones running east to west: the north including the high Himalaya; the Middle Hills; and the Terai. Each group has adapted its lifestyle and farming practices to its environment but, thanks largely to Nepal's tortured topography, has retained its own traditions. Social taboos, especially among caste Hindus, have limited further assimilation between groups.

Nepal's diverse ethnic groups speak somewhere between 24 and 100 different languages and dialects depending on how finely the distinctions are made. Nepali functions as the unifying language, though less than half of Nepal's people speak Nepali as their first language.

People of Nepal, by Dor Bahadur Bista, describes the many diverse ethnic groupings found in the country and is written by the country's foremost anthropologist.

Himalayan Zone

The hardy Tibetan peoples who inhabit the high Himalaya are known in Nepal as Bhotias (Bhotiyas), a slightly derogatory term among caste Hindus. Each group remains distinct but their languages are all Tibetan-based and, with a few exceptions, they are Tibetan Buddhists.

The Bhotiyas' names combine the region they came from with the suffix 'pa' and include the Sherpas (literally 'easterners') of the Everest region, the Dolpopas of the west and the Lopas, or Lobas (literally 'southerners'), of the Mustang region.

The withering of trans-Himalayan trade routes and the difficulty of farming and herding at high altitude drives these people to lower elevations during winter, either to graze their animals or to trade in India and the Terai. Yak herding and the barley harvest remain the economic bedrocks of the high Himalaya.

Changes in trading patterns and traditional culture among Nepal's Himalayan people are examined in *Himalayan Traders*, by Von Fürer-Haimendorf.

THAKALIS

Originating along the Kali Gandaki Valley in central Nepal, the Thakalis have emerged as the entrepreneurs of Nepal. They once played an important part in the salt trade between the subcontinent and Tibet, and today they are active in many areas of commercial life. Originally Buddhist, many pragmatic Thakalis have now adopted Hinduism. Most Thakalis have small farms, but travellers will regularly meet them in their adopted roles as hoteliers and lodge owners, especially on the Annapurna Circuit.

TAMANGS

The Tamangs make up one of largest groups in the country. They live mainly in the hills north of Kathmandu and have a noticeably strong Tibetan influence, from their monasteries, known as *ghyang*, to the mani walls that mark the entrance to their villages.

According to some accounts, the Tamang's ancestors were horse traders and cavalrymen from an invading Tibetan army who settled in Nepal. They are well known for their independence and suspicion of authority, probably caused by the fact that in the 19th century they were relegated to a low status and seriously exploited, with much of their land distributed to Bahuns and Chhetris. As bonded labourers they were dependent upon menial work such as portering. Many of the 'Tibetan' souvenirs, carpets and thangkas (religious paintings) you see in Kathmandu are made by Tamangs.

TIBETANS

About 12,000 of the 120,000 Tibetans in exile around the world live in Nepal. The heavy hand of the Chinese during the 1950s and the flight of the Dalai Lama in 1959 resulted in waves of refugees who settled mainly in Kathmandu or Pokhara.

Although their numbers are small, Tibetans have a high profile, partly because of the important role they play in tourism. Many hotels and restaurants in Kathmandu are owned or operated by Tibetans. They are also responsible for the extraordinary success of the Tibetan carpet industry (see the boxed text, p62).

Tibetans are devout Buddhists and their arrival in the valley has rejuvenated a number of important religious sites, most notably the stupas at Swayambhunath (p164) and Bodhnath (p174). A number of large, new Buddhist monasteries have been constructed on the outskirts of Kathmandu in recent years.

High Religion, by Sherry B Ortner, is probably the best introduction to Sherpa history, culture, religion and traditional society, though it was written in 1989 and is a little dated. Also worth looking for is Sherpa of the Khumbu by Barbara Brower.

SHERPAS

The Sherpas who live high in the mountains of eastern and central Nepal are probably the best-known Nepali ethnic group. These nomadic Tibetan herders moved to the Solu Khumbu region of Nepal 500 years ago from eastern Tibet, bringing with them their Tibetan Buddhist religion and building the beautiful gompas (monasteries) that dot the steep hillsides. They are strongly associated with the Khumbu region around Mt Everest, although only 3000 of the total 35,000 Sherpas actually live in the Khumbu; the rest live in the lower valleys of the Solu region.

Tourism stepped in after the collapse of trade over the Nangpa La pass in 1959, following the Chinese invasion of Tibet, and these days the Sherpa name is synonymous with mountaineering and trekking. Potatoes were introduced to the region in the late 19th century and are now the main Sherpa crop. Sherpas are famously hard drinkers.

Sherpas: Reflections on Change in Himalayan Nepal, by James F Fisher, offers an anthropological snapshot of how tourism and modernisation has affected Sherpa religious and cultural life. Fisher worked with Edmund Hillary in the Khumbu in the 1960s, bringing the first schools and airstrip to the region.

Midlands Zone

The Middle Hills of Nepal are the best places to witness village life at its most rustic. In the east are the Kirati, who are divided into the Rai and Limbu groups. The Newari people dominate the central hills around the Kathmandu Valley, while the Magars and Gurungs inhabit the hills of the Kali Gandaki northwest of Pokhara.

Moving west, the Bahun and Chhetri are the dominant groups, although the lines between castes have become blurred over time.

RAIS & LIMBUS

The Rais and Limbus are thought to have ruled the Kathmandu Valley in the 7th century BC until they were defeated around AD 300. They then moved into the steep hill country of eastern Nepal, from the Arun Valley to the Sikkim border, where many remain today. Others have moved to the Terai or India as economic migrants. Many Rai work as porters in the Middle Hills.

Describing themselves as Kirati, these tribes are easily distinguishable by their Mongolian features. They are of Tibeto-Burmese descent and their

NEPALI NAMES

You can tell a lot about a Nepali person from their name, including often their caste, profession, ethnic group and where they live. Gurung and Sherpa are ethnic groups as well as surnames. The surname Bista or Pant indicates that the person is a Brahman, originally from western Nepal; Devkota indicates an eastern origin. Thapa, Pande and Bhasnet are names related to the former Rana ruling family. Shrestha is a high-caste Newari name. The initials KC often stand for Khatri Chhetri, a mixed-caste name. The surname Kami is the Nepali equivalent of Smith.

Sherpa names even reveal which day of the week the person was born – Dawa (Monday), Mingmar (Tuesday), Lhakpa (Wednesday), Phurba (Thursday), Pasang (Friday), Pemba (Saturday) and Nyima (Sunday). Ironically the one thing you can't tell from a Sherpa name is their sex – Lhakpa Sherpa could be a man or a woman!

traditional religion is distinct from Buddhism and Hinduism, although the latter is exerting a growing influence. Himalayan hunter-warriors, they are still excellent soldiers and are well represented in the Gurkha regiments.

Many of the men still carry a large khukuri (traditional curved knife) tucked into their belt and wear a *topi* (traditional Nepali cap). Some communities in upper Arun live in bamboo houses.

NEWARS

The Newars of the Kathmandu Valley number about 1.1 million and make up 6% of the population. Their language, Newari, is distinct from Tibetan, Nepali or Hindi, and is one of the world's most difficult languages to learn. The Newars are excellent farmers and merchants, as well as skilled artists, famed across Asia. The Kathmandu Valley is filled with spectacular examples of their artistic work and their aesthetic influence was felt as far away as Lo Manthang and Lhasa.

Their origins are shrouded in mystery: most Newars have Mongoloid and Caucasian physical characteristics. It's generally accepted that their ancestors were migrants of varied ethnicity who settled in the Kathmandu Valley over centuries – possibly originating with the Kiratis, or an even earlier group.

Newars lead a communal way of life and have developed several unique customs, including the worship of the Kumari, a girl worshipped as a living god (see p123), and the annual chariot festivals that provide the high point of the valley's cultural life. Living so close to the centre of power has also meant there are many Newars in the bureaucracies of Kathmandu.

Newari men wear *surwal* (trousers with a baggy seat that are tighter around the calves, like jodhpurs), a *daura* (thigh-length double-breasted shirt), a vest or coat and the traditional *topi* hat. Newari castes include the Sakyas (priests), Tamrakar (metal casters) and the Jyapu (farmers). Jyapu women wear a black sari with a red border, while the men often wear the traditional trousers and shirt with a long piece of cotton wrapped around the waist.

See the boxed text, p50, for more on this group.

GURUNGS

The Gurungs, a Tibeto-Burmese people, live mainly in the central midlands, from Gorkha and Baglung up to Manang and the southern slopes of the Annapurnas, around Pokhara. One of the biggest Gurung settlements is Ghandruk, with its sweeping views of the Annapurnas and Machhapuchhare. The Gurungs have made up large numbers of the Gurkha regiments, and army incomes have contributed greatly to the economy of their region. For more on the Gurkha forces see the boxed text, p259. Gurung women wear nose rings, known as *phuli,* and coral necklaces.

Despite associations in the West, Sherpas actually do very little portering, focusing mostly on high-altitude expedition work. Most of the porters you meet on the trails are Tamang, Rai or other groups.

NEWARI RITES OF PASSAGE

Newari children undergo a number of *samskaras* (rites of passage) as they grow up, many of which are shared by other Nepali Hindus. The *namakarana* (naming rite) is performed by the priests and chief of the clan and the family astrologer gives the child its public and secret name. The next rite is the *machajanko* or *pasni* (rice feeding), which celebrates the child's presence on earth and wishes them a smooth life. Next for boys comes the *busakha,* performed between the ages of three and seven, when the head is shaved, leaving just a small tuft known as a *tupi.* This is followed by the fixing of a *kaitapuja* (loincloth), which marks a commitment by the boy to bachelorhood and self-control. Girls undergo *Ihi* (a symbolic marriage to Vishnu) between the ages of five and 11 and at this time they begin to wear a thick cotton thread. The *Ihi samskara* venerates chastity and guarantees the girl a choice of husband. This is followed by a *barha* (menarche rite), which protects the girl's virginity and safeguards against passion.

Weddings are usually negotiated through a *lami* (mediator) and take place at times deemed auspicious by the family astrologer. The bride is taken in a noisy procession to the groom's house where she is received with an oil lamp and key to the house. The *chipka thiyeke samskara* involves the serving of 84 (!) traditional dishes and is a symbol of the couple's union.

The first *janko* (old-age *samskara*) takes place at 77 years, seven months and seven days, the second at 83 years, four months and four days and the third at 99 years, nine months and nine days. The final *samskara* is *sithan* (cremation), which marks the body's move to its final destination.

The Gurungs (who call themselves Tamu, or highlanders) originally migrated from western Tibet, bringing with them their animist Bön faith. One distinctive aspect of village life is the *rodi,* a cross between a town hall and a youth centre, where teenagers hang out and cooperative village tasks are planned.

MAGARS

The Magars, a large group (around 8% of the total population), are a Tibeto-Burmese people who live in many parts of the midlands zone of western and central Nepal. With such a large physical spread there are considerable regional variations.

The Magars are also excellent soldiers and fought with Prithvi Narayan Shah to help unify Nepal. Their kingdom of Palpa (based at Tansen) was one of the last to be incorporated into the unified Nepal. They make up the biggest numbers of Gurkhas, and army salaries have greatly improved their living standards.

The Magars generally live in two-storey, rectangular or square thatched houses washed in red clay. They have been heavily influenced by Hinduism, and in terms of religion, farming practices, housing and dress, they are hard to distinguish from Chhetris.

BAHUNS & CHHETRIS

The Hindu caste groups of Bahuns and Chhetris are dominant in the Middle Hills, making up 30% of the country's population.

Even though the caste system was formally abolished in 1963 these two groups remain the top cats of the caste hierarchy. Although there is no formal relationship in Hinduism between caste and ethnicity, Nepal's Bahuns and Chhetris (Brahmin priests and Kshatriya warriors respectively) are considered ethnic groups as well as the two highest castes.

Bahuns and Chhetris played an important role in the court and armies of Prithvi Narayan Shah and after unification they were rewarded with tracts of land. Their language, Khas Kura, then became the national language of Nepal and their high-caste position was religiously, culturally and legally enforced. Ever since, Bahuns and Chhetris have dominated the government in Kathmandu, making up over 80% of the civil service.

A number of Bahuns and Chhetris had roles as tax collectors under the Shah and Rana regimes and to this day many are moneylenders with a great deal of power. Outside the Kathmandu Valley, the majority of these groups are simple peasant farmers, indistinguishable in most respects from their neighbours.

The Bahuns tend to be more caste-conscious and orthodox than other Nepali Hindus, which sometimes leads to difficulties in relationships with 'untouchable' Westerners. Many are vegetarians and do not drink alcohol; marriages are arranged within the caste.

Terai Zone

Until the eradication of malaria in the 1950s, the only people to live in the valleys of the inner Terai and along much of the length of the Terai proper were Tharus and a few small associated groups, who enjoyed a natural immunity to the disease. After the Terai opened for development, large numbers of people from the midlands settled – every group is represented and around 50% of Nepali people live in the region.

A number of large groups straddle the India–Nepal border. In the eastern Terai, Mithila people dominate; in the central Terai, there are many Bhojpuri-speaking people; and in the western Terai, Abadhi-speaking people are significant. All are basically cultures of the Gangetic plain and Hindu caste structure is strictly upheld.

THARUS

One of the most visible groups is the Tharus, who are thought to be the earliest inhabitants of the Terai. About one million Tharu speakers inhabit the length of the Terai, including the inner Terai around Chitwan, although they mainly live in the west. Caste-like distinctions exist between different Tharu groups or tribes. Most have Mongoloid physical features.

Nobody is sure where they came from although some believe they are the descendants of the Rajputs (from Rajasthan), who sent their women and children away to escape Mughal invaders in the 16th century. Others believe they are descended from the royal Sakya clan, the Buddha's family, although they are not Buddhist. Tharu clans have traditionally lived in thatched huts with wattle walls or in traditional long houses. Their beliefs are largely animistic, involving the worship of forest spirits and ancestral deities, but they are increasingly influenced by Hinduism.

More recently, many Tharus were exploited by *zamindars*, fell into debt and entered into bonded labour. In 2000 the *kamaiyas* (bonded labourers) were freed by government legislation, but little has been done to help these now landless and workless people. Consequently, in most Terai towns in western Nepal you will see squatter settlements of former *kamaiyas*.

MEDIA

The introduction of private FM radio stations after the multiparty democratic system began in 1990 revolutionised the Nepali media, breaking the monopoly enjoyed by Radio Nepal since the 1950s. There are three private TV stations, including Kantipur TV and Channel Nepal.

Freedom of the press was one of many victims during the People's War, particularly when King Gyanendra seized power in 2005. The palace banned FM stations from presenting news stories or criticising the king, a move that led to 1000 journalists losing their jobs. Between 2002 and 2005 more journalists were arrested in Nepal than in any other country and in 2005 Reporters

Bahun and Chhetri men can be recognised by their sacred thread – the janai, worn over the right shoulder and under the right arm – which is changed once a year during the Janai Purnima festival (see p24).

According to the most recent (2001) census, Nepal's population is made up of the following groups: Chhetri 15.5%, Brahman-Hill 12.5%, Magar 7%, Tharu 6.6%, Tamang 5.5%, Newar 5.4%, Muslim 4.2%, Kami 3.9%, Yadav 3.9%, other 32.7%, unspecified 2.8%.

Sans Frontiers described Nepal's media as the world's most censored. Things have improved somewhat since then but journalists still face violence and intimidation in the Terai region.

RELIGION

From the simple early morning puja (worship; see the boxed text, opposite) of a Kathmandu housewife at a local Hindu temple to the chanting of Buddhist monks in a village monastery, religion is a cornerstone of Nepali life. In Nepal, Hinduism and Buddhism have mingled wonderfully into a complex, syncretic blend. Nowhere is this more evident than in Kathmandu where Tibetan Buddhists and Nepali Hindus often worship at the same temples.

The Buddha was born in Nepal over 25 centuries ago but the Buddhist religion first arrived in the country later, around 250 BC. It is said to have been introduced by the great Indian-Buddhist emperor Ashoka. Buddhism eventually lost ground to Hinduism, although the Tantric form of Tibetan Buddhism made its way full circle back into Nepal in the 8th century AD. Today Buddhism is practised mainly by the people of the high Himalaya, such as the Sherpas and Tamangs, and by Tibetan refugees.

Take the concepts of Hinduism and Buddhism, add some Indian and Tibetan influence and blend this with elements of animism, faith healing and a pinch of Tantric practice and you get a taste of Nepal's fabulous spiritual stew. Thanks to this tendency towards assimilation and synthesis there is little religious tension in Nepal and religion has long played little part in politics.

This situation has changed somewhat in recent years with the election of Maoists into the government and the abolition of the monarchy, with its strong ties to Nepal's rich Hindu tradition. The president of Nepal has replaced the king at all religious events and festivals and the Maoists are keen to remove any institution that retains a royal connection, including the centuries-old link between the king and the Kumari, or living goddess; see p123.

It is joked that Nepal has three religions – Hinduism, Buddhism and Tourism.

Hinduism

Hinduism is a polytheistic religion that has its origins in the Aryan tribes of central India about 3500 years ago.

Hindus believe in a cycle of life, death and rebirth with the aim being to achieve *moksha* (release) from this cycle. With each rebirth you can move closer to or further from eventual *moksha*; the deciding factor is karma, which is literally a law of cause and effect. Bad actions during your life

---

SADHUS

Sadhus are Hindu ascetics who have left their homes, jobs and families and embarked upon a spiritual search. They're an easily recognised group, usually wandering around half-naked, smeared in dust with their hair matted, and carrying nothing except a *trisul* (trident) and a begging bowl.

Sadhus wander all over the subcontinent, occasionally coming together in great religious gatherings such as the Maha Shivaratri festival (p23) at Pashupatinath in Kathmandu and the Janai Purnima festival (p24) at the sacred Hindu lakes of Gosainkund. You may also see sadhus wandering around Thamel and posing for photos in Kathmandu's Durbar Sq.

A few sadhus are simply beggars using a more sophisticated approach to gathering donations, but most are genuine in their search. Remember that if you take a picture of a sadhu, or accept a *tika* blessing from him, you will be expected to pay some *baksheesh* (tip), so negotiate your photo fee in advance to avoid any unpleasantness.

PUJA & SACRIFICE

Every morning Hindu women all over Nepal can be seen walking through the streets carrying a plate, usually copper, filled with an assortment of goodies. These women are not delivering breakfast but are taking part in an important daily ritual called puja. The plate might contain flower petals, rice, yoghurt, fruit or sweets, and it is an offering to the gods made at the local temple. Each of the items is sprinkled onto a temple deity in a set order and a bell is rung to let the gods know an offering is being made. Once an offering is made it is transformed into a sacred object and a small portion (referred to as prasad) is returned to the giver as a blessing from the deity. Upon returning home from her morning trip, the woman will give a small portion of the blessed offerings to each member of the household.

Marigolds and sweets don't cut it with Nepal's more terrifying gods, notably Kali and Bhairab, who require a little extra appeasement in the form of bloody animal sacrifices. You can witness the gory executions, from chickens to water buffalo, at Dakshinkali (p218) in the Kathmandu Valley, Manakamana Temple (p237) and the Kalika Temple at Gorkha (p239), or during the annual Dasain festival, when these temples are literally awash with blood offerings.

---

result in bad karma, which ends in a lower reincarnation. Conversely, if your deeds and actions have been good you will reincarnate on a higher level and be a step closer to eventual freedom from rebirth. Buddhism later adapted this concept into one of its core principles.

Hinduism has a number of holy books, the most important being the four Vedas, the 'divine knowledge' that is the foundation of Hindu philosophy. The Upanishads are contained within the Vedas and delve into the metaphysical nature of the universe and soul. The Mahabharata is an epic 220,000-line poem that contains the story of Rama. The famous Hindu epic, the Ramayana, is based on this.

The Hindu religion has three basic practices. These are puja (worship; see the boxed text, above), the cremation of the dead, and the rules and regulations of the caste system.

There are four main castes: the Brahmin (of the Brahman ethnic group), or priest caste; the Kshatriya (Chhetri in Nepali), or soldiers and governors; the Vaisyas, or tradespeople and farmers; and the Sudras, or menial workers and craftspeople. These castes are then subdivided, although this is not taken to the same extreme in Nepal as it is in India. Beneath all the castes are the Harijans, or untouchables, the lowest, casteless class for whom the most menial and degrading tasks are reserved.

Despite common misconceptions, it is possible to become a Hindu, although Hinduism itself is not a proselytising religion. Once you are a Hindu you cannot change your caste – you're born into it and are stuck with your lot in life for the rest of that lifetime.

HINDU GODS

Westerners often have trouble getting to grips with Hinduism principally because of its vast pantheon of gods. The best way to look upon the dozens of different Hindu gods is simply as pictorial representations of the many attributes of the divine. The one omnipresent god usually has three physical representations: Shiva the destroyer and reproducer, Vishnu the preserver and Brahma the creator.

Most temples are dedicated to one of these gods, but most Hindus profess to be either Vaishnavites (followers of Vishnu) or Shaivites (followers of Shiva). A variety of lesser gods and goddesses also crowd the scene. The cow is, of course, the holy animal of Hinduism, and killing a cow in Nepal brings a jail term.

'The best way to look upon the dozens of different Hindu gods is simply as pictorial representations of the many attributes of the divine.'

INCARNATIONS, MANIFESTATIONS, ASPECTS & VEHICLES

There's a subtle difference between these four concepts. Vishnu has incarnations – 10 of them in all. They include Narsingha the man-lion, Krishna the cowherd and the Buddha. Shiva, on the other hand, may be the god of 1000 names, but these are manifestations – what he shows himself as – not incarnations. When you start to look at the Buddhist 'gods' their various appearances are aspects rather than incarnations or manifestations.

Each god also has an associated animal known as the *vahana* (vehicle) on which they ride, as well as a consort with certain attributes and abilities. You can normally pick out which god is represented by identifying either the vehicle or the symbols held in the god's hand.

The oldest deities are the elemental Indo-European Vedic gods, such as Indra (the god of war, storms and rain), Suriya (the sun), Chandra (the moon) and Agni (fire). Added to this is a range of ancient local mountain spirits, which Hinduism quickly co-opted. The Annapurna and the Ganesh Himal massifs are named after Hindu deities, and Gauri Shankar and Mt Kailash in Tibet are said to be the residences of Shiva and Parvati (Shiva's shakti, or female energy).

The definitions that follow include the most interesting and frequently encountered 'big names', plus associated consorts, vehicles and religious terminology.

Shiva

As reproducer and destroyer, Shiva is probably the most important god in Nepal – so it's important to keep on his good side! Shiva is often represented by the phallic lingam, symbolic of his creative role. His vehicle is the bull Nandi, which you'll often see outside Shiva temples. The symbol most often seen in Shiva's hand is the trident.

Shiva is also known as Nataraja, whose dance shook the cosmos and created the world. Shiva's home is Mt Kailash in the Himalaya and he's supposed to be keen on smoking hashish.

In the Kathmandu Valley Shiva is most popularly worshipped as Pashupati, the lord of the beasts. As the keeper of all living things, Pashupati is Shiva in a good mood. The temple of Pashupatinath (p170) outside Kathmandu is the most important Hindu temple in the country.

Shiva appears as bushy-eyebrowed Bhairab when he is in his fearful or 'terrific' manifestation. Bhairab can appear in 64 different ways, but none of them is pretty. Typical of Tantric deities, he has multiple arms, each clutching a weapon; he dances on a corpse and wears a headdress of skulls and earrings of snakes. More skulls dangle from his belt, and his staring eyes and bared fangs complete the picture. Usually Bhairab is black, carries a cup made from a human skull and is attended by a dog. The gruesome figure near the Hanuman Dhoka palace entrance in Kathmandu is a good example of this fearsome god at his worst. Bhairab's female counterparts are the Joginis, wrathful goddesses whose shrines can be found near Sankhu in the eastern end of the Kathmandu Valley, at Guhyeshwari near Pashupatinath and at Pharping.

Outside of the Kathmandu Valley, Shiva is most commonly worshipped as Mahadeva (Great God), the supreme deity.

Vishnu

Vishnu is the preserver in Hindu belief, although in Nepal (where he often appears as Narayan) he also is seen to have played a role in the creation of the universe. Narayan is the reclining Vishnu, sleeping on the cosmic ocean, and from his navel appears Brahma, who creates the universe. The kings of Nepal long enjoyed added legitimacy because they were considered an incarnation of Vishnu.

Vishnu has four arms and can often be identified by the symbols he holds: the conch shell or sankha, the disclike weapon known as a chakra, the sticklike weapon known as a *gada*, and a lotus flower or padma. Vishnu's vehicle is the faithful man-bird Garuda; a winged Garuda will often be seen kneeling reverently in front of a Vishnu temple. Garuda has an intense hatred of snakes and is often seen destroying them. Vishnu's shakti is Lakshmi, the goddess of wealth and prosperity, whose vehicle is a tortoise.

Vishnu has 10 incarnations, starting with Matsya, the fish. Then he appeared as Kurma, the tortoise on which the universe was built. Number three is his boar incarnation as Varaha, who bravely destroyed a demon who would have drowned the world. Vishnu was again in a demon-destroying mood in incarnation four as Narsingha (or Narsimha), a half-man and half-lion (see p216 for an explanation of the legend behind this incarnation).

Vishnu's next incarnation was Vamana (or Vikrantha), the dwarf who reclaimed the world from the demon-king Bali. The dwarf politely asked the demon for a patch of ground upon which to meditate, saying that the patch need only be big enough that he, the dwarf, could walk across it in three paces. The demon agreed, only to see the dwarf swell into a giant who strode across the universe in three gigantic steps. In his sixth incarnation Vishnu appeared as Parasurama, a warlike Brahmin who proceeded to put the warrior-caste Chhetris in their place.

Incarnation seven was Rama, the hero of the Ramayana who, with help from Hanuman the monkey god, rescued his beautiful wife Sita from the clutches of Rawana, evil king of Lanka. Sita is believed to have been born in Janakpur and this is also where she and Rama married (a temple marks the site of the marriage; see p317). Incarnation eight was the gentle and much-loved Krishna, the fun-loving cowherd, who dallied with the gopis (milkmaids), danced, played his flute and still managed to remain devoted to his wife Radha.

For number nine Vishnu appeared as the teacher, the Buddha. Of course, Buddhists don't accept that the Buddha was just an incarnation of another religion's god. Incarnation 10? Well, we haven't seen that one yet, but it will be as Kalki the destroyer, when Vishnu wields the sword that will destroy the world at the end of the Kaliyuga, the age we are currently in.

Brahma

Despite his supreme position, Brahma appears much less often than Shiva or Vishnu. Like those gods, Brahma has four arms, but he also has four heads, to represent his all-seeing presence. The four Vedas (ancient or Hindus Hindu scriptures) are supposed to have emanated from his mouths.

> The Kathmandu Valley has the world's densest collection of Unesco World Heritage sites.

TIKA

A visit to Nepal is not complete without being offered a *tika* by one of the country's many sadhus (Hindu holy men; see p52) or Hindu priests. The ubiquitous *tika* is a symbol of blessing from the gods and is worn by both women and men. It can range from a small dot to a full-on mixture of yoghurt, rice and sindur (a red powder) smeared on the forehead. The *tika* represents the all-seeing, all-knowing third eye, as well as being an important energy point, and receiving this blessing is a common part of most Hindu ceremonies. It is an acknowledgment of a divine presence at the occasion and a sign of protection for those receiving it. Shops these days carry a huge range of tiny plastic *tikas*, known as *bindi*, that women have turned into an iconic fashion statement.

Parvati

Shiva's shakti is Parvati the beautiful and she is the dynamic element in their relationship. Just as Shiva is also known as Mahadeva, the Great God, she is Mahadevi (or just Devi), the Great Goddess. Shiva is often symbolised by the phallic lingam, so his shakti's symbol is the yoni, representing the female sex organ. Their relationship is a sexual one and it is often Parvati who is the energetic and dominant partner.

Shiva's shakti has as many forms as Shiva himself. She may be peaceful Parvati, Uma or Gauri, but she may also be fearsome Kali, the black goddess, or Durga, the terrible. In these terrific forms she holds a variety of weapons in her hands, struggles with demons and rides a lion or tiger. As skeletal Kali, she demands blood sacrifices and wears a garland of skulls.

Actress Uma Thurman is named after the beautiful Hindu goddess Uma, a manifestation of Parvati. Uma forms half of the Uma-Maheshwar image, a common representation of Shiva and Parvati.

Ganesh

With his elephant head, Ganesh is probably the most easily recognised and popular of the gods. He is the god of prosperity and wisdom and there are thousands of Ganesh shrines and temples across Nepal. His parents are Shiva and Parvati and he has his father's temper to thank for this elephant head. After a long trip, Shiva discovered Parvati in bed with a young man. Not pausing to think that their son might have grown up a little during his absence, Shiva lopped his head off! Parvati then forced Shiva to bring his son back to life, but he could only do so by giving him the head of the first living thing he saw – which happened to be an elephant.

Chubby Ganesh has a super sweet tooth and is often depicted with his trunk in a mound of sweets and with one broken tusk; one story tells how he broke it off and threw it at the moon for making fun of his weight, another tale states that Ganesh used the tusk to write the India epic, the Mahabharata.

Hanuman

The monkey god Hanuman is an important character from the Ramayana who came to the aid of Rama to help defeat the evil Rawana and release Sita from his grasp. Hanuman's trustworthy and alert nature is commemorated by the many statues of the god guarding palace entrances, most famously the Hanuman Dhoka.

Hanuman also has an important medicinal connection in Nepal and other Hindu countries. The Ramayana recounts a legend of how Rama desperately needed a rare herb that was grown only in the Himalaya region and sent Hanuman to procure it for him. Unfortunately, by the time he finally arrived in the mountains, Hanuman had forgotten which particular herb he had to bring back to Rama, but he got around the problem by simply grabbing a whole mountain, confident the plant would be somewhere on it.

Machhendranath

A strictly Nepali Hindu god, Machhendranath (also known as Bunga Dyo) has power over the rains and the monsoon and is regarded as protector of the Kathmandu Valley. It is typical of the intermingling of Hindu and Buddhist beliefs in Nepal that, in the Kathmandu Valley at least, Machhendranath has come to be thought of as an incarnation of Avalokiteshvara, the Buddhist's Bodhisattva of Compassion.

There are two forms of Machhendranath based on colour and features: Seto (White) Machhendranath of Kathmandu and Rato (Red) Machhendranath of Patan. Some scholars say that they are the same god, others say they are distinct. Both deities feature in the Kathmandu Valley's spectacular chariot festivals – for Kathmandu's festival see p136 and for Patan's see p189.

Tara
The goddess Tara is another deity who appears in both the Hindu and Buddhist pantheons. There are 108 different Taras but the best known are Green Tara and White Tara. Tara is generally depicted sitting with her right leg hanging down and her left hand in a *mudra* (hand gesture).

Saraswati
The goddess of learning and consort of Brahma, Saraswati rides upon a white swan and holds the stringed musical instrument known as a *veena*.

Buddhism
Strictly speaking, Buddhism is not a religion, as it is centred not on a god but on a system of philosophy and a code of morality. Buddhism was founded in northern India in about 500 BC when prince Siddhartha Gautama achieved enlightenment. According to some, Gautama Buddha was not the first Buddha but the fourth and he is not expected to be the last 'enlightened one'.

The pipal tree, under which the Buddha gained enlightenment, is also known by its Latin name, *ficus religious*.

The Buddha never wrote down his dharma (teachings) and a schism that developed later means that today there are two major Buddhist schools. The Theravada (Doctrine of the Elders), or Hinayana, holds that the path to nirvana is an individual pursuit. In contrast, the Mahayana school holds that the combined belief of its followers will eventually be great enough to encompass all of humanity and bear it to salvation. To some, the less austere and ascetic Mahayana school is considered a 'soft option'. Today it is practised mainly in Vietnam, Japan and China, while the Hinayana school is followed in Sri Lanka, Myanmar (Burma) and Thailand. There are still other, sometimes more esoteric, divisions of Buddhism, including the Tantric Buddhism of Tibet, which is the version found in Nepal.

The Buddha renounced material life to search for enlightenment but unlike other prophets found that starvation did not lead to discovery. He developed his rule of the Middle Way (moderation in all things). The Buddha taught that all life is suffering, and that suffering comes from our desires and the illusion of their importance. By following the 'eightfold path' these desires will be extinguished and a state of nirvana, where we are free from their delusions, will be reached. Following this process requires going through a series of rebirths until the goal is reached and no more rebirths into the world of suffering are necessary. The path that takes you through this cycle of births is karma, but this is not simply fate. Karma is a law of cause and effect; your actions in one life determine what you will have to go through in your next life.

The first images of the Buddha date from the 5th century AD, 1000 years after his death (stupas were the symbol of Buddhism previous to this). The Buddha didn't want idols made of himself but a pantheon of Buddhist gods grew up regardless, with strong iconographical influence from Hinduism. As in Hinduism, the many Buddhist deities reflect various aspects of the divine, here called 'Buddha-nature'. Multiple heads convey multiple personalities, *mudras* convey coded messages, and everything from eyebrows to stances indicate the nature of the god.

There are many different types of Buddha images, though the most common are those of the past (Dipamkara), present (Sakyamuni) and future (Maitreya) Buddhas. The Buddha is recognised by 32 physical marks,

---

A BUBBLE IN A STREAM

The core Buddhist vision of impermanence is summed up perfectly in these lines from the *Diamond Sutra*:

Thus shall you think of all this fleeting world,
A star at dawn, a bubble in a stream,
A flash of lightning in a summer cloud,
A flickering lamp, a phantom, and a dream

---

including a bump on the top of his head, his third eye and the images of the Wheel of Law on the soles of his feet. In his left hand he holds a begging bowl and his right hand touches the earth in the witness *mudra*. He is often flanked by his two disciples.

Bodhisattvas are beings who have achieved enlightenment but decide to help everyone else gain enlightenment before entering nirvana. The Bodhisattva Manjushri has strong connections to the Kathmandu Valley. The Dalai Lama is considered a reincarnation of Avalokiteshvara (Chenresig in Tibetan), the Bodhisattva of Compassion.

'Nepal's Hindu and Muslim communities coexist peacefully.'

Tibetan Buddhism also has a host of fierce protector gods, called *dharmapalas*.

TIBETAN BUDDHISM

There are four major schools of Tibetan (Vajrayana) Buddhism, all represented in the Kathmandu Valley: Nyingmapa, Kargyupa, Sakyapa and Gelugpa. The Nyingmapa order is the oldest and most dominant in the Nepal Himalaya. It origins come from the Indian sage Padmasambhava (or Guru Rinpoche), who is credited with the establishment of Buddhism in Tibet in the 8th century. (He is a common image in Nyingmapa monasteries and is recognisable by his *katvanga* staff of human heads and his fabulously curly moustache.)

The Dalai Lama is the head of the Gelugpa school and the spiritual leader of Tibetan Buddhists.

In some texts the Gelugpa are known as the Yellow Hats, while the other schools are sometimes collectively identified as the Red Hats. Nepal has small pockets of Bön, Tibet's pre-Buddhist animist faith, now largely considered a fifth school of Tibetan Buddhism.

Islam

Nepal's small population of Muslims (about 4% of the total population) are mainly found close to the border with India, with a large population in Nepalganj.

The first Muslims, who were mostly Kashmiri traders, arrived in the Kathmandu Valley in the 15th century. A second group arrived in the 17th century from northern India and they primarily manufactured armaments for the small hill states.

The largest Muslim group are the Terai Muslims, many of whom still have strong ties with the Muslim communities in the Indian states of Bihar and Uttar Pradesh. Religious tension is a major problem in India, but Nepal's Hindu and Muslim communities coexist peacefully.

Shamanism

Shamanism in practised by many mountain peoples throughout the Himalaya and dates back some 50,000 years. Its ancient healing traditions are based on a cosmology that divides the world into three main levels: the Upper World where the sun, moon, stars, planets, deities and spirits important to the shaman's healing work abide; the Middle World of human life; and the Lower World, where powerful deities and spirits exist.

Faith healers protect against a wide range of spirits, including headless *mulkattas*, who have eyes in their chest and signify imminent death; the *pret*, ghosts of the recently deceased that loiter in crossroads; and *kichikinni,* the ghost of a beautiful and sexually insatiable siren who is recognisable by her sagging breasts and the fact that her feet are on backwards.

During ceremonies the shaman or faith healer (jhankri) uses techniques of drumming, divination, trances and sacrifices to invoke deities and spirits, which he or she wishes to assist in the ritual. The shaman essentially acts as a broker between the human and spirit worlds.

> Traditional prejudice against daughters is reflected in the bitter Nepali proverb: 'Raising a girl is like watering your neighbour's garden.'

WOMEN IN NEPAL

Women have a hard time of it in Nepal. Female mortality rates are higher than men's, literacy rates are lower and women generally work harder and longer than men, for less reward. Women only truly gain status in traditional society when they bear their husband a son. Bearing children is so important that a man can legally take a second wife if the first has not had a child after ten years.

Nepal has a strongly patriarchal society, though this is less the case among Himalayan communities such as the Sherpa, where women often run the show (and the lodge). Boys are strongly favoured over girls, who are often the last to eat and the first to be pulled from school during financial difficulties. Nepal has a national literacy rate of 49%, with the rate among women at 35%.

The traditional practice of *sati,* where a woman was expected to throw herself on her husband's funeral pyre, was outlawed in the 1920s. Nepal legalised abortion in 2002. In 2005 landmark rulings gave women under the age of 35 the right for the first time to apply for a passport without their husband's or parent's permission, and safeguarded their right to inherited property. The rural custom of exiling women to cowsheds for four days during their period was made illegal in 2005.

On the death of her husband, a widow is often expected to marry the brother of the deceased and property is turned over to her sons, on whom

> The lives and roles of Nepali women are examined in the insightful *The Violet Shyness of their Eyes: Notes from Nepal,* by Barbara J Scot, and *Nepali Aama,* by Broughton Coburn, which details the life of a remarkable Gurung woman.

HUMAN TRAFFICKING IN NEPAL

Trafficking of girls is a major problem in Nepal's most impoverished rural areas. Some 10,000 to 15,000 girls are tricked or sold every year into servitude, either as domestic, factory or sex workers. Brokers called *dalals* sell Nepali girls for around US$2500 into the brothels of Mumbai. It is believed that over 100,000 Nepali women work in Indian brothels, often in conditions resembling slavery, and around half of these women are thought to be HIV positive. When obvious AIDS symptoms force these women out of work, some manage to return to Nepal. However, they are shunned by their families and there is virtually no assistance available for them or their children.

Particularly common in the Tharu areas of Dang and Bardia is the tradition of selling young daughters, aged seven to 10, to work as *kamlaris,* or indentured slaves, in the families of wealthy high-caste households. One organisation, the **Nepalese Youth Opportunity Programme** (www .nyof.org), has come up with an ingenious way of persuading families to hold on to their daughters: they give them a piglet and kerosene stocks for every girl they keep at home. The organisation also pays the US$100-a-year costs to send a child to school. So far the organisation has steered 2500 girls away from slavery.

she is then financially dependant. In the far western hills the traditional system of polyandry (one woman married to two brothers) emerged over centuries in response to limited amounts of land and the annual trading trips that required husbands to leave their families for months at a time. The practice kept population levels down and stopped family land being broken up between brothers. All children born into the family are considered the elder brother's. In recent years the system has started to break down.

The annual festival of Teej is the biggest festival for women, though ironically this honours their husbands. The activities include feasting, fasting, ritual bathing (in the red and gold saris they were married in) and ritual offerings.

Before you start to visit the Kathmandu Valley's many temples, get a great overview on Buddhist and Nepali art at the Patan Museum (p186) and at Kathmandu's National Museum (p166), both of which explain the concepts behind Buddhist and Hindu art and iconography in an insightful and accessible way.

ARTS

Wander around the towns of the Kathmandu Valley and you'll come across priceless woodcarvings and sculptures at every turn, in surprisingly accessible places. Nepal's artistic masterpieces are not hidden away in dusty museums but are part of a living culture, to be touched, worshipped, feared or ignored.

Architecture & Sculpture

The oldest architecture in the Kathmandu Valley has faded with history. Grassy mounds are all that remain where Patan's four Ashoka stupas once stood and the impressive stupas of Swayambhunath (p164) and Bodhnath (p174) have been rebuilt many times over the centuries. Magnificent stonework is one of the lasting reminders of the Licchavi period (4th to 9th centuries AD) and you will discover beautiful pieces scattered around the temples of the Kathmandu Valley. The Licchavi sculptures at the temple of Changu Narayan near Bhaktapur (p210) are particularly good examples, as is the statue of Vishnu asleep on a bed of serpents at Budhanilkantha (p179).

No wooden buildings and carvings are known to have survived from before the 12th century, although Newari craftsmen were responsible for parts of the Jokhang Temple in Lhasa, which still survive.

The famed artistic skills of the valley's Newari people reached their zenith under the Mallas, particularly between the 15th and 17th centuries. Squabbling and one-upmanship between the city states of Kathmandu, Patan and Bhaktapur fuelled a competitive building boom as each tried to outdo the other with even more magnificent palaces and temples.

Nepal, by Michael Hutt, is an excellent guide to the art and architecture of the Kathmandu Valley. It outlines the main forms of art and architecture and describes specific sites within the valley, often with layout plans. It has great colour plates and black-and-white photos.

Their skills extended far beyond the woodwork for which they are so well known and included fine metalwork, terracotta, brickwork and stone sculptures. The finest metalwork includes the stunning images of the two Tara goddesses at Swayambhunath (p165), and the Golden Gate (Sun Dhoka) in Bhaktapur (p202).

Statues were created through two main techniques – the repoussé method of hammering thin sheets of metal (see p177) and the 'lost wax' method. In the latter, the statue is carved in wax, this is then encased in clay and left to dry. The wax is then melted, metal is poured into the clay mould and the mould is then broken, leaving the finished statue.

The Nepali architect Arniko can be said to be the father of the Asian pagoda. He kick-started the introduction and reinterpretation of the pagoda in China and eastern Asia when he brought the multiroofed Nepali pagoda design to the court of Kublai Khan in the late 13th century. The great age of Nepali architecture came to a dramatic end when Prithvi Narayan Shah invaded the valley in 1769.

NEPAL'S STOLEN HERITAGE

In the last 20 years Nepal has seen a staggering amount of its artistic heritage spirited out of the country by art thieves – 120 statues were stolen in the 1980s alone. Much of the stolen art languishes in museums or private collections in European nations and in the US, while in Nepal the remaining temple statues are increasingly kept under lock and key.

One of the reasons that photography is banned in some temples in Nepal is that international thieves often put photos of temple artefacts in their underground 'shopping catalogues'. Pieces are then stolen to order, often with the aid of corrupt officials, to fetch high prices on the lucrative Himalayan art market. UN conventions against the trade exist but are weakly enforced.

Several catalogues of stolen Nepali art have been produced in an attempt to locate these treasures, and in 2000 and 2003 several pieces were given back to Kathmandu's National Museum, marking the slow return of Nepal's heritage to its rightful home. Most recently, a Buddha statue stolen from Patan was returned after a dealer tried to sell it to an ethnographic museum in Austria for a cool US$200,000.

These days traditional building skills are still evidenced in the extensive restoration projects of the Hanuman Dhoka in Kathmandu and the Tachupal Tole buildings in Bhaktapur, which were completed in the 1970s. Today some young architects are attempting to incorporate traditional features into their buildings, particularly hotels.

If you are interested in the architectural conservation of Kathmandu check out the website of the Kathmandu Valley Preservation Trust at www.kvptnepal.org.

NEWARI PAGODA TEMPLES

The distinctive Newari pagoda temples are a major feature of the Kathmandu Valley skyline, echoing, and possibly inspired by, the horizon's pyramid-shaped mountain peaks. While strictly speaking they are neither wholly Newari nor pagodas, the term has been widely adopted to describe the temples of the valley.

The temples are generally square in design, and may be either Hindu or Buddhist (or both, as is the nature of Nepali religion). On occasion temples are rectangular or octagonal; Krishna can occupy an octagonal temple, but Ganesh, Shiva and Vishnu can only inhabit square temples.

The major feature of the temples is the tiered roof, which may have one to five tiers, with two or three being the most common. In the Kathmandu Valley there are two temples with four roofs and another two with five (Kumbeshwar at Patan and Nyatapola at Bhaktapur). The sloping roofs are usually covered with distinctive *jhingati* (baked clay tiles), although richer temples will often have one roof of gilded copper. The bell-shaped *gajur* (pinnacle) is made of baked clay or gilded copper.

The temples are usually built on a stepped plinth, which may be as high as or even higher than the temple itself. In many cases the number of steps on the plinth corresponds with the number of roofs on the temple.

The temple building itself has a small sanctum, known as a *garbha-griha* (literally 'womb room'), housing the deity. Worshippers practise individually, with devotees standing outside the door to make their supplications. The only people permitted to actually enter the sanctum are pujari (temple priests).

In Power Places of Kathmandu, by Kevin Bubriski and Keith Dowman, Bubriski provides photos of the valley's most important sacred sites and temples, while noted Buddhist scholar Dowman provides the interesting text.

Perhaps the most interesting feature of the temples is the detailed decoration, which is only evident close up. Under each roof there are often brass or other metal decorations, such as *kinkinimala* (rows of small bells) or embossed metal banners. The metal streamer that often hangs from above the uppermost roof to below the level of the lowest roof (such as on the Golden Temple in Patan) is called a *pataka*. Its function is to give the deity a way to descend to earth.

TIBETAN CARPETS

One of most amazing success stories of the last few decades is the local Tibetan carpet industry. Although carpet production has long been a cottage industry inside Tibet, in 1960 the Nepal International Tibetan Refugee Relief Committee, with the support of Toni Hagen and the Swiss government, began encouraging Tibetan refugees in Patan to make and sell carpets.

Tibetan and New Zealand wool is used to make the carpets. The exuberant colours and lively designs of traditional carpets have been toned down for the international market, but the old ways of producing carpets remain the same. The intricacies of the senna loop method are hard to pick out in the blur of hands that is usually seen at a carpet workshop; each thread is looped around a gauge rod that will determine the height of the carpet pile, then each row is hammered down and the loops of thread split to release the rod. To finish it off the pile is clipped to bring out the design.

The carpet industry has declined somewhat over recent years, largely because of political instability and negative publicity about the exploitative use of child labour and the use of carcinogenic dye. Still, today Nepal exports more than 130,000 sq metres of rugs (down from a peak of 300,000 sq metres in the 1990s), valued at around US$100 million. The industry accounts for around 50% of the country's exports of manufactured goods to countries other than India, and employs 200,000 workers directly, and up to a million indirectly. Thanks to the efforts of groups such as **Rugmark** (www.rugmark.org), child labour in Nepal's carpet production has dropped from 11% in 1996 to 3% today.

The other major decorative elements are the wooden *tunala* (struts) that support the roofs. The intricate carvings are usually of deities associated with the temple or of the *vahana* (deity's vehicle) but quite a few depict explicit sexual acts (see the boxed text, p121, for more on Nepali erotic art).

The cultural organisation Spiny Babbler (www .spinybabbler.org) has an online Nepali art museum and articles on Nepali art. It is named after Nepal's only endemic species of bird.

SHIKHARA TEMPLES

The second-most common temples are the shikhara temples, which have a heavy Indian influence. The temples are so named because their tapering tower resembles a shikhara (mountain peak, in Sanskrit). Although the style developed in India in the 6th century, it first appeared in Nepal in the late Licchavi period.

The main feature is the tapering, pyramidal tower, which is often surrounded by four similar but smaller towers, and these may be located on porches over the shrine's entrances.

The Krishna Mandir and the octagonal Krishna Temple, both in Patan's Durbar Sq, and the spire of the Mahabouddha Temple in Patan are all excellent examples.

Painting

The CD *Rough Guide to the Music of the Himalayas* has a range of traditional music, from Bill Laswell–produced traditional Tibetan chants to Nepali flutes and drums. You can't exactly sing along but the tracks evoke the mountains.

Chinese, Tibetan, Indian and Mughal influences can all be seen in Nepali painting styles. The earliest Newari paintings were illuminated manuscripts dating from the 11th century. Newari *paubha* paintings are iconic religious paintings similar to Tibetan thangkas. Notable to both is a lack of perspective, symbolic use of colour and strict iconographic rules. See p374 for more on thangkas.

Modern Nepali artists struggle to make a living, although there are a few galleries in Kathmandu that feature local artists. Some artists are fortunate enough to get a sponsored overseas exhibition or a posting at an art college outside the country to teach their skills. Commissioning a painting by a local artist is a way to support the arts and take home a unique souvenir of your trip.

The eastern Terai has its own distinct form of colourful mural painting called Mithila art – see the boxed text, p319.

Music & Dance

The last few years have seen a revival in Nepali music and songs, both folk and 'Nepali modern'. The staple Hindi film songs have been supplanted by a vibrant local-music scene thanks to advances made in FM radio.

In the countryside most villagers supply their own entertainment. Dancing and traditional music enliven festivals and family celebrations, when villages erupt with the energetic sounds of *bansari* (flutes), *madal* (drums) and cymbals, or sway to the moving soulful sounds of devotional singing and the gentle twang of the four-stringed *sarangi*. Singing is one important way that girls and boys in the hills can interact and flirt, showing their grace and wit through dances and improvised songs.

You can see 'for-tourist' versions of Nepal's major dances at Newari restaurants in Kathmandu (see p152 for more information).

There are several musician castes, including the *gaine*, a dwindling caste of travelling minstrels, the *ghandarba*, whose music you can hear in Kathmandu, and the *damai*, who often perform in wedding bands. Women generally do not perform music in public.

Nepali dance styles are as numerous and varied as its ethnic groups. They range from the stick dances of the Tharu in the Terai to the linedancing style of the mountain Sherpas. Joining in with an enthusiastic group of porters from different parts of the country at the end of a trekking day is a great way to learn some of the moves. Masked dances are also common, from the Cham dances performed by Tibetan Buddhist monks to the masked Hindu dances of Nava Durga in Bhaktapur (p203).

The website www .mountainmusicproject .blogspot.com has links to radio and video clips of several Nepali musicians, including Rubin Gandharba – the 'Nepali Bob Dylan'.

A good introduction to popular Nepali folk music is the trio (flute, sitar and tabla) of Sur Sudha, Nepal's de facto musical ambassadors, whose evocative recordings will take you back to the region long after you've tasted your last daal bhaat. Try their *Festivals of Nepal* and *Images of Nepal* recordings. You can listen to track excerpts at www.amazon.com and check out the band at www.sursudha.com.

One of Nepal's most famous singers is the Tibetan nun Choying Drolma, who is based in Pharping in the Kathmandu Valley and who can count Tracey Chapman among her fans. Her CDs *Cho* and *Selwa*, recorded with guitarist Steve Tibbets, are transcendentally beautiful and highly recommended.

The folk song that you hear everywhere in Nepal (you'll know which one we mean when you get there) is 'Resham Pheeree Ree' ('My Heart is Fluttering Like Silk in the Wind').

The Kathmandu International Mountain Film Festival (www .himalassociation.org /kimff) screens over 60 Nepali and international films every December.

Film

The Nepali film industry has come a long way since the 1980s and early '90s, when only four or five films were produced annually. In the late '90s the Kathmandu film industry ('Kollywood') was making up to 70 films per year, although this bubble burst in 2001 when government-imposed curfews caused audience numbers to plummet and finances to dry up.

Film South Asia (www .himalassociation.org/fsa) is a biennial (odd years) festival of South Asian documentaries.

According to John Whelpton in his *History of Nepal*, the first film shown in Kathmandu depicted the wedding of the Hindu god Ram. The audience threw petals and offerings at the screen as they would do at a temple or if the god himself were present.

The Oscar-nominated Nepali-French film *Caravan*, directed by Eric Valli, is the most famous 'Nepali' film and played to packed houses in Kathmandu. It features magnificent footage of the Upper Dolpo district of western Nepal as it tells the tale of yak caravaners during a change of generations. It was renamed for distribution abroad as *Himalaya*.

NEPALI NOVELS

The last few years have seen a bounty of novels written by Nepali writers. Pack one of them in your backpack for added insights into the country.

Arresting God in Kathmandu, by Samrat Upadhyay, is an engaging and readable series of short stories set in Kathmandu by an author billed as the first Nepali writer writing in English (he is now living in the US). His follow-ups include the novel *Guru of Love* and *The Royal Ghosts*, a series of short stories set against the backdrop of the Maoist uprising.

Mountains Painted With Turmeric by Lil Bahadur Chettri is a classic 1958 short novel, recently translated into English by Michael Hutt. The novel realistically portrays the struggles of a farming family trapped in a cycle of poverty and social conservatism in eastern Nepal.

Several novels have tried to make sense of the political chaos in Nepal's recent history. *Palpasa Café*, by Narayan Wagle, tells the story of an artist, an expat Nepali and a guerrilla set against the backdrop of the war, revolution and political violence that has dominated life in rural Nepal for the last 10 years. The author is the editor of the *Kantipur* newspaper.

The Tutor of History, by Manjushree Thapa, is a portrait of a rural Nepali village in western Nepal during the run-up to elections. It's worth a read for its insights into modern Nepal. Thapa is also the author of *Tilled Earth*, a collection of short stories.

Kagbeni, by Bhushan Dahal, is Nepal's first ever HD movie. A creepy supernatural tale adapted from the short story *The Monkey's Paw*, by WW Jacobs, it is set in the foothills around Annapurna. You can view the trailer at www.kagbeni.us.

Himalayan Voices: an Introduction to Modern Nepali Literature, by Michael Hutt, includes work by contemporary poets and short-story writers.

Basantpur by Neer Shah, the coproducer of *Caravan*, is a recent Nepali film depicting the intrigues and conspiracies of life at the Rana court. Another Nepali film to look out for is *Mukundo* (Mask of Desire), directed by Tsering Rita Sherpa, which explores secular and spiritual desires in Kathmandu. Tulsi Ghimire is another popular Nepali director. Perhaps the best-known film shot in Nepal is Bernado Bertolucci's *Little Buddha*, which was partly filmed at Bhaktapur's Durbar Sq and the Gokarna Forest.

Literature

Nepal's literary history is brief, dating back to just the 19th century. The written language was little used before then, although religious verse, folklore, songs and translations of Sanskrit and Urdu dating back to the 13th century have been found.

One of the first authors to establish Nepali as a literary language was Bhanubhakta Acharya (1814–68), who broke away from the influence of Indian literature and recorded the Ramayana in Nepali; this was not simply a translation but a Nepali-ised version of the Hindu epic. Motiram Bhatta (1866–96) also played a major role in 19th-century literature, as did Lakshmi Prasad Devkota (1909–59) in the 20th century.

Nepal's literary community has always struggled in a country where literacy levels are extremely low. However, today a vibrant and enthusiastic literary community exists, meeting in teashops, brew houses and bookstalls in Kathmandu and other urban centres.

Food & Drink

You can eat like a king in Kathmandu and Pokhara, but sadly, this cannot always be said for the rest of the country. Most Nepali cooks do not have the luxury of expensive ingredients or the time to make complicated meals, and most Nepalis eat rice and vegetables twice a day, every day. If you are used to a varied diet with lots of meat and dairy, eating in some areas of Nepal can feel like slow death for your taste buds.

There are two local forms of porridge in the mountains – *tsampa*, made from roasted barley flour, and *dhedo*, a thick doughlike paste made from grain or millet flour.

The good news is that over the years international travellers have brought dishes from home to Nepal. As a result, restaurants in tourist areas are a world map of cuisines, with dishes from Tibet, China, India, Japan, Thailand, Mexico, Italy, France and the Middle East. Take advantage of these offerings – once you start trekking it's rice and vegetables, all day, every day…

STAPLES & SPECIALITIES

Most Hindu Nepalis are vegetarians, some out of choice and some out of necessity. The staple meal of Nepal is *daal bhaat tarkari* – literally 'lentil soup', 'rice' and 'curried vegetables'. If you are lucky it will be spiced up with *achar* (pickles) and maybe some *chapati* (unleavened Indian bread), *dahi* (curd or yoghurt) or *papad* (pappadam – crispy fried lentil-flour pancake). The most common vegetables are potato, green leaves and chayote (a kind of squash, introduced from South America). Only very occasionally does it come with *masu* (meat).

To eat daal bhaat the local way, pour the soupy daal onto the rice, mix it into balls with your fingers, add a pinch of pickle and vegetables and shovel it into your mouth with your right hand.

However, the Newars of the Kathmandu Valley are great meat eaters – *buff* (water buffalo) is the meat of choice, as cows are sacred and never eaten, but goat is also common. Spices feature heavily in Newari food, especially chilli, and Newari dishes are usually served with *chiura* (dry, beaten rice). One cheap and cheerful dish you'll find everywhere is chow mein (thin noodles fried with vegetables or meat).

Many of the best Newari dishes are only eaten at celebrations or family events. However, several upmarket restaurants in Kathmandu serve good Newari cuisine (see p152). Nepal is also one of the best places to try Tibetan cuisine, though most dishes are simple variations on momos (stuffed dumplings) or *thuk* (noodles, typically served in soups).

Garam masala (hot mix) is a blend of cardamom, cloves, fenugreek, coriander, cinnamon, cumin, fennel and pepper. Serious chefs make their own – you can buy all the ingredients around the Asan Tole area in Kathmandu.

See p68 for a rundown of common dishes.

Desserts

Like their Indian neighbours, Nepalis enjoy a huge range of sticky sweets, mostly based on milk curd, *jaggery* (palm sugar) and nuts. Top treats include *barfi* (milk fudge), *rasbari* (milk balls), *lal mohan* (deep-fried milky dough balls), *khir* (rice pudding) and *julebi* (orange-coloured, syrupy fried dough swirls).

Anyone who visits Bhaktapur should try the *juju dhau* (king of curds), a wonderfully creamy thick yoghurt. Because of the vagaries of refrigeration, avoid ice cream except in upmarket tourist restaurants.

A CAUTIONARY TALE… *Joe Bindloss*

Where meat is served in the mountains, it is often dried and marinated with chilli, ginger and other spices to create a form of meat jerky known as *sukuti*. Although delicious, *sukuti* is the living embodiment of the phrase 'tough as old leather'. While researching this book, I cracked a molar on a particularly tough piece of *sukuti* and had to walk for five days to reach a dentist who performed an emergency root canal operation without anaesthetic! My advice is chop your *sukuti* up into small bits and chew gently…

DRINKS
Nonalcoholic

The golden rule in Nepal is *don't drink the water* (see p398). Cheap bottled water is available everywhere but every bottle contributes to Nepal's mountain of waste plastic. You can purify your own water if you carry a canteen or water bottle and iodine drops or tablets.

Tea is almost always safe. Tourist restaurants often serve the world's weakest tea – typically an ineffectual Mechi tea bag dunked into a glass of sweet, hot milk. For proper Nepali *chiya* (sometimes called masala tea), the leaves are boiled with milk, sugar and spices. If you want Western-style tea, ask for 'milk separate'.

In Tibetan-influenced areas the drink of choice is black tea churned with salt and (sometimes iffy) butter. It's an acquired taste – locals often pour it over their *tsampa* (roasted barley flour). In Indian-influenced areas, look out for *lassi* – a refreshing drink of curd (yoghurt) mixed with sugar and what may be untreated water (proceed with caution).

> Tibetans take their tea with butter and salt, rather than milk and sugar – providing useful metabolites for dealing with cold weather.

Alcoholic

Nepali beer – lager, of course – is pretty good, especially after a hard day's walking. Tuborg (Danish), Carlsberg (Danish), Löwenbräu (German) and San Miguel (Spanish) are brewed under licence in Nepal; local brands include Gorkha and Everest. Nepal Distilleries produces a variety of bottled spirits that claim to be rum, whisky, brandy and gin. Most are pretty grim, but Kukhri Rum goes down well with mixers. For more local alcoholic drinks, see opposite.

Officially alcohol is not sold by retailers on the first two days (full moon days) and the last two Saturdays of the Nepali month, but this rarely affects tourist restaurants.

> *The Nepal Cookbook*, by the Association of Nepalis in the Americas, is a good collection of home recipes, or try *Taste of Nepal*, by Jyoti Pathak.

CELEBRATIONS

At festival time, animal sacrifices are followed by feasts known as *bhoj* where the carcasses are put to good use in the cookpot. Certain festivals are associated with specific foods. During the Janai Purnima festival, Newars make up batches of *kwati*, a soup made from up to a dozen types of sprouted beans. During the Tibetan Buddhist festival of Lhosar (Tibetan New Year), a special dumpling stew called *gutuk* is served and the leftover dumplings are ceremonially cast away, representing the casting away of bad luck.

WHERE TO EAT & DRINK
Restaurants

In 1955 Kathmandu had only one restaurant. These days, every other building in Kathmandu is a restaurant, serving food from across the globe. However, travel outside Kathmandu and Pokhara and you'll find that menus quickly shrink to chow mein, fried rice, fried potatoes and daal bhaat.

At local restaurants, known as bhojanalayas, the custom is to eat with your right hand. If you order daal bhaat, someone will come around offering free extra helpings of rice, daal or *tarkari* (vegetable curry). Also look out for the vegetarian restaurants known as misthan bhandars, which serve Indian sweets and *dosas* (fried lentil-flour pancakes).

In small local restaurants and trekking lodges, the cooking equipment is often limited to a simple gas burner or a cooking fire. To save firewood and time, order the same food as your companions and order together.

> Nepal has a long history of drinking milk and eating products made from milk curd, but fermented cheese was only introduced (from Switzerland) in the 1950s!

FARANGI (FOREIGN) FOOD

Many restaurants in Kathmandu try to serve something from everywhere – pizzas, momos, Indian curries, a bit of Thai here, some Mexican tacos there. Predictably, some places do this better than others.

THE LOCAL FIREWATER

On trekking routes, look out for the traditional homebrews of the hills. One drink you'll find everywhere is *chang*, a mildly alcoholic concoction made from fermented rice (or occasionally barley or millet) and water, which may be untreated. It can be drunk hot or cold – local connoisseurs take it hot with a raw egg in it…

In eastern Nepal, look out for *tongba*, a Himalayan brew made by pouring boiling water into a wooden (or metal) pot full of fermented millet. The liquid is slurped through a bamboo straw and more hot water is added periodically to seep extra alcohol from the mash. Harder spirits include *arak*, fermented from potatoes or grain, and *raksi*, a distilled rice wine that runs the gamut from smooth sipping schnapps to headache-inducing paint stripper.

For the best international food, head to the specialist restaurants of Kathmandu. Among other dishes, you'll find spectacular Sicilian pizzas, Sichuan chicken, flawless Korean bulgogi, sublime sushi, brilliant burritos, terrific tandoori chicken and perfect pad thai.

Quick Eats

Nepali towns have a range of snack foods, from muffins in bakeries to grilled corn cobs on the street. A couple of *samsa* (samosas – potato curry, fried in a lentil-dough parcel) or *papad* (fried lentil-flour crisps) make a great snack. Newari beer snacks are legendary – try a plate of *sekuwa* (spiced, barbecued meat) or 'masala peanuts' (with chilli and spices) when you have a beer.

HABITS & CUSTOMS

When following the Nepali eating schedule, the morning begins with a cup of sweet tea and a light snack such as *samsa*, *puri* (fried bread), or *sel* (rice-flour doughnuts) with spiced chickpeas. This is followed by a more substantial meal in the late morning. Dinner is generally just before going to bed.

Hindus have strict rules about keeping food and drink ritually pure and unpolluted. A high-caste Brahmin cannot eat food prepared or touched by a lower-caste individual as it is considered to be *jhuto* (polluted).

In general, when eating in a group, no one gets up until everyone has finished their food. If you have to leave early, make your apologies by saying *bistaai khaanus*, or 'please eat slowly'.

COOKING COURSES

There are a handful of cooking courses in Nepal:

Sadhana Yoga Centre (Map p273; ☎ 061-694041; www.sadhana-asanga-yoga.com) Courses in Nepali cooking at a popular yoga centre near Pokhara.

Trekkers Holiday Inn (☎ 01-4480334; www.trekkersholidayinn.com; Chuchepati, Bodhnath) This Swiss-run centre offers a Nepali cookery course on Saturday afternoons – call or email for the latest prices and venue.

Via Via Café (Map p140; ☎ 01-4700184; www.viaviacafe.com; Kathmandu) This Belgian-Nepali restaurant (see p151) runs weekly cookery courses for €5.

EAT YOUR WORDS

For pronunciation guidelines and other general language phrases see p401.

Useful Phrases

I'm a vegetarian
ma sāhkāhari hun
I don't like spicy food
ma piro khandina/piro nahahlnuhos

Most Nepalis round off a meal with a *digestif* of *pan* (betel nut and leaf mixture). Those little spots of red on the pavement that look like little pools of blood are (generally) *pan*.

Food Nepal (www .food-nepal.com) offers an excellent introduction to Nepali food and ingredients, with recipes from mango *lassi* to chicken chilli.

Members of the Brahmin caste will not eat chicken, buffalo, onion, tomatoes, mushrooms or eggs, or anything prepared by somebody from another caste. Conversely, food prepared by Brahmins can be eaten by people of any caste.

Can I have the bill?
bill pauna sakchhu?
Please bring me a spoon
malai chamchah lyaunuhos

Food Glossary

alu	potato
badam	peanut
bhaat	cooked rice
bhanta	eggplant
daal	lentils
dahi	yoghurt
dudh	milk
gobi	cauliflower
kerah	banana
khasi	mutton
kukhara	chicken
maachha	fish
masu	meat
murgh	chicken
phul	egg
ram toriya	okra (lady's finger)
roti	bread
sag	spinach

Nepali uses different words for 'clean' *(saphaa)* and 'ritually clean' *(choko)*.

DRINKS

(chiso) biyar	(cold) beer
chini	sugar
chiya	tea
sodamah kagati	lemon soda
tato panimah kagati	hot lemon
umaahleko pani	boiled water

In rural areas Nepalis often greet each other with *khaanaa khaiyo?* or 'have you eaten yet?'

NEPALI & NEWARI FOOD

aloo tahmah	stew made from potatoes, bamboo shoots and beans
aloo tareko	fried potato with cumin, turmeric and chilli
chatamari	rice-flour pancake topped with meat and/or egg
chiura	beaten rice, served as an alternative to rice
choyla or *choila*	roasted spiced *buff* (water buffalo) meat, usually eaten with *chiura*
daal bhaat tarkari	rice, lentil soup and vegetables – the staple food of Nepal

DOS & DON'TS

- Food becomes ritually *jhuto* (polluted) if touched by someone else's hand, plate or utensils, so only eat off your own plate and never use your own fork or spoon to serve food off a communal plate.
- When using water from a communal jug or cup, pour it straight into your mouth without touching the sides (and without pouring it all over your shirt!).
- Don't use your left hand for eating or passing food to others as this hand is used for personal ablutions.
- Do wait to be served.
- Do leave your shoes outdoors when dining in someone's house.
- Do wash your hands and mouth before dining.
- Do ask for seconds when eating at someone's home.

WE DARE YOU!

In Newari eateries you can find dishes made from just about every imaginable part of an animal. Dishes for the brave include *jan-la* (raw steak with the skin attached), *bul-la* (dregs of rice wine with diced spleen and pieces of bone), *ti-syah* (fried spinal bone marrow) and the aptly named *swan-puka* (lung filled through the windpipe with spicy batter and then boiled, sliced and fried) topped off with some *cho-hi* (steamed blood pudding). Oh...my...God... Still hungry?

dayakula	meat curry
gundruk	traditional Nepali sour soup with dried vegetables
gurr	grilled pancake made from raw potatoes ground and mixed with spices
khasi kho ledo	lamb curry
kwati	a special festival soup made from a dozen types of sprouted beans
mis mas tarkari	seasonal mixed vegetables
samay baji	ritual feast of *chiura, choyla,* black soybeans and other side dishes
sandeko	cold pickles
sekuwu	spiced, barbecued meat, fish or chicken
sikarni	sweet whipped yoghurt dessert with nuts, cinnamon and dried fruit
sukuti	extremely spicy nibble of dried buffalo or goat meat
tama	traditional Nepali soup made from dried bamboo shoots
wo	lentil-flour pancake

TIBETAN DISHES

gacok	Tibetan hotpot; usually for a group of people
kapse	fried Tibetan bread, often served with honey
kothe (*kothe*)	fried momos
momo	meat, cheese or vegetables wrapped in dough and steamed
phing	glass noodles, vermicelli
pingtsey	wontons
richotse	momos in soup
sha-bhalay	meat in a deep-fried pastie *(sya-bhakley)*
shabrel	meatballs
talumein	egg noodle soup
thentuk	similar to *thukpa* but with noodle squares
thukpa	traditional thick Tibetan meat soup (also *thugpa*)
ting-mo	steamed Tibetan bread
tsampa	ground roasted barley, eaten in place of rice; often mixed with tea, water or milk
tserel	vegetable balls

The Nepali word for eating is *khanu*, which is also used for the verbs 'to drink' and 'to smoke'.

INDIAN DISHES

bhaji	vegetable fritter
biryani	steamed rice with meat or vegetables
channa masala	chickpea curry
chicken tikka	skewered chunks of marinated chicken
korma	currylike braised dish, often quite sweet
makani	any dish cooked with butter, often daal or chicken
malai kofta	potato and nut dumplings in a rich gravy
matter paneer	unfermented cheese with peas
nan	baked bread
pakora	fried vegetables in batter
palak paneer	unfermented cheese with spinach in a gravy
pilau	rice cooked in stock and flavoured with spices
rogan josh	Kashmiri-style lamb curry
samosa	pyramid-shaped, deep-fried and potato-filled pasties

Responsible Tourism

In the 50 years since Nepal opened its borders to outsiders, tourism has brought many benefits, in terms of wealth generation, employment opportunities, infrastructure, health care, education and transport, creating a level of social mobility that would have been unthinkable in the past. Many of the Nepalis who own trekking companies today worked as porters themselves 20 years ago.

Sadly, the negative effects of tourism are also clear to see. Begging is widespread and litter chokes mountain trails. New hotels and lodges are being built at an unprecedented rate, and forests are vanishing as lodge owners collect ever more firewood to keep trekkers supplied with warm showers and hot meals.

There is endless discussion among travellers about the most environmentally and culturally sensitive way to travel. What is certain is that making a positive contribution is as much about the way you behave as the money you spend. Independent travellers may spend less money, but they have a much greater impact on poverty alleviation by contributing directly to the local economy.

The following sections cover some of the issues you will need to think about, but drop into the Kathmandu office of **Kathmandu Environmental Education Project** (KEEP; Map p140; ☎ 01-4216775; www.keepnepal.org; Thamel; ⊙ 10am-5pm Sun-Fri) for more advice.

For tips on responsible trekking in Nepal see p335.

> Trekkers in Nepal leave behind an estimated 100 tonnes of unrecyclable water bottles every year. Plastic bottles don't have to end up in landfill – the clothing firm Patagonia is one of several organisations spinning discarded bottles into fleeces. It takes just 25 plastic water bottles to make a new fleece jacket for an adult.

SUSTAINABLE TOURISM INITIATIVES

Following the lead of international development organisations, the Nepal Tourism Board has established the **Tourism For Rural Poverty Alleviation Programme** (TRPAP; ☎ 01-4269768; www.welcome2nepal.com.cn/index-3.htm), which aims to develop new community-based environmental and cultural tourism projects in rural areas. Profits from homestay accommodation and handicrafts are funnelled into village social funds. The programs change from year to year – see their website for details.

A smaller village homestay program operates in the Gurung village of Sirubari (p275), about 56km from Pokhara.

Dolma Ecotourism (www.dolmatours.com) runs 14-day trips to Briddim in the Langtang area, during which you stay in village-houses, learn the local language and take cookery classes. Profits help fund local development and education projects – for more on this area see Tamang Heritage Trail, p233.

> World Expeditions (www.worldexpeditions.net) has a useful online booklet on responsible tourism – follow the 'Responsible Travel' links.

CONTRIBUTING WHILE YOU TRAVEL

A number of trekking and tour agencies use the proceeds from their trips to support charitable projects around Nepal, and many travellers also undertake sponsored treks and climbing expeditions in Nepal to raise money for specific charities and projects. Organisations that set up expeditions of this kind include:

Community Action Treks (www.catreks.com) Offers various treks that contribute to the work of Community Action Nepal (www.canepal.org.uk).

Dolma Ecotourism (www.dolmatours.com) Runs tours and treks which help fund the Dolma Development Fund, which manages a variety of social, education and health-care projects.

Exodus (www.exodus.co.uk/responsible-travel) UK agency offering various treks; proceeds help fund tree-planting in Mustang and an orphanage in Patan.

Explore Nepal (Map p126; www.xplorenepal.com.np) Trek and tour agency with commendable ethical policies; money from trips helps fund litter clearing and other environmental projects.
Himalayan Travel (www.himalayantravel.co.uk) UK agency offering treks to support the Nepal Trust (www.nepaltrust.org).
Sponsortrek Nepal (www.sponsortrek.nl) Dutch agency offering various treks with a donation to medical projects in Nepal.

VOLUNTEER WORK

Hundreds of travellers volunteer in Nepal every year, working on an incredible range of development and conservation projects, covering everything from volunteering with street children in Kathmandu to counting the tracks of endangered animals in the high Himalaya.

However, it is important to remember the principles of ethical volunteering – good volunteer agencies match volunteers to suitable projects, rather than offering the chance to do whatever you want, wherever you want, for as long as you like. See www.ethicalvolunteering.org for more tips on selecting an ethical volunteer agency.

Although you give your time for free, you will be expected to pay for food and lodging, and you may also be asked to pay a placement fee. Fees paid to local agencies tend to be much lower than the huge fees charged by some international volunteer agencies, and you can be confident that the money will be used locally.

When looking for a volunteer placement, a good place to start is the Kathmandu office of Kathmandu Environmental Education Project (KEEP; see opposite).

This highly regarded organisation places volunteers with a variety of local NGOs (nongovernmental organisations) and offers one-month placements in Kathmandu teaching English and other skills to porters and guides in December/January and July/August. A minimum two-month time commitment is preferred and there's a US$50 administration fee which covers you for one year.

Other organisations that arrange volunteer placements and volunteer treks include.
Balthali Resort (www.balthalivillageresort.com) This resort near Panauti can arrange all sorts of volunteer opportunities at local villages.
Butterfly Foundation (www.butterflyfoundation.org) Accepts volunteers to help with administration and child care at its orphanage in Pokhara; linked to Butterfly Lodge (p262).
Child Environment Nepal (www.cennepal.org.np) Takes child-care volunteers in its orphanage at Naya Bazaar in Kathmandu.
Crooked Trails (www.crookedtrails.com) Runs fundraising treks and volunteer programs that can be combined with treks.
Cultural Destination Nepal (www.volunteernepal.org.np) A cultural immersion package, combining a homestay and Nepali language course with a one- to three-month volunteer placement.
Cultural Tourism Restoration Project (www.crtp.net) Paying volunteer treks to Mustang to help with the restoration of Chairro Gompa.
Esther Benjamins Trust (www.ebtrust.org.uk) Can arrange placements working to improve the lives of trafficked and abandoned children.
Ford Foundation (www.fordnepal.org) Arranges volunteer work focusing on teaching and child care; accommodation is provided by a host family.
Global Vision International (www.gvi.co.uk, www.gviusa.com) Offers one-month volunteer placements on educational and conservation projects in the Everest region.
Global Volunteer Network (www.volunteer.org.nz/nepal) A Kiwi organisation offering placements in health care, education, child care and social development.

British climber Doug Scott is one of dozens of mountaineers who have returned to Nepal to establish development projects for the people who helped them to the top. Doug now runs treks to support the charity Community Action Nepal (www.canepal.org.uk).

For more on the general issues behind responsible tourism, check out Tourism Concern (www.tourismconcern.org.uk).

Some of the best work done by volunteers is arranged through VSO (www.vso.org) in the UK, which arranges long-term placements (lasting up to two years) for skilled professionals.

Helping Hands (www.helpinghandsusa.org) Places medical volunteers at clinics around Nepal.

Himalayan Encounters (Map p140; ☎ 01-4700426; www.himalayanencounters.com; Kathmandu Guest House courtyard, Thamel, Kathmandu) This trekking and rafting agency can arrange volunteer placements at schools and orphanages.

Himalayan Healthcare (www.himalayan-healthcare.org) Arranges medical and dental treks around Nepal.

Himshikhar Socio-Cultural Society (www.hopenhome.org) Nepali NGO placing volunteers on health, teaching and child-care programs.

Insight Nepal (www.insightnepal.org.np) Combines a cultural and education program near Pokhara with a volunteer placement and a trek in the Annapurna region; the package lasts seven weeks or three months.

Journeys International (www.journeys.travel) American agency offering tree-planting treks in the foothills west of Kathmandu.

Kanchenjunga School Project (www.kangchenjunga.org) Arranges treks with volunteer placements in health and education at villages in the Kanchenjunga region.

Mount Everest Foundation (www.everestparivar.com/mount) Runs an annual service trek providing health care in remote parts of Solu Khumbu.

Mountain Fund (www.mountainfund.org) Offers various volunteer opportunities, including an annual volunteer medical trek.

Mountain Trust Nepal (www.mountain-trust.org) British NGO that can arrange volunteer placements in social projects around Pokhara.

Nepal Sathi (www.nepalsathi.ws) Places volunteers on projects at villages near the Arniko Hwy in central Nepal.

Nepali Children's Trust (www.nepalichildrenstrust.com) Runs an annual trek for volunteers and disabled Nepali children from the Annapurna region.

Prison Assist Nepal (www.panepal.org) Kathmandu-based organisation that needs volunteers to help look after children whose parents are in prison.

Rainbow Children Home (www.orphancarenepal.org) Accepts volunteers at its Pokhara children's home, and also arranges fund-raising treks.

Rokpa (www.rokpa.org) Swiss-Tibetan organisation that needs volunteers for its soup kitchen and medical tent at Bodhnath for six or more weeks (December-March).

Rural Community Development Programme (www.rcdpnepal.org) Arranges placements on volunteer projects that can be combined with organised treks.

Social Tours (www.socialtours.com) Can arrange volunteer placements as part of treks around Nepal.

Sustainable Agriculture Development Programme (www.sadpnepal.org) Arranges placements in sustainable and organic agriculture and other social programs near Pokhara.

Volunteer Nepal National Group (www.volnepal.np.org) Places volunteers on a variety of teaching, conservation and development programs.

Volunteer Service Nepal (VSN; www.vsnnepal.org) Places volunteers on social and educational projects around Nepal.

For details on fair-trade organisations and the crafts they produce, see p157 and p193. See also the boxed text about the Janakpur Women's Development Centre (p319).

ECONOMIC CHOICES

Don't underestimate your power as an informed consumer. You can maximise the impact of the money you spend by frequenting locally owned restaurants and lodges and by shopping at fair-trade craft stores. By choosing local trekking agencies, tour companies and lodges that have a policy of reducing their environmental and cultural impact, you are providing an example to other travellers and an incentive for other companies to adopt the same practices.

Entry fees to historical sights contribute to their preservation, and the growth of 'ecotourism' in Nepal's national parks and conservation areas has encouraged the government to make environmental protection a priority. Hiring guides on treks also helps; as well as improving your cultural understanding, it provides employment for local people, infusing money into the hill economy.

Ethical Shopping

Many species in Nepal are being driven towards extinction by the trade in animal parts. Although most products made from endangered species are sent to China or Tibet for use in traditional medicine, travellers also contribute to the problem by buying souvenirs made from wild animals.

In particular, avoid anything made from fur, and the metal-inlaid animal skulls and tortoise shells sold as cultural souvenirs. Another item to avoid is the *shahtoosh* shawl – endangered *chiru,* or Tibetan antelope, are killed to provide the wool.

Also be aware of the threat posed to Nepal's cultural heritage by the illegal trade in antiquities (see the boxed text, p61). The export of real antiques is banned but local artisans still use traditional techniques, so you can avoid any problems by buying modern reproductions.

FAIR TRADE

Fair trade principles can make a genuine difference in Nepal, a nation where 90% of the population live in underdeveloped rural areas. A number of non-profit organisations support local cooperatives that pay artisans a fair wage to produce traditional crafts in safe working conditions, using sustainable materials, without child labour. Many of these organisations provide work, training and education for workers from neglected economic groups, including women, the disabled and members of the 'untouchable' castes.

Established by the Nepali philanthropist Tulsi Mehar, **Mahaguthi** (www .mahaguthi.org) provides support, employment and rehabilitation for destitute women, funded through the sale of quality handicrafts at its fair-trade shops in Patan and Lazimpat (Kathmandu). See p193 for information on Mahaguthi and other fair-trade stores in Patan.

The workshops run by Tibetan refugees at Jawalakhel in Patan also contribute directly to the welfare of disadvantaged people – see p193 for details.

More information on fair trade can be found on the websites of the Fair Trade Group Nepal (www.fairtradegroup nepal.org) and the World Fair Trade Organisation (www.ifat.org).

Begging

Hinduism and Buddhism have a long tradition of giving alms to the needy. However, begging in Nepal today is also fuelled by the perception that foreigners will hand out money on demand. In areas frequented by tourists, groups of beggars work specific street corners using tried-and-tested scams to separate tourists from their money. Among all this, there are also many people who are genuinely in need.

At many religious sites you will see long lines of beggars, and pilgrims customarily give a coin to everyone in the line (there are special money-changers nearby who will change notes for loose change). Sadhus (holy men) are also dependent on alms, though there are plenty of con artists among their ranks.

In tourist areas, you can expect to be harassed with requests for 'one pen, one bonbon, one rupee' by children and even sometimes by adults. Don't encourage this behaviour. Most Nepalis find it offensive and demeaning (as do most visitors), and it encourages a whole range of unhealthy attitudes.

Haggling is a way of life in Nepal (see p373) but wrangling over the last Rs 10 may lead to the vendor making a loss to save face; while paying over the odds will drive up local inflation (especially for the next tourist).

Ways to Help

You only need to look at the standards of dentistry in Nepal to realise that handing out sweets to children is neither appropriate or responsible. If you want to give something to local people, make the donation to an adult, preferably someone in authority, like a teacher or a lama at a local monastery. Appropriate gifts include toothbrushes and toothpaste, pens and paper, biodegradable soap and school books, preferably with lessons in Nepali or other local languages.

If you must give money, consider making a donation to a local or international NGO that is working in the area. Sir Edmund Hillary's **Himalayan Trust** (☎ 01-4412168; www.himalayan-trust.org; Dilli Bazaar) supports education, health care, cultural projects and afforestation across the Himalaya, and similar work is carried out by the **Sir Edmund Hillary Foundation** (www.thesiredmundhillaryfoundation.ca) in Canada and the **American Himalayan Foundation** (www.himalayan-foundation.org) in the USA. The American Himalayan Foundation also runs various social and cultural projects to benefit Sherpas and Tibetan refugees.

The following organisations also may accept donations.

If you have any clothes or medicines left at the end of your trip, don't haul them home. Instead donate them to the clothing bank run by the Mountain Fund (www.mountainfund.org).

DEVELOPMENT ORGANISATIONS
Community Action Nepal (www.canepal.org.uk) Charity founded by mountaineer Doug Scott, working in porter villages in the Middle Hills.
Eco Himal (www.ecohimal.org) Austrian organisation, running development projects across Nepal, including an ecotourism scheme in the Rolwaling Valley.
Ford Foundation Nepal (www.fordnepal.org) Runs education, development and cultural projects across Nepal.
Global Action Nepal (www.gannepal.org) Sponsors various development projects in Nepal, and has run volunteer programs in the past.
Himalayan Light Foundation (www.hlf.org.np) Provides solar power and renewable energy to villages across Nepal.
Himalayan Projects (www.himalayanprojects.org) Belgian organisation that supports education and health projects in the Annapurna region.
Nepal Trust (www.nepaltrust.org) Runs integrated development programs in northwestern Nepal.
Room to Read (www.roomtoread.org) Establishes libraries and other educational facilities around Nepal.

CHILDREN'S ORGANISATIONS
APC Nepal (www.pommecannelle.org) Operates a home for street kids in Basantapur, Kathmandu.
Child Welfare Scheme (www.childwelfarescheme.org) Provides support for impoverished and homeless children in Pokhara and around Nepal.
Educate the Children Nepal (www.etc-nepal.org) Provides education and training opportunities for children and women in rural areas.
Read Nepal (www.readglobal.org/nepal.asp) Provides education at village level across Nepal.
Street Children of Nepal Trust (www.streetchildrenofnepal.org) UK organisation providing health care, education and support for disadvantaged children.

HEALTH ORGANISATIONS
Britain-Nepal Medical Trust (www.britainnepalmedicaltrust.org.uk) Joint venture providing health care in Nepal since 1968.
Himalayan Cataract Project (www.cureblindness.org) Works to cure blindness caused by cataracts.
Himalayan Rescue Association (www.himalayanrescue.org) Provides emergency medicine to villagers and trekkers at high altitude.
The Fred Hollows Foundation (www.hollows.com.au) Australian organisation treating cataract blindness in Nepal.
Tilganga Eye Centre (www.tilganga.org) Provides eye-care services to the poorest of the country's poor.

CULTURAL CONSIDERATIONS
Travellers may find the traditional lifestyle of people in Nepal to be picturesque, but in many places it is a meagre, subsistence-level existence that could be improved in numerous ways. The challenge faced by the numerous charitable organisations working in Nepal is how to bring a modern standard of living without destroying the traditional culture of the mountains.

You can do your bit by showing respect for local traditions – this will also demonstrate to local people that the relationship between locals and foreigners is one of equals. Many of the problems experienced by travellers in Nepal have been caused by past travellers who have treated locals as second-class citizens.

Visiting Religious Sites

When visiting monasteries or temples, avoid smoking and remove your shoes before you enter. Always walk clockwise around Buddhist stupas (bell-shaped religious structures), chörtens (Tibetan-style stupas) and mani (stone carved with a Tibetan-Buddhist chant) walls, even if this involves detouring off the trail. Some Hindu temples are closed to non-Hindus (this is normally indicated by a sign) and others will not allow you to enter with any leather items. Locals always leave a donation in a gompa or temple and you should follow their example.

Buddhism has a number of taboos which you should avoid. The head is regarded as the 'highest part of the body', so avoid touching children on the head, particularly young monks. Similarly, the feet are the 'lowest' part of the body – never sit with the soles of your feet pointing towards a person or a Buddha image, and don't step over someone's outstretched legs.

If you are introduced to a Buddhist lama (teacher) it is customary to give a *kata* (white scarf) to the Buddhist lama. Place it in the lama's hands, not around their neck.

Public Modesty

Follow the lead of locals when it comes to appropriate clothing. Short shorts, sleeveless tops and other revealing items of clothing are unsuitable for women or men. Nudity is unacceptable anywhere. Public displays of affection between men and women are frowned upon, so tone down the public intimacy. Nepali men often walk around hand in hand, but this does not carry any sexual overtones.

Manners

Nepalis rarely shake hands – the *namaste* greeting (placing your palms together in a prayer position) is a better choice. When giving or receiving money, use your right hand and touch your right elbow with your left hand, as a gesture of respect. If you are invited into a Nepali home, always remove your shoes before you enter. Do not throw rubbish onto any fire used for cooking – fire is considered sacred.

Nepalis do not like to give negative answers and will always try to give some answer, even if they do not know the answer to your question. If you are given incorrect information, this may be through fear of disappointing you. Raising your voice or shouting shows extremely bad manners and will not solve your problem, whatever it might be. Always try to remain cool, calm and collected.

A sideways tilt or wobble of the head, accompanied by a slight shrug of the shoulders, conveys agreement in Nepal, not a 'no'.

Photography

The behaviour of some photographers at places such as Pashupatinath (the most holy cremation site in Nepal) is shameful – imagine the outrage if a busload of scantily clad, camera-toting tourists invaded a family funeral in the West. Do not intrude with a camera, unless it is clearly OK with the people you are photographing. Ask first, and respect the wishes of local people. Photography is prohibited at many temples and

Smoking is forbidden at Buddhist monasteries and other sacred sites across Nepal. As legend has it, even the great Guru Rinpoche believed the demon weed was an obstacle to enlightenment!

monasteries, and it is plainly inappropriate at cremations or where people are washing in public at riverbanks or cisterns. If you attend any religious ritual, get explicit permission from senior participants before you start clicking.

USEFUL ORGANISATIONS

There are a number of organisations based in Nepal that are involved in grassroots initiatives to minimise the impact of tourism. Contact the following:

Annapurna Conservation Area Project (ACAP; Map p126; ☎ 01-4222406; www.ntnc.org.np; Pradarshanti Marg, Kathmandu; 9am-5pm Sun-Fri, 9am-2pm Sat) Nongovernmental, nonprofit organisation that exists to improve local standards of living, to protect the environment and to develop more sensitive forms of tourism. ACAP also administers the Annapurna Conservation Area and Manaslu Conservation Area. There are branches in Kathmandu, Patan and Pokhara.

Kathmandu Environmental Education Project (KEEP; Map p140; ☎ 01-4216775; www.keepnepal.org; Jyatha, Thamel; 10am-5pm Sun-Fri) This excellent educational organisation offers advice on reducing the environmental impact of tourism. Drop into the Kathmandu office for tips and purified water refills.

National Trust for Nature Conservation (☎ 01-5526571; www.ntnc.org.np) Manages and oversees the Annapurna Conservation Area and Manaslu Conservation Area and promotes conservation and sustainable development.

The Sagarmatha Pollution Control Committee (SPCC; spcc@mail.com.np) was set up to combat the growing problem of pollution in the Everest region – drop into its office in Lukla or Namche Bazaar for information on current issues and campaigns.

Environment

Nepal is blessed by, and is hostage to, its incredible environment. Its economy, its history, its resources and its culture are all intrinsically linked to the string of mountains that rise like icy giants above the plains. Often, this daunting landscape is as much a hindrance as a benefit – development has been massively set back by the logistical problems of bringing roads, electricity, health care and education to remote mountain communities.

If there is one lesson that can be drawn from Nepal, it is that man underestimates the power of nature at his peril. Many of the natural disasters that blight Nepal year after year – floods, forest fires, droughts and landslides – are directly linked to human activity. Faced by environmental issues of this scale, you may feel that one person cannot make a difference, but the reality is that every traveller who carries a piece of litter downhill is making a genuine difference to the environment of the Himalaya.

See the Responsible Tourism chapter (p70) for more ways you can help while travelling in Nepal.

margin notes:

Nepalis divide the year into six, not four, seasons: Basanta (spring), Grisma (premonsoon heat), Barkha (monsoon), Sharad (post-monsoon), Hemanta (autumn) and Sheet (winter).

The Terai makes up only 17% of Nepal's area but holds 50% of its population and 70% of its agricultural land.

For reasons that are not entirely clear, the official height of Everest in Nepal is 2m lower than the accepted height in the rest of the world.

THE LAND

Nepal is a small, landlocked strip of land, 800km long and 200km wide. However, it fits a lot of terrain into just 147,181 sq km. Heading north from the Indian border, the landscape rises from just 150m above sea level to 8850m at the tip of Mt Everest. Around 64% of the country is covered by mountains, yet almost half the population live on the flat plains of the Terai, which accounts for just 17% of the landmass of Nepal.

This dramatic landscape provides a habitat for an incredible range of plants, animals and people – Nepal is home to 59 recognised tribes, who make up 37% of the total population. In Nepal, it is not just the flora and fauna that has adapted to life in this epic terrain. The Sherpas and other hill tribes have a unique physiology that enables them to carry more oxygen in their blood than people from the plains.

Geology

Imagine the space currently occupied by Nepal as an open expanse of water, and the Tibetan plateau as the coast. This was the situation until 60 million years ago, when the Indo-Australian plate collided with the Eurasian continent, bucking the earth's crust up into mighty ridges and forming the mountains we now call the Himalaya.

The upheaval of mountains caused the temporary obstruction of rivers that once flowed unimpeded from Eurasia to the sea. Simultaneously, new rivers arose on the southern slopes of these young mountains as moist winds from the tropical seas to the south rose and precipitated. For the next 60 million years, the mountains moved up and rivers and glaciers cut downwards, creating the peaks and valleys seen across Nepal today.

The modern landscape of Nepal – a grid of four major mountain systems, incised by the north–south gorges of rivers – is not the final story. The Indo-Australian plate is still sliding under the Eurasian Himalaya at a rate of 27mm per year and pushing the Himalaya even higher. As fast as the mountains rise, they are being eroded by glaciers, rivers and landslides, and chipped away by earthquakes and the effects of cold and heat.

Nepal is still an active seismic zone. A huge earthquake caused devastation around the country in 1934 and a similar-sized quake today would

---

MT EVEREST

Everest has gone by a number of different names over the years. The Survey of India christened the mountain 'Peak XV', but it was renamed Everest after Sir George Everest, the surveyor general of India in 1865. It was later discovered that the mountain already had a name – Sherpas call the peak Chomolungma, after the female guardian deity of the mountain, who rides a red tiger and is one of the five sisters of long life. There was no Nepali name for the mountain until 1956 when the historian Babu Ram Acharya invented the name Sagarmatha, meaning 'head of the sky'.

Using triangulation from the plains of India, the Survey of India established the elevation of the summit of Everest at 8839m. In 1954, this was revised to 8848m using data from 12 different survey stations around the mountain. In 1999, a team sponsored by National Geographic used GPS data to produce a new elevation of 8850m, but in 2002, a Chinese team made measurements from the summit using ice radar and GPS systems and produced a height of 8844.43m.

So is Everest shrinking? Not exactly; the Chinese calculated the height of the bedrock of the mountain, without the accumulated snow and ice. In fact, Everest is still growing at a rate of 6mm a year as plate tectonics drives the Indian subcontinent underneath Eurasia. To complicate things, Nepal still prefers to use the old 8848m elevation.

---

cause unimaginable damage to the tall, densely packed and poorly constructed buildings that dominate the Kathmandu Valley.

Physiographic Regions

Nepal consists of several physiographic regions, or natural zones: the southern plains, the four mountain ranges, and the valleys and hills in between. Most people live in the fertile lowlands or on the sunny southern slopes of mountains. Above 4000m, the only residents are yak herders, who retreat into the valleys with the onset of winter.

The Kali Gandaki Valley between the Annapurna and Dhaulagiri massifs is considered the world's deepest gorge, with a vertical gain of 7km.

THE TERAI & CHURE HILLS

The only truly flat land in Nepal is the Terai (or Tarai), a patchwork of paddy fields, sal forests, tiny thatched villages and sprawling industrial cities. The vast expanse of the Gangetic plain extends for 40km into Nepal before the land rises to create the Chure Hills. With an average height of 1000m, this minor ridge runs the length of the country, separating the Terai from a second low-lying area called the inner Terai or the Dun.

MAHABHARAT RANGE

Saligrams (fossilised squidlike ammonites) are found throughout the Himalaya and are regarded as symbols of Vishnu – they also provide clear proof that the Himalaya used to lie beneath the ancient Tethys Sea.

North of the inner Terai, the land rises again to form the Mahabharat Range, or the 'Middle Hills'. These vary between 1500m and 2700m in height, and form the heartland of the inhabited highlands of Nepal. Locals raise rice, barley, millet, wheat, maize and other crops on cascades of terraced fields set among patches of tropical and temperate forest. These hills are cut by three major river systems: the Karnali, the Narayani and the Sapt Kosi.

PAHAR ZONE

Between the Mahabharat Range and the Himalaya lies a broad, extensively cultivated belt called the Pahar zone. This includes the fertile valleys of Kathmandu, Banepa and Pokhara, which were once the beds of lakes, formed by trapped rivers. After the Terai, this is the most inhabited part of Nepal and the expanding human population is putting a massive strain on natural resources. Only a few areas of forest have escaped the ravages of firewood collectors.

The stunningly located Pokhara area, right at the foot of the Annapurna massif, is unique because there is no major barrier to the south to block the path of spring and monsoon rain clouds. As a result Pokhara receives an exceptionally high level of rainfall, limiting cultivation to below 2000m.

THE HIMALAYA

One-third of the total length of the Himalaya lies inside Nepal's borders and the country claims 10 of the world's 14 tallest mountains. The Himalayan range is broken up into groups of massifs divided by glaciers and rivers draining down from the Tibetan plateau.

Because of the southerly latitude (similar to that of Florida) and the reliable rainfall the mountains are cloaked in vegetation to a height of 3500m to 4000m. Humans mainly inhabit the areas below 2700m – from here to the tree line (around 3900m), the forests are fairly well preserved.

THE TRANS-HIMALAYA

North of the first ridge of the Himalaya is a high-altitude desert, similar to the Tibetan plateau. This area encompasses the arid valleys of Mustang, Manang and Dolpo, as well as the minor peaks of the Tibetan marginals. The moisture-laden clouds of the monsoon drop all their rain on the south side of the mountains, leaving the trans-Himalaya in permanent rain shadow. Surreal crags, spires and badlands eroded by the scouring action of the wind are characteristic of this bleak landscape.

> The Sanskrit word Himalaya means abode (*alaya*) of the snows (himal). There is no such thing as the Himalayas. To pronounce it correctly, as they do in the corridors of the Royal Geographical Society, emphasise the second syllable – hi*m-aaar*-liya, darling…

WILDLIFE

Nepal is a region of exceptional biodiversity, with a unique variety of landscapes and climatic conditions. The following is a guide to the species that travellers are likely to see – or would like to see. If you are a nature buff, it's worth carrying a spotters' guide; see the sidebars in this chapter for some suggestions.

Animals

The diverse environments of the Himalaya and the Middle Hills provide a home for a remarkable array of birds, reptiles, amphibians and mammals. However, many mammal and bird species are threatened by poaching and hunting. Your best chances for spotting wildlife are in national parks and conservation areas, or high in the mountains far away from human habitation.

SIGNATURE SPECIES

Nepal has a number of 'signature species' that every visitor wants to see. Unfortunately, these also tend to be the species most threatened by poaching and habitat loss. Opportunities to view the following animals are usually restricted to national parks, reserves and sparsely populated areas of western Nepal. For more on signature species see the boxed text, p286.

At the top of the food chain is the royal Bengal tiger (*bagh* in Nepali), which is solitary and territorial. Chitwan National Park and Bardia National Park in the Terai protect sufficient habitat to sustain viable breeding populations (Chitwan has around 110 tigers, Bardia 22). The main threat to tigers is poaching to supply skins for Tibetan traditional costumes and tiger parts for Chinese medicine.

The spotted leopard (*chituwa*) is more common than the tiger and a major threat to domestic livestock. Like the tiger, this nocturnal creature has been known to target humans when it is unable, through old age or illness, to hunt for its normal prey species. The endangered snow leopard is so rare that it is almost a legend, but there are thought to be 300 to 500 snow leopards surviving in the high Himalaya, particularly around Dolpo.

> There are estimated to be less than 500 surviving snow leopards, spread across a territory of 30,000 sq km, which could be one reason they are so rarely seen.

Snow leopards are so elusive that many locals believe the animals have the power to vanish at will.

Found in the *phanta* (grass plains) of the Terai region, the one-horned rhinoceros (gaida) is the largest of the three Asian rhino species. Rhino populations plummeted due to poaching during the Maoist insurgency but they have recovered slightly since 2005 – today there are around 408 rhinos in Chitwan and smaller populations in Bardia National Park and Sukla Phanta Wildlife Reserve.

Soul of the Rhino, by Hemanta R Mishra, is an intriguing peek into the world of the one-horned Indian rhinoceros and the human beings who share its habitat.

The only wild Asian elephants (hathi) in Nepal are in the western part of the Terai and Chure Hills. However, herds of domesticated elephants are found at all the national parks in the Terai, where they carry tourists on wildlife-spotting safaris.

The predator most commonly seen in the hills is the Himalayan black bear. This large omnivore frequently raids crops on the edge of mountain villages. In the rare event of an attack by a bear, the best defence is to lie face down on the ground. All of Nepal's bears are threatened by the trade in animal parts for Chinese medicine.

Perhaps the rarest animal of all is the endangered river dolphin. This mammalian predator is almost blind and hunts its way through the murky waters of lowland rivers using sonar. There are thought to be fewer than 100 dolphins left in Nepal, with the largest population living in the Karnali River.

MONKEYS

International activists are campaigning to stop Nepal shipping rhesus macaque monkeys overseas to be used for animal experimentation. Neighbouring India banned the export of monkeys in 1977.

Because of Hanuman, the monkey god from the Ramayana, monkeys are considered holy and are well protected in Nepal. You will often see troops of muscular rhesus macaques harassing tourists and pilgrims for food scraps at monuments and temples. These monkeys can be openly aggressive and they carry rabies, so appreciate them from a distance (and if that doesn't work, carry a stick).

You may also spot the slender common langur, with its short grey fur and black face, in forested areas up to 3700m. This species is more gentle than the thuggish macaque but again, watch your bananas.

HERBIVORES

Deer are abundant in the lowlands, providing a food source for tigers, leopards and other predators. Prominent species include the sambar and the spotted deer, the main prey of the royal Bengal tiger.

In forests up to 2400m, you may hear the screamlike call of the *muntjac* (barking deer), the oldest species of deer on earth. At higher altitudes, watch for the pocked-sized musk deer, which stands just 50cm high at the shoulder. These animals have been severely depleted by hunting for the musk gland found in the abdomen of male deer.

Nature Treks (www .nature-treks.com) offers organised walks with expert naturalists at Shivapuri National Park, Chitwan National Park, Bardia National Park and in the Langtang area.

In high mountain areas, look out for the Himalayan tahr, a shaggy mountain goat, and the blue sheep (*naur* in Tibetan, *bharal* in Nepali), which is genetically stranded somewhere between goats and sheep.

SMALL MAMMALS

The boulder fields and forests of the Himalaya provide shelter for several small rodents. The *pika* (mouse-hare) is commonly spotted scurrying nervously between rocks on trekking trails. You must climb higher to the trans-Himalayan zone in western Nepal to see the Himalayan marmot, related to the American groundhog.

Various species of squirrels and chipmunks live in the forests, including rare flying squirrels, which glide through the canopy using extended flaps of skin between their legs. Noisy colonies of fruit bats can be spotted roosting in trees in the Terai and the Kathmandu Valley, particularly near the new Royal Palace in Kathmandu. Although these 'flying foxes' look quite fearsome, their diet consists entirely of fruit.

BIRDS

More than 850 bird species are known in Nepal and almost half of these can be spotted in the Kathmandu Valley. March to May is the main breeding season and the best time to spot birds. Resident bird numbers are augmented by migratory species, which arrive in the Terai in February and March en route from Siberia. The best places in Nepal for birdwatching are Koshi Tappu Wildlife Reserve (p321) and Chitwan National Park (p281). The best spots in the Kathmandu Valley are Pulchowki Mountain (p221), Nagarjun Forest Reserve (p179) and Shivapuri National Park (p180).

Eight species of stork have been identified along the watercourses of the Terai, and demoiselle cranes fly down the Kali Gandaki and Dudh Kosi for the winter, before returning in spring to their Tibetan nesting grounds. The endangered sarus crane can be spotted in Bardia National Park and the privately funded Lumbini Crane Sanctuary near Lumbini (p299).

Raptors or birds of prey of all sizes are found in Nepal. In the Kathmandu Valley and Terai, keep an eye out for the sweeping silhouettes of vultures and fork-tailed pariah kites circling ominously in the haze. In the mountains, watch for golden eagles and the huge Himalayan griffon and lammergeier.

There are six species of pheasant in Nepal, including the national bird, the *danphe*, also known as the Himalayan monal or impeyan pheasant. Females are a dull brown, while males are an iridescent rainbow of colours. In areas frequented by trekkers, these birds are often quite tame, though they will launch themselves downhill in a falling, erratic flight if disturbed.

Nepal hosts 17 species of cuckoo, which arrive in March, heralding the coming of spring. The call of the Indian cuckoo is likened to the Nepali phrase *kaphal pakyo*, meaning 'the fruit of the box myrtle is ripe'. The call of the common hawk cuckoo sounds like the words 'brain fever' – or so it was described by British *sahibs* (gentlemen) as they lay sweating with malarial fevers.

While trekking through forests, keep an eye out for members of the timalid family. The spiny babbler is Nepal's only endemic species, and the black-capped sibia, with its constant prattle and ringing song, is frequently heard in wet temperate forests. In the Pokhara region, the Indian roller is conspicuous when it takes flight, flashing the iridescent turquoise on its wings. Local superstition has it that if someone about to embark on a journey sees a roller going their way it is a good omen.

Another colourful character is the hoopoe, which has a retractable crest, a long curved bill, eye-catching orange plumage, and black-and-white stripes on its wings. Nepal is also home to 30 species of flycatchers and 60 species of warblers, as well as bee-eaters, drongos, minivets, parakeets and sunbirds.

Around watercourses, look out for thrushes, such as the handsome white-capped river chat and the delightfully named plumbeous redstart.

Nepal covers only 0.1% of the world's surface area but is home to nearly 10% of the world's species of birds, including 72 critically endangered species.

Bird Conservation Nepal (www.birdlife nepal.org) is an excellent Nepali organisation based in Kathmandu that organises birdwatching trips and publishes books, birding checklists and a good quarterly newsletter.

Birds of Nepal, by Robert Fleming Sr, Robert Fleming Jr and Lain Singh Bangdel, is a field guide to Nepal's many hundreds of bird species. *Birds of Nepal*, by Richard Grimmett and Carol Inskipp, is a comprehensive paperback with line drawings.

DINNER AT THE ROTTING CARCASS

Three of Nepal's nine species of vultures are critically endangered and thousands more birds die every year after scavenging dead cows that have been treated with the anti-inflammatory drug diclofenac. A new scheme to feed vultures with uncontaminated meat has yielded remarkable results. Nicknamed the 'vulture restaurant', the project has doubled the vulture population of Nawalparasi district in the western Terai in just two years. Plans are now afoot to open vulture bistros across the country to save these magnificent birds from extinction.

ENDANGERED SPECIES

You might think that the mountains and jungles would provide some protection for wildlife, but many of Nepal's most famous animals are on the list of endangered species. In the mountains, time is running out for the snow leopard, clouded leopard, red panda, wild yak, musk deer, great Tibetan sheep and hispid hare. In the Terai, the Bengal tiger, Asian elephant, one-horned rhinoceros, Gaur bison, swamp deer, gharial crocodile and Gangetic dolphin are clinging on in the face of extinction.

The greatest threat to Nepal's wildlife comes from hunting for food and from poaching to supply animal parts for Chinese medicine and Tibetan traditional costumes. In just one raid in 2005, the Nepali army seized five tiger skins, 36 leopard skins, 238 otter skins and 113kg of tiger and leopard bones, destined for sale in China and Tibet. International organisations such as the World Wide Fund for Nature (WWF; www.wwf.org) are attempting to ensure the preservation of these wonderful, endangered animals.

Scan the surrounding trees or electricity cables for the black-and-white pied kingfisher and the white-breasted kingfisher with its iridescent turquoise jacket.

Different species of crows have adapted to different altitudes. The yellow-billed blue magpie and Himalayan tree pie are commonly seen in the temperate zone. Above the tree line, red- and yellow-billed choughs gather in flocks, particularly in areas frequented by humans. In the trans-Himalayan region you will also see the menacing black raven, which scours the valleys looking for scavenging opportunities.

Nepal Nature (www .nepalnature.com) is a tour company run by Nepali conservationists and nature experts. It runs birdwatching tours to Shivapuri National Park and crane sanctuaries around Lumbini.

REPTILES & AMBHIBIANS

As well as hundreds of species of frogs and lizards, Nepal is home to two indigenous species of crocodile. The endangered gharial inhabits rivers, hunting for fish with an elongated snout lined with sharp teeth – fossils of similar crocodiles have been found that date back 100 million years. The gharial was hunted to the brink of extinction, but populations have recovered since the establishment of a hatchery in Chitwan.

The stocky marsh mugger prefers stagnant water and is omnivorous, feeding on anything within reach, including people. In fact, the Western word 'mugger' comes from the Hindi/Nepali name for this skulking predator. Many species of snake survive in the Terai, including cobras, vipers and kraits; travellers rarely encounter these animals, but keep an eye out for pythons in Nepal's national parks.

Plants

And the Wildest dreams of Kew are but the facts of Kathmandu
Rudyard Kipling

Himalayan Flowers & Trees, by Dorothy Mierow and Tirtha Bahadur Shrestha, is the best available field guide to the plants of Nepal.

There are about 6500 known species of trees, shrubs and wildflowers in Nepal, but perhaps the most famous is *Rhododendron arboreum* (*lali gurans* in Nepali), the national flower of Nepal. It might better be described as a tree, reaching heights of 18m and forming whole forests in the Himalaya region. More than 30 other species of rhododendrons are found in the foothills of the Himalaya and the rhododendron forests burst into flower in March and April, painting the landscape in swathes of white, pink and red.

The best time to see the wildflowers of the Himalaya in bloom is during the monsoon, when the trails are muddy and the skies overcast. The views may be obscured but the ground underfoot will be a carpet of mints, scrophs, buttercups, cinquefoils, polygonums, ephedras, cotoneasters, saxifrages and primulas.

Many of the alpine species found above the tree line bear flowers in autumn, including irises, gentians, anemones and the downy-petalled edelweiss. In subtropical and lower temperate areas, look for aree pink luculia, mauve osbeckia and yellow St John's wort, as well as flowering cherry trees. Marigolds are grown in gardens and plantations across Nepal to provide the garlands offered at Hindu temples. In the Kathmandu Valley, silky oak with its spring golden inflorescence, and bottlebrush and eucalyptus, are planted as ornamentals.

In the foothills of the Himalaya, as well as in the plains, look for the magnificent mushrooming canopies of banyan and pipal trees, which often form the focal point of villages. The pipal tree has a special religious significance in Nepal – the Buddha gained enlightenment under a pipal tree and Hindus revere various species of pipals as symbols of Vishnu and Hanuman.

Sal, a broad-leaved, semideciduous hardwood, dominates the low-lying tropical forests of the Terai. Sal leaves are used as disposable plates and the wood is used for construction. On the flat plains, many areas are covered by *phanta* – this giant grass can grow to 2.5m high and is used by villagers for thatching.

> Bis Hajaar Tal (literally '20,000 lakes') in Chitwan National Park (p281) and the Koshi Tappu Wildlife Reserve (p321) are both Ramsar sites (www.ramsar .org), designated as wetlands of international importance.

NATIONAL PARKS & CONSERVATION AREAS

Nepal's first national park was established in 1973 at Chitwan National Park in the Terai. There are now nine national parks, three wildlife reserves, three conservation areas and, somewhat incongruously, one hunting reserve, protecting 18% of the land in Nepal. Entry fees apply for all the national parks and reserves, including conserved areas on trekking routes in the mountains – see the National Parks & Conservation Areas boxed text (p84) for a breakdown.

The main agency overseeing national parks and conservation areas is the **Department of National Parks and Wildlife Conservation** (Map p126; www.dnpwc.gov.np). However, the last few years have seen a shift in the management of protected areas away from the Nepali government to international nongovernmental organisations (NGOs). The **National Trust for Nature Conservation** (www.ntnc.org .np), formerly the King Mahendra Trust for Nature Conservation, runs the Annapurna Conservation Area Project and Manaslu Conservation Area, and the **Mountain Institute** (www.mountain.org) runs a number of conservation projects in the Makalu-Barun and Kanchenjunga areas.

> Nepal's national parks and conservation areas are described in detail at www.visitnepal .com/nepal_information /nepalparks.php.

The first protected areas were imposed by the government with little partnership with locals and initially without their cooperation. Recent initiatives have concentrated on educating local people and accommodating their needs, rather than evicting them completely from the land.

The community forest model has been particularly successful in Nepal – many protected areas are surrounded by a buffer zone of communityowned forests, whose owners harvest natural resources and thus have a stake in their continued existence. See the website of the **Federation of Community Forest Users** (www.fecofun.org) for more information.

> For more on Nepal's environment check out www.iucnnepal.org and www.wwfnepal.org.

ENVIRONMENTAL ISSUES

The ecology of Nepal is fragile and a rapidly growing population is constantly adding to the pressure on the environment. Much of the land between the Himalaya and the Terai has been vigorously modified by humans to provide space for crops, animals and houses. Forests have been cleared, wildlife populations depleted and roads have eaten into valleys that were previously accessible only on foot. As a result, Shangri La is hovering on the edge of environmental collapse.

NATIONAL PARKS & CONSERVATION AREAS

Name	Location	Features	Best time to visit	Entry fee (Rs)	Page
Annapurna CA	north of Pokhara	most popular trekking area in Nepal, high peaks, diverse landscapes & varied culture	Oct-Apr, May	2000	p352
Bardia NP	far western Terai	sal forest, tiger, one-horned rhinoceros, over 250 species of birds	Oct-early Apr	500	p309
Chitwan NP	central Terai	tropical & subtropical forests, rhinoceros, tiger, gharial crocodile, 450 species of birds, World Heritage site	Oct-Feb	500	p281
Dhorpatan HR	west-central Nepal	Nepal's only hunting reserve (access is difficult), blue sheep	Mar-Apr	500	
Kanchenjunga CA	far eastern Nepal	third-highest mountain in the world, prolific wildlife, blue sheep & snow leopards	Mar-Apr, Oct-Nov	1000	
Khaptad NP	far western Nepal	core area is important religious site	Mar-Apr	1000	
Koshi Tappu WR	eastern Nepal	grasslands, often flooded during monsoon, 439 species of birds, wild water buffalo	Oct-Nov, Mar-Apr	500	p321
Langtang NP	northeast of Kathmandu	varied topography, diverse culture, a stop on the migratory route for birds travelling between India & Tibet	Mar-Apr, Sep-mid Dec	1000	p346
Makalu-Barun NP	eastern Nepal	bordering Sagarmatha NP, protecting high mountains & diverse hill landscapes	Oct-May	1000	p360
Manaslu CA	west-central Nepal	rugged terrain, 11 types of forest, bordering Annapurna CA	Oct-Nov, Mar-Apr	2000	p360
Parsa WR	central Terai	inside Chitwan NP, sal forests, wild elephants, 300 species of birds	Oct-Apr	500	p281
Rara NP	northwestern Nepal	Nepal's biggest lake, little visited, many migratory birds	Oct-Dec, Mar-May	1000	p312
Sagarmatha NP	Everest region	highest mountains on the planet, World Heritage sites, monasteries & Sherpa culture	Oct-May	1000	p343
Shey Phoksumdo NP	Dolpo, western Nepal	trans-Himalayan ecosystem, alpine flowers, high passes, snow leopard & musk deer	Jun-Sep	1000	
Shivapuri NP	northeast of Kathmandu	close to Kathmandu, many bird & butterfly species, good hiking & biking	Oct-May	250	p180
Sukla Phanta WR	southwestern Nepal	riverine flood plain, grasslands, endangered swamp deer, wild elephants	Oct-Apr	500	p312

NP = National Park, CA = Conservation Area, WR = Wildlife Reserve, HR = Hunting Reserve

Population growth is the biggest issue facing the environment in Nepal. More people need more land for agriculture and more natural resources for building, heating and cooking. The population of Nepal is increasing at a rate of 2.1% every year and tourism is providing a financial incentive for the settlement of previously uninhabited mountain areas.

There have also been some environmental successes in Nepal. Foreign and Nepali NGOs have provided solar panels, biogas and kerosene powered stoves and parabolic solar heaters for thousands of farms, trekking lodges, schools and monasteries across Nepal.

Deforestation

Almost 80% of Nepali citizens rely on fuel wood for heating and cooking, particularly in the mountains, leading to massive problems with deforestation. Nepal has lost more than 70% of its forest cover in modern times and travellers are contributing to the problem by increasing the demand for firewood in mountain areas.

As well as robbing native species of their natural habitat, deforestation drives animals directly into conflict with human beings and the loss of tree cover is a major contributing factor to the landslides that scar the valleys of the Himalaya after every monsoon. Many locals were killed in severe landslides at Khobang in eastern Nepal in 2002 and in Mustang in 2006.

It's not all doom and gloom though – in recent years, a number of community forests have been established on the boundaries of national parks. The forests are communally owned and the sustainable harvest of timber and other natural resources provides an economic alternative to poaching and resource gathering inside the parks.

Poaching

Nepal's 10-year Maoist insurgency did not only affect human beings. Soldiers were withdrawn from national park checkpoints, leading to a massive upsurge in poaching. Nepal's rhino population fell by 30% between 2000 and 2005 and elephants, tigers, leopards and other endangered species were also targeted.

The main engines driving poaching are the trade in animal parts for Chinese medicine and the trade in animal pelts to Tibet for the manufacture of traditional costumes known as *chubas*. Travellers can avoid contributing to the problem by rejecting souvenirs made from animal products – see p73 for more information.

Hydroelectricity

On the face of things, harnessing the power of Nepal's rivers to create electricity sounds like a win-win situation, but the environmental impact

> Pressure cookers make an unlikely contribution to the environment in Nepal – water boils below 100°C at altitude, and cooks can reduce cooking times, and therefore firewood consumption, by cooking in a pressurised pot.

> More than 30% of the world's total one-horned rhino population lives in Nepal's Chitwan National Park. Frighteningly, the population of rhinos at Chitwan dropped by 30% from 2000 to 2005 due to poaching.

USEFUL ENVIRONMENTAL ORGANISATIONS

Contact the following organisations for more information on environmental issues in Nepal:

Bird Conservation Nepal (www.birdlifenepal.org)
Himalayan Nature (www.himalayannature.org)
International Centre for Integrated Mountain Development (www.icimod.org)
National Trust for Nature Conservation (www.ntnc.org.np)
Resources Himalaya (www.resourceshimalaya.org)
Wildlife Conservation Nepal (www.wcn.org.np)
World Conservation Union (www.iucnnepal.org)
World Wildlife Fund Nepal (www.wwfnepal.org)

FLOODING IN THE HIMALAYA

Every year, the Terai faces severe flooding problems because of increased drainage from the mountains caused by the monsoon rains. In recent years, these problems have been exacerbated by deforestation, which increases drainage from mountain slopes, and by high rainfall, linked to climate change. In August 2008, unusually heavy rainfall caused the Sapt Kosi River to burst its banks near Loki, displacing millions of people in Nepal and Bihar (see p320).

In the mountains, the flood risk comes from a different source. Rising global temperatures are melting the glaciers that snake down from the Himalaya, swelling glacial lakes to dangerous levels.

In 1985, a natural dam collapsed in the Thame Valley, releasing the trapped waters of the Dig Tsho lake and sending devastating floods roaring along the Dudh Kosi Valley.

Scientists are now watching the Imja Tsho in the Chhukung Valley with alarm. Since 1960, the lake has grown by 35 million cu metres – when it ruptures, experts are predicting a 'vertical tsunami' that will affect one of the most heavily populated and heavily trekked parts of the Himalaya.

---

of building new hydroelectric plants can be devastating. Entire valleys are flooded to create new reservoirs and most of the energy is diverted to the overpopulated Kathmandu Valley or exported to China and India.

As well as displacing local people and damaging the local environment, large hydro schemes affect the flow of water downstream, disrupting the passage of nutrient-rich silt to agricultural land in the plains. Concerns about the huge new hydroelectric plants on the Kali Gandaki and West Seti Rivers have been exacerbated by the 2008 floods in Nepal.

For information on alternative energy projects in Nepal, visit the websites of the Centre for Rural Technology (www .crtnepal.org), the Foundation for Sustainable Technologies (www.fost-nepal.org) and Drokpa (www .drokpa.org).

Tourism

Tourism has brought health care, education, electricity and wealth to some of the most remote, isolated communities on earth, but it has also had a massive impact on the local environment.

Forests are being cleared at an unprecedented rate to provide timber for the construction of new lodges and fuel for cooking and heating, and trekkers contribute massively to the build-up of litter and the erosion of mountain trails.

Even the apparent benefits of tourism can have environmental implications – the wealth that tourism has brought to villages in the Himalaya has allowed many farmers to increase the size of their herds of goats, cows and yaks, leading to yet more deforestation as woodland is cleared to provide temporary pastures.

You can read the government take on the controversy over hydroelectricity on the website of the West Seti Hydro project (www .wsh.com.np).

Water Supplies

Despite the natural abundance of water, water shortages are another chronic problem in Nepal, particularly in the Kathmandu Valley. Where water is available, it is often contaminated with heavy metals, industrial chemicals, bacteria and human waste. In Kathmandu, the holy Bagmati River has become one of the most polluted rivers on earth; see www.friendsofthebagmati .org.np for more on this sorry story.

In the Terai, one of the biggest problems is arsenic poisoning from contaminated drinking water. Up to 1.4 million people are thought to be at risk from this deadly toxin, which is drawn into wells and reservoirs from contaminated aquifers.

In the mountains, the problem is often too much, rather than too little water – see the boxed text, above.

Himal South Asia (www .himalmag.com) is a bimonthly magazine mainly devoted to development and environmental issues. It's an excellent publication with top-class contributors.

Outdoor Activities

Despite what Kiwis will tell you, Nepal is probably the world's greatest outdoors destination. The towering mountains offer some of the Himalaya's most awe-inspiring walking but there's also some spectacular mountain biking, and its mighty mountain rivers fuel some of the best white-water rafting you'll find anywhere. An added bonus is that all this fun comes in at less than half the price of places like the US or New Zealand. For an added thrill try bungee jumping 160m into a Himalayan gorge or abseiling *into* a thundering 45m waterfall. Oh, and did we mention that Pokhara is one of the best paragliding spots in the world? Pack a spare pair of underpants – you're going to need them.

BUNGEE JUMPING

The 'ultimate bungee' straddles a mighty 160m drop into the gorge of the Bhote Kosi at the Last Resort, just 12km from the Tibetan border. It's one of the world's longest bungee jumps (higher than the highest bungee in New Zealand) and the roars and squeals of free-falling tourists echo up and down the valley for miles.

The swing or bungee costs US$80 from Kathmandu (including return transport from Kathmandu and lunch) or US$70 if you are already up at the Last Resort. Extra jumps cost US$25, or add on a swing to a bungee for an extra US$20. Every fourth jump is free. For US$15 you can reveal your inner wisdom and travel up to watch someone else jump and enjoy the looks on everyone else's faces when they catch their first glimpse of how deep a 160m gorge really is. The price includes whatever lunch you can muster, wisely served up *after* the jump.

Visit the office of the **Last Resort** (Map p140; ☎ 01-4439525; www.tlrnepal.com) in Kathmandu for details of current packages. A two-day bungee and rafting package with overnight accommodation and four meals and transport costs around US$130.

As if the tallest bungee in Asia wasn't enough, the fiendish minds at the Last Resort have devised the 'swing', a stomach-loosening eight-second free fall, followed by a Tarzanlike swing and then three or four pendulum swings back up and then down the length of the gorge. We feel ill just writing about it.

HOW MUCH TIME DO YOU HAVE?

One day Bungee jump at the Last Resort (above); paraglide at Sarangkot (p88); take a mountain flight (p387).
Two days Go canyoning at Borderlands or the Last Resort (p88); raft the Bhote Kosi (p107) or Trisuli River (p106); trek Nagarkot to Sundarijal (p223).
Three days Mountain hike Kathmandu–Dhulikhel Namobuddha–Lakuri Bhanjyang (p95); raft the Kali Gandaki (p108).
Four days Learn to kayak at a kayak clinic (p104); do a canyoning and Bhote Kosi rafting combo (p88); raft the Kali Gandaki (p108) or Marsyangdi (p108); go to Chitwan from Kathmandu and then take a safari excursion in the park (p288); experience the views on the Annapurna Skyline Trek (Royal Trek; p276).
Six days Trek from Borderlands or the Last Resort to the Tibetan border (p231); hike the Tamang Heritage Trail near Langtang (p233); complete the Ghorepani to Ghandruk loop trek (p276).
Seven days Fly in to Lukla then trek to Thame, Namche Bazaar and Tengboche on the Everest Base Camp Trek (p340); walk the Langtang Valley trek (p346).
Eight days Trek the Helambu trek (p351).
Nine days Raft the Sun Kosi River (p110).
10 days Do a Karnali River trip (p109).
15 days Trek up to Everest Base Camp with flights in and out of Lukla (p340).
18 days Complete the Annapurna Circuit (p352).
21 days Combine the Everest Base Camp and Gokyo treks (p340).

CANYONING

This exciting sport is a wild combination of rappelling/abseiling, climbing, sliding and swimming that has been pioneered in the canyons and waterfalls near the Last Resort and Borderlands (see p231).

Both companies run two-day canyoning trips for about US$100, or you can combine two days canyoning with a two-day Bhote Kosi rafting trip for US$200 (half this for one day's canyoning and one day's rafting). On day one you drive up from Kathmandu, have lunch, get some basic abseiling training and then practise on nearby cascades. Day two involves a trip out to more exciting falls, with a maximum abseil of up to 45m. Most canyons involve a short hike to get there.

The Last Resort uses Panglong canyon early in the season and to train novices. After December the action moves to higher and more exciting canyons such as Kanglang, Kahule and Bhukute (a 60m drop), once the water flow has subsided to safe levels. Canyoning is not possible during the monsoon.

Borderlands uses Old and New Jombo canyons. Old Jombo (also called Big Jombo) is the more challenging of the two (only possible from late November) and involves a flying fox cable ride across the Bhote Kosi River and then a 30-minute walk up to the first of four waterfalls and a short water slide.

It's best to bring a pair of closed-toe shoes that can get wet as these are better than sandals. Hiking shoes, a water bottle and bathing suits are also required and a waterproof camera is a real bonus. After November wetsuits are a must and are provided.

> The Nepal Open Paragliding Championships are held every year over five days in January in Sarangkot and attract competitors from around the world.

PARAGLIDING

Pokhara is the place to head for if you want to hurl yourself off a cliff at nearby Sarangkot and glide in majestic silence above the Himalaya, either on a tandem paragliding flight or solo after a multiday course. November, December and January bring perfect flying conditions and stunning views of Phewa Tal and the Himalayan peaks that have inspired gliders to rank Sarangkot as one of the best paragliding spots in the world.

Frontiers Paragliding (☎ 061-461706, 9804125096; www.nepal-paragliding.com) is the leading company. It offers short tandem flights (20 to 30 minutes, €70) in the morning and late afternoon, longer distance cross-country flights (60 to 90 minutes, €100) that take advantage of midday thermals and even multiday 'treks' that journey from valley to valley. For something a lot scarier try the 20-minute acrobatic tandem flights. If you want to learn to fly yourself, a nine-day paragliding course costs €900. Most flights start with a short jeep ride up to Sarangkot.

> Nepa Maps and Himalayan Maphouse produce a fairly useful map, *Paragliding the Annapurna Region*.

Paragliding pioneer **Sunrise Paragliding** (Map p263; ☎ 061-463174; www.sunrise-paragliding.com; ☉ 8am-9pm) offers identical flights and prices.

In conjunction with Frontiers, **Himalayan Frontiers** (Map p263; www.himalayanfrontiers.co.uk, www.parahawking.com) has pioneered parahawking, an intriguing mix of paragliding and hawking that uses trained steppe eagles and pariah kites to lead gliders to the best thermals, enabling them to glider higher and further. You can experience this glorious blending of man and nature on a tandem flight or learn on a multiday parahawking course (November to February). Glider and ultralight flights are also available, as are falconry lessons. Less brave souls can see the avian guides at their roost at Maya Devi Village on the northern shore of Phewa Tal.

The Nepali-Swiss operation **Blue Sky Paragliding** (☎ 61-463747; www.paragliding-nepal.com) offers similar flights, courses and multiday 'paratrekking'. See the website for course dates. In Kathmandu you can contact it through the **Hotel Northfield** (☎ 01-470078; www.hotelnorthfield.com; Thamel).

ALL FOR THE SAKE OF RESEARCH *Bradley Mayhew*

'Its the most exciting thing you can do in a day from Kathmandu' was what Megh Ale told me when I mentioned I might try some canyoning up at the Borderlands Resort. Sure, I thought, it'll be fun but how exciting can a day trip from the capital really be?

The first day was pretty relaxed, meeting my fellow canyoners (experienced abseilers, just what the insecure novice in me needed…), learning how to abseil down a large boulder (I had to stifle a yawn) and then some small cascades. This is nice, I thought, but not quite the underpants-soiling adrenalin Megh had promised me.

So the next day, as I stood astride a small stream and shuffled backwards towards a drop-off, it came as a bit of a shock to see the water fall away into vertical nothingness. It takes a certain leap of faith to trust all your weight to a harness but I eventually learned that the key to canyoning is to lean right back, with your weight all on the rope 'brake', in order to position your legs at 90 degrees from the rock face. This stops your legs slipping quite so much on the mossy, water-polished rock face.

The challenge of the first drop was to avoid slipping into the waterfall just to the side. The second involved a backwards jump of about 5m into a churning pool of uncertain depth. It took several 'one, two, THREE!'s from the guides and some considerable swearing on my part before I let myself fall backwards into the narrow rock pool.

The scariest thing about the third descent was that I couldn't see the bottom of the drop (and there's nothing worse than the thousand-foot gorge of my imagination). After about 10m of descent, the rock overhang meant I had to lower myself down into mid-air, dangling like bait on a hook.

That freaked me out a bit but it wasn't until the last fall, as I stood astride Big Jombo (the name of the waterfall, unfortunately), that the fear really hit me like, well, a 50-tonne waterfall. This was a 45m drop and when you are leaning back over the slippery lip of a waterfall, that's a BIG drop! Even the instructors were looking a bit nervous… There was no way out, no way back up the last waterfall. The only option was to go down Big Jombo (again, let's be clear, the waterfall).

As I lowered myself down the cliff the angle between the rope and the waterfall began to narrow until there was only one harrowing choice; straddle the waterfall or enter it. Apparently there was one other option – slip on some wet moss, swing into the full force of the water and scream like a girl. I chose the latter. Actually, there was no chance of screaming because the full crashing force of the icy water made it hard to breathe. I tried to keep calm and lower myself down the chute but at one point I remember thinking 'Holy crap! This is too much pressure, I'm going to fall – and I don't even know how far it is!'.

After a serious pummelling, I felt a tug on the rope and swung out of the waterfall, scrambling on the rock face like Buster Keaton in a wetsuit. I stood there shaking for a while, before lowering myself down the last 10m. *'Jesus!'* I shouted at the main guide. *'That was frickin' GREAT!!* Now *that* I can recommend in a guidebook!'.

Avia Club Nepal (Map p263; ☎ 061-465944; www.aviaclubnepal.com; Lakeside, Pokhara) operates microlight flights from Pokhara between October and May. The 15-/30-/60-minute flights cost around US$65/112/198.

ROCK CLIMBING

If you need to polish up or learn some climbing skills before heading off into the mountains, try the **Pasang Lhamu Climbing Wall** (Map pp114-15; ☎ 01-4370742; www.pasanglhamu.org; ☺ 10am-5.30pm) on the outskirts of Kathmandu. A day's membership costs Rs 350 and equipment can be rented for Rs 100. Week-long climbing courses are available (Rs 4799). See p133 for details.

The **Shreeban Nature Camp** (www.shreeban.com.np) in Dhading, on the road from Kathmandu to Pokhara, offers climbing from December onwards on the roped rock wall behind its camp. See p236.

Borderlands offers a day's climbing tuition at Nagarjun just outside Kathmandu for US$50, including lunch. The Last Resort offers a brief introduction to rock climbing at its resort for US$13.

The **Nepal Mountaineering Association** (Map p126; ☎ 01-4434525; www.nepalmountaineering .org; Naxal, Kathmandu) runs month-long climbing courses in Manang or Langtang every August (introductory) and December (advanced). These are really aimed at Nepali guides but also accept foreigners for a fee of US$2000. It also runs occasional rock-climbing courses in Nagarjun.

For mountaineering and climbing on Nepal's trekking peaks see p111.

MARATHONS

The annual **Kathmandu International Marathon** (www.nepalmarathon.com) attracts over 6000 runners in September, with courses ranging from 5km to 42km. Registration costs US$30 for foreigners. Amazingly, the police hold back Kathmandu's revving traffic for a full five hours to let the race take place.

As if a normal marathon wasn't enough, several marathons are held in the Everest region at an altitude of over 5000m. Participants get to enjoy a two-week acclimatisation trek to base camp, before running all the way back to Namche Bazaar in around five hours.

The annual **Tenzing Hillary Everest Marathon** (www.everestmarathon.com) on 29 May commemorates the first ascent of Mt Everest on 29 May 1953 with the world's highest marathon (42km), starting at Everest Base Camp. The similar **Everest Marathon** (www.everestmarathon.org.uk) is run every other November (next in 2009) from Gorak Shep to Namche Bazaar, to raise money for charities working in Nepal.

If those don't sound challenging enough, go for psychological testing and then consider the annual **Annapurna Mandala Trail**, a nine-day, 340km foot race from Annapurna Base Camp to Jomsom, over the 5400m Thorung La and remote Tilicho Lake. Alternatively, consider the **Everest Lafuma Sky Race**, a 10-stage, 250km race from Lukla and back over three 5000m-plus passes.

The even crazier **Himal Race** started in 2002 as a 955km, 22-day run from Annapurna to Everest Base Camp. It was put on hold for a few years, due to a temporary bout of sanity, but competitors returned with a vengeance in 2007, running from Kathmandu to Dolpo (!), and it is scheduled again for 2010, this time routing 1000km from Kanchenjunga Base Camp to Kathmandu in 23 days. The races are organised by extreme runner Bruno Poirier and Nepali company **Base Camp Trekking** (www.basecamptrek.com). They all clearly need help.

The madness continues. **Extreme World Challenges** (www.extremeworldchallenges .com) is currently planning the world's highest triathlon at Tilicho Lake in the Annapurna region, as well as a 150km duathlon to Mt Everest called the 'Sweaty Yeti', scheduled for 2010.

For something a bit more relaxed, the Nepal branch of **Hash House Harriers** (www.aponarch.com/hhhh) meets for a run every Saturday afternoon. Check the website for details.

TREKKING

Nepal is the world's greatest trekking destination, even (and perhaps especially) if the only camping you do at home is lip-synching to Kylie Minogue and Queen songs (we know you do it!). For an overview of the most popular multiday teahouse treks, see the Trekking chapter, p328.

Short Treks & Day Hikes

If you don't have time for a big trek, there are several shorter treks which give you a taste of life on Nepal's trails – see the boxed text, p87. In particular, there are several short treks from Pokhara in the southern foothills of the

---

For details on elephant-back jungle safaris in Chitwan National Park see p287, in Bardia National Park see p310 and in Koshi Tappu Wildlife Reserve see p321.

The League of Adventurists International (http://rickshawrun .theadventurists .com) operates an annual Rickshaw Run, a two-week dash across the subcontinent in a 147cc three-wheeled autorickshaw. The 2008 itinerary traversed Nepal and future trips may do so again.

Annapurnas (see p275), or you could easily cobble together a trek of several days around the rim of the Kathmandu Valley (p170).

You can also throw in a couple of flights here and there to speed up the trekking process. As an example, fly in to Jomsom, overnight in Marpha (to aid acclimatisation) and take a few days to hike to the surrounding villages of Kagbeni and Muktinath before flying back to Pokhara for a four- or five-day trip.

There are also plenty of great day hikes around Nepal, particularly around Bandipur, Tansen and Pokhara. We have detailed many of these throughout this chapter.

MOUNTAIN BIKING

Strong wheels, knobbly tyres, a soft padded seat and 17 more gears than the average Nepali bike – the mountain bike is an ideal, go anywhere, versatile machine for exploring Nepal. These attributes make it possible to escape sealed roads, and to ride tracks and ancient walking trails to remote, rarely visited areas of the country. Importantly, they allow independent travel – you can stop whenever you like – and they liberate you from crowded buses and claustrophobic taxis.

For information on some of the golfing opportunities in Nepal see p260.

Nepal's tremendously diverse terrain and its many tracks and trails are ideal for mountain biking. In recent years Nepal has rapidly gained recognition for the biking adventures it offers – from easy village trails in the Kathmandu Valley to challenging mountain roads that climb thousands of metres to reach spectacular viewpoints, followed by unforgettable, exhilarating descents. For the adventurous there are large areas of the country still to be explored by mountain bike.

The Kathmandu Valley offers the best and most consistent biking in Nepal, with a vast network of tracks, trails and backroads. A mountain bike really allows you to get off the beaten track and discover idyllic Newari villages that have preserved their traditional lifestyle. Even today it's possible to cycle into villages in the Kathmandu Valley that have rarely seen a visitor on a foreign bicycle. Each year more roads are developing, opening trails to destinations that were previously accessible only on foot.

Many trails are narrow, century-old walkways that are not shown on maps, so you need a good sense of direction when venturing out without a guide. To go unguided entails some risks, and you should learn a few important words of Nepali to assist in seeking directions. It's also important to know the name of the next village you wish to reach.

Transporting Your Bicycle

If you plan to do a mountain biking trip of more than a day or two it may be a good idea to bring your own bicycle from home. Your bicycle can be carried as part of your baggage allowance on international flights. You are required to deflate the tyres, turn the handlebars parallel with the frame and remove the pedals. Passage through Nepali customs is quite simple once you reassure airport officers that it is 'your' bicycle and it will also be returning with you, though this requirement is never enforced.

The Yak Attack is a six-day, 240km mountain-bike race around the Annapurna Circuit, including over the 5416m Thorung La. The 13-day trip costs £1400; see www.yak-attack .co.uk for details.

On most domestic flights if you pack your bicycle correctly, removing wheels and pedals, it is possible to load it in the cargo hold. Check with the airline first.

Local buses are useful if you wish to avoid some of the routes that carry heavy traffic. You can place your bicycle on the roof for an additional charge (Rs 50 to Rs 100 depending on the length of the journey and the bus company). If you're lucky, rope may be available and the luggage boy will assist you. Make sure the bicycle is held securely to cope with the rough roads and that it's lying as flat as possible to prevent it catching low wires or tree branches. Unless you travel with foam padding it is hard to avoid the scratches to the frame. Supervise its loading and protect the rear derailleur from being damaged. Keep in mind that more baggage is likely to be loaded on top once you're inside. A lock and chain is also a wise investment.

Equipment

Most of the bicycles you can hire in Nepal are low-quality Indian so-called mountain bikes, not suitable for the rigours of trail riding. The better operators like Himalayan Mountain Bikes or Dawn Till Dusk rent high-quality front-shock, 18-gear mountain bikes for around US$10 per day, with discounts for a week's hire. Cheaper companies offer battered front-suspension bikes for Rs 450, with discounts for a week's hire. The better rental shops can supply helmets and other equipment.

If you bring your own bicycle it is essential to bring tools and spare parts, as these are largely unavailable outside of Kathmandu. Established mountain-bike tour operators have mechanics, workshops and a full range of bicycle tools at their offices in Kathmandu. Dawn Till Dusk also has a separate repair workshop near Kilroy's restaurant in Thamel (see Map p140).

Although this is not a complete list, a few items that may be worth considering bringing with you:

■ bicycle bell
■ cycling gloves, tops and padded shorts (or even your own seat)
■ energy bars and electrolyte water additives
■ face mask and gloves
■ fleece top for evenings and windbreaker
■ helmet
■ lightweight clothing (eg Coolmax or other wicking materials)
■ medium-sized money bag for valuables
■ minipump
■ spare parts (including inner tubes)
■ stiff-soled shoes that suit riding and walking
■ sun protection and sunglasses
■ water bottles or hydration system (eg CamelBak)

Road Conditions

Traffic generally travels on the left-hand side, though it's not uncommon to find a vehicle approaching you head-on or even on the wrong side of the road. In practice, smaller vehicles give way to larger ones, and bicycles are definitely at the bottom of the hierarchy. Nepali roads carry a vast array of vehicles: buses, motorcycles, cars, trucks, tractors, holy cows, wheelbarrows, dogs, wandering children and chickens, all moving at different speeds and in different directions.

The centre of Kathmandu is a particularly unpleasant place to ride because of pollution, heavy traffic and the increasingly reckless behaviour of young motorcyclists.

Extreme care should be taken near villages as young children play on the trails and roads. The onus seems to fall on the approaching vehicle to avoid an incident.

A good bicycle helmet is a sensible accessory, and you should ride with your fingers continually poised on the rear brake lever.

A few intrepid mountain bikers have taken bicycles into trekking areas hoping to find great riding but these areas are generally not suitable for mountain biking and you have to carry your bicycle for at least 80% of the time. Trails are unreliable, and are subject to frequent rock falls. In addition,

The Trans Himalayan Mountain Bike Race is a 1000km race from Lhasa to Kathmandu via Everest Base Camp that runs most years – contact Himalayan Marathons (www.everestmarathon.com/bikerace) for details.

there are always trekkers, porters and local people clogging up the trails. Sagarmatha National Park doesn't allow mountain bikes. Courtesy and care on the trails should be a high priority when biking.

Trail Etiquette

Arriving in a new country for a short time where social and cultural values are vastly different from those of your home country does not allow much time to gain an appreciation of these matters. So consider a few pointers to help you develop respect and understanding. For more information, see p74.

CLOTHING

Tight-fitting lycra bicycle clothing might be functional, but is a shock to locals, who maintain a very modest approach to dressing. Such clothing is embarrassing and also offensive to Nepalis.

A simple way to overcome this is by wearing a pair of comfortable shorts and a T-shirt over your bicycle gear. This is especially applicable to female bicyclists, as women in Nepal generally dress conservatively.

SAFETY

Trails are often filled with locals going about their daily work. A small bell attached to your handlebars and used as a warning of your approach, reducing your speed, and a friendly call or two of *'cycle ioh!'* (cycle coming!) go a long way in keeping everyone on the trails happy and safe. Children love the novelty of the bicycles, the fancy helmets, the colours and the strange clothing, and will come running from all directions to greet you. They also love to grab hold of the back of your bicycle and run with you. You need to maintain a watchful eye so no one gets hurt.

Guided Tours

A small number of Nepali companies offer guided mountain-bike trips. They provide high-quality bicycles, local and Western guides, helmets and all the necessary equipment. There is usually a minimum of four bicyclists per trip, although for shorter tours two is often sufficient. For the shorter tours (two to three days) vehicle support is not required, while for longer tours vehicles are provided at an extra cost.

Local group tours range from US$25 to US$35 for a simple day trip, such as the loop routes north from Kathmandu to Tinpiple, Tokha and Budhanilkantha; or south to the traditional village of Bungamati.

A downhill day trip with vehicle support costs around US$55 per person. Options include driving to Nagarkot and riding down to Sankhu and Bodhnath or Bhaktapur, or driving to Kakani and taking the Scar Rd down. Dawn Till Dusk offers exhilarating downhill runs from the top of Phulchowki and Nagarjun peaks.

Multiday trips around the Kathmandu Valley cost around US$45 per day without vehicle backup, or US$65 with vehicle support and range from two to 10 days. Prices include bike hire, a guide, hotel accommodation and meals.

A few companies have recently started operating trips down the Kali Gandaki Valley, along the new unpaved road (and former trek route). Tours take around a week, with overnights in Ghasa, Tatopani, Beni and Pokhara, plus two days in Muktinath and Jomsom. An all-inclusive tour with flights and guide costs around US$1000, or you can organise a guide and bike only for around US$400. A few die-hards even attempt the full Annapurna Circuit (see p352), though even the hardiest biker ends up carrying their bike 70% of the time on the Manang side.

The most detailed Kathmandu Valley map is commonly referred to as the 'German map' (also Schneider and Nelles Verlag), and is widely available in Kathmandu.

When it comes to caring for the environment, the guidelines that apply to trekkers also apply to mountain bikers. For more detailed information, see p335.

The following routes rank among the most popular organised itineraries:

- Budhanilkantha–Chisopani–Nagarkot and back
- Nagarkot–Kathmandu downhill (overnight)
- Kathmandu to Chitwan National Park via Daman and Hetauda; the most interesting route leads via the backroads west of Dakshinkali
- Bhaktapur–Dhulikhel–Namobuddha–Panauti (three days)
- Nagarkot–Dhulikhel–Panauti–Lakuri Bhanjyang–Sisneri (three days)
- Tibet border (four days)
- Jomsom to Pokhara (nine days)

Nepa Maps and Himalayan Maphouse (www.himalayan-maphouse.com) produce the useful maps Mountain Biking the Kathmandu Valley *and* Biking around Annapurna, *though they aren't to be relied on completely.*

TOUR COMPANIES

The following companies have good-quality imported mountain bikes that can also be hired independently of a tour. Any others fall a long way back in standards and safety.

Bike Nepal (Map p140; ☎ 01-4240633; www.bikenepal.com; Thamel, Kathmandu) Day trips US$25. Located next to Adrenaline Rush.

Dawn Till Dusk (Map p140; ☎ 01-4700286, 4215046; www.nepalbiking.com; JP School Rd, Thamel, Kathmandu) Contact Chhimi Gurung. Local tours, rentals and servicing at the Kathmandu Guest House office; for bike repairs and servicing see the workshop a five-minute walk east, near Kilroy's restaurant. Day trips US$35, multiday trips around US$65/45 with/without transport backup.

Himalayan Mountain Bikes (HMB; www.bikingnepal.com, www.bikeasia.info) Kathmandu (Map p140; ☎ 01-4212860; hmb@bikeasia.info) Kathmandu Valley tours US$50 per day with accommodation but no transport. Full service and repairs, bike hire RS 700 per day, guide US$40 per day.

Nepal Mountain Bike Tours (Map p140; ☎ 01-4701701; www.bikehimalayas.com) Day trips from US$30, bike rentals Rs 700. Next to Green Hill Tours. Contact Ranjan.

Path Finder Cycling (Map p140; ☎ 01-4700468; www.tibetbiking.com; Thamel, Kathmandu) Offers day- and multiday tours, bike hire (Rs 700 per day) and guides. Located across from La Dolce Vita Restaurant.

Routes

THE SCAR ROAD FROM KATHMANDU
Distance 70km
Duration Six hours, or two days overnighting in Kakani
Start Kathmandu
Finish Kathmandu
Brief description Fine views and a challenging descent through a national park, after a tough initial climb of around 700m

The Scar Rd is considered one of the Kathmandu Valley's classic mountain-bike adventures but it's a challenging ride for experienced riders only. Route-finding can be tricky so a guide is recommended.

Leaving Kathmandu (elevation 1337m), head towards Balaju on the Ring Rd 2km north of Thamel, and follow the sealed Trisuli Bazaar road towards Kakani, 23km away at an altitude of 2073m. You start to climb out of the valley as the road twists and turns past the **Nagarjun Forest Reserve** (p179), which provides the road with a leafy canopy. Once you're through the initial pass and out of the valley, the road continues northwest and offers a view of endless terraced fields to your left. (If you don't fancy the climb you can avoid cycling on the road by putting your bike on the roof of the early morning bus to Dhunche and getting off here.) On reaching the summit of the ridge, take a turn right (at a clearly marked T-junction), instead of continuing down to Trisuli Bazaar. (If you go too far you reach a checkpoint just 100m beyond.) At this point magnificent views of the Ganesh Himal (himal means a range with permanent snow) provide the inspiration required to complete the remaining 4km of steep and deteriorating blacktop to the crown of the hill at **Kakani** (p233) for a well-deserved rest. It's an excellent idea to overnight here at the Tara Gaon or other such guest house and savour the dawn views over the Himalaya.

After admiring the view from a road-side teashop, descend for just 30m beyond the gate and take the first left onto a 4WD track. This track will take you through the popular picnic grounds frequented on Saturday by Kathmandu locals. Continue in an easterly direction towards Shivapuri. The track narrows after a few kilometres near a metal gate on your left. Through the gate, you are faced with some rough stone steps and then a 10-minute push/carry up and over the hilltop to an army checkpoint. Here it's necessary for foreigners to pay an entry fee of Rs 250 to the Shivapuri National Park. Exit the army camp, turning right where the Scar Rd is clearly visible in front of you. You are now positioned at the day's highest point – approximately 2200m.

Taking the right-hand track you start to descend dramatically along an extremely steep, rutted single trail with several water crossings. The trail is literally cut into the side of the hill, with sharp drops on the right that challenge a rider's skill and nerve. As you hurtle along, take time to admire the view of the sprawling Kathmandu Valley below – it's one of the best. In recent years the trail has become quite overgrown so you may have to carry your bike for several stretches and seek out the correct path. A guide would be useful for this section.

For more ideas on biking around the Kathmandu Valley see p169.

The trail widens, after one long gnarly climb before the saddle, then it's relatively flat through the protected Shivapuri watershed area. This beautiful mountain-biking section lasts for nearly 25km before the trail descends into the valley down a 7km spiral on a gravel road. This joins a sealed road, to the relief of jarred wrists, at **Budhanilkantha** (p179), where you can buy refreshments. Take a moment to see the Sleeping Vishnu just up on your left at the main intersection. From here the sealed road descends gently for the remaining 15km back into the bustle of Kathmandu.

KATHMANDU TO DHULIKHEL
Distance 90km
Duration Two days
Start Kathmandu
Finish Kathmandu
Brief description A circular route past a classic selection of the valley's cultural sights

This circular tour (see Map p168) takes you along valley backroads to Dhulikhel on the first day (32km), and then to Namobuddha and back to Kathmandu via the busy Arniko Hwy (58km).

From Thamel, head east out of town in the direction of **Pashupatinath** (p170). Proceed along the northern fringe of the Pashupatinath complex, on the south side of the Bagmati River, and look for the road running off to the right near the northern end of the airport runway. From the northeast corner join the road running north–south and then the road running east to the town of **Bhaktapur** (p194). This road runs parallel to the much busier Arniko Hwy and is a much better option to Bhaktapur, via the northern tip of Thimi.

You can also access this road from the Arniko Hwy; take a left off the main highway, just past the bridge over the Manohara River, onto a narrower sealed road that heads back towards the airport on its east side. At the next main intersection (1.8km on) is the turn right to Bhaktapur, 16km away.

You could spend time in this wonderfully preserved former kingdom, but if you intend to cycle straight through, you'll save yourself the Rs 750 entry fee by taking the roads around the town, to the north and east. Make your way to the town's eastern gate, join a tarmac road and then bear southeast.

The asphalt ends and the road continues in the form of a compacted track towards the rural village of **Nala**, 9km away through a beautiful corner of the valley. The track climbs gradually to a minor pass and army checkpoint. A gentle 2km downhill gradient brings you past the Buddhist Karunamaya Temple (dedicated to Machhendranath) to rural Nala, with its pretty four-roofed Bhagwati Temple in the central square.

From Nala head right and continue for 3km to **Banepa** (p225), riding through the old town before hitting the main Arniko Hwy. Turn left at the highway and continue along the sealed main road for a further 4km uphill to **Dhulikhel** (p226). This completes the first day (32km).

Dhulikhel to Namobuddha & Kathmandu (37km)

The trail to Namobuddha is a popular detour from Dhulikhel, and offers superb trail riding with spectacular views of the Himalaya. See p228 for a description of the route.

From Panauti you join a sealed road that's a flat run along the valley to the main road at Banepa. From this point you can return to Kathmandu, 26km via the Arniko Hwy, or ride the 3.5km back to Dhulikhel. The loop from Dhulikhel via Namobuddha is 37km; if you return to Kathmandu it's a total run of 58km via Namobuddha. For something wilder, take the adventurous alternative route back to Kathmandu via Lakuri Bhanjyang (see below).

THE BACK DOOR TO KATHMANDU
Distance 30km
Duration Half-day
Start Panauti
Finish Patan/Kathmandu
Brief description Remote and difficult mountain route with almost zero traffic. A good motorbike route.

Don't let the heavenly first 4.5km of tarmac lull you into a false sense of security. The road soon deteriorates into 3km of dirt road to the village of Kushadevi, followed by 2.5km of bone-jarring stony track to Riyale. From here the valley really starts to close in and gets increasingly remote – this is definitely not the place to blow a tyre! It's amazing how remote the route is, considering it is so close to Kathmandu. If you're not an experienced mountain biker, you're probably better off considering this as a motorbike route.

The next 8.5km is on a smooth dirt road that switchbacks up the hillsides to the pass of **Lakuri Bhanjyang** (1960m). You may find some basic food stalls but the actual summit is currently occupied by the army. In the past, travel companies have set up tented camp accommodation near here but this depends on tourism numbers and the levels of army presence. Figure on two to three hours to here.

From here on it's all downhill. The first section drops down the back side of the hill, blocking the views, but you soon get great views of the Annapurna and Ganesh Himal massifs – particularly spectacular in sunset's pink glow.

A further 5km of descent, rough at times, brings you to the turn-off left to Sisneri and the first village on this side of the pass. Soon the asphalt kicks in again, shortly followed by the pleasant village of **Lubbhu**, with its impressive central three-tiered Mahalakshmi Mahadev Temple. Traffic levels pick up for the final 5km to the Kathmandu ring road near Patan; be prepared for the 'civilisation' to come as a bit of a shock after such a beautiful, peaceful ride.

DHULIKHEL TO THE TIBETAN BORDER
Distance 83km one way
Duration Four days return
Start Dhulikhel
Finish Kodari
Brief description A long descent followed by a gradual climb alongside the white water of the Bhote Kosi to the border with Tibet

This backroads track offers a great alternative return route to Kathmandu, bypassing the busy, dangerous and polluted main Arniko Hwy. It's a surprisingly remote route (see Map p168), so make sure you take enough water, food and spare parts as there's nothing en route.

Dhulikhel to Lamosangu (49km)

From Dhulikhel you immediately begin an adrenaline-filled descent (almost 900m) into the Panchkhal Valley, on a slick sealed road, with majestic views of the Himalaya adding to a thrilling ride. A couple of short climbs interrupt the descent as you cycle to Dolalghat, on the Indrawati River, a popular starting point for Sun Kosi rafting trips (see p110 for more information). On the downhill watch for overtaking buses on the blind corners.

From Dolalghat (around 53km from Kathmandu) you cross the bridge over the Indrawati River and climb out of the Panchkhal Valley to join the Bhote Kosi, which you follow for the rest of the journey. Owing to landslide damage there is a mixture of surfaced and unsurfaced roads. Traffic can be quite heavy along this section. The road climbs at a gentle gradient as it follows the river.

A couple of kilometres past the turn-off to Jiri is Lamosangu, 27km from Dolalghat, where there are a couple of fish restaurants.

Lamosangu to Tatopani & Kodari (34km)

The next section of the ride continues for around 7km to Barabise, where the road changes into a compacted dirt track with a top layer of dust that is transformed into choking clouds when buses pass; in wet weather it all turns to mud. Care should be taken during heavy rains as this section of the road is particularly susceptible to landslides. The valley's sides begin to get steeper and it gradually changes into a beautiful gorge with spectacular waterfalls.

The track climbs practically the entire 23km to Tatopani and a further 4km to Kodari (p232), at the edge of the Friendship Bridge and the border with Tibet. The section of the ride that climbs from Tatopani to the Friendship Bridge is probably the most beautiful.

It should be possible to return as far as Borderlands the same day, taking advantage of a mainly downhill ride. Otherwise, you can stay in Tatopani (p232) and visit the hot springs there.

Tatopani to Dhulikhel (79km)

The ride back to Dhulikhel is around 80km and includes the long climb out of Dolalghat, for which you should allow plenty of time. An option here is to jump on a local bus with your bicycle. Depending on how you feel after the climb, you can stay in Dhulikhel or complete the trip by returning the 32km to Kathmandu.

THE RAJPATH FROM KATHMANDU

Distance 150km
Duration Two days
Start Kathmandu
Finish Hetauda
Brief description Classic but gruelling on-road ride over a 2488m pass, culminating with incomparable Himalayan views at Daman. For a regional overview see the map, pp314–15.

The ride begins on the Kathmandu–Pokhara (Prithvi) Hwy, which gives the only access to the valley. After leaving the valley, the highway descends to Naubise, at the bottom of the Mahesh Khola Valley, 27km from Kathmandu, where the Rajpath intersects with the Prithvi Hwy. Take the Rajpath, which forks to the left and is well signposted, for Hetauda. Start a 35km climb to Tistung (2030m) past terraced fields, carved into steep hillsides. On reaching the pass at Tistung you descend for 7km into the beautiful Palung Valley before the final steep 9km climb to **Daman** (p306), at a height of 2322m.

Add the trip from Dhulikhel to the Friendship Bridge at Kodari onto the previous itinerary for a great four- or five-day run from Kathmandu.

It may be possible (but dependent on border guards) for border junkies to cycle beyond the bridge and climb a rough, winding and steep track to the Chinese customs checkpoint (8km), just outside of Zhangmu (Nepali: Khasa), which is visible from the bridge.

Accommodation options are at Barabise, Borderlands Resort (a further 16km from Lamosangu, on a dirt road), and the Last Resort (4km further). See p231 for more on accommodation options in this area.

This day's ride (almost all climbing) takes between six and nine hours in the saddle. Thus, with an early start it is possible to stay in Daman, which will give you the thrill of waking up to the broadest Himalayan panorama Nepal has to offer. The following day the road climbs a further 3km to the top of the pass, at 2488m. At this point you can savour the very real prospect of an exhilarating 2300m descent in 60km!

As you descend towards the Indian plains, laid out before you to the south, notice the contrast with the side you climbed, as the south side is lush and semitropical. With innumerable switchbacks and a bit of speed you should watch out for the occasional bus and truck looming around blind corners. The road eventually flattens out after the right turn to cross a newly constructed bridge and the first main river crossing. The rest of the journey is a gently undulating route alongside a river; a further 10km brings you to **Hetauda**. (See p306 for details on accommodation; note that there are useful cyclists' notebooks in the Motel Avocado.) After a night's rest you can continue along the Rajpath towards India or turn right at the statue of the king in the centre of town and head towards Chitwan National Park.

The switchbacking Tribhuvan Hwy (or Rajpath) was the first highway to connect Kathmandu with the rest of the world. Most traffic from the Terai and India uses the highway that runs to the west between Narayangarh (Narayanghat) and Mugling, so traffic along the Rajpath is relatively light.

HETAUDA TO NARAYANGARH & MUGLING
Distance 91km to Narayangarh, 105km via Sauraha
Duration One to 1½ days
Start Hetauda
Finish Narayangarh or Mugling
Brief description Tropical ride across the Terai plains, best during winter and combined with a visit to Chitwan

Hetauda is just to the east of Chitwan National Park, which has a wide selection of accommodation, both in the park and in the town of Sauraha – see p288. You are prohibited from riding inside the park, but are allowed to ride directly to your resort.

This is vastly different riding from that of the other rides described in this chapter, and in the summer months (May to September) it can be a very hot and humid ride. From Hetauda, as you cycle along the flat, smooth road towards Narayangarh enjoying the lush subtropical scenery, watch for resort signposts on your left. Machan Wildlife Resort's (p290) turn-off is 40km from Hetauda, and the resort is reached after a further 4km of beautiful trail riding with three river crossings. Alternatively, a further 23km from the Machan turn-off brings you to the Chitwan Jungle Lodge (p290) turn-off. A further 14km brings you to Tadi Bazaar and the turn-off for Sauraha, reached by an interesting 6km-long 4WD track.

From Narayangarh (p279), on the banks of the Narayani River 20km from Sauraha, you can return to either Kathmandu or Pokhara via Mugling. Although some may say this section from Narayangarh to Mugling is best avoided on a bicycle because of heavy bus and truck traffic, it is nonetheless a very beautiful section of road to ride, and traffic during many times of the day can be light. The alternative is to catch a bus. If you're heading to Pokhara (96km) it may be a good idea to miss the busy highway between Mugling and Pokhara by catching a bus in Mugling (p238). Here, the road is much improved and vehicles travel a lot faster in what are still quite dusty conditions.

At Mugling you'll find plenty of food and accommodation (see p238), or break the trip at the idyllic River Side Springs Resort (p238), just before Mugling, at Kurintar.

KATHMANDU TO POKHARA VIA THE PRITHVI HIGHWAY
Distance 216km
Duration Two days
Start Kathmandu
Finish Pokhara
Brief description Riverside views, changing scenery and plenty of traffic separate Nepal's two tourist magnets

It's theoretically possible to make Pokhara in 12 to 14 hours of steady biking, but it's a much better idea to break the trip at the wonderful but little-visited sights of Bandipur and Gorkha, both of which are a short detour off the road and offer decent accommodation. For details of the sights along this road see the Kathmandu to Pokhara chapter, p235.

After leaving the valley on the Prithvi Hwy during the climb to Thankot, the highway descends to Naubise, at the bottom of the Mahesh Khola Valley, 27km from Kathmandu, where the Rajpath intersects with the Prithvi Hwy.

Following the thrilling, if not hair-raising, descent (watching for oil slicks after on-the-spot truck repairs), Mugling is about the halfway mark at 120km, four to five hours' ride from Kathmandu. There are also lots of simple food stops along the way at some very scenic spots.

From Mugling you keep to the right as you exit the town and within 300m you will cross the Trisuli River bridge. The second half of your journey to Pokhara is mostly uphill, but still offers some excellent downhills. From Mugling there's an overall altitude gain of about 550m over 96km. Again there are numerous roadside cafes and food stops to keep the carbohydrates supplied. The final approach to Pokhara, with the Annapurnas as a backdrop, will pick you up after a long day of biking.

A surprisingly large number of bicyclists show an interest in this ride, perhaps due to the riverside views, and the attractions at either end. You are almost guaranteed to see the remains of a truck or bus crash en route. The message is obvious – take care on this notorious stretch of road.

POKHARA TO SARANGKOT & NAUDANDA

Distance 54km
Duration Seven hours, or an overnight trip
Start Pokhara
Finish Pokhara
Brief description Work up a sweat to two of Pokhara's best Himalayan viewpoints, followed by a great downhill coast

Leave early and ride along Lakeside (towards the mountains) to the last main intersection and sealed road. Turn right; this is the road that returns to central Pokhara. After 2km you turn left and continue straight on (north). This intersection is the zero kilometre road marker. After a further 2km there is a smaller sealed road to the left, signposted as the road to Sarangkot.

This winds its way along a ridge into Sarangkot, providing outstanding views of the Himalaya, which seems close enough to reach out and touch. After 6km a few tea shops make a welcome refreshment stop just where the stone steps mark the walking trail to the summit. From here it's a 4WD track that closely hugs the edge of the mountain overlooking Phewa Tal. Continue until you join a Y-intersection that doubles back sharply to the right and marks the final climb to Sarangkot Point. You can turn this ride into a relaxed overnight trip by staying in lodges here (see p272).

From Sarangkot continue straight ahead, riding the narrower motorcycle trails leading to Kaski and Naudanda. After the Sarangkot turn-off the trail soon begins to climb to Kaski, towards the hill immediately in front of you. The section to Kaski takes around 30 to 60 minutes, and you may need to push your bicycle on the steeper section near the crown of the hill. Over the top you follow the trail through to Naudanda. You are now at around 1590m, having gained around 840m altitude from Pokhara. The trail is rocky in parts and will test your equipment to the extreme, so do not consider riding this trail on a cheap hire bicycle.

From Naudanda it's a 32km downhill run to Pokhara along the smooth asphalt highway. This route starts with a twisting 6km descent into the Mardi Khola Valley then descends gently as it follows the river, allowing an enjoyable coast almost all the way back to Pokhara.

The ride to Sarangkot, visible directly north from Pokhara Lakeside, provides an excellent, challenging day trip. This is in fact the bicycle leg of the Annapurna Triathlon. For a map of the area see p273.

The view from the ridge at Naudanda is particularly beautiful. Dhaulagiri, Manaslu, the Annapurnas and Machhapuchhare create a classic Himalayan panorama, especially on a cool, clear morning. To the south you can look down over Pokhara and Phewa Tal.

RAFTING & KAYAKING

Nepal has a reputation for being one of the best places in the world for rafting and kayaking, with outstanding river journeys ranging from steep, adrenaline-charged mountain streams to classic big-volume wilderness expeditions. Warm water, a subtropical climate (with no bugs!) and huge white sandy beaches that are ideal for camping just add to the appeal.

There has also been a continuous increase in the number of kayakers coming to Nepal and it is justifiably recognised as a mecca for paddlers. Several companies offer trips that cater specifically to kayakers, where you get to explore the river with rafts carrying all your gear and food, and often camp near choice play spots.

Several adventure camps offer tented accommodation, superb locations and a range of outdoor activities from rafting to canyoning. For details see Borderlands (www.borderlandresorts.com; p231), the Last Resort (www.tlrnepal.com; p232) and the Royal Beach Camp (www.royalbeachnepal.com; p237).

When to Go

The best times for rafting and kayaking are September to early December, and March to early June. From early September to early October, and May to June, the rivers can be extremely high with monsoon runoff. Any expeditions attempted at this time require a very experienced rafting company with an intimate knowledge of the river and strong teams, as times of high flows are potentially the most dangerous times to be on a river.

From mid-October onwards is one of the most popular times to raft or kayak, with warm settled weather and exciting runs. In December many of the rivers become too cold to enjoy unless you have a wetsuit, and the days are short with the start of winter – the time to consider shorter trips. The summer season from March to early June has long hot days and lower water flows to begin with, which generally means the rapids are a grade lower than they are from September to November. The rivers rise again in May with the pre-monsoon storms and some snowmelt.

From June to August the monsoon rains arrive. The rivers carry 10 times their low-water flows, and can flood with 60 to 80 times the low-water levels, making most rivers insanely difficult. Only parts of the Seti, upper Sun Kosi and Trisuli are commercially run during the monsoon. River levels can fluctuate dramatically at any time, although as a general rule weather patterns in Nepal are quite stable.

What to Bring

The website www.raftnepal.org offers an excellent overview of rafting options across Nepal, as well as advice about other extreme sports.

If you go on an organised rafting or kayaking trip all specialised equipment is supplied, as well as tents. Roll-top dry bags keep your gear dry even if the vessel flips.

Usually you will only need light clothing, with a warmer change for cool nights. A swimsuit, a towel, a sunhat, insect repellent, sunscreen and light tennis shoes or sandals (that will stay on your feet) are all necessary, but can be bought in Kathmandu. Overnight trips require a sleeping bag, but these can be hired. In winter you will need thermal clothing, especially on rivers like the Bhote Kosi. Check if companies provide paddle jackets and wetsuits.

Organised Trips

There are dozens of companies in Kathmandu claiming to be rafting and kayaking operators. A few are well-established companies with good reputations, and the rest are newer companies, often formed by guides breaking away and starting their own operations, and sometimes by people with very little experience of rivers. Although these new companies can be enthusiastic and good, they can also be shoestring operations that may not have adequate equipment and staff. Most of the small travel agencies simply sell trips on commission; often they have no real idea about the details of what they are selling and are only interested in getting bums on seats.

THE FUTURE OF RIVER-RUNNING IN NEPAL

In the past 20 years, a number of Nepali rivers have stopped flowing freely because of construction of hydroelectric projects. Around 90% of Nepal's power comes from hydroelectricity, much of it exported to India, and the government's vision of using hydro development to stimulate economic growth has put it on a collision course with environmental and rafting groups. A recent project on the Marsyangdi cut the river into a series of shorter sections and more dams are planned. There are further projects planned for the Karnali, Arun, Budhi Gandaki, West Seti, Tamur and Bhote Kosi Rivers.

The Nepal River Conservation Trust (NRCT) was formed by a group of concerned river guides in 1995 to raise awareness of the plight of Nepal's rivers, to lobby governments and to promote responsible use of rivers. The NRCT trains river guides in best environmental practice and organises river restoration projects. The NRCT organises the Bagmati River Festival from June to August (main events mid-August), which involves clean-up and environmental awareness campaigns, and rafting trips on the Bagmati from Sundarijal to Sankhamul. Contact the **NRCT** (☎ 01-4361995; www.nepalrivers.org.np) for more information.

If a group has recently returned from a trip, speak to its members. This will give you reliable information about the quality of equipment, the guides, the food and the transportation. Question the company about things such as how groups get to and from the river, the number of hours spent paddling or rowing, where the camps are set up, food provided (rafting promotes a very healthy appetite), who does the cooking and work around the camp, the cooking fuel used (wood isn't convenient or responsible), what happens to rubbish, hygiene precautions, and nighttime activities. Many companies have a photo file or video in their office, which can give you an impression of the equipment, safety and how trips are operated.

Check how many people have booked and paid for a trip, as well as the maximum number that will be taken.

The quality of the rafting and kayaking equipment is another variable, and can make a huge difference to the comfort and safety of participants. Modern self-bailing rafts, good life jackets and helmets are essential. Check how old the equipment is (modern plastic and alloy paddles are preferable to locally made wooden ones, for example) and ask what first-aid gear, supplies, spare parts and repair equipment are carried.

If your time is limited you may choose to book a trip before you leave home, though all Kathmandu operators accept walk-in bookings. Shorter trips depart every few days but the longer rafting trips only depart every week or so, so it's worth contacting a company in advance to see when they are planning a trip. The best companies will refer you to a friendly competitor if they don't have any suitable dates.

Rafting and kayaking trips vary from quite luxurious trips where you are rowed down the river and staff do everything for you (pitch camp, cook and so on), to trips where you participate in the running of the expedition including pitching tents, loading the rafts and helping with the cooking.

Generally you'll be rafting or kayaking for around five to six hours a day, and you can expect to be running rapids about 30% of the time depending on the river. The first and last days will most likely be half days. Longer trips of a week or more will probably have one rest day when you can relax or explore the surroundings.

Trips booked in Nepal range in price from US$30 to US$80 a day, depending on the standard of service, number of people on the trip and the river. On the Trisuli and Kali Gandaki the better operators charge US$35 to US$40 per day

Nepa Maps and Himalayan Maphouse (www.himalayan-maphouse.com) produce fairly useful rafting maps of the Bhote Kosi, Sun Kosi and Trisuli Rivers.

The annual Himalayan Whitewater Challenge, or rodeo, is a kayaking competition that runs for three days in November, either on the Trisuli or the Bhote Kosi Rivers.

RIVER GRADING SYSTEM

Rivers are graded for difficulty on an international scale from class 1 to 6, with class 1 defined as easy-moving water with few obstacles, and class 6 as nearly impossible to negotiate and a hazard to life. Anyone who is in reasonable physical shape and isn't afraid of water can safely go on rivers graded class 1 to 3. For more difficult and exciting class 4 rivers, you should be active, confident in water and have rafting experience. Class 5 is a very large step up from class 4; expect long continuous sections of powerful white water, strenuous paddling, steep constricted channels, powerful waves and the possibility of overturning a raft. Swimming in a class 5 rapid poses a significant risk.

---

while other river trips cost US$45 to US$55 per day. Expect to pay US$10 to US$20 per day on a more remote expedition with more difficult and expensive logistics. Generally you get what you pay for. It is better to pay a bit more and have a good, safe trip than to save US$100 and have a lousy, dangerous trip. Bear in mind that trips in Nepal are generally less than half the cost of similar trips in the US, so in relative terms all the prices are extremely reasonable. If you plan to do a more difficult trip it's particularly important to choose a company that has the experience, skills and equipment to run a safe and exciting expedition. As one rafting company says, 'saving you a little can cost you a lot'.

With the constant change in rafting and kayaking companies it's difficult to make individual recommendations; the fact that a company is not recommended here does not necessarily mean it will not deliver an excellent trip. Nonetheless, the following companies have been recommended for their professionalism.

Adrenaline Rush (Map p140; ☎ 01-4700961; www.adrenalinenepal.com; Thamel) All kinds of rafting and kayaking trips, including in a 'ducky' (inflatable kayak).

Drift Nepal (Map p140; ☎ 01-4700797; www.driftnepal.com.np) Contact Samir Thapa.

Equator Expeditions (Map p140; ☎ 01-4700782; www.equatorexpeditionsnepal.com, www .nepalgate.com; Thamel, Kathmandu) This company specialises in long participatory rafting/kayaking trips and kayak instruction.

Himalayan Encounters Kathmandu (Map p140; ☎ 01-4700426; www.himalayanencounters .com; Kathmandu Guest House courtyard, Thamel, Kathmandu) This company has earned a solid reputation through many Trisuli and Sun Kosi trips. Its Trisuli trips stay at its Trisuli Center camp, near Big Fig beach, while its Seti trips hike in from Bandipur.

Mountain River Rafting (Map p140; ☎ 01-4700770; www.mountainriverrafting.com; Thamel, Kathmandu)

Paddle Nepal (www.paddlenepal.com) Kathmandu (Map p140; ☎ 01-4700239; Thamel) Pokhara (Map p263; ☎ 061-207077) Tiny office in Thamel under Nargila Restaurant, with a main office in Pokhara; also offers kayak clinics.

Ultimate Descents Nepal (www.udnepal.com) Kathmandu (Map p140; ☎ 01-4701295); Pokhara (Map p263; ☎ 061-463240) Near Northfield Cafe and part of the Borderlands group. Specialises in long participatory rafting trips as well as kayak instruction and clinics on the Seti River.

Ultimate Rivers (Map p140; ☎ /fax 01-4700526; info@urnepal.wlink.com.np; Thamel, Kathmandu) Ultimate Rivers is associated with the New Zealand company Ultimate Descents International (www.ultimatedescents.com) and specialises in multiday expedition rafting and kayaking. The Kathmandu office is just north of the Kathmandu Guest House.

Safety

Safety is the most important part of any river trip. Safety is a combination of the right technical skills, teamwork, planning and local knowledge. Unfortunately, there are no minimum safety conditions enforced by any official body in Nepal. This makes it very important to choose a professional rafting and kayaking company.

Anyone who is seriously interested in rafting and kayaking should get White Water Nepal *by Peter Knowles. It has very detailed information on river trips, with 60 maps, river profiles and hydrographs, plus advice on equipment and health. Get a copy in Kathmandu, or check out www.riverpublish ing.co.uk.*

Waterproof camera containers allow you to take photos all the way down the river – ask your company if they have any for rent or, better, bring your own.

NUMBERS

There should be a minimum of two rafts per trip. If anyone falls out of a raft the second raft can help with the rescue. In higher water three rafts are safer than two. Many experts agree that one or two safety kayakers can replace the second raft, though the kayakers need to be white-water professionals with the training, skill and experience not only to run the most difficult rapids on the river, but also to be able to perform rescues in these rapids. Good safety kayakers are invaluable on steeper rivers where they can often get to swimmers in places no other craft could manage.

GUIDES

The most important aspects of rafting safety are both the skills and judgment of the guides and the teamwork of the group on the trip. If possible, speak with the guide who will lead the trip to get an impression of the people you will be spending time with and the type of trip they run. Ask them about their previous experience. Overseas experience or training allows the guides to keep up with the latest advances and safety training. Kayaking experience adds additional depth to a rafting guide's skills.

All guides should have a current first-aid certificate and be trained in cardiopulmonary resuscitation. Reputable companies with reliable guides will seek international accreditation such as the Swiftwater Rescue Technician (SRT) qualification.

ON THE RIVER

Your guide should give you a comprehensive safety talk and paddle training before you launch off downstream. If you don't get this it is probably cause for concern.

- Listen to what your guide is telling you. Always wear your life jacket in rapids. Wear your helmet whenever your guide tells you, and make sure that both the helmet and jacket are properly adjusted and fitted
- Keep your feet and arms inside the raft. If the raft hits a rock or wall and you are in the way, the best you'll escape with is a laceration.
- If you do swim in a rapid, get into the 'white-water swimming position'. You should be on your back, with your feet downstream and up where you can see them. Hold on to your paddle as this will make you more visible. Relax and breathe when you aren't going through waves. Then turn over and swim at the end of the rapid when the water becomes calmer. Self-rescue is the best rescue.

Kayaking

The opportunities for kayak expeditions are exceptional. Apart from the rivers discussed later in this chapter, of note at the right flows are the Mardi Khola, Tamba Kosi, Karnali headwaters, Thuli Bheri, Balephi Khola and tributaries of the Tamur.

The upper Modhi Khola is also good for experienced kayakers. The side creek of the Bhurungdi Khola, by Birethani village, hides several waterfalls which are runable by experienced kayakers.

TRANSPORTING YOUR OWN KAYAK

Most airlines will carry short kayaks on the same basis as surfboards or bicycles; there's no excess baggage charge, as long as you are within the weight limits. If you are a group, negotiate a deal at the time of booking. If there are only one or two of you, just turn up, put all your bulky light gear in the kayak, with heavy items in your carry-on luggage, and smile sweetly!

www.raftingassociation .org.np is the website of the Nepal Association of Rafting Agents and has information on the annual Himalayan Whitewater Challenge, contact details of rafting companies and overviews of river routes.

If you phone the airline in advance they have to quote the rulebook and start talking air cargo, which is expensive.

KAYAK CLINICS

Nepal is an ideal place to learn to kayak and several rafting companies offer learner kayak clinics. For the communication required to teach, the best instruction clinics tend to be staffed with both Western and Nepali instructors. Kayak clinics normally take about four days, which gives you time to get a good grounding in the basics of kayaking, safety and river dynamics.

The clinics are a pretty laid-back intro to kayaking, with around four to six hours of paddling a day. On day one you'll learn self-rescue, T-rescue and Eskimo roll, which will help you to right yourself when you capsize. Day two sees you on the river, learning to ferry glide (cross the river), eddy in and eddy out (entering and leaving currents) and perfecting your paddling strokes. Day three is when you start really having fun on the river, running small (class 2) rapids and journeying down the river, learning how to read the rapids. The key is to relax your upper body to move with the kayak, and not to panic if you tip over. Physical flexibility is a real plus. Expect one instructor for every three people.

'Nepal is an ideal place to learn to kayak and several rafting companies offer learner kayak clinics.'

Equator Expeditions and Ultimate Rivers (see rafting companies, p102) operate clinics on the upper Sun Kosi. Equator runs the Sukute Beach Resort, just north of Sukute village between kilometre markers 69 and 70. It's fairly comfortable but isn't as luxurious as Borderlands or the Last Resort, with squat toilets and cold showers. Still, it has a great spot on the river, with a private beach, a bar area with pool tables and a lovely stretch of river nearby. It also has a pool which is a real bonus when learning Eskimo rolls.

Ultimate Rivers uses the Riverside Camp, between kilometre markers 83 and 84, which is a similarly basic camp, made up of dome tents. Both companies charge around US$160 for the four-day clinic, though you can often negotiate a cheaper price if you take the local bus. For both trips check what kind of transportation is included. You may find yourself flagging down local buses and putting your kayak on the roof for short rides after a trip down the river. For US$40 you can tag on a day's kayaking to a bungee jump at the Last Resort.

The **Royal Beach Camp** (www.royalbeachnepal.com) offers two- to seven-day kayak clinics from its camp on the Trisuli River. Add-ons include canyoning and rafting trips. Contact it at the office in Kathmandu just north of the Kathmandu Guest House.

Ultimate Descents Nepal and Mountain River Rafting (see rafting companies, p102) operate their four-day clinics on the gentle Seti River, for around US$250, from Pokhara to Pokhara. The first day's training takes place on Phewa Tal and the remaining three days are on the Seti, with two nights' riverside camping. The kayak route follows the rafting route (see p108), putting in at Damauli and taking out at Ghaighat, at the junction with the Trisuli River. The advantage to learning on the Seti is that you get to journey down a wilderness river. Upper Sun Kosi kayak clinics can be structured for instruction from one to four days.

Kayak-clinic accommodation is more basic than luxury tented camps like Borderlands or the Last Resort. Nose plugs are useful for those practice Eskimo rolls and you should bring a warm change of clothes as you are going to get wet.

The bulk of kayak clinics operate in late October, November, March and April. December to February clinics are still possible, but with shorter days, and there's a lot less sunlight to warm you up at the beginning and end of the day.

Choosing a River

Before you decide on a river, you need to decide what it is that you want out of your trip. There are trips available from two to 12 days on different rivers, all offering dramatically different experiences.

First, don't believe that just because it's a river it's going to be wet 'n' wild. Some rivers, such as the Sun Kosi, which is a full-on white-water trip in September and October, are basically flat in the low water of early spring. On the flip side, early spring can be a superb time to raft rivers such as the Marsyangdi or Bhote Kosi, which would be suicidal during high flows. The Karnali is probably the only river that offers continually challenging white water at all flows, though during the high-water months of September and May it's significantly more challenging than in the low-water months.

Longer trips such as the Sun Kosi (in the autumn), the Karnali and the Tamur offer some real heart-thumping white water with the incredible journeying aspect of a long river trip. With more time on the river, things are more relaxed, relationships progress at a more natural pace, and memories become entrenched for a lifetime. Long after the white water has blurred into one white-knuckled thrill ride, the memories of a moonrise over the river and the friends you inevitably make will remain. River trips are much more than gravity-powered roller-coaster rides; they're liquid journeys traversed on very special highways. For many people they become a way of life.

If a long trip is simply impossible because of financial or time constraints, don't undervalue the shorter ones. Anyone who has ever taken a paddle-raft or kayak down the Bhote Kosi (at any flow) would be hard pressed to find anything better to do with two days in Nepal. There are also medium-length options that are perfect for people who want to experience a river journey but have limited time.

Ganesh Kayak Shop (www.ganeshkayak.com) in Pokhara is the only place to hire kayaks by the day – see p260.

River Routes

This section describes the main commercially rafted rivers in Nepal. It is by no means a complete list, and private boaters who have the experience, equipment and desire to run their own expeditions are best advised to consult the guidebook, *White Water Nepal* (see sidebar, p102).

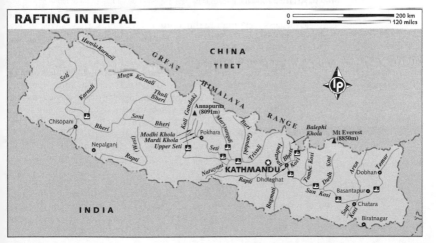

RAFTING IN NEPAL

RIVER TRIPS IN NEPAL

Note that in the 'Season/Grade' column, the number in brackets refers to the grade when the high river flows, which is normally at the beginning and end of the season.

River	Trip duration (days)	Approx cost	Transport	Season/Grade	Add-ons
Bhote Kosi	2	US$80-110	3hr from Kathmandu	late Oct-May/ 4 (5-)	bungee jump, canyoning, kayak clinics
Upper Sun Kosi	2	US$80-90	2hr from Kathmandu	Oct-May/3 (4), Jun-Sep/4 (4+)	
Trisuli	2	US$80-90	2hr from Kathmandu	Oct-May/3 (4), Jun-Sep/4 (4+)	excursions to Bandipur or Pokhara
Seti	3	US$140-170	1½hr from Pokhara	Sep-May/2 (3+)	kayak clinics are popular here
Kali Gandaki	3	US$120-160	2hr from Pokhara	late Sep-May/ 3 (4)	Chitwan National Park
Marsyangdi	4	US$220-250	5hr from Kathmandu	late Oct-Apr/ 4 (5-)	Annapurna Circuit Trek
Sun Kosi	8-9	US$350-450	3hr from Kathmandu 16hr bus back to Kathmandu or fly from Biratnagar	Sep-Nov/3+ (4+), Dec-Apr/3 (4)	Koshi Tappu Wildlife Reserve or continue onto Darjeeling in India
Karnali	10	US$500-550	16hr bus ride or flight and 4hr bus ride	late Sep-May/ 3 (4+)	Bardia National Park
Tamur	12	US$650-800	18hr bus or flight, then 3-day trek; flight or 16hr bus back (6 days of rafting total)	Oct-Dec/4 (5-)	trek to Kanchenjunga

TRISULI
Distance 40km
Duration One to two days
Start Baireni
Finish Multiple locations
Brief description Popular introduction to rafting, a wild ride during the monsoon

With easy access just out of Kathmandu, the Trisuli is where many budget river trips operate.

This is an obvious choice if you are looking for a short introduction to rafting at the cheapest possible price.

The Trisuli has some good rapids and scenery but with the main busy road to Kathmandu beside the river it is not wilderness rafting. Some operators have their own fixed campsites or lodges, ranging from safari-style resorts to windblown village beaches complete with begging kids and scavenging dogs. The two most established locations are the Royal Beach Camp (see p104) and the Trisuli Centre, part of Himalayan Encounters (see p102). Both are sited in the best of the white water and have good facilities and food. The Trisuli Centre is next to Big Fig beach, a charming village and a 160m suspension bridge across the river.

When booking, ask where the put-in point is: anything starting at Kuringhat or Mugling will mainly be a relaxing float. During the mid-monsoon months (August to early October) the Trisuli changes character completely as huge runoffs make the river swell and shear like an immense ribbon of churning ocean, especially after its confluence with the Bhodi

A rafting trip on the Trisuli is a convenient and fun add-on to travelling between Kathmandu and Pokhara, Chitwan, Bandipur or the start of the Annapurna Circuit.

Gandaki. At these flows it provides a classic big-volume Himalayan river so make sure you choose a reputable company to go with.

BHOTE KOSI
Distance 18km
Duration Two days
Start 95km from Kathmandu, near the Tibetan border
Finish Lamosangu
Brief description Just three hours from Kathmandu, the Bhote Kosi is one of the best short raft trips to be found anywhere in the world

The Bhote Kosi is the steepest river rafted in Nepal – technical and totally committing. With a gradient of 15m per kilometre, it's a full eight times as steep as the Sun Kosi, which it feeds further downstream. The rapids are steep and continuous class 4, with a lot of continuous class 3 in between.

This river is one of the most fun things you can do right out of Kathmandu and a great way to get an adrenaline fix during the low-water months, but it should only be attempted with a company that has a lot of experience on the Bhote Kosi, and is running the absolute best guides, safety equipment and safety kayakers.

The normal run is from around 95km northeast of Kathmandu (north of Barabise) to the dam at Lamosangu. The river has been kayaked above this point, but a raft trip here would not be recreational. At high flows several of the rapids become solid class 5, and the consequences of any mistakes become serious.

Most trips are two days. At higher flows the first day is normally on the easier waters of the Upper Sun Kosi, graduating to the Bhote Kosi on the second day. At lower flows both days are on the Bhote Kosi. If you are already up here then the whole Bhote Kosi River can be done as a day trip.

Camping on the Bhote Kosi is limited, with few good beaches, so most groups stay at comfortable river camps like Borderlands and the Last Resort (see p231).

Rafting the Bhote Kosi out of one of these camps makes for a less hectic trip and means you can relax at the end of the day in pristine surroundings and comfort.

The environmental impact of trips is limited by staying at fixed camps, which also create local employment and business. They also offer other activities, so you can mix and match what you do.

The best white water is found on the section between Charaudi and Mugling and can be done as a full-on half-day. Trips on the Trisuli can be combined with excursions to Pokhara or Chitwan.

You can get an idea of what you are in for by looking at the names of some of the rapids – Gerbil in the Plumbing, Frog in a Blender, Carnal Knowledge of a Deviant Nature, Exlax and Liquid Bliss!

UPPER SUN KOSI
Distance 20km
Duration One day
Start Khadichour
Finish Dolalghat
Brief description A great place for a short family trip or learner kayak clinics

The top section of the Upper Sun Kosi from below the dam to near Sukute Beach is a class 3 white-water run offering an easier alternative when the Bhote Kosi is too high.

The lower section is a mellow scenic float, with forest down to the river, and it is a popular river for kayak clinics. At high flows during and just after the monsoon rains the Upper Sun Kosi is a full-on high class 3 to 4 high-adrenaline day trip.

SETI
Distance 32km
Duration Two days
Start Damauli
Finish Gaighat
Brief description A quieter river that is perfect for beginners, birdwatchers, families and learner kayakers

The Seti is an excellent two-day trip in an isolated area, with beautiful jungle, white sandy beaches and plenty of class 2 to 3 rapids. The warm water also makes it a popular place for winter trips and kayak clinics. During the monsoon (June to August) the river changes radically as monsoon runoff creates big-volume class 3 to 4 rapids.

The logical starting point is Damauli on the Prithvi Hwy between Mugling and Pokhara. This would give you 32km of rafting to the confluence with the Trisuli River. From the take-out at Gaighat it's just a one-hour drive to Chitwan National Park.

> Beware if you decide to try the upper section of the Seti River, as it disappears underground above Dule Gouda! Perhaps this is what they refer to as class 6...

KALI GANDAKI
Distance 90km
Duration Three days (two days rafting)
Start Baglung
Finish Andhi Khola
Brief description Diverse trip down the holy river, through deep gorges and past waterfalls

The Kali Gandaki is an excellent alternative to the Trisuli, as there is no road alongside, and the scenery, villages and temples all combine to make it a great trip.

The rapids on the Kali Gandaki are much more technical and continuous than those on the Trisuli (at class 3 to 4 depending on the flows), and in high water it's no place to be unless you are an accomplished kayaker experienced in avoiding big holes. At medium and lower flows it's a fun and challenging river with rapids that will keep you busy.

The Kali Gandaki is one of the holiest rivers in Nepal, and every river junction is dotted with cremation sites and above-ground burial mounds. If you've been wondering what's under that pile of rocks, we recommend against exploring. Because of the recent construction of a dam at the confluence with the Andhi Khola, what was once a four- to five-day trip has now become a three-day trip, starting at Baglung and taking out at the dam site. At very high flows it will probably be possible to run the full five-day trip to Ramdhighat by just portaging the dam site. This option would add some great white water and you could visit the fantastic derelict palace at **Ranighat** (p303).

> Kayakers have the option of descending the Modhi Khola on the first day to its confluence to the Kali Gandaki, to join up with the rafting group at the end of the first day.

If you can raft to Ramdhighat beside the Siddhartha Hwy between Pokhara and Sunauli, you could continue on to the confluence with the Trisuli at Devghat. This adds another 130km and three or four more days. The lower section below Ramdhighat doesn't have much white water, but it is seldom rafted and offers a very isolated area with lots of wildlife.

MARSYANGDI
Distance 27km
Duration Four days (two days rafting)
Start Ngadi
Finish Phaliya Sanghu (Phalesangu)
Brief description A magnificent blue white-water river with a spectacular mountain backdrop

The Marsyangdi is steeper and offers more continuous white water than most other rivers in Nepal; it's not called the 'Raging River' for nothing! You can drive by bus to Khudi or Bhulbule, from where it is a short but scenic walk up to the village of Ngadi, with great views of Manaslu ahead of you the whole time.

From Ngadi downstream to the dam side above Phaliya Sanghu, it's pretty much solid white water. Rapids are steep, technical and consecutive, making the Marsyangdi a serious undertaking. Successful navigation of the Marsyangdi requires companies to have previous experience on the river and to use the best guides and equipment. Rafts must be self-bailing, and should be running with a minimum of weight and gear on board. Professional safety kayakers should be considered a standard safety measure on this river.

A hydro project has severely affected this world-class rafting and kayaking river but it is still possible to have a two-day run on the rapids before reaching the dam. You could divert around the dam and continue on the lower section for another two days but at this stage it is hard to tell how much water will be released and whether it will be worth doing. Future dams are planned for the river so you might want to raft this one soon.

KARNALI

Distance 180km
Duration 10 days (seven days rafting)
Start Sauli
Finish Chisopani
Brief description A classic wilderness trip in far western Nepal down Nepal's largest and longest river

The Karnali is a gem, combining a short (two-hour) trek with some of the prettiest canyons and jungle scenery in Nepal. Most experienced river people who have paddled the Karnali find it one of the best all-round river trips they've ever done. In high water the Karnali is a serious commitment, combining huge, though fairly straightforward, rapids with a seriously remote location. At low water the Karnali is still a fantastic trip. The rapids become smaller when the river drops, but the steeper gradient and constricted channel keep it interesting.

Being the longest and largest river in all of Nepal, the Karnali drains a huge and well-developed catchment. Spring snowmelts can drive the river up dramatically in a matter of hours – as the river rises, the difficulty increases exponentially. The river flows through some steep and constricted canyons where the rapids are close together, giving little opportunity to correct for potential mistakes. Pick your company carefully.

The trip starts with a long, but interesting, two-day bus ride to the remote far west of Nepal. If you're allergic to bus rides, it's possible to fly to Nepalganj and cut the bus transport down to about four hours on the way over, and two hours on the way back. New roads now run from the hill town of Surkhet to Sauli, from where it is a two-hour trek to the Karnali River. Once you start on the Karnali it's 180km to the next road access at Chisopani, on the northern border of the Bardia National Park.

The river section takes about seven days, giving plenty of time to explore some of the side canyons and waterfalls that come into the river valley. Better-run trips also include a layover day, where the expedition stays at the same campsite for two nights. The combination of long bus rides and trekking puts some people off, but anyone who has ever done the trip raves about it. Finish with a visit to the Bardia National Park for an unbeatable combination.

SUN KOSI
Distance 270km
Duration Eight to nine days (seven days rafting)
Start Dolalghat
Finish Chatara
Brief description A self-sufficient expedition through central Nepal from the Himalaya to the Gangetic Plain

This is the longest river trip offered in Nepal, traversing 270km through the beautiful Mahabharat Range on its meandering way from the put-in at Dolalghat to the take-out at Chatara in the far east of the country. It's quite an experience to begin a river trip just three hours out of Kathmandu, barely 60km from the Tibetan border, and end the trip looking down the hot, dusty gun barrel of the north Indian plain just eight or nine days later. Because it's one of the easiest trips logistically, it's also one of the least expensive for the days you spend on a river.

Many rafters consider the Sun Kosi to be one of the world's 10 classic river journeys.

The Sun Kosi (River of Gold) starts off fairly relaxed, with only class 2 and small class 3 rapids to warm up on during the first couple of days. Savvy guides will take this opportunity to get teams working together with precision. The river volume increases with the air temperature as several major tributaries join the river and from the third day the rapids become more powerful and frequent. During high-water trips you may well find yourselves astonished at just how big a river wave can get.

While the lower sections of large-volume rivers are usually rather flat, the Sun Kosi reserves some of its biggest and best rapids for the last days, and the last section is nonstop class 4 before a final quiet float down the Sapt Kosi. Some companies add on an extra day's rafting on the lower section of the Tamur, from Mulghat down.

At the right flow it's an incredible combination of white water, scenery, villages, and quiet introspective evenings.

Note that a new highway is being built alongside the top 40km of the Sun Kosi; once complete (and no one knows when this will be), it'll allow shorter six-day trips on the river and will also probably halve the return time from the take-out.

TAMUR
Distance 120km
Duration 11 days
Start Dobhan
Finish Chatara
Brief description Remote expedition in the foothills of Kanchenjunga in the far east of the country; includes a three-day trek

Way out in the far east, this river combines one of the best short treks in Nepal with some really challenging white-water action. The logistics of this trip make it a real expedition, and while it is a little more complicated to run than many rivers in Nepal, the rewards are worth the effort.

First you have to get to Basantapur, a 15-hour drive from Kathmandu or a one-hour flight to Biratnagar and then a five-hour drive. Most expeditions begin with a stunning three- or four-day trek from Basantapur up over the Milke Danda Range, past the alpine lake of Gupha Pokhari to Dobhan. At Dobhan three tributaries of the Tamur join forces, combining the waters of the mountains to the north (including Kanchenjunga, the world's third-largest mountain). The first 16km of rapids is intense, with rapid after rapid, and the white water just keeps coming through towering canyons until the big finale. The best time to raft is at medium flows between mid-October and mid-November.

OTHER RIVERS

The **Upper Seti River**, just outside Pokhara, makes an excellent half-day trip when it is at high flows. Trips operate in mid-September and October (class 3+) and cost US$40 to US$45 return from Pokhara.

The **Balephi Khola** (above the Bhote Kosi) is run by a few companies from Jalbire to its confluence with the upper Sun Kosi. Trips normally run only when the river is high from mid-September to early November and in May, and cost US$90 to US$110 for a two day trip that combines this river with the Upper Sun Kosi.

The **Bheri River**, which is in the west, is a great float trip with incredible jungle scenery and lots of wildlife, making it a possible family trip. This is also one of Nepal's best fishing rivers and can be combined with a visit to the Bardia National Park.

The powerful **Arun River** from Tumlingtar makes an excellent three-day wilderness trip with good class 3 rapids and pristine canyons, although the logistics of flying into the start of the river and getting gear there makes it an expensive trip.

CLIMBING & TREKKING PEAKS

Bivouacked somewhere between trekking and mountaineering are Nepal's 'trekking peaks'. The name 'trekking peak' can be quite deceiving; they vary in their level of difficulty but most include significant mountaineering challenges. They are the natural first step if you are interested in progressing from trekking and scrambling onto crampon and rope work.

Organised Climbs

Because of the bureaucracy involved (see p112), it is easiest to use an adventure travel company to organise the climb, rather than do the running around yourself. Trip permit fees are included in all the prices listed in this section.

Equator Expeditions (p112) is one company that organises mountaineering courses and ascents of Mera and Island Peaks in the Solu Khumbu region. If you sign up for a climb you can often get discounts on its other trips, such as a free two-day Bhote Kosi raft or US$50 off a kayak clinic.

Equator operates a six-day course and ascent of Island Peak, properly known as Imja Tse (6189m), from a base in Chhukung. After acclimatisation, briefing, training and a half-day hike to base camp, the peak is generally climbed in a single eight hour day, departing early in the morning. It's physically demanding but not technically difficult – only the last section is on ice and snow. The north ridge offers a slightly more difficult route option. Trips run weekly in season (mid-October to mid-November, end March to May) and cost US$700. Climbing guides report that Island Peak is becoming more of a technical climb because of ice melting caused by global warming. Sections that it used to be possible to cover with jumars (ascenders) on fixed ropes, and limited use of crampons and ice axes, now require some actual technical rock climbing.

The second most popular option is to the false summit of Lobuche East (6119m), a more technically difficult ascent that requires two days' training. Climbers generally depart from a high camp at 1.30am and are back by noon. The six-day round trip from Dzongla costs around US$700. Trips operate in November and from mid-April to mid-May.

Nepa Maps produces several trekking peak maps, including to Paldor, Island Peak, Mera Peak, Chulu, Pisang and Naya Kanga, with scales ranging from 1:30,000 to 1:80,000.

Also in the Everest region, Mera Peak (6476m) involves more trekking than climbing, though it is the highest of the trekking peaks. It's a minimum 15-day trip from Lukla and involves trekking up to the 5415m Mera La, from where the climbing begins. Trips from Kathmandu cost around US$2000 and run in November, April and May. Don't confuse Mera Peak with Mehra Peak (Kongma Tse), further north.

Other possible trekking peak ascents in the Everest region include Phari Lapche (6017m), Macchermo (6273m) and Kyozo/Kyajo Ri (6186m), all in the stunning Gokyo Valley.

For all of these trips you will need to hire your own plastic climbing boots and gaiters, either from Kathmandu (Shona's rents climbing boots; see p160) or Namche Bazaar. Prices include permits, equipment, guides, tent accommodation and food. Expect a group size of around six to eight climbers.

In the Annapurna region, Pisang Peak (6091m) and Chulu East (6584m) are both five-day excursions from Manang; the former is more common, with an organised trip costing around US$1200, with a minimum of three climbers. A few companies, such as the UK's **Himalayan Frontiers** (www.himalayanfrontiers.co.uk), run climbing trips to Tharpu Chuli/Tent Peak (5663m) from Machhapuchhare Base Camp in the Annapurna Sanctuary.

Several companies, including Mountain Monarch, run trekking peaks as part of a standard trek. In the Everest region this includes the Everest Base Camp Trek and Island Peak (21 to 23 days, US$1750) or Lobuche East (25 days, US$1990). Pisang Peak or Chulu West can be combined with the Annapurna Circuit Trek (24 to 25 days, US$1650 to US$1950). Yala Peak (5500m) can be included as part of a 16-day Langtang trek (US$1500).

Trekking companies in Kathmandu that organise ascents of trekking peaks include the following:

Climb High Himalaya (☎ 01-4372874; www.climbhighhimalaya.com; Kathmandu)

Equator Expeditions (Map p140; ☎ 01-4700782; www.equatorexpeditionsnepal.com, www.nepalgate.com; Thamel, Kathmandu)

Himalayan Ecstasy (Map p140; ☎ 01-4700795; www.himalayanecstasy.com; Kathmandu) Offers Island and Lobuche Peaks together in one trip for US$1000.

Mountain Monarch (☎ 01-4361668; www.mountainmonarch.com; Lazimpat, Kathmandu)

Namaste Adventure (☎ 01-4700239; www.namasteadventure.com) From trekking peaks to full-on mountaineering trips.

Nepal Mountain Trekking (Map p140; ☎ 01-4700006; www.nepalmountain.com) Across from Northfield Cafe; generally a bit more expensive.

Permits & Fees

To arrange your own climbing trip, a permit is required from the **Nepal Mountaineering Association** (NMA; Map p126; ☎ 01-4434525; www.nepalmountaineering.org; PO Box 1435, Nag Pokhari, Kathmandu). Permits must be applied for in advance and are only valid for one month, although weekly extensions are available for 25% of the total fee. All people ascending trekking peaks must be accompanied by a *sirdar* (leader) who is registered with the NMA.

Of the 33 'trekking peaks' the 15 'new' peaks designated in 2002 are classified as 'A' peaks, the original 18 (including all those covered earlier) are 'B' peaks. The fees for climbing trekking peaks depend on the group size and the classification. For group 'B' peaks the fees are: one to four people US$350; five to eight people US$350 for the group plus US$40 per person; nine to 12 people (the maximum group size) US$510 plus US$25 per person. For group 'A' peaks the fees are: one to seven people US$500; eight to 12 people US$500 plus US$100 per person.

Bill O'Connor's book *The Trekking Peaks of Nepal* gives a detailed description of the climb to each of the 18 traditional peaks plus the approach trek to the mountain. Equipment, applications, procedures and other matters are comprehensively covered but there's little information on the new 'A' trekking peaks.

Kathmandu

For many, stepping off a plane into Kathmandu is a pupil-dilating experience, a riot of sights, sounds, colours and smells that can quickly lead to sensory overload. Whether you're barrelling down the atmospheric winding streets of the old town in a rickshaw, marvelling at the exquisite medieval temples of Durbar Sq or dodging the tiger balm sellers and trekking touts in Thamel, Kathmandu can be an intoxicating, amazing and exhausting place.

As the largest city in the country, Kathmandu is regularly paralysed by political ferment, electricity cuts and traffic seizures on a scale that is almost apocalyptic. Town planning is not Kathmandu's greatest strength. The fact that the city keeps moving at all is a testament to the patience and equanimity of its people. Take a walk through the backstreets, however, and the capital's rich cultural and artistic heritage reveals itself in hidden temples overflowing with marigolds, courtyards full of drying chillies and rice, and tiny hobbit-sized workshops.

Since the 1960s Kathmandu has been supplying the closest thing backpackers have to Disneyland and, with over 2500 tourist-related business in 5 sq metres, Thamel boasts a collection of hotels, restaurants, trekking agencies, bakeries and shops that is rivalled only by Bangkok's Khao San Rd. This endlessly fascinating, sometimes infuriating, city is well worth a week of your time, but it's easy to spend too much time stuck in touristy Thamel. Enjoy the internet cafes, the espresso and the lemon cheesecake, but make sure you also get out into the 'real Nepal' before your time runs out.

HIGHLIGHTS

- Follow our walking tours through the labyrinthine backstreets of the **old town** (p134), bursting with hidden courtyards and little-known temples
- Soak up the amazing architectural monuments of **Durbar Square** (p119), an artistic and architectural tradition that rivals the great cities of Europe
- Dine on momos and wild boar to the beat of *madal* drums and *bansari* flutes at one of the city's superb **Newari restaurants** (p152)
- Ensure the enduring love of friends and family by snapping up the bargains in Thamel's excellent **shops** (p157)
- Chill out in one of Thamel's rooftop garden **restaurants** (p149), with a good book, a pot of masala tea and a slice of chocolate cake
- Take a day trip to the nearby Unesco World Heritage site of **Swayambhunath** (p163)

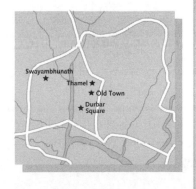

| ■ TELEPHONE CODE: 01 | ■ POPULATION: 1 MILLION | ■ ELEVATION: 1337M |

KATHMANDU

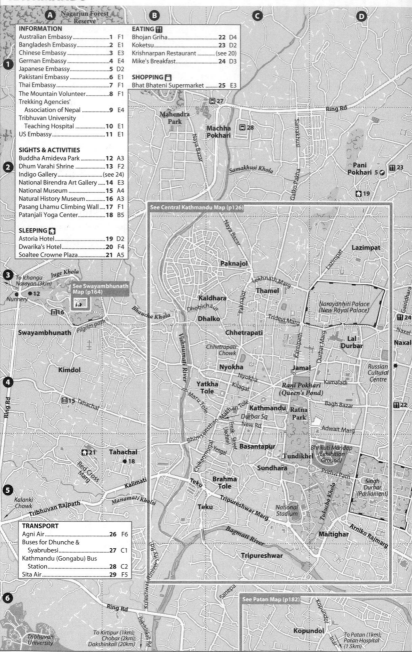

INFORMATION

Australian Embassy	**1** F1
Bangladesh Embassy	**2** E1
Chinese Embassy	**3** E3
German Embassy	**4** E4
Japanese Embassy	**5** D2
Pakistani Embassy	**6** E1
Thai Embassy	**7** E1
The Mountain Volunteer	**8** F1
Trekking Agencies' Association of Nepal	**9** E4
Tribhuvan University Teaching Hospital	**10** E1
US Embassy	**11** E1

SIGHTS & ACTIVITIES

Buddha Amideva Park	**12** A3
Dhum Varahi Shrine	**13** F2
Indigo Gallery	(see 24)
National Birendra Art Gallery	**14** E3
National Museum	**15** A4
Natural History Museum	**16** A3
Pasang Lhamu Climbing Wall	**17** F1
Patanjali Yoga Center	**18** B5

SLEEPING

Astoria Hotel	**19** D2
Dwarika's Hotel	**20** F4
Soaltee Crowne Plaza	**21** A5

EATING

Bhojan Griha	**22** D4
Koketsu	**23** D2
Krishnarpan Restaurant	(see 20)
Mike's Breakfast	**24** D3

SHOPPING

Bhat Bhateni Supermarket	**25** E3

TRANSPORT

Agni Air	**26** F6
Buses for Dhunche & Syabrubesi	**27** C1
Kathmandu (Gongabu) Bus Station	**28** C2
Sita Air	**29** F5

See Central Kathmandu Map (p126)

See Swayambhunath Map (p164)

See Patan Map (p182)

Nagarjun Forest Reserve

Mahendra Park

Machha Pokhari

Ring Rd

Pani Pokhari

Naya Bazar

Samakhusi Khola

Juge Khola

To Ichangu Narayan (3km)

Nunnery

Swayambhunath

Pilgrim path

Bhaucha Khola

Kimdol

Vishnumati River

Tahachal

Red Cross Marg

Ring Rd

Tahachal

Kalanki Chowk

Tribhuvan Rajpath

Manamati Khola

Kalimati

Kuleshwar Dhobi Khola Rd

To Kirtipur (1km); Chobar (2km); Dakshinkali (20km)

Tribhuvan University

Ring Rd

Balkhu Rd

Paknajol

Kaldhara

Dhobichaur

Dhalko

Chhetrapati

Chhetrapati Chowk

Nyokha

Nyokha

Yatkha Tole

Kilagal

Maru Tole

Marti Tole

Bhimsensthan

Chikanmugal

Yengal

Teku

Brahma Tole

Teku

Tripureshwar Marg

Bagmati River

Tripureshwar

Thamel

Lekhnath Marg

Tridevi Marg

Kantipath

Makhan Tole

Kathmandu Durbar Sq

New Rd

Basantapur

Ratna Park

Rani Pokhari (Queen's Pond)

Jamal

Kamaladi

Bagh Bazar

Adwait Marg

Tundikhel

Sundhara

Prithvi Path

Bhrikuti Mandap (Exhibition Ground)

National Stadium

Bhairava Khola

Sanepa

Lazimpat

Narayanhiti Palace (New Royal Palace)

Lal Durbar

Russian Cultural Centre

Naxal

Galidhara

Durbar Marg

Singh Durbar (Parliament)

Arnika Rajmarg

Maitighar

See Patan Map (p182)

Kopundol

To Patan (1km); Patan Hospital (1.5km)

Samakhusi

Galfutola

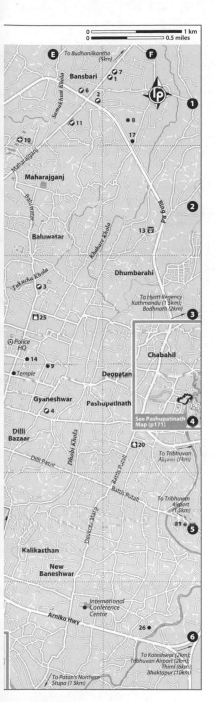

HISTORY

The history of Kathmandu is really a history of the Newars, the main inhabitants of the Kathmandu Valley. While the documented history of the valley goes back to the Kiratis, around the 7th century BC, the foundation of Kathmandu itself dates from the 12th century AD, during the time of the Malla dynasty.

The original settlements of Yambu and Yangala, at the confluence of the Bagmati and Vishnumati Rivers in what is now the southern half of the old town, grew up around the trade route to Tibet. Traders and pilgrims stayed at resthouses such as the Kasthamandap (see p120), which later lent its name to the city.

Originally known as Kantipur, the city flourished during the Malla era, and the bulk of its superb temples, buildings and other monuments date from this time. Initially, Kathmandu was an independent city within the valley, but in the 14th century the valley was united under the rule of the Malla king of Bhaktapur. The 15th century saw division once more, this time into the three independent kingdoms: Kathmandu, Patan and Bhaktapur. Rivalry between the three city-states led to a series of wars that left each state weakened and vulnerable to the 1768 invasion of the valley by Prithvi Narayan Shah.

The ensuing Shah dynasty unified Nepal and made the expanded city of Kathmandu its new capital – a position the city has held ever since.

ORIENTATION

The most interesting part of Kathmandu is the crowded backstreets of the rectangular-shaped old town. This is bordered to the north by the main tourist and backpacker district of Thamel (pronounced tha-*mel*) and to the east by the sprawling modern new town.

In the centre of the old town is historic Durbar Sq and Hanuman Dhoka (the old royal palace). Freak St, the focus of Kathmandu's overland scene during the hippie era, runs south from here. Thamel is 15 to 20 minutes' walk north from Durbar Sq.

Running east from Durbar Sq is New Rd, constructed after the great earthquake of 1934, and one of the main shopping streets in town. At the eastern end are the offices of Nepal Airlines. South of the junction of New Rd and Kantipath is the main post office and Sundhara district, easily located by the minaretlike Bhimsen Tower.

The street known as Kantipath forms the boundary between the older and newer parts of the city. On the east side of Kantipath is a large, open parade ground known as Tundikhel, and on the eastern edge of this is the Ratna Park (City) bus station for buses around the Kathmandu Valley.

North of the Tundikhel is Durbar Marg, a wide street flanked by airline offices, restaurants and expensive hotels; at its northern end is the New Royal Palace, which is slated to become a museum. Further north are the embassy and NGO districts of Lazimpat and Maharajganj. To the south of town is Patan (see p181), an historically distinct city, which has now partially merged with Kathmandu's southern sprawl.

Both Kathmandu and Patan are encircled by the Ring Rd. The main Kathmandu bus station is on this road in the north of the city; Tribhuvan Airport is on its eastern edge.

Addresses

In old Kathmandu, streets are only named after their district, or *tole*. The names of these districts, squares and other landmarks (perhaps a monastery or temple) form the closest thing to an address. For example, the address of everyone living within a 100m radius of Thahiti Tole is Thahiti Tole. 'Thamel' is now used to describe a sprawling area with at least a dozen roads and several hundred hotels and restaurants.

Given this anarchic approach it is amazing that any mail gets delivered – it does, but slowly. Most businesses have post office boxes. If you're trying to find a particular house, shop or business, make sure you get detailed directions. Otherwise, the interactive online map at www.mapmandu.com can sometimes help.

INFORMATION
Bookshops

Kathmandu has excellent bookshops with a great selection of Himalaya titles, including books that are not usually available outside the country. Most dealers will buy back books for 50% of what you paid.

Barnes & Noble Bookhouse (Map p140; Thamel)
Mandala Bookpoint (Map p140; Kantipath) Excellent selection, with a good range in French.
Nepal Book Depot (Map p140; Thamel) Some of the best prices.
New Tibet Book Store (Map p140; ☎ 4415788; Tridevi Marg) The best collection of Tibet-related titles but few discounts.

Pilgrims Book House (Map p140; ☎ 4424942; www .pilgrimsbooks.com, www.pilgrimsonlineshop.com) A couple of doors north of the Kathmandu Guest House; the best in town and particularly strong on antiquarian travelogues. There are a couple of smaller branches around town.
United Books (Map p140; Thamel) Well-chosen selection and sensible prices, run by Danish Lars. Branches across town at Northfield Cafe and elsewhere.
Vajra Books (Map p140; ☎ 4220562; www.vajrabooks .com.np; Jyatha) This knowledgeable local publisher offers an excellent selection of academic books and will post books internationally. There's a branch across the road.

Emergency
Ambulance service (☎ 4521048) Provided by Patan Hospital.
Fire Brigade (☎ 101, 4221177)
Police (Map p120; ☎ 100, 4223011; Durbar Sq)
Red Cross Ambulance (☎ 4228094)
Tourist Police Bhrikuti Mandap (☎ 4247041); Thamel (☎ 4700750)

Internet Access

Cybercafes are everywhere in Thamel. The best have scanners and printers (Rs 10 per page) plus, importantly, power backup. Connection speeds are generally fast and the rates are standard at around Rs 50 per hour.

If you have your own laptop you can get free wireless internet access at a few places such as the New Orleans Cafe (see p153). Alternatively, invest in a WorldLink wireless card (Rs 250 for five hours online) and access wi-fi at dozens of places across town, including Himalayan Java and the Garden of Dreams. Other places such as the Kathmandu Guest House offer their own wi-fi for variable rates.

Laundry

Several laundries across Thamel will machine wash laundry for Rs 50 per kilo. Get it back the next day or pay double for a three-hour service. Amazingly, it all comes back relatively clean, even after a three-week trek. Power cuts can delay wash times so don't cut it too fine by handing in your laundry the day before your flight.

Libraries
Kaiser Library (Map p140; ☎ 4411318; Ministry of Education & Sports compound, cnr Kantipath & Tridevi Marg; ☒ 10am-5pm Sun-Thu, 10am-3pm Fri) Also known as the Keshar Library, this place is definitely worth a visit. The main reading room has antique globes, a stuffed tiger

and suits of armour that you expect to spring to life at any moment. The library has a remarkable collection of antique travel books, with Nepal titles on the upper floor.

Medical Services

Bir Hospital (Map p126; ☎ 4221119) Government hospital where terminally ill Nepalis come to die; not recommended.

CIWEC Clinic Travel Medicine Center (Map p126; ☎ 4424111; www.ciwec-clinic.com; ⏰ 9am-noon & 1-4pm Mon-Fri) Just across from the British embassy, to the northeast of Thamel and used by many foreign residents. It has operated since 1982 and has developed an international reputation for research into travellers' medical problems. The clinic is staffed mostly by foreigners and a doctor is on call around the clock. A consultation costs around US$55. Credit cards are accepted and they are used to dealing with insurance claims.

CIWEC Dental Clinic (Map p126; ☎ 4440100, emergency 4424111; ciwecdental@subisu.net.np) US dentist on the top floor of CIWEC Clinic (see above).

Healthy Smiles (Map p126; ☎ 4420800; www.smilenepal.com) UK-trained dentist, opposite the Hotel Ambassador.

Nepal International Clinic (Map p126; ☎ 4434642, 4435357; www.nepalinternationalclinic.com; ⏰ 9am-1pm & 2-5pm) Just south of the New Royal Palace, east of Thamel. It has an excellent reputation and is slightly cheaper than the CIWEC Clinic. A consultation costs about US$40 (US$50 at weekends). Credit cards accepted.

NORVIC Hospital (Map p126; ☎ 4258554; www.norvichospital.com; Thapathali) Private Nepali hospital with a good reputation for cardiology.

Patan Hospital (Map p182; ☎ 5522295; www.patanhospital.org.np) Probably the best hospital in the Kathmandu Valley, in the Lagankhel district of Patan. Partly staffed by Western missionaries.

Tribhuvan University Teaching Hospital (Map pp114-15; ☎ 4412808, 4412363; Maharajganj) Reasonably well equipped (and carrying a ventilator); northeast of the centre.

There are several good pharmacies in Thamel, including the **KB Drug Store** (Map p140; ☎ 4251567; ⏰ 8am-9pm), on Chhetrapati Chowk, which offers knowledgeable English-speaking advice and all the cheap antibiotics you can pronounce.

Money

It is worth checking banks' exchange rates and commission – both vary. There are also dozens of licensed moneychangers in Thamel. Their hours are longer than those of the banks (until 8pm, later if things are busy) and rates

---

KATHMANDU IN...

Two Days

Start off with the two-hour **walking tour** (p134), 'South from Thamel to Durbar Square'. Grab lunch overlooking Basantapur Sq or in nearby **Freak St** (p153) and then spend the afternoon taking in the architectural grandeur of **Durbar Square** (p119). Finish the day with a cold beer and dinner in Thamel.

Next day walk out to **Swayambhunath** (p163) in the morning and spend the afternoon **shopping** (p157) in Thamel. For your final meal splurge at one of the blowout Newari restaurants like **Bhojan Griha** or **Nepali Chulo** (see p152).

Four Days

If you have an extra couple of days, take a short taxi ride out to **Patan** (p181) for a full day exploring its **Durbar Square**, **Patan Museum** (the best in the country) and more fascinating backstreets.

After an early lunch on day four, take a taxi to **Pashupatinath** (p170) and then make the short walk out to **Bodhnath** (p173) to soak up some Tibetan culture as the sun sets.

If you are in town on a Friday, splurge on the Friday barbecue at **Dwarika's Hotel** (p155).

One Week

With a week up your sleeve you can spend a day at **Bhaktapur** (p194). At the beginning of the week sign up for a two-day rafting or canyoning trip up at **Borderlands** (p231) or **Last Resort** (p232). When stress levels build, fit in some quiet time at the delightful **Garden of Dreams** (p131).

Seven days gives you the chance to gorge on Thai (Krua Thai), Indian (Third Eye), Korean (Hankook Sarang), South Indian *dosas* (Dudh Sagar), yak steak (K-Too), felafel (Or2k) and maybe even some Nepali food! Don't get us started on lunch...

are pretty consistent, though slightly lower than the banks. See p370 for information on exchange rates, commissions and transfers.

Himalayan Bank (Map p140; ☎ 4250208; www .himalayanbank.com; Tridevi Marg; ☯ 8am-8pm Sun-Fri) The most convenient bank for travellers in Thamel is in the basement of the Sanchaya Kosh Bhawan shopping centre. You can change cash (no commission) and travellers cheques (commission of 0.75%, minimum Rs 150), get cash advances on a Visa card and access its nearby ATM, in front of the Tridevi Temples.

Sita World Travel (Map p140; ☎ 4248556; wu@ sitanepal.com; Tridevi Marg; ☯ 9am-6pm Sun-Fri, 9am-1pm Sat) One of hundreds of local agents for Western Union money transfers and the closest to Thamel.

Standard Chartered Bank (Map p126; ☎ 4418456; Lazimpat; ☯ 9.45am-7pm Sun-Thu, 9.45am-4.30pm Fri, 9.30am-12.30pm Sat & holidays) Has well-located ATMs – opposite the Third Eye Restaurant and in the compound of the Kathmandu Guest House – and others around town. The main branch in Lazimpat charges 1.5% (minimum Rs 300) to change travellers cheques and Rs 200 per transaction for cash. There's no charge for a rupee cash advance on a credit card but you pay 2% to get the cash in US dollars.

Yeti Travels (Map p126; ☎ 4226172; amexrep@wlink .com.np; Kantipath; ☯ 10am-1pm & 2-4pm Sun-Fri) American Express (AmEx) agent, located on the 3rd floor of the Annapurna Arcade, above Thai Airways. It provides AmEx cash advances, encashment of travellers cheques, client mail services and is the place to come if your travellers cheques are stolen.

Other useful ATMs in the Thamel area are located beside Yin Yang Restaurant, United Books and Himalayan Java (Map p140).

Post

Most bookshops in Thamel, including Pilgrims Book House (p116), sell stamps and deliver postcards to the post office, which is much easier than making a special trip to the post office yourself. Pilgrims charges a 10% commission for this service.

Everest Postal Care (Map p140; ☎ 4417913; Tridevi Marg; ☯ 9.30am-5.30pm Sun-Fri) Convenient private post office near Thamel, which posts letters and parcels at the same rates as the post office.

Foreign post office (Map p126; Sundhara; ☯ 10am-5pm Sun-Fri) Parcels can be sent from here, in a separate building just north of the main post office. Parcels have to be examined and sealed by a customs officer. Start the process before 2pm.

Main post office (Map p126; Sundhara; ☯ 7am-6pm Sun-Thu, 7am-3pm Fri) Close to the Bhimsen Tower. Stalls in the courtyard sell air mail and padded envelopes. Poste restante is here. Get stamps at counter 12. You can post packages up to 2kg at counter 16; beyond that you need to go to the foreign post office.

Sending parcels from the foreign post office is something of an ordeal so, if you're short of time, you're best off using a cargo agency like **Diki Continental Exports** (Map p140; ☎ 4256919; www.dikiexports.com; JP School, Thamel).

Courier agencies include:

DHL Kamaladi (Map p126; ☎ 4496248; www.dhl.com .np); Thamel (Map p140; ☎ 2012221; ☯ 11am-7pm Sun-Fri) The Thamel address is the less reliable of the two.

FedEx (Map p140; ☎ 4269248; www.fedex.com/np; Kantipath; ☯ 9am-6pm Sun-Fri, 9am-1pm Sat)

Telephone

You can make international telephone calls and send faxes from any of the dozens of 'communication centres' in Thamel and elsewhere throughout the city. The cheapest places charge around Rs 20 per minute, with internet phone calls as low as Rs 10. See p376 for more information.

Tourist Information

There are a number of good notice boards in Thamel that are worth checking for information on apartments, travel and trekking partners, courses and cultural events. The Kathmandu Guest House has a good notice board, as do the Pumpernickel Bakery and Fire & Ice Restaurant.

For Kathmandu-based offices that offer trekking-related information see p337.

Kathmandu Environmental Education Project (KEEP; Map p140; ☎ 4216775; www.keepnepal.org; ☯ 10am-5pm Sun-Fri) A good place for trekking reports, occasional lectures, a small collection of reference books, a cafe and a mineral-water refill service (Rs 10 per litre). They also sell biodegradable travel products such as anti-leech oil (Rs 90) and fair-trade beeswax lip balm, as well as water purification tablets (Rs 500). It's also a good place to find a trek partner. Leave your shoes outside.

Tourist Service Centre (Map p126; ☎ 4256909 ext 223, 24hr tourism hotline 4225709; www.welcomenepal .com; Bhrikuti Mandap; ☯ 10am-1pm, 2-5pm Sun-Fri) On the eastern side of the Tundikhel parade ground, the centre has a few brochures and maps but the location of the office is inconvenient. Get your TIMS card here (see p335).

Travel Agencies

Kathmandu has a great number of travel agencies, particularly along Durbar Marg,

Kantipath and in Thamel. See p332 for details of trekking agencies. Reliable places include:

Flight Connection International (Map p140; ☎ 4258282; www.flightconnectionintl.com; Jyatha, Thamel) Good for flight tickets.

President Travel & Tours (Map p126; ☎ 4220245; www.president-travels.com; Durbar Marg) Professional agency favoured by expats and wealthy Nepalis; particularly good at getting seats on heavily booked flights.

Wayfarers (Map p140; ☎ 4266010; www.wayfarers .com.np; Thamel; ☉ 9am-7pm Mon-Fri, 9am-5pm Sat & Sun) For straight-talking travel and ticketing (particularly international air tickets) this is the place. The staff also book domestic Indian air and train e-tickets and offer Kathmandu Valley walking trips (see p170).

Visa Extensions

Central Immigration Office (Map p126; ☎ 4223590, 4222453; www.immi.gov.np; Maitighar; ☉ 10am-4.30pm Sun-Thu, 10am-3pm Fri, 11am-1pm Sat) Recently relocated to southeastern Kathmandu, this office offers relatively painless visa extensions. Get a form, join the queue, supply one photo and then join a separate queue to pay the fee. If you apply before 2pm you should get your passport back the same day at 3.30pm. See p377 for more on visa extensions.

DANGERS & ANNOYANCES

Kathmandu is sometimes the focus of political demonstrations, strikes and even occasional curfews. These generally just affect transport but they can turn violent so are best avoided. Bandhs (strikes) paralyse the city every now and then, closing shops and shutting down transport. See p366 and p18.

There aren't many capital cities in the world where electricity is unavailable for up to 16 hours a day. Electricity cuts ('load shedding') are a fact of life in Kathmandu, especially in winter when water and thus hydro power levels are at their lowest. Electricity is currently rationed across the city, shifting from district to district every eight hours or so. Most hotels post a schedule of planned electricity cuts. Try to choose a hotel with a generator and make sure your room is far away from it.

The main annoyances in Thamel are the crazy motorcyclists, the pollution and the limpetlike hash/tiger balm/chess set sellers. Durbar Sq has some persistent wannabe guides. Note that the colourful sadhus (itinerant holy men) who frequent Durbar Sq will expect *baksheesh* (a tip) if you take a photo.

The Thamel 'holy men' who anoint you with a *tika* on your forehead also expect a donation.

SIGHTS

Most of the interesting things to see in Kathmandu are clustered in the old part of town, focused around the majestic Durbar Sq and its surrounding backstreets.

Durbar Square

Kathmandu's **Durbar Square** (Map p120; foreigner/ SAARC Rs 200/25, no student tickets) was where the city's kings were once crowned and legitimised, and from where they ruled (durbar means 'palace'). As such, the square remains the traditional heart of the old town and Kathmandu's most spectacular legacy of traditional architecture, even though the king no longer lives in the Hanuman Dhoka – the palace was moved north to Narayanhiti about a century ago.

It's easy to spend hours wandering around the square and watching the world go by from the terraced platforms of the towering Maju Deval; it's a wonderful way to get a feel for the city. Although most of the square dates from the 17th and 18th centuries (many of the original buildings are much older), a great deal of damage was caused by the great earthquake of 1934 and many were rebuilt, not always in their original form. The entire square was designated a Unesco World Heritage site in 1979.

The Durbar Sq area is actually made up of three loosely linked squares. To the south is the open Basantapur Sq area, a former royal elephant stables that now houses souvenir stalls and off which runs Freak St. The main Durbar Sq area, with its popular watch-the-world-go-by temples, is to the west. Running northeast is a second part of Durbar Sq, which contains the entrance to the Hanuman Dhoka and an assortment of temples. From this open area Makhan Tole, at one time the main road in Kathmandu and still the most interesting street to walk down, continues northeast.

A good place to start an exploration of the square is with what may well be the oldest building in the valley, the unprepossessing Kasthamandap.

INFORMATION

The admission ticket to Durbar Sq is valid only for the date stamped. If you want a longer duration you need to go to the **site office** (Map p120;

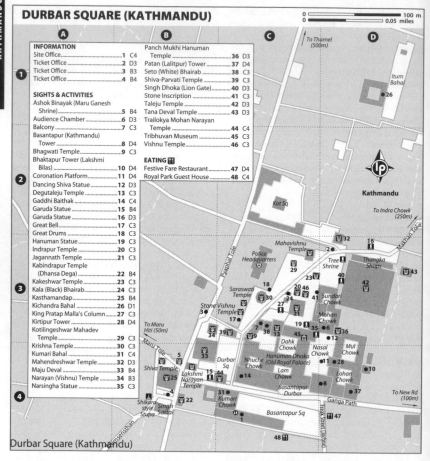

DURBAR SQUARE (KATHMANDU)

0 — 100 m
0 — 0.05 miles

INFORMATION
Site Office.............................**1** C4
Ticket Office........................**2** D3
Ticket Office........................**3** B3
Ticket Office........................**4** B4

SIGHTS & ACTIVITIES
Ashok Binayak (Maru Ganesh
  Shrine).............................**5** B4
Audience Chamber..............**6** D3
Balcony...............................**7** C3
Basantapur (Kathmandu)
  Tower...............................**8** D4
Bhagwati Temple.................**9** C3
Bhaktapur Tower (Lakshmi
  Bilas)...............................**10** D4
Coronation Platform...........**11** D4
Dancing Shiva Statue..........**12** D3
Degutaleju Temple..............**13** C3
Gaddhi Baithak...................**14** C4
Garuda Statue.....................**15** B4
Garuda Statue.....................**16** D3
Great Bell...........................**17** C3
Great Drums.......................**18** C3
Hanuman Statue.................**19** C3
Indrapur Temple.................**20** C3
Jagannath Temple...............**21** C3
Kabindrapur Temple
  (Dhansa Dega)..................**22** B4
Kakeshwar Temple..............**23** C3
Kala (Black) Bhairab............**24** C3
Kasthamandap.....................**25** B4
Kichandra Bahal..................**26** D1
King Pratap Malla's Column..**27** C3
Kirtipur Tower.....................**28** D4
Kotilingeshwar Mahadev
  Temple.............................**29** C3
Krishna Temple...................**30** C3
Kumari Bahal......................**31** C4
Mahendreshwar Temple......**32** D3
Maju Deval.........................**33** B4
Narayan (Vishnu) Temple....**34** B3
Narsingha Statue.................**35** C3

Panch Mukhi Hanuman
  Temple.............................**36** D3
Patan (Lalitpur) Tower........**37** D4
Seto (White) Bhairab...........**38** C3
Shiva-Parvati Temple..........**39** C3
Singh Dhoka (Lion Gate).....**40** D3
Stone Inscription................**41** C3
Taleju Temple.....................**42** D3
Tana Deval Temple.............**43** D3
Trailokya Mohan Narayan
  Temple.............................**44** C4
Tribhuvan Museum..............**45** C3
Vishnu Temple....................**46** C3

EATING 🍴
Festive Fare Restaurant.......**47** D4
Royal Park Guest House........**48** C4

To Thamel
(500m)

Itum
Bahal
● 26

Kathmandu

To Indra Chowk
(250m)

Kot Sq

Mahavishnu
Temple

🗼 32
16

Police
Headquarters

Tree
Shrine

Thangka
Shops

🗼 43

29
23
40
42

18
20 46
41

Saraswati
Temple
30
24
Sundari
Chowk

Stone Vishnu
Temple
27
21

Mohan
Chowk

17
7
19
35
6 36
12

34
39
9
38 13
45

Dahk
Chowk

Nasal
Chowk

Mul
Chowk

5
33

Durbar
Sq

Nhuche
Chowk

Hanuman Dhoka
(Old Royal Palace)

11 28

10

Shiva Temple
25
15
44
14
Lam
Chowk

Basantapur
Durbar

8

Lohan
Chowk
37

To New Rd
(100m)

Ganga Path

31
Kumari
Chowk

Lakshmi
Narayan
Temple

To Maru
Hiti (50m)

Maru Tole

Shikara
style
Stupa

Singh
Sattal

4
22

Basantapur Sq

47

1

48

Durbar Square (Kathmandu)

☎ 4268969; www.kathmandu.gov.np; 🕑 7am-6.30pm),
on the south side of Basantapur Sq, to get a
free visitor pass, which allows you access for as
long as your visa is valid. You will need your
passport and one photo (no photo required
for less than three days) and the process takes
about two minutes. You generally need to
show your ticket even if you are just transit-
ing the square to New Rd or Freak St.

There is a toilet near the site office.

KASTHAMANDAP
Kathmandu owes its name to the **Kasthamandap**
(Pavilion of Wood; Map p120). Although
its history is uncertain, local tradition says
the three-roofed building was constructed
around the 12th century from the wood of a

single sal tree. It first served as a community
centre where visitors gathered before major
ceremonies (a *mandap* is a 16-pillared pilgrim
shelter), but later it was converted to a temple dedicated to Gorakhnath, a 13th-century
ascetic who was subsequently linked to the
royal family.

The last disciples were kicked out in
the 1960s.

A central wooden enclosure houses the
image of the god, which is noteworthy since
Gorakhnath is usually represented only by his
footprints. In the corners of the building are
four images of Ganesh.

The squat, medieval-looking building is
especially busy in the early morning hours
when the valley's vegetable sellers set up shop

and porters sit awaiting customers. Piles of smoked fish, banana leaves and marigolds spill into the surrounding alleyways.

Across the square is the **Kabindrapur Temple** (Map p120), or Dhansa Dega, an ornate 17th-century performance pavilion that houses the god of music.

ASHOK BINAYAK

On the northern side of Kasthamandap, at the top of Maru Tole, stands the tiny golden **Ashok Binayak** (Map p120), or Maru Ganesh Shrine. The small size of this shrine belies its importance, as this is one of the four most important Ganesh shrines in the valley. Ganesh is a much-loved god and there is a constant stream of visitors, helping themselves to the self-serve *tika* dispenser and then ringing the bells at the back. A visit to this shrine is thought to ensure safety on a forthcoming journey so make an offering here if you are headed on a trek.

It's uncertain how old the temple is, although its gilded roof was added in the 19th century. Look for the golden shrew (Ganesh's vehicle) opposite the temple.

MARU TOLE

This *tole* leads you away from Durbar Sq down to the Vishnumati River, where a footbridge continues the pathway to Swayambhunath (see p163). This was a busy street in the hippy era but the famous pastry shops that gave it the nickname 'Pie Alley' have long gone. Just 30m from Durbar Sq down Maru Tole is **Maru Hiti** (off Map p120), one of the finest sunken water conduits in the city.

MAJU DEVAL

A pleasant half hour can easily be spent sitting on the steps of this Shiva temple. In fact the nine-stage ochre platform of the **Maju Deval** (Map p120) is probably the most popular meeting place in the city. From here you can watch the constant activity of fruit and vegetable hawkers, the comings and goings of taxis and rickshaws, and the flute and other souvenir sellers importuning tourists. The large, triple-roofed temple has erotic carvings on its roof struts and offers great views over the square and across the roofs of the city. Marigold sellers set up shop on the ground level.

The temple dates from 1690 and was built by the mother of Bhaktapur's king Bhupatindra Malla. The temple has a Shiva lingam (phallic symbol) inside.

At the bottom of the temple stairway on the east side is a small white temple to Kam Dev, a 'companion' of Shiva. It was built in the Indian shikhara style, with a tall corncoblike spire.

EROTIC ART (OR HOW THEY DID IT IN ANCIENT TIMES)

The most eye-catching decorations on Nepali temples are the erotic scenes, often quite explicit, that decorate the roof struts, or *tunala*. These scenes are rarely the central carving on the strut; they're usually the smaller carving at the bottom of the strut, like a footnote to the larger image. Nor are the carvings sensuous and finely sculptured like those at Khajuraho and Konark in India. In Nepal the figures are often smaller and cruder, even cartoonlike.

The themes have a Tantric element, a clear connection to the intermingling of Tibetan Buddhist and Hindu beliefs in Nepal, but their real purpose is unclear. Are they simply a celebration of an important part of the life cycle? Are they a more explicit reference to Shiva's and Parvati's creative roles than the enigmatic lingams and yonis scattered around so many temples? Or are they supposed to play some sort of protective role for the temple? It's popularly rumoured that the goddess of lightning is a shy virgin who wouldn't dream of striking a temple with such goings-on, although that's probably more a tourist-guide tale than anything else.

Whatever the reason for their existence, these Tantric elements can be found on temples throughout the valley. Some temples reveal just the odd sly image, while others are plastered with the 16th-century equivalent of hard-core pornography, ranging from impressively athletic acts of intercourse to medieval *ménages à trois*, scenes of oral or anal intercourse or couplings with demons or animals.

The temples you may want to avoid showing your kids include Kathmandu's Jagannath Temple, Basantapur Tower and Ram Chandra Temple; Patan's Jagannarayan Temple; and Bhaktapur's Erotic Elephants and Pashupatinath temples.

TRAILOKYA MOHAN NARAYAN TEMPLE

The other temple standing in the open area of the square is the smaller five-roofed **Trailokya Mohan Narayan Temple** (Map p120), just to the south. Dating from 1680, it is easily identified as a temple to Narayan/Vishnu by the fine Garuda kneeling before it. This powerful stone figure was a later addition, erected by King Prithvibendra Malla's widow soon after his death. Look for the Vaishnavite images on the carved roof struts and the window screens with their decoratively carved medallions. Dances depicting the 10 incarnations of Vishnu are performed on the platforms to the east of the temple during the Indra Jatra festival.

SHIVA-PARVATI TEMPLE

From the steps of the Maju Deval you can look north across to the **Shiva-Parvati Temple** (Map p120), also known as the Nawa Jogini Temple, where the much-photographed white images of Shiva and his consort look out from the upstairs window on the chaos below them. The temple was built in the late 1700s by Bahadur Shah, the son of Prithvi Narayan Shah. Although the temple is not very old by Kathmandu standards, it stands on a two-stage platform that may have been an open dancing stage hundreds of years earlier. A **Narayan (Vishnu) temple** (Map p120) stands to the west side.

KUMARI BAHAL

At the junction of Durbar and Basantapur Sqs is a red brick, three-storey building with some incredibly intricate carved windows. This is the **Kumari Bahal** (House of the Living Goddess; Map p120), home to the Kumari, the girl who is selected to be the town's living goddess (see opposite) until she reaches puberty and reverts to being a normal mortal. The building, in the style of the Buddhist *viharas* (monastic abodes) of the valley, was built in 1757 by Jaya Prakash Malla.

Inside the building is the three-storey courtyard, or Kumari Chowk. It is enclosed by magnificently carved wooden balconies and windows, making it quite possibly the most beautiful courtyard in Nepal. Photographing the goddess is forbidden, but you are quite free to photograph the courtyard when she is not present.

The Kumari went on strike in 2005, refusing to appear at her window for tourists, after authorities denied her guardians' request for a 10% cut of the square's admission fees!

The courtyard contains a miniature stupa carrying the symbols of Saraswati, the goddess of learning. Non-Hindus are not allowed to go beyond the courtyard.

The large yellow gate to the right of the Kumari Bahal conceals the huge chariot that transports the Kumari around the city during the annual Indra Jatra festival (see p138). Look for the huge wooden runners in front of the Kumari Bahal that are used to transport the chariot. The wood is painted at the tips and considered sacred. You can see part of the chariot from the top of the nearby Trailokya Mohan Narayan Temple steps.

GADDHI BAITHAK

The eastern side of Durbar Sq is closed off by this white neoclassical **building** (Map p120). With its imported European style, it was built as part of the palace in 1908 during the Rana period and makes a strange contrast to the traditional Nepali architecture that dominates the square. It is said to have been modelled on London's National Gallery following Prime Minister Jung Bahadur's visit to Europe.

BHAGWATI TEMPLE

On the northwest corner of the Gaddhi Baithak, this triple-storey, triple-roofed **temple** (Map p120) is easily missed since it surmounts the building below it, which currently has thangka (Tibetan religious painting) shops along its front. The temple is actually part of the palace courtyard. The best view of the temple and its golden roofs is probably from the Maju Deval, across the square. The temple was built by King Jagat Jaya Malla and originally had an image of Narayan. This image was stolen in 1766 so, when Prithvi Narayan Shah conquered the valley two years later, he simply substituted it with an image of the goddess Bhagwati. In April each year the image of the goddess is conveyed to the village of Nuwakot, 65km to the north, then returned a few days later.

GREAT BELL

On your left as you leave the main square along Makhan Tole is the **Great Bell** (Map p120), elevated atop a white building erected by Rana Bahadur Shah (son of Prithvi Narayan Shah) in 1797. The bell's ring drives off evil spirits, but it is only rung during puja (worship) at the Degutaleju Temple (p124).

KUMARI DEVI

Not only does Nepal have countless gods, goddesses, deities, bodhisattvas, Buddhas, avatars (incarnations of deities) and manifestations – which are worshipped and revered as statues, images, paintings and symbols – but it also has a real living goddess. The Kumari Devi is a young girl who lives in the building known as the Kumari Bahal, right beside Kathmandu's Durbar Sq.

The practice of having a living goddess probably came about during the reign of Jaya Prakash Malla, the last of the Malla kings of Kathmandu, whose reign abruptly ended with the conquest of the valley by Prithvi Narayan Shah in 1768. As usual in Nepal, where there is never one simple answer to any question, there are a number of legends about the Kumari.

One such legend relates that a paedophile Malla king had intercourse with a prepubescent girl. She died as a result of this and, in penance, he started the practice of venerating a young girl as a living goddess. Another tells of a Malla king who regularly played dice with the goddess Taleju, the protective deity of the valley. When he made an unseemly advance she threatened to withdraw her protection, but relented and promised to return in the form of a young girl. Yet another tells of a young girl who was possessed by the goddess Durga and banished from the kingdom. When the furious queen heard of this she ordered her husband to bring the young girl back and keep her as a real goddess.

Whatever the background, in reality there are a number of living goddesses around the Kathmandu Valley, although the Kumari Devi, or Royal Kumari (as she was known for centuries) of Kathmandu is the most important. The Kumari is selected from a particular caste of Newari gold- and silversmiths. Customarily, she is somewhere between four years old and puberty and must meet 32 strict physical requirements ranging from the colour of her eyes and shape of her teeth to the sound of her voice. Her horoscope must also be appropriate, of course. Once suitable candidates have been found they are gathered together in a darkened room where terrifying noises are made, while men dance by in horrific masks and 108 gruesome buffalo heads are on display. These goings-on are unlikely to frighten a real goddess, particularly one who is an incarnation of Durga, so the young girl who remains calm and collected throughout this ordeal is clearly the new Kumari. In a process similar to the selection of the Dalai Lama, as a final test the Kumari then chooses items of clothing and decoration worn by her predecessor.

Once chosen as the Kumari Devi, the young girl moves into the Kumari Bahal with her family and makes only a half dozen ceremonial forays into the outside world each year. The most spectacular of these occasions is the September Indra Jatra festival, when she travels through the city on a huge temple chariot over a three-day period. For centuries the Kumari customarily blessed the king of Nepal but now blesses the president.

The Kumari's reign ends with her first period, or any serious accidental loss of blood. Once this first sign of puberty is reached she reverts to the status of a normal mortal, and the search must start for a new Kumari. During her time as a goddess the Kumari is supported by the temple income and, on retirement, she is paid a handsome dowry. It is said that marrying an ex-Kumari is unlucky, but it's believed more likely that taking on a spoilt ex-goddess is likely to be too much hard work!

For an account of the life of a Kumari, check out *From Goddess to Mortal*, the story of Rashmilla Shakya, Kathmandu's Kumari between 1984 and 1991, cowritten with Scott Berry. It's available in Kathmandu bookstores.

Across from the great bell is a very ornate corner **balcony** (Map p120), decorated in gorgeous copper and ivory, from where members of the royal court could view the festival action taking place in Durbar Sq.

KRISHNA TEMPLE (CHYASIN DEGA)

The history of the octagonal **Krishna Temple** (Map p120) is well documented. It was built in 1648–49 by Pratap Malla, perhaps as a response to rival Siddhinarsingh's magnificent Krishna Temple in Patan. Inside there are images of Krishna and two goddesses, which, according to a Sanskrit inscription, are modelled on the king and his two wives. The temple's Newari inscription neglects to mention the king's little act of vanity. The temple is a favourite of

KATHMANDU

sadhus who pose (and expect to be paid) for photos here.

GREAT DRUMS & KOT SQUARE

Just beyond the temple are the **Great Drums** (Map p120), to which a goat and a buffalo must be sacrificed twice a year. In front of these is the police headquarters building. Beyond here is the closed-off Kot Sq, where Jung Bahadur Rana perpetrated the famous 1846 massacre that led to a hundred years of Rana rule (see p36). Kot means 'armoury' or 'fort'. During the Dasain festival each year, blood again flows in Kot Sq as hundreds of buffaloes and goats are sacrificed. Young soldiers are supposed to lop off each head with a single blow.

KING PRATAP MALLA'S COLUMN

Across from the Krishna Temple is a host of smaller temples and other structures, all standing on a slightly raised platform in front of the Hanuman Dhoka and the towering Taleju Temple behind. The square stone pillar, known as the Pratap Dhvaja, is topped by a **statue** (Map p120) of the famous King Pratap Malla (1641–74), seated with folded hands and surrounded by his two wives and his five (including an infant) sons. He looks towards his private prayer room on the 3rd floor of the Degutaleju Temple. The column was erected in 1670 by Pratap Malla and preceded the similar columns in Patan and Bhaktapur.

This area and its monuments are usually covered in hundreds if not thousands of pigeons; you can buy packets of grain to feed them.

SETO (WHITE) BHAIRAB

Seto (White) Bhairab's horrible face is hidden away behind a grille opposite King Pratap Malla's column. The huge **mask** (Map p120) dates from 1794, during the reign of Rana Bahadur Shah, the third Shah-dynasty king. Each September during the Indra Jatra festival the gates are opened to reveal the mask for a few days. At that time the face is covered in flowers and rice; at the start of the festivities beer is poured through the horrific mouth as crowds of men fight to get a drink of the blessed brew (see p138). At other times of the year you can peek through the lattice to see the mask, which is used as the symbol of Nepal Airlines.

JAGANNATH TEMPLE

This **temple** (Map p120), noted for the erotic carvings on its roof struts, is the oldest structure in this part of the square. Pratap Malla claimed to have constructed the temple during his reign, but it may actually date back to 1563, during the rule of Mahendra Malla. The temple has a three-tiered platform and two storeys. There are three doors on each side of the temple, but only the centre door opens.

DEGUTALEJU TEMPLE

This triple-roofed **temple** (Map p120) is actually part of the Hanuman Dhoka, surmounting the buildings below it, but is most easily seen from outside the palace walls. The painted roof struts are particularly fine. Degutaleju is another manifestation of the Malla's personal goddess Taleju. This temple was built by Shiva Singh Malla.

KALA (BLACK) BHAIRAB

North of the Jagannath Temple is the figure of **Kala (Black) Bhairab** (Map p120). Bhairab is Shiva in his most fearsome aspect, and this huge stone image of the terrifying Kala Bhairab has six arms, wears a garland of skulls and tramples a corpse, which is symbolic of human ignorance. The figure is said to have been brought here by Pratap Malla, having been found in a field to the north of the city. The image was originally cut from a single stone but the upper left-hand corner has since been repaired. It is said that telling a lie while standing before Kala Bhairab will bring instant death and it was once used as a form of trial by ordeal.

INDRAPUR TEMPLE

Immediately east of the horrific Bhairab stands the mysterious **Indrapur Temple** (Map p120). This puzzling temple may be of great antiquity but has been renovated recently and little is known of its history. Even the god to which it is dedicated is controversial – the lingam inside indicates that it is a Shiva temple but the Garuda image half-buried on the southern side indicates that it is dedicated to Vishnu. To compound the puzzle, however, the temple's name clearly indicates it is dedicated to Indra! The temple's unadorned design and plain roof struts, together with the lack of an identifying torana (pediment above the temple doors), offer no further clues.

KAKESHWAR TEMPLE

This **temple** (Map p120) just to the north was originally built in 1681 but, like so many other structures, was rebuilt after it was badly damaged in the 1934 earthquake. It may have been considerably altered at that time as the temple is a strange combination of styles. It starts with a Newari-style floor, above which is an Indian shikhara-style upper storey, topped by a spire shaped like a *kalasa* (water vase), indicative of a female deity.

STONE INSCRIPTION

On the outside of the white palace wall, opposite the **Vishnu Temple** (Map p120), is a long, low **stone inscription** (Map p120) to the goddess Kalika written in 15 languages, including one word of French. King Pratap Malla, renowned for his linguistic abilities, set up this inscription in 1664 and a Nepali legend tells that milk will flow from the spout in the middle if somebody is able to decipher all 15 languages!

KOTILINGESHWAR MAHADEV TEMPLE

This distinctive early stone Malla **temple** (Map p120) dates from the reign of Mahendra Malla in the 16th century. The three-stage plinth is topped by a temple in the *gumbhaj* style, which basically means a square structure topped by a bell-shaped dome. The bull facing the temple on the west side indicates that it is dedicated to Shiva.

MAHENDRESHWAR TEMPLE

At the extreme northern end of the square, this popular **temple** (Map p120) dates from 1561, during the reign of Mahendra Malla, and is always bustling with pilgrims. The temple was clumsily restored with marble in 1963 and is dedicated to Shiva. A small image of Shiva's bull Nandi fronts the temple to the west and at the northeastern corner there is an image of Kam Dev. The temple has a wide, two-level plinth and a spire topped by a golden umbrella.

TALEJU TEMPLE

The square's most magnificent **temple** (Map p120) stands at its northeastern extremity but is not open to the public. Even for Hindus admission is restricted; they can only visit it briefly during the annual Dasain festival.

The Taleju Temple was built in 1564 by Mahendra Malla. Taleju Bhawani was originally a goddess from the south of India, but she became the titular deity, or royal goddess, of the Malla kings in the 14th century, after which Taleju temples were erected in her honour in Patan and Bhaktapur, as well as in Kathmandu.

The temple stands on a 12-stage plinth and reaches more than 35m high, dominating the Durbar Sq area. The eighth stage of the plinth forms a wall around the temple, in front of which are 12 miniature temples. Four more miniature temples stand inside the wall, which has four beautifully carved wide gates. If entry to the temple were permitted it could be reached from within the Hanuman Dhoka or from the Singh Dhoka (Lion Gate) facing Durbar Sq.

On the west side of the compound wall look for the small shrine that has been crushed by the tree that sprouted from its roof decades ago, looking like something out of Cambodia's Angkor Wat.

TANA DEVAL TEMPLE & MAKHAN TOLE

Directly across from the Taleju Temple is a 10th-century kneeling **Garuda statue** (Map p120), facing a small Vishnu Temple.

To your right, in a walled courtyard just past the long row of stalls, is the neglected **Tana Deval Temple** (Map p120), with three carved doorways and multiple struts, the latter of which show the multi-armed Ashta Matrikas (Mother Goddesses). It's possible to enter the temple. Nearby shops sell brightly coloured Tibetan thangkas and their Newari equivalents, called *paubhas*.

Crowded and fascinating **Makhan Tole** (*makhan* is the Nepali word for butter, *tole* means street) starts from here and runs towards the busy marketplace of Indra Chowk (see p131). Makhan Tole was at one time the main street in Kathmandu and the start of the main caravan route to Tibet.

From here you can either head south to visit the Hanuman Dhoka or continue northeast up Makhan Tole back towards Thamel.

Hanuman Dhoka

The inner palace complex of the **Hanuman Dhoka** (Map p120; foreigner/SAARC Rs 250/25; ☑ 10.30am-4pm Tue-Sat Feb-Oct, 10.30am-3pm Tue-Sat Nov-Jan, 10.30am-2pm Sun) was originally founded during the Licchavi period (4th to 8th centuries AD) but, as it stands today, most of it was constructed by King Pratap Malla in the 17th century. The royal palace has been renovated many times over the

KATHMANDU

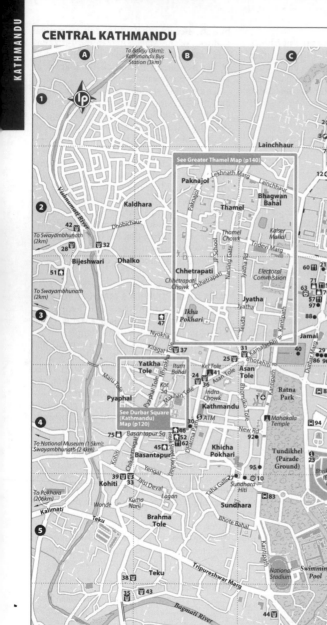

CENTRAL KATHMANDU

To Balaju (3km);
Kathmandu Bus
Station (3km)

Lainchhaur

Lazimpat

See Greater Thamel Map (p140)

Paknajol

Thamel

Bhagwan
Bahal

Kaldhara

Kaiser
Mahal

Narayanhiti Palace
(New Royal Palace)

To Swayambhunath
(2km)

Bijeshwari   Dhalko

Chhetrapati

Tridevi Marg

Electoral
Commission

To Swayambhunath
(2km)

Chhetrapati
Chowk

Jyatha

Lal
Durbar

To Naxal (500m); Tribhuvan
Airport (5km); Bodhnath (6km)

Ikhu
Pokhari

Jyatha

Kamal Pokhari

Jamal

Kamaladi

Yatkha
Tole

Dilli Bazar

Pyaphal

Asan
Tole

Ratna
Park

Dilli
Bazaar

See Durbar Square
(Kathmandu)
Map (p120)

Kathmandu

Indra
Chowk

Mahakala
Temple

Bag Bazar

Adwait Marg

Basantapur Sq

Khicha
Pokhari

New Rd

To National Museum (15km);
Swayambhunath (24km)

Basantapur

Tundikhel
(Parade
Ground)

Bhrikuti Mandap
(Exhibition
Ground)

Pradarshanti Marg

Kohiti

Jaisi Deval

Sundhara
Hiti

To Pokhara
(206km)

Brahma
Tole

Sundhara

Prithvi Path

Kalimati

Teku

Singha
Durbar
(Parliament)

Teku

National
Stadium

Swimming
Pool

Maitighar

Bagmati River

Thapathali

To Tribhuvan
Airport (4km);
Bhaktapur (10km)

Tripureshwar

Tripureshwar Marg

To Kirtipur (3km);
Dakshinkali (14km)

To Patan; Patan
Hospital (2km)

years. The oldest parts are the smaller Sundari Chowk and Mohan Chowk at the northern part of the palace (both closed). The complex originally housed 35 courtyards and spread as far as New Rd, but the 1934 earthquake reduced the palace to today's 10 chowks (courtyards). Cameras are allowed only in the courtyards, not inside the buildings of the complex.

Hanuman's brave assistance to the noble Rama during the exciting events of the Ramayana has led to the monkey god's appearance guarding many important entrances.

Here, cloaked in red and sheltered by an umbrella, a **Hanuman statue** (Map p120) marks the *dhoka* (entrance) to the Hanuman Dhoka and has even given the palace its name. The statue dates from 1672; the god's face has long disappeared under a coating of orange vermillion paste applied by generations of devotees.

Standards bearing the double-triangle flag of Nepal flank the statue, while on each side of the palace gate are stone lions, one ridden by Shiva, the other by his wife Parvati. Above the gate a brightly painted niche is illustrated with a central figure of a ferocious Tantric version of Krishna. On the left side is the gentler Hindu Krishna in his traditional blue colour accompanied by two of his comely gopi (milkmaids). On the other side are King Pratap Malla and his queen.

NASAL CHOWK
From the entrance gate of the Hanuman Dhoka you immediately enter its most famous chowk. Although the courtyard was constructed in the Malla period, many of the buildings around the square are later Rana constructions. During that time Nasal Chowk was used for coronations, a practice that continued until as recently as 2001 with the crowning of King Gyanendra. The **coronation platform** (Map p120) is in the centre of the courtyard, while the nine-storey **Basantapur (Kathmandu) Tower** (Map p120) looms over the southern end of the courtyard.

The rectangular courtyard is aligned north–south and the entrance is at the northwestern corner. Just by the entrance there is a surprisingly small but beautifully carved doorway, which once led to the Malla kings' private quarters.

Beyond the door is the large **Narsingha Statue** (Map p120), Vishnu in his man-lion incarnation, in the act of disembowelling a demon. The stone image was erected by Pratap Malla in 1673 and the inscription on the pedestal explains that he placed it here for fear that he had offended Vishnu by dancing in a Narsingha costume. The Kabindrapur Temple in Durbar Sq was built for the same reason.

Next is the Sisha Baithak or **Audience Chamber** (Map p120) of the Malla kings. The open verandah houses the Malla throne and contains portraits of the Shah kings.

PANCH MUKHI HANUMAN TEMPLE
At the northeastern corner of Nasal Chowk stands the **Panch Mukhi Hanuman** (Map p120) with its five circular roofs. Each of the valley towns has a five-storey temple, although it is the great Nyatapola Temple of Bhaktapur (p198) that is by far the best known. Hanuman is worshipped in the temple in Kathmandu, but only the priests may enter.

DANCING SHIVA STATUE
In Nepali *nasal* means 'dancing one', and Nasal Chowk takes its name from this **Shiva** statue (Map p120) hidden in the whitewashed chamber on the eastern side of the square.

TRIBHUVAN MUSEUM
The part of the palace west of Nasal Chowk, overlooking the main Durbar Sq area, was constructed by the Ranas in the middle to late part of the 19th century. Ironically, it is now home to a **museum** (Map p120) that celebrates King Tribhuvan (ruled 1911–55) and his successful revolt against their regime, along with memorials to Kings Mahendra (1955–72) and Birendra (1972–2001).

Exhibits with names such as 'the Royal Babyhood' include some fascinating recreations of the foppish king's bedroom and study, with genuine personal effects that give quite an eerie insight into his life. Some of the exhibits, such as the king's favourite stuffed bird (looking a bit worse for wear these days!), his boxing gloves, the walking stick with a spring-loaded sword hidden inside and his dusty, drained aquarium, add some surreal moments. There are several magnificent thrones, plenty of hunting photos and the obligatory coin collection.

Halfway through the museum you descend before ascending the steep stairways of the nine-storey (*or nau tale*) **Basantapur Tower** (1770), which was extensively restored prior to King Birendra's coronation. There are superb views over the palace and the city from the top. The struts along the facade of the Basantapur Tower, particularly those facing out to Basantapur Sq, are decorated with erotic carvings.

It's hard not to rush through the second half of the museum, full of dull press clippings about the rather Peter Sellers-looking King Mahendra, before conveniently glossing over the massacre of King Birendra by his son in 2001 (see the boxed text, p42). The museum exits into Lohan Chowk.

LOHAN CHOWK
King Prithvi Narayan Shah was involved in the construction of the four red-coloured towers around Lohan Chowk. The towers represent the four ancient cities of the valley: the Kathmandu or Basantapur Tower, the Kirtipur Tower, the Bhaktapur Tower or Lakshmi Bilas, and the Patan or Lalitpur Tower (known more evocatively as the Bilas Mandir, or House of Pleasure).

KATHMANDU'S ROYAL PALACES

Kathmandu is littered with hidden Rana-era palaces, some still in use, others crumbling in neglect. The most impressive is the royal palace of the **Singh (or Singha) Durbar**, built in 1907 and now home to Nepal's government. With over 1700 rooms, it was once the largest private residence in Asia, until fire destroyed 90% of the complex in 1973. It's not open to visitors.

The **Keshar Mahal Palace** (1895) still retains some atmosphere thanks to its creaky Kaiser Library (p116) and recently restored palace grounds (see p131), though its western wing was sold off long ago and developed as part of Thamel. One other notable former palace is the **Electoral Commission Building**, visible from Kantipath. At one point the building housed Kathmandu's first hotel, the Royal, established by Boris Lissanevitch. Other notable palace conversions include the restaurants of 1905 (p154), Nepali Chulo and Gaddhi Baithak (both p152).

Kathmandu's most impressive palace is the huge **Narayanhiti Palace**, home to the royal family until 2008. The palace is currently being turned into a museum.

OTHER CHOWKS

The palace's other courtyards are currently closed to visitors, but you can get glimpses of them from the Tribhuvan Museum and they might reopen at a future date.

North of Lohan Chowk, **Mul Chowk** was completely dedicated to religious functions within the palace and is configured like a *vihara*, with a two-storey building surrounding the courtyard. Mul Chowk is dedicated to Taleju Bhawani, the royal goddess of the Mallas, and sacrifices are made to her in the centre of the courtyard during the Dasain festival.

A smaller Taleju temple stands in the southern wing of the square and the image of the goddess is moved here from the main temple during the Dasain festival.

North of Nasal Chowk is **Mohan Chowk**, the residential courtyard of the Malla kings. It dates from 1649 and, at one time, a Malla king had to be born here to be eligible to wear the crown. (The last Malla king, Jaya Prakash Malla, had great difficulties during his reign, even though he was the legitimate heir, because he was born elsewhere.) The golden waterspout, known as Sundhara, in the centre of the courtyard delivers water from Budhanilkantha in the north of the valley. The Malla kings would ritually bathe here each morning.

North of Durbar Square

Hidden in the bustling and fascinating backstreets north of Durbar Sq is a dense sprinkling of colourful temples, courtyards and shrines.

The best way to get a feel for this district is on the walking tour 'South from Thamel to Durbar Square' (see p134).

KATHESIMBHU STUPA

The most popular Tibetan pilgrimage site in the old town is this lovely **stupa** (Map p140), a small copy dating from around 1650 of the great Swayambhunath complex. Just as at Swayambhunath, there is a two-storey pagoda to Harti, the goddess of smallpox, behind and to the right (northwest) of the main stupa. The entrance is flanked by metal lions atop red ochre concrete pillars, just a couple of minutes' walk south of Thamel.

Various statues and a few smaller chaityas (small stupas) stand around the temple, including a fine standing Avalokitesvara statue enclosed in a glass case and protective metal cage in the northeast corner. Avalokitesvara carries a lotus flower in his left hand, and the Dhyani Buddha Amitabha is seen in the centre of his crown.

ASAN TOLE

From dawn until late the junction of **Asan Tole** (Map p126) is jammed with vegetable and spice vendors, making it the busiest square in the city. Every day, produce is carried to this popular marketplace from all over the valley, so it is fitting that the three-storey **Annapurna Temple** (Map p126) is dedicated to the goddess of abundance; Annapurna is represented by a *purana* bowl full of grain. At most times, but especially Sundays, you'll see locals walk around the shrine, touch a coin to their heads, throw it into the temple and ring the bell above them.

Nearby the two-storey **Ganesh shrine** (Map p126) is coated in bathroom tiles. South is the Yita Chapal (Southern Pavilion) which was once used for festival dances (the dance platform out front is still visible). Cat Stevens

QUIRKY KATHMANDU

Kathmandu has more than its fair share of quirk and, as with most places in the subcontinent, a 10-minute walk in any direction will throw up numerous curiosities.

The corridors of the **Natural History Museum** (see p166) are full of bizarre moth-eaten animals and jars that lie somewhere between a school science experiment and *The Texas Chainsaw Massacre*. The 20ft python skin and nine-month old baby rhino in a jar are guaranteed to give you nightmares. The other exhibits are a bit slapdash, including the line of stuffed birds nailed carelessly to a bit of wood to indicate their distribution, or the big pile of elephant dung deposited randomly in the front corner. After all this fun the section on algae is a bit dull...

For items of personal quirkiness, the **Tribhuvan Museum** (see p128) in the Hanuman Dhoka palace offers up such gems as the king's personal parachuting uniform, the king's personal film projector and the king's personal walking stick with a spring-loaded sword inside – very '007'.

The **National Museum** (see p166) also houses more than its fair share of weirdness, including the mandible of a whale (?), a portrait of King Prithvi Narayan Shah giving everyone the finger (apparently symbolising the unity of the nation...), and a man poking a fox in the arse with a stick, the significance of which passed us by completely.

Compared to all this funkiness, Kathmandu's old town is pretty docile. Look for the antique **fire engines** (Map p126) hidden behind a grille just west of the junction of New Rd and Sukra Path. If you get a toothache during your trip, be sure to visit the old town's **toothache god** (see 'wood with coins' in the South from Thamel to Durbar Square walk, p134) – a raggedy old stump of wood covered with hundreds of nails and coins.

Finally, the roguish Indian **snake charmers** who set up shop on Tridevi Marg always raise a smile, as does the crazy sadhu, dressed as the god Hanuman in a very unrealistic monkey suit, who occasionally haunts Durbar Sq.

wrote his hippie-era song *Kathmandu* in a smoky teahouse in Asan Tole, penning the lines: 'Kathmandu I'll soon be seeing you, and your strong bewildering time will hold me down.'

On the western side of the square are spice shops. Near the centre of the square, sandwiched between two potted trees, is a small **Narayan shrine** (Narayan is a form of Vishnu).

SETO MACHHENDRANATH TEMPLE (JAN BAHAL)

Southwest of Asan Tole at the junction known as Kel Tole, this **temple** (Map p126) attracts both Buddhists and Hindus – Buddhists consider Seto (White) Machhendranath to be a form of Avalokitesvara, while to Hindus he is a rain-bringing incarnation of Shiva. The temple's age is not known but it was restored during the 17th century. The arched entrance to the temple is marked by a small Buddha figure on a high stone pillar in front of two metal lions.

In the courtyard there are lots of small shrines, chaityas and statues, including a mysteriously European-looking female figure

surrounded by candles who faces the temple. It may well have been an import from Europe that has simply been accepted into the pantheon of gods. Facing the other way, just in front of the temple, are two graceful bronze figures of the Taras seated atop tall pillars. Buy some grain to feed the pigeons and boost your karma.

Inside the temple you can see the white-faced image of the god covered in flowers. The image is taken out during the Seto Machhendranath festival in March/April each year and paraded around the city in a chariot; see p136. You can follow the interior path that circles the central building.

In the courtyard you may see men standing around holding what looks like a bizarre string instrument. This tool is used to separate and fluff up the downlike cotton padding that is sold in bulk nearby. The string is plucked with a twang by a wooden double-headed implement that looks like a cross between a dumb-bell and a rolling pin.

As you leave the temple, to the left you'll see the small, triple-roofed **Lunchun Lunbun Ajima**, a Tantric temple that's red-tiled around the lower level and has some erotic carvings at the base of the struts at the back.

INDRA CHOWK

The busy street of Makhan Tole spills into Indra Chowk, the courtyard named after the ancient Vedic deity, Indra. Locals crowd around the square's newspaper sellers, scanning the day's news.

On the west side of the square is the façade of the **Akash Bhairab Temple** (Map p126), or Bhairab of the Sky Temple. From the balcony four metal lions rear out over the street. The temple's entrance is at the right-hand side of the building, guarded by two more brass lions, but non-Hindus cannot enter. The silver image inside is visible through the open windows from out in the street, and during important festivals, particularly the Indra Jatra festival (September; see p138), the image is displayed in the square. A large lingam is also erected in the centre of the square at that time.

In a small niche just to the left of the Akash Bhairab Temple is a very small but much-visited brass Ganesh shrine.

Indra Chowk is traditionally a centre for the sale of blankets and cloth, and merchants cover the platforms of the **Mahadev Temple** (Map p126) to the north. The next-door stone **Shiva Temple** (Map p126) is a smaller and simplified version of Patan's Krishna Temple (see p185).

ITUM BAHAL

The long, rectangular courtyard of the **Itum Bahal** (Map p120) is the largest Buddhist bahal (courtyard) in the old town and remains a haven of tranquillity in the chaotic surroundings. A small, white-painted stupa stands in the centre of the courtyard. On the western side of the courtyard is the **Kichandra Bahal** (Map p120) or 'Keshchandra Paravarta Mahar Bihar', one of the oldest bahals in the city, dating from 1381 and renovated in 2007. A chaitya in front of the entrance has been completely shattered by a Bodhi tree, which has grown right up through its centre. In autumn and winter the square is decorated in ornate swirling patterns of drying grain.

Inside the Kichandra Bahal is a central pagodalike sanctuary, and to the south is a small chaitya decorated with graceful standing bodhisattvas. On the northern side of the courtyard are four brass plaques mounted on the upper-storey wall. The one on the extreme left shows a demon known as Guru Mapa taking a misbehaving child from a woman and stuffing it greedily into his mouth. Eventually the demon was bought off with the promise of an annual feast of buffalo meat, and the plaque to the right shows him sitting down and dipping into a pot of food. With such a clear message on juvenile misbehaviour it is fitting that the courtyard houses a primary school – right under the Guru Mapa plaques!

To this day, every year during the festival of Holi the inhabitants of Itum Bahal sacrifice a buffalo to Guru Mapa on the banks of the Vishnumati River, cook it in the afternoon in the courtyard and in the middle of the night carry it in huge cauldrons to a tree in the Tundikhel parade ground where the demon is said to live.

NARA DEVI TEMPLE

Halfway between Chhetrapati and Durbar Sq, the **Nara Devi Temple** (Map p126) is dedicated to Kali, Shiva's destructive consort. It's also known as the Seto (White) Kali Temple. It is said that Kali's powers protected the temple from the 1934 earthquake, which destroyed so many other temples in the valley. A Malla king once stipulated that a dancing ceremony should be held for the goddess every 12 years, and dances are still performed on the small dance platform that is across the road from the temple.

East of Thamel
THREE GODDESSES TEMPLES

Next to the modern Sanchaya Kosh Bhawan Shopping Centre in Thamel are the often ignored **Three Goddesses Temples** (Map p140). The street on which the temples are located is Tridevi Marg – *tri* means 'three' and *devi* means 'goddesses'. The goddesses are Dakshinkali, Manakamana and Jawalamai, and the roof struts have some creative erotic carvings.

GARDEN OF DREAMS

Just two minutes' walk, but a million miles from Thamel, is the beautifully restored Swapna Bagaicha, or **Garden of Dreams** (Map p140; ☎ 4425340; www.asianart.com/gardenofdreams; adult/child Rs 160/40, no student tickets; 🕙 9am-10pm), one of the most serene and beautiful enclaves in Kathmandu.

Field marshal Kaiser Shamser (1892–1964), whose palace the gardens complement, built the Garden of Dreams in the 1920s after a visit to several Edwardian estates in England, using funds won from his father (the prime minister) in an epic Rs 100,000 game of cowrie shells. The gardens and its pavilions suffered neglect to the point of collapse before they were lovingly brought back to life over a six-year period by the same Austrian-financed team that created the Patan Museum.

There are dozens of gorgeous details in the small garden, including the original gate, a marble inscription from Omar Khayam's *Rubaiyat*, the new fountains and ponds, and a quirky 'hidden garden' to the south. Of the original four acres and six pavilions (named after the six Nepali seasons), only 1.2 acres and three pavilions remain. To truly savour the serenity, come armed with a book or picnic and relax on one of the supplied lawn mats. Wi-fi is available.

Dwarika's operates the swanky Kaiser Cafe here (see p154) and there are occasional cultural events and exhibitions.

RANI POKHARI

This large fenced **tank** (Map p126) just off Kantipath is said to have been built by King Pratap Malla in 1667 to console his queen over the death of their son (who was trampled by an elephant). The pool (pokhari means pool or small lake) was apparently used during the Malla era for trials by ordeal and later became a favourite suicide spot.

Perhaps because of the high suicide rate, the gate to the tank and its central Shiva Temple is unlocked only one day each year, on the fifth day of the Tihar festival. The footbridge over the nearby chowk has the best views of Rani Pokhari. The chowk has rather optimistically been declared a no-horn zone!

Across Kantipath is a long imposing building originally known as the Durbar School, which was the first school in Nepal (1854). It has since been renamed the Bhanubhakta School, after the Nepali poet of that name.

South of Durbar Square
JAISI DEVAL TEMPLE

The south of Kathmandu's old city was the heart of the ancient city in the Licchavi period (4th to 8th centuries) and its major temple is the tall, triple-roofed **Jaisi Deval Temple** (Map p126), built just two years before Durbar Sq's famous Maju Deval (which is one platform higher). It's a Shiva temple, as indicated by the bull on the first few steps and the mildly erotic carvings on some of the temple struts. Right across the road from the temple is a natural stone lingam rising a good 2m from a yoni (female equivalent of a phallic symbol). The monolith is definitely a god-sized phallic symbol and a prayer here is said to aid fertility.

In its procession around the town during the Indra Jatra festival (see p138), the Kumari Devi's chariot pauses here. During its stop, dances are held on the small dance platform across the road from the temple.

West of the temple, enter the courtyard of the **Ram Chandra Temple** (Map p126), named after Ram, an incarnation of Vishnu and the hero of the Hindu epic, the Ramayana. This small temple is notable for the tiny erotic scenes on its roof struts; it looks as if the carver set out to illustrate 16 different positions, starting with the missionary position, and just about made it before running out of ideas (there's one particularly ambitious, back-bending position). The north side of the courtyard is used as a cow stable, highlighting the wonderful mix of the sacred and profane in Nepal!

The temple is best visited as part of the walking tour 'South from Durbar Square' (see p137).

BHIMSEN TOWER (DHARAHARA)

Towering like a lighthouse over the labyrinthine old town, this white, minaretlike **tower** (Map p126; ☎ 4215616; foreigner/SAARC Rs 299/49, over 65 & under 5 years free, no student tickets; ◷ 8am-8pm) is a useful landmark near the post office. The views from 61.88m up – 213 steps above the city – are the best you can get. There is a small Shiva shrine right at the very top.

The tower was originally built in 1826 by the Rana prime minister, Bhimsen Thapa, for Queen Lalit as part of the city's first European-style palace. It was rebuilt with nine storeys, two less than the original building, after it was severely damaged in the 1934 earthquake. The nearby Sundhara water tank is the largest in the city and lends its name to the district.

PACHALI BHAIRAB &
THE SOUTHERN GHATS

The northern banks of the Bagmati River south of the old town are home to little-visited temples and shrines, as well as the worst urban poverty in Kathmandu; rarely do such splendour and squalor sit so close.

Between Tripureshwar Marg and the Bagmati River at **Pachali Bhairab** (Map p126) a huge, ancient pipal tree forms a natural sanctuary for an image of Bhairab Pachali, surrounded by tridents (Pachali is a form of Shiva). To the side lies the brass body of Baital, one of Shiva's manifestations. Worshippers gather here on Tuesday and Saturday. It is particularly busy here during the festival of Pachali Bhairab Jatra (see p25).

From the temple you could explore the temples and ghats that line the holy, polluted Bagmati River. Head south of Pachali Bhairab to the ghats on the riverbank to find a collection of lovely statuary. To the south is the Newari-style pagoda of the **Lakshmi Mishwar Mahadev** (Map p126); to the southeast is the interesting **Tin Deval Temple** (Map p126), easily recognisable by its three shikhara-style spires.

From here you can continue west along footpaths to cremation ghats and a temple at the holy junction of the Bagmati and Vishnumati Rivers; or east past some of Kathmandu's poorest and lowest-caste communities to the triple-roofed **Tripureshwar Mahadev Temple** (Map p126), currently under restoration to become a centre for street children. Further east is the Mughal-style **Kalmochan Temple** (Map p126) built in 1873.

Dhum Varahi Shrine

In an unprepossessing schoolyard just inside Kathmandu's Ring Rd to the northeast of Kathmandu, a huge pipal tree encloses a small **shrine** (Map pp114–15) and a dramatic 5th-century sculpture of Vishnu as a wild boar with a human body, holding Prthivi, the earth goddess, on his left elbow.

The statue is one of the earliest depictions of an animal-human, created before iconographic rules were established, which perhaps contributes to the unusual sense of movement and vitality that the statue possesses. The statue shows Vishnu rescuing Prithvi from the clutches of a demon.

To get here head north along the Ring Rd from Pashupatinath and take a left about 200m north of the bridge over the Dhobi River. The statue lies 100m down the dirt track, in the grounds of the Shridhumrabarah Primary School.

ACTIVITIES

See p87 for the various rafting, canyoning, climbing and bungee-jumping trips that you can arrange from Kathmandu.

For golfing near the capital, see the Gokarna Forest Resort, p213.

Climbing

If you need to polish your climbing skills before heading to the mountains, try the **Pasang Lhamu Climbing Wall** (Map pp114–15; ☎ 4370742; www.pasanglhamu.org; ⏰ 10am-5.30pm) on the city's northeastern edge. A day's membership costs Rs 350 and equipment rental costs Rs 100. Week-long climbing courses and private tuition are available.

The wall is on the Ring Rd, near the Bangladesh embassy, and is part of the Pasang Lhamu Mountaineering Federation, named after the first Nepali woman to summit Everest, in 1993. A taxi here from central Kathmandu costs around Rs 200.

Pools & Fitness Centres

Generally, pools in the major hotels can be used by friends of hotel guests, or at some hotels by outsiders, for a charge. Yak & Yeti Hotel (p148) charges Rs 500 for a one-time use of its pools, plus Rs 500 for its health club.

The **Clark Hatch Fitness Center** (Map p126; ☎ 4411818) at the Radisson charges Rs 1050 for a day pass to its gym, while the Hyatt Regency charges Rs 1000 for its gym, pool, sauna, steam and Jacuzzi.

A decent health club for aerobics addicts is **Banu's Total Fitness** (Map p126; ☎ 4434024; banu94@ yahoo.com; Kamal Pokhari; ⏰ 6am-9pm Sun-Fri, 6-11am Sat), hidden down an alleyway southeast of the New Royal Palace. There are aerobics classes

---

DAY TRIPS FROM KATHMANDU

The great thing about Kathmandu is that there are so many fantastic sights just a couple of kilometres outside the city centre. You can check out any of the following sites and still be back in Thamel for the start of happy hour:

- Bhaktapur – see p194
- Patan – see p181
- Bodhnath – see p173
- Budhanilkantha – see p179

at 7am, 10.30am (women only) and 5.30pm, and regular yoga lessons (Rs 1500 per month). A visit costs Rs 200 for nonmembers, or Rs 375 with cardio machines and sauna.

The **Kamma Healing Centre** (Map p126; ☎ 4256618; Babar Mahal Revisited) offers classes in t'ai chi, yoga, transcendental meditation and anything else you can dream up. Yoga classes cost Rs 400 per hour, t'ai chi Rs 4000 per month, or join the free meditation class at 4pm on Saturdays.

For more on other yoga, meditation and massage classes in Kathmandu, see p364.

WALKING TOURS

A stroll around Kathmandu's backstreets will lead the casual wanderer to dozens of hidden temples, shrines and sculptures, especially in the crowded maze of streets and courtyards in the area north of Durbar Sq. The fast-paced succession of sights, colours and sounds makes these walking tours a highlight of any visit to Kathmandu.

Both of the walks will take you to a number of markets, temples, *toles,* bahals, *bahil* (courtyard with accommodation) and chowks, which remain the focus of traditional Nepali life. You only really appreciate Kathmandu's museumlike quality when you come across a 1000-year-old statue – something that would be a prized possession in many Western museums – being used as a plaything or a washing line in some communal courtyard.

The walks can be made as individual strolls or linked together into one longer walk. The first walking tour gives you a taste of the crowded and fascinating shopping streets in the oldest part of Kathmandu and takes you to some of the city's most important temples. The second walking tour takes you to a lesser-known section of southern Kathmandu, without spectacular sites but where the everyday life of city dwellers goes on and tourists are much rarer.

If these walking tours leave you wanting more, pick up Annick Holle's book *Kathmandu The Hidden City* (Rs 250), which details dozens of backstreet courtyards across town.

South from Thamel to Durbar Square

This walk is best made en route from Thamel to Durbar Sq, or vice versa. To get to Thahiti Tole, walk south from Thamel on the road from the main Thamel Chowk; the first square you come to is Thahiti.

Thahiti Tole wraps around a central **stupa (1)**, whose stone inscription indicates that it was constructed in the 15th century. Legends relate that it was built over a pond plated with gold and that the stupa served to keep thieves at bay. Or perhaps the pond was full of dangerous snakes and the stupa kept the snakes in their place – the legends vary!

Nateshwar Temple (2), on the northern side of the square, is dedicated to a form of Shiva that doubles as the local Newari god of music; the metal plates that surround the renovated doors show creatures busily playing a variety of musical instruments.

Take the road heading south past shops selling prayer flags and Buddhist brocade, then bear west to the impressive **Kathesimbhu Stupa (3**; p129), radiating colourful prayer flags. There are lots of *malla* (prayer beads) stalls in the square, as well as a little teahouse if energies are already flagging.

Just 10m further on your right, a single broken stone lion (his partner has disappeared) guards a passageway to the small enclosed courtyard of the **Nag Bahal (4)**, signed as the 'Ratna Mandal Mahabihar', with painted murals above the shrine.

Further down on the left, past a Ganesh statue, is a small recessed area and a dark grilled doorway marking a small but intricate central **stone relief (5)** dating from the 9th century. It shows Shiva sitting with Parvati on Mt Kailash, her hand resting proprietarily on his knee in the pose known as Uma Maheshwar. Various deities and creatures, including Shiva's bull Nandi, stand around them. To the right of the door is an almost unrecognisable orange-coloured Ganesh head. Incidentally, the impressive wooden balcony across the road is said to have had the first glass windows in Kathmandu (it looks like it's the same glass!).

Continue south past a string of dentists' shops (the reason will soon become clear), advertised by signs showing a grinning mouthful of teeth. When you hit a square you'll see a small, double-roofed **Sikha Narayan Temple (6)**, easily identified by the kneeling Garuda figure facing and the modern clock on the wall. The temple houses a beautiful 10th- or 11th-century four-armed Vishnu figure that you might be able to see through the grill. Just to the north is a fine image of the goddess Saraswati playing her lute at the **Saraswati shrine (7)**, with a Shiva shrine beside it.

WALKING TOUR: SOUTH FROM THAMEL TO DURBAR SQUARE

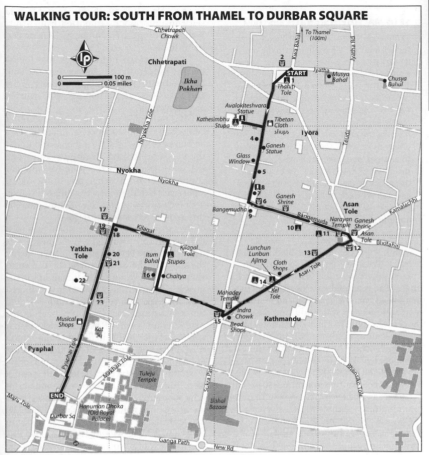

WALK FACTS

Start Thahiti Tole
Finish Durbar Sq
Distance 2km
Duration two hours

In the middle of the nondescript northern frontage, directly beneath the 'Raj Dental Clinic' sign, is a standing **Buddha statue (8)** framed by modern blue and white tilework. The image is only about 60cm high but dates from the 5th or 6th century. It's a reminder of the casual treatment of artistic treasures.

At the southern end of the area, just across the crossroads on the corner, you will see a lump of **wood with coins (9)** into which thousands of coins have been nailed. The coins are offerings to the toothache god, which is represented by a tiny image in the grotesque lump of wood. The square at the junction is known as Bangemudha, which means 'Twisted Wood'.

Head east to the triple-roofed **Ugratara Temple (10)** by a small square known as Nhhakantalla; a prayer at the shrine is said to work wonders for the eyes. Just further on your right you will pass the Krishna Music Emporium (maker and repairer of harmoniums), before spotting a gated entrance on the right that leads into **Haku Bahal (11)**. Look for the sign that advertises 'Opera Eye Wear'. This tiny bahal has a finely carved wooden window overlooking the courtyard.

SETO MACHHENDRANATH FESTIVAL

Kathmandu's Seto (White) Machhendranath festival kicks off a month prior to the much larger and more important Rato (Red) Machhendranath festival in Patan (see p189). The festival starts with removing the image of Seto Machhendranath from the temple at Kel Tole and placing it on a towering and creaky wooden temple chariot known as a *rath*. For the next four evenings, the chariot proceeds slowly from one historic location to another, eventually arriving at Lagan in the south of Kathmandu's old town. There the image is taken down from the chariot and carried back to its starting point in a palanquin while the chariot is disassembled and put away until next year.

You'll soon come to the bustling chowk of Asan Tole (see p129), old Kathmandu's busiest junction and a fascinating place to linger. The diagonal southwest-to-northeast main road was for centuries the main commercial street in Kathmandu, and the start of the caravan route to Tibet. It was not replaced as Kathmandu's most important street until the construction of New Rd after the great earthquake of 1934. The main shrine here is the **Annapurna Temple (12)**.

The street continues southwest past the octagonal **Krishna Temple (13)**, jammed between gleaming brass shops. It looks decrepit, but the woodcarvings on this temple are very elaborate, depicting beaked monsters and a tiny Tibetan protector, holding a tiger on a chain like he's taking the dog for a walk. Look for the turn-of-the-century plaques depicting marching troops on the building to the left.

The next square is Kel Tole, where you'll find one of the most important and ornate temples in Kathmandu, the **Seto (White) Machhendranath Temple** (14; see p130). Just to the north of the temple on the side street known as Bhedasingh is a collection of shops selling *topi* (cloth hats) and the Nepali traditional dress known as a *daura suruwal,* (a long shirt over tapered drainpipe trousers), including adorable miniature versions for children.

The busy shopping street spills into Indra Chowk, marked by the stepped Mahadev Temple and **Akash Bhairab Temple (15**; see p131). From the south of the square, wide Sukra Path

leads to New Rd; the shops along this road sell consumer goods imported from Hong Kong and Singapore, and many of them end up in India.

Before you leave Indra Chowk, look for the market hidden in the alleyways to the east, crowded with stalls selling the glass bangles and beads that are so popular with married Nepali women.

Take the quiet alleyway west from Indra Chowk and, after 200m or so, look for a tiny entryway to the right, by a shrine and under the sign for 'Jenisha Beauty Parlour'. The entryway leads into the long, rectangular courtyard of Itum Bahal, one of the oldest and largest bahals in the city, with some lovely architecture and stupas. See p131 for more on this and the **Kichandra Bahal (16)**.

Exit the courtyard at the north and turn left (west). On your right at the next junction is the **Nara Devi Temple (17**; p131). Just to the south of the **dance platform (18)** is a small shop occupied by one of Kathmandu's many marching bands, mainly used for weddings – look for gleaming tubas, red uniforms and tuneless trumpeting. Just visible across the road is a three-roofed **Narsingha Temple (19)** but it's almost impossible to find through a maze of small courtyards (you can see the roof from the dance platform).

At the Nara Devi corner, turn left (south); after 30m or so you come to a nondescript photocopy/magazine shop on your left with an utterly magnificent **wooden window (20)** above it. It has been called *deshay madu* in Nepali, which means 'there is not another one like it'. Next door in a small courtyard is the recently restored triple-roofed **Bhulukha Dega Temple (21)**, dedicated to Shiva.

Further south, on the right is the entrance to the **Yatkha Bahal (22)**, a huge open courtyard with a central stupa that looks like a mini-Swayambhunath. Directly behind it is an old building, whose upper storey is supported by four superb carved-wood struts. Dating from the 12th to 13th century, they are carved in the form of *yakshas* (attendant deities or nymphs), one of them gracefully balancing a baby on her hip. The struts were restored in 2002 by the Department of Architecture, Unesco and the Kathmandu Valley Preservation Trust.

Back on the road you'll see the deep red brick **temple (23)** to Chaumanda, a Newari mother goddess, that features a six-pointed star on the side. Head south again, past the music shops on the right, to Durbar Sq, your final destination for this walk.

South from Durbar Square

Starting from the Kasthamandap in Durbar Sq (see p119), a circular walk can be made to the older parts in the south of the city. This area is not as packed with historical interest as the walk north of Durbar Sq, but the streets are less crowded and you are unlikely to run into other tourists.

Starting from the **Kasthamandap (1;** p120) in the southwestern corner of Durbar Sq, the road out of the square forks almost immediately around the **Singh Sattal (2)**, built with wood left over from the Kasthamandap Temple. The squat building has some fascinating stalls and curd shops on the ground floor and golden-winged lions guarding each corner of the upper floor and is a popular place for *bhajan* (devotional music) in the mornings and evenings. The building was originally called the Silengu Sattal (*silengu* means 'left over wood' and a *sattal* is a pilgrim hostel) until the addition of the *singh* (guardian lions).

Take the road running diagonally to the right of this building, past a Shiva temple with a finely carved pilgrim shelter, and you eventually come to the large stone **hiti (3)**, or water tank, where people will usually be washing clothes.

Immediately beyond is the highly decorated **Bhimsen Temple (4)**, which is fronted by a brass lion on a pedestal ducking under the electric wires and has white-painted snow lions guarding the two front corners. Bhimsen is supposed to watch over traders and artisans, so it's quite appropriate that the ground floor of this well-kept temple should be devoted to shop stalls. An image of Bhimsen used to be carried to Lhasa in Tibet every 12 years to protect those vital trade routes, until the route was closed by Chinese control and the flight of the Dalai Lama in 1959. In front of

> **WALK FACTS**
>
> **Start** Durbar Sq
> **Finish** Durbar Sq
> **Distance** 2km
> **Duration** one hour

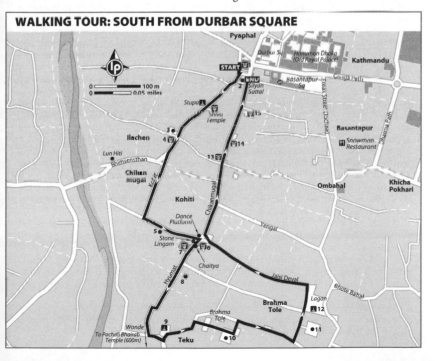

WALKING TOUR: SOUTH FROM DURBAR SQUARE

the temple there are some lovely chaityas set on a lingam base. Tourists are not allowed in the temple.

Continue south beyond the Bhimsen Temple then turn sharp left (uphill) at the junction and lose the traffic, passing the deep and ornate **Kohiti water tank (5)** en route. At the top of the hill you'll come out by the tall, triple-roofed, 17th-century **Jaisi Deval Temple (6; p132)**, which stands on a seven-level base. Nearby is the **Ram Chandra Temple (7)**.

Heading southwest there is a series of bahals, but most are of little interest apart from the small and very much lived-in courtyard of **Tukan Bahal (8)**. The Swayambhunath-style 14th-century stupa in the centre is surprisingly impressive.

The road continues with a few bends, then turns sharply left (east) at Wonde junction, which is marked by several temples, including a taller white **shikhara temple (9)**. If you take the downhill road leading south from this junction (off the Walking Tour map) you emerge onto Tripureshwar Marg from where you can continue to the Pachali Bhairab Temple (see p132).

Our walk continues past Brahma Tole to the **Musum Bahal (10)**, with its phallic-shaped Licchavi-style chaityas, an enclosed well and surrounding interconnecting bahals. Turn sharp left (north) at the next main junction and, after 25m, look out for the spacious and sunny **Ta Bahal (11)**, with its lovely chaityas, down an alley on the right.

The road opens into an open square, known as Lagan, featuring the white 5m-high **Machhendranath Temple (12)**, as well as the occasional neighbourhood cricket match. During the annual Seto Machhendranath festival (see the boxed text Seto Machhendranath Festival, p136, for more information), the image of the white-faced god is transported here from the Seto Machhendranath Temple in Kel Tole (see p130). The final stage of the procession is to pull the god's chariot three times around the temple, after which the image is taken back

---

KATHMANDU'S INDRA JATRA FESTIVAL

Indra, the ancient Aryan god of rain, was once captured in the Kathmandu Valley while stealing a certain flower for his mother, Dagini. He was imprisoned until Dagini revealed his identity and his captors gladly released him. The festival celebrates this remarkable achievement (villagers don't capture a real god every day of the week). In return for his release Dagini promised to spread dew over the crops for the coming months and to take back with her to heaven all those who had died in the past year.

The Indra Jatra festival thus honours the recently deceased and pays homage to Indra and Dagini for the coming harvests. It begins when a huge, carefully selected pole, carried via the Tundikhel, is erected outside the Hanuman Dhoka in Kathmandu. At the same time images and representations of Indra, usually as a captive, are displayed and sacrifices of goats and roosters are made; the screened doors obscuring the horrific face of Seto (White) Bhairab are also opened and for the next three days his gruesome visage will stare out at the proceedings.

The day before all this activity, three golden temple chariots are assembled in Basantapur Sq, outside the home of the Kumari (a living goddess; see p123). In the afternoon, with Durbar Sq packed with colourful and cheerful crowds, two boys emerge from the Kumari's house. They play the roles of Ganesh and Bhairab and will each ride in a chariot as an attendant to the goddess. Finally, the Kumari herself appears, either walking on a rolled-out carpet or carried by attendants so that her feet do not touch the ground.

The chariots move off and the Kumari is greeted from the balcony of the old palace by the president. The procession then continues out of Durbar Sq towards Hanuman Dhoka where it stops in front of the huge Seto Bhairab mask. The Kumari greets the image of Bhairab and then, with loud musical accompaniment, beer starts to pour from Bhairab's mouth! Getting a sip of this beer is guaranteed to bring good fortune, but one lucky individual will also get the small fish that has been put to swim in the beer – this brings especially good luck (though probably not for the fish).

Numerous other processions also take place around the town until the final day when the great pole is lowered and carried down to the river. A similar pole is erected in Bhaktapur as part of the Bisket Jatra Festival (p206), celebrating the Nepali New Year.

to its starting point on a palanquin while the chariot is dismantled here.

Turn left out of Lagan and walk back to the tall Jaisi Deval Temple, then turn right (northeast) back towards Durbar Sq.

At the next crossroads the slender triple-roofed **Hari Shankar Temple (13)** stands to the left of the road. Built in 1637 the temple's deity is a fusion of Shiva and Vishnu.

Continue north past a **Vishnu (Narayan) Temple (14)** to a second Vishnu temple, the **Adko Narayan Temple (15)**. Although it's not all that large, it is one of the four most important Vishnu temples in Kathmandu. Twin feathered Garudas front the temple while lions guard each corner. There's a particularly ornate *path* (pilgrim's shelter) on the street corner.

Beyond the temple you pass the Singh Sattal building again and arrive back at the starting point. Alternatively, head east through the backstreets for a reviving chocolate cake and milk tea at Freak St's Snowman Restaurant (see p153).

COURSES

See p363 and p67 for details of meditation classes, language courses, cookery classes and massage courses available in Kathmandu.

KATHMANDU FOR CHILDREN

Pilgrims Book House (see p116) has a fine collection of kids' books, including colouring books. Away from the tourist areas highchairs are virtually nonexistent but finding nonspicy food that children will eat may be more of a problem.

Kids will probably enjoy the zoo in nearby Patan (see p190) and older kids will get a thrill from spotting the monkeys at Swayambhunath (p163).

FESTIVALS & EVENTS

Kathmandu has many festivals, of which the most outrageous is probably Indra Jatra (see opposite) in September, closely followed by the Seto Machhendranath chariot festival (see p136) in March/April, Dasain in October, and the Pachali Bhairab Jatra, also in October. See p23 for details.

The annual **Jazzmandu Festival** (www.kathmandujazzfestival.com; tickets around Rs 900) is a week-long program of local and international jazz acts that plays in venues across town in late-October/November. See the website for details.

SLEEPING

Kathmandu has a great range of places to stay, from luxurious international-style hotels to cheap and cheerful lodges, and although prices have risen considerably in recent years, almost all offer competitive prices.

It's difficult to recommend hotels, especially in the budget and middle brackets, as rooms in each hotel can vary widely. Many of these hotels have multiple wings and, while some rooms may be very gloomy and run-down, others (generally the upper floors) might be bright and pleasant. A friendly crowd of travellers can also make all the difference.

In general, roadside rooms are brighter but noisier than interior rooms, and top-floor rooms are the best as you stand a chance of getting a view and have easy access to the roof garden.

Budget places generally don't have heating so in winter you'll want the warmer south-facing rooms and garden access, as it's always pleasant to sit outside during the cool, but sunny, autumn and winter days.

Quite a few hotels bridge the budget and midrange categories by having a range of room standards – these places have been grouped according to their lowest price.

Normal high-season rates are listed here, but it's always worth asking for a discount, particularly during low season when most places offer discounts of between 20% and 40%. If you email a reservation in advance you probably won't get the largest discount but you should get a free airport pick-up. Remember that most places will add on 23% tax.

Most budget and some midrange places are found in the bustling Thamel district. Midrange and top end places are widely scattered around Kathmandu, some quite a way from the centre.

Some travellers base themselves further afield, outside Kathmandu in Patan or Bodhnath, to escape the traffic, pollution and commercialism of Thamel (see p177 and p190 for details), and this isn't a bad idea. For something quieter still, there is an increasing number of mostly top-end resorts around the Kathmandu Valley that offer a peaceful rural atmosphere less than an hour from the centre of Kathmandu.

The following listings are divided by location and then by price category.

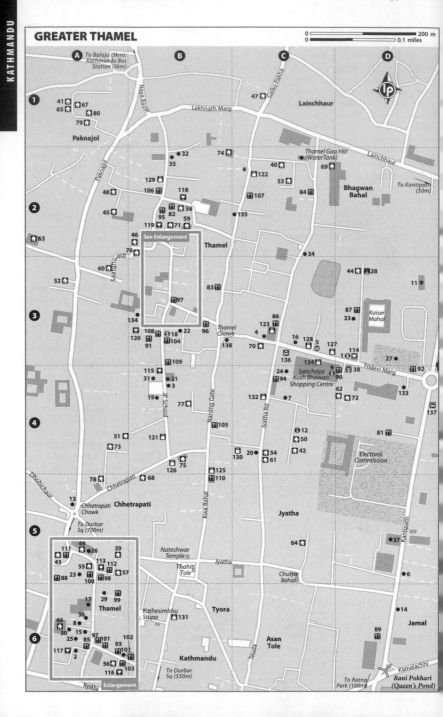

Thamel

For budget and midrange places the tourist ghetto of Thamel is the main locale. It's a convenient and enjoyable area to stay for a short time, especially to meet fellow travellers or indulge in some budget-priced apple crumble, but you are likely to tire of the place in a couple of days.

In an attempt to establish some order, we have somewhat arbitrarily divided the Greater Thamel area into: Thamel, around the two main intersections; Paknajol, to the north; Bhagwan Bahal, to the northeast; Jyatha, to the southeast; and Chhetrapati, to the southwest.

BUDGET
Central Thamel

Kathmandu Guest House (Map p140; ☎ 4700800; www.ktmgh.com; r without bathroom US$2-14, r with bathroom US$14-50, deluxe r US$55-120; ⚡ 🖳) The KGH is a bit of an institution. A former Rana palace, it was the first hotel to open in Thamel and still serves as the central landmark – everything in Thamel is 'near the Kathmandu Guest House'. In strictly dollar terms you can get better rooms elsewhere, but most people enjoy the bustling atmosphere and it's often booked out weeks in advance during the high season. The wi-fi enabled front courtyard and very pleasant rear garden acts as a haven from the Thamel mayhem. This is budget travel with a deluxe twist.

A vast range of rooms are available. The cheapest rooms without bathroom form part of the original 13-room guest house and really aren't up to much – you can get better-value rooms elsewhere – but at least the common showers are clean and hot. In the newer wing, the best-value rooms are probably the garden-facing rooms (single/double US$30/35).

Marco Polo Guest House (Map p140; ☎ 4251914; marcopolo@wlink.com.np; r Rs 300-600) There's a certain boarding school feel here but it's a popular place with a convenient location on the eastern edge of Thamel, near traffic-soaked Tridevi Marg. The rooms at the top and back are surprisingly quiet and bright, especially the spacious deluxe rooms; others are noisier and darker.

Hotel Potala (Map p140; ☎ 4700159; www.potalahotel.com; s/d without bathroom Rs 350/450, s/d with bathroom Rs 450/550, deluxe r Rs 900-1125) Bang in the beating heart of Thamel, this small backpacker place has recently been revitalised by switched-on new management. The rooms are simple and

smallish but clean and decent, though some are smaller and darker than others. Internet terminals, a nice rooftop area and a convenient restaurant overlooking Thamel's main drag are nice extras. It's down an alleyway near the Maya Cocktail Bar.

Student Guest House (Map p140; ☎ 4251448; krishna@student.wlink.com.np; s/d with bathroom Rs 350/600; 🖳) It's right next door to Marco Polo and a similar deal. It's quiet and clean but the buildings are so crammed in that there's little natural light and no views. The rooms out the back are much better and solo travellers can often get these double rooms for a single price, which is as good a deal as you're going to get in central Thamel.

Hotel Red Planet (Map p140; ☎ 4700879; red planet_thamel@hotmail.com; s/d from Rs 500/700, deluxe s/d Rs 650/850) Tucked away by the bend in the road just north of Kathmandu Guest House, this is a good Thamel cheapie, and not too noisy despite its central location. There's no glamour here but most rooms are clean and good value with decent bathrooms; try to get a garden-side room with a balcony.

Hotel Horizon (Map p140; ☎ 4220904; www.hotelhorizon.com; economy s/d US$8/10, standard s/d US$10/15, deluxe s/d US$15/20; 🖳) A good choice down an alley off the main street in southern Thamel, making it a quiet and central option. All rooms have a bathroom, most of which are bright and spacious, if a little old-fashioned, and there are some nice communal seating areas. The mid-priced rooms are the best value; more than this and you are really just paying for a bath tub.

Acme Guest House (Map p140; ☎ 4700236; www.acmeguesthouse.com; economy s/d US$8/10, standard s/d US$15/20, garden-facing s/d US$20/25) Next to the Hotel Red Planet, the rooms here are quite large and there is an open lawn area, which is something of a rarity in crowded Thamel. The rooms with a balcony overlooking the lawn are the best value; those at the back can be dark. Recent price hikes have made the rooms poorer value.

Thorong Peak Guest House (Map p140; ☎ 4253458; www.thorongpeak.com; s/d without bathroom US$8/12, standard s/d US$14/18, deluxe s/d US$20/24, superior s/d US$26/30; 🖳) A clean and well-looked-after place, off the main street in a small cul de sac. Most rooms are spacious, light and airy, if a little bland, with super-clean bathrooms. Plus points include nice communal balconies and a decent courtyard restaurant, though without discounts it's a bit overpriced.

DECLAN MURPHY

Declan Murphy is the director of the children's charity Just One (www.just-one.org) in Nepal.

What drives children onto the streets of Kathmandu? Many children on the streets of Kathmandu are there because of poverty and domestic violence. Although illegal, child labour is commonly accepted in Nepal and is often seen as a good escape from poverty – both for the children themselves and for the families that send them away. Kids often come to the streets of Kathmandu in search of better fortune, either of their own accord or under the influence of friends or family. Far away hills are always greener though, and many kids discover that life in the capital is not as glittering as it might have seemed from their home village.

Perhaps a more important question is what 'keeps' these children on the street? Bizarrely, kindness is often the answer. Consider the following scenario – a child is sent to Kathmandu to work by poor and uneducated parents and discovers that the 'boss' is unkind, uncaring and often quite cruel. Seeing how other children seem able to survive on the street, the child decides to try their luck and falls under the influence of older street kids – kids who've learnt that begging can be a lucrative game, who know the escape of solvent abuse, who no longer have the tension of living with impoverished and over-stressed parents, and who are prepared to put up with various hardships in return for what they see as a life of total freedom.

What can travellers do to help? More often than not doing nothing probably won't make the traveller feel better about a particular situation, but that should never be their reason for wanting to help. The best thing travellers can do to help is to do nothing. There are many organisations working to help Nepal's street children, and handing out food, money and other gifts in the street never provides a lasting solution to the child's problems. What it will do is give the child a reason to stay on the street – at home, parents rarely give them biscuits, or bananas, or chocolate, or cola, or cream doughnuts, or Rs 10 notes, or any of the random gifts that countless travellers regularly bestow on street children. When organisations, like Just-One, offer assistance to these young and vulnerable kids, what they are actually being asked is to choose between 'normal' life of school, learning, family, routine, structure, rules and day-to-day hardships, and a life of comparative freedom that the random acts of kindness of countless kind-hearted people make possible.

Are there any organisations that travellers can donate to or volunteer with to help children in Kathmandu? There are thousands of organisations here and many welcome volunteers and donations. However, aside from being prohibited on a tourist visa, the volunteering industry is unregulated and travellers should look very carefully at any organisation that they donate time or money to. When volunteering, think about your own skills and experience and look for an organisation that can use those skills in its work.

Paknajol (Northern Thamel)

This area lies to the north of central Thamel and can be reached by continuing north from the Kathmandu Guest House, or by approaching from Lekhnath Marg to the north.

Not far from the steep Paknajol intersection with Lekhnath Marg (northwest of Thamel) are a few pleasant guest houses grouped together in a district known as Sorakhutte. They're away from traffic, a short walk from Thamel (but it could be a million miles), and they have fine views across the valley towards Balaju and Swayambhunath.

Tibet Peace Guest House (Map p140; ☎ 4381026; www.tibetpeace.com; r without bathroom Rs 200-400, r with bathroom Rs 400-800) Friendly and family-run, this is a quiet and mellow hang out with a very nice

garden and small restaurant. There's a wide range of rooms, some ramshackle and others with private balconies, so have a dig around before committing.

Yellow House (Map p140; ☎ 4381186; theyellowhouse2007@gmail.com; r without bathroom Rs 250-350, r with bathroom Rs 500-600) This friendly new place across the road is an excellent addition to the expanding Paknajol scene. The 20 rooms are bright, there's lots of garden space and the house restaurant dishes up good Thai food.

Kathmandu Garden House (Map p140; ☎ 4381239; www.hotel-in-nepal.com; s/d without bathroom Rs 200/300, s/d with bathroom Rs 500/700) A small and intimate guest house that is cosy and deservedly popular. The views from the roof are excellent and there are nice sitting areas and a lovely garden, where you can sit back and marvel at the staff cutting the grass by hand (literally!).

Family Peace House (Map p140; ☎ 4381138; peace_family@hotmail.com; s/d without bathroom Rs 250/300, s/d with bathroom Rs 400/500) Next door, Family Peace House is a similar deal: it's a notch down in quality but still good value.

Hotel Encounter Nepal (Map p140; ☎ 4440534; www.encounternepal.com; old block s/d without bathroom US$4/8, s/d with bathroom from US$8/10, new block s/d from US$15/20, deluxe r US$30-65; 🖳) This faded place to the north of Thamel suffers from crummy decor and overpriced rates but has some OK rooms. The best old-block rooms are sunny and spacious, and the spiffier new block across the garden has some nice air-conditioned deluxe corner rooms with balcony views over the valley. You take your life in your hands crossing diabolical Lekhnath Marg to get here.

Hotel Down Town (Map p140; ☎ 4700471; www.hotel-downtown-nepal.com; r without bathroom Rs 300-400, with bathroom Rs 400-800) This decent Thamel cheapie has a wide range of rooms; some dark, others (especially those clustered around the rooftop) bright and pleasant. There are a couple of nice communal sitting areas and balconies. The website makes it look much more glamorous than it actually is…

Holy Lodge (Map p140; ☎ 4700265; s/d from Rs 300/400, with bathroom Rs 750/900) This place offers neat, clean rooms, but there's a sad lack of garden, sitting areas or views, especially in the warrenlike back building, which has the cheaper rooms. Deluxe rooms are spacious but the hideous carpets are a serious style violation.

Annapurna Guest House (Map p140; ☎ 4420159; www.annapurnaguesthouse.com; s/d without bathroom Rs 350/400, s/d with bathroom Rs 500/600) Further north near the Hotel Norbu Linka, this somewhat dour family guest house is down a side alley. The rooms are smallish but clean and most come with a private bathroom, though some are dark. The rooftop restaurant is pleasant. This area is quieter than Thamel proper and has not yet been completely taken over by restaurants, souvenir shops and travel agencies.

Hotel Florid (Map p140; ☎ 4701055; www.hotelflorid.com.np; s/d without bathroom US$5/6.50, s/d with bathroom US$10/12, deluxe r US$15; 🖳) This is one of several small guest houses just north of central Thamel, down a lane west of Advanced Photo Finisher. There is a pleasant garden restaurant at the rear and no buildings behind, so there's a feeling of space that is often lacking

in Thamel. The suitelike deluxe rooms overlooking the garden are sunny and spacious. Doubles overlooking the road are noisier but come with a shared balcony. You'll need to negotiate a discount to get good value here.

Pilgrims Guest House (Map p140; ☎ 4440565; pilgrimsghouse@yahoo.com; s/d without bathroom US$6/9, s with bathroom US$10, d $15-20; 🖳) The first thing that appeals about this secluded place in northern Thamel is the outdoor garden restaurant and bar. The wide range of rooms fit most budgets, from top-floor rooms with a sofa and balcony, to the cheapest singles, which are little more than a box. It's a popular place so you may have to take what you can get for the first night and then upgrade as rooms become available.

Prince Guest House (Map p140; ☎ 4700456; princeguesthouse@hotmail.com; s/d US$8/12) Across the road from Down Town, this passable budget place is cheered up by potted plants and a pleasant rooftop. Rooms have small hot-water bathrooms but are pretty charmless. The upper-floor rooms are much brighter.

Hotel Shree Tibet (Map p140; ☎ 4700902; sritibet@ccsl.com.np; s/d US$10/15, deluxe r US$20) It's easy to miss this upper-budget, Tibetan-run place and most people do (it's often deserted). It's a clean, quiet and friendly place with cosy rooms, although some are dark and smallish due to the buildings being very close together. As always, the back rooms on the higher floors are best. The small restaurant serves decent Tibetan food. For some reason 85% of the guests are French.

Kathmandu Peace Guest House (Map p140; ☎ 4380369; www.ktmpeaceguesthouse.com; s with/without bathroom US$12/8, d with/without bathroom US$16/12, deluxe s/d with bathroom US$14/18) Along the road from the Tibet Peace Guest House, this is a little more upmarket, offering rooms with satellite TV in either the slightly ramshackle old wing or the fresher pine-clad new block. There are fine views from the rooftop towards Nagarjun.

Hotel Tashi Dhargey (Map p140; ☎ 4700030; www.hoteltashidhargey.com; s/d US$12/15, deluxe s/d US$20/25; 🌂) A pretty good upper budget choice in the heart of things, down a back alley with entrances on two different roads. It has a wide range of slightly old-fashioned but spacious rooms, the best of which are on the upper floors and on the sunny south side. Deluxe rooms come with air-con/heating and have a large bathroom; they are good value at the discounted rate of US$12/15.

Hotel Metropolitan Kantipur (Map p140; ☎ 4266518; www.kantipurhotel.com; s/d US$15/20, deluxe s/d US$25/30) Just west of the Thamel action, this is a decent find with a scruffy garden of pomelo trees, rooftop seating and friendly staff. Rooms are spacious, though levels of maintenance vary; upper-floor rooms are best. There's even a small Kumari Temple in the corner of the grounds. Without the discounts it's overpriced.

Mustang Guest House (Map p140; ☎ 4700053; www .mothersland.com; s/d without bathroom Rs 250/300, s with bathroom Rs 300, d $450-500) Another acceptable cheapie, this place is the tucked away down an inconspicuous laneway with decent, quiet rooms but a dearth of natural light.

Chhetrapati (South Thamel)

This area is named after the important five-way intersection (notable by its distinctive bandstand) to the southwest of Thamel. The further you get from Thamel, the more traditional the surroundings become.

Khangsar Guest House (Map p140; ☎ 4260788, www.khangsarguesthouse.com; s Rs 400-600, d Rs 500-750) This is a friendly and central option, though recent price hikes mean you can now find better value elsewhere. The threadbare rooms come with an anorexically thin but clean bathroom with (generally) hot water, plus there's a Korean restaurant and a pleasant rooftop bar for cold beers under the stars. The upper-floor rooms are best.

our pick **Hotel Ganesh Himal** (Map p126; ☎ 4243819, 4263598; www.ganeshhimal.com; standard s/d US$11/14, deluxe s/d US$16/19; 🛋 🖵) Our pick for comfort on a budget is this well-run and friendly place, a 10-minute walk southwest of Thamel – far enough to be out of range of the tiger balm salesmen but close enough to restaurants for dinner. The rooms are among the best value in Kathmandu, with endless hot water, satellite TV and lots of balcony and garden seating, plus a sunny rooftop. The deluxe rooms are more spacious, a little quieter and come with a bath tub. Throw in free internet access, free airport pick-up and cheap mountain bike hire (the manager is a keen biker) and this place is hard to beat. Here's a tip – bring earplugs, as the residential neighbourhood can be a bit noisy.

MIDRANGE
Central Thamel

Hotel Garuda (Map p140; ☎ 4700766; www.garuda -hotel.com; s/d US$10/15, standard s/d US$15/20, deluxe s/d US$25/30) There's a definite mountaineering connection going on here – there are lots of signed expedition photos on the walls (including those of Scott Fisher and Rob Hall) and John Krakauer mentions staying here in his bestseller *Into Thin Air*. It's very central, right in the eye of the Thamel storm, but that means you suffer from either road noise or the plain and dark interior rooms. It probably feels great after two weeks bivouacked on the side of Everest; for everyone else there are better options.

Hotel Blue Horizon (Map p140; ☎ 4421971; www .hotelbluehorizon.com; Tridevi Marg; s US$15-25, d US$20-30, deluxe r US$50-60; 🛋 🖵) There's good and bad news here. Pluses include a nice rooftop seating, a quiet neighbourhood and a secluded location down an alleyway off Tridevi Marg that makes it super easy for transport around the city. Downers include a disinterested management. The mid-priced corner rooms offer best value and the top-priced suites are good for families, but all are a bit overpriced.

Paknajol (North Thamel)

our pick **International Guest House** (Map p140; ☎ 4252299; www.ighouse.com; s/d with bathroom US$16/20, deluxe s/d US$22/28, superior deluxe s/d US$30/35, ste US$45) West from the Hotel Tradition in an area known as Kaldhara, this is a highly recommended and quite stylish place that boasts century-old carved woodwork, terraced sitting areas, a spacious garden and one of the best rooftop views in the city. The superior deluxe rooms in the renovated wing are bright, spacious and well decorated, while the deluxe rooms come with a garden view. Standard rooms vary. This area is quieter and much less of a scene than Thamel but still close to plenty of restaurants. Rates include breakfast, wi-fi and airport pick-up. Keep an eye out for the stuffed yak...

Hotel Tradition (Map p140; ☎ 4700217; www.hotel tradition.com; standard s/d US$30/40, deluxe s/d US$55/65) At eight storeys, this is probably the tallest building in the area and a good choice. The rooms are comfortable and well furnished (though some are a bit small) and the views from the 6th-floor terrace restaurant are sensational. The hotel is located on the snaking side road known as Saatghumti, or 'Seven Bends'. Reservations are a good idea in high season.

Hotel Courtyard (Map p140; ☎ 4700648; www.hotel courtyard.com; s/d US$35/40, deluxe r US$65, ste US$90) For something more stylish, this well-run hotel is one of the few boutique options in

Thamel. Built in a traditional style with oil bricks, Newari-style carved wooden lintels and stone waterspouts, it's well insulated from the Thamel madness; there are pleasant seating areas and the rooms are big enough to tango in. A small spa, library and bar enhance the lush, romantic mood.

Bhagwan Bahal (Northeastern Thamel)

Hotel Norbu Linka (Map p140; ☎ 4410630; www.hotel norbulinka.com; s/d US$45/50, deluxe s/d US$60/80, ste US$85-100) A modern, secluded place, down an alley opposite the interesting Thamel Gaa Hiti (water tank). The spacious modern rooms aren't as Tibetan as you'd think from the name but they are clean and comfortable, and there are a couple of rooms on the rooftop garden area. The opulent suites are great for families and the restaurant is open 24 hours, so if you are jetlagged and with kids, look no further. Credit cards are accepted.

Jyatha (Southeastern Thamel)

The neighbourhood southeast of Thamel is traditionally known as Jyatha, but the word is also used to describe the main north–south road that runs into the western end of Tridevi Marg.

Turn east a short way down Jyatha Rd, and a couple of twists and turns will bring you to a neat little cluster of modern guest houses, whose central but quiet location feels a million miles from the Thamel hustle.

Fuji Hotel (Map p140; ☎ 4250435; www.fujiguesthouse .com; s with/without bathroom US$10/6, d with/without bathroom US$15/10, standard r US$15-30, deluxe r US$30-45) A well-run place in the same lane as the Holy Himalaya. It's popular with Japanese travellers and rooms are neat, quiet and spotlessly clean; the more expensive rooms have balconies, towels and bath tubs. The economy rooms with shared bathroom are a good deal.

Imperial Guest House (Map p140; ☎ 4249339; imperial _guesthouse@hotmail.com; s/d US$12/15) Further east and across the road from Mustang Holiday Inn, this place is cheap and plain but it has a few good rooms. There's a rooftop sitting area that overlooks a small shrine.

Mustang Holiday Inn (Map p140; ☎ 4249041; www .mustangholiday.com; s/d with bathroom US$15/20, deluxe s/d US$22/28, super deluxe s/d US$30/40) Really, how many times do you get to stay in a hotel owned by the king of a remote Himalayan kingdom? The dimly lit rooms are looking a bit old these days but the Tibetan decor is still hanging on,

with thangkas decked in khatas (silk scarfs), and some come with a balcony. It's quiet, has a restaurant and nice terrace seating and, yes, it really is leased from the King of Mustang!

Hotel Utse (Map p140; ☎ 4228952; www.hotelutse.com .np; Jyatha Rd; standard s/d US$15/21, deluxe s/d US$19/25, super deluxe s/d US$24/30) This comfortable Tibetan hotel is owned by Ugyen Tsering, one of the original Thamel tourism pioneers, with his long-running and popular Utse Restaurant (see p151). It's solid in an old-school way, with a good rooftop area (with library) and Tibetan-influenced foyer. Deluxe rooms have nice Tibetan touches, with air-con and satellite TV, but the standard rooms probably offer best value. Rooms tend to be very dark; the roadside rooms are brighter but noisy.

Hotel Norling (Map p140; ☎ 4240734; www.hotel norling.com; Jyatha Rd; standard s/d US$15/20, deluxe d US$25-30) A thin slice of a hotel next door to the Hotel Utse that is a good-value option. Also Tibetan-run, it has small but neat rooms set around an interior courtyard and boasts a rooftop garden with real lawn. The small interior single rooms are worth avoiding; the back rooms with a window are best. Deluxe rooms are slightly larger.

Hotel Holy Himalaya (Map p140; ☎ 4263172; www.holy himalaya.com; s/d US$24/34, deluxe s/d US$49/69; ☒ ▢) Tucked away in a lane behind the Hotel Utse, this is a good midrange find frequented by small in-the-know tour groups. It's a modern, well-run place that feels like a 'real' hotel, down to the marbly lobby and lift. The rooms are bland but reassuring and some come with a balcony. The spacious deluxe rooms are the best value. Perks include free internet access, organic coffee and a nice rooftop. Formerly known as the Hotel Dynasty.

ourpick Kantipur Temple House (Map p140; ☎ 4250131; www.kantipurtemplehouse.com; s/d US$55/66, deluxe s/d US$85/125) Hidden down an alley on the edge of the old town, at the southern end of Jyatha, this boutique-style hotel has been built in traditional Newari-temple style with meticulous attention to detail. The spacious rooms are tastefully decorated, with traditional carved wood, window seats and specially commissioned fair-trade dhaka (hand-woven) cloth bedspreads. Due to the traditional nature of the building rooms tend to be a little dark. This place is doing its best to be eco-friendly – guests are given cloth bags to use when shopping and bulk mineral water is available free of charge, so you don't need to buy plastic bottles. In fact there's no plastic anywhere in the hotel. The new block encircles a traditional brick courtyard and there's garden and rooftop seating. The old town location is close to almost anywhere in town, but taxi drivers might have a hard time finding it.

Chhetrapati (South Thamel)

Potala Guest House (Map p140; ☎ 4220467; www .potalaguesthouse.com; s US$10, d US$15-20, dcluxe r US$38; 🖾) At the quiet southern end of Thamel is this large, fairly popular hotel. The garden is small but pleasant, with a lovely terrace and a rooftop garden. The quiet deluxe rooms with air-con and wooden floors are the best bet; the other rooms are older and much plainer, especially the singles.

Tibet Guest House (Map p140; ☎ 4254888; www .tibetguesthouse.com; s/d US$16/20, standard s/d US$25/30, deluxe s/d US$35/40, superior s/d US$50/55, ste s/d US$65/75; 🖾 🖳) You can't go wrong at this well-run and popular hotel, so book in advance. All the rooms are comfortable, though lower floors can be dark; the deluxe rooms have a much larger bathroom. There's a lovely breakfast patio and the superb views of Swayambhunath from the rooftop garden just cry out to be appreciated at sunset with a cold beer. The standard rooms come with a balcony and are in a separate block across the street. Free wi-fi is a perk.

Nirvana Garden Hotel (Map p140; ☎ 4256200; www .nirvanagarden.com; s/d US$40/50, deluxe s/d US$50/60) The relaxing garden here may not quite be nirvana but it is the closest you'll find to bliss in Thamel and it's a real oasis, making this hotel a very relaxing choice close to the centre. The clean and fresh deluxe rooms with private balcony are the ones to opt for (ask for a garden view) and offer great midrange value. The standard rooms are much smaller.

Freak Street (Jochne) & Durbar Square

Although Freak St's glory days have passed, a few determined rock-bottom budget restaurants and lodges have clung on. Staying here offers two pluses – you won't find much cheaper, there are fewer crowds and you're right in the heart of the fascinating old city. On the downside, the pickings are slimmer and the lodges are generally grungier than in Thamel.

Century Lodge (Map p126; ☎ 4247641; www.century lodge.4t.com; s/d without bathroom Rs 200/400, s/d with bathroom Rs 350/450) One of Freak St's long-term survivors, this ramshackle place treads a tightrope between atmospheric and dingy but remains fairly popular. The creaky old-wing rooms haven't changed since 1972 (be warned, neither have the mattresses); the new top-floor rooms are cleaner but disappointingly concrete. The nicest rooms come with a balcony.

Annapurna Lodge (Map p126; ☎ 4247684; r with/ without bathroom Rs 350/250) Simple but well kept, cheerful and cosy, this is probably the best budget option in Freak St. The attached Diyalo Restaurant (p153) is a good place to eat and there are evening movies and a laundry service.

Monumental Paradise (Map p126; ☎ 4240876; mparadise52@hotmail.com; s/d with bathroom Rs 400/650) A newish place that's a lot more modern than the rest of Freak St. Rooms are clean, fresh and spacious, with a tiled bathroom, and the upper-floor back rooms come with a private balcony and lots of natural light.

FREAK STREET – THE END OF THE ROAD

Running south from Basantapur Sq, Freak St dates from the overland days of the late 1960s and early 1970s, when it was one of the great gathering places on 'the road east'. In its hippy prime, this was the place for cheap hotels (Rs 3 a room!), colourful restaurants, hash and 'pie' (pastry) shops, the sounds of Jimmy and Janis blasting from eight-track players and, of course, the weird and wonderful foreign 'freaks' who gave the street its name. Along with Bodhnath and Swayambhunath, Freak St was a magnet for those in search of spiritual enlightenment, cheap dope and a place where the normal boundaries no longer applied.

Times change and Freak St (better known these days by its real name, Jochne) is today only a pale shadow of its former funky self. While there are still cheap hotels and restaurants, it's the Thamel area in the north of the city that is the main gathering place for a new generation of travellers. However, for those people who find Thamel too slick and commercialised, Freak St retains a faint echo of those mellower days.

KATHMANDU

There's an excellent rooftop bar/restaurant and one suite (Rs 1000) in the crow's nest has its own balcony and hammock! A good choice.

Central Kathmandu

Most of the following hotels are within walking distance of Durbar Marg and the Thamel area and fall into the top-end price range.

Shanker Hotel (Map p126; ☎ 4410151; www.shanker hotel.com.np; s/d incl breakfast US$90/105; ❷) There's nowhere in town quite like this former Rana palace – the kind of place where you expect some whiskered old Rana prince to come shuffling around one of the wooden corridors. The renovated rooms are quirky rather than luxurious (some are split level); for real grandeur you'll have to track down the dining halls and Durbar Hall conference space. The entry columns of neoclassical whipped cream overlook a palatial manicured garden and swimming pool.

Malla Hotel (Map p140; ☎ 4418385; www.hotelmalla .com; s/d US$130/156, club deluxe s/d US$150/182; ❷ ❷) On the northeastern edge of Thamel, west of the New Royal Palace but still only a five-minute walk to all the Thamel restaurants, the Malla is solid four-star comfort. The slightly anaemic rooms enjoy either pool or garden views. There's a good swimming pool, a new casino and, best of all, a superb garden complete with a mini-stupa and even a peacock enclosure.

Yak & Yeti Hotel (Map p126; ☎ 4248999; www .yakandyeti.com; Newari wing d US$185, Durbar wing d US$205, executive club US$250; ❷ ❷) This hotel is probably the best-known in Nepal, due to its connections with the near-legendary Boris Lissanevitch, its original owner. The oldest section of the hotel is part of the Lal Durbar, a Rana palace that houses restaurants and a casino; these retain traces of an overblown but spectacular baroque decor (the foyer is decorated with excellent old black-and-white photos of Rana royalty). The actual rooms are in two modern wings: the older Newari wing incorporates Newari wood-carvings, oil brick walls and local textiles, while the Durbar wing is modern and stylish with better bathroom facilities. Request a garden-facing room. Business people will find an executive floor and a well-equipped business centre. There's also a beautiful garden, two pools, tennis courts and a fitness centre.

Lazimpat

North of central Kathmandu is the Lazimpat embassy area. The options in this area are generally popular with nongovernment organisation (NGO) staff, repeat visitors and business people.

MIDRANGE

Astoria Hotel (Map pp114-15; ☎ 4436180; www.astoria -hotel.com; s/d incl breakfast US$28/35, deluxe s/d US$50/60; ❷) North along Lazimpat, signposted down a secluded alley to the side of the Hotel Shangri-La, is this excellent find. The light and airy rooms are spotlessly clean, and have TV, carpet and nice home touches. The spacious standard rooms are in the block out back; deluxe rooms are bigger and come with air-con and an internet port. The stylish Swiss-French restaurant, switched-on staff and pleasant garden are icing on the cake. Take a left after the Shangri-La and then a right at the fork.

Hotel Manaslu (Map p126; ☎ 4410071; www.hotel manaslu.com; standard s/d incl breakfast US$45/50; ❷ ❷) Just beyond Hotel Tibet, the big draw at this nice modern hotel is the pleasant garden and pool fed by Newari-style fountains. The glorious carved windows in the restaurant were brought in from Bhaktapur. After this initial splendour, the rooms themselves are ho-hum; try to get a room overlooking the garden. The slightly inconvenient location explains the relatively low rates.

Hotel Tibet (Map p126; ☎ 4429085; www.hotel-tibet .com; s/d US$70/80; ❷) Tibetophiles and tour groups headed to or from Tibet like this recommended midrange choice, run by a friendly Tibetan family and with a very Tibetan vibe. The 56 quiet and comfortable rooms are a bit plain compared to the opulent lobby, but the larger front-facing rooms have a balcony. There's also a great rooftop terrace, a garden and even a meditation chapel. It's just in front of the Radisson Hotel.

TOP END

Hotel Shangri-La (Map p126; ☎ 4412999; www.hotel shangrila.com; superior s/d incl breakfast US$120/130, executive s/d US$150/160; ❷) Recent renovations have added a new casino, fitness centre and an alleged fifth star, but unfortunately more attention has been spent on the shopping arcades than the superior rooms, which are looking pretty tired. The real draw is the large relaxing garden, with a kids' play area and twice-weekly barbecues (Rs 500). Try a High Lama cocktail at the Lost Horizon Bar. Nice, but not top-notch.

Radisson Hotel (Map p126; ☎ 4423888; www.radisson.com/kathmandune; superior/deluxe/club r US$185/200/250; 🏊 🖳 ⛷) North of the city in the Lazimpat embassy area, the Radisson is modern, fresh and well maintained, with a 5th-floor pool and a good gym operated by Clark Hatch. The instant coffee supplied with the coffee maker doesn't exactly scream five stars, though.

Elsewhere
MIDRANGE
Hotel Vajra (Map p126; ☎ 4271545; www.hotelvajra.com; s/d without bathroom incl breakfast US$14/16, s/d with bathroom from US$33/38, new wing s/d from US$53/61) Across the Vishnumati River in the Bijeshwari district, this is one of Kathmandu's most interesting hotels in any price category. The complex feels more like an artists' retreat than a hotel, with an art gallery, a library of books on Tibet and Buddhism, a fine rooftop bar and an Ayurvedic massage room. The cheapest rooms in the old block have shared bathrooms but are still good value. All the rooms in the old wing are unique so take a look at more than one. The only catch is the location, which, though peaceful, makes it tricky for getting a taxi.

TOP END
Soaltee Crowne Plaza (Map pp114-15; ☎ 4273999; s/d US$180/190, deluxe s/d US$220/230; ⛷) Space and tranquillity are precious commodities in Kathmandu but the Soaltee has acres of both; 11 acres, to be precise, so take a map if you go for a stroll. Spread around the palatial grounds (the hotel is owned by former King Gyanendra) are some excellent restaurants, a lovely poolside area, a casino and even a bowling alley. The price you pay is the crummy location on the western edge of town, a 15-minute taxi ride from the centre.

Hyatt Regency Kathmandu (☎ 4491234; www.kathmandu.regency.hyatt.com; d from US$210; ⛷) No expense has been spared on this superb palace-style building, from the dramatic entrance of Newari water tanks to the modern Malla-style architecture. It's worth popping in en route to Bodhnath just to admire the gorgeous stupas in the foyer, which set the stylish tone for the hotel (there's a lamp-lighting ceremony at dusk). As you'd expect, the rooms are furnished tastefully and many

have views over nearby Bodhnath stupa. The large swimming pool, good restaurants and Sunday brunch make this the perfect spot for a splurge. After a tough day's sightseeing unwind with a *shirodhara* (oil pouring) Ayurvedic treatment at the spa. The Hyatt is a couple of kilometres outside Kathmandu, on the road to Bodhnath.

ourpick **Dwarika's Hotel** (Map pp114-15; ☎ 4470770; www.dwarikas.com; s/d US$220/230, ste US$330-385; ⛷) For stylish design and sheer romance, this outstanding hotel is unbeatable; if you're on honeymoon, this is the place to choose. Over 40 years the owners have rescued thousands of woodcarvings from around the valley (from buildings facing demolition or collapse) and incorporated them into the hotel design, which consists of clusters of traditional Newari buildings (including a library and pool) separated by brick-paved courtyards. The end result is a beautiful hybrid – a cross between a museum and a boutique hotel, with a lush, pampering ambience. Each room is unique and some have sexy open-plan granite bathrooms. Its only disadvantage is its location – on a busy street in the east of town – but finding a taxi is never a problem.

EATING
Kathmandu has an astounding array of restaurants. Indeed, with the possible exception of the canteen at the UN building, there are few places where you have the choice of Indian, Chinese, Japanese, Mexican, Korean, Middle Eastern, Italian or Irish cuisines, all within a five-minute walk. And there are even some Nepali restaurants! After long months on the road in India or weeks trekking in the mountains Kathmandu feels like a culinary paradise.

Thamel's restaurant scene has been sliding upmarket for a few years now, with a slew of places now costing US$5 per main course, plus 23% tax – still a great bargain but unthinkable a few years ago. A bottle of beer will nearly double your bill in a budget restaurant.

Thamel
Thamel restaurants spill into Paknajol, Jyatha and Chhetrapati, just like the hotels. The junction outside the Kathmandu Guest House is the epicentre of Thamel dining and you'll find dozens of excellent restaurants within a minute's walk in either direction.

Beyond the restaurants listed here, there are dozens of other budget restaurants, all offering the same standard menu of, well, pretty well anything, and all serving remarkably similar and often very bland food. What marks the difference between these places is the atmosphere, music, service and who happens to be there on the night.

BUDGET

Yangling Tibetan Restaurant (Map p140; Saatghumti Chowk; momos Rs 60-80; ☺ closed Sat) Both locals and tourists flock to this unpretentious family-run place for possibly the best momos (dumplings) in town (try the chicken ones). The kitchen here is a nonstop momo production line.

Shree Lal House of Vegetarian Restaurant (Map p140; ☎ 2093021; mains Rs 60-120) Vegetarians and vegans love this bright and modern family-run place for its vegetarian Indian dishes, South Indian *dosas* (fried lentil-flour pancakes) and open kitchen. The food is tasty and good value for a light meal. The lababdar roll comes with nuts, onion, pepper, carrot and paneer (cottage cheese).

Nargila Restaurant (Map p140; ☎ 4700712; mains Rs 60-150; ☺ 1-10pm) Across from the Northfield Cafe, on the 1st floor, this somewhat dour budget favourite is a quiet place to just take a break from the bustle outside. Try a *shwarma* (grilled meat and salad in a pitta; Rs 185) or hummus served with pitta (Rs 105), washed down by a mint tea. The hot waffle with fruit and yoghurt (Rs 125) is simply the best in Kathmandu.

Zaika (Map p140; ☎ 4701785; mains Rs 60-160) Finding a really cheap meal is getting harder and harder in Kathmandu, so this new cheapie is a useful addition. The Indian dishes, momos, baguette sandwiches and Newari snacks aren't exactly haute cuisine but the food is cheap and tasty.

Yak Restaurant (Map p140; mains Rs 70-155) An unpretentious and reliable Tibetan-run place at the other end of Thamel. The booths give it a 'Tibetan diner' vibe and the clientele is a mix of trekkers, Sherpa guides and local Tibetans who come to shoot the breeze over a cigarette and a tube of *tongba* (hot millet beer). The menu includes Tibetan dishes, with good *ko-*

they (fried momos), and some Indian dishes, at unbeatable prices. It feels just like a trekking lodge, down to that familiar electronic sound of a chicken being strangled every time a dish leaves the kitchen.

Chang Cheng Restaurant (Map p140; Centre Point Hotel; veg dishes Rs 80-120, meat Rs 180-300) The real deal for Chinese food, and often full of visiting Chinese business people and Chinese Tibetans who shout, smoke, slurp and burp their way through large portions of wonderfully spicy Sichuanese food.

Dahua Restaurant (Map p140; ☎ 4410247; dishes Rs 80-150) In contrast, this definitely isn't 'real' China – sticky sweet-and-sours and egg foo yong are the rule here – but it's quiet, cosy and tasty, and the price is right. It's on the eastern edge of Thamel.

Old Tashi Delek Rest (Map p140; mains Rs 90-140) This place, a long-time favourite, feels like a trekking lodge that's been transplanted from Everest into a Thamel time warp. Prices are decent, the Tibetan momos (especially the *richosse* momo soup) are authentic, and the spinach mushroom enchilada (Rs 140) is surprisingly good for Tibetan-Mexican food (Tib-Mex?). It's down a corridor, slap bang in the centre of the Thamel action.

Thakali Kitchen (Map p140; ☎ 4701910; veg/nonveg daal bhaat Rs 95/140; ☺ 10am-10pm) If, after having travelled all the way to Nepal, you actually fancy some Nepali food (!), this upstairs restaurant is a modern place popular with local Thamel workers on their lunch break. Most opt for daal bhaat but there's also a range of Thakali food such as *aa lang kho*, a dried meat, cheese and radish soup.

Delima Garden Cafe (Map p140; mains Rs 100-250) If you can't decide whether you want baked beans or Thai coconut chicken, this garden restaurant down an alleyway away from the traffic in Paknajol covers all the bases. The lush garden surroundings are nice but the food can be a bit hit and miss. There are plenty of breakfast choices.

Pilgrims Feed 'N Read (Map p140; ☎ 4700942; mains Rs 110-180, set meal Rs 250) Keep walking past the self-help section of Pilgrims Book House and you'll end up in this quiet and classy cafe, with indoor and garden seating. The focus is on herbal teas (Rs 60 per pot) and vegetarian

Indian food (including *dosas*) and there's no shortage of reading material.

Utse Restaurant (Map p140; mains Rs 120-160) In the hotel of the same name, this is one of the longest-running restaurants in Thamel and it turns out excellent Tibetan dishes, including unusual Tibetan desserts that you won't find anywhere else. The decor feels lifted straight from Lhasa. For a group blowout, *gacok* (also spelt *gyakok*) is a form of hotpot named after the brass tureen that is heated at the table and from which various meats and vegetables are served (Rs 720 for two). The set meals are a worthy extravagance.

Or2k (Map p140; ☎ 4422097; www.or2k.com; mains Rs 130-200) This popular Israeli-run vegetarian restaurant is our current favourite for fresh and light Middle Eastern dishes. The menu spreads to crêpes, soups, zucchini pie, coconut tofu and *ziva* (pastry fingers filled with cheese). The mood is bright and buzzy. All seating is on cushions on the floor; you have to take your shoes off so make sure you're wearing your clean pair of socks. A small stand at street level serves takeaway felafel wraps (Rs 110).

Hankook Sarang (Map p140; ☎ 4256615; mains Rs 150-300) Currently our favourite Asian food fix, the Hankook is that rare combination of authentic taste and good value. Korean staples like *bibambap* and *bulgogi* (barbecued beef cooked at your table and eaten with lettuce) come with crunchy *kimchi*, salad, soup, dried fish, sweet beans and green tea. *Bibambap* is rice and vegetables in a stone pot, to which you add the egg and sweet chilli sauce and mix it all together. The service is excellent and there's a pleasant alfresco garden. It's down a courtyard near Tamas Lounge.

KC's Restaurant (Map p140; ☎ 4701387; mains Rs 190-290) One of Thamel's first restaurants, KC's has been going since 1976 and is still one of the best places in town. The oatmeal pumpkin pie (Rs 190) is sweet but tasty, the salads and pasta are excellent, and there's a good range of breakfasts, including sausage and beans in a bun. The terrace seating is very pleasant.

A good option for local Thakali daal bhaat is the **Mustang Thakal** (daal bhaat Rs 140), above the

Shree Lal House of Vegetarian Restaurant, and popular with local Manangis.

MIDRANGE
Northfield Cafe (Map p140; breakfast Rs 115-220, mains Rs 240-350; ⊙ 7am-10.30pm) Next door to Pilgrims, this open-air spot is the place for serious breakfast devotees (huevos rancheros included), with the option of half or full portions. The Mexican and Indian tandoori dishes (dinner only) are excellent and the sunny garden is a real plus in winter. It's also one of the few places to offer kids' meals.

Dechenling (Map p140; ☎ 4412158; mains Rs 150-260, fixed meal Rs 410) Quality Tibetan and Indian food is served up in this attractive beer garden, and it's one of the few places in town to offer interesting Bhutanese dishes such as *kewa dhatsi* (potatoes and cheese curry). The *thukpa* (Tibetan noodle soup; Rs 150) is the best in Thamel. If you can't decide, opt for a Tibetan or Bhutanese set meal washed down with a draught Everest Beer. No wonder the Tibetan name means Place of Joy.

K-Too Beer & Steakhouse (Map p140; ☎ 4700043; www.kilroygroup.com; mains Rs 160-450, glass of wine Rs 160-245) Run by the same people who run Kilroy's, the decor and furnishings here are deliberately rough-and-ready pub style, and the food and atmosphere are excellent. Dishes range from Irish stew to spinach and potato salad with honey mustard dressing, and the excellent pepper steak (Rs 420) followed by fried apple momos is already a post-trekking classic. Live European football is broadcast on the TV. For a quieter vibe head for the garden.

Third Eye Restaurant (Map p140; mains Rs 200-230) Next door to Yin Yang, and run by the same people, this is a long-running favourite that retains something of the old Kathmandu atmosphere. There's a sit-down section at the front, and a more informal section with low tables and cushions at the back and a rooftop terrace. Indian food is the speciality and the tandoori dishes are especially good.

Krua Thai Restaurant (Map p140; ☎ 4701291; mains Rs 200-280) North of Sam's Bar, this is another good open-air Thai place. The food is reasonably authentic (ie spicy), with good curries,

NEPALI & NEWARI RESTAURANTS

A growing number of restaurants around town specialise in Nepali (mostly Newari) food (see p68 for a rundown of Newari dishes). These run the gamut from unobtrusive little places in Thamel to fancy converted palaces with cultural shows, linen tablecloths and 15-course banquets. Most places offer a set meal, either veg or nonveg, and you dine on cushions at low tables. The 'cultural shows' consist of musicians and dancers performing 'traditional' song and dance routines. The whole thing is pretty touristy, but it's a fun night out nonetheless. At most places it's a good idea to make a reservation during the high season.

Thamel House Restaurant (Map p140; ☎ 4410388; www.thamelhouse.com.np; dishes Rs 225, veg/nonveg set meal Rs 550/650) In Paknajol, this place is set in a traditional old Newari building and has bags of atmosphere. The food is traditional Nepali and Newari. Ask for the à la carte menu and choose individual dishes or go for the blowout set meal. It's also open for lunch.

Baithak (Map p126; ☎ 4267346; 12-course set menu Rs 945, snacks Rs 200; ⏲ 10am-10pm) At Babar Mahal Revisited, southeast of the centre (see p158), this restaurant has a dramatic and regal, almost Victorian, setting, with crystal and linens, and where diners are attended by waiters dressed in royal costume and watched over by looming portraits of various disapproving Ranas. The menu features 'Rana cuisine', a courtly cuisine created by Nepali Brahmin chefs and heavily influenced by north Indian Mughal cuisine. The setting is probably the most memorable part of the restaurant. Vegetarians will find plenty to eat here. The attached K2 Bar has a delightful terrace for a pre-dinner drink. A *baithak* is a royal suite or state room.

Nepali Chulo (Map p126; ☎ 4220475; set menu Rs 960, mains Rs 280) Closer to Thamel is this 157-year-old former Rana palace, the Phora Durbar. Most people choose the fixed menu of 11 dishes.

Bhojan Griha (Map pp114-15; ☎ 4416423; www.bhojangriha.com; set menu Rs 997) In the same vein as Bhanchha Ghar (below), but perhaps more ambitious, Bhojan Griha is located in a recently restored 150-year-old mansion in Dilli Bazaar, just east of the city centre. It's worth eating here just to see the imaginative renovation of this beautiful old building, once the residence of the caste of royal priests. Most of the seating is traditional (ie on cushions on the floor), although these are actually legless chairs, which saves your back and knees. In an effort to reduce waste, plastic is not used in the restaurant and mineral water is bought in bulk and sold by the glass.

Bhanchha Ghar (Map p126; ☎ 4225172; per person Rs 1000, beer Rs 250; ⏲ 11am-10pm) You'll find Bhanchha Ghar in a traditional three-storey Newari house in Kamaladi, just east of Durbar Marg, next to a Ganesh Temple. There is an upstairs loft bar where you can stretch out on handmade carpets and cushions for a drink, snacks and the obligatory cultural show (try to arrive before 7pm). You can then move downstairs to take advantage of an excellent set menu of traditional Nepali dishes and delicacies. Musicians stroll between the tables playing traditional Nepali folk songs.

Krishnarpan Restaurant (Map pp114-15; ☎ 4470770; www.dwarikas.com; 6-course meal US$24, 22-course meal US$37; ⏲ dinner only) One of the best places for Nepali food is the Krishnarpan Restaurant at Dwarika's Hotel, east of the centre near the Ring Rd. The atmosphere is superb and the food gets consistent praise from diners. Bookings are advisable. If you are coming on Friday, arrive in time for the 6pm dance show in the hotel courtyard and take advantage of happy hour.

tom yam soup and papaya salad, although some dishes taste more Chinese than Thai.

Ciao Ciao (Map p140; ☎ 4413724; Bhagwan Bahal; mains Rs 200-300) Further out on the fringes of Thamel, this restaurant is good for authentic Italian food, including interesting antipasti dishes and desserts like tiramisu, served in the garden or on the terrace.

La Dolce Vita (Map p140; ☎ 4700612; pizzas Rs 210-350, pasta Rs 250) Life is indeed sweet at Thamel's best Italian bistro, offering up delights such as parmesan gnocchi; excellent antipasti; goat's cheese, spinach and walnut ravioli; sinfully rich chocolate torte and wines by the glass. Choose between the rustic red-and-white tablecloths and terracotta tiles of the main restaurant, a rooftop garden, the yummy-smelling espresso bar (real Lavazza coffee) or sunny lounge space; either way the atmosphere and food are excellent. It's right on the corner opposite Kathmandu Guest House.

Four Season Restaurant (Map p140; ☎ 4701715; Trilok Plaza; dishes Rs 250-310) A great location and some of the tastiest Thai and Indian food in town make this a good compromise if you fancy a chicken tikka masala but your date wants a green papaya salad. You can sit overlooking the road or on the rooftop under what looks like an aircraft hangar. One of the chefs is Thai, the other worked at the Rum Doodle for 17 years, so they know their stuff.

New Orleans Cafe (Map p140; ☎ 4700736; mains Rs 270-425) Hidden down an alley near the Brezel Bakery, New Orleans boasts a relaxed and intimate candlelit vibe and a great selection of music, often live. It's a popular spot for a drink but the menu also ranges far and wide, from Thai curries and good burgers to Creole jambalaya and oven-roasted vegies, plus good breakfasts.

Yin Yang Restaurant (Map p140; ☎ 4425510; Thai curries Rs 280) Just south of the intersection, this is one of Thamel's most highly regarded restaurants. It serves authentic Thai food cooked by a Thai chef with either garden or floor seating. It's not cheap but the food is a definite cut above the imitation Thai food found elsewhere. The green curry is authentically spicy – the massaman curry (with onion, peanut and potato) is sweeter. There's a good range of vegetable choices.

Fire & Ice Restaurant (Map p140; ☎ 4250210; 219 Sanchaya Kosh Bhawan, Tridevi Marg; pizzas Rs 320-380; ⏰ 8am-11pm) Rumour has it that this was a favourite of Prince Dipendra and his girlfriend, before he massacred his entire family in 2001 (don't worry, no one's blaming the pizza). Regardless, it's an excellent and informal Italian place, serving some of the best pizzas in Kathmandu, imported Italian soft-serve ice cream, seriously good Illy espresso and rousing opera – Italian, of course. It's very popular and you'll need a reservation in the high season.

Roadhouse Cafe (Map p140; ☎ 4267005, Arcadia Bldg; pizzas Rs 320-400) The big attraction here is the pizzas from the wood-fired oven. The pizzas are pretty darn good, and the decor, especially the courtyard out back, is warm and intimate. The salads, soups (tomato coconut soup), desserts (sizzling brownie with ice cream) and espresso coffees are all top-notch, though some say the service has slipped recently. Credit cards are accepted.

Kilroy's (Map p140; ☎ 4250441; www.kilroygroup.com; mains Rs 345-700; ⏰ 9am-10pm) Named after the Irish founder and chef, this place is a definite cut above the average Thamel restaurant. The menu ranges from Balti chicken

(Rs 345) to Irish stew (Rs 355) and interesting hybrids such as seafood *thukpa* with lemongrass (Rs 400), plus great desserts, especially the bread-and-butter pudding (Rs 195). The menu is posted online. You can sit inside, or outside in the shady garden, complete with waterfall.

Freak Street (Jochne)

Freak St has a number of budget restaurants where you can find good food at lower prices than Thamel. Even if you're staying in other areas of the city it's nice to know there are some good places for lunch if you're sightseeing around Durbar Sq.

Snowman Restaurant (Map p126; cakes Rs 50) A long-running and mellow, if slightly dingy, place, this is one of those rare Kathmandu hang-outs that attracts both locals and backpackers. The chocolate cake has been drawing overland travellers for close to 40 years now. When John Lennon starts singing 'I am the Walrus' on the stereo it suddenly feels like 1967 all over again...

Diyalo Restaurant (Map p126; mains Rs 70-130) At the Annapurna Lodge, this is a cosy little garden restaurant with a large menu, including tasty crêpes, burgers and a few Chinese, Mexican and Indian dishes, all for less than Rs 130.

Kumari Restaurant (Map p126; mains Rs 80-200, set Nepali meals Rs 160-195) Next to the Century Lodge, this friendly hang-out attracts the densest collection of dreadlocked travellers in Kathmandu and is one of few places that seems to have hung onto some of the mellowness of times past. All the travellers' favourites are here.

Royal Park Guest House (Map p120; ☎ 4247487; mains Rs 150-250) For a good-value lunch with a view over Basantapur Sq, try the rooftop restaurant of this budget hotel on the square's south side.

Festive Fare Restaurant (Map p120; ☎ 4232004; mains Rs 375; ⏰ 9am-5pm) Overlooking Basantapur Sq, this restaurant has unsurpassed views from its top-floor terrace and attracts a mainly tour-group crowd. Prices are about double those of the Freak St cheapies.

Central Kathmandu

The restaurants in the Kantipath and Durbar Marg areas are generally more expensive than around Thamel, although there are a few exceptions. See the last few listings here and the boxed text, opposite, for some of Kathmandu's worthwhile splurges.

KATHMANDU

BUDGET

Dudh Sagar (Map p140; ☎ 4232263; Kantipath; dosas Rs 40-70; ☺ 8am-8pm) This is the place to reacquaint yourself with South Indian vegetarian snacks like *dosas* and *idly* (pounded rice cakes), topped off with Indian sweets like *barfi* (fudge) and *gulab jamun* (deep-fried milk balls in rose-flavoured syrup). A *masala dosa* followed by *dudh malai* (cream cheese balls in chilled pistachio milk) makes a great meal for less than Rs 80.

MIDRANGE & TOP END

Kaiser Cafe (Map p126 ☎ 4425341; Garden of Dreams, Tridevi Marg; mains Rs 240-700; ☺ 9am-10pm) This cafe/restaurant in the Garden of Dreams is run by Dwarika's (see p149) so quality is high. It's a fine place for a light meal (such as crêpes stuffed with mushroom, asparagus and grated cheese) or to linger over a pot of tea or something stiffer at the stylish bar. The Austrian dishes are a nod to the country that financed and oversaw the garden's restoration. You have to pay the garden's admission fee to eat here.

Koto Restaurant (Map p126; ☎ 4226025; Durbar Marg; dishes Rs 250-300, set menu Rs 530; ☺ 11.30am-3pm & 6-9.15pm) Koto has long been a favourite of ours and, now that the Thamel branch is dead, you'll have to head to pricier Durbar Marg for your fresh mackerel fix. There's a wide range of decent Japanese dishes, from cold soba noodles to sukiyaki, plus several set menus.

1905 (Map p140; ☎ 4225272; www.1905restaurant .com; Kantipath; mains Rs 400-800) You can dine with ambassadors and ministers in this classy top-end restaurant set in a charming former Rana summer palace. The tables on a bridge over a wonderful lily pond add a definite colonial Burmese feel, so it's fitting that there are several Southeast Asian dishes on offer. Lunch is light and casual, with sandwiches and salads. Dinner is a more serious affair, so dress up for dishes such as beef Wellington or salmon mousse layered in rainbow trout ratatouille and tomato hollandaise sauce. If nothing else, it's a very romantic place for drinks.

Ghar-e-Kebab (Map p126; dishes Rs 425-800; ☺ 6.30-11pm) Inside the Hotel de l'Annapurna on Durbar Marg, this has some of the best north Indian and tandoori food in the city. Indian miniatures hang on the walls and in the evenings classical Indian music is played and traditional Urdu *ghazals* (love songs) are sung. Try the pistachio sherbet for dessert.

Chimney (Map p126; ☎ 4248999; mains Rs 600-1100; ☺ 6.30-10pm) At the Yak & Yeti Hotel, northwest of the centre, this is one of Kathmandu's most famous restaurants, named after the famous open fireplace. It now serves mostly continental cuisine, with the excellent borscht and chicken à la Kiev two of the last links with its Russian roots.

Elsewhere
BUDGET

Lazimpat Gallery Cafe (Map p126; ☎ 4428549; Lazimpat; mains Rs 90-150; ☺ 9am-8pm Sun-Fri) This friendly place occupies a unique niche, somewhere between a greasy spoon and an art cafe, with a menu boasting both beans on toast and fresh carrot and coriander soup. Everything from the cakes to the juices is made fresh on the spot. It's great for a cheap, light lunch, especially if you're out in Lazimpat and suddenly need a cheese-and-ham toastie. It's run by a British former VSO worker so it's a popular hideaway for local volunteers. Friday night is film night and there's free wi-fi all the time.

MIDRANGE & TOP END

Mike's Breakfast (Map pp114-15; ☎ 4424303; breakfasts Rs 160-290; ☺ 7am-9pm) As the name suggests, this place specialises in big American-style breakfasts (Mike was a former Peace Corps worker), served up to a mix of expats and well-heeled locals. It's a bit out of the way but it's certainly a laid-back way to start (and occupy most of) the day, in the attractive, leafy garden of an old Rana house. The breakfast menu includes excellent waffles, fresh juices and great eggs Florentine (Rs 345); all prices include organic Nepali coffee from Palpa. Lunch extends to Mexican quesadillas and daily salad/soup combos; the barbecue fires up on Sunday evenings (Rs 550). While you're here take a wander through the excellent Indigo Gallery (see p157). The restaurant is in the suburb of Naxal, about 15 minutes' walk from the top end of Durbar Marg.

Koketsu (Map pp114-15; ☎ 6218513; Panipokhari; teppanyaki Rs 200-400, sushi Rs 300-1000; ☺ noon-3pm, 5-10pm) If your focus is more on eating than soaking, then Koketsu is probably the best Japanese place in town. It takes a brave person to order sushi in the Himalaya but the seafood here is flown in fresh from Thailand, as are the *takosu* (marinated octopus), squid and roe. The focal point of the restaurant is definitely the central teppanyaki grill. It's no coincidence that the Japanese embassy is across the road.

Royal Hana Garden (Map p126; ☎ 4416200; Lazimpat; mains Rs 260-420; ⏰ 10am-10pm) This place is a bit of a secret – there are two outdoor hot-spring baths (admission Rs 340, includes towel and shampoo, Thursday to Saturday from 3pm only) where you can luxuriate for as long as you like before heading inside for a very reasonably priced Japanese meal. It's perfect for small groups and it's worth ringing ahead to book a soak. The restaurant is in Lazimpat, just north of the Hotel Ambassador.

Chez Caroline (Map p126; ☎ 4263070; mains Rs 450-1150; ⏰ 9.30am-10pm) In the Babar Mahal Revisited complex (p158), Caroline's is a swanky outdoor cafe/restaurant popular with expat foodies. It offers French-influenced main courses such as wild mushroom tart with walnut sauce, quiche, salads and crêpes, plus imported cheese, daily specials and a wide range of desserts, teas and wines. Try a swift glass of pastis (liquorice-flavoured liqueur) with mint syrup: it's the perfect aperitif to an afternoon's shopping.

Dwarika's Hotel (p149) has a candlelit Friday night poolside barbecue (Rs 899) and dance show that makes for a great splurge. See the boxed text, p152, for details of the hotel's Krishnarpan Restaurant.

There are also several excellent midrange and top-end dining options in Patan (see p191), a short taxi ride away.

Quick Eats

Curry Kitchen/Hot Bread (Map p140; pastries Rs 40-70) This bakery on the main Thamel junction does a roaring trade in sandwiches, bread rolls, pizza slices and pastries. Add an espresso and head upstairs to the sunny terrace for a leisurely breakfast. The ham-and-cheese rolls (Rs 65) make a great lunch on the run. Bakery items are discounted by 50% after 9.30pm.

Bakery Cafe (Map p140; ☎ 4422616; www.nanglos .com; Rs 60-150 snacks; Tridevi Marg; ⏰ 7am-9.30pm) With branches on the eastern edge of Thamel, on Durbar Marg and in Patan (see p192), this buzzy chain offers excellent-value coffees and snacks for when you just need to take a break over an Americano and a plate of momos. The management have commendably hired deaf staff, which is perhaps one reason why the music is so bad.

Pumpernickel Bakery (Map p140; mains Rs 80-250) Bleary-eyed tourists crowd in here every morning for fresh croissants, yak-cheese sandwiches, pastries and filter coffee in the pleasant garden area at the back. The restaurant is self-service.

BK's Place (Map p140; chips Rs 110-160) This place has a well-deserved reputation for good old-fashioned chips (French fries), with a variety of sauces, as well as good momos. It's a tiny place, west of the Rum Doodle.

Weizen Bakery (Map p140; mains Rs 150-280) Down from the Yin Yang, this bakery restaurant serves good vegetarian food. It has a pleasant garden and is a nice quiet place for breakfast, with newspapers to read and music playing in the background. The bakery out front has decent cakes, breads (particularly the pretzels) and pastries, with bakery goods (but not cakes) discounted by 50% after 8pm.

Self-Catering

For trekking food such as noodles, nuts, dried fruit and cheese, there are a number of small supermarkets in Thamel, including the Best Shopping Centre (Map p140) on the edge of Thamel at the end of Tridevi Marg.

The Bluebird Supermarkets (Map p126) have a wide variety of goods. The largest branch is by the main bridge across the Bagmati River to Patan and has a decent food court; there's another branch in Lazimpat, near the French embassy. The Kasthamandap Bazaar Supermarket (Map p126), just off the southern end of Durbar Marg, also has a good selection.

Bhat Bhateni Supermarket (Map pp114-15; ☎ 4419181) is the largest in the city, though it has a slightly inconvenient location south of the Chinese embassy.

DRINKING

There are a few bars scattered around Thamel, all within a short walk of each other. Just poke your nose in to see which has the crowd and style that appeals. Most places have a happy hour between 5pm and 8pm, with two-for-one cocktails. Thamel's bar scene was hit recently by a government decision to close bars at 11pm, though this may change.

Rum Doodle Restaurant & Bar (Map p140; ☎ 4701208; mains Rs 270-500; ⏰ 10am-10pm) Named after the world's highest mountain, the 40,000½ft Mt Rum Doodle (according to WE Bowman, author of *The Ascent of Rum Doodle*, a spoof of serious mountaineering books), this famous bar is still milking a dusty (1983!) *Time* magazine accolade as 'one of the world's best bars'. It's long been a favourite meeting place for mountaineering expeditions – Edmund Hillary, Reinhold Messner, Ang Rita Sherpa and Rob Hall have left their mark on the walls – and a visit here feels like a bit of a pilgrimage for mountain lovers. Trekking groups can add their own yeti footprint trek report to the dozens plastered on the walls. The restaurant serves up decent steaks, pasta and pizza and there's often live music. You can eat here free for life – the only catch is that you have to conquer Everest first! It's worth a visit but is somewhat overrated.

Maya Cocktail Bar (Map p140; cocktails Rs 200; ☻ 4-11pm) A long-running favourite; the two-for-one cocktails between 4pm and 7pm are a guaranteed jump-start to a good evening. The associated and nearby Pub Maya (Map p140) is somewhat more boisterous.

Tom & Jerry Pub (Map p140; pool per half hr Rs 50) Close to Nargila Restaurant, this is a long-running, rowdy upstairs place that has pool tables and a dance floor. Thursday is ladies' night.

Jatra (Map p140; ☎ 4211010; mains Rs 160-220) An intimate and pretty cool venue for a beer or dinner, with indoor and outdoor seating. Friday nights bring live music jams; on Wednesdays ladies get a free cocktail.

Tamas Lounge (Map p140; ☎ 4275658; drinks Rs 300) *Sex and the City* fans will enjoy this glam lounge bar, decked out with plush, velvety sofas and a lush palette of cool creams. Take a seat in the courtyard or the old Rana house and indulge your inner princess with a sparkling Bellini or espresso martini. Live music livens things up on Saturday and Wednesday and a basement spa is on the way. The entrance is suitably low-key, hidden down an alleyway just south of Yin Yang Restaurant.

J-Bar (Map p140; ☎ 4418209; drinks Rs 250-300; ☻ 6pm-midnight Tue-Fri & Sun, 3pm-2am Sat) At the back of Himalayan Java, the J-Bar is more like a New York club than a Nepal bar, with cream leather interiors and pricey drinks; it's a place to rub shoulders with Nepal's beautiful set. Expect a cover charge on Fridays. After 10pm access is via the side alley.

Himalayan Java (Map p140; ☎ 4422519; Tridevi Marg; coffee Rs 60-100, breakfast Rs 110-200; ☻ 8am-9pm) Above the Bakery Cafe, this modern and buzzing coffeehouse serves good espresso

and fine paninis and cakes, in addition to decent breakfasts. There's a sunny balcony, lots of sofas and big-screen TV for the football, but from certain angles it feels a bit like a hotel foyer. It's popular with hip middle-class Nepalis and there's wi-fi.

Other long-timers include **Sam's Bar** (Map p140; ☻ 4-11pm), a cosy place with reggae every Saturday, and **Full Moon** (Map p140; beer Rs 175; ☻ 6-11pm), a tiny chill-out bar and den of iniquity that draws a mixed Nepali-foreign clientele.

ENTERTAINMENT

Nepal is an early-to-bed country and even in Kathmandu you'll find few people on the streets after 10pm, especially when the capital's political situation is tense. Most bars close their doors by 11pm, though a few keep serving those inside.

Duelling cover bands compete for aural supremacy at various Thamel restaurants on Friday and Saturday nights in the high season, particularly at Jatra and New Orleans Cafe – just follow your ears.

Beyond this, you could take in a Bollywood blockbuster or try to earn back your flight money at one of half a dozen casinos. Major sporting events such as Premier League football and Formula 1 grand prixs are televised in all the major bars.

There are also several cultural performances, which generally involve local youths wearing a variety of dress over their jeans and performing traditional dances from Nepal's various ethnic groups, accompanied by a live band that includes a tabla, harmonium and singer.

Casinos

Kathmandu's casinos are all attached to up-market hotels and open 24 hours. Pull your tuxedo out of your backpack, polish up your best Sean Connery impersonation ('Aaah, Mish Moneypenny…') and make a beeline for the **Casino Royale** (Map p126; ☎ 4271244), set in a former Rana palace at the Yak & Yeti Hotel. Hang around the tables (not the slots) long enough and staff will ply you with free drinks and a dinner buffet, though sadly the Russian dancing girls have gone back to Moscow.

The other casinos, like **Casino Anna** (Map p126; ☎ 4225228) at the Hotel de l'Annapurna, attract a mainly Indian crowd. New casinos have opened recently at the Shangri-La and Malla hotels.

KATHMANDU ART

If you have a particular interest in Nepali art the following galleries might be worth visiting. Check the websites to see what's being exhibited.

Indigo Gallery (Map pp114-15; ☎ 4424303; Naxal; ⏲ 8.30am-5pm) An upmarket gallery at Mike's Breakfast (see p154) set in a lovely old Rana building; excellent exhibits of modern thangkas, photography and prints, most for sale at top-end prices.

National Birendra Art Gallery (Map pp114-15; ☎ 4411729; admission Rs 75; ⏲ 9am-5pm Sun-Fri) The offbeat location in a crumbling old Rana palace is probably more interesting than the dusty collection of Nepali oils and watercolours.

Siddhartha Art Gallery (Map p126; ☎ 4218048; www.siddharthaartgallery.com; Babar Mahal Revisited; ⏲ 11am-6pm Sun-Fri, noon-4pm Sat) The best in the city, with a wide range of top-notch exhibitions.

At all casinos you can play in either Indian rupees or US dollars, and winnings (in the same currency) can be taken out of the country when you leave. The main games offered are roulette and blackjack. Most clients are Indian; Nepalis are officially forbidden from entering.

Music & Dance

There are a few performances of Nepali music and dancing in the restaurants of the top-end hotels but little is scheduled. The best live music is to be found by heading further afield to Moksh in Patan (p193).

Kalamandapa Institute of Classical Nepalese Performing Arts (Map p126; ☎ 4271545; admission incl tea Rs 400) Nepali dances (and occasional theatre) are performed here at the Hotel Vajra most Tuesdays at 7pm. Phone ahead to check schedules. There are authentic Newari music concerts (Rs 500) on Sunday, and sometimes Friday, evenings.

Gandharba Culture and Art Organisation (Map p140; ☎ 4700292; http://gandharbas.nyima.org) This is an organisation for the city's musician caste. There are informal music jams between 5pm and 7pm at their offices on the 3rd floor above Equator Expeditions (tourists are welcome), but they also play in local restaurants such as the Northfield Cafe (see p151). Individual musicians offer music lessons for around Rs 200 per hour (see p363) and they also sell their own CDs.

Upstairs Jazz Bar (Map p126; ☎ 4410436; cover Rs 200) It's worth schlepping out to Lazimpat on a Wednesday and Saturday night (from 8pm) to catch the live jazz in this tiny upstairs bar. The clientele is an interesting mix of locals and expats.

Weekly sitar concerts accompany dinner every Sunday at the Pilgrims Feed 'N Read restaurant in Pilgrims Book House, and fusion music concerts are planned for Thursdays.

Cinemas

Sadly the video cafes made famous by the title of Pico Iyer's book *Video Night in Kathmandu* have almost disappeared, with only a couple hanging on in Freak St.

Kathmandu Guest House Minitheatre (Map p140; admission Rs 100) The Kathmandu Guest House still shows nightly films in its 25-seat theatre.

Jai Nepal Cinema (Map p126; ☎ 4442220; www.jainepal.com; Narayanhiti Marg; stalls Rs 100-150, balcony Rs 200), on the south side of the New Royal Palace, and its branch the Kumari Cinema (Map p126) show some foreign films in English and are the best in town.

Elsewhere, Bollywood-style Hindi and Nepali films are the usual fare. Admission charges are minimal and the films are worth attending, since understanding the language is only a minor hindrance to enjoying these comedy-musical spectaculars. Indians call them 'masala movies' as they have a little bit of everything in them.

SHOPPING

Everything that is turned out in the various centres around the valley can be found in Kathmandu, although you can often find a better choice, or more unusual items, in the centres that produce the items – Jawalakhel (southern Patan) for Tibetan carpets; Patan for cast-metal statues; Bhaktapur for woodcarvings; and Thimi for masks. For more tips on shopping see p373.

Thamel in particular can be a pretty stressful place to shop, what with all the tiger balm sellers, rickshaw drivers and high-speed motorbikers. Dive into a side street or garden haven when stress levels start to rise.

KATHMANDU

Amrita Craft Collection (Map p140; ☎ 4240757; www.amrita.com.np) This is a good place to start, with a broad collection of crafts and clothing. Subtract 20% from its fixed prices and you get a good benchmark for what you should aim to pay on the street if you don't mind haggling. The branch across the road has a larger selection.

Aroma Garden (Map p140; ☎ 4420724) As the name suggests, this is Thamel's sweetest-smelling shop. It's a good one-stop shop for incense, essential oils, soaps and almost anything else that smells great.

Originally built in 1919, **Babar Mahal Revisited** (Map p126) is a unique complex of old Rana palace outbuildings that has been redeveloped to house a warren of chic clothes shops, designer galleries and handicraft shops, as well as a couple of top-end restaurants and bars. It's aimed squarely at expats and wealthy locals so prices are as high as the quality. It's southeast of the city near the Singh Durbar government offices.

There are dozens of shops in Thamel that sell handmade paper products from photo albums to paper lamps. One of the better shops is **Paper Park** (Map p140; ☎ 4700475; www.handmade paperpark.com), next to the Hotel Marshyangdi.

Bronze Statues

Patan is the place to shop for statues (see p194). This is one area where research is vitally important, as quality and prices do not necessarily correlate. The best shops in central Kathmandu are on Durbar Marg; **Curio Arts** (Map p126; ☎ 4224871; www.devasarts.com) is a good place to start.

Clothing

Kathmandu is the best place for ready-to-wear Western clothes. Embroidered T-shirts are a popular speciality (our favourite has '*Same Same...*' on the front and '*...But Different*' on the back!) and you can custom any design or logo, preferably on your own higher-quality T-shirt. Expect it to shrink in the wash.

A few tailors in central Thamel and Lazimpat stock Chinese silks and can make pretty much anything that you can explain, including copies of your favourite shirt or dress. There are lots of funky hats, felt bags, jumpers etc, particularly on the twisting road known as Saatghumti, but *please* think twice before buying those red stripy juggling pants… Always try clothes on before handing over the cash.

DZI BEADS

Wherever you find Tibetan Buddhism, you'll find the striped agate beads known as *dzi*. First recorded in 2000 BC, these beads are believed to act as amulets, protecting the wearer from spiritual and physical harm. Special properties are linked to the patterns of stripes and 'eyes' that are etched onto the surface of the beads and collectors have been known to pay more than US$5000 for a single bead. Some *dzi* even have marks where stone has been chipped away to be used as medicine. Interestingly, similar beads have been found in Neolithic tombs in Persia and the Mediterranean.

Popular and unique items include felt bags (from Rs 250) and impossibly cute baby-sized North Face fleeces (Rs 300) or Tibetan jackets.

Curios

An endless supply of curios, art pieces and plain old junk is churned out for the tourist trade. Most does not come from Tibet but from the local Tamang community and doesn't date back much further than, well, last month, but that doesn't put most people off. Basantapur Sq in old Kathmandu's Durbar Sq is the headquarters for this trade, but before you lock wits with these operators, visit the **Amrita Craft Collection** (Map p140; ☎ 4240757).

Gems & Jewellery

Buying gems is always a risky business unless you know what you're doing – see p366 for a warning on gem scams. Be immediately suspicious of anyone who tells you that you will be able to make an enormous profit – if this was possible and legal they would do it themselves.

There are dozens of jewellery shops in Kathmandu – including in Thamel, on New Rd and Durbar Marg. When walking between Thamel and Durbar Sq you'll often come across tiny silver workshops.

The prices for silver jewellery are very low compared with what you'd pay at home, and many people have jewellery made to order. You buy the stones or draw the design and they'll make it up, usually in just a day or two. The quality is usually excellent, but be sure to agree on a price before giving the go-ahead.

If you feel like making your own adornments, many shops sell loose Tibetan beads, including ceremonial *dzi* beads (see the boxed text, opposite).

Fair-Trade Handicrafts

For general handicrafts such as handmade paper, ceramics and woodwork – much of it made by disadvantaged or minority groups – the best places are the showrooms of the nonprofit development organisations that are based in the Kopundol district of Patan. See p193 for details. One of these shops, **Mahaguthi** (Map p126; ☎ 4438760; ⏰ 10am-6.30pm Sun-Fri, 10am-5pm Sat), has an outlet in Lazimpat.

Other nearby fair trade shops include **Folk Nepal** (Map p126; ☎ 4414670; www.folknepal.org; ⏰ 9am-7pm Sun-Fri, 10am-5pm Sat) and **Third World Craft Nepal** (Map p126; ☎ 2090500; www.thirdworldcraft .com), which, although not as interesting, are worth a quick look.

Indian Goods

Since the insurgency in Kashmir killed the tourist trade there, many Kashmiris have migrated to Nepal to sell traditional crafts such as carpets, cushions, tapestry, woollen shawls and papier mâché. These guys are excellent salespeople, so buy with caution.

You'll also find a fair amount of embroidered clothing, cushions and bed linen from Gujarat and Rajasthan. Prices are higher than if you buy in India, but considerably less than if you buy in the West. Tridevi Marg is lined with colourful Indian bedspreads.

Photography

Dozens of photo shops in Thamel sell film and can process film or print out digital shots from around Rs 10 per print.

Digimax Tridevi Marg (Map p140; ☎ 4250163); Lazimpat (Map p126; ☎ 4429284) Fairly reliable, Digimax can handle colour prints and E-6 or Ektachrome slides. Mounted slide processing will cost you around Rs 500 for 36 slides. Passport photos are available on the spot (Rs 200 for nine photos).

Ganesh Photo Lab (Map p126; ☎ 4216898) In an alley southwest of Durbar Sq, Ganesh is an unlikely looking but reputedly good place for B&W processing.

New camera equipment can be a good deal in Nepal and the range of cameras and lenses is good. New Rd in central Kathmandu is the best place to look. Be sure to ascertain whether what you are buying has an international warranty.

Tea & Spices

Kathmandu is a good place to expand your home spice collection. Plenty of shops and supermarkets in Thamel sell small packets of spices, from momo mixes to chai spices, or head to Asan Tole (see p129), where the locals buy their freshly ground masalas.

Thangkas

The main centre for thangkas is just off Durbar Sq, and this is where you'll find the best salespeople (not necessarily the best thangkas). For modern work there are plenty of places in Thamel.

Phaba Chengreshi Thangka Art School (Map p140; ☎ 4220428) You can see thangkas being painted on the spot at this school in Thamel.

Dharmapala Thangka Center (Map p126; ☎ 4223715; www.thangka.de) Down an arcade, off Durbar Marg, this is a showroom for a local school of thangka painting. You can see the thangkas being painted at the nearby workshop (Map p126).

Tibetan Thangka Gallery (Map p126; ☎ 4428863) Just past the Hotel Ambassador, this is another good little place. Thangkas are painted on the spot (you can watch the artists at work) and many pieces from here end up in the Durbar Sq shops with higher price tags.

Tibetan Antiques

Kathmandu seems to be the global clearing house for a continual stream of antiques from Tibet, including thangkas, carpets, jewellery, storage chests, religious objects, saddles and clothing. Considering the cultural damage that Tibet has endured over the last half century, removing some of what remains to safety is perhaps more morally acceptable than some other 'collecting' that goes on in Nepal (see the boxed text, p61, for information on stolen Nepali artefacts). There are a number of good shops on Durbar Marg, but don't go without a very healthy wallet.

For prayer flags (Map p140) and Tibetan and Bhutanese cloth, the best place is the street in front of the Kathesimbhu Stupa south of Thamel. Choose between cheaper polyester and better-quality cotton flags and remember, this is your karma that we are talking about.

Trekking Gear

Thamel has some excellent trekking gear for sale, but don't think that you are getting the genuine article. Most of the 'Columbia' fleeces and 'North Face' jackets are made locally but with imported fleece and Gore-Tex, though most knick-knacks are imported. See p334 for details on hiring and buying trekking gear. For reliable rentals and purchase try **Shona's Alpine Rental** (Map p140; ☎ 4265120), which makes its own sleeping bags and offers unbiased advice on the best trek gear for your trip.

The better trekking gear shops are at the southern end of Thamel. **Holyland Hiking Shop** (Map p140; ☎ 4248104) and **Everest Adventure Mountaineering** (Map p140; ☎ 4259191) have been recommended.

A collection of *pukka* (authentic) gear shops on Tridevi Marg, including **Mountain Hard Wear** (Map p140; www.mountainhardwear.com .np) and the North Face, offer imported gear at foreign prices, These shops sell everything from Black Diamond climbing gear to proper Thermarests.

GETTING THERE & AWAY

See p379 for details of getting to/from Kathmandu both by air and by land from neighbouring countries.

Air

Even if your airline does not officially require you to reconfirm the return leg of your flight, you should check if this is required for flights out of Kathmandu. This goes double for the notoriously unreliable Nepal Airlines; at peak times you should reconfirm when you first arrive in Nepal and reconfirm again towards the end of your stay. Even this may not guarantee you a seat – make sure you get to the airport very early as people at the end of the queue can still be left behind.

DOMESTIC AIRLINES

The various domestic airlines have sales offices around the city but locations and phone numbers seem to change with the weather. Anyway, it's far less hassle to buy tickets through a travel agency, and you'll probably get a better deal this way. See p379 for an overview of domestic airlines.

The **Nepal Airlines domestic office** (Map p126; ☎ 4227133; ⏰ 10am-1pm & 2-5pm) has computerised booking on five routes: Pokhara, Jomsom, Lukla, Bharatpur and Manang. Other domestic

flights are booked in a much more haphazard manner, with the booking clerk happy to issue tickets as long as people keep fronting up with money. Book these tickets at the office to the side of the main Nepal Airlines international booking centre (the entrance is around the back). A special tourist counter here avoids the bulk of the booking chaos and often offers discounts of around 20% on domestic fares. The other domestic carriers are much more reliable.

Bus

LONG-DISTANCE BUSES

The **Kathmandu bus station** (Map pp114-15; Ring Rd, Balaju) is north of the city centre. It is officially called the Gongabu Bus Park, but is generally known as the Kathmandu Bus Terminal, or simply 'bus park'. This bus station is basically for all long-distance buses, including to Pokhara and destinations in the Terai. It's a huge and confusing place and there are very few signs in English, but most of the ticket sellers are very helpful. There's often more than one reservation counter for each destination. Bookings for long trips should be made a day in advance – Thamel travel agents will do this for a fee.

Bus No 23 (Rs 12) runs to the bus station from Lekhnath Marg on the northern edge of Thamel but takes an age. A taxi from Thamel costs around Rs 100.

Note that buses to Dhunche and Syabrubesi run from both the Kathmandu bus station and the stand diagonally across from it.

The exceptions to this are the popular tourist buses to Pokhara (Rs 400 to Rs 450, seven hours) that depart daily at around 7am from a far more convenient location at the Thamel end of Kantipath (see Map p140). Buses are

BUSES FROM RATNA PARK BUS STATION			
Destination	Departures	Duration	Cost (Rs)
Banepa		2hr	35
Barabise	last bus 4pm	4hr	135
Dhulikhel		2hr	43
Jiri	5.30-8.45am	10-12hr	360
Kodari	7am	4½hr	240-280
Panauti		2hr	45
Patan		20min	13
Shivalaya	6am	12-14hr	550
Unless otherwise noted, buses depart when full			

BUSES FROM KATHMANDU BUS STATION

Destination	Km	Departures	Duration (hr)**	Cost (Rs)	Ticket window
Besi Sahar	150	6.30-11am	6	350	25
Bhairawa/Sunauli	282	5am-noon, 4-8pm	7-10	425/440-480*	23, 24, 29
Bharatpur	150	hourly	5	300	17
Biratnagar	541	afternoon	14	1000	9
Birganj	298	6.30-9am, 7.30pm	9	350/400*	15 & 17
Butwal	237	6.20am, 7.20am, 5.30pm	7-9	415	22, 23, 24
Dhunche	119	6.30am, 7.30am	8-9	180-230	30
Gorkha	141	6.15am, 11am	5	150-180	25
Hile	635	afternoon	24	900*	8
Kakarbhitta	610	4pm	17	1500	26
Nepalganj	531	5.45am, 6.30am, 7am, plus hourly night buses	12	857*	19
Pokhara	202	every 30 mins until 2pm, 6.30pm & 7.30pm	6-8	300/330* (minibus 450)	25
Syabrubesi	135	6.30am & 7.30am	10	250-290	30
Tansen (Palpa)	302	6.20am, 7.20am, 5.30pm	10-12	475-500	23 & 24

* Night bus
** Duration is daytime driving time; night buses take around 50% longer, with a sleep stop

comfortable and you get a fixed seat number with your ticket. For more details see p270.

There are also tourist buses to Sauraha for Chitwan National Park (Rs 400 to Rs 450, five to seven hours). For details see p293.

Greenline (Map p140; ☎ 4253885; www.greenline .com.np; Tridevi Marg; ☻ 7am-5.30pm) offers air-con deluxe services that are considerably more expensive than the tourist buses (but include lunch). There are daily morning buses at 7.30am to Pokhara (US$18, seven hours) and Chitwan (US$15, six hours), with a lunch break and bus change in Kurintar. A service to Lumbini (US$25) is currently on hold but may resume. You should book a day in advance.

Golden Travels (Map p126; ☎ 4220036; Woodlands Complex, Durbar Marg) runs similar services, departing at 6.30am from Kantipath to Pokhara (US$15 with lunch) and 6.30am from Sundhara to Sunauli (US$14), the latter changing buses in Kalanki.

TO/FROM THE KATHMANDU VALLEY

Buses for destinations within the Kathmandu Valley, and for those on or accessed from the Arniko Hwy (for Jiri, Barabise and Kodari on the Tibetan border), operate from the **Ratna Park bus station** (Map p126), also known as the old bus stand, in the centre of the city on the eastern edge of Tundikhel parade ground. The station is a bit of a horror, drenched in diesel fumes, with no English signs and not much English spoken. Keep shouting out your destination and someone will eventually direct you to the right bus.

As with anything in Nepal, however, there are exceptions to the rule. Buses to Bhaktapur (Rs 20, one hour) run from a stand (Map p126) on Bagh Bazar.

Buses to Pharping (Rs 21, two hours) and Dakshinkali (Rs 32, 2½ hours) leave from Shahid Gate (Martyrs' Memorial) at the southern end of the Tundikhel parade ground (Map p126), as well as the Ratna Park station.

Buses heading to Bungamati, Godavari and Chapagaon in the southern valley leave from Patan – see p194.

Car

Although you cannot rent cars on a drive-yourself basis, they can be readily rented with a driver from a number of operators. The rental cost is high, both in terms of the initial hiring charge and fuel. Charges are as high as US$50 per day, although they can be lower, especially if you are not covering a huge distance.

Wayfarers (see p119) can arrange car hire for a one-way drop to Pokhara (Rs 6875) or Chitwan (Rs 6200). Sightseeing around the Kathmandu Valley costs around Rs 1100/2100 for a half/full day, depending on the itinerary.

KATHMANDU

Taxi

A better option than hiring a car is to hire a taxi for the day. Between several people, longer taxi trips around the valley, or even outside it, are affordable. A half-/full-day sightseeing trip within the valley costs around Rs 800/1500.

For longer journeys outside the valley count on about Rs 2500 per day plus fuel, which is generally cheaper than hiring a car through a travel agency.

GETTING AROUND

The best way to see Kathmandu and the valley is to walk or ride a bicycle. Most of the sights in Kathmandu itself can easily be covered on foot, and this is by far the best way to appreciate the city. If and when you run out of steam, there are plenty of reasonably priced taxis available.

The closest taxi stand to Thamel is on Tridevi Marg, close to the junction with Jyatha Rd (Map p140).

To/From the Airport

Kathmandu's international airport is called **Tribhuvan Airport** (Map pp114-15; ☎ 4472256) after the late king; the area's former name Gaucher (literally 'cow pasture') speaks volumes about Kathmandu's rapid urban expansion. See p379 for details of arrival and departure procedures.

Getting into town is quite straightforward. Both the international and domestic terminals offer a fixed price pre-paid taxi service, currently Rs 500 to Thamel.

Once outside the international terminal you will be confronted by hotel touts, who are often taxi drivers making commission on taking you to a particular hotel. Many hold up a signboard of the particular hotel they are connected with and, if the one you want is there, you can get a free lift. The drawback with the taxis is that the hotel is then much less likely to offer you a discount, as it will be paying a hefty commission (up to 50% of the room) to the taxi driver.

If you book a room in advance, most hotels will pick you up direct for free and there's no commission.

Public buses leave from the main road – about 300m from the terminal – but they're only really practical if you have very little luggage and know exactly how to get to where you want to go.

From Kathmandu to the airport you should be able to get a taxi for Rs 250 during daylight hours, a bit more for a late or early flight.

For departure formalities see p379.

Bicycle

Once you get away from the crowded streets of Kathmandu, cycling is a pleasure and, if you're in reasonable shape, this is the ideal way to explore the valley. See p91 for general information on biking and some route ideas.

Mountain bikes cost around Rs 250 to Rs 350 per day for simple models. For longer trips around the valley, the major mountain bike companies such as Dawn Till Dusk, Himalayan Mountain Bikes and Path Finder Cycling hire out high-quality bikes with front suspension for around Rs 700. See p94 for company details.

If you want to make an early start, most places are happy to give you the bike the evening before. For all bikes, negotiate discounts for rentals of more than a day. Check the brakes before committing and be certain to lock the bike whenever you leave it.

Bus

Buses are very cheap, but often unbelievably crowded and limited in where they can go to in Kathmandu. The smaller minibuses are generally quicker and can be useful to places like Bodhnath and Patan if you can work out the routes.

Cycle-Rickshaw

Cycle-rickshaws cost Rs 30 to Rs 50 for most rides around town – because you have to negotiate all fares they can actually be more expensive than going by taxi. The tourist rate from Thamel to Durbar Sq is Rs 50. You *must* agree on a price before you start.

Motorcycle

There are a number of motorcycle rental operators in Thamel. You will have to leave a deposit of either your passport or air ticket. For Rs 350 per day you'll get a 125cc Indian-made Honda road bike, which is generally fine for road trips in the Kathmandu Valley. A 250cc trail bike costs around Rs 600 per day.

Officially, you need an international driving licence to ride a motorbike in Nepal. This regulation hasn't been enforced for years but recent reports suggest traffic police are targeting foreigners on this and other hitherto disregarded traffic violations in an attempt to raise funds. A traffic fine will set you back around Rs 1050.

Singh Motorbike Centre (Map p140; ☎ 4418594; 🕙 8am-7pm) is a reliable place for bike hire. Choose from a Hero Honda (Rs 250 per day), Yamaha 125cc (Rs 350) or Pulsar 150cc (Rs 500).

Pheasant Transportation Service (Map p140; ☎ 4701090) in a side street off the central Thamel junction has somewhat slippier prices, ranging from Rs 400 for a Yamaha 125cc to Rs 800 for a Hero Honda or Rs 1200 for an Enfield Bullet.

Motorcycles can be great fun outside the town, once you master the traffic. The main problem is getting out of Kathmandu, which can be a stressful, choking and dangerous experience. You will need a pair of goggles and some kind of face mask (available in most pharmacies).

Fuel currently costs Rs 100 (and rising) per litre; you'll only need a couple of litres for a day trip. Beyond the ring road petrol stations are few and far between.

Safa Tempos

These electric and ecofriendly three-wheeled vans serve various routes around town from a confusing collection of stands alongside the main post office on Kantipath (Map p126). Unfortunately, few drivers speak English, there are few English signs and the routes can be fiendishly complicated. Blue signs marked with the white outline of a tempo indicate a stop – fares start from Rs 10.

Taxi

Taxis are quite reasonably priced. The charge for a metered taxi is Rs 10 flagfall and Rs 4.00 for every 200m; drivers don't usually take too much convincing to use the meter for short trips, although from major tourist centres you may have to negotiate. Shorter rides around town (including to the bus station) rarely come to more than Rs 100. Night-time rates (between 10pm and 6am) cost 50% more.

Most taxis are tiny Suzuki Marutis, which can just about fit two backpackers and their luggage.

Taxis can be booked in advance ☎ 4420987; at night call ☎ 4224374.

Other approximate taxi fares from Thamel include:

Pashupatinath Rs 150
Swayambhunath Rs 150
Bodhnath Rs 200
Patan Rs 200
Budhanilkantha Rs 500
Bhaktapur Rs 700
Changu Narayan Rs 1000
Nagarkot Rs 2500

AROUND KATHMANDU

There are several outlying attractions inside the ring road that surrounds Kathmandu. All can be reached by taxi or rickshaw, by rented bicycle or motorcycle, or on foot. For sights and spectacles outside the ring road, see p170.

SWAYAMBHUNATH

A journey up to the Buddhist temple of Swayambhunath is one of the definitive experiences of Kathmandu. Mobbed by monkeys and soaring above the city on a lofty hilltop, the 'Monkey Temple' is a fascinating, chaotic jumble of Buddhist and Hindu iconography.

The compound is centred around a gleaming white stupa, topped by a gilded spire painted with the eyes of the Buddha. Depictions of these eyes appear all over the Kathmandu Valley.

Coming to Swayambhunath is an intoxicating experience, with ancient carvings jammed into every spare inch of space and the smell of incense and butter lamps hanging heavy in the air. The mystical atmosphere is heightened in the morning and evening by local devotees who make a ritual circumnavigation of the stupa, spinning the prayer wheels set into its base. It is a great place to watch the sun set over Kathmandu.

According to legend, the Kathmandu Valley was once a lake – geological evidence supports this – and the hill now topped by Swayambhunath rose spontaneously from the waters, hence the name *swayambhu*, meaning 'self-arisen'.

The emperor Ashoka allegedly visited 2000 years ago, but the earliest confirmed activity here was in AD 460. During the 14th century, Mughal invaders from Bengal broke open the stupa in the search for gold, but the stupa was restored and expanded over the following centuries.

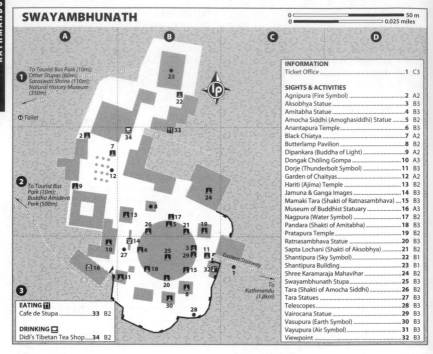

SWAYAMBHUNATH

0   50 m
0   0.025 miles

INFORMATION

Ticket Office	1 C3

SIGHTS & ACTIVITIES

Agnipura (Fire Symbol)	2 A2
Aksobhya Statue	3 B3
Amitabha Statue	4 B3
Amocha Siddhi (Amoghasiddhi) Statue	5 B2
Anantapura Temple	6 B3
Black Chiatya	7 A2
Butterlamp Pavilion	8 B2
Dipankara (Buddha of Light)	9 A2
Dongak Chöling Gompa	10 A3
Dorje (Thunderbolt Symbol)	11 B3
Garden of Chaityas	12 A2
Hariti (Ajima) Temple	13 B2
Jamuna & Ganga Images	14 B3
Mamaki Tara (Shakti of Ratnasambhava)	15 B3
Museum of Buddhist Statuary	16 A3
Nagpura (Water Symbol)	17 B2
Pandara (Shakti of Amitabha)	18 B3
Pratapura Temple	19 B2
Ratnasambhava Statue	20 B3
Sapta Lochani (Shakti of Aksobhya)	21 B2
Shantipura (Sky Symbol)	22 B1
Shantipura Building	23 B1
Shree Karamaraja Mahavihar	24 B2
Swayambhunath Stupa	25 B3
Tara (Shakti of Amocha Siddhi)	26 B2
Tara Statues	27 B3
Telescopes	28 B3
Vairocana Statue	29 B3
Vasupura (Earth Symbol)	30 B3
Vayupura (Air Symbol)	31 B3
Viewpoint	32 B3

EATING 🍴

Cafe de Stupa	33 B2

DRINKING 🍷

Didi's Tibetan Tea Shop	34 B2

Map labels: To Tourist Bus Park (10m); Other Stupas (60m); Saraswati Shrine (110m); Natural History Museum (350m); Toilet; To Tourist Bus Park (10m); Buddha Amideva Park (500m); Eastern Stairway; To Kathmandu (1.8km)

Sights

EASTERN STAIRWAY

There are two ways to approach **Swayambhunath temple** (foreigner/SAARC 100/50), but by far the most atmospheric is the stone pilgrim stairway that climbs the eastern end of the hill. Constructed by King Pratap Malla in the 17th century, this steep stone staircase is mobbed by troops of rhesus macaques, who have made an artform of sliding down the steep handrails. A word of advice: keep foodstuffs out of sight of these simian hoodlums!

From a collection of brightly painted Buddha statues at the bottom of the hill, the steps climb past a series of chaityas and bas-reliefs, including a stone showing the birth of the Buddha, with his mother Maya Devi grasping a tree branch. You can often see Tibetan astrologers reading fortunes here. At the top, the steps are lined with pairs of Garudas, lions, elephants, horses and peacocks, the 'vehicles' of the Dhyani Buddhas. Near the end of the climb is the ticket office (there's another one at the western entrance, near the tourist bus park). When you reach the top, remember to walk around the stupa in a clockwise direction.

GREAT THUNDERBOLT

At the top of the eastern stairway is an enormous, brass-plated dorje (celestial thunderbolt), one of the core symbols of Tibetan Buddhism. Known as the *vajra* in Sanskrit, the thunderbolt is a symbol of the power of enlightenment, which destroys ignorance, but is itself indestructible. In rituals the dorje is used to indicate male power, while female power is represented by a ceremonial bell.

Around the pedestal supporting the symbol are the animals of the Tibetan calendar; flanking the plinth are the **Anantapura** and **Pratapura** temples, two slender, Indian-style shikharas built by King Pratap Malla in the 17th century. Nearby is a viewpoint and a raised area with telescopes for hire.

SWAYAMBHUNATH STUPA

The Swayambhunath stupa is one of the crowning glories of Kathmandu Valley architecture. This perfectly proportioned monument seems to hint at some celestial perfection with its gleaming, gilded spire and white-washed dome. From the spire, four faces of the Buddha stare out across the valley in the cardinal directions. The nose-like squiggle below the piercing eyes is actually the Nepali number *ek* (one), signifying unity, and above is a third eye signifying the insight of the Buddha. The entire structure of the stupa is symbolic – the white dome represents the earth, while the 13-tiered, beehivelike structure at the top symbolises the 13 stages that man must pass through to achieve nirvana.

The base of the central stupa is ringed by prayer wheels embossed with the sacred mantra *om mani padme hum* ('hail to the jewel in the lotus'). Pilgrims circuiting the stupa spin each one as they pass by. Fluttering above the stupa are thousands of prayer flags, with similar mantras, which are said to be carried to heaven by the winds. Set in ornate plinths around the base of the stupa are statues representing the Dhyani Buddhas – Vairocana, Ratnasambhava, Amitabha, Amocha Siddhi (Amoghasiddhi) and Aksobhya – and their shaktis (consorts). These deities represent the five qualities of Buddhist wisdom.

STUPA PLATFORM

The great stupa is surrounded on all sides by a veritable sculpture garden of religious monuments. At the rear of the stupa, next to a small, poorly lit **museum** of Buddhist statuary, is the Kargyud-school **Dongak Chölling gompa**, set above a brick *path*. Take your shoes off to view the murals inside.

North of the pilgrim shelter is the pagoda-style **Hariti (Ajima) Temple**, with a beautiful image of Hariti, the goddess of smallpox. This Hindu goddess, who is also responsible for fertility, illustrates the seamless interweaving of Hindu and Buddhist beliefs in Nepal.

Mounted on pillars near the Hariti Temple are figures of **Tara** making the gesture of charity, with an upturned palm. In fact, there are two Taras, Green Tara and White Tara, said to be the Chinese and Nepali wives of King Songtsen Gampo, the first royal patron of Buddhism in Tibet. The Taras are also female consorts to two of the Dhyani Buddhas.

Nearby, bronze images of the river goddesses **Jamuna** and **Ganga** guard an eternal flame in a cage. Northwest of these statues is a garden of ancient chaityas, and at the back of this group is a slick black statue of **Dipankara**, carved in the 7th century. Also known as the 'Buddha of Light', Dipankara is one of the 'past Buddhas' who achieved enlightenment

before the time of Siddhartha Gautama, the historical Buddha. Also note the **black chaitya** at the north end of the courtyard, set atop a yoni – a clear demonstration of the mingling of Hindu and Buddhist symbology.

Back at the northeast corner of the complex is the **Shree Karmaraja Mahavihar**, a Buddhist temple enshrining a 6m-high figure of Sakyamuni, the historical Buddha. A prayer service takes place every day at around 4pm, accompanied by a cacophony of crashing cymbals, honking horns and the rumbling chanting of Sutras (Buddhist texts).

Symbols of the five elements – earth, air, water, fire and ether – can be found around the hilltop. Behind the Anantapura temple are shrines dedicated to **Vasupura**, the earth symbol, and **Vayupura**, the air symbol. **Nagpura**, the symbol for water, is a stone set in a muddy pool just north of the stupa, while **Agnipura**, the symbol for fire, is the red-faced god on a polished boulder on the northwestern side of the platform. **Shantipura**, the symbol for the sky, is north of the platform, in front of the Shantipura building.

WESTERN STUPA

If you follow either path leading west from the main stupa, you will reach a smaller **stupa** near the car park for tourist buses. Just behind is a **gompa** surrounded by rest houses for pilgrims and an important **shrine** to Saraswati, the goddess of learning. At exam time, many scholars come here to improve their chances, and school children fill the place during Basanta Panchami, the Festival of Knowledge.

Eating & Drinking

If you need a break, you can grab a reviving cup of *chiya* (milk tea) at the hole-in-the-wall **Didi's Tibetan Tea Shop** (drinks from Rs 20) or stop and get lunch at tourist-oriented **Cafe De Stupa** (dishes from Rs 100).

Getting There & Away

You can approach Swayambhunath by taxi (Rs 150), by bicycle or as part of an easy stroll from Kathmandu. Taxis can drop you at the tourist bus park at the western end of the hill or the steep pilgrim stairway at the eastern end of the hill.

Safa tempo No 20 (Rs 10) shuttles between Swayambhunath's eastern stairway and Kathmandu's Sundhara district (near the main post office).

WALKING & CYCLING

There are two popular walking or bicycle routes to Swayambhunath – using both offers a pleasant circuit, either in the direction described or in reverse.

Starting at the Chhetrapati Tole junction near Thamel, the road runs west to the Vishnumati River (with Swayambhunath clearly visible in the distance), passing the pagoda-style **Indrani Temple**, which is surrounded by ghats (riverside steps) used for cremations.

Cross the river and detour right to the **Shobabaghwati Temple**, with its gaudy painted statues of Shiva and other Hindu deities. Return to the bridge and follow the steps uphill past the courtyard-style **Bijeshwori Temple**, following an arcade of religious shops to the statue-lined stairway at the east end of Swayambhunath hill.

You can return to the centre of Kathmandu via the National Museum (see right). From the bottom of the eastern stairway, go west around the base of the hill and turn left at the first major junction, then left again at the large T-junction to reach the museum. Continue southeast along this road to reach Tankeshwor, then turn left again and cross the Vishnumati River. On the other side, it's a short walk north to the bottom of Durbar Sq.

AROUND SWAYAMBHUNATH

There are several other sights scattered around Swayambhunath. Before moving on, join the Tibetan pilgrims on a clockwise *kora* or *parikrama* (pilgrim circuit) around the base of the hill, passing a series of gigantic *chörtens* (reliquary shrines), *mani dungkhor* (giant prayer wheels) and Buddhist chapels.

Starting from the eastern gateway to Swayambhunath, walk around the southwest side of the hill, passing the turn-off to the tourist bus park and the Natural History Museum (see below). The path meets the Ring Rd at **Buddha Amideva Park** (Map pp114–15), a compound containing three enormous shining gold statues of Sakyamuni, Chenresig and Guru Rinpoche, constructed in 2003. Return past the string of chörtens and chapels along the north side of the hill.

Natural History Museum

Below Swayambhunath, on the road to the tourist bus park, the **Natural History Museum** (Map pp114-15; admission Rs 30; 10am-4pm Sun-Fri, closed government holidays) offers a faded but quirky collection of exhibits, including varnished crocodiles, model dinosaurs and mounted animal heads that look suspiciously like hunting trophies. The museum provides a valuable service to local school children and it could use more support.

National Museum

Around 800m south of Swayambhunath at Chhauni, the **National Museum** (Map pp114-15; 4271504; Tahachal; foreigner/SAARC Rs 100/40, camera foreigner Rs 50; 10.30am-5pm Wed-Mon Apr-Oct, 10.30am-3.30pm Wed-Sun, 10.30am-2pm Mon Nov-Mar) faces onto a huge army barracks. The walled compound looks a little moth-eaten and overgrown, but there are some interesting treasures on display and the museum is never crowded.

As you enter the compound, turn left to reach the Judda Art Gallery, which contains some exquisite stone, metal and terracotta statues of Nepali deities and fabulous Hindu cloth paintings. Look out for the statue of buffalo-headed Sukhavara Samvara with 34 arms, 16 feet and 10 faces! You can climb to the top of the building for great views of Swayambhunath, but watch your footing as there are no guard rails.

At the back of the compound is the temple-style Buddha Art Gallery. As well as Buddhist statues, votive objects, thangkas, photos and manuscripts as big as coffee tables, there are some informative displays on the ancient mandalas (geometric Buddhist diagrams) dotted around the Kathmandu Valley. In the centre of the building is a three-dimensional mandala made up of flags.

To the north of the main compound, housed in a handsome Rana-era palace, is the Historical Museum, which displays a blood-thirsty collection of weapons, including the personal *kukris* (daggers), *katars* (punch-daggers), *tulwars* (curved swords) and *khandas* (hatchet swords) of such national heroes as Prithvi Narayan Shah, the founder of Nepal. Note the leather cannon seized in the 1792 Nepal-Tibet War.

In the same building, the Natural History Museum displays stuffed animals and old bones, including, bizarrely for this landlocked location, the jaws of a whale. Upstairs are the rather matter-of-fact Numismatic Museum, with old coins and banknotes, and Philatelic Museum, with lots of Nepali first-day covers.

Ticket sales stop an hour before closing time; bags must be left in the free lockers at the gate. See Getting There & Away under Swayambhunath (p165) for directions to the museum.

Around the Kathmandu Valley

Once upon a time, the valley surrounding Kathmandu was a vast lake, trapped by the uprising of the Himalaya. According to legend, the yogi Manjushree saw a sacred lotus rising from the waters and opened a channel with his sword to drain the waters. So the Kathmandu Valley was born. Today, this natural basin is a patchwork of terraced fields and sacred temple towns that showcase the glory of the architects and artisans of Nepal. If Kathmandu is the head of Nepal, the valley could be its heart.

Few visitors leave Nepal without seeing at least the Unesco World Heritage–listed towns of Patan and Bhaktapur, which once jostled for power with Kathmandu. However, the whole valley is a living museum of Nepali culture. It is hard to go more than a few hundred metres without stumbling upon a medieval village or centuries old temple.

There's so much to see here – just set out from Kathmandu and explore. Buses are frequent and inexpensive and all of the attractions in this chapter can be explored by rented mountain bike or motorcycle, or even on foot, utilising a series of shortcuts that can shave hours off the journey by road.

As well as Patan and Bhaktapur, be sure to make time for Pashupatinath, the sacred funeral compound beside the Bagmati River, and Bodhnath, the gigantic stupa that acts as a spiritual lodestone for Nepal's Tibetan Buddhists. Between these famous sights are smaller Newari towns and villages that lie well off the mainstream tourist circuit. In fact, you'll see fewer tourists just 10km outside Kathmandu than you will if you trek for days through the Himalaya!

HIGHLIGHTS

- Have your mind blown by the glorious Newari architecture of Patan's **Durbar Square** (p181)
- Get lost in the fascinating backstreets of **Bhaktapur** (p194), Nepal's best-preserved medieval town
- Join the pilgrims on the *parikrama* (clockwise circuit) around the enormous **Bodhnath Stupa** (p174)
- Have a mini-adventure in the little-visited towns of the Southern Valley – **Kirtipur** (p215), **Bungmati** (p219) and **Chobar** (p216)
- Wake up to bedside views of the Himalaya from your hotel in **Nagarkot** (p222), **Dhulikhel** (p226) or **Kakani** (p233)
- Escape the crowds and find the real spirit of Nepal in the temple town of **Panauti** (p229)

■ TELEPHONE CODE: 03	■ POPULATION: 4.7 MILLION	■ AREA: 227,420 SQ KM

KATHMANDU VALLEY

HISTORY

The legend that the Kathmandu Valley was formed from a vanished lake is in fact quite true. The uprising of the Himalaya trapped rivers draining south from Tibet, creating a vast lake that eventually burst its banks and drained away around 10,000 years ago.

As the valley was settled by people from the north and south, it became an important entrepôt on the trade route from India to Tibet. Hinduism and Buddhism were introduced from India and transported north across the Himalaya by saints such as Padmasambhava (Guru Rinpoche). In time, migrating Tibeto-Burman tribes carried Buddhism back into Nepal, fusing Tantric Indian beliefs with the ancient Bön religion of Tibet. This has resulted in a fascinating hybrid culture, where Hindu and Buddhist beliefs infuse every aspect of Nepali life.

Historically, the Kathmandu Valley was the homeland of the Newars, a mixed tribe of Indian and Tibeto-Burman origin. Much of the iconography, architecture and culture associated with Nepal today is actually Newari culture. For more on the customs and traditions of the Newars, see p49.

The first formal records of Newari history come from the Licchavi era (AD 400 to 750), but the golden age of the Newars came in the 17th century when the valley was dominated by three rival city-states – Kantipur (Kathmandu), Lalitpur (Patan) and Bhadgaon (Bhaktapur) – all competing to outshine each other with architectural brilliance. The reign of the Malla kings (see p34) saw the construction of many of Nepal's most iconic palaces, temples and monuments.

The unification of Nepal in 1768–69 by Prithvi Narayan Shah signalled the end of his three way struggle for supremacy. Nepali, an Indo-European language spoken by the Khas of western Nepal, replaced Newari as the country's language of administration and Kathmandu became the undisputed capital of the nation.

CLIMATE

The Kathmandu Valley is best visited before or after the monsoon. The summer – May to September – is hot and humid, with regular rainfall and temperatures exceeding 30°C. From November to February night-time temperatures plummet and early-morning bus rides become a chilly ordeal. It never snows at the bottom of the Kathmandu Valley, but the valley rim often gets a dusting from December to February – wear appropriate clothing if you visit Nagarkot, Dhulikhel or any of the other Himalayan viewpoints.

DANGERS & ANNOYANCES

Since the Maoists formed government, political violence has dropped off markedly. There are occasionally violent exchanges between the youth wing of the Maoists and the youth wings of opposition parties, but these only affect travellers if political leaders call a bandh (general strike) – see p366 for more information.

If you explore the Kathmandu Valley on a rented motorcycle, be wary of the traffic police, particularly after dark. Locals are routinely stung with fines for trumped up traffic offences and foreigners are being increasingly targeted.

Women in particular should avoid hiking alone in remote corners of the valley. For general security advice see p367.

GETTING AROUND

If you intend to do any biking, hiking or motorcycling, it's worth investing in Nepa Maps' rather useful 1:50,000 Around the Kathmandu Valley or Himalayan Maphouse's Biking Around Kathmandu Valley. Both are available from bookstores in Kathmandu.

Bicycle & Motorbike

By far the easiest and most economical way of getting around the valley is by rented bicycle or motorbike – see p162 for rental companies. On day trips, give yourself time to get back to Kathmandu by nightfall – you really don't want to ride these roads after dark.

Once you get beyond the Kathmandu Ring Rd, there is surprisingly little traffic and the valley offers some spectacular riding country. However, take corners slowly as buses and trucks will not give way. Be sure to securely lock your bike or motorcycle when you stop and carry plenty of petrol from Kathmandu as rural petrol stations regularly run dry.

See the Outdoor Activities chapter (p94) for details of some of the excellent cycling routes around the Kathmandu Valley.

Bus & Taxi

From Kathmandu's Ratna Park (City) bus station, inexpensive public buses run to every town in the valley, though you may need to change in Patan or Bhaktapur. However, the buses can be incredibly crowded, and ye gods are they slow. As a more comfortable alternative, consider hiring a car or taxi (Rs 800 per half-day, or Rs 1500 per full day) – this can be quite economical if you share the costs with other travellers.

Foot
There are many interesting day hikes and overnight treks around the valley, allowing you to take shortcuts that are not accessible by bicycle or motorcycle.

Organised Tours
Many of the travel agents in Thamel can arrange day trips around the valley, but standards vary. One reliable operator is **Wayfarers** (Map p140; ☎ 4266010; www.wayfarers .com.np; Thamel, Kathmandu). Guided walks through Kirtipur, Khokana, Bungmati and Chapagaon (US$35 per person) leave on Wednesday and Saturday. Three-day trips to Panauti, Namobuddha, Dhulikhel, Nagarkot and Sankhu (US$135 per person) leave on Thursday and Sunday.

See p93 for information on organised mountain-bike trips around the valley.

AROUND THE RING ROAD

There are several interesting sights just outside the Kathmandu Ring Rd, all accessible by public transport, on foot, or by rented bike or motorcycle.

PASHUPATINATH
Nepal's most important Hindu temple stands on the banks of the holy Bagmati River, surrounded by a bustling market of religious stalls selling marigolds, prasad, incense, rudraksha beads, conch shells, pictures of Hindu deities and temples, *tika* powder in rainbow colours, glass lingams, models of Mt Meru and other essential religious paraphernalia.

At first glance, Pashupatinath might not look that sacred – the temple is just a few hundred metres from the end of the runway at Tribhuvan International Airport, overlooking a particularly polluted stretch of the Bagmati. However, in religious terms, this is a powerhouse of Hindu spiritual power.

Elsewhere in Nepal, Shiva is worshipped in his wrathful form as the destructive Bhairab but at Pashupatinath, he is celebrated as Pashupati, the lord of the beasts.

Devotees of Shiva and sadhus flock to Pashupatinath from across the subcontinent and many Nepalis choose to be cremated on the banks of the holy river. Even the kings of Nepal used to come here to ask for a blessing from Pashupati before commencing any important journey. Nepal's Dalit (untouchable) community was only allowed access to the shrine in 2001!

Non-Hindus cannot enter the main temple, but the surrounding complex of Shaivite shrines, lingams and ghats (stone steps) is fascinating and highly photogenic. Groups of 'photo me' sadhus loiter around in outlandish paraphernalia hoping to make a little extra money posing for tourist photos. Be respectful with your camera at the funeral ghats – you wouldn't take snaps of bereaved relatives at a funeral back home, so don't do it here.

You can visit Pashupatinath as a half day trip from central Kathmandu and walk on easily to Bodhnath. There are ticket booths near the southern entrance to the main Pashupatinath temple and next to the Guhyeshwari Temple, where foreigners must pay the entrance fee. Guides can be hired from the office of the **Guide Association of Pashupatinath** (1½hr tours Rs 500; ⊙ 9am-5pm) close to the main temple.

Sights
PASHUPATINATH TEMPLE
Only Hindus are allowed to enter the compound of this famous **temple** (admission Rs 250 child under 10yr free; ⊙ 24hr), but you can catch

---

TOP VALLEY HIKES

Get the blood moving with these excellent half-day hikes.

- Nagarkot to Nala and Banepa (p223)
- Dhulikhel to Panauti via Namobuddha (p228)
- Gokarna Mahadev Temple to Bodhnath, via Kopan Monastery (p214)
- Nagarkot to Sundarijal (p223)
- Nagarkot to Sankhu (p223) and Changu Narayan (p222)

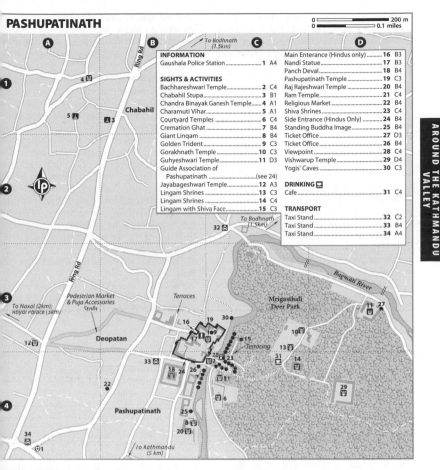

PASHUPATINATH

INFORMATION	
Gaushala Police Station	**1** A4
SIGHTS & ACTIVITIES	
Bachhareshwari Temple	**2** C4
Chabahil Stupa	**3** B1
Chandra Binayak Ganesh Temple	**4** A1
Charamuti Vihar	**5** A1
Courtyard Temples	**6** C4
Cremation Ghat	**7** B4
Giant Linqam	**8** B4
Golden Trident	**9** C3
Gorakhnath Temple	**10** C3
Guhyeshwari Temple	**11** D3
Guide Association of Pashupatinath	(see 24)
Jayabageshwari Temple	**12** A3
Lingam Shrines	**13** C3
Lingam Shrines	**14** C4
Lingam with Shiva Face	**15** C3

Main Enterance (Hindus only)	**16** B3
Nandi Statue	**17** B3
Panch Deval	**18** B4
Pashupatinath Temple	**19** C3
Raj Rajeshwari Temple	**20** B4
Ram Temple	**21** C4
Religious Market	**22** B4
Shiva Shrines	**23** C4
Side Entrance (Hindus Only)	**24** B4
Standing Buddha Image	**25** B4
Ticket Office	**27** D3
Ticket Office	**26** B4
Viewpoint	**28** C4
Vishwarup Temple	**29** D4
Yogis' Caves	**30** C3
DRINKING	
Cafe	**31** C4
TRANSPORT	
Taxi Stand	**32** C2
Taxi Stand	**33** B4
Taxi Stand	**34** A4

tantalising glimpses of what is going on inside from several points around the perimeter wall. From the main gate on the west side of the compound, you can view the mighty golden behind of an enormous brass statue of **Nandi**, Shiva's bull. Inside the shrine, hidden from view, is a black, four-headed image of Pashupati, Lord of the Beasts.

The pagoda-style temple was constructed in 1696 but Pashupatinath has been a site of Hindu and Buddhist worship for far longer. If you climb between the terraces and ceremonial cisterns to the west of the temple, you can look down on the gilded rooftop, which cascades down in two wide tiers. There are more views from the top of the terraces on the east side of the Bagmati.

If you follow the road running south from the side entrance to the temple, you will pass the **Panch Deval** (Five Temples), a former temple complex that now acts as a social welfare centre for destitute old people. A donation box offers a way for visitors to directly contribute.

THE RIVERBANKS OF THE BAGMATI

Despite being clogged with garbage and black with pollution, the Bagmati is an extremely sacred river and Pashupatinath is the Nepali equivalent of Varanasi on the sacred River Ganges. The **cremation ghats** along the Bagmati are used for open-air cremations, but only members of the royal family can be cremated immediately in front of the Pashupatinath Temple. The funerals of 10 members of the

Nepali royal family took place here after the massacre in 2001 (see boxed text, p42). At the north end of the ghats, best viewed from across the river, are a series of **yogis' caves** used as shelters in medieval times.

Funerals of ordinary Nepalis take place daily on the ghats to the south of the temple. Bodies are wrapped in shrouds and laid out along the riverbank, then cremated on a wooden pyre in a surprisingly businesslike way. It's a powerful place to contemplate notions of death and mortality. Needless to say, this is a personal and traumatic time for relatives, and tourists intruding with cameras is just not appropriate.

Between the two groups of ghats on the west bank of the Bagmati is the small, 6th-century **Bachhareshwari Temple**, decorated with Tantric figures, skeletons and erotic scenes. It is said that human sacrifices were once made at this temple as part of the Maha Shivaratri Festival (opposite).

If you walk south along the west bank, you will pass a huge uprooted **lingam** and a small 7th-century **standing Buddha image**, next to the **Raj Rajeshwari Temple**, with its unusual rounded stucco outbuildings.

THE EAST BANK

Two footbridges cross the Bagmati in front of the Pashupatinath Temple, entering a garden of stone terraces covered in dozens of small **Shiva shrines**. These one-room temples are often used as lodgings by wandering sadhus and each contains a central Shiva lingam. Although the shrines are built in many styles, all share certain design features – note the mask of Bhairab, Shiva's fearsome incarnation, on the south wall, and the Nandi statue and animal-head water spout to the north.

Two flights of steps lead up the hillside between the shrines, passing the elaborately frescoed **Ram Temple**, which is often thronged by visiting sadhus, especially during Maha Shivaratri Festival (see opposite). At the top, where the path enters the forest, a side track leads north along the top of the terraces to an excellent **viewpoint** over the Pashupatinath Temple. Look for the enormous **golden trident** on the northern side of the temple and the golden figure of the king kneeling in prayer under a protective hood of naga to the north.

On the ghats below this terrace, devotees ritually bathe in the dubious-looking waters of the Bagmati and holy men perform rituals on the stone steps. Look out for children retrieving coins from the murky river using a magnet on the end of a string.

GORAKHNATH & VISHWARUP TEMPLES

The steps continue up the hill from the terraces to a convenient cafe and another huge complex of **Shiva shrines** on the edge of the forest that is well worth exploring. There are more than 50 shrines here and the variety of architectural forms is quite stunning.

If you bear right at the top of the hill, you will reach the courtyard-style **Vishwarup Temple**, topped by a Mughal-style onion dome. You can peek through the gates but only Hindus may enter. Turning left at the top of the hill will take you to the towering red-and-white shikhara of the **Gorakhnath Temple**, dedicated to the 11th-century yogi who founded the Shaivite monastic tradition and invented Hatha yoga.

Past the Gorakhnath Temple, the path drops down through the forest, passing the **Mrigasthali Deer Park**, a fitting blending of nature and religion, as Shiva is said to have frolicked here once in the shape of a golden deer.

GUHYESHWARI TEMPLE

The path drops out of the forest to the side of the large, courtyard-style Guhyeshwari Temple, built by King Pratap Malla in 1653 and dedicated to Parvati (the wife of Shiva) in her terrible manifestation as Kali. Entry is banned to non-Hindus, but you can peek into the compound from the path to see the four huge gilded snakes that support the roof finial.

The riverbank in front of the temple is lined with Shiva shrines and octagonal plinths for ritual bathing.

The temple's curious name comes from the Nepali words *guhya* (vagina) and *ishwari* (goddess) – literally, it's the temple of the goddess' vagina! According to legend, the father of Parvati insulted Shiva and the goddess become so incensed that she burst into flames, providing the inspiration for the practice of *sati*, where widows were burned alive on the funeral pyres of their husbands. The grieving Shiva wandered the earth with the disintegrating corpse of Parvati and her genitals fell at Guhyeshwari. However, Indian Hindus

nake the same claim for the Kamakhya
Temple at Guwahati in Assam.

Festivals & Events
Pashupatinath is generally busiest (with
genuine pilgrims rather than tourists) from
4am to 10am and again from 6pm to 7.30pm,
especially on *ekadashi,* which falls 11 days
after the full and new moon each month. As
night falls, pilgrims release butter lamps on
boats made of leaves onto the Bagmati as part
of the *arati* (light) ceremony.

In the Nepali month of Falgun (in
February or March), pilgrims throng to
Pashupatinath from all over Nepal and India
to celebrate Shiva's birthday at the **Maha
Shivaratri** Festival. It's an incredible spectacle, and a chance to see members of some of
the more austere Shaivite sects performing
rituals through the night.

Another auspicious date on the calendar
is **Bala Chaturdashi** in November/December,
when pilgrims hold a lamplit vigil and
bathe in the holy Bagmati the following
morning.

Pilgrims then scatter sweets and seeds
around the compound for their deceased
relatives to enjoy in the afterlife.

Getting There & Away
The most convenient way to Pashupatinath
is by taxi (Rs 150 to Rs 200 from Thamel) –
taxis usually drop off by the police station at
Gaushala, but you can ask to be dropped off
closer to the temples.

If you are walking or cycling, head east
from the Royal Palace through Naxal, meeting the Ring Rd near the Jayabageshwari
Temple, with its fine painting of Bhairab.
To reach the temple, cross the Ring Rd and
follow the winding lanes lined with religious
stalls towards the Bagmati.

If you want to walk on from Pashupatinath
to Bodhnath, it's a pleasant 20-minute walk
through villages and farmland, offering a window onto ordinary life in the Kathmandu
burbs. Take the footbridge across the river
in front of the Guhyeshwari Temple and head
north for five minutes, then turn right at the
signposted junction, by a temple surrounding
a large pipal tree. At the next junction follow
the Buddha's example and take the middle
(straight) path, which eventually emerges on
the main Bodhnath road, right across from
the stupa.

CHABAHIL
East of the centre, on the way to Bodhnath,
the suburb of Chabahil (see Map p171) has
a number of historic temples and shrines.
Right on the Ring Rd is the imposing **Chabahil
Stupa** (free admission), the fourth largest stupa
in the Kathmandu area after Bodhnath,
Swayambhunath and the Kathesimbhu Stupa
near Thahiti Chowk. According to legend,
the stupa was constructed by Charumati,
the daughter of Ashoka, but it has been re
built numerous times, most recently in 2002,
when the tower cracked because of vibrations
from passing traffic. The spire is covered
by brass plates and the surrounding courtyard has some graceful chaityas from the
Licchavi period.

If you take the lane just north of the stupa,
and turn left, you will reach the **Charamuti Vihar**,
a medieval Buddhist monastery that used
to house the monks who tended the stupa.
Continuing past this turning will take you
to the revered **Chandra Binayak Ganesh Temple**,
enshrining a tiny silver image of Ganesh. The
courtyard is full of *tika*-powder-covered statues – note the Budhanilkantha-style statue of
Narayan reclining on his serpent bed, next to a
human figure made of beaten brass panels.

BODHNATH (BOUDHA)
There is nowhere quite like Bodhnath. This
enormous stupa pulses with life as thousands
of pilgrims gather daily to make a ritual circumnavigation of the dome, beneath the
watchful eyes of the Buddha, which gaze out
from the gilded central tower. This is one of
the few places in the world where Tibetan
Buddhist culture is accessible and unfet-
tered, and the lanes around the stupa are
crammed with monasteries and **workshops**
producing butter lamps, ceremonial horns,
Tibetan drums, singing bowls, plumed hats
for lamas and other essential paraphernalia
for Buddhist life.

Historically, the stupa was an important
staging post on the trade route between
Lhasa and Kathmandu, and Tibetan traders would pray here for a safe journey
before driving their yaks on to the high
passes of the Himalaya. Today, most of the
Tibetans living in the village of Boudha
(pronounced *boe*-da) are refugees who fled
China after 1959, but the stupa also attracts
many Sherpas, descendants of Tibetan
tribal people who migrated to Nepal in

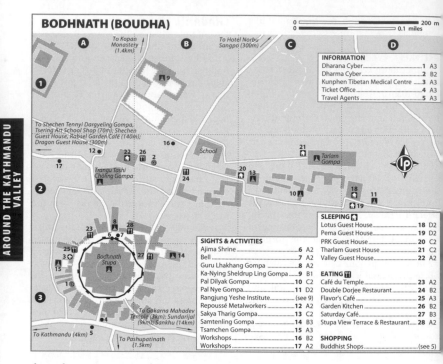

BODHNATH (BOUDHA)

the 16th century. Many of the monasteries around the stupa have opened their doors to foreign students, so you'll see plenty of Westerners in maroon robes as you stroll around the backstreets.

The best time to visit Bodhnath is late afternoon, when the group tours depart and local Buddhists stroll down to the stupa to light butter lamps, spin prayer wheels, chant mantras, shop for household goods, socialise and perform a ritual clockwise circuit of the monument. Try to visit on the evening of the full moon, when the plaza surrounding the stupa is lit up by thousands of butter lamps.

Information

There are numerous internet cafes and ISD phone offices around the stupa and on the lane leading north. Try **Dharana Cyber** (per hr Rs 30; 7am-9pm), on the west side of the stupa, or **Dharma Cyber** (per hr Rs 25; 9am-7pm), just north of the stupa.

The ticket office is at the main southern entrance to the stupa. Various travel agents along the main road here can arrange flights, long-distance bus tickets and other services,

but be wary of 'direct buses' to India – se boxed text, p384.

If you fancy trying out Tibetan trad itional medicine – where diagnosis is base on the speed and regularity of the puls and the condition of the tongue, and ill nesses are treated with Himalayan herbs - visit the **Kunphen Tibetan Medical Centr** (4251920; 9am-noon & 2-5pm) near th Tsamchen Gompa.

Sights
THE BODHNATH STUPA

The first **stupa** (admission foreigner/SAARC Rs 100/20 at Bodhnath was built sometime after AD 600, when the Tibetan king, Songtsen Gampo converted to Buddhism. According to legend the king constructed the stupa as an act o penance after unwittingly killing his father Unfortunately, the first stupa was wrecked by Mughal invaders in the 14th century, so the current stupa is a more recent construction.

In terms of grace and purity of line, no other stupa in Nepal comes close to Bodhnath From its whitewashed dome to its gilded tower painted with the eyes of the Buddha

VISITING TIBETAN MONASTERIES

Most Tibetan Buddhist monasteries welcome visitors and entering these atmospheric buildings can be a powerful and evocative experience. During the morning and evening prayers, the lamas and novices gather to chant passages from the Sutras (Buddhist texts), normally accompanied by a cacophony of crashing cymbals, thumping drums and honking Tibetan horns. The ceremony is often followed by a meal of *tsampa* (roasted barley flour) and butter tea, and you may see monks making temporary sand mandalas (geometrical representations of the path to enlightenment) or butter sculptures, which are then destroyed as a reminder of the impermanence of human existence.

Gompas follow a remarkably consistent layout, linked to the complex symbology of Tibetan Buddhism. The main prayer hall is invariably decorated with intricate murals depicting Buddhist deities from the past, present and future, who also appear on dangling thangkas edged with brocade. The focal point of the monastery is the collection of statues depicting Buddhas and bodhisattvas, usually painted in vivid colours – pick up the booklet *Short Description of Gods, Goddesses and Ritual Objects of Buddhism and Hinduism in Nepal* (published by the Handicraft Association of Nepal and available in Nepali bookshops) for a guide to the myriad Buddhist deities.

Many gompas also have a library of cloth-wrapped Buddhist manuscripts set into alcoves around the altar, which is frequently covered in offerings, including butter lamps and seven bowls of water. The throne of the head lama (who may be living, or dead and pending the discovery of his reincarnation) is often surrounding by pictures of past abbots and the Dalai Lama, the spiritual leader of Tibetan Buddhism and the representation on earth of Avalokiteshvara, the deity of compassion.

As you enter a monastery you will see murals of the four guardian protectors – fearsome-looking deities who scare away ignorance – and the Wheel of Life, a highly complex diagram representing the Buddha's insights into the way humans are chained by desire to the endless cycle of life, death and rebirth.

For a detailed breakdown of the elements of the Wheel of Life, see www.buddhanet.net/wheel1.htm.

The front of a monastery may also feature enormous *mani dungkhor* – giant prayer wheels stuffed with thousands of copies of the Buddhist mantra *om mani padme hum* ('praise to the jewel in the lotus').

This mantra also appears on the smaller prayer wheels around the outer wall and on the fluttering prayer flags outside. Each spin, or gust of wind, carries these prayers to heaven. On the monastery roof you may see a statue of two deer on either side of the Wheel of Law, symbolising the Buddha's first sermon at the deer park of Sarnath.

Cultural Considerations

Visitors are welcome in most monasteries, but please stick to the following guidelines:

- Remove your shoes and hat before you enter a gompa.
- Ask before taking photos and avoid taking photos during a service.
- Do not smoke anywhere in the main compounds.
- Do not step over or sit on the monks' cushions, even if no one is sitting on them.
- During ceremonies, enter quietly and stand by the wall near the main entrance; do not walk around while monks are engaged in rituals.
- Always walk around stupas and chörtens (Tibetan-style stupa) in a clockwise direction.
- It is appropriate to make an offering – a khata is traditional, but cash donations will help fund the monastery and its charitable works in the community.

the monument is perfectly proportioned and every part of the stupa has a specific religious significance – see boxed text, below.

Many ancient stupas were built to house holy relics and some claim that Bodhnath contains a piece of bone from the skeleton of Siddhartha Gautama, the historical Buddha. Around the base of the stupa are 108 small images of the Dhyani Buddha Amitabha (108 is an auspicious number in Tibetan culture) and a ring of prayer wheels, set in groups of four or five into 147 niches.

To reach the top of the plinth, look for the gateway at the north end of the stupa, beside a **small shrine** dedicated to Ajima, the goddess of smallpox. The plinth is open from 5am to 6pm (till 7pm in summer), offering a raised viewpoint over the tide of pilgrims surging around the stupa. Note the committed devotees prostrating themselves full-length on the ground in the courtyard on the east side of the stupa.

THE GOMPAS

Since the Chinese invasion of Tibet, a number of new monasteries have been constructed at Bodhnath by refugees. All welcome visitors but many close their doors in the middle of the day. See boxed text, p175, for some guidelines on visiting gompas.

Facing the stupa from the west side of the square, **Tsamchen Gompa** contains some delicate mural work and a magnificent statue of Maitreya (Jampa in Tibetan), the Future Buddha, covered in embroidered robes. Note the murals of King Mahendra and Queen Ratna in the doorway and the massive *mani dungkhor* (prayer wheel shrine) to the left of the entrance.

Immediately north of the stupa is the newly constructed **Guru Lhakhang Gompa** which offers perfect views over the stupa from its upper balcony. The prayer hall has some fine ceiling mandalas and huge statues of Guru Rinpoche, Sakyamuni and Avalokiteshvara. In front is a huge **bell** inscribed with Tibetan mantras.

Take the alley running northeast from the stupa, past the small Gelugpa **Samtenling Gompa**, and turn right to reach the **Sakya Tharig Gompa** (www.sakyatharig.org.np). This sprawling complex includes a large Buddhist school and the prayer hall at the back contains a huge statue of Sakyamuni inlaid with turquoise, red coral, *dzi* beads (see boxed text p158) and other precious materials.

Continue east along this path to reach the Kargyud school **Pal Dilyak Gompa**, with another large monastic school and a huge prayer hall full of musical instruments that create a rousing soundtrack during afternoon prayers. Follow the same path past the Lotus Guest House to reach the **Pal Nye Gompa**, with around 80 young novices and the loudest gong and horn section in the area.

To the west and down the alley leading to the Dragon Guest House, the huge **Shechen Tennyi Dargyeling Gompa** (www.shechen.org) was established by the famous Nyingmapa lama Dilgo Khyentse Rinpoche to replace the destroyed Shechen Gompa in eastern Tibet. Today, the monastery has a thriving com-

---

STUPA SYMBOLISM

There are many complicated rules governing the layout of Buddhist stupas. Each part of a stupa has a specific significance, creating a three-dimensional representation of important elements of Buddhist philosophy to remind devotees of the path towards enlightenment. Key features of stupa architecture include the following:

Plinth The lowest level of the stupa is a square or terraced plinth, representing the earth. The four sides or four terraces represent the four states of mindfulness and the four immeasurables – love, compassion, joy and equanimity.

Kumbha Above the plinth is a hemispherical dome, resembling an upturned pot of rice (*kumbha* literally means 'pot'). The dome symbolises water and is freshly whitewashed each year and decorated with a pattern of yellow paint to represent lotus petals.

Harmika Above the dome is a square tower, symbolising fire, usually painted on each side with the eyes of the Buddha.

Spire Topping the harmika is a tapering spire, representing the air. The 13 levels of the tower represent the 13 stages that a human being must pass through to achieve nirvana.

Umbrella At the very top of the stupa is a protective umbrella that symbolises the void beyond space.

REPOUSSÉ METALWORK

Many of the richly decorated objects used for religious rituals in Nepal make use of the ancient technique of repoussé – where a design is hammered into the metal from the back using hammers and punches. First the metal shape is set into a bed of *jhau* (a mixture of resin and brick dust) then the design is painstakingly applied and the resin is melted away, allowing finishing touches to be added from the front using engraving tools.

This style of metalwork has been produced since at least the second millennium BC and the technique is still practiced today in the alleyways around Bodhnath, particularly near the Shechen Gompa.

munity of over 300 monks and novices and the main prayer hall features fabulous murals by artists from Bhutan. The attached **Tsering Art School** produces Buddhist crafts that are sold in the monastery shop (see p178).

Further north, down a side alley, the handsome 'white gompa' of **Ka-Nying Sheldrup Ling** features ornamental gardens and a richly decorated interior with some exquisite paintings and thangkas. The attached **Rangjung Yeshe Institute** (www.shedra.org) runs classes in Tibetan, Sanskrit, Nepali and Buddhist studies (see p365).

Festivals & Events

Bodhnath goes into spiritual overdrive every year in February or March for **Losar**, the Tibetan New Year. Long copper horns are blown, a portrait of the Dalai Lama is paraded around, thousands of pilgrims throng the stupa, and monks from the surrounding monasteries perform masked *chaam* dances.

Another good time to be here is **Buddha Jayanti** in April/May, which celebrates the birth of the Buddha. Thousands of butter lamps are lit by devotees and an image of the Buddha is paraded by elephant around the stupa.

Sleeping

The guest houses in the tangle of lanes north and east of the stupa offer an interesting and more peaceful alternative to basing yourself in Kathmandu.

Lotus Guest House (☎ 4472320; s/d Rs 300/450, without bathroom Rs 250/400, tr Rs 600, deluxe r Rs 700) This calm, contemplative guest house is close to Pal Dilyak Gompa. Rooms are spread over two floors around a marigold-fringed garden lawn and the bathrooms are so clean they sparkle.

Pema Guest House (☎ 4495662; pemaguesthouse@hotmail.com; r with/without bathroom from Rs 550/300, deluxe r with TV Rs 700) Behind the Sakya Tharig Gompa, this tidy house is set in a neat courtyard garden. The spacious rooms on the upper levels get lots of natural light and there are sitting terraces on each level where you can sit and ponder. Ground-floor rooms are darker and therefore cheaper.

Tharlam Guest House (☎ 4496878; tharlamgh@yahoo.com; s/d from Rs 350/500) Part of the Tharlam Gompa, this huge place looks a bit like a Spanish holiday villa. Rooms have rather bright carpets but are large and well appointed, and there are stupa views from the rooftop.

Dragon Guest House (☎ 4479562; dragon@ntc.net.np; d Rs 600, s/d without bathroom Rs 350/450) This friendly, family-run place is set in a peaceful location north of the Shechen Gompa, and staff keep the place looking spick and span. To get here, walk north through the gate beside the Shechen Guest House.

PRK Guest House (Pal Rabten Khansar; ☎ 4465055; www.sakyatharig.org.np; s/d/tw Rs 600/1000/800) This surprisingly stylish guest house is run by the Sakya Tharig Gompa next door, and its capacious, well-appointed rooms are very comfortable indeed. Out back is an ornamental garden with bench seats and a large stupa.

our pick **Shechen Guest House** (☎ 4479009; www.shechenguesthouse.com.np; s/d/tr Rs 750/1030/1430) At the back of the Shechen Tennyi Dargyeling Gompa, this agreeable guest house caters to a mix of dharma students and ordinary travellers. Tibetan fabrics add a dash of colour to the uncluttered bedrooms, and you can rent a heater for Rs 150 per night. The attached Rabsel Garden Café cooks up some excellent vegetarian food. To get here, enter the monastery compound and turn left, then right beside a line of giant chörten (Tibetan-style stupa). Discounts of Rs 100 are available from May to August.

Valley Guest House (☎ 4471241; www.thevalleyguesthouse.com; s/d from Rs 1000/1500, ste Rs 2500, f Rs 2700) Owned by a Dutch-Nepali couple, this modern and tasteful place doubles as a family

AROUND THE KATHMANDU VALLEY

home. It's popular with long-term dharma students and there are excellent rooftop views to the stupa. For a splurge, try the single air-conditioned suite.

Hotel Norbu Sangpo (☎ 4482500; www.hotel norbusangpo.com; s/d from US$15/24, apt per month from US$350) Hidden away in the backstreets northeast of the stupa, this very private place has a cute, flowery garden and big rooms with all mod cons. There are balconies on every level and long-stay guests can rent apartments with kitchens (but no appliances) and living rooms.

Eating

Buddhist Bodhnath is nirvana for vegetarians and there are traveller-oriented restaurants around the stupa taking advantage of the views. For cheaper eats, head to the back-lanes radiating out from the stupa – any building with a curtain across an open door is a local cafe serving momos, *thukpa* (noodle soup) and other Tibetan staples. Unless otherwise stated, the following restaurants open from 8am to 9pm.

Double Dorjee Restaurant (☎ 4488947; dishes Rs 50-180) On the lane north of the stupa, this cosy Tibetan-run place targets backpackers and the dharma crowd with good prices, tasty Tibetan and Western food and soft sofas to relax in.

Garden Kitchen (☎ 4470760; mains Rs 50-150) A partly open-air place near the Shechen Tennyi Dargyeling Gompa, serving the usual globetrotting menu in pleasing surroundings. Reasonable prices attract many long-term dharma students.

Saturday Café (☎ 2073157; mains Rs 60-200) Looking more like something you'd find in Portland, Oregon, this multistorey cafe serves excellent vegetarian meals, snacks and cakes. There's a bookshop full of holistic titles and it even serves organic coffee. Come early for a seat with a view on the rooftop.

Café du Temple (☎ 2143256; www.cafedutemple .com.np; mains Rs 120-300) Run by the same people as the Café du Temple in Patan, this smart and efficient place targets tour groups with a solid menu of international food, plus grand views.

Stupa View Terrace & Restaurant (☎ 4480262; mains Rs 140-350; ☻ from 9am) The views are as good as they claim at this superior traveller-oriented place to the north of the stupa, with good vegetarian food and proper clay-oven pizzas.

our pick **Flavor's Café** (☎ 4498748; meals Rs 200-400) Formerly New Orleans, this upscale place has

changed its name but not its menu, which covers everything from Nepali *choyla* (spiced meat curry) to Cajun chicken and steaks. There's wireless internet, and tables are set in a calm, covered courtyard, or upstairs on the roof, for stupa views.

Shopping

The stupa is ringed by shops selling Tibetan crafts, thangkas, votive objects and Tibetan cowboy hats, but prices are high compared to other parts of Kathmandu so bargain hard. For tea bowls, butter lamps, prayer flags and other essential items for the Tibetan home, try the shops on the alleyway leading north from the stupa.

Tsering Art School Shop (Shechen Tennyi Dargyeling Gompa; ☻ 9am-5pm Mon-Fri, to noon Sat) The shop at Shechen Gompa has an on-site tailor and a workshop that produces thangkas, incense and sculptures. The shop also sells Buddhist reference books and CDs.

Getting There & Away

The easiest way to reach Bodhnath is by taxi (Rs 200 to Rs 250 one way), but you can also come by cycle (watch the traffic), by bus from Kathmandu's Ratna Park bus station (Rs 15, 30 minutes) or by tempo from Kantipath in Kathmandu (Rs 15, routes 2 and 28).

There's also an interesting short walk between Bodhnath and Pashupatinath (see p173), or you could combine Bodhnath with a visit to Gokarna Mahadev Temple and Kopan Monastery (see boxed text, p214).

AROUND BODHNATH
Kopan Monastery

On a hilltop north of Bodhnath, **Kopan Monastery** (☎ 4821268; www.kopan-monastery.com) was founded by Lama Thubten Yeshe, who died in 1984, leading to a worldwide search for his reincarnation. A young Spanish boy, Osel Torres, was declared to be the reincarnated lama, providing the inspiration for Bernardo Bertolucci's film *Little Buddha*. Lama Tenzin Osel Rinpoche no longer resides at Kopan, but visitors are welcome to explore the monastery and many people come here to study Buddhist psychology and philosophy (see p364 for more details).

You can visit Kopan on the pleasant walk between Bodhnath and the Gokarna Mahadev Temple (see boxed text, p214).

THE NORTHWESTERN VALLEY

There are several interesting detours to the north and west of the capital, which can easily be visited by bus, tempo, taxi, rented bicycle or motorcycle, or even on foot.

ICHANGU NARAYAN

About 3km northwest of Swayambhunath, **Ichangu Narayan** (admission free; ☾ dawn-dusk) is one of several important temples dedicated to Vishnu in his incarnation as Narayan, the 'eternal man'. Built in the two-tiered pagoda style, the temple was founded in around 1200 and its courtyard is dotted with ancient Garuda statues and other Vaishnavite symbols.

The walk here starts opposite the Buddha Amideva Park on the Ring Rd and climbs steeply through small villages to reach the temple compound. On the way you'll pass a line of handsome lotus-bud-style Shiva shrines.

Getting here from Kathmandu by bike is a long hard slog, but it's an easy freewheel on the way back down.

BALAJU

You will have to use your imagination to envision the former glory of the 18th-century gardens at Balaju, now known as **Mahendra Park** (admission Rs 5; ☾ 7am-7pm). Although the gardens are faded and untidy, many local Hindus swing by to pay their respects at the cluster of shrines in the northeast corner of the park.

In the centre of the compound is a sunken tank containing a handsome floating Vishnu image that pays tribute to the older and more famous image at Budhanilkantha. Nearby is the 19th-century, pagoda-style **Shitala Mai Temple**, fronted by some ancient statues of Ganesh, Buddha and other deities. A line of 22 painted waterspouts from which the park takes its name, **Bais Dhara**, is at the back of the park.

Getting There & Away

The village is 3km north of Thamel, just beyond the Ring Rd. Tempos and minibuses (No 1, Rs 12) go to Balaju from Lekhnath Marg; a taxi from Thamel costs around Rs 150.

NAGARJUN FOREST RESERVE

If you continue uphill from Balaju on the road towards Trisuli Bazaar, you'll reach the **Nagarjun Forest Reserve** (admission per person Rs 10, per bicycle/motorcycle/car Rs 10/30/100; ☾ entry 7am-2pm, visitors must exit by 5pm), also known as the Rani Ban (Queen's Forest). This protected forest is one of the last undamaged areas of woodland in the valley, providing a home for pheasants, deer and monkeys. It's a popular picnic spot, but female visitors are banned from walking here alone after two foreign tourists were murdered in the reserve in 2005.

The 2095m summit of the hill – accessible by the winding unpaved road or a two-hour hike on the footpath leading directly up the hill – is a popular Buddhist pilgrimage site and there's a small shrine to Padmasambhava. The viewing tower offers one of the valley's widest mountain panoramas, stretching all the way from the Annapurnas to Langtang Lirung (a plaque identifies the peaks).

It's a peaceful spot but its proximity to the capital means that safety has to be a consideration. Don't trek here alone and be sure to register at the main gate and sign out afterwards.

Getting There & Away

The main entrance to the reserve is at Phulbari, about 2km north of Balaju. Depending on the current whim of the authorities, it may be possible to exit at the Mudkhu Bhanjyang gate, 3km northwest of Phulbari, but check this when you register.

BUDHANILKANTHA

The Kathmandu Valley is awash with ancient temples and sacred sites, but Budhanilkantha is a little bit special. For one thing, it lies off the main traveller circuit, so most visitors are local devotees. This gives Budhanilkantha a uniquely mystical air – butter lamps flicker in the breeze, incense curls through the air, and devotees toss around *tika* powder like confetti.

The focal point of the devotions at Budhanilkantha is a vast **reclining statue** (admission free; ☾ dawn to dusk) of Vishnu as Narayan, the creator of all life, who floats on the cosmic sea. From his navel grew a lotus and from the lotus came Brahma, who in turn created the world. The 5m-long Licchavi-style image was created in the 7th or 8th century from one monolithic piece of black stone and hauled here from outside the valley by devotees.

It's one of the most impressive pieces of sculpture in Nepal, and that's saying something!

Only Hindus can approach the statue to leave offerings of fruit and flower garlands, but visitors can view the statue through the fence that surrounds the sacred tank. Narayan slumbers peacefully on the knotted coils of Ananta (or Shesha), the 11-headed snake god who symbolises eternity. In each hand, Narayan holds one of the four symbols of Vishnu: a chakra disc (representing the mind), a conch shell (the four elements), a mace (primeval knowledge), and a lotus seed (the moving universe).

Vaishnavism (the worship of Vishnu) was the main sect of Hinduism in Nepal until the early Malla period, when Shiva became the most popular deity. The Malla king Jayasthithi is credited with reviving the Vishnu cult by claiming to be the latest incarnation of this oft-incarnated god. Every subsequent king of Nepal has made the same claim, and because of this they are forbidden, on pain of death, from seeing the image at Budhanilkantha.

Vishnu is supposed to sleep through the four monsoon months and a great festival takes place at Budhanilkantha for **Haribodhini Ekadashi** – the 11th day of the Hindu month of Kartik (October–November) – when Vishnu is said to awaken from his annual slumber (see p26).

Sleeping & Eating

There are no budget sleeping options in the area. The road to the sacred pavilion is lined with bhojanalayas serving *sel roti* (riceflour donuts), *channa puri* (fried bread with chickpeas), pakora (battered vegetables) and outsized pappadums.

Park Village Hotel (☎ 4375280; www.ktmgh.com; s/d from US$60/70, cottages from US$60) Part of the Kathmandu Guest House group, this delightful hotel feels like a country retreat, despite being smack in the middle of Budhanilkantha. The tidy rooms and self-contained, comfortable cottages are surrounded by leafy gardens full of meditation spaces and statuary, and there's a lovely pool and spa. The hotel also offers various spa treatments and activities, including bird-spotting tours to Shivapuri National Park. A free daily shuttle bus runs

to and from the Kathmandu Guest House in Thamel.

our pick **Shivapuri Heights** (☎ 4372518, 9841371927; www.shivapuricottage.com; two-/three-bedroom cottage US$200/300, r US$120-150) Perched on the hillside above Budhanilkantha, Shivapuri Heights offers a peaceful, private bolthole away from the chaos of Kathmandu. There are two cottages for hire – one with two bedrooms, one with three – both decked out with tasteful furniture and modern conveniences. You can rent the whole cottage or just a room either way, all meals are included and staff are on hand to lead you on guided forest walks. Staff will arrange transport when you make a booking (essential).

Getting There & Away

No 5 minibuses run from the northern end of Kantipath to the main junction in Budhanilkantha (Rs 15, 35 minutes). There are also tempos (from Sundhara) and buses (from the Kathmandu Ratna Park bus station). The shrine is about 100m uphill from the junction. From Thamel, a taxi costs around Rs 500 one way.

By bicycle it's a gradual, uphill haul of 15km – you could pause to rest at the Dhum Varahi shrine (see p133).

SHIVAPURI NATIONAL PARK

The northern part of the Kathmandu Valley rises to the sprawling forests of **Shivapuri National Park** (☎ 4370355; www.shivapuri.com.np /nationalpark.php; admission foreigner/SAARC Rs 250/25, motorbike Rs 15, car Rs 75), upgraded to national park status in 2002 to protect the valley's main water source, as well 177 species of birds and numerous rare orchids. This is one of the last areas of woodland left in the valley, and the forest is alive with monkeys, and maybe even leopards and bears.

In the past the park was mainly visited by trekkers en route to Helambu (see p351), but today the reserve is a popular destination for birdwatching tours from Kathmandu. Several good trekking and mountain-bike routes criss-cross the park, including the excellent Scar Rd cycle path – see p94.

You can combine a nature-spotting tour with a trip to the Tibetan nunnery of **Nagi Gompa**, about 3km uphill from the main gate above Budhanilkantha. Around 100 nuns are resident and there are soaring valley views – you can walk here in 1½ hours or drive here in 20 minutes by motorcycle or hired 4WD. Bodhnath's Ka-Nying Sheldrup Ling Gompa holds **retreats** here for foreign students every November.

From the gompa it's possible to climb steeply for about three hours to reach **Shivapuri Peak** (2725m), via Baghdwar (where the source of the holy Bagmati River pours out of two stone tiger mouths), returning to the park entrance via the Pani Muhan water tank, for a very long day of around seven hours.

This is a serious hike that you shouldn't do alone. Take a map, plenty of water and preferably a guide.

There are several easier **walks** from Nagi Gompa. Consider the relaxing downhill stroll to Budhanilkantha, or continue south along the ridgeline for three hours to reach Kopan Monastery (p178) and Bodhnath. Another good option on foot or by mountain bike is to follow the dirt track east to Mulkarkha and then descend to Sundarijal – a mostly level 11km trip.

PATAN

☎ 01 / pop 190,000

Once a fiercely independent city-state, Patan (*pah*-tan) is now almost a suburb of Kathmandu, separated only by the murky Bagmati River. Many locals still call the city by its original Sanskrit name, Lalitpur (City of Beauty) or by its Newari name, Yala. Almost everyone who comes to Kathmandu also visits Patan's spectacular Durbar Sq – arguably the finest collection of temples and palaces in the whole of Nepal.

Another good reason to come here is to take advantage of the shops and restaurants set up to cater to the aid workers and diplomats who live in the surrounding suburbs. Then there are Patan's fair-trade shops, selling superior handicrafts at fair prices and channelling tourist dollars to some of the most needy people in Nepal.

Most people visit Patan on day trips from Kathmandu and, as a result, the accommodation offerings are rather limited. On the flip side, Patan becomes a different place once the crowds of day-trippers retreat across the Bagmati. If you stay here, you'll be able to explore the myriad *toles* and bahals at your leisure.

HISTORY
Patan has a long Buddhist history, which has even had an influence on the town's Hindu temples. The four corners of the city are marked by stupas said to have been erected by the great Buddhist emperor Ashoka in around 250 BC.

The town was ruled by local noblemen until King Shiva Malla of Kathmandu conquered the city in 1597, temporarily unifying the valley. Patan's major building boom took place under the Mallas in the 16th, 17th and 18th centuries.

ORIENTATION
Durbar Sq forms the heart of Patan. From the square, four public thoroughfares will lead you north, south, east and west to the four Ashoka stupas (see boxed text Ashoka Stupas, p185). The main bus stand is south of Durbar Sq at Lagankhel, however, buses from Kathmandu run to Patan Dhoka (City Gate), which is a short walk northwest of Durbar Sq.

Most road traffic bypasses the centre. The main road from Kathmandu crosses the Bagmati River and passes west of the old town through the districts of Kopundol, Pulchowk and Jawalakhel, the centre for Patan's Tibetan refugee community. South of Jawalakhel is the Kathmandu Ring Rd.

INFORMATION
There are banks with ATMs at Mangal Bazar, at the south end of Durbar Sq, and at Pulchowk and Jawalakhel. **Patan Hospital** (Map p182; ☎ 5522295; www.patanhospital.org.np), in the Lagankhel district, is the best in the Kathmandu Valley.

SIGHTS
Most of the famous sights are centred on Durbar Sq. Don't miss the walking tour of the courtyards to the north (see boxed text, p184).

Patan Durbar Square
As in Kathmandu, the ancient Royal Palace of Patan faces on to a magnificent **Durbar Square** (Royal Square; Map p186; admission foreigner/SAARC Rs 200/25; ☉ ticket office 7am-7pm). This concentrated mass of temples is perhaps the most visually stunning display of Newari architecture to be seen in Nepal. Temple construction in the

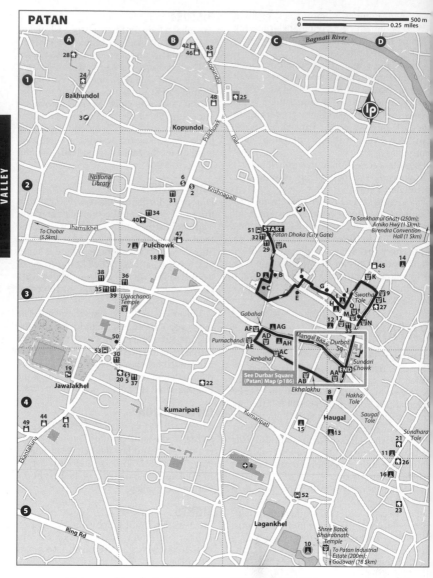

PATAN

square went into overdrive during the Malla period (14th to 18th centuries), particularly during the reign of King Siddhinarsingh Malla (1619–60).

The entry fee is payable at the southern end of Durbar Sq – for repeated visits ensure that your visa validity date is written on the back of your ticket.

BHIMSEN TEMPLE

At the northern end of Durbar Sq, the Bhimsen Temple (Map p186) is dedicated to the god of trade and business, which may explain its prosperous appearance. One of the five Pandavas from the Mahabharata, Bhimsen is credited with superhuman strength – he is often depicted as a red muscleman, lifting a horse or crushing an elephant under his knee.

The three-storey pagoda has an unusual rectangular plan which marks it out from other temples in Patan.

The current temple was completely built in 1682 after a fire and later restored after the 1934 earthquake, and again in 1967. Non-Hindus can enter and climb to the upper level (the inner sanctum is usually upstairs in Bhimsen temples) to view the wild-eyed statue of Bhimsen.

MANGA HITI
Immediately across from Bhimsen Temple is the sunken Manga Hiti (Map p186), one of the water conduits with which Patan is liberally endowed.

The tank contains a cruciform-shaped pool and three wonderfully carved dhara in the shape of makara. Overlooking the tank are two wooden pavilions known as the **Mani Mandap**, which were built in 1700 for use in the elaborate ceremonies at royal coronations – one of the shelters features a serpent-backed throne.

VISHWANATH TEMPLE
South of the Bhimsen Temple stands the Vishwanath Temple (Map p186), sacred to Shiva. This elaborately decorated two-tiered pagoda was built in 1627 and it features some particularly ornate woodcarving, particularly on the friezes above the colonnade. Also note worthy are the fine stone carvings of Ganesh set into the brick walls. On the west side is a statue of Shiva's loyal mount, Nandi the bull, while the east side features two stone elephants with mahouts, one crushing a man beneath its foot. When the doors are open, you can view the enormous lingam inside.

KRISHNA MANDIR
Continuing into the square, you can't miss the splendid Krishna Mandir (Map p186) built by King Siddhinarsingh Malla in 1637. Constructed from carved stone – in place of the usual brick and timber – this fabulous architectural confection shows the clear influence of Indian temple design. The temple is one of the most distinctive monuments in the valley and it is often depicted on the ornate brass butter lamps hung in Nepali homes.

WALKING TOUR

Duration 1¾ hours
Start Patan Dhoka
Finish Durbar Sq

This route gives a great insight into the communal lifestyle and traditional layout of Newari villages, with their bahal, hiti and *tun* (wells). The walk starts at Patan Dhoka, ends at Durbar Sq and takes under two hours (see Map p182).

Southeast Patan

From Patan Dhoka, stroll southeast to a handsome **Ganesh shrine (A)**, then turn right into **Sulima Square (B)**, a crumbling brick-lined square with a 17th-century Mahadev (Shiva) shrine. On the east side of the square is the derelict house of a famous 16th-century Tantric master. Continue south to the **Pim Bahal Pokhari (C)** pond and go round it anticlockwise, past the three-tiered **Chandeswari Temple (D)** built in 1663. In front is a bell supported by stone columns on the backs of turtles. Nearby is a 600-year-old whitewashed stupa that was damaged by Muslim invaders in the 14th century.

At the road junction, walk northeast past fine wooden windows to a large square at Nakabhil. On the south side is the courtyard-style **Lokakirti Mahavihar (E)**, a former Buddhist monastery now used to store parts of the Rato Machhendranath (see p189). Masked dances are performed on the *dabali* (platform) in front of the monastery for festivals. An alley leads north off the square, signposted 'Bhaskar Varna Mahavihar', to the **Nyakhuchowk Bahal (F)**. The courtyard is full of ancient chaitya and in the centre is a white stupa and a gaudy 4m statue of Sakyamuni.

Head past a row of stupas to the eastern wall and go through the covered entrance, across an alley, into another chaitya-filled courtyard, the **Naga Bahal (G)**. Walk past the statue of a golden bull to a painting of a naga on the wall, repainted every five years during the Samyak festival.

Go through the eastern passageway to a further courtyard with the red-walled Harayana Library in one corner. Follow a diagonal path past the carved wooden frontage of an ancient monastery then go east beneath a wooden torana to reach the **Golden Temple (H; see p187)**.

After visiting the temple, exit east onto the main street, then turn left. You'll soon see a sign for the courtyard-style **Manjushri Temple (I)**. From here continue north past a group of ancient **megaliths (J)**, possibly the oldest objects of worship in the Kathmandu Valley, and continue to the **Kumbeshwar Temple (K; see p188)**.

From this temple, head east and turn south back to Durbar Sq. This road is lined with shrines to different incarnations of Vishnu, including a north Indian–style **Krishna Temple** and the two-tiered **Uma Maheshwar Temple (L; see p188)**. Further south, at Swotha Tole, are the pagoda-style **Rada Krishna Temple (M)**, the Garuda-fronted **Narayan Temple (N)** and another Indian-influenced **Krishna Temple (O)**. A few more steps will take you to Durbar Sq.

Southwest Patan

There are more interesting temples and bahal in the southwest of Patan, which you can visit on the following walking tour (40 minutes) starting and finishing at Durbar Sq. This tour is marked on the Patan map, p182.

Start by walking south from Durbar Sq then take the lane leading west near the **Bishwakarma Temple (AA)**. At the first junction, Ekhalakhu, there are several Nepali-style **Vishnu shrines (AB)**, one with a Garuda statue. Continue past a Ganesh shrine and Shiva shrine to Jenbahal and a brightly painted, three-tiered **Ganesh Temple (AC)**. From here, stroll west past a stone shikhara-style **Narayan Temple (AD)**. At Purnachandi, detour south to see a substantial, three-tiered **Kali Temple (AE)** in front of a large tank, then walk north past another small **Vaishnavite temple (AF)** to the junction at Gabahal.

Turn right and look for a small gateway on the left leading to **Bubahal (AG)**, a courtyard full of Buddhist statues and chaityas in front of the restored Yasodhara Mahavihar temple. Continue east along the main road then duck right into **Haka Bahal (AH)**, the courtyard of the Ratnakar Mahavihar, linked to Patan's Kumari (living goddess) cult. Continue east through Mahapal to finish at the south end of Durbar Sq.

The temple consists of three tiers, fronted by columns and supporting a north Indian style-shikhara. Non-Hindus cannot enter to view the statue of Vishnu as Krishna, the goatherd, but you'll often hear temple musicians playing upstairs. Vishnu's mount, the man-bird Garuda, kneels with folded arms on top of a **column** facing the temple. The delicate stone carvings along the beam on the 1st-floor recount events from the Mahabharata, while the beam on the 2nd floor features scenes from the Ramayana.

A major festival, **Krishna Jayanta**, also known as Krishnasthami, is held here in the Nepali month of Bhadra (August–September) for Krishna's birthday.

JAGANNARAYAN TEMPLE

Fronted by a pair of barrel-chested lions, the two-storey Jagannarayan (or Char Narayan) Temple (Map p186) is dedicated to Vishnu as Narayan, the creator of the universe. Dating from 1565, it is said to be the oldest temple in the square, and its roof struts are alive with carvings of couples engaged in saucy goings-on.

KING YOGANARENDRA MALLA'S STATUE

South of the Jagannarayan Temple is a tall column (Map p186) topped by a striking brass statue of King Yoganarendra Malla (1684–1705) and his queens, installed in 1700. Above the king's head is a cobra, and above the cobra is a small brass bird – legend has it that as long as the bird remains the king may still return to his palace. Accordingly, the door and window of the palace are always kept open and a hookah is kept ready should the king ever decide to come back. A rider to the legend adds that when the bird flies off, the elephants in front of the Vishwanath Temple will stroll over to Manga Hiti for a drink!

Behind the statue of the king are three smaller **Vishnu temples**, including a brick-and-plaster shikhara temple, built in 1590 to enshrine an image of Narsingha, Vishnu's man-lion incarnation.

HARI SHANKAR TEMPLE

The three-storey temple to Hari Shankar (Map p186), a curious hybrid deity that has half the attributes of Vishnu and half the attributes of Shiva, has roof struts carved with scenes of the tortures of the damned. This is a strange contrast to the erotic scenes more commonly seen on temple roofs. It was built in 1704–05 by the daughter of King Yoganarendra Malla.

TALEJU BELL

South of the Hari Shankar Temple is a huge, ancient bell (Map p186), hanging between two stout pillars, erected by King Vishnu Malla in 1736. Petitioners could ring the bell to alert the king to their grievances. The huge brass chains attached to the bell look almost as solid as the stone columns that support them. Behind the bell pavilion is a fountain crossed by an ornamental bridge.

KRISHNA TEMPLE

This attractive, octagonal stone temple (Map p186) completes the 'front line' of temples in the square. Also known as the Chyasim Deval, it has strong architectural similarities to the Krishna Temple at the north end of the square. The tiered structure was built in 1723 in a style clearly influenced by the stone temples of northern India.

Behind the Krishna Temple stands the squat and rather plain **Bhai Dega Temple**, dedicated to Shiva. Nearby is a stone shikhara-style temple dedicated to **Uma Maheshwar**, in a similar style to the two Krishna temples. Note the ornate carvings in the faux windows on the upper level.

ROYAL PALACE

Forming the whole eastern side of the Durbar Sq, the Royal Palace of Patan (Map p186) was originally built in the 14th century, but expanded massively during the 17th and 18th centuries by Siddhinarsingh Malla,

---

ASHOKA STUPAS

Legend claims that the four stupas marking the boundaries of Patan were built when the great Buddhist emperor Ashoka visited the valley 2500 years ago. The Northern Stupa is just beyond the Kumbeshwar Temple, on the way to the Sankhamul ghats; the Southern Stupa is just south of the Lagankhel bus stop; the Western Stupa is beside the main road from Kathmandu at Pulchowk; and the tiny Eastern Stupa is well to the east of centre, across Kathmandu's Ring Rd. Buddhist and Tibetan pilgrims walk around all four stupas in a single day during the auspicious full moon of August.

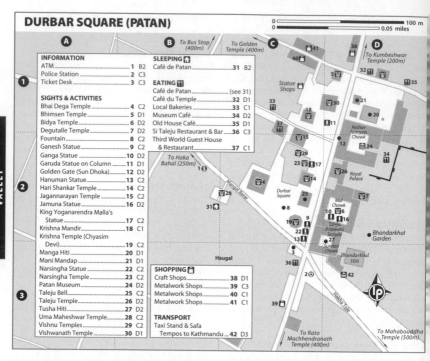

DURBAR SQUARE (PATAN)

INFORMATION

ATM	1	B2
Police Station	2	C3
Ticket Desk	3	C3

SIGHTS & ACTIVITIES

Bhai Dega Temple	4	C2
Bhimsen Temple	5	D1
Bidya Temple	6	D2
Degutalle Temple	7	D2
Fountain	8	C2
Ganesh Statue	9	C2
Ganga Statue	10	D2
Garuda Statue on Column	11	D1
Golden Gate (Sun Dhoka)	12	D2
Hanuman Statue	13	C2
Hari Shankar Temple	14	C2
Jagannarayan Temple	15	C2
Jamuna Statue	16	D2
King Yoganarendra Malla's Statue	17	C2
Krishna Mandir	18	C1
Krishna Temple (Chyasim Devi)	19	C2
Manga Hiti	20	D1
Mani Mandap	21	D1
Narsingha Statue	22	C2
Narsingha Temple	23	C2
Patan Museum	24	D2
Taleju Bell	25	C3
Taleju Temple	26	D2
Tusha Hiti	27	D2
Uma Maheshwar Temple	28	C2
Vishnu Temples	29	C2
Vishwanath Temple	30	D1

SLEEPING

Café de Patan	31	B2

EATING

Café de Patan	(see 31)	
Café du Temple	32	D1
Local Bakeries	33	C1
Museum Café	34	D2
Old House Café	35	D1
Si Taleju Restaurant & Bar	36	C3
Third World Guest House & Restaurant	37	C1

SHOPPING

Craft Shops	38	D1
Metalwork Shops	39	C3
Metalwork Shops	40	C1
Metalwork Shops	41	C1

TRANSPORT

Taxi Stand & Safa		
Tempos to Kathmandu	42	D3

Srinivasa Malla and Vishnu Malla. The Patan palace predates the palaces in Kathmandu and Bhaktapur and it was severely damaged during the conquest of the valley by Prithvi Narayan Shah in 1768. More restoration was done after the great earthquake of 1934, but the palace remains one of the architectural highlights of Nepal.

Behind the extravagant facade, with its overhanging eaves, carved windows and delicate wooden screens, are a series of connecting courtyards and three **temples** dedicated to the valley's main deity, the goddess Taleju. The **Bhairab gateway** leading to the central courtyard – known as Mul Chowk – is flanked by two stone lions and colourful murals of Shiva in his wrathful incarnation as Bhairab. Strings of buffalo guts are hung above the door in his honour.

The northern courtyard is reached through the **Golden Gate** (Map p186), or Sun Dhoka. Installed in 1734, this finely engraved and gilded gateway is topped by a golden torana showing Shiva, Parvati, Ganesh and Kumar (an incarnation of Skanda, the God of War). Directly above the gateway is a window made

from gold foil wrapped around a timber frame, where the king once made public appearances. The gateway now forms the entrance to the Patan Museum.

PATAN MUSEUM

Formerly the residence of the Malla kings, the section of the palace surrounding Keshav Narayan Chowk now houses one of the finest collections of religious art in Asia. Partly funded by the Austrian government, the **Patan Museum** (Map p186; ☎ 5521492; www.patanmuseum .gov.np; admission foreigner/SAARC Rs 250/75; ☷ 10.30am-4.30pm, last admission 4pm) is a national treasure, and a visit should form part of any trip to Patan's Durbar Sq.

The collection is displayed in a series of brick and timber rooms, linked by steep and narrow stairways. There are informative labels on each of the hundreds of statues, carvings and votive objects, allowing you to put a name to many of the deities depicted at temples around the valley.

There are also some interesting displays on the techniques used to create these wonderful objects, including the art of repoussé (see boxed text, p177) and the 'lost-wax' method of casting. Gallery H at the back of the complex, near the cafe, houses some fascinating photos of Patan at the turn of the 19th and 20th centuries.

You need at least an hour, and preferably two, to do this place justice, and it's worth taking a break at the excellent Museum Café (see p193) before diving in for another round. The museum also has a shop selling reproductions of some of the works displayed inside. For a sneak preview of the museum's highlights and the story of its renovation go to www.asianart.com/patan-museum.

MUL CHOWK

South of the Patan Museum, a gateway opens onto the stately Mul Chowk (Map p186), the largest and oldest of the palace's three main chowks (squares). The original buildings were destroyed by fire in 1662 but rebuilt just three years later by Srinivasa Malla. If the doors happen to be open when you visit, you can enter the square to view the exquisitely carved windows and balconies and the three temples dedicated to Taleju, the personal deity of the Malla kings.

As you enter through the Bhairab gate (see the Royal Palace, p185), the first thing you will notice is the small, gilded **Bidya Temple** in the middle of the square, beside a wooden post used to secure animals for sacrifices. To the south is the **Taleju Bhawani Temple**, flanked by statues of the river goddesses Ganga, on a tortoise, and Jamuna, on a makara.

At the northeastern corner of the square is the tall **Degutalle Temple**, topped by an octagonal triple-roofed tower. The larger, triple-roofed **Taleju Temple** is directly north, looking out over Durbar Sq. This temple has been destroyed almost as many times as it has been rebuilt.

The latest incarnation was reconstructed out of the wreckage of the 1934 earthquake. All three temples are closed to non-Hindus and actually rarely open to anyone.

SUNDARI CHOWK

South of Mul Chowk is the smaller Sundari Chowk (Map p186), arranged around a superbly carved sunken water tank known as the Tusha Hiti. Unfortunately the courtyard is closed to the public, but swing by the gateway to view the gilded metal window over the entrance, which is flanked by windows of carved ivory. Nearby are three magnificent statues of **Hanuman** (barely recognisable beneath layers of orange paint), **Ganesh** and Vishnu as **Narsingha**, the man-lion.

North of Durbar Square

The following sights are north of Durbar Sq. They can be visited as part of the Patan Walking Tour (see boxed text, p184).

GOLDEN TEMPLE (KWA BAHAL)

Also known as the Hiranya Varna Mahavihara, this unique Buddhist **monastery** (Map p182; admission Rs 50; ☉ dawn-dusk) is just north of Durbar Sq. The monastery was allegedly founded in the 12th century, and it has existed in its current location since 1409. Entry is via a narrow stone doorway to the east or a wooden doorway to the west, inside one of the interlinked bahal on the north side of Nakabhil.

Entering from the east, note the gaudy painted lions and the signature of Krishnabir, the master stonemason who sculpted the fine doorway with its frieze of Buddhist deities. This second doorway leads to the main courtyard in front of the Golden Temple, so named because of the gilded metal plates that cover most of its frontage. Slums and other leather

---

KARTIK DANCES

Every year in Kartik (October–November), Patan's Durbar Sq fills with music and dancers for a festival that can trace its origins back to the time of King Siddhinarsingh Malla in the early 17th century. As the story goes, the king was frustrated at the unhappiness of his citizens compared to the inhabitants of neighbouring Kantipur (Kathmandu) and Bhadgaon (Bhaktapur), so he came up with a plan for a human sacrifice. Dancers filled Durbar Sq for eight days and on the last day, a dancer dressed as the demon Hiranyakashipu was ritually killed by a dancer dressed as Narsingha. History failed to record whether the ceremony improved happiness in the greater Patan area, but the tradition endured in a less violent form through the annual Kartik Dance, which is still performed by dancers wearing masks to represent Narsingha and Hiranyakashipu.

articles must be removed if you enter the inner courtyard. Look for the tortoises pottering around the compound – these are the temple guardians. The main priest of the temple is a young boy under the age of twelve, who serves for 30 days before handing the job over to another young boy.

The temple itself is a magnificent example of courtyard temple architecture. Two elephant statues guard the doorway and the facade is covered by a host of gleaming Buddhist figures. Inside the main shrine is a beautiful statue of Sakyamuni (no photos allowed). To the left of the courtyard is a statue of Green Tara and to the right is a statue of the Bodhisattva Vajrasattva wearing an impressive silver-and-gold cape. Nearby is a mural depicting the parable of the 'Four Harmonious Friends' – the elephant, monkey, rabbit and bird who worked together to reach the highest fruit on the tree.

Facing the main temple is a smaller shrine containing a 'self-arisen' *(swayambhu)* chaitya. The four corners of the courtyard have statues of four Lokeshvaras (incarnations of Avalokitesvara) and four monkeys, which hold out jackfruits as an offering. A stairway leads to an upper-floor chapel dedicated to the Amitabh Buddha, lined with Tibetan-style frescoes. Finally, as you leave the temple, look up to see an embossed Kalachakra mandala mounted on the ceiling.

It's worth ducking south towards Durbar Sq to see the small, two-tiered **Uma Maheshwar Temple** (Map p186) and the handsome stone **Gauri Shankar Temple** (Map p186), in the Indian shikhara style. Across the road, the Buddhist **Maru Mandapa Mahavihar** (Map p182) is set in a small courtyard.

KUMBESHWAR TEMPLE

Due north of Durbar Sq is the eye-catching Kumbeshwar Temple (Map p182), one of the valley's three five-storey temples. This tall, thin mandir features some particularly artistic woodcarving, and it seems to defy gravity as it towers above the surrounding houses. A large Nandi statue indicates that the shrine is sacred to Shiva.

The temple platform has two ponds whose water is said to come straight from the holy lake at Gosainkund, a long trek north of the valley (see p350 for more information about the trek). Bathing in the tank at Kumbeshwar Temple is said to be as meritorious as making the arduous walk to Gosainkund.

The surrounding square is dotted with temples sacred to Bhairab and Baglamukhi (Parvati). Local women gather at the tank known as **Konti Hiti** to socialise, wash clothes and fill up their water jugs. To the north of the temple is the Kumbeshwar Technical School (p193).

From here you can detour north to see the Northern Stupa, one of four marker shrines showing the old city limits of Patan.

UMA MAHESHWAR TEMPLE

En route from Kumbeshwar Temple to Durbar Sq, the small, inconspicuous double-roofed Uma Maheshwar Temple (Map p182) is on the eastern side of the road. Peer inside the temple to see a very beautiful black-stone relief of Shiva and Parvati in the pose known as Uma Maheshwar – the god sitting cross-legged with his shakti leaning against him rather seductively. There are several other temples dedicated to Vishnu along this road.

South of Durbar Square

The following sights are south of Durbar Sq in the backstreets south of Mangal Bazar, the main local shopping street. If you continue south, you will reach the busy marketplace surrounding the Lagankhel bus stand.

BISHWAKARMA TEMPLE

Walk south from Durbar Sq past brassware shops and workshops and keep an eye out for a small lane leading off to the right (west). A short distance down this lane is the Bishwakarma Temple (Map p182), with its entire facade covered in sheets of embossed copper. The temple is dedicated to

---

JANAI PURNIMA AT KUMBESHWAR

Thousands of pilgrims visit the Kumbeshwar Temple during the **Janai Purnima Festival** in July or August, when members of the Brahmin and Chhetri castes replace the sacred thread they wear looped over their left shoulder. A silver-and-gold lingam is set up in the tank and devotees take a ritual bath in the cloudy waters while jhankri in colourful headdresses and skirts dance around the temple beating drums. Needless to say, it's quite a spectacle.

RATO MACHHENDRANATH FESTIVAL

The image in the Rato Machhendranath Temple may look like a crudely carved piece of painted wood, but each year it forms the centrepiece for the **Rato Machhendranath Festival** in the Nepali month of Baisakh (April–May). Immediately prior to the festival, the scattered timbers of Rato Machhendranath's chariot are gathered and assembled and the statue is installed on his awesome coach on the fourth day of the light fortnight of Baisakh. It takes a full month to move the chariot across Patan to Jawalakhel, where the chariot is finally dismantled. Machhendranath is considered to have powers over rain and, since the monsoon is approaching at this time, this festival is essentially a plea for generous rains.

The towering main chariot is accompanied for much of its journey by a smaller chariot, which contains the image of Rato Machhendranath's companion, Jatadhari Lokesvara, which normally resides in the nearby Minnath Temple. The highlight of the festival is the Bhoto Jatra, or showing of the sacred vest. According to the legend, the jewelled vest was given to the god for safe keeping after a dispute between two potential owners. Every year, the vest is displayed three times in order to give the owner the chance to claim it – although this does not actually happen. The king of Nepal attends this ceremony, which is also a national holiday.

From Jawalakhel, Rato Machhendranath is conveyed on a khat (palanquin) to his second home in the village of Bungamati, 6km to the south, where he spends the next six months of the year, before returning to Patan. The main chariot is so large and the route is so long that the Nepali army is often called in to help transport it.

the patron deity of carpenters and craftspeople, which is appropriate, as you can hear many of them banging hammers in the surrounding workshops.

I BAHA BAHI

Further south, another tiny doorway leads to the quiet bahal containing the I Baha Bahi (Map p182). This handsome Buddhist monastery was founded in 1427 and the structure was restored in the 1990s by a team of archaeologists from Japan.

MINNATH TEMPLE

Further south, another gateway leads to a courtyard strewn with wooden beams. In the centre is the brightly painted, two-tiered Minnath Temple (Map p182), dedicated to the Budhisattva Jatadhari Lokesvara, who is considered to be the little brother of Rato Machhendranath.

The temple was founded in the Licchavi period (3rd to 9th centuries) but the multiarmed goddesses on the roof struts were added much later. Note the metal pots and pans nailed to the temple rafters by devotees. The timbers lying around the courtyard are assembled into a chariot every year to haul the statue of Minnath around town as part of the Rato Machhendranath Festival.

RATO MACHHENDRANATH TEMPLE

Almost directly across the road, another gateway leads to the wide, open square containing the revered Rato Machhendranath Temple (Red Machhendranath Temple; Map p182). Dedicated to the god of rain and plenty, the temple straddles the line between Buddhism and Hinduism. Buddhists regard Rato Machhendranath as an incarnation of Avalokitesvara, while Hindus see him as an incarnation of Shiva.

Set inside a protective metal fence, the towering three-storey temple dates from 1673, but there has been some kind of temple on this site since at least 1408. The temple's four ornate doorways are guarded by stone lions and at ground level on the four corners of the temple plinth are curious yeti-like demons known as *kyah*.

Mounted on freestanding pillars at the front of the temple is a curious collection of metal animals, including peacocks, Garudas, horses, buffalos, lions, elephants, fish and snakes. Look up to see the richly painted roof struts of the temple, which show Avalokitesvara standing above figures being tortured in hell.

The temple comes into its own during the Rato Machhendranath Festival in April–May.

MAHABOUDDHA TEMPLE

To reach the Mahabouddha Temple (Temple of a Thousand Buddhas; Map p182), you must walk southeast from Durbar Sq along Hakha Tole, passing a series of small Vaishnavite and Shaivite temples.

When you reach Sundhara Tole, with its sunken hiti with three brass waterspouts, turn right and look for the tiny doorway leading to the temple.

As you step through, the temple suddenly looms above you, crammed into a tiny courtyard. Built in the Indian shikhara style, the shrine takes its name from the hundreds of terracotta tiles that cover it, each bearing an image of the Buddha. The temple is loosely modelled on the Mahabouddha Temple at Bodhgaya in India, where the Buddha gained enlightenment.

The temple dates from 1585, but it was ruined by the 1934 earthquake and totally rebuilt. Unfortunately, without plans to work from, the builders ended up with a different-looking temple, and had enough bricks and tiles left over to construct a smaller shrine to Maya Devi, the Buddha's mother, in the corner of the courtyard!

The surrounding lanes are full of shops selling high-quality Patan-style metal statues of Hindu and Buddhist deities, and these even spill into the square around the temple. The roof terrace of the shop at the back of the courtyard has a good view of the temple and there's no undue pressure to buy.

UKU BAHAL (RUDRA VARNA MAHAVIHAR)

South of the Mahabouddha Temple, this ancient Buddhist monastery (Map p182) is one of the best known in Patan.

The main courtyard is jam-packed with statuary and metalwork – dorjes, bells, peacocks, elephants, Garudas, rampant goats, kneeling devotees, a regal-looking statue of a Rana general, and, rather incongruously, a pair of Victorian-style British lions that look like they would be mush more at home in Trafalgar Sq than in a Buddhist monastery in Nepal!

The monastery has been used for centuries, and the wooden roof struts are some of the oldest in the valley, but much of what you can see today dates back to the 19th century. Behind the monastery is a large stupa in the Swayambhunath style.

LAGAN STUPA

South of the noisy Lagankhel Bus Stand, crowning a hilltop in a small park, the Lagan Stupa (Map p182) is one of the four stupas marking the historical city limits of Patan (see boxed text, p185). It's a scenic spot and a good vantage point from which to look out over the southern part of Patan.

Zoo

Nepal's only **zoo** (Map p182; ☎ 5528323; admission adult/child Rs 150/100, paddle boats Rs 40; ⏲ 10am-5pm) is in the southwestern part of Patan by the Jawalakhel roundabout. Although there is definitely room for improvement, the animals live in better conditions than you might expect and there are always crowds of local kids being wowed by such exotic creatures as elephants, tigers, leopards, hyenas, guar, deer, blue bulls, gharials, giant tortoises, langur monkeys and some very noisy hippos. Stoners routinely get freaked out by the giant 60cm-long squirrels.

Western Temples

To the north of the Jawalakhel roundabout is a group of temples clustered around the busy road to Kathmandu. Next to the St Xavier School is the stately, Newari-style **Ugrachandi Temple** (Map p182), dedicated to Parvati in the form she adopted to drive the buffalo-demon Mahisasura from heaven. Further north at Pulchowk is the **Western Stupa** (Map p182), marking the western city limits of Patan, set on a grassy knoll. A set of steps leads uphill to the **Aksheshwor Mahavihar** (Map p182), a courtyard-style Buddhist monastery on the hilltop.

FESTIVALS & EVENTS

Patan's most dramatic festival is the **Rato Machhendranath Festival** (p189) in April–May followed by the **Janai Purnima Festival** (p188) at Kumbeshwar Temple in July–August.

SLEEPING

There's a small but decent spread of accommodation for all budgets in Patan.

Budget

Durbar Guest House (Map p182; ☎ 5540034; www.durba guesthouse.com; s without bathroom Rs 200-250, d with bathroom Rs 500-600) Close to Sundhara Tole, this place is set back from the road behind a statue shop. Rooms are not too exciting but they are functional and cheap.

Mahabuddha Guest House (Map p182; ☎ 5540575; mhg@mos.com.np; s/d Rs 450/600; ☐) Southeast of Durbar Sq, across the road from the Mahabuddha Temple, this is a good budget choice, with tidy, cared-for rooms and an internet cafe. Rooms can be dark so aim for a room higher up.

Café de Patan (Map p186; ☎ 5537599; www.cafede patan.com; r with/without bathroom Rs 800/600) This courtyard hotel is almost on Durbar Sq and there's a rooftop garden and a pleasant downstairs cafe (p192). The neat, modern rooms get plenty of light, but only two have bathrooms.

Midrange & Top End

Patan has a good selection of more expensive hotels and all accept international credit cards.

ourpick Newa Chén (Map p182; ☎ 5533532; www .newachen.com; s with/without bathroom US$25/20, d with/without bathroom US$40/30) Housed inside the Unesco-restored Shestha House mansion, this charming boutique hotel offers a window onto what it must have been like to be a well-to-do resident of Patan in centuries past. Rooms are decked out in traditional style with divan seating areas and coir matting on the floors.

Hotel Goodwill (Map p182; ☎ 5514520, www.hotel goodwillpatan.com; s/d from US$25/30; ☒) South of Uku Bahal, this comfortable midrange hotel is a spin-off from a metal workshop and the owners have filled it with an outrageous bestiary of statues. The wood-floored rooms are large and inviting, and the pool makes this a good choice for families.

Aloha Inn (Map p182; ☎ 5522796; www.alohainn .com; s/d with air-conditioning US$30/35, s/d without air-conditioning US$25/30; ☒ ☐) Where they got the Hawaiian name from is anyone's guess, but the Aloha is calm, friendly and blissfully air-conditioned. Rooms are slightly chintzy, but good value, with TVs and bathrooms, plus fridges in the air-conditioned rooms.

Hotel Clarion (Map p182; ☎ 5524512; www.hotel clarion.com; s/d from US$30/40; ☒) At first glance the Clarion looks a bit dated, but the rooms are comfortable and well appointed, with parquet floors and marble bathrooms. Central air-conditioning is another bonus and there's a good restaurant with unusual round doors. Room rates fluctuate with demand so see if it is offering discounts.

ourpick Summit Hotel (Map p182; ☎ 5521810; www.summit-nepal.com; budget s/d US$15/20, s/d from US$45/55; ☒ ☒ ☐) Expats and NGOs like to keep the Summit secret so that there is room when relatives and friends come to visit. The hotel is built in mock-Newari style, with lots of red brick and carved timber, and the atmosphere is uniquely calm and relaxed. The swimming pool comes into its own in summer, while open fires keep things snug in winter. The budget rooms in Holland House are pretty plain, but the Himalayan View rooms and the Garden View rooms are delightful. The Summit Hotel is tucked away in the lanes west of Kopundol.

Hotel Greenwich Village (Map p182; ☎ 5521780; www.godavariresort.com.np; s/d from US$60/70; ☒ ☒) In the same area as the Summit Hotel, the oddly named Greenwich Village is peaceful and secluded, through less luxurious than the rates might suggest. Rooms are smart and comfortable but you'll probably spend most of your time at the lovely poolside terrace and cafe. Foreign exchange and free airport pick-up are useful perks.

Hotel Himalaya (Map p182; ☎ 5523900; www .himalayahotel.com.np; s/d from US$140/160; ☒ ☐ ☒) Patan's only truly top-end hotel, the Himalaya is the haunt of wealthy businessmen and Nepali wedding parties. Expect lots of marble, concierge service and comfortable, well-appointed rooms that are arranged around a pool.

EATING

Most of Patan's restaurants overlook Durbar Sq and are aimed at day-tripping tour groups. Unless otherwise stated, the following restaurants are open from 8am to 8pm.

For a quick sweet or savoury snack, pop into one of the bustling local bakeries on the alley behind the Vishnu Temple on Durbar Sq. More substantial meals of tandoori chicken and roti (oven baked bread) are available from the 'oscillatory chicken' restaurants by the Jawalakhel roundabout.

For a classy dinner for two while in Patan, consider the expat-oriented restaurants around Pulchowk (see p192).

Anmol Sweet (Map p182; ☎ 4423576; snacks Rs 20-100) A convenient misthan bhandar, serving tasty bhujia (crisp lentil noodles), Indian sweets, dosas and other South Indian snacks, to eat-in or takeaway.

Si Taleju Restaurant & Bar (Map p186; ☎ 5538358; mains Rs 100-240) A narrow, towering place with

EXPAT EATS

The area around the UN compound at Pulchowk is a favourite hang-out of diplomats, aid-workers and other expats, and it's well worth coming here to escape the crowds in Thamel (a few kilometres north). There are all sorts of restaurants and cafes here and you may find yourself starting some interesting conversations with fellow diners.

Bakery Café (Map p182; ☎ 5522949; mains Rs 50-200; www.nanglos.com; ☻ 10.30am-9.30pm; ☐) All the branches of the excellent Bakery Café chain provide work for deaf Nepalis who would otherwise struggle to find employment. Patan has two Bakery Cafés – one by the zoo at Jawalakhel and one opposite UN House at Pulchowk. Both have wireless internet access and momos, sizzlers, salads and sandwiches on the menu.

Singa Ma Food Court (Map p182; ☎ 5509092; mains Rs 100-220; ☻ 8.30am-9pm Sun-Fri) For the authentic tastes of Malaysia, head to this busy food court south of Pulchowk. The noodle soups, nasi lemak (coconut rice with anchovies) and beef rendang (dry coconut curry with lime leaves) are the real *mamak* (Malay Tamil) deal.

Masala (Map p182; ☎ 5009205; mains Rs 100-300; ☻ 11am-10pm) Quality Indian food is surprisingly hard to find in Kathmandu, but this sophisticated place plugs the gap, with an excellent menu of Mughlai and tandoori dishes. It's a stylish choice for a dinner date.

Red Dingo (Map p182; ☎ 6914960; www.thereddingo.com; mains from Rs 200; ☻ 7am-9pm Sat-Thu, to 4pm Sun) No prizes for guessing the origins of the owners of this Aussie bistro near the Jawalakhel roundabout. Come for hearty meat pies, elegant salads and mains in the modern-Australian mould.

New Orleans (Map p182; ☎ 5522708; mains Rs 200-300; ☻ 8am-10pm; ☐) Set around a lovely courtyard that is always full of expats with laptops, this branch of the popular Thamel bar and restaurant serves everything from Nepali *choyla* to stuffed pittas and Mongolian beef.

our pick **La Soon** (Map p182; ☎ 5537166; www.lasoon.com.np; mains Rs 200-385; ☻ noon-10pm) Down a quiet side alley near Pulchowk, this charming garden restaurant and wine bar is run by a Swiss-Ghanaian couple, and the menu is an interesting fusion of Asian, French and African influences. The regular 'Africa Nights' with live music and fashion shows always pull in a crowd.

Roadhouse Café (Map p182; ☎ 5521755; pizzas from Rs 260; ☻ 11am-10pm) A branch of the ever-popular Thamel pizza parlour, with a relaxed, family vibe. As well as pizzas from the wood-fired oven, the menu runs to good burgers and grills.

New York Pizza (Map p182; ☎ 5520294; Kopundol; pizzas from Rs 350) This delivery-only pizza company makes good 12-inch American-style pizzas and it offers free delivery anywhere in Patan.

For something extra special, the Friday-night barbecues (Rs 750) at the Summit Hotel (p191) are a treat. The hotel also hosts an organic produce market on Sundays, from 10am to 1.30pm.

four floors, each with a different look and feel. Best is the top-floor dining room with jaw-dropping views north across Durbar Sq to the mountains beyond. You'll find all your favourites on the menu – momos, chow mein, Indian curries and those ubiquitous 'Continental' dishes.

Café de Patan (Map p186; ☎ 5537599; www.cafedepatan.com; dishes Rs 100-250) Southwest of Durbar Sq behind a small Uma Maheshwar temple, this is place is a long-running travellers' favourite. There's a pleasant open-air courtyard and a rooftop garden (with one table right at the very top of the building). The menu runs to pizza, Newari dishes and cold beers.

Kwalkhu Café (Map p182; ☎ 6212154; mains Rs 100-250) An island of calm in the courtyard of the restored Rajbhandari House, this peaceful cafe has a terracotta-tiled terrace and a solid menu of Nepali, Tibetan, Chinese and Continental food.

Café du Temple (Map p186; ☎ 5527127; www.cafedutemple.com.np; mains Rs 100-300) A tour-group favourite at the north end of Patan's Durbar Sq. The rooftop tables are covered by red-and-white sun umbrellas and the menu runs from fried rice to daal bhaat, via chicken stroganoff. There's a branch in Bhaktapur.

Dhokaima Café (Map p182; ☎ 5522113; mains Rs 100-300) A pleasant cafe in the New Orleans mould set inside a Rana-era storehouse by the Patan

Dhoka gateway. Shaded by a sprawling walnut tree, the courtyard garden is a great place to enjoy such varied international dishes as Mexican nachos, Italian pizzas and Japanese *edamame* (soy beans).

our pick **Museum Café** (Map p186; light meals Rs 130-240; 9am-5pm) In the rear courtyard of the Patan Museum, this stylish open-air place is run by the team behind the Summit Hotel. Prices are high but so is the quality of the food, and the garden terrace setting feels elegant and refined. You don't need to buy a museum ticket to eat at the cafe.

Nearby are the similar **Old House Café** (Map p186; 5555027; mains from Rs 100), set in an old Newari house in the northeastern corner of the square, and **Third World Restaurant** (Map p186; 5522187; mains from Rs 100), on the quiet western side of the square, with good rooftop views of the Krishna Mandir.

DRINKING

Moksh Bar (Map p182; 5526212; 11am-11pm Tue-Sun) Across from La Soon, Moksh has some of the best live rock, funk and folk music in town (not just the standard cover bands) on Tuesday, Friday and Saturday. Other nights, it can be pretty quiet.

SHOPPING

Patan is packed with small handicraft shops and is the best place in the valley for statuary and fair-trade products. The Jawalakhel area around the zoo is great for Tibetan crafts and carpets.

Patan Industrial Estate (Map p182; 5521367; www.patan.com.np; 10am-5pm Sun-Fri) Despite the dubious-sounding name, this tourist-oriented crafts complex boasts a number of workshop showrooms selling high-quality carpets, wood carvings and metalwork. It's around 500m south of Lagenkhel Bus Stand.

Namaste Supermarket (Map p182; 5520026; Pulchowk; 8.30am-8pm). Sharing a building with the Hotel Narayani, this is where expats come to stock up on quality local produce and the tastes of home.

Carpets

Anyone who appreciates carpets should visit Jawalakhel, the former Tibetan refugee camp where Nepal's enormous carpet industry was born. Tibetan-run carpet shops line the approach road south of the zoo and there are several stores that sell imported tribal rugs

from Afghanistan. For more on Tibetan carpets see boxed text, p62.

The **Jawalakhel Handicraft Centre** (5521305; www.jhcnepal.com; 9am-5pm Sun-Fri, 10am-5pm Sat peak season), established in 1960, is a large cooperative workshop where you can watch the carpet-makers at work and buy the finished article. The quality is high, there is a great selection, the prices are fixed, credit cards are accepted and staff can arrange shipping for you.

Fair-Trade Shops

For the some of the best and certainly the most ethical souvenirs in the valley, head to the fair-trade shops of Kopundol, just south of the bridge linking Kathmandu and Patan. Lined up along the road are a series of emporiums that support the work of craft cooperatives around the country, channelling money directly from travellers to disadvantaged and neglected communities.

Mahaguthi (Map p182; 5521607; www.mahaguthi.org; 10am-6.30pm, to 5pm Sat) was founded by a Nepali disciple of Mahatma Gandhi and its Kopundol showroom is a treasure house of dhaka weavings, handmade paper, ceramics, block prints, pashminas, woodcrafts, jewellery, knitwear, statues, singing bowls, embroidery and Mithila paintings (see boxed text, p319). There's a second branch in Kathmandu's Lazimpat district (see p159).

Another shop worth looking at is **Dhukuti** (Map p182; 5535107; www.acp.org.np; 9am-7pm), which represents the artisans of the Association of Craft Producers. Browse several floors of clothes, batiks, bags, paintings, toys, woodcarvings, felt slippers and even Christmas decorations, produced by over 1200 low-income women.

Other recommended fair-trade emporiums include **Sana Hastakala** (Map p182; 5522628; www.sanahastakala.org; 9.30am-6pm, to 5pm Sat) for paper, batiks, Mithila crafts, felt products and clothing woven from natural fibres; and **Dhankuta Sisters** (Map p182; 5203209; 11am-5.30pm Sun-Fri) for tablecloths, cushion covers and clothing made from dhaka cloth from eastern Nepal.

Near to the Kumbeshwar Temple in the backstreets of Patan, the **Kumbeshwar Technical School** (Map p182; 5537484; www.kumbeshwar.com; 9am-5pm Sun-Fri) provides disadvantaged low-caste families with training, education and a livelihood, making carpets, knitwear and

AROUND THE KATHMANDU VALLEY

woodcarvings. Sales from the showroom help fund the work of the attached school.

Metalwork & Woodwork

Patan is a famous centre for bronze casting, repoussé work and other metal arts. Most of the statues of the Buddha, Mahakala and other Tantric deities that you see on sale in Kathmandu are actually made in Patan, and you can save money by buying them at their source.

There are numerous metalwork shops north and south of Durbar Sq, and more around the Mahabouddha Temple. The price of a bronze statue of a Buddhist or Hindu deity can range from Rs 3000 to more than Rs 100,000, depending on the size, the complexity of the casting, the level of detail and the amount of gilding and enamelling on the finished statue.

Woodcarving Studio (☎ 5000077, 9741028053; www .leebirch.com; Jawalakhel; ◷ 10am-5pm Sun-Fri) Artist Lee Birch's studio displays some of the best carvings in the valley, made on site by Newar woodcarvers. Prices are generally high, but so is the quality. It's best to call ahead to check it is open.

GETTING THERE & AWAY

You can get to Patan from Kathmandu by bicycle, taxi, bus or tempo. The trip costs around Rs 200 by taxi. If you come under your own steam, go south from the Tundikhel to the National Stadium in Tripureshwar, passing the striking, lion-topped Tripureshwar Mahadev Temple, and cross the Bagmati to Kopundol. At the top of the hill, bear right after the Hotel Himalaya to reach Patan Dhoka.

Safa (electric) tempos (Rs 10, route 14A) leave from Kantipath, near the Kathmandu main post office. Double-check the destination when getting in, as some run to Mangal Bazar/Durbar Sq while others to Lagankhel bus station. In the reverse direction, ask for Kantipath. Local buses and minibuses run frequently between Kathmandu's Ratna Park bus station and Patan Dhoka or the chaotic Lagankhel bus stand in the south of the city (Rs 13, 20 minutes).

Buses and faster minibuses to the southern valley towns leave when full from Lagankhel. There are regular services till nightfall to Godavari (Rs 16, one hour), Bungamati (Rs 13, 40 minutes) and Chapagaon (Rs 12, one

hour). There are also fast and frequent services to Bhaktapur (Rs 20, 30 minutes).

An interesting route back to Kathmandu is to continue northeast from the Northern Stupa down to the riverside ghats at Sankhamul, across the footbridge over the Bagmati River and then up to the Arniko Hwy near the big convention centre, from where you can take a taxi or minibus back to Thamel.

BHAKTAPUR

☎ 01 / pop 65,000

The third of the medieval city-states in the Kathmandu Valley, Bhaktapur is also the best preserved. Many Nepalis still use the old name of Bhadgaon (pronounced *bud*-gown) or the Newari name Khwopa, meaning City of Devotees. The name fits - Bhaktapur has not one but three major squares full of towering temples that comprise some of the finest religious architecture in the country. This grandeur is set against a surprisingly rural backdrop - many locals still make a living farming the fields around Bhaktapur and the streets are full of drying crops and farmers winnowing rice and wheat using wicker baskets and electric fans.

From a visitors' perspective, this is a place to wander around aimlessly, soaking up the atmosphere. Narrow cobblestone streets wind between the red-brick houses, joining a series of squares and courtyards that are peppered with temples, statues, cisterns and wells. The contents of any one of these historic squares could fit out a decent-sized museum and the streets are blissfully traffic free, apart from the occasional tractor hauling in crops from the surrounding fields.

The town's cultural life is also proudly on display. Artisans weave cloth and chisel timber by the roadside, squares are filled with drying pots and open kilns and locals gather in communal courtyards to bathe, collect water and socialise – often over intense card games. Visitors must pay a steep entry fee to view this tapestry of Nepali life, but it's worth every paisa.

HISTORY

As with many other towns in the valley, Bhaktapur grew up to service the old trade route from India to Tibet, but the city became a formal entity under King Ananda Malla in the 12th century. The oldest part of town, around Tachupal Tole, was laid out at this time.

From the 14th to the 16th century, Bhaktapur became the most powerful of the valley's three Malla kingdoms, and a new civic square was constructed at Durbar Sq in the west of the city.

Many of the city's most iconic buildings date from the rule of King Yaksha Malla (1428–82), but there was another explosion of temple-building in the reign of King Bhupatindra Malla in the 17th century. At its peak the city boasted 172 temples and monasteries, 77 water tanks, 172 pilgrim shelters and 152 wells.

The 15th-century royal palace in Durbar Sq was the principal seat of power in the valley until the city was conquered by Prithvi Narayan Shah in 1768 and relegated to the status of a secondary market town. An earthquake that hit in 1934 caused major damage to the city but locals were able to restore most of the buildings, though you can still see the occasional unoccupied temple plinth.

Bhaktapur's streets were paved and extensively restored in the 1970s by the German-funded Bhaktapur Development Project, which also established proper sewerage and wastewater management facilities.

ORIENTATION

Bhaktapur rises up on the northern bank of the Hanumante River, hemmed in to the north by the road to Nagarkot. Public buses, minibuses and taxis from Kathmandu stop near Guhya Pokhari, a short walk from the Lion Gate at the western end of town. Tour buses unload at the Tourist Bus Park, just north of Durbar Sq. From either point it's just a short walk to the centre.

Most of the sights in Bhaktapur are spread out along one long, curving road – the old trade route to Tibet – that runs from the Lion Gate at the west end of town through Taumadhi Tole to Tachupal Tole. Bhaktapur's Durbar Sq is just north of this road, reached by numerous side-lanes.

INFORMATION

To enter Bhaktapur, you must pay a hefty fee of Rs 750 (US$10). SAARC nationalities pay Rs 50 and children under 10 are free. This fee is collected at over a dozen entrances to the city and your ticket will be checked whenever you pass one of the checkpoints. If you are staying here for up to a week, you need only pay the entrance fee once, but you must ask the ticket desk to write your passport number on the back of the ticket.

For longer stays (up to one year), a Bhaktapur Visitor Pass is available within a week of purchasing your entry ticket. Passes are issued by the Bhaktapur Municipality at the **ticket office** (Map pp196-7; ☎ 6610310) by the Tourist Bus Park. You need two passport photos and a photocopy of your visa and passport details.

Around Taumadhi and Tachupal Tole, there are moneychangers and several internet cafes charging Rs 20 per hour – try **Surfer's Edge** (Map pp196-7; 9am-10pm) just north of Potters' Sq, or **Namaste Cyber Café** (Map p200; 8.30am-10pm) by Taumadhi Tole.

Guides touting their services around Durbar Sq charge Rs 200 per hour. Look out for the booklet *Bhaktapur: A Guide Book* (Rs 175) published by the **Bhaktapur Tourism Development Committee** (www.btdc.org.np) and sold in local shops. Its website is quite useful too.

SIGHTS

The following sights will lead you on a walk from west to east through the old town. To dive into the backstreets follow the walking tour (p198).

The Western Gate to Taumadhi Tole

The main road through Bhaktapur forks by the Siddha Pokhari – the left (northern) fork goes directly to Durbar Sq, but it's more interesting to follow the right (southern) fork which winds east to Taumadhi Tole.

Starting from the bus stand at Guhya Pokhari, walk south down the alley to the entrance fee booth by the brilliant white **Lions' Gate**, (Map pp196-7), decorated with the stucco head of a lion, then follow the wide brick road east.

LION'S GATE TO POTTERS' SQUARE

Heading east from Lion's Gate, you will pass a small tank on your right and then the much larger **Teka Pokhari** (pp196-7). Just before the next major junction, to your left, look for the tiny, tunnel-like entrance to the tiny **Ni Bahal** (Map pp196-7), or Jet Barna Maha Bihar,

AROUND THE KATHMANDU VALLEY

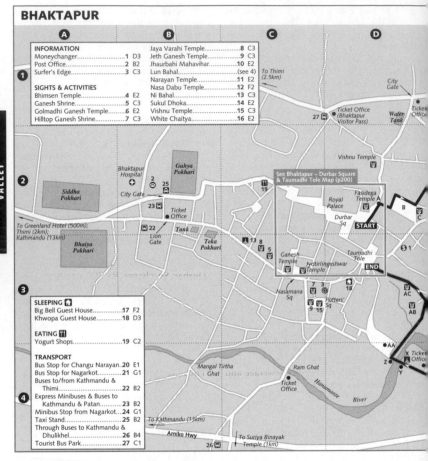

BHAKTAPUR

INFORMATION
Moneychanger.....................1 D3
Post Office.............................2 B2
Surfer's Edge.........................3 C3

SIGHTS & ACTIVITIES
Bhimsen Temple...................4 E2
Ganesh Shrine.......................5 C3
Golmadhi Ganesh Temple....6 E2
Hilltop Ganesh Shrine............7 C3

Jaya Varahi Temple................8 C3
Jeth Ganesh Temple..............9 C3
Jhaurbahi Mahavihar............10 E2
Lun Bahal........................(see 4)
Narayan Temple...................11 E2
Nasa Dabu Temple...............12 F2
Ni Bahal...............................13 E2
Sukul Dhoka.........................14 E2
Vishnu Temple......................15 C3
White Chaitya.......................16 E2

SLEEPING
Big Bell Guest House..............17 F2
Khwopa Guest House............18 D3

EATING
Yogurt Shops.......................19 C2

TRANSPORT
Bus Stop for Changu Narayan.20 E1
Bus Stop for Nagarkot...........21 G1
Buses to/from Kathmandu &
  Thimi...............................22 B2
Express Minibuses & Buses to
  Kathmandu & Patan...........23 B2
Minibus Stop from Nagarkot..24 G1
Taxi Stand...........................25 B2
Through Buses to Kathmandu &
  Dhulikhel..........................26 B4
Tourist Bus Park....................27 C1

dedicated to Maitreya Buddha, the future Buddha. The courtyard contains a very old whitewashed chaitya and several Buddhist shrines. Next to the gatehouse to the courtyard is an enormous pilgrims' rest-house with finely carved timbers.

Cross the junction, where the road runs downhill to the Mangal Tirtha Ghat, and look left to see the fabulous frontage of the red-brick **Jaya Varahi Temple** (Map pp196–7), dedicated to Parvati as the boar-headed Varahi. Look for two very different depictions of the goddess on the torana above the central doorway and the torana over the window above. At the eastern end of the temple is the entrance to the upper floor, flanked by stone lions and banners.

A few more steps bring you to a small **Ganesh shrine** (Map pp196–7), jutting out into the street and covered in bathroom tiles. Continue to **Nasamana Square** (Map pp196–7) which lost its temples in the 1934 quake, but still has a large Garuda statue praying to a vanished Vishnu shrine. Also here is a stone hiti with a spout in the shape of a goat being eaten by a makara.

Nearby is the **Jyotirlingeshwar Temple** (Map pp196–7), a tall shikhara housing an important linga, and two small Shiva shrines by a tank filled with alarmingly green algae. Continue straight and you will pass a turning on the right to Potters' Sq.

Walk a little further on and you will come to Taumadhi Tole.

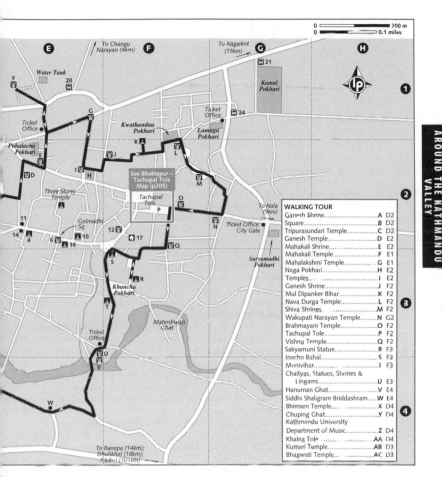

WALKING TOUR	
Ganesh Shrine.................................A	D2
Square...B	D2
Tripurasundari Temple.................C	D2
Ganesh Temple..............................D	E2
Mahakali Shrine............................E	E2
Mahakali Temple...........................F	E1
Mahalakshmi Temple.........G	E1
Naga Pokhari..................................H	E2
Temples..I	E2
Ganesh Shrine................................J	F2
Mul Dipanker Bihar.......................K	F2
Nava Durga Temple......................L	F2
Shiva Shrines..................................M	F2
Wakupati Narayan Temple.........N	G2
Brahmayani Temple......................O	F2
Tachupal Tole................................P	F2
Vishnu Temple...............................Q	F2
Sakyamuni Statue.........................R	F3
Inacho Bahal..................................S	F3
Munivihar..T	F3
Chaityas, Statues, Shrines &	
Lingams...U	E3
Hanuman Ghat...............................V	E4
Siddhi Shaligram Briddashram.....W	E4
Bhimsen Temple.............................X	D4
Chuping Ghat..................................Y	D4
Kathmandu University	
Department of Music....................Z	D4
Khalna Tole.................................AA	D4
Kumari Temple.............................AB	D3
Bhagwati Temple.........................AC	D3

POTTERS' SQUARE

Hidden by the alleyways leading south from the curving road to Taumadhi Tole, the Potters' Sq is exactly what you would expect – a huge public square, full of treadle-power potters' wheels and rows of clay pots drying in the sun. This is the centre of Bhaktapur's ceramic industry, and it's a fascinating place to wander around. Several shops sell the finished article, and you can see the firing process at the back of the square, which is lined with mud-covered straw kilns. During the harvest in October, everywhere that is not covered by pots is covered by drying rice.

On the northern side of the square a small hillock is topped by a shady pipal tree and a **Ganesh shrine** (Map pp196–7), surrounded by piles of straw for the pottery kilns. In the square itself is a solid-brick **Vishnu Temple** (Map pp196–7), constructed from remnants of temples destroyed in the 1934 quake, and the double-roofed **Jeth Ganesh Temple** (Map pp196–7), whose priest is chosen from the Kumal (potters') caste.

Taumadhi Tole

Beyond Potters' Sq, the main street turns north and emerges into the bottom of Taumadhi Tole (Map p200), the first of Bhaktapur's grand civic squares. Here you'll find the Nyatapola Temple, the highest in the valley, and Café Nyatapola (p208), which offers a great vantage point to view the temple.

AROUND THE KATHMANDU VALLEY

WALKING TOUR

Duration Two hours
Start Durbar Sq
Finish Taumadhi Tole
See Map pp196–7 for the route of this circular walking tour. The letters following the sights correspond to the map position.

North of Durbar Square

Starting from the northeastern corner of Durbar Sq, walk to the east of the Fasidega Temple, passing a multicoloured **Ganesh shrine (A)**, where the god is worshipped in the form of a rock that naturally resembles an elephant's head. Turn to the right to reach a **square (B)** with disused palace buildings and a ruined temple plinth.

Walk around the north side of the square and exit at the northeast corner, by the strut-roofed **Tripurasundari Temple (C)**, sacred to one of the Nava Durgas (see boxed text, p203). Continue northeast, then turn right, then left, and look for a weathered **Ganesh temple (D)** with fine figures of the elephant-headed deity on its torana and an unusual terracotta Ganesh window above the door.

At the next junction take a right, past some lovely carved windows, and then swing left past a small **Mahakali shrine (E)** and the Pohalacha Pokhari tank to a city ticket office. Make a short detour north to the Bhaktapur–Nagarkot road and climb the small hillock to a large **Mahakali Temple (F)**, with an eccentric collection of statues inside a gated pavilion. Note the buffalo guts draped over the guardian statues.

Return to the ticket office and walk northeast until you reach a brick square containing a tiny, yellow-roofed **Mahalakshmi Temple (G)**, sacred to the goddess of wealth. Turn right (south) and continue straight to another large tank, the **Naga Pokhari (H)**, where saffron colour threads are dried on large racks beside the lurid green waters. On the western side of the tank are a cluster of small **temples (I)** to various Hindu deities, and in the middle is a statue of a rearing cobra.

Pass along the north side of the tank, turn left and look for a tiny low doorway on the right (marked by three steps), just before a crumbling **Ganesh shrine (J)**. Cross a tiny courtyard with lovely woodcarvings and a central chaitya, and continue out the far end past another courtyard. On the left you'll see the white stucco pillars that mark the entrance to the **Mul Dipanker Bihar (K)**, enshrining an image of Dipankar, the Buddha of Light. There are some old chaityas in the courtyard and the statue of the deity wears a richly decorated silver-and-gold cape.

Continue east to the road junction, and turn left by a lotus-roofed Vishnu shrine, to reach the large Kwathandau Pokhari. Head right at the tank and you'll pass the **Nava Durga Temple (L)**, a Tantric Shaivite temple with a fine gilded torana.

Continue southeast through a wide square full of drying pots, brick **Shiva shrines (M)** and houses with carved balconies. Follow the lanes south to reach a junction by a stupa and a dance platform, on the main east–west road. Turn right and immediately on your left you'll see the elaborate entrance to the **Wakupati Narayan Temple (N)**, built in 1667. The courtyard is full of spinners and wood-whittlers and women winnow rice here in the harvest season using flat

NYATAPOLA TEMPLE

You will be able to see the sky-high rooftop of the Nyatapola Temple (Map p200) long before you reach the square. With five-stories towering 30m above Taumadhi Tole, this is the highest temple in all of Nepal and one of the tallest buildings in the Kathmandu Valley. If you look over the city from the hillside above Suriya Binayak (see p209), the temple looms over the city like a giant fir tree, with the snow-capped Himalaya as a picturesque and dramatic backdrop.

This perfectly proportioned temple was built in 1702 during the reign of King Bhupatindra Malla in 1702, and the construction was so sturdy that the 1934 earthquake caused only minor damage. The temple is reached by a stairway flanked by stone figures of the temple guardians.

At the bottom are the legendary Rajput wrestlers Jayamel and Phattu, depicted kneel-

baskets as fans. The ornate, golden temple is fronted by an entourage of five Garudas supported on pillars on the backs of turtles.

Continue from here past the centuries-old wooden frontage of the **Brahmayani Temple (O)**, sacred to the patron goddess of Panauti (see p230) then on to **Tachupal Tole (P)**.

South of Tachupal Tole

From Tachupal Tole turn left down the side of the Pujari Math, passing the famous Peacock Window (p205). Follow the road round south and turn right at the small square with a **Vishnu Temple (Q)** on an octagonal plinth.

Go straight down an atmospheric alley lined with brick houses and follow it round to the left, then to the right into a large square. Detour south from this square down a wide cobbled road to reach a large statue of **Sakyamuni (R)**, the historical Buddha, overlooking the river from the east end of the Khancha Pokhari tank.

Return to the square and walk west towards the main road linking Taumadhi Tole and Tachupal Tole. Just before the junction is the unassuming gateway to the ornate **Inacho Bahal (S)**, containing the narrow Sri Indravarta Mahavihar, a 17th-century Buddhist temple topped by a lopsided miniature pagoda roof. From here, the walk gets really interesting. Rather than following the road to Taumadhi Tole, walk south towards the Hanumante River, passing the other end of the Khancha Pokhari and the **Munivihar (T)**, a rapidly expanding modern Buddhist temple. At the bottom of the hill is one of the most remarkable sights in the valley, an astonishing collection of **chaityas, Shiva statues, Shaivite shrines and lingams (U)**, including a bas-relief of a nude Shiva (obviously pleased to see you!) beside what could well be the two largest Shiva lingams in Nepal.

Duck left beside the Ram Janaki Mandir to another splendid collection of statues at **Hanuman Ghat (V)**. Note the exquisitely carved images of Ganesh, Sakyamuni, Ram and Sita, Hanuman and Vishnu/Narayan, reclining on a bed of snakes. Hindu yogis often come here to meditate.

Cross the bridge and follow the road uphill, then turn sharply right after the Happy Home School onto a brick-lined path that runs west along the riverbank. You'll soon pass the **Siddhi Shaligram Briddhashram (W)**, the first old-people's home in Bhaktapur. Look north to see the tower of the Nyatapola Temple rising above the rooftops across the river as you pass another ticket booth and a **Bhimsen Temple (X)** fronted by a carved tiger on a column.

Follow this wide road to the river past some modern cremation plinths at **Chuping Ghat (Y)**. Just across the river, turn left past a Hanuman statue on the riverbank and nip into the campus of the **Kathmandu University Department of Music (Z)**, where the sound of traditional music wafts over the ornamental gardens.

Above the river is the wide open square of **Khalna Tole (AA)**, the setting for the spectacular Bisket Jatra Festival (see boxed text, p206). In the middle of the square, note the huge stone yoni where the giant lingam is erected (you may have to pick your way through mountains of drying rice and grain to get here).

To finish, walk north along the river at the bottom of the square and follow the curving path uphill past the modern **Kumari Temple (AB)** and the **Bhagwati Temple (AC)**, emerging on the southern side of Taumadhi Tole.

ng with hefty maces. Subsequent levels are guarded by elephants with floral saddles, lions adorned with bells, beaked griffons with rams' horns and finally two goddesses – Baghini and Singhini. Each figure is said to be 10 times as strong as the figure on the level below.

The temple is dedicated to Siddhi Lakshmi, a bloodthirsty incarnation of the goddess Durga (Parvati). The idol of the goddess is so fearsome that only the temple's priests are allowed to enter the inner sanctum, but less brutal incarnations of the goddess appear on the torana above the door, beneath a canopy of braided snakes, and also on the temple's 180 carved roof struts. In a classic piece of religious crossover, the Buddhist eight lucky signs are carved beside the temple doorways.

BHAIRABNATH TEMPLE

The broad-fronted, triple-roofed Bhairabnath Temple (also known as the Kasi Vishwanath

(vertical side text) AROUND THE KATHMANDU VALLEY

AROUND THE KATHMANDU VALLEY

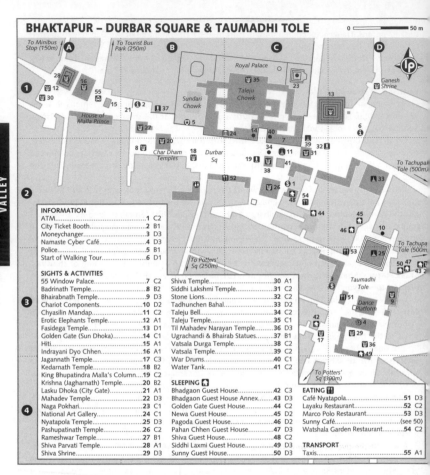

BHAKTAPUR – DURBAR SQUARE & TAUMADHI TOLE

0 ⸺ 50 m

or Akash Bhairab; Map p200) is dedicated to Bhairab, the fearsome incarnation of Shiva, whose consort occupies the Nyatapola Temple across the square. The first temple on this site was a modest structure built in the early 17th century, but King Bhupatindra Malla added an extra storey in 1717 and a third level was added when the temple was rebuilt after the 1934 earthquake. The final version of the temple has a similar rectangular plan to the Bhimsen Temple in Patan's Durbar Sq.

Casually stacked against the north wall of the temple are the enormous wheels and runners from the chariot used to haul the image of Bhairab around town during the Bisket Jatra Festival in mid-April – see boxed text, p206. More chariot runners are piled up on the north side of the Nyatapola Temple.

Despite Bhairab's fearsome powers and his massive temple, the deity is depicted here as a disembodied head just 15cm high! A small hole in the central door (below a row of carved boar snouts) is used to push offerings into the temple's interior, but priests gain entry through the small Betal Temple, on the south side of the main pagoda.

The temple's facade is guarded by two brass lions holding the Nepali flag, the only national flag that is not rectangular or square. To the right of the door is an image of Bhairab painted on rattan, decorated with a gruesome garland of buffalo guts. Head here at dusk to hear traditional devotional music. Next to the temple is a sunken hiti with a particularly fine spout in the form of a makara.

TIL MAHADEV NARAYAN TEMPLE

The third interesting temple at Taumadhi Tole is hidden away behind the buildings at the south end of the square. The Til Mahadev Narayan Temple (Map p200) is set in an untidy courtyard but this is actually an important place of pilgrimage and one of the oldest temples in the city. An inscription states that the site has been in use since 1080 and that the image of Til Mahadev was installed here in 1170.

The double-tiered temple is fronted by an elegant kneeling Garuda statue on a pillar and two columns bearing the sacred sankha and chakra symbols of Vishnu. In case Shiva was feeling left out, a lingam symbol on a yoni base (the Shaivite symbol for the male and female genitals) stands behind a grill in front and to one side of the temple. A plaque to the right of the door depicts the Buddhist deity Vajrayogini in characteristic pose with her left leg high in the air.

Durbar Square

Bhaktapur's Durbar Sq was once much more crowded than it is today. Victorian-era illustrations show the square packed with temples and buildings, but the disastrous earthquake of 1934 reduced many of the temples to empty brick plinths, with lion-guarded stairways leading to nowhere. If we were asked to rank the square against the others in the valley, it would come behind Kathmandu or Patan, but it's still an impressive sight. Expect to be approached by a string of would-be guides and thangka painting school touts as you walk around.

EROTIC ELEPHANTS TEMPLE

Coming from the public bus stand, it's worth ducking right before the main Durbar Sq entrance gate to observe a little piece of architectural whimsy on the roof of the small **Shiva Temple** (Map p200). Giving graphic representation to the lyric 'birds do it, bees do it…', the temple roof struts feature camels, cows and even elephants engaged in the act of making sweet love, usually in the missionary position! Nearby are another large **Shiva Parvati Temple** (Map p200) and the **Indrayani Dyo Chhen** (Map p200), a former Hindu monastery.

UGRACHANDI & BHAIRAB STATUES

As you enter Durbar Sq through the western gate, look left to a gateway flanked by two stocky stone lions, erected by King Bhupatindra Malla in 1701. On either side are statues of the terrible Bhairab (Map p200), the rending, sundering incarnation of Shiva, and his consort, the equally terrible Ugrachandi (Durga). It is said that the unfortunate sculptor had his hands cut off afterwards, to prevent him from duplicating his masterpieces.

Ugrachandi has 18 arms holding various Tantric weapons symbolising the multiple aspects of her character. She is depicted casually killing a demon with a trident to symbolise the victory of wisdom over ignorance. Bhairab gets by with just 12 arms, one holding two heads impaled on a spear and another holding a cup made from a human skull. The statues originally guarded a courtyard destroyed in the 1934 quake.

CHAR DHAM

Hinduism has always been very accommodating when it comes to pilgrimages. The sacred lake at Gosainkund is spiritually represented by the tank at Patan's Kumbeshwar Temple (see p188) and devotees who are unable to trek all the way to India to visit the famed Char Dham temples can visit local branches of these auspicious shrines in Bhaktapur.

Standing at the western end of Durbar Sq, the four Char Dham temples (Map p200) were constructed to provide spiritual merit for pilgrims who were unable to make the journey to the temples of Kedarnath, Badrinath, Gangotri and Yamunotri, in the Himalayan state of Uttaranchal. Most impressive are the **Kedarnath Temple** (Map p200), dedicated to Shiva, and the **Badrinath Temple** (Map p200), sacred to Vishnu in his incarnation as Narayan.

KING BHUPATINDRA MALLA'S COLUMN

King Bhupatindra Malla was the best known of the Malla kings of Bhaktapur and a bronze statue of the king (Map p200) gazes in eternal wonderment at his palace from the top of a column in front of the Vatsala Durga Temple. The statue was created in 1699 and it mirrors the similar statues in the Durbar Sqs of Kathmandu and Patan.

VATSALA DURGA TEMPLE & TALEJU BELL

Beside the king's statue and directly in front of the Royal Palace is the stone **Vatsala**

BHAKTAPUR'S PONDS

Around the outskirts of Bhaktapur are a series of enormous tanks, constructed in the medieval period to store water for drinking, bathing and religious rituals. The tanks still play an important role in the social life of Bhaktapur – in the mornings and afternoons, locals gather by the ponds to bathe, socialise, take romantic walks and feed the giant carp and turtles that keep the water free from detritus. The most impressive tank is the ghat-lined **Siddha Pokhari** near the main bus park. This rectangular reservoir is set inside an enormous wall broken by rest-houses and towers that have been consumed by the roots of giant fig trees. You can buy bags of corn and rice to feed the fish for a few rupees.

During the annual festival of **Naga Panchami** in the Nepali month of Saaun (July–August), residents of Bhaktapur offer a bowl of rice to the nagas (serpent spirits who control the rain) who live in the Siddha Pokhari. According to legend, a holy man once attempted to kill an evil naga who lived in the lake by transforming himself into a snake. An attendant waited by with a bowl of magical rice to transform the yogi back into human form, but when the victorious holy man slithered from the water, his terrified assistant fled, taking the holy rice with him, leaving the yogi trapped for eternity in his scaly form. To this day, locals leave a bowl of rice out at Naga Panchami in case the snake-yogi decides to return.

Other significant tanks include the nearby Bhaiya Pokhari (across the road to the south), the Guhya Pokhari (across the road to the west) and the Kamal Pokhari (at the northeast end of Bhaktapur on the road to Nagarkot).

Durga Temple (Map p200), which was built by King Jagat Prakash Malla in either 1672 or 1727 (depending on which inscriptions you trust). This is Bhaktapur's answer to the Krishna Mandir in Patan, and it follows similar Indian architectural rules. Note the mythical beasts bursting out from the sides of the shikhara and the detailed carvings of multi-armed deities in the false windows on the second level.

In front of the temple is the large **Taleju Bell** (Map p200), which was erected by King Jaya Ranjit Malla in 1737 to mark morning and evening prayers at the **Taleju Temple** (Map p200). A smaller bell on the plinth to the Taleju Temple is known as 'the barking bell'. According to legend, it was erected by King Bhupatindra Malla in 1721 to counteract a vision he had in a dream, and to this day dogs are said to bark and whine if the bell is rung – which could have a physical explanation in terms of resonance frequencies.

ROYAL PALACE

The northern half of the square is taken up by Bhaktapur's Royal Palace (Map p200). This vast compound was founded by Yaksha Malla (r 1428–82) and added to by successive kings, but only half a dozen of the 99 courtyards survived the 1934 earthquake. The only parts of the palace open to visitors are the western wing, which houses the National Art Gallery,

and a section of the eastern wing, reached through the Golden Gate.

NATIONAL ART GALLERY

The western end of the palace contains Nepal's **National Art Gallery** (Map p200; admission foreigner/SAARC Rs 100/40, camera/video Rs 50/200; ⏰ 10am-5pm Wed-Mon), the best of the three museums in Bhaktapur. The entrance to the gallery is flanked by two huge guardian lions, one male and one female (with almost human breasts). Beside the lions are some imposing 17th-century statues of Hanuman the monkey god, in his four-armed Tantric form, and Vishnu, as the gut-ripping Narsingha.

Inside the gallery you can view an extensive collection of Tantric cloth paintings – the Hindu version of Buddhist thangkas – as well as palm-leaf manuscripts and metal, stone and wooden votive objects. Look out for depictions of the nightmarish Maha Sambhara, with 21 faces and unbelievable numbers of arms. Also here are portraits of all the Shah kings, except Gyanendra, who has been neatly excised from the gallery. Keep hold of your ticket as this also covers the Woodcarving Museum (p205) and Brass & Bronze Museum in Tachupal Tole (p205).

GOLDEN GATE

You can't miss the magnificent Golden Gate (Map p200), or Sun Dhoka, the entrance to he **55 Window Palace**. This fabulous portal, opped by a frieze of Hindu deities, is set nto a bright red gatehouse surrounded by he white palace walls. Construction of the gate and palace began during the reign of King Bhupatindra Malla (r 1696–1722), and he project was completed by his successor, aya Ranjit Malla, in 1754. The death of Jaya Ranjit Malla marked the end of the Malla dynasty and the end of the golden age of Newari rchitecture in Nepal.

The level of detail on the repoussé work on he Golden Gate is extraordinary. The gilded orana features a fabulous Garuda (the mount of Vishnu) wrestling with a number of supernatural serpents, his sworn enemies. Below s a four-headed and 10-armed figure of the goddess Taleju Bhawani, the family deity of he Malla kings. There are temples to Taleju n the royal palaces in Kathmandu and Patan s well as Bhaktapur.

The Golden Gate opens to the inner courtyards of the palace, passing a pair of enormous var drums, used to rouse the city in the event of attack. Only Hindus can enter the main courtyard to view the Taleju Temple, built n 1553, but non-Hindus can view the **Naga Pokhari**, a 17th-century water tank used for he ritual immersion of the idol of Taleju. The pool is encircled by a writhing stone cobra and more serpents rise up in the middle and at the end of the tank, where water pours from a magnificent dhara in the form of a goat being eaten by a makara. The sides of the spout are overed by an incredible frieze of wild animals nd monsters.

CHYASILIN MANDAP

Beside Vatsala Durga Temple is an ornate unken water tank containing a fine stone lhara in the form of a makara, topped by a rocodile and a frog. Just in front is the octagonal pavilion known as Chyasilin Mandap Map p200). In fact, the pavilion is a fantasy, created in 1990 using components from a emple that was destroyed in the 1934 earthquake, reassembled around a metal frame!

PASHUPATINATH TEMPLE

Behind the Vatsala Durga Temple, the Pashupatinath Temple (Map p200) is dedicated to Shiva as Pashupati and is a replica of he main shrine at Pashupatinath. Originally built by King Yaksha Malla in 1475 (or 1482), t is the oldest temple in the square. The roof

struts here verge on pornography – unexpected humour is provided by one boredlooking woman who multitasks by washing her hair while pleasuring her husband at the same time. And as for what the dwarf with the bowl is doing…

SIDDHI LAKSHMI TEMPLE

By the southeastern corner of the palace stands the 17th-century Siddhi Lakshmi Temple (Map p200), also known as the Lohan Dega, or Stone Temple. The steps up to the temple are flanked by male and female attendants, each leading a child and a rather eager-looking dog. On successive levels the stairs are flanked by horses, garlanded rhinos, human-faced lions and camels. The temple itself is a built in the classic shikhara style, commonly seen in the north of India.

Behind the temple is a neglected corner of the square containing a small red-brick **Vatsala Temple** and a pair of lost-looking curlyhaired **stone lions** who are guarding the site of a temple that crumbled to dust in the 1934 earthquake.

FASIDEGA TEMPLE

The large and plain Fasidega Temple (Map p200) is notable more as a landmark than for any great architectural merit. If you look towards Bhaktapur from vantage points such as Changu Narayan (p210) the white bulk of the Fasidega is always an easy landmark

NAVADURGA DANCERS

The colourful masks sold around Bhaktapur and Thimi are not just souvenirs. Every year, as part of the Dasain celebrations in September or October, local residents perform fiendish dances in Bhaktapur's public squares, during which they are said to be possessed by the spirits of the Nava Durga, the nine incarnations of the fearsome consort of Shiva. The masks worn by dancers are cremated ever year and new masks are made from the ashes, mixed with black clay from the fields around Bhaktapur. Although most of the masks for sale in Bhaktapur are made for the tourist market, they are full of Tantric symbolism. Popular figures include Ganesh, Kali, Bhairab, boar-headed Varahi, red-faced Kumari and roaring Sima and Duma, the eerie harbingers of death.

to pick out. The shrine is dedicated to Shiva and it sits atop a six-level plinth with guardian elephants, lions and cows. Inside is a substantial lingam.

TADHUNCHEN BAHAL

Walking east from Durbar Sq, you'll pass the gateway to the restored Tadhunchen Bahal monastery (Map p200), tucked between souvenir shops. Also known as the Chatur Varna Mahavihara, this Buddhist temple is linked to the cult of the Kumari, Bhaktapur's living goddess. Bhaktapur actually has three Kumaris but they lack the political importance of Kathmandu's (see boxed text, p123).

In the inner courtyard the roof struts on the eastern side have unusual carvings showing the tortures of the damned. In one a snake is wrapped around a man, another shows two rams butting an unfortunate's head, while a third strut shows a nasty tooth extraction being performed with a large pair of pliers! Locals use the courtyard as a quiet place to practice traditional crafts such as spinning and copper chasing.

Taumadhi Tole to Tachupal Tole

The curving main road through Bhaktapur runs from beside the Bhairabnath Temple in Taumadhi Tole to Tachupal Tole, the old centre of town, passing the following sights.

The first stretch of the street is a busy shopping thoroughfare selling everything from porters' tumplines (the straps worn across the forehead to support loads carried on the back) to Hindi movie DVDs. At the start of the road, in front of the Bhadgaon Guest House Annex, is a tall **Mahadev Temple** (Map p200), and nearby are several small temples to different incarnations of Vishnu and Shiva.

After passing several local confectionery shops selling milk-based Indian sweets, the road bends right at a brick **Narayan shrine** (Map pp196–7). On the south side of the road is the **Sukul Dhoka** (Map pp196–7), a math (Hindu priest's house), with overhanging balconies and finely carved wooden screens over its windows. Past the next alley, a doorway leads into a cramped bahal containing a small **Bhimsen Temple** (Map pp196–7), which was created from remains of the Lun Bahal, a 16th-century Buddhist monastery. Note

the pots and pans nailed to the roof strut by devotees.

A little further along, the road joins **Golmadhi Square** (Map pp196–7). In the left corner, behind two brick temples, is a fine house with ornate timbers and rounded windows. In front is a deep stepped hiti, and on the right side of the square is a three-tiered **Ganesh temple** (Map pp196–7), with flying human figures carved at the ends of its beams. Just beyond is a large white chaitya.

To the east of the square, on the right, is the well-restored facade of the **Jhaurbahi Mahavihar** (Map pp196–7), which has a mixture of Hindu and Buddhist symbols carved on its timbers. On the lion-flanked main doors, the bottom panels feature all eight Buddhist lucky symbols combined into a single motif!

A further 100m brings you to an open area containing a brick Vishnu temple, a tank and, just behind it, the gateway to **Inacho Bahal** (Map pp196–7). A few more steps will take you past the gatewaylike **Nasa Dabu Temple** (Map pp196–7) to Tachupal Tole.

Tachupal Tole

Tachupal Tole was the original central square of Bhaktapur and it formed the official seat of Bhaktapur royalty until the late 16th century. South of this square, a maze of narrow laneways, passageways and courtyards runs down to the ghats beside the Hanumante River. The following sights are shown on the Map p205.

DATTATREYA TEMPLE

At the east end of the square, the eye-catching Dattatreya Temple (Map p205) was originally built in 1427, supposedly using the timber from a single tree. The slightly mismatched front porch was added later. The temple is dedicated to Dattatreya, a curious hybrid deity, blending elements of Brahma, Vishnu and Shiva. Judging from the Garuda statue and the conch and chakra disc mounted on pillars supported by stone turtles in front of the temple, Vishnu seems to have come out on top.

The three-storey temple is raised above the ground on a brick and terracotta base, which is carved with erotic scenes, and the main steps to the temple are guarded by statues of the same two Malla wrestlers who watch over the first plinth of the Nyatapola Temple.

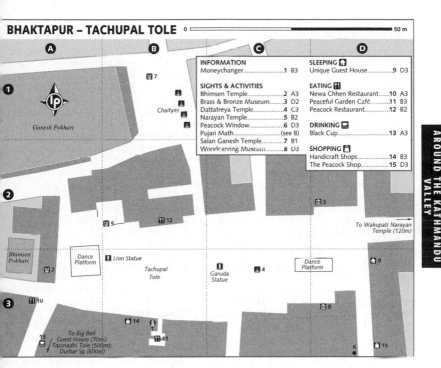

BHAKTAPUR – TACHUPAL TOLE

INFORMATION		SLEEPING
Moneychanger.....................1 B3		Unique Guest House.............9 D3
SIGHTS & ACTIVITIES		**EATING**
Bhimsen Temple...................2 A3		Newa Chhen Restaurant......10 A3
Brass & Bronze Museum.......3 D2		Peaceful Garden Café..........11 B3
Dattatreya Temple................4 C3		Peacock Restaurant.............12 B2
Narayan Temple....................5 B2		
Peacock Window..................6 D3		**DRINKING**
Pujari Math.........................(see 8)		Black Cup...........................13 A3
Salan Ganesh Temple............7 B1		
Woodcarving Museum..........8 D3		**SHOPPING**
		Handicraft Shops.................14 B3
		The Peacock Shop..............15 D3

BHIMSEN TEMPLE

At the other end of the square, this two-storey 17th-century temple (Map p205) is sacred to Bhimsen, the god of commerce. The squat rectangular structure has an open ground floor and an inner sanctum on the second level. In front is a platform with a small double-roofed Vishnu/Narayan Temple and a pillar topped by a brass lion with his right paw raised. Steps lead down behind it to the deeply sunken Bhimsen Pokhari tank.

THE TACHUPAL MUSEUMS

The square is flanked by a series of ornate brick-and-timber buildings that were originally used as maths. The best known is the **Pujari Math** (Map p205), which was constructed in the 15th century during the reign of King Yaksha Malla, but rebuilt in 1763. Until the 20th century, an annual caravan brought tributes to the monastery from Tibet. German experts renovated the building in 1979 as a wedding gift for the then King Birendra.

The most famous feature of this handsome mansion is the superb 15th-century **Peacock Window**, visible from the narrow alley on the right-hand side. This is widely regarded as the finest carved window in the valley and it appears on countless postcards. Many surrounding shops sell miniature wooden copies of the window as souvenirs.

The Pujari Math now houses the small **Woodcarving Museum** (Map p205; admission foreigner/SAARC Rs 100/40, camera/video Rs 50/200; 9am-5pm Wed-Sun, 10am-3pm Mon, to 5pm winter), with some fine examples of Bhaktapur woodcarving displayed in dark, creaky rooms. There isn't enough light to justify paying the camera fee, but it's worth a visit, not least for the extravagantly carved windows in the inner courtyard. Head upstairs to see the mechanism that operates the window shutters. The same ticket covers entry to the nearby Brass & Bronze Museum (below) and the National Art Gallery (p202).

Directly across the square, in another old math with similar lighting problems, is the **Brass & Bronze Museum** (Map p205; admission foreigner/SAARC Rs 100/40, camera/video Rs 50/200; 9am-5pm Wed-Sun, 10am-3pm Mon, to 5pm winter). It has some excellent examples of traditional metalwork,

AROUND THE KATHMANDU VALLEY

BISKET JATRA AT KHALNA TOLE

Held annually in the Nepali month of Baisakh (typically in the middle of April), the dramatic Bisket Jatra Festival heralds the start of the Nepali New Year. The focal point of the celebrations is the mighty chariot of Bhairab, which is assembled from the timbers scattered beside the Bhairabnath Temple and Nyatapola Temple in Taumadhi Tole. As the festival gets underway, the ponderous chariot is hauled through the streets by dozens of devotees to Khalna Tole, with Betal, Bhairab's sidekick from the tiny temple behind the Bhairabnath Temple, riding out front like a ship's figurehead. Bhadrakali, the consort of Bhairab, follows behind in her own chariot.

The creaking and swaying chariots lumber around the town, pausing for a huge tug of war between the eastern and western sides of town. The winning side is charged with looking after the images of the gods during their week-long sojourn in Khalna Tole's octagonal *path* (pilgrim shelter). The chariots then skid down the steep road leading to Khalna Tole, where a huge 25m-high lingam is erected in a stone base shaped like a yoni.

As night falls the following day (New Year's day), the pole is pulled down in another violent tug of war, and as the pole crashes to the ground, the new year officially commences. Bhairab and Betal return to Taumadhi Tole, while Bhadrakali goes back to her shrine by the river. It certainly beats Auld Lang Syne…

---

including ceremonial lamps and ritual vessels from around the valley.

On the north side of Tachupal Tole is another open area, with the small **Salan Ganesh Temple** (Map p205), dating from 1654. Backed by a large tank, the open temple is ornately decorated, but the image is a natural rock with only the vaguest elephant-head shape.

FESTIVALS & EVENTS

Bhaktapur celebrates **Bisket Jatra** (Nepal's New Year's Day) in mid-April with a stupendous chariot festival (see boxed text, above). The nearby town of Thimi celebrates the dramatic **Balkumari Jatra** at the same time (see boxed text, p209).

Bhaktapur is also the best place to witness the antics of **Gai Jatra** (see p24), where cows and boys dressed as cows are paraded through the streets. It's not quite the running of the bulls at Pamplona, but it's all good fun.

SLEEPING

Despite the comparatively high prices, it's worth staying overnight to appreciate this gem of a city without the crowds. Remember to get your Bhaktapur entrance ticket marked with your passport number for overnight stays.

Budget

Big Bell Guest House (Map pp196–7; ☎ 6611675; s/d without bathroom Rs 400/500) Down an alley south of Tachupal Tole, this is a solid, well-run

cheapie. You won't find rooms this cheap in a better location. Common bathrooms are clean and the best rooms overlook the small garden restaurant.

Khwopa Guest House (Map pp196–7; ☎ 6614661; www.khwopa-guesthouse.com.np; s/d from US$5/10) Just south of Taumadhi Tole, this pocket-sized family-run guest house is a rare budget choice in expensive Bhaktapur. Tall travellers may struggle with the low ceilings, but the vibe is easygoing and friendly.

Siddhi Laxmi Guest House (Map p200; ☎ 6612500; siddhilaxmi.guesthouse@gmail.com; r Rs 500-750) Sharing a courtyard with the Til Mahadev Narayan Temple, this tiny five-roomed guest house is built in the modern-Newari style seen all over the valley. The best rooms are up on the top floor – lower rooms get less light and have tiny bathrooms.

Shiva Guest House (Map p200; ☎ 6613912; www .shivaguesthouse.com; s/d US$15/20, without bathroom US$6/8) You pay a mark-up for this well-maintained place on Durbar Sq, but the rooms are comfy and the welcome heartfelt. There's a small restaurant where you can escape the Durbar crowds on the ground floor. Ask for a corner room if you want a view. Discounts of 20% are available from December to August.

Golden Gate Guest House (Map p200; ☎ 6610534; www.goldengateguesthouse.com; d US$25-30, s/d without bathroom from US$7/10) A quiet courtyard and attentive staff are the drawcards at this brick-built guest house between Durbar Sq and Taumadhi Tole. Rooms won't win any design awards, but they are clean and some have balconies. The rooftop offers views towards the Fasidega Temple in one direction and the Nyatapola Temple in the other.

Pagoda Guest House (Map p200; ☎ 6613248; www pagodaguesthouse.com.np; r with/without bathroom from US$20/8) A cute family-run place in the north-west corner of Taumadhi Tole, set back from the hubbub and piled high with pot plants. There are only six rooms, all different but all well appointed – the deluxe rooms with plinth beds come with TV. There's also a decent rooftop restaurant.

Midrange

Unique Guest House (Map p205; ☎ 6611575; unique@ col.com.np; s/d US$10/15) Above a souvenir shop, this creaky and slightly claustrophobic old building is nevertheless convenient for Tachupal Tole. There is one room per floor, and barely room to swing a shopping bag on the stairs.

Greenland Guest House (off Map pp196-7; ☎ 6618115; greenland@ntc.net.np; d/ste Rs 1200/2000) Set on the edge of the forest on the west-ern side of Bhaktapur, this midrange resort is surrounded by lovely quiet lawns and trees full of flying foxes (fruit bats). The Greenland's rooms are smart, clean and comfortable and the showers are set in giant beaten copper dishes.

our pick **Sunny Guest House** (Map p200; ☎ 6616094; sunnyres@hotmail.com; r Rs 1300, deluxe r with TV Rs 2500) This long-established place scores extra points for the sunny disposition of its staff and an excellent location at the north end of Taumadhi Tole. There's a superior rooftop restaurant (p208) and rooms have screen-printed bedspreads and carved wooden lattice windows.

Pahan Chhen Guest House (Map p200; ☎ 6612887; srp@mos.com.np; r Rs 2000) One of a cluster of guest houses at the northeastern corner of Taumadhi Tole, offering naturally cool, well-shaded rooms with terracotta tiled floors. Black-and-white photos lend a dash of style and the views from the roof are as good as you'll get.

Bhadgaon Guest House (Map p200; ☎ 6610488; www.bhadgaon.com.np; Taumadhi Tole; s/d from US$25/30) An update of a traditional Newari building, this place has it all – a courtyard restaurant, a rooftop balcony with perfect views and a coveted deluxe room with a private balcony overlooking Taumadhi Tole. Rooms are modern-looking rather than traditional,

but they are excellent value. The nine-roomed annex across the square is just as good, but you miss out on the restaurant. Do not be put off by the note on its website announcing 'Our Facilities Will Blow Out Your Mind!'

Newa Guest House (Map p200; ☎ 6916335; r US$30) Run by the same owners as the Pagoda, this crisp new guest house is a little expensive, but the tasteful rooms have rattan furni-ture, sparkling white linen and immacu-late bathrooms. Some rooms have good Nyatapola views.

EATING & DRINKING

Bhaktapur is certainly no competition for Kathmandu when it comes to restaurants. Most places have an almost identical menu of tried and tested local and Western dishes – burgers, chow mein, fried rice, Nepali set meals, you know the drill. Unless otherwise stated, the following restaurants are open 8am to 9pm.

Black Cup (Map p205; coffee or tea Rs 30-80) Staffed by enthusiastic local students, this small cof-feehouse serves decent espressos, lattes etc. It's a handy retreat from Tachupal Tole.

Newa Chhen Restaurant (Map p205; snacks Rs 30-70) Tachupal Tole's answer to the Nyatapola Café has a single corner table with killer views over the square. Grab it early and don't let go. The menu covers the usual bases but does it competently.

Marco Polo Restaurant (Map p200; mains Rs 70-120) On the corner of the square beside the Nyatapola Temple, Marco Polo offers cheaper food than the competition, from a very similar menu, but you don't get such good views.

KING OF CURDS

While in Bhaktapur, be sure to try the town's great contribution to the world of desserts – *juju dhau*, 'the king of curds'. Just how spe-cial can yoghurt be, you might ask? Well, this could just be the richest, creamiest yo-ghurt in the world! You'll find this delicacy in many tourist restaurants, but the best places to try it are the hole-in-the-wall res-taurants between Durbar Sq and the public bus stand (look for the pictures of bowls of curd outside). King curd comes set in an earthenware bowl for Rs 25.

ourpick **Café Nyatapola** (Map p200; ☎ 6610346; mains Rs 100-300, set meals from Rs 450; ⊙ to 7pm) Out in the square at Taumadhi Tole, this place is touristy and pricey, but what a setting! Tables are set on the balconies of a former pagoda temple – there are even erotic carvings on the roof struts. The menu covers the usual Nepali, Chinese, Continental standards and a portion of the profits supports a local hospital.

Watshala Garden Restaurant (Map p200; ☎ 6610957; mains Rs 100-250) Set in a pot-plant-filled courtyard behind the Shiva Guest House, this place is a genuine retreat from the Durbar Sq crowds. Sit back with a cold beer and gently exhale…

Layaku Restaurant (Map p200; ☎ 6614812; mains Rs 120-350) Opposite the Royal Palace on the stately balcony of a wooden mansion, this place offers the chance to dine in front of the kind of view that used to be reserved for the Malla kings.

Sunny Café (Map p200; mains Rs 140-200) Set above the guest house of the same name, this place has one of the best terraces for views of Taumadhi Tole. Look for local dishes like the Newari set meal and Bhaktapur king curd.

Other dining options in Tachupal Tole (serving similar menus) include the sleepy **Peaceful Garden Café** (Map p205; dishes from Rs 80), in a courtyard behind the souvenir shops on the south side of the square, and the touristy **Peacock Restaurant** (Map p205; mains Rs 100-325) in the wood-fronted math on the north side of the square.

SHOPPING

Bhaktapur is famed for its pottery and woodcarving, which is sold from a staggering number of souvenir shops around the main squares, particularly at Tachupal Tole and Taumadhi Tole. There's also some good metalwork on sale – look out for beaten metal dishes embossed with Buddhist symbols and ornate brass butter lamps in the shape of the Krishna Temple in Patan's Durbar Sq.

Paper

Many small factories in Bhaktapur produce handmade paper from the pulp of the *lokta* (daphne) bush, which is sold in the form of cards, notepads, photo-albums, envelopes and other stationary items all over town.

One good paper emporium is **The Peacock Shop** (Map p205; ☎ 6610820; ⊙ 9am-6.30pm, factory closed Sat), near the Peacock Window down the side of Pujari Math. Prices are higher than some other stores, but so is the quality and you can visit the workshop to observe the pressing, drying, smoothing, cutting and printing of the paper.

Woodcarving & Puppets

Bhaktapur has long been renowned for its woodcarving and this craft is now used to make objects that fit well into Western homes. Some of the best work is sold from the stalls around Tachupal Tole and the alley beside the Pujari Math. Miniature models of the famous Peacock Window are always popular souvenirs.

Like nearby Thimi, Bhaktapur is a major centre for the manufacture of masks and puppets in the form of Bhairab, Ganesh, Kali and other deities. However, prices may be higher than in Patan's excellent fair-trade shops (see p193).

GETTING THERE & AWAY

Bicycle

The Arniko Hwy to Bhaktapur carries a lot of bellowing, belching buses and trucks so it's better to follow the parallel road to Bhaktapur past the northern end of Thimi. See p95 for a description of the route.

Bus, Minibus & Taxi

Taxis from Kathmandu cost around Rs 700 one way. Minibuses run extremely frequently from Kathmandu's Bagh Bazar bus stand (Rs 20, one hour) until nightfall, dropping off next to the Guhya Pokhari, a short walk west of Durbar Sq. For Thimi (Rs 12, 20 minutes), take a local bus rather than an express bus. Buses also run along the highway south of Bhaktapur from the Lagankhel bus stand in Patan (Rs 20, 30 minutes).

Kathmandu buses also leave from a stand at the northeastern edge of Bhaktapur by the Lamuga Pokhari. The stand for buses to Nagarkot (Rs 27, one hour) is nearby, beside the Kamal Pokhari tank. Buses to Changu Narayan (Rs 13, 30 minutes) leave every 30 minutes or so from the junction with the Changu Narayan road.

For Dhulikhel or anywhere further east, you'll have to walk 20 minutes south across the river to the Arniko Hwy to catch a (probably packed) through bus from Kathmandu.

AROUND BHAKTAPUR

SURIYA BINAYAK TEMPLE

South of Bhaktapur, on the south side of the Arniko Hwy, Suriya Binayak is an important Ganesh temple dating back to the 17th century. The white shikhara-style temple contains some interesting statuary, but the main attraction is the peaceful setting and the walk uphill above the temple to a hillside with sweeping views over Bhaktapur.

To get here, take the road south from Potters' Sq to Ram Ghat (where there are areas for ritual bathing and cremations) and cross the river to the Arniko Hwy. On the other side, it's a 1km walk along the road to the start of the steps to the temple, then a 10-minute climb. Bank on around an hour from Taumadhi Tole.

The temple is on the north side of the hill flanked by statues of Malla kings and a large statue of Ganesh's vehicle, the rat. There are twice-weekly puja ceremonies on Tuesday and Saturday mornings; get here early and grab a tea-and-omelette breakfast at one of the surrounding pilgrim stalls.

If you take the steps to the right of the temple entrance, you'll reach a dirt path climbing steeply into the forest, passing a small modern temple. A 10-minute climb will take you to a superb viewpoint where you can see the Fasidega Temple and Nyatapola Temple sticking up above the dun-coloured rooftops of Bhaktapur.

THIMI

Thimi, known historically as Madhyapur, was once the fourth-largest town in the valley. Today, it's a sleepy backwater but its winding, brick-lined streets are lined with medieval temples. The town takes its modern name from the Newari phrase for 'capable people', which is fitting as the town is major centre for the production of pottery and papier-mâché masks. You'll pass a string of mask shops on the road that cuts across the north end of town toward Bhaktapur.

Sights

The town's winding main street runs north–south between the old Bhaktapur road and the Arniko Hwy. From the southern gate, walk uphill to the large, 16th-century **Balkumari Temple**, dedicated to one of Bhairab's shaktis. The goddess' peacock vehicle is depicted on a column in front of the temple and the temple's entrance is plastered in feathers from past sacrifices. Stroll north past a **Lokeshwar temple**, kept safe behind four sets of locked doors, a **school** flanked by painted images of Bhairab, and a 16th-century Newari-style **Narayan Temple**.

Walk past two dry tanks to a square on the left with a two-tiered **Bhairab Temple** with erotic carvings on its roof struts and a small brass plaque of Bhairab's face. Continue

---

BALKUMARI JATRA

While Bhaktapur goes wild for Bisket Jatra Festival, Thimi welcomes the new year with the Balkumari Jatra, a festival that has been celebrated since the time of King Jagat Jyoti Malla in the early 1600s. Honouring Balkumari, one of Bhairab's consorts, the festival is centred on the Balkumari Temple. As dusk falls hundreds of chirags (ceremonial oil lamps) are lit and some devotees even lie motionless around the temple all night with burning oil lamps balanced on their legs, arms, chests and foreheads.

The next morning men come from the various *toles* of Thimi and from surrounding villages, each team carrying a khat with images of different gods. As the 32 khats whirl around the temple, red powder is hurled at them and the ceremony reaches fever pitch as the khat bearing Ganesh arrives from the village of Nagadesh. The festivities last until late morning, when the palanquin bearing Ganesh, borne by hundreds of men, makes a break for home, pursued by the other khats. Sacrifices are then made to Balkumari.

In the nearby village of Bode a smaller khat festival takes place at the Mahalakshmi Temple, where one brave volunteer is shaved of his hair and eyebrows and subjected to the 'tongue-boring ceremony' where an iron spike is driven through his tongue. The penitent then walks around the streets so all can see and admire his devotion. Successful completion of this painful rite brings merit to the whole village as well as the devotee.

TOP FIVE TEMPLES IN THE KATHMANDU VALLEY

The following are our five favourite temples in the valley:

- **Changu Narayan** (right) A treasure house of sculpture at this Unesco World Heritage site.
- **Gokarna Mahadev Temple** (p212) A visual A to Z of Hindu iconography.
- **Indreshwar Mahadev Temple** (p230) A perfect temple by a mystical river confluence south of the highway to Tibet.
- **Budhanilkantha** (p179) Impressive monolithic stone carving of a sleeping Vishnu.
- **Dakshinkali** (p218) Spooky place of blood sacrifices and wrathful goddesses.

---

north past a **Buddhist temple** flanked by two yellow lions to a large courtyard on the left containing the colourful **Chitikari Temple**. A passage on the south side of the square leads to Thimi's **potters' square**, which is full of kilns made from straw covered with ash. Return to the main road and walk north past a string of Ganesh shrines to reach a group of large **stupas** and the northern road to Bhaktapur.

At the crossroads, turn left, and head downhill past a small shrine and water tank, where a road branches off to the right to the village of **Nagadesh**. Go through the tall gatehouse with a square tower and ornate torana, and turn right to reach an open square and the triple-roofed **Ganesh Dyochen** (a *dyochen* is a Tantric temple), whose facade is often smeared with sacrificial blood.

Return to the northern crossroads in Thimi and walk north for 15 minutes to the village of **Bode**. Where the tarmac road turns sharply right by some shops, walk down the lane to the left and turn right just before the first tank to reach a small **Shiva temple** in front of another small tank. From here, go west for one block and turn right to reach an open square full of drying crops and the 17th-century **Mahalakshmi Temple**, with a small image of Narayan reclining on his snake bed just behind. To get back to the road, stroll south past the junction where you turned left,

passing a shikhara-style **Narayan Temple**, then go left past two tanks to get back to where you started.

Getting There & Away

Any of the Bhaktapur-bound minibuses from Kathmandu will be able to drop you at Thimi (Rs 15, 40 minutes), either at the southern gateway on the Arniko Hwy or on the back road at the north end of Thimi. A taxi from Kathmandu to the southern gateway costs around Rs 350.

If you are continuing by bike to Bhaktapur the northern (old) road offers a far more pleasant ride. The road branches off the Arniko Hwy to the east of the runway at Tribhuvan Airport.

CHANGU NARAYAN TEMPLE

Perched atop a narrow ridge due north of Bhaktapur, the beautiful and historic temple of **Changu Narayan** (admission Rs 100; ☉ dawn-dusk) is a living museum of carvings from the Licchavi period (4th to 9th centuries). The temple is a Unesco World Heritage site and rightly so because the statues, and the temple itself, are genuine works of art. Despite being only 6km from Bhaktapur and 22km from Kathmandu the temple attracts relatively few visitors which is part of its appeal.

The single brick-lined street in Changu village climbs from the car park and bus stand past the **Changu Museum** (admission Rs 140; ☉ 7am-6pm), which offers a quirky introduction to traditional village life. The displays are scattered around a 169-year-old house and the owner will give you a whistlestop tour of such oddities as a rhino-skin shield, leather coins from the 2nd century and some 225-year-old rice!

Just uphill, past some shops selling thangkas, masks and wooden toys, is a *path* (pilgrim shelter) containing a Ganesh shrine, and just beyond is the courtyard of the **Changu Narayan Temple**. Built in the two-tiered pagoda style, the shrine is guarded on all sides by pairs of mythical beasts – lions, elephants and ram-horned griffons – and its roof struts feature some amazingly intricate carvings of Tantric deities. The statue inside shows Vishnu as Narayan the creator of all life, but the beautifully decorated metal-plate doors are only opened for rituals and only Hindus may enter.

Facing the west door is a kneeling figure of Garuda said to date from the 5th century

CHANGU NARAYAN TEMPLE

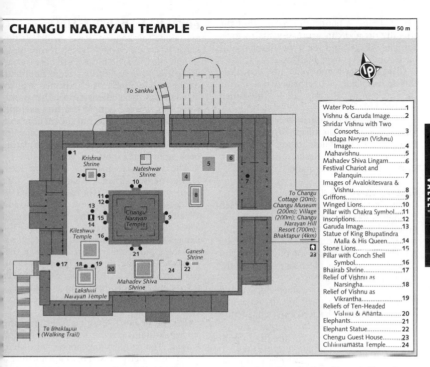

0 — 50 m

Water Pots....................................1
Vishnu & Garuda Image........2
Shridar Vishnu with Two
   Consorts.................................3
Madapa Naryan (Vishnu)
   Image......................................4
Mahavishnu...............................5
Mahadev Shiva Lingam..........6
Festival Chariot and
   Palanquin................................7
Images of Avalokitesvara &
   Vishnu....................................8
Griffons.......................................9
Winged Lions..........................10
Pillar with Chakra Symbol....11
Inscriptions..............................12
Garuda Image..........................13
Statue of King Bhupatindra
   Malla & His Queen..........14
Stone Lions..............................15
Pillar with Conch Shell
   Symbol.................................16
Bhairab Shrine.........................17
Relief of Vishnu as
   Narsingha............................18
Relief of Vishnu as
   Vikrantha.............................19
Reliefs of Ten-Headed
   Vishnu & Ananta.............20
Elephants.................................21
Elephant Statue......................22
Chengu Guest House...........23
Chhinnamasta Temple.........24

In front of this statue is the oldest stone inscription in the valley, dating from AD 464, which recalls how the king persuaded his mother not to commit *sati* (ritual suicide) after his father's death. Two large pillars carry a conch and chakra disc, the traditional symbols of Vishnu.

Dotted around the courtyard are a series of extraordinary carvings dating from the Licchavi era, showing Vishnu in his various avatars (incarnations). In the southwest corner of the compound, Vishnu appears as Narsingha (his man-lion incarnation), disembowelling a demon with his fingers, and as Vikrantha (Vamana), the six-armed dwarf who transformed himself into a giant capable of crossing the universe in three steps to defeat King Bali (look for his outstretched leg).

To the side of these images is a broken slab showing a 10-headed and 10-armed Vishnu, with Ananta reclining on a serpent below. The scenes are divided into three sections – the underworld, the world of man and the heavens. In the northwest corner of the compound is an exquisite 7th-century image of Vishnu

astride Garuda, which is illustrated on the Rs 10 banknote.

The squat temple in the southeast corner of the complex is dedicated to the Tantric goddess Chhinnamasta, who beheaded herself to feed the bloodthirsty deities Dakini and Varnini.

Down the steps leading east from the temple complex are the one-storey Bhimsen Pati, with its stone guardians, and the remains of a Malla-era royal palace.

Sleeping & Eating

There are two guest houses in the village and one just outside.

Changu Narayan Hill Resort (☎ 6617691; r with/without bathroom Rs 300/240) About 600m before the village on the track to Nagarkot, this secluded modern guest house has good views and a peaceful setting.

Look for the dirt track leading east where the road bends (the smaller track to the left runs down to Sankhu).

Chengu Guest House (☎ 6616652; saritabhatta@ hotmail.com; r lower fl Rs 300, r upper fl Rs 500) Close to the temple entrance, this brick courtyard place has just a handful of rooms, but the friendly owners can arrange visits to local Tamang villages and the upper-floor rooms have good views over Bhaktapur.

Changu Cottage (r from Rs 400) Just downhill, this faded place is overpriced but handy for the temple. Rooms are in tin-roofed A-frame huts.

There are several tourist-oriented restaurants at the start of the village, or you can grab a meal at one of the guest houses. Try Binayak Restaurant, New Hill Restaurant or Rooftop Restaurant near the car park.

Getting There & Away

Regular public buses run the 6km between Changu Narayan and Bhaktapur (Rs 13, 30 minutes), with the last bus around sunset. A taxi from Kathmandu costs around Rs 1500 return, or Rs 800 from Bhaktapur. If you come by motorcycle, there's a Rs 5 toll at the entrance to the village.

By bike or on foot, it's a steep climb uphill from Bhaktapur (one hour), but an easy downhill trip on the way back. If you're headed to Nagarkot you can take the footpath east to Tharkot and catch a bus for the final uphill stretch – see below for details of the hike.

THE NORTHEASTERN VALLEY

Most travellers miss this corner of the valley, which means things are blissfully peaceful and quiet. The attractions here are strung out along the road to Sundarijal, which is the starting point for the Helambu trek (p351).

GOKARNA MAHADEV TEMPLE

Set beside the Bagmati River, which at this stage is a comparatively clear mountain stream, the Gokarneshwar (Lord of Gokarna) Temple is an easy 6km trip from Bodhnath on the road to Sundarijal. Dedicated to Shiva as Mahadev (the Great God), this handsome three-tiered temple is a fine example of Newari pagoda style, but the main reason to come is to see the exquisite stone carvings dotted around the compound, some dating back more than a thousand years.

The sculptures provide an A to Z of Hindu deities, from as Aditya (the Sun God) and Chandra (the Moon God) to Indra (the elephant-borne God of War and Weather) and Ganga (with four arms and a pot on her head from which pours the Ganges). Vishnu is depicted as Narsingha, making a particularly thorough job of disembowelling the demon Hiranyakashipu (see boxed text, p216), while Shiva makes several appearances, including as Kamadeva, the God of Love, complete with an erect celestial wang.

The god Gauri Shankar is interesting since it contains elements of both Shiva and Parvati. The goddess appears on her own in a particularly elegant **statue** in the northwest corner of the compound. The **Brahma figure** in the southwest corner appears to have only three heads (he should have four) until you peer around the back and discover the hidden head. Many of the deities have one foot on their *vahana*, or spiritual vehicle. Shiva's vehicle **Nandi** appears as a large statue made from brass panels laid over a stone base, in front of the main temple, and Shiva is venerated in the form of an enormous lingam inside the main chamber.

HIKING THE SHORTCUT BETWEEN CHANGU NARAYAN & SANKHU

From Changu Narayan there's an interesting shortcut north to the Bodhnath–Sankhu road, allowing a detour to Sankhu and Bodhnath on your way back to Kathmandu. From the northern entrance of the Changu Narayan Temple, follow the obvious path that drops to Manohara River, which is crossed by wading or by a temporary bridge during the dry season (crossing is impossible in the monsoon). This brings you out to the Sankhu road at Bramhakhel, about 4km southeast of Gokarna. Frequent minibuses head east and west from here.

Coming from the other direction, you'll see a small sign for Changu Narayan on a building wall on the south side of the road as you enter Bramhakhel. It's a five-minute walk across fields to the river and temporary bridge, then a steep and tiring 45-minute scramble up the hill to the temple – look for the golden rooftop on the final bump of the spur running down from the eastern edge of the valley.

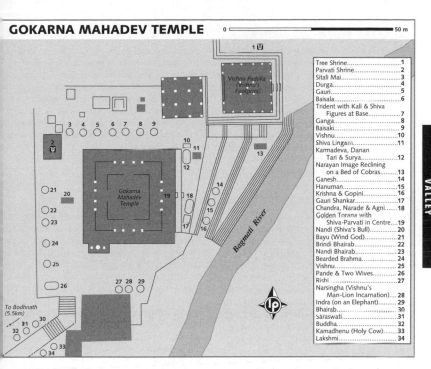

GOKARNA MAHADEV TEMPLE

0 — 50 m

AROUND THE KATHMANDU VALLEY

Nepalis who have recently lost a father often visit the temple, particularly during Gokarna Aunsi, the Nepali equivalent of Father's Day, which falls in September.

Behind the temple, just above the river, is the **Vishnu Paduka**, a low pavilion enshrining a metal plate with a footprint of Vishnu. Just in front is an image of **Narayan** reclining on a bed of snakes, just like the images at Budhanilkantha and Balaju. To the north of the pavilion is a remarkable **shrine** that has almost been consumed by a fig tree that must have started as a seed on its roof.

Getting There & Away

You can walk, cycle, take a minibus (easiest from Bodhnath) or hire a taxi (Rs 700 one way from Kathmandu or Rs 400 from Bodhnath). For a great day out on a mountain bike you can combine a visit to the temple with a trip to Sankhu (p214).

GOKARNA FOREST

The 470-acre forest at Gokarna was formerly set aside as a hunting reserve for the Nepali royal family, which saved it from the wood-cutters. Today, the sound of gunshots has been replaced by the sudden thwack of flying golf balls.

The forest forms part of the **Gokarna Forest Resort** (☎ 01-4451212; www.gokarna.com; ☼ 7.30am-sunset), which was designed by the team behind the famous Gleneagles in Scotland. A change of ownership from Le Meridien to a local group has not affected the high standards at the resort. Green fees for 18 holes are Rs 3400 on weekdays and Rs 4200 at weekends, and you can rent clubs, shoes and caddies.

If you stay here, you can pamper yourself with all sorts of luxury spa treatments, and the resort can arrange guided forest walks to the Bandevi (Forest Goddess) Temple and the Gokarna Mahadev Temple (one hour; see opposite).

At the entrance to the resort spa is a 200-year old pipal tree, where the Buddha (played by Keanu Reeves, of all people) in Bertolucci's film *Little Buddha* was tempted by the demon Mara and called the earth to witness his victory. Not a lot of people know that…

AROUND THE KATHMANDU VALLEY

GOKARNA–KOPAN–BODHNATH WALK

There's a pleasant walking or biking route between Gokarna and Bodhnath via the monastery at Kopan. The obvious trail starts just opposite the Gokarna Mahadev Temple, to the right of a roadside statue, and branches left at the Sahayogi Higher Secondary School. After five minutes, turn right onto a dirt road as it follows the side of a pine-clad hill. You will see the yellow walls of Kopan Monastery ahead atop a hill and the Bodhnath Stupa down below in the valley.

After another 10 minutes, branch left onto a paved road which soon becomes a footpath. After another five minutes, branch left, passing below a new monastery and follow the hillside to a saddle on the ridge. Where the path forks, take the trail heading uphill to the right, passing another small monastery before reaching the entrance to Kopan (45 minutes).

From Kopan, follow the main road south for 40 minutes to Bodhnath, or jump on one of the frequent minibuses. Travelling on foot, branch off to the left before you hit the built-up area of Bodhnath to reach the stupa.

Sleeping

Gorkana Forest Resort (☎ 4451212; www.gokarna.com; s/d from US$120/140) Top-of-the-line accommodation is provided in this sublimely peaceful former-Meridien property. Wicker furniture and dark timber lends a colonial feel, and the surrounding forest is alive with deer and monkeys. The new block is luxurious, but for real character, book a room in the Rana-era Hunter's Lodge. A taxi from Kathmandu will cost around Rs 700 one way.

SANKHU

The red-brick town of Sankhu was once an important stop on the old trade route from Kathmandu to Lhasa (Tibet), and you can still see signs of its former prosperity. The main attraction is the imposing Vajrayogini Temple on the hillside north of the village, but it's worth taking time to explore the winding brick alleyways (there's a faded map by the bus stand).

Vajrayogini Temple

To reach Sankhu's most famous temple, you should walk north from the bus stand under a deity-covered archway, passing Dhalna Tole. As you leave the village, an interesting collection of lingam shrines and finely crafted statues of Ganesh, Vishnu and Hanuman will show you are on the right path. Where the road forks, turn left to reach the pedestrian steps to the temple or right to reach the parking area about halfway up.

Having found the steps, join the pilgrims climbing the hill to reach a gorgeous complex of temples, surrounded by Newari-style mansions and set in a grove of gnarled trees. The stately, three-tiered Vajrayogini Temple has an amazing gilded doorway flanked by images of Bhairab, Garuda and other celestial beings, but the image of the revered female yogi is only visible when the priest opens the doors for devotees. Although the goddess Vajrayogini is nominally a Buddhist deity, the complex also features plenty of Hindu iconography. The other temple in the main courtyard enshrines a huge chaitya and its roof struts are decorated with images of the Buddhist protector deities. Immediately behind this temple is a chaitya with four Buddha images mounted on a yoni base – a striking fusion of Hindu and Buddhist iconography.

The climb up the stone steps to the temples is steep and hot but there are dhara along the route where you can cool off. About halfway up is a shelter with carvings of a withered-looking Kali and an orange Ganesh. A natural **stone lingam** represents Bhairab, and sacrifices are made at its foot. If you climb the stairway above the Vajrayogini temple, you will reach a rest house for pilgrims and several small tea-stands.

Getting There & Away

Buses and minibuses on route 30 run to Sankhu from Kathmandu's Ratna Park bus station (Rs 28, one hour). The last bus back to Kathmandu leaves Sankhu around 6pm. Minibuses on route 4 pass by Patan.

It's an easy 20km cycle to Sankhu from Kathmandu, or an even easier motorcycle ride. Head to Bodhnath and turn right at Jorpati, then skirt around the Gokarna Forest. If you are walking, you can continue from Sankhu to Changu Narayan by crossing the Manohara River near Bramhakhel – see boxed text, p212.

THE SOUTHERN VALLEY

There are some fascinating temples and Buddhist monasteries in the southern part of the Kathmandu Valley, but it's hard to see too many together in a single day-trip as the villages are strung out on four different roads branching south from the Kathmandu Ring Rd. There's a useful dirt-road short-cut linking the roads to Godavari and Chapagaon and a walking-only route linking the road to Bungmati and Chobar on the way to Dakshinkali.

KIRTIPUR

Just 5km southwest of Kathmandu, the sleepy town of Kirtipur has a wonderful sense of faded grandeur thanks to the impressive medieval temples dotted around its backstreets. When Prithvi Narayan Shah stormed into the valley in 1768, he made a priority of capturing Kirtipur to provide a base for his crushing attacks on the Malla kingdoms. Kirtipur's resistance was strong, but eventually, after a bitter siege, the town was taken. The inhabitants paid a terrible price for their brave resistance – the king ordered that the nose and lips be cut off every male inhabitant in the town, sparing only those who could play wind instruments for his entertainment.

As you approach Kirtipur from the Ring Rd, the old town is up the hill straight ahead, best approached by following the main road to the right and climbing the hillside on a wide flight of steps. Many of the town's 9000 inhabitants are weavers or farmers and you will often see dyed yarn drying from windows and hear the clatter of the town's handlooms. For Nepalis, the town is most famous as the location of the Tribhuvan University campus.

Sights

Everything of interest in Kirtipur is at the top of the hill above the road into town. Before you head uphill, follow the left fork of the main road around the base of the hill to the **Nagar Mandap Sri Kirti Vihar**, a classic Thai-style *wat* (Buddhist monastery) inaugurated by the Supreme Patriarch of Thailand in 1995.

Return to the fork and go right, taking the obvious stairway up the hillside. At the top, turn right and walk past a water tank into a large square with several chaitya. Exit at the top right corner and walk northwest on a curving brick lane, passing a semi-ruined **temple archway** covered in Hindu deities. You'll soon reach the main square, which is ringed by the former residences of the royal family of Kirtipur.

In the middle of the square is a large tank and a white-washed **Narayan Temple** guarded by lions and griffons, but the main attraction is in a courtyard off the north side of the square. The frontage of the imposing **Bagh Bhairab Temple** is decorated with an incredible armoury of *tulwars* (swords) and shields belonging to the soldiers defeated by Prithvi Narayan Shah. Befitting the militaristic mood, animal sacrifices are made here early on Tuesday and Saturday mornings.

From the temple exit, go right heading west through the village to a Ganesh shrine and a stone stairway that climbs to the triple-roofed **Uma Maheshwar Temple**, flanked by two stone elephants that wear spiked saddles to discourage disrespectful children! The temple was originally built in 1673 with four roofs, but one was lost in the earthquake of 1934. This was the spot where Kirtipur's residents made their last stand during the 1768 siege.

Return to the main square and turn right, exiting at the southeast corner of the square to reach the 16th-century stone shikhara-style **Lohan Dehar**. Turn left, then right through a brick gate and cross a large square. The next right will take you to a shrine gripped by the roots of an enormous fig tree, and opposite, the gateway to the **Chilanchu Vihara**. Built in 1515, this stately stupa crowns the hilltop and the harmika above the dome is painted a rich blue. The main stupa is surrounded by a garden of chaity and fronted by a giant dorje symbol.

Return to the square with the brick gate and go right to reach the carved archway you passed on the way into town, then walk south-east to the steps leading down to the main road, where you can flag down a minibus to Kathmandu.

Getting There & Away
BUS, MINIBUS & TAXI
Minibuses on route 21 leave regularly for Kirtipur from Kathmandu's Ratna Park bus station (Rs 12, 30 minutes). Taxis charge around Rs 500.

It takes around one hour to Kirtipur by mountain bike from Kathmandu; turn south off the Ring Rd at Balkhu and follow the tarmacked Chobar road to the turn-off to Kirtipur.

CHOBAR

The tiny little village of Chobar, 6km from Kathmandu, tops a hill overlooking the Bagmati River where it flows through the Chobar Gorge, allegedly chopped out by the sacred sword of Manjushree. The village itself is lovely, with a tangle of old streets surrounding a famous temple, but the gorge has been ravaged by mining to supply cement for construction in Kathmandu.

To reach Chobar, follow the road that turns south off the Kathmandu Ring Rd at Balkhu and follow the Bagmati River. The side road to Chobar climbs to a small square beside the curious **Adinath Lokeshwar Temple**, originally built in the 15th century. This handsome three-tiered Newari temple is dedicated to red-faced Rato Machhendranath – see p189 – and its roof struts, walls and courtyard are adorned with hundreds of metal plates, cups, jugs, dishes, knives, ladles and ceremonial vessels, nailed there by newlyweds to ensure a happy married life. The temple is sacred to both Hindus and Buddhists and in front is an octagonal stone shikhara temple fronted by a gilded dorje symbol.

A tangle of lanes leads off the square in front of the temple to the main part of the village and a small Tibetan Buddhist monastery, tucked behind the Le Village resort. Even if you don't stay here, it's worth swinging by the resort to see the modernist sculptures created by the owner.

The Chobar Gorge is 1km southeast of Chobar village. This was once a beauty spot but the now-defunct cement factory has

LEGEND OF THE CHOBAR GORGE

Geologists and theologians rarely find common ground but everyone agrees that eons ago the Kathmandu Valley was a lake and the hill of Swayambhunath was an island. Around 10,000 years ago the lake burst its banks and dried up, leaving the fertile valley floor we see today. Local legends recall a much more dramatic turn of events. The Buddhist deity Manjushree is said to have taken his mighty sword and cut open the valley wall with a single blow to release the pent-up waters, creating the Chobar Gorge. Countless nagas were washed out of the valley with the departing waters, but many, including Kartotak, 'king of the snakes', made it to the nearby Taudaha Pond, beside the road to Pharping.

scarred the landscape. The newly created **Manjushree Park** (admission adult Rs 50; daylight hr) is seeking to repair the damage, but it will take a few years for the ornamental gardens to bed down. Note the boulder shaped like Ganesh on the roadside uphill from the park.

If you duck down the dirt road at the bottom of the hill, beneath the giant conveyor belt of the old cement factory, you will reach a cluster of restaurants and some steps leading down to the **Jal Binayak Temple**, one of the valley's most important Ganesh shrines.

Built in 1602, the tall, triple-tiered temple enshrines another natural rock resembling Ganesh.

The temple's roof struts depict eight Bhairabs and the eight Ashta Matrikas (Mother Goddesses) with whom Ganesh often appears.

NARSINGHA

The image of Vishnu in his man-lion incarnation as Narsingha (or Narsimha) can be seen all over the Kathmandu Valley. The deity is normally depicted gleefully disembowelling the demon Hiranyakashipu with his bare hands, recalling a famous legend from the Bhagavata Purana. Because of a deal made with Brahma, the demon was granted special powers – he could not be killed by man or beast, either inside or outside, on the ground or in the air, by day or by night, nor by any weapon. Vishnu neatly got around these protections by adopting the form of a man-lion and killing the demon with his fingernails, at dusk, on his lap, on the threshold of the house. You can see statues of Narsingha at his grisly work at Gokarna Mahadev Temple (p212), in front of the palace in Patan (p187) and just inside the Hanuman Dhoka entrance in Kathmandu (p128).

Sleeping & Eating

our pick **Chobar Le Village Resort** (☎ 4333555; www
.nepalvillageresort.com; s/d Rs 1200/1800, group room per
person Rs 1500) Up the steps opposite the entrance
to the Adinath Lokeshwar Temple, this little
charmer feels like a Mediterranean artists'
retreat. Rooms are set in a 200-year-old stone
house, amongst sublimely peaceful gardens
full of sculptures. There are just three tasteful
rooms, but one can sleep up to 12 people (it's
priced on a per person basis).

On the wide lane south of the temple is
Hira's Coffee Shop (snacks from Rs 50), a quaint cafe in
a village house. Reached by turning north off
the road into Chobar, **Kathmandu View Cottage**
(mains Rs 60-150) is a tasteful garden restaurant
with tables in bamboo huts looking out over
the rooftops of Kathmandu.

Getting There & Away

There are no direct buses to Chobar, but any
bus to Pharping or Dakshinkali can drop you
at the turn-off, a 10-minute walk below the
village. A taxi will cost Rs 500. You can also
walk here from Kirtipur in around an hour,
via the village of Panga, which has several
old temples, including the revered Vishnu
Devi Mandir.

If you feel like walking back to Kathmandu,
cross the suspension bridge by the Jal Binayak
Temple and turn left on the other side to meet
the Kathmandu Ring Rd at Nakthu. Heading
straight here will take you to Jawalakhel and
on to Kathmandu. Alternatively, turn right
after the bridge and follow a convoluted path
to reach Khokana and the Bungamati road.

PHARPING

About 19km south of Kathmandu, Pharping
is a thriving Newari town whose ancient
Buddhist pilgrimage sites have been taken
over by large numbers of Tibetans. Pharping
lies on the road to Dakshinkali and it's easy to
visit both villages in a day by bus or bicycle.
En route you'll pass the pond at Taudaha,
allegedly home to the nagas released from the
Kathmandu lake. More Buddhist monasteries
are opening up around here every year, some
of which accept foreign dharma students.

Sights

The temples in the middle of Pharping can be
reached on an easy pilgrim circuit taking one
to two hours. The interesting Shesh Narayan
Temple complex is about 600m downhill

from the main junction at Pharping, which
is marked by the village football ground.

THE PILGRIMAGE ROUTE

The best way to visit the sights of Pharping
is to join the other pilgrims on a clockwise
pilgrimage circuit (a *parikrama* in Nepali,
or *kora* in Tibetan). As you enter the town
from the main road, take the first right and
head uphill, passing a **Guru Rinpoche statue** in a
glass case. Next to the statue is the **Auspicious
Pinnacle Dharma Centre of Dzongsar**, a giant
chörten containing 16 enormous prayer
wheels. Elderly Tibetans spend the afternoons
turning these enormous prayer wheels from
comfortable armchairs.

Continue uphill past a line of Tibetan restaurants to reach the large white **Ralo Gompa**
with a brightly painted chörten. Next door is
the **Sakya Tharig Gompa**, with another enormous
chörten – step inside to see hundreds of miniature chörten and statues of Guru Rinpoche
set into alcoves in the walls.

Walk onwards to a set of steps on the right,
climbing up to a temple signposted 'Pharping
Ganesh and Saraswati Temple'. Also known
as the **Drölma Lhakhang**, the shrine is sacred
to both Hindus and Buddhists, who identify
Saraswati as Tara or Drölma, one of the wives
of the first Buddhist king of Tibet.

To the right of this chapel is the **Rigzu
Phodrang Gompa**, which contains an impressive frieze of statues, with Guru Rinpoche
(Padmasambhava) surrounded by his fearsome incarnations as Dorje Drolo (riding
a tiger) and Dorje Porba (with three faces,
Garuda-like wings and a coupling consort).

Climb the steps between the two temples,
passing a rocky fissure jammed full of *tsha
tsha* (stupa-shaped clay offerings) and cracks
stuffed with little bags of wishes and human
hair. Eventually you'll come to the walls of a
large white monastery, inside which is the **Guru
Rinpoche Cave** (also known as the Gorakhnath
Cave). Take off your shoes and duck between
the monastery buildings to reach the soot-
darkened cavern, which is illuminated by
butter lamps and a Liza Minnelli–style row
of coloured light bulbs.

Continue out of the cave enclosure down
a flight of stairs to the 17th-century Newari-
style **Vajra Yogini Temple**, sacred to the Tantric
goddess Vajrayogini. One of the few female
deities in Buddhist mythology, Vajra Yogini
was a wandering ascetic who achieved a level

of enlightenment almost equivalent to the male Buddhas. Note the lovely Rana-style buildings around the courtyard.

Before you return to the main road, take the path leading uphill to the left through a scrubby forest to the Nyingmapa school **Do Ngak Chöling Gompa**. The main chapel features colourful statues of Sakyamuni flanked by Padmasambhava and Vajrasattva, and there are views from the entrance towards the imposing hilltop monastery at Dollu (see right). Finally, head downhill for a post-pilgrimage cup of butter tea at one of the Tibetan restaurants on the main road.

SHESH NARAYAN TEMPLE

About 600m downhill from the main junction at Pharping, in the direction of Kathmandu, the Shesh (or Sekh) Narayan Temple is a highly revered Vishnu shrine surrounded by ponds and statues, tucked beneath a rocky cliff wall and a **Tibetan monastery**. The main temple was built in the 17th century, but it is believed that the cave to the right (now dedicated to Padmasambhava, or Guru Rinpoche) has been a place of pilgrimage for far longer.

There are some artfully carved Licchavi-era statues in the courtyard, including lively depictions of Ganesh and Hanuman. The surrounding ponds are full of koi carp and semi-submerged carvings, including an image of Aditya, the sun god, framed by a stone arch. If you are lucky you might catch devotional religious music being played in the pavilion by the pools.

Sleeping & Eating

Family Guest House (☎ 4710412; r with/without bathroom Rs 600/400) The only choice in the middle of Pharping, this well-run guest house is right on the pilgrim circuit and there's a good rooftop restaurant.

Hotel Ashoka (☎ 4710057; r in bungalow Rs 500, r in lodge Rs 600-700) On the road that passes around Pharping to Dakshinkali, this place is good value. Take your pick from rooms in the modern main building or in bungalows near the stone-walled restaurant.

Dakchhinkali Village Inn (☎ 4710053; www.dakch hinkali.com; s/d/tr from US$30/40/45) At the far end of Pharping by the gate marking the route to Dakshinkali, this midrange resort has an inviting garden restaurant but heinously overpriced rooms. Discounts of 20% or more are usually available.

Hattiban Resort (☎ 4710122, city office 4371397; s/d US$44/60) Perched on a ridge high above the valley, but rather inaccessible, this small resort has 24 good-quality rooms, most with balconies that make the most of the views. From the resort you can make an excellent two-hour hike up to the peak of Champa Devi (2249m). To get here you must travel 2km on a steep, rutted dirt road that branches off about 3km north of Pharping. The condition of the road varies so ask the hotel about arranging transfers by taxi.

Along the main road uphill from Pharping bazaar are numerous Tibetan restaurants serving momos, *thukpa* and butter tea to hungry pilgrims.

Getting There & Away

Buses on route 22 leave throughout the day for Pharping from Kathmandu's Ratna Park bus station (Rs 21, two hours), continuing to Dakshinkali. The last bus back to Kathmandu leaves around 5.30pm.

AROUND PHARPING

Dollu

About 3km before Pharping, a side road turns north along a small valley to the village of Dollu, passing several huge Tibetan Buddhist monasteries, including the **Rigon Tashi Choling**, which contains some fine murals and statuary, including a fearsome image of Guru Dorje Drolo and his tiger. The same road continues up the valley to the **Dakshinkali Hill Resort** (☎ 4710072; www.dakhillresort.com; s/d from Rs 1200/1600), a comfortable, quiet place with rooms and bungalows in a big garden centred on a pool.

If you walk a few hundred metres back towards Kathmandu from the Dollu junction, you will reach a cluster of houses tucked into a hairpin bend, where a track leads uphill to the enormous **Neyndo Tashi Choling** monastery. This newly constructed gompa looms over the surrounding landscape like *Howl's Moving Castle* and the main prayer hall contains some stunning mural-work and a 15m-high statue of Sakyamuni. There are nearly 200 monks here, so the morning and evening prayer ceremonies are quite an experience.

Dakshinkali

The road from Pharping continues south to the blood-soaked temple of **Dakshinkali**, a favourite Hindu pilgrimage destination. Set at the confluence of two sacred streams in a rocky cleft in the forest, the temple is dedicated to the goddess Kali, the most bloodthirsty incarnation of Parvati, consort of Shiva. To satisfy the blood-lust of the goddess, pilgrims drag a menagerie of chickens, ducks, goats, sheep, pigs and even the occasional buffalo up the path to the temple to be beheaded and transformed into cuts of meat by the temple priests, who are also skilled butchers.

Once the sacrifice is made, the meat goes in the pot – pilgrims bring all the ingredients for a forest barbecue and spend the rest of the day feasting in the shade of the trees. Saturday is the big sacrificial day, and the blood also flows freely on Tuesday. For the rest of the week Dakshinkali is very quiet. During the annual celebrations of Dasain in October the temple is washed by a crimson tide and the image of Kali is bathed in the gore.

The approach to the temple from the bus stand winds through a religious bazaar which is often hazy with smoke from barbecue fires. Locals farmers sell their produce here to go into the post-sacrifice feasts, along with piles of marigolds, coconuts and other offerings for the goddess. Only Hindus can enter the temple courtyard where the image of Kali resides, but visitors can watch from the surrounding terraces. However, remember that the sacrifices are a religious event, with profound spiritual significance for local people, and not just an excuse to snap gruesome photos.

A pathway leads off from behind the main temple uphill to the small **Mata Temple** on the hilltop, which offers good views over the forest. Several snack stalls at the Dakshinkali bus park serve reviving tea and pappadums.

GETTING THERE & AWAY

Buses on route 22 run to Dakshinkali regularly from Kathmandu's Shahid Gate (Martyrs' Memorial) and Ratna Park bus station (Rs 32, 2½ hours). There are extra buses on Tuesday and Saturday to accommodate the pilgrimage crowds. From Pharping it's an easy 1km downhill walk or ride, but a steep uphill slog in the other direction.

BUNGAMATI

Across the Bagmati River from Chobar, Bungamati is another classic medieval village, dominated by the massive shikhara of its main temple. Exploring the pedestrian-only streets is a great way to pass a few hours, and

tourists have yet to arrive here en masse, so tread lightly. Many locals make a living as woodcarvers and there are several workshops and showrooms around the main square.

Sights

Bungamati is the birthplace of Rato Machhendranath, the patron god of Patan. For six months of the year, the deity resides in the enormous shikhara of the **Rato Machhendranath Temple** in the main village square (he spends the rest of his time at the Rato Machhendranath Temple in Patan). The process of moving him backwards and forwards between Patan and Bungamati is central to one of the most important festivals in the valley – see boxed text, p189.

The solid mass of the temple dominates the village – you can get an awesome view of the temple from a viewpoint on the main road above the village, near two garden restaurants. The chowk around the temple is one of the most beautiful in the Kathmandu Valley – here you can see the beating heart of a functioning Newari town. On one side of the square is a double-tiered **Bhairab Temple**, enshrining a ferocious-looking brass mask of Bhairab in front of a brass vessel in the shape of a *kapala* (human skull bowl). Around the square you'll hear the tap-tap of woodcarvers' chisels.

To get here from the bus stand, follow the wide road south, then turn right, and then right again at an obvious junction by a Ganesh shrine. Almost immediately you'll pass the small **Bungmati Culture Museum** with cultural objects from the local area. Bear left at the next junction and you'll reach the Rato Machhendranath Temple.

If you leave the main square by the northern gate (opposite the Bhairab temple), you'll pass a crumbling Buddhist courtyard monastery and an assortment of chaityas and shrines, then the brick-lined water tank of the **Dey Pukha** (Central Pond). Continue to the village gates – a right turn will take you back to the bus stand, while a left turn will take you north to the village of **Khokana**.

Halfway between Bungmati and Khokana, the **Karya Binayak Temple** is dedicated to Ganesh and local pilgrims flock here on Saturdays for a *bhoj* (feast) and some *bhajan* (devotional music) – the Newari version of a barbecue and singalong. To reach the temple, turn left when the path from Bungmati meets a larger track by a school.

If you bear right at this junction, you'll join a tarmac road and soon arrive at the village of **Khokana**, another Newari town that was seriously damaged in the 1934 earthquake. The main road through the village is a window back in time, with mattress-makers stuffing cases with cotton, farmers baling straw, tailors stitching and women spinning wool and winnowing rice. In the main village square is the triple-tiered **Shekala Mai Temple**, with carved balconies covered by fretwork screens.

You can return to Patan by bus from the stand you passed on the way into Khokana (Rs 13, 30 minutes) or turn left by the large pool to rejoin the main Patan–Bungamati road.

Getting There & Away

Buses to Bungamati leave frequently from Patan's Lagankhel station (Rs 13, 40 minutes), or you can get here easily by bike or motorcycle, turning off the Kathmandu Ring Rd at Nakhu.

CHAPAGAON

Chapagaon is a typical Newari village of tall brick houses but its central square is cut in two by the road to Tika Bhairab and the rumbling gravel lorries rather destroy the atmosphere. Beside the road are a number of shrines, including temples to Bhairab, Krishna and Narayan, but the main attraction here is the **Vajra Varahi Temple** (parking Rs 5), about 500m east of the main road on the back route to Godavari (turn left by the Narayan temple).

Set in a peaceful wood, this important Tantric temple was built in 1665 and it attracts lots of wedding parties, pilgrims and picnickers who descend en masse on Saturdays. Visitors pour milk and offerings over the statue of a bull in front of the temple and make similar offerings to the image of Vajra Varahi, an incarnation of the 'female Buddha' Vajrayogini. There are lots of wild birds in the forest – check the sign by the car park for a list of species.

Getting There & Away

Local minibuses leave from Lagankhel in Patan to Chapagaon (Rs 12, one hour) but you can cycle from the Kathmandu Ring Rd in around the same time (the turn-off is south of Patan near Satdobato).

The road to the Vajra Varahi Temple continues through peaceful countryside to meet the Godavari road just south of Bandegaon. You can walk it in about an hour or cycle it in 20 minutes.

AROUND CHAPAGAON
Lele Valley

For a bit of exploring, point your feet or wheels towards the Lele Valley, which runs east off the valley of the Nakhu Khola, about 5km south of Chapagoan. Few tourists make it out here and the valley offers a window onto a way of life that is fast vanishing in other parts of the Kathmandu Valley.

To get to Lele, follow the trucking road south from Chapagaon to the **Tika Bhairab**, a large rock shrine with a multicoloured painting of Bhairab, set at the confluence of two rivers. Once you pass the gravel mines, things get quieter and you can loop around the hill, passing a lonely memorial for the people killed in a Pakistan International Airlines crash in 1992.

The only place to stay is the Malla Alpine Resort at Kalitar, up a dirt road 3km beyond the Tika Bhairab. The resort was closed at the time of writing but contact the Malla Hotel in Kathmandu for the latest information (p148).

GODAVARI

Godavari is best known for the green fingers of its inhabitants. The village is home to Nepal's Royal Botanical Gardens and the approach road is lined with the nurseries that supply Kathmandu with flowers and potted plants. There are no must-sees here, but few tourists visit and you can take some peaceful walks in the surrounding community forests. The 10km road from the Kathmandu Ring Rd forks in the middle of Godavari – the left fork goes to the botanical gardens while the right fork climbs past the Pulchowki Mai Temple and turns into a dirt track running up to Pulchowki Mountain.

Sights

The verdant **Royal Botanic Gardens** (☎ 5560546; admission foreigner/SAARC Rs 100/25, camera/video Rs 10/100, child under 10yr 50% discount; ☀ 10am-5pm, to 4pm mid–Nov-mid–Feb) is a quiet and peaceful spot for a walk or picnic, except on Friday and Saturday when the place is overrun with schoolkids. The visitor centre has some good exhibits on Nepal's flora and in the middle is the decorative Coronation Pond with its 7m commemorative pillar.

If you turn to the right at the junction before the gardens, you'll reach a cluster of local restaurants and the **Godavari Kunda** – a sacred spring marked by a neat line of Shaivite shrines. Every 12 years (the next is 2015) thousands of pilgrims come here to bathe and gain spiritual merit.

On the other side of the road is a Tibetan monastery and beside it is the entrance to the **Godavari Kunda Community Forest** (admission Rs 20), a 363-acre woodland managed by local people, that provides a haven for 300 species of birds.

If you follow the main road back to the junction by St Xavier's School and turn left, you'll reach a marble quarry opposite the entrance to the **Pulchowki Mai Temple**. The three-tiered pagoda is dedicated to one of the Tantric mother goddesses and the two large pools before the temple compound are fed by nine spouts (known as the Naudhara Kunda) that represent the nine streams that flow from Pulchowki Mountain. The temple sits at the mouth of the **Naudhara Community Forest** (admission Rs 20), another 363 acres of locally managed woodland, established with support from **Bird Conservation Nepal** (www.birdlifenepal.org).

On the hillside above Godavari is the **Shanti Ban Buddha** (www.shantiban.com), an enormous golden Buddha image, created by local Buddhists who were inspired by the Japanese Peace Pagoda movement. To reach the statue, take the signposted road to the right at the end of the village.

Sleeping & Eating

Hotel View Bhrikuti (☎ 5560471; www.hotelview bhrikuti.com.np; s/d US$30/40) A modern and so phisticated place about 2km from the main Godavari junction. The surprisingly swanky rooms have minibars, bathrooms and TVs and there's a good, if chintzy, restaurant and a faux waterfall by the entrance.

our pick **Godavari Village Resort** (☎ 5560675; www.godavariresort.com.np; s/d US$150/165; 🖭) The best option at Godavari is off the main road, on the dirt track running west to the Vajra Varahi Temple and Chapagaon. It's a comfortable modern escape for city dwellers, sprawling down a hillside with views across paddy fields to the mountains. The excellent facilities – including a great big pool, a sauna

and spa, tennis courts, a swish restaurant and a program of guided treks and mountain biking tours – are reflected in the prices (ask about discounts). The weekend barbecues (Rs 499/599 veg/nonveg) always pull in a crowd. To get here look for the signposted road, about 3km south of Godavari.

There are several cheap restaurants in front of the Godavari Kunda where you can grab a bite of lunch for not too many rupees – the Godawari Restaurant and Evergreen Restaurant are good choices.

Getting There & Away

Local minibuses (No 5) and buses (No 14) run between Lagankhel in Patan and Godavari (Rs 16, one hour). The road is in good condition for cycling or motorcycling, but watch for trucks headed for the mines near Tika Bhairab.

AROUND GODAVARI
Harisiddhi

About 7km northwest of Godavari, on the main road, Harisiddhi is notable for the towering, four-tiered **Harisiddhi Bhagwan Temple** on its brick-lined market square. Dedicated to one of the fearsome incarnations of Durga, the temple has been painted in bright colours by local devotees. Any bus bound for Godavari can drop you here.

Bishankhu Narayan

If you're looking for an excuse to get off the beaten track, the shrine of Bishankhu Narayan may do nicely. Dedicated to Vishnu, this chain-mail-covered shrine is reached by a steep stairway that climbs to the temple and then drops into a narrow fissure in the rock, where pilgrims test their sin levels by trying to squeeze through the tiny gap. If you get stuck, the sin in question is either gluttony or pride...

The unsealed 3km road to Bishankhu Narayan starts at Bandegaon on the Godavari road, and runs southeast over a small stream. At Godamchowr village, take the left fork at the football ground and climb for about 2km to reach the shrine.

Pulchowki Mountain

This 2760m-high mountain is the highest point around the valley and there are magnificent views from the summit. It's also home to over 570 species of flowering plants and one third of all the bird species in Nepal. There have been rumours that the government will turn this into a national park for years. The mountain is famous for its springtime (March–April) flowers, in particular its magnificent red and white rhododendrons.

To get here, the only options are a full-day hike along dirt tracks from the Pulchowki Mai Temple, or a very rough unsealed road that is only suitable for 4WDs, mountain bikes or trail motorcycles. There are no facilities so bring water, food, a compass and fellow travellers for company (solo trekkers have been robbed here in the past).

THE VALLEY FRINGE

Beyond Bhaktapur the landscape starts to rise, revealing views north to the rugged mountain wall of the Himalaya, which is rarely visible from the bottom of the valley. Technically, most of the following towns are outside the valley, on the roads to Langtang or the Tibetan border, but it is easy to visit these places on day-trips or overnight sorties from Kathmandu. See p94 for possible cycling routes through the eastern valley.

NAGARKOT

☎ 01 / elev 2175m

Competing with Dhulikhel (p226) and Kakani (p233), Nagarkot is perhaps the best place to view the Himalaya from the comfort of your hotel balcony. Just 32km from Kathmandu, the village is packed with hotels, stacked up on a ridge facing one of the broadest possible views of the Himalaya. Between October and March a trip to Nagarkot will nearly always be rewarded with a view, but the mountains melt into cloudy skies from June to September. It can get very cold at Nagarkot in autumn and winter, so bring warm clothing.

Nagarkot is very much a one-night stand, and few visitors stay longer. The best way to leave Nagarkot is on foot, on the downhill hikes west to Sundarijal, Sankhu or Changu Narayan, north to Chisopani or south to Banepa.

Orientation & Information

Buses stop on the highway, where a dirt road turns towards the edge of the ridge

and drops down to Sankhu. All the hotels are scattered along this road, but the hotel area is a good 15-minute walk from where the buses drop off.

Sights

Nagarkot only exists because of the views and there is not much to the village. But what views! From any clear point on the ridge, you can take in a panorama from Dhaulagiri in the west to Mt Everest (little more than a dot on the horizon) and Kanchenjunga in the east, via Ganesh Himal (7406m), Langtang Lirung (7246m), Shisha Pangma (8012m), Dorje Lakpa (6975m) and Gauri Shankar (7146m).

The only other thing to see in the hotel area is the small hilltop **Mahakali Temple**. An hour's walk (4km) south from the village will give an even better 360-degree view from a **lookout tower** on a ridge, passing a former Rana palace (now part of the army camp).

Activities

HIKING & CYCLING

There are a number of hiking routes in this area, best walked downhill from Nagarkot. Nepa Maps' 1:25,000 *Nagarkot – Short Trekking on the Kathmandu Valley Rim* is useful, though its 1:50,000 *Around the Kathmandu Valley* is probably good enough.

If you fancy following these routes by mountain bike, you can rent bikes from Club Himalaya for Rs 150 per hour or Rs 1000 per day.

To Changu Narayan (1½ Hours From Tharkot)

From Nagarkot, it's an easy stroll along the spur to Changu Narayan. The trail runs parallel to the road to Bhaktapur along the ridge, branching off at the sharp hairpin bend at **Tharkot** (marked on some maps as Deuralibhanjhang). Catching a bus to here from Nagarkot will save you the tedious first half of the walk.

From the bend, follow the middle dirt road up into the forest and keep to the left. The track climbs uphill through a pine forest for about 20 minutes to the top of the ridge and then follows the ridgeline, dropping gently down to Changu Narayan. On clear days there are good views of the Himalaya.

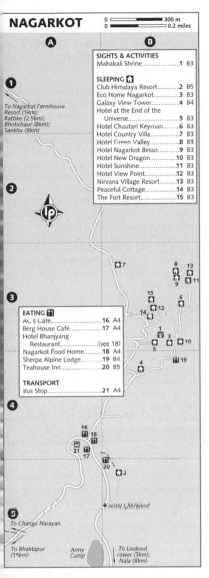

NAGARKOT

0 ——————— 300 m
0 ——————— 0.2 miles

SIGHTS & ACTIVITIES
Mahakali Shrine....................1 B3

SLEEPING
Club Himalaya Resort............2 B5
Eco Home Nagarkot..............3 B3
Galaxy View Tower...............4 B4
Hotel at the End of the
Universe............................5 B3
Hotel Chautari Keyman..........6 B3
Hotel Country Villa................7 B3
Hotel Green Valley................8 B3
Hotel Nagarkot Besso............9 B3
Hotel New Dragon...............10 B3
Hotel Sunshine....................11 B3
Hotel View Point..................12 B3
Nirvana Village Resort..........13 B3
Peaceful Cottage.................14 B3
The Fort Resort...................15 B3

EATING
AC's Café............................16 A4
Berg House Café.................17 A4
Hotel Bhanjyang
Restaurant....................(see 18)
Nagarkot Food Home............18 A4
Sherpa Alpine Lodge.............19 B4
Teahouse Inn......................20 B5

TRANSPORT
Bus Stop............................21 A4

To Nagarkot Farmhouse
Resort (1km);
Kattike (2.5km);
Bhotichaur (8km);
Sankhu (8km)

Army Checkpost

To Changu Narayan

To Bhaktapur
(15km)

Army
Camp

To Lookout
Tower (3km);
Nala (8km)

AROUND THE KATHMANDU VALLEY

You can follow this track on foot or on a mountain bike or motorcycle.

In the reverse direction, pick up the track near the Changu Narayan Hill Resort, and take the middle road where the track splits. See p210 for details of the temple and onward hikes to Bhaktapur or Bodhnath.

To Sankhu (2½ Hours From Nargakot)
From Nagarkot a dirt road leads all the way to Sankhu, offering an easy route back to Kathmandu on foot or by bike. Take the northwest road down to the Nagarkot Farmhouse Resort and follow switchbacks down to the village of **Kattike**, which has a teahouse for refreshments. Go left at the junction at the edge of town. You can continue all the way down this track, or take a minor road that turns off sharply to the right after 15 minutes. Follow this track for 20 minutes as it shrinks to a trail and then take a sharp left downhill past several houses to rejoin the main track. From here it's an hour's slog to Sankhu village.

To Banepa (3½ Hours From Nargakot)
The town of Banepa is outside the valley on the Arniko Hwy, and you can continue by bus or on foot to Dhulikhel (p226) or the delightful village of Panauti (see p229). From Nagarkot, follow the road south for an hour to a lookout tower, then take the dirt road leading west and then south for another 1¾ hours, following the western ridge downhill all the way to **Nala** (you can also follow a tangle of dirt paths to Nala through the village of Ghimiregaon). At Nala, visit the four-roofed Newari-style **Bhagwati Temple** in the centre of town and then walk or catch a bus for the remaining 3km to Banepa.

To Sundarijal (One to Two Days From Nargakot)
It takes two easy days – or one very long day – to skirt around the valley rim to Sundarijal, from where you can travel by road to Gokarna, Bodhnath and Kathmandu, trek for another day along the valley rim to Budhanilkantha (p179), or start the circuit trek to Helambu (see p351). Accommodation is available at Bhotichaur and Sundarijal in local guest houses, but the trails can be confusing so ask for directions frequently.

Start by following the Sankhu trail as far as Kattike (about one hour), then turn right (north) to Jorsim Pauwa. Walk further down through Bagdhara to Chowki Bhanjyang (about one hour) and on for one more hour through Nagle to **Bhotichaur**, a good place to stop overnight in a village inn.

On day two, walk back up the trail towards Chowki Bhanjyang and take the fork leading uphill by a chautara (porters' resting place). This path climbs uphill to cross a ridge line before dropping down on the middle of three trails to Chule (or Jhule). Here the path enters the Shivapuri National Park (see p180) and contours around the edge of the valley for several hours, before dropping down to Mulkarkha, on the first stage of the Helambu trek (see p351). From Mulkharka, it's an easy descent beside the water pipeline to Sundarijal.

An alternative route runs northwest from Bhotichaur to **Chisopani**, the first overnight stop on the Helambu trek, which has several trekking lodges. The next day, you can hike southwest over the ridge through Shivapuri National Park to Sundarijal.

Sleeping

Nagarkot has numerous guest houses and hotels that take advantage of the views on the north side of the ridge, and charge a premium for the privilege. However, most of the hotels offer significant discounts so always ask when you book or check in.

Note that Nagarkot has been hit by a number of strikes by hotel workers since the Maoists came to power. If this happens, it can shut the hotels in town for days at a time.

BUDGET

Hotels in this price bracket miss out on the best of the views, but you only have to walk to the ridge to see the peaks.

Nirvana Village Resort (☎ 9841272325; r Rs 400) There are good cheap rooms at this ramshackle place at the end of the hotel track. It's got a laid-back traveller feel and some rooms have sweeping valley views.

Galaxy View Tower (☎ 6680122; r Rs 400-800) Where the road leading up from the highway splits, this solid cheapie has a cosy restaurant, and rooms in cottages scattered around a slightly unkempt garden. The rooms at the top of the hill sneak a peek of the peaks.

our pick **Hotel at the End of the Universe** (☎ 6680011; www.endoftheuniverse.com.np; r without bathroom Rs 400-700, cottage Rs 1500, ste Rs 2500-4000) As well as a great name, this eclectic resort offers an intriguing selection of cottages, bamboo cabins and gingerbread-style cottages, set in a verdant garden. The gigantic suites have multiple bedrooms and huge lounges – perfect for families. There's an appealing hippy-style restaurant and the hotel runs a car to Bodhnath every Friday morning (Rs 250).

Hotel New Dragon (☎ 6680179; hotelnewdragon@gmail.com; r Rs 800, f Rs 2000) A decent hotel with an above-average restaurant. There are no mountain views, but rooms are clean, bright and decent value. Family rooms come with TVs.

Peaceful Cottage (☎ 6680077; peacefulcottage@hotmail.com; r US$20-30, without bathroom US$10) The best of a group of cheapies on a side track leading north off the dirt road to Kattike. It's an architectural hodgepodge but there are good views from the top of the octagonal tower. The plywood box rooms are fairly gloomy, but the deluxe rooms with carved bedsteads and bathrooms are more inviting.

Eco Home Nagarkot (☎ 6680180, r from Rs 800) A funky new place inspired by Tibetan architecture, opposite the Hotel Dragon. It's owned by a famous Nepali athlete and the rooms have flagstone floors and colourful Tibetan curtains, carpets and bedspreads. The roaring open fire in the restaurant will keep out the evening chills.

Hotel Sunshine (☎ 6680105; www.sunshinehotel.com.np; r Rs 800-2000) A typical modern Nepali hotel, where room rates correspond directly to the quality of the view. The best rooms on the upper levels have windows on three sides, facing directly onto the panorama.

There are more hotels at the end of the dirt road, including the **Hotel Green Valley** (☎ 6680078; r Rs 700, deluxe Rs 1000), where the deluxe rooms have eye-watering carpets but good balcony views. Nearby **Hotel Nagarkot Besso** (☎ 6680119; nagarkotbesso@yahoo.com; r Rs 800, deluxe Rs 1200-1500) offers slightly more tasteful interior decor and yet more giddying views.

MIDRANGE & TOP END

Hotel View Point (☎ 6680123; www.hotelviewpoint.com.np; s/d US$24/30, deluxe US$55/65) On a track branching off near the Hotel New Dragon, this place is slowly climbing skywards to stay ahead of the competition. It's not the most architecturally sensitive development, but the views are awesome and the wood-lined rooms have a certain Swiss-chalet charm. You have to go deluxe to get a view from your room.

Hotel Chautari Keyman (☎ 6680075; keyman@wlink.com.np; r old/new block US$30/60) Sprawling across a series of buildings below the Fort Resort, this expanding resort obviously has some wealthy backers. The old rooms are a bit overpriced but the swish new rooms have patio doors opening onto the view.

AROUND THE KATHMANDU VALLEY

Nagarkot Farmhouse Resort (☎ 6202022; www
.nagarkotfarmhouse.com; s/d incl all meals from US$40/60)
Well away from the main hotel sprawl, this
highly recommended place feels like an exclu-
sive country retreat. The best rooms are in the
Newari-inspired brick complex on the edge
of the garden, with tiled floors, spotless bathrooms and deck chairs on the balconies, which
face a sensational sweep of peaks. Room 15
has windows on two sides. The resort is about
2km past the Hotel Country Villa down the
dirt track to Sankhu.

Hotel Country Villa (☎ 6680128; www.hotelcountry
villa.com; s/d US$60/75) Down the dirt road to
Sankhu, this tasteful place feels like a modern resort, with a stylish dining room and
bedrooms livened up by prints of Robert
Powell's paintings of Nepal. The bright
rooms have blond-wood details and modernist carpets hand-woven in the Kathmandu
Valley.

Club Himalaya Resort (☎ 6680080; www.nepalshotel
.com; s/d from US$65/80; 🏊) A big, luxury resort
like this does nothing for the rural ambience
of Nagarkot, but this is still the most comfortable place in town. Staggered along the ridge
and set around a stylish glass-fronted restaurant and foyer, this place offers little luxuries
like a heated pool and a private helipad. The
views from the terraces and rooms are probably the best in town. It's just uphill from the
bus stand on the main road. Inside the hotel is
the Teahouse Inn restaurant (see right).

ourpick The Fort Resort (☎ 6680149; www.mountain
-retreats.com; s/d US$70/75, ste US$150) At the end of
the track branching off near the Hotel New
Dragon, this is perhaps the most stylish resort
in the main tourist enclave. It's a towering
place, built in the Newari red-brick style,
and the immaculately trimmed garden terrace looks out over a natural amphitheatre of
peaks. This was the location of the fort (kot)
that gave Nagarkot its name and the dignified
rooms and suites are set in stylish cottages or
in the main building.

Eating

Most people eat at the lodges, but there are a
few independent restaurants.

Berg House Café (dishes Rs 100-200) By the main
junction on the highway, this colourful cafe is
packed with fossils, gnarled tree roots and other
found bits of bric-a-brac, and the traveller-
oriented menu runs to pizzas, sandwiches
and steaks.

Sherpa Alpine Lodge (meals Rs 100-250) Ignore the
rooms here and focus on the pleasant al fresco
restaurant, with tables in little huts around a
terraced garden overlooking the valley.

Hotel New Dragon (mains Rs 100-350) This spick
and span restaurant has a broad menu of local
and Continental dishes to match the broad
views from the back terrace. The modern open
kitchen is a legacy of the times when Kilroy's
of Kathmandu ran the show.

Teahouse Inn (mains Rs 150-250, set meals Rs 350)
Inside the Club Himalaya Resort, this day-
tripper-oriented place has a great terrace
with mountain views. Food is good and not
too expensive.

At the junction, Nagarkot Food Home,
Hotel Bhanjyang Restaurant and AC's Café
offer similar food at similar prices to Berg
House Café, but have less atmosphere.

Getting There & Away

A tourist minibus runs daily to Nagarkot
from Kathmandu's Narsingh Chowk (Rs 200,
two hours) at about 12.30pm, but this can be
hard to find – call your hotel ahead of time
and they will tell the driver to expect you.
Return buses depart from the Galaxy View
Tower at 3pm.

Outside the tourist season, the only option is to take a bus to Bhaktapur (Rs 20,
one hour), then walk to the east end of town
and take a second bus to Nagarkot (Rs 27,
one hour).

A one-way taxi to Nagarkot costs around
Rs 1500 from Kathmandu, or Rs 2500 for a return trip with an hour or so to view the peaks.
Walking to, or preferably from, Nagarkot is
an interesting alternative. For route ideas
see p222.

BANEPA
pop 16,000

The first major town you reach heading east
out of the valley, Banepa is a busy crossroads
with interesting brick-lined backstreets snaking north from the highway. The temples were
built in the 14th and 16th centuries, when
Banepa was an important stop on the trade
route to Tibet, boasting trade links as far
afield as the Ming dynasty on the east coast
of China. The town is an easy cycle or motorcycle ride from Kathmandu (29km) and you
can continue east along the Arniko Hwy to
Dhulikhel (5km), or go south to the wonderful temple town of Panauti (7km). The places

covered in the Banepa section can be found on Map p227.

Take an hour or two to explore the backstreets. From the main junction with the empty statue plinth, walk north to two large water tanks (one surrounded by interesting statues) and take the path leading uphill to the right past the hospital. After about 700m, you'll reach the cobbled street leading down to the **Chandeshwari Temple**. Legend has it that the people of this valley were once terrorised by a demon known as Chand, who was defeated by one of the fearsome incarnations of Parvati, earning the goddess a new title – Chandeshwari, 'Slayer of Chand'.

The temple used to be famous for the enormous mural of Bhairab on its wall, but this was lost during the recent renovations – nevertheless, this is a popular pilgrimage spot and animals are sacrificed here on feast days. In front of the temple is a row of columns supporting statues of a menagerie of animals, and the struts supporting the triple-tiered roof show the eight Ashta Matrikas and eight Bhairabs. On the north side of the approach road is a smaller **temple** dedicated to the 'Mother of Chandeshwari'.

Returning to the junction by the two tanks, turn right along Banepa's cobbled main shopping street, passing a string of **Shiva shrines** and chaityas and a two-tiered **Narayan temple**. Continue past a square with a *tindhara* (three spouts) and bear right to reach the **Lokeshwar Karma Temple**, with an ornate pagoda turret and a collection of ancient Buddha statues out front. Follow the road past a Ganesh shrine on the right and look for a set of steps on the left leading to a bahal with a disused Buddhist monastery and a stupa almost consumed by the roots of a pipal tree. About 20m past the entrance to the square is another courtyard on the right containing a pair of Newari-style **Narayan temples** and a solid-looking statue of Garuda.

For a snack before moving on, there are numerous roadhouses along the highway around the main junction.

Getting There & Away

Regular buses leave from Kathmandu's Ratna Park bus station (Rs 35, two hours) and continue on to Dhulikhel and beyond. Buses to Panauti (Rs 10, 20 minutes) turn-off the Arniko Hwy at the main Banepa junction.

DHULIKHEL

☎ 011 / pop 9800 / elev 1550m

Only 3km southeast of Banepa (32km from Kathmandu), Dhulikhel is a quieter, less developed place to observe the high Himalaya, and the views easily compete with Nagarkot. From the edge of the ridge, a stunning panorama of peaks unfolds, from Langtang Lirung (7246m) in the east, through Dorje Lakpa (6966m) to the huge bulk of Gauri Shankar (7145m) and nearby Melungtse (7181m) and as far as Numbur (5945m) in the east.

Dhulikhel has one big advantage over Nagarkot – it's a real Newari town, with a temple-lined village square and a life outside of exposing tourists to the views. This is also a good base for short walks, including the stroll up to the Kali temple on the hilltop above the village and the longer walk to the stupa at Namobuddha (see boxed text, p228). Ask at your hotel about treks to local villages.

A new Japanese-funded highway from Dhulikhel to Bardibas has recently been constructed, offering a shorter alternative route to the Eastern Terai (see p229).

Also be aware that Dhulikhel has what is referred to in Nepal as 'Maoist problems' – strikes over pay and conditions for workers, agitated by Maoist politicians, that can shut the resort down for days at a time.

Sights

The old part of the town, west of the bus stop, is an interesting area to wander around. The main square contains a triple-roofed **Hari Siddhi Temple** and a three-tiered **Vishnu Temple** fronted by two worshipful Garudas in quite different styles. Just south is a small **Buddha shrine**. Northwest of the square are the modern **Gita Temple** and the tiered, Newari-style **Bhagwati Shiva Temple**.

If you take the road leading southeast from the bottom of the square for 2km, you'll pass a playing field and the turn-off of the road to the Kali Temple. Just beyond this junction, a Ganesh shrine marks the path down to a picturesque little **Shiva Temple** at the bottom of a gorge. A trickling stream flows through the site, and the temple enshrines a four-faced lingam topped by a metal dome with four nagas arching down from the pinnacle. Note the statues of a Malla royal family in the courtyard.

AROUND THE KATHMANDU VALLEY

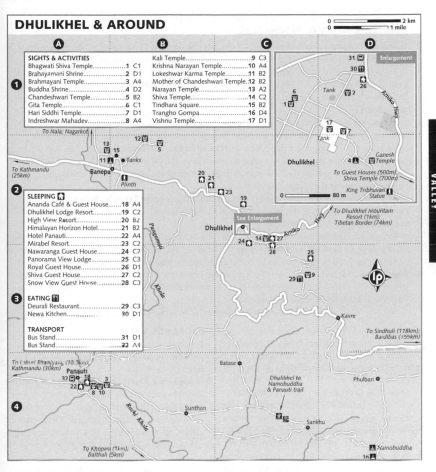

DHULIKHEL & AROUND

0 — 2 km
0 — 1 mile

If you don't mind a steep 30-minute uphill climb, you can continue up a series of short-cuts on concrete steps to reach the modern hilltop **Kali Temple**, and excellent mountain views.

The site is occupied by the army but it attracts hordes of local sightseers at weekends and villagers sell *suntala* (small oranges) beside the path in autumn. The peaceful Deurali Restaurant (see p229) is just below the temple.

Sleeping

There are two clusters of accommodation at Dhulikhel. The expensive places with good views are strung out on dirt roads leading off the highway. The cheapies are down the winding back-road that leads southeast from the main square.

BUDGET

Nawaranga Guest House (☎ 490226; s/d Rs 250/400, without bathroom Rs 200/300) A real blast from the past, this arty guest house has been around for nearly 40 years. Rooms are basic but the price is right and the organic restaurant and communal areas are full of paintings by the owner, Purna (for sale at fair prices). The guest house is southeast of the main chowk, on the back road towards the Shiva Temple.

Shiva Guest House (☎ 9841254988; d Rs 700, without bathroom Rs 300-500) Reached via a dirt track behind the Shiva temple, this family-run

DHULIKHEL TO NAMOBUDDHA HIKE

The hike or mountain-bike trip from Dhulikhel to Namobuddha is a fine leg-stretcher. It takes about three hours each way, or you can continue to Panauti (opposite) in around two more hours.

From Dhulikhel the trail first climbs up to the Kali Temple lookout (p226) then drops down to the left after the Deurali Restaurant for half an hour to the village of **Kavre**, by the new road to Sindhuli. Cross the road and walk down beside prayer flags for around an hour to the village of **Phulbari**.

As you crest the ridge, you'll see a Tibetan monastery on a hilltop, with Namobuddha just below it. To reach the stupa, take the right branch where the path forks.

Very little is known about the stupa at **Namobuddha** but legend relates that one of the past Buddhas came across a tigress close to death from starvation and unable to feed her cubs. The sorrowful Buddha allowed the hungry tigress to consume him, an act of compassion that transported him to the higher realms of existence.

You can see a marble tablet depicting the event in the nearby **Trangho Gompa** (10 minutes up the path to the left of the stupa). There are several teahouses by the stupa where you can get a basic lunch.

From Namobuddha, one trail descends from the right side of the stupa through forest to the small village of **Sankhu**, with temples and riverside ghats. Shortly after, the track splits – the right fork leads back to Batase and Dhulikhel, while the left fork winds past terraced fields to **Sunthan** and **Panauti**, about two hours from Namobuddha. As you approach Panauti, cross the stream over a suspension bridge to the ghats and then follow the road as it curves round to the Indreshwar Mahadev Temple (see opposite).

---

farmhouse has five clean, fresh rooms and great views from the upper floors and rooftop. Food comes fresh from the organic garden and you can pick mandarins right off the trees in autumn.

Snow View Guest House (☎ 661229, 9841482487; d with/without bathroom Rs 600/400) Probably the cheapest place with a proper mountain view, the Snow View is an annex to a family home, set beside a pleasant garden restaurant. Only two rooms look directly onto the mountains but the rooftop has enough views for everybody.

Royal Guest House (☎ 490010; r with/without bathroom Rs 600/400) Despite the noisy location by the highway, this is a good budget place, with a trekking lodge–style restaurant. You can even sneak a peak of the mountains from the roof.

Panorama View Lodge (☎ 680786; www.panorama viewlodge.com.np; r lower/upper fl Rs 500/1200) A proper retreat for those who really want to get away from it all, this place offers the full 'panorama view' plus good food and inviting rooms. Rates include breakfast but don't expect crowds of people for company. The hotel is 2km above town on the dirt track to the Kali Temple.

MIDRANGE & TOP END

Discounts are often available at the more expensive resorts in Dhulikhel so ask when you book or check in.

High View Resort (☎ 490048; www.highviewresort .com; deluxe s/d US$60/65) A 1980s atmosphere pervades this secluded place, about 700m past the Himalayan Horizon, then a stiff five-minute climb up some steps. The styling is a little dated but the huge deluxe rooms come with a private balcony and the views are superb. Discounts can bring rates down by as much as 50%.

Himalayan Horizon Hotel (☎ 490296; www.himalayan horizon.com; s/d from US$62/66) Also known as the Hotel Sun-n-Snow, this huge place uses traditional brickwork and woodcarving to create a Newari ambience. It's not quite 'old Dhulikhel' but the restaurant and garden terrace are great and the rooms have sublime views to the snow peaks.

Dhulikhel Lodge Resort (☎ 490114; www.dhulikhel lodgeresort.com; s/d from US$70/80) A rather clunky name for a rather appealing resort. Modern but built in a vaguely traditional style, this place has cracking views (particularly from the top floor rooms) and the great circular fireplace in the bar provides an après-ski atmosphere.

ourpick **Dhulikhel Mountain Resort** (☎ 420774; www.catmando.com/dhulikhel-mt-resort; s/d/tw US$76/78/78) You'll need transport to reach this hilltop escape, about 4km downhill from Dhulikhel towards the Tibetan border. Consisting of tasteful thatched cottages scattered over the hillside in a lovingly tended garden, the resort offers uninterrupted views across the valley to the peaks. Ring in advance and staff will pick you up in Dhulikhel.

Mirabel Resort (☎ 490972; www.mirabelresorthotel .com; s/d US$90/100) This large, comfortable resort would look more at home on a Balearic island, with its tiled white villas and hacienda vibe. Rooms have balconies facing the Himalayan vista, and you can also admire the peaks from the rooftop and gardens.

Eating

The hotels offer the best places to eat, but if you're staying near the centre, the **Newa Kitchen** (dishes Rs 50-200) by the bus stand has a full menu of Nepali, Indian, Chinese and European standards and an internet cafe (Rs 25 per hour).

If you're headed to the Kali Temple you could grab breakfast or a snack at the nearby **Deurali Restaurant**.

Getting There & Away

Frequent buses to Dhulikhel leave from Kathmandu's Ratna Park bus station (Rs 43, two hours).

The last bus goes back to Kathmandu at around 6pm. A taxi from Kathmandu costs about Rs 1500, or about Rs 800 from Bhaktapur.

The walk to Dhulikhel from Nagarkot is an interesting alternative. After watching the sunrise at Nagarkot you can walk down through Nala to Banepa, from where you can take a bus the last 4km to Dhulikhel (see opposite for details).

Schedules for buses on the new Japanese-funded road to Sindhuli and Bardibas in the Terai are only just being decided – enquire locally for the latest information.

PANAUTI

Tucked away in a side valley off the Arniko Hwy, about 7km south of Banepa, Panauti sits at the sacred confluence of the Roshi Khola and Pungamati Khola. A third 'invisible river' called the Padmabati is said to join the other two rivers at Panauti, making this a particularly sacred spot (see boxed text, below). Accordingly, there are some fabulously ancient temples which have stood the test of time partly because of Panauti's legendary resistance to earthquakes. Sadly, this didn't help in 1988 when a tremor damaged several buildings in the village. The places covered in the Panauti section can be found on Map p227.

Panauti was once a major trading centre with its own royal palace but today the village is a serene backwater, and all the more appealing for that. Most people visit on day-trips, but we recommend staying over and exploring the streets at dawn and dusk, when they are at their most magical. As well as its ornate temples, the village has some striking Rana-era mansions, which have been restored with assistance from the French government.

Information & Orientation

Panauti is squeezed between two brick lanes along the banks of the wedge of land running down to the confluence of the Roshi Khola and Pungamati Khola. Buses stop on the highway at the village's west end.

TRICKERY & REPENTANCE AT PANAUTI

Legend has it that Ahilya, the beautiful wife of a Vedic sage, was seduced by the god Indra, who tricked her by assuming the shape of her husband. When the sage returned and discovered what had happened he took his revenge by causing Indra's body to become covered in yonis – female sexual organs! Naturally, Indra was somewhat put out by this and for many years he and his wife Indrayani repented at the auspicious *sangam* (river confluence) at Panauti.

Parvati, Shiva's consort, took pity upon Indrayani and turned her into the invisible river, Padmabati, but it was some years before Shiva decided to release Indra from his strange affliction. The god appeared in Panauti in the form of a giant lingam and when Indra bathed in the river, his extranumerary yonis disappeared. Locals maintain that this miraculous Shiva lingam is the one enshrined in the Indreshwar Mahadev Temple.

For tourist information, you can visit the **information office** (☎ 01-6209707; www.welcome panauti.com) by the gateway at the start of the northern lane.

Sights

INDRESHWAR MAHADEV TEMPLE

Panauti's most famous temple is set in a vast courtyard full of statuary in the middle of the isthmus between the two rivers. Topped by a three-storey pagoda roof, the temple is a magnificent piece of Newari architecture. The first temple here was founded in 1294 but the shrine was rebuilt in its present form in the 15th century. The lingam enshrined here is said to have been created personally by Shiva (see boxed text, p229).

The woodcarvings on the temple's windows, doorways and roof struts are particularly fine, and the erotic carvings here are subtle and romantic rather than pornographic. To the south of the main temple is the rectangular **Unamanta Bhairab Temple**, with three faces of the demon deity peering out of the upstairs windows. A small, double-roofed Shiva temple stands in one corner of the courtyard, and a second shrine containing a huge black image of Vishnu as Narayan faces the temple from the west.

OTHER TEMPLES

The rest of Panauti's temples are grouped around the confluence at the east end of the village. Take the northern brick lane under the town gate, passing a series of pilgrim's rest-houses, brick temples and sunken tanks. Note the shops selling large ceramic pots with holes in the base, used to distil *raksi* (rice brandy).

At the end of the path, cross a small suspension bridge to the north bank of the Pungamati Khola to reach the three-tiered **Brahmayani Temple**, built in the 17th century to honour Brahmayani, the chief goddess of the village. The image from the temple is hauled around town during the lively annual chariot festival, marking the end of the monsoon.

Cross back to the south bank over the weir, then take another bridge back to the end of the spur, which is covered by the shrines and statues of the **Krishna Narayan Temple**. There are temples to various incarnations of Vishnu here – the largest temple has roof struts depicting Vishnu

as the carefree, flute-playing Krishna. Many of the shrines are embellished with Rana-era stucco-work.

There are more interesting buildings in the middle of the village. Walk west along the northern brick lane and turn right just before you reach the main road. You'll soon come to a large **civic square** with a music platform, a large white stupa, a Brahmayan Temple and the stately Municipality Offices built in classic Newari style.

Festivals & Events

Panauti holds a lively **chariot festival** at the end of the monsoon each year (usually in September), when images of the gods from the town's various temples are drawn around the streets in wooden chariots, starting from the town's main square.

Every year, pilgrims come to Panauti to bathe at the confluence of the two rivers as part of the festival of **Maghe Sankranti** in the Nepali month of Magh (usually in January). This celebrates the end of the month of Poush, a dark time when religious ceremonies are forbidden. Every 12 years – next in 2010 – this is accompanied by a huge *mela* (fair) attracting devotees and sadhus from all over Nepal.

Sleeping & Eating

Opposite the western entrance to the Indreshwar Mahadev Temple, **Ananda Cafe & Guest House** (☎ 01-6211924; s/d Rs 250/500) is set in an authentic village house, complete with drying corncobs in the windows. The rooms are creaky and full of character, the cafe serves delicious spiced *chiya* (tea), and the owner can arrange homestays in surrounding villages.

Back on the main road, south of the two brick lanes, the above-average **Hotel Panauti** (☎ 011-440055; panauti@wlink.com.np; r with/without bathroom Rs 1000/400) has a superior rooftop restaurant, set under a thatched canopy. The giant rooms without bathrooms are better value than the rooms with bathrooms and TVs.

Getting There & Away

Buses run frequently between Panauti and Kathmandu's Ratna Park bus station (Rs 45, two hours); the last bus leaves Panauti around 6pm. For Dhulikhel you'll have to change in Banepa (Rs 10, 20 minutes). See p228 for information on walking to Panauti from Dhulikhel.

If you are travelling by mountain bike or motorcycle, you could return to Kathmandu along the remote, little-used dirt road over the Lakuri Bhanjyang – see p96 for a description of the 30km route.

AROUND PANAUTI

Many of the small villages dotted around the valley have Newari-style temples and traditional brick architecture. Get hold of Nepa Maps' 1:50,000 *Around Kathmandu Valley* map and explore. One place to check out is the village of **Shrikandapur**, just off the Banepa–Panauti road. On the hilltop is a three-tiered Bhairab Temple with good views over the valley.

At Balthali, 7km southeast of Panauti, the **Balthali Resort** (☎ 01-4108210; www.balthalivillage resort.com; s/d US$35/45, half board US$47/69) can arrange all sorts of volunteering and cultural immersion activities and treks to the surrounding villages. The resort is perched on the hilltop above Balthali village, with sweeping Himalayan views.

To get to Balthali from Panauti, take a bus (Rs 10, 15 minutes) or walk along the road for an hour, crossing the river after Khopasi.

BEYOND THE VALLEY

The following destinations lie outside the Kathmandu Valley on the roads north to Syabrubesi and Kodari, on the Tibetan border. You can only cross into Tibet on an organised tour, but a trickle of independent travellers come up this way on overnight trips so they can say they've been there, done that.

ARNIKO HIGHWAY TO TIBET

The Arniko Hwy provides Nepal's overland link with Tibet and China. Beyond Barabise, the road is particularly vulnerable to landslides and sections are likely to be closed temporarily during the monsoon months (May to August). Even when the highway is open it's of limited use in breaking India's commercial stranglehold on Nepal, as it's still cheaper to ship Chinese goods via Kolkata (Calcutta) than to truck them through Tibet. For a more detailed description of this route see p96. The main towns covered

in the Arniko Hwy section can be found on Map p342.

Barabise

Strung out along the Arniko Hwy, Barabise is the region's main bazaar town but there's no real reason to visit except to change buses. If you get stuck overnight, there are several guest houses along the main road. **Mata Chandeshwori Hotel** (☎ 011-489188; d Rs 250) is right opposite the ticket desk for buses to Kodari and it serves good fried momos. Similar rooms at similar prices can be found at the Him Shrinkhala Guest House and Roshan Guest House.

Buses run frequently from the north end of town to Kodari (Rs 65, three hours, last bus 5pm) and from the south end of town to Kathmandu (Rs 135, four hours, last bus 4pm).

Borderlands Resort

Tucked away in a bend of the Bhote Kosi River, 97km from Kathmandu, the superb **Borderlands Resort** (Map p342; ☎ 01-4701295; www .borderlandresorts.com; adventure packages from US$40 per night) is one of Nepal's top adventure resorts. Adrenaline-charged activities include rafting, trekking and canyoning but you can also just kick back and enjoy the peace and quiet. The resort is centred on an attractive bar and dining area, surrounded by luxury thatch-roofed safari tents dotted around a lush tropical garden.

Most people visit on a package that includes activities, accommodation, meals and transport from Kathmandu – drop in to the

---

OFF THE BEATEN TREK

Both Borderlands and Last Resort offer trekking trips to the Tibetan border. A four- or five-day trek takes in the ruins of Duganagadi Fort, built in 1854 to defend Nepal during the Nepal-Tibet war, the Tibetan monastery at Bagam, the nunnery at Gumba and the villages of Yemershing, Tasitham and Listikot. Longer treks also visit Bhairab Kunda, a holy lake at 4080m with great views of the Langtang range. Thousands of pilgrims trek up to the lake during the full moon of August. Prices hover around US$50 per person per day for the fully supported camping trek.

resort's Kathmandu office (Map p140) next to the Northfield Cafe in Thamel to discuss the options.

Last Resort

Thrill-seekers also drop off the Kodari road – quite literally – at the **Last Resort** (Map p342; ☎ 01-4700525; www.thelastresort.com.np; accommodation only standard/deluxe US$21/24, day trips from US$62, two-day trips from US$104). Set in a gorgeous spot on a ridge above the Bhote Kosi River, 12km from the Tibetan border, the resort is reached by a vertiginous suspension bridge that acts as a launch pad for Nepal's only bungee jump (see p87).

Accommodation at the resort is in comfortable standard (four-person) or deluxe (two-person) safari tents, set around a soaring stone-and-slate dining hall and bar. Most people visit on all-inclusive adventure packages – as well as swinging from a giant elastic band, you can go rafting, trekking, mountain biking, canyoning, rock climbing, abseiling, rafting and kayaking.

For less endorphin-motivated travellers, there are gas-heated showers, a plunge pool and a sauna and spa. Package rates include activities, accommodation, meals and transport to and from Kathmandu – drop into the Kathmandu office (Map p140) near the Kathmandu Guest House for more information and to book. Bring mosquito repellent and a torch (flashlight).

Tatopani

About 4km downhill from the border, Tatopani is famous for its natural hot springs, hence the name – *tato* (hot) *pani* (water). The **springs** (entry Rs 10; ☺ 4am-8pm) have been quite tastefully developed, with a riverside restaurant and clean concrete bathhouses for men and women with running hot showers. There is a small **gompa** on the southern edge of town and a large *mani lhakhang* (shrine with a prayer wheel) on the rocky bluff above the village.

Several simple guest houses are strung out along the highway offering basic box rooms for Rs 200.

It is worth paying a little extra for the superior comforts of the large, modern **New Family Guest House** (☎ 011-690439; r with bathroom Rs 600-1200, r without bathroom Rs 400; meals from Rs 150), which is located just downhill from the springs.

Kodari

The road linking Kathmandu and Lhasa was constructed in the 1960s, but political wrangles and the ever-present risk of landslides prevented the Arniko Hwy from ever becoming a mainstream route between the two countries. Even today, traffic on the road from Barabise to Kodari is mainly limited to freight trucks and the occasional overland jeep tour. However, big changes are afoot on the Chinese side of the border, with the construction of a huge new immigration complex, so everything could change in the next couple of years.

It is not possible for foreigners to enter Tibet here except as part of an organised tour with a Chinese visa and Tibetan travel permit. However, quite a few people traipse up to the border to pose for photos on the **Friendship Bridge** that separates the two countries. From here, everything to the north is Tibet, though at this elevation, there is no real difference in the landscape. The nearest Tibetan town is Khasa (Zhangmu), about 8km uphill from the border.

It's worth taking the steps beside the Ganesh shrine to the hilltop **Liping Gompa** for views over the Chinese side of the border, with long lines of trucks snaking up the hill towards Khasa.

INFORMATION

Just before the Friendship Bridge, the **immigration office** (☺ 8am-5pm) can provide you with a visa on arrival at the usual rates, but you should pay in US dollars and you'll need one photo. You can change cash and travellers cheques at the **Nepal Bangladesh Bank** (☺ 10am-3.30pm Sun-Thu, to 1.30pm Fri) or the **Bank of Kathmandu** (☺ 10am-3pm Sun-Thu, to 1pm Fri), about 20m before the immigration office.

SLEEPING & EATING

Accommodation options are fairly bleak, but the **Kailash Tashi Delek Guest House** (☎ 011-63302; d Rs 400) has OK rooms and a nice river view from its timber-lined restaurant (mains Rs 100 to Rs 180). The nearby **Namguel Guesthouse** (r Rs 200) is another passable cheapie.

GETTING THERE & AWAY

There are four daily buses to Kathmandu (Rs 240 to Rs 280, 4½ hours) – the 1.30pm service

---

TAMANG HERITAGE TRAIL

The Nepal Tourism Board has established an interesting village tourism project in the Tibetan-influenced Rasuwa district bordering Langtang (Map pp348–9), providing income for local people and offering an alternative to the more commercialised Langtang area. The best option is a five- or six-day loop starting from Syabrubesi – accommodation is available in Gotlang, Briddim, Goljung, Tatopani, Timure and Thuman for around Rs 150 per person per night, plus Rs 100 per meal. Guides in Syabrubesi charge around Rs 1000 per day, which includes their food and accommodation.

Here's a sample itinerary:

Day One Climb on steep switchbacks, gaining 720m to Rongga Bhanjyang and continuing along the dirt road to Gotlang, the largest Tamang village in the area. From Gotlang make the short detour to Parvati Kund Lake.

Day Two Trek to the community-run hot-spring pools at Tatopani via Chilime and Gonggang, an ascent of 840m.

Day Three Climb 560m to the ridge of Nagthali Ghyang for fine mountain views, then descend 820m to Thuman.

Day Four Follow the ridge then descend another 640m to cross the Bhote Kosi and hike north to Timure. Alternatively, head south to stay in a traditional homestay in Briddim (a 400m ascent).

Day Five It's all downhill to Syabrubesi via Wangal (a 770m descent), or you can link up with the Langtang trek by taking the high northern route via Syarpagaon.

---

runs express. Otherwise take a local bus to Barabise (Rs 65, three hours), and change.

After 2pm your only option to get to Kathmandu the same day is to take a taxi for around Rs 3000 (Rs 800 a seat), but you'll struggle to find a willing driver after 5pm. Hitching is possible on this route, though you'll probably have to pay for your ride.

THE ROAD TO LANGTANG

A tarmac road heads northwest out of Kathmandu towards Dhunche, offering fantastic views of the Ganesh Himalaya as it gains the ridge at Kakani. Beyond Trisuli Bazaar, the road deteriorates and is travelled mainly by mountain bikers and trekkers headed for the Langtang region (see p346).

There are police checkpoints at Mudkhu and Kaulithana but foreigners are usually waved straight through. Just before Malekhu, on the Kathmandu–Pokhara (Prithvi) Hwy, a road branches north over the Trisuli to Dhading and east to Trisuli Bazaar. This opens up the possibility of a circular bicycle ride taking in Kakani, Trisuli Bazaar, Dhading and Malekhu. See Map pp236–7 for this route.

Kakani

Most of the towns around Kathmandu sit at the bottom of the valley – you have to travel to the valley rim to get decent views of the Himalaya. Set atop a ridge at 2073m, just off the road to Trisuli Bazaar, Kakani is the quieter, more peaceful cousin of Dhulikhel and Nagarkot. From a series of high points along the ridge, there are magnificent views towards the Ganesh Himal range. Part of the fun is getting here – the 24km road that winds uphill from Balaju makes for a great cycle ride and an even better motorcycle trip.

Apart from staring open-mouthed at the view, there's not much to do. In the middle of the village, the meticulously tended **Thai Memorial Park** commemorates and provides a final resting place for the 113 passengers of a Thai Airlines plane that crashed near Gosainkund in 1992. On the other side of the hill is the **International Mountaineer Memorial Park**, with an artificial climbing wall used by local school groups. The handsome colonial mansion at the start of the village was built as a summer villa for the British embassy, but it's closed to visitors.

SLEEPING & EATING

Kakani Guest House (☎ 01-2173325; r without bathroom Rs 250) At the start of the main path through the village, this trekking-lodge-style place offers simple rooms. The nearby Hotel Kakani Inn and Lama Guesthouse are very similar.

View Himalaya Guesthouse (☎ 01-6915706; r Rs 600) Above the path, this place does what is says on the label. The garden offers great mountain views, and the rooms are OK for the price.

Tara Gaon Hotel (☎ 061-520255; s/d US$12/16) Formerly occupied by the army, the Tara Gaon offers good food and sublime views from its lawns but very tired and overpriced rooms.

GETTING THERE & AWAY

Kakani is 1½ hours from Kathmandu by bus or motorcycle but you'll burn plenty of calories powering up here by bicycle. It's uphill all the way, but there are numerous 'garden restaurants' where you can rest. In the other direction, it's a thrilling freewheel back to Kathmandu (just watch for trucks or buses on the corners). See p94 for details of the route to Kakani and on through Shivapuri National Park.

The road to Kakani turns off the Kathmandu–Trisuli Bazaar road just before the Kaulithana police checkpoint, at the crest of the hill. Buses bound for Trisuli Bazaar can drop you at the junction at Kaulithana (Rs 40, 1½ hours) and you can walk the 4km to Kakani in around one hour. A taxi costs Rs 3000 return.

Nuwakot

The small village of Nuwakot, just southeast of Trisuli Bazaar, is one of those sprawling Newari townships that seems to float somewhere between the 17th and 21st centuries. Centred on the **Saat Tale Durbar**, a 16th-century fortress built by Prithvi Narayan Shah, this was also where the great king died in 1775.

In the fortress compound is a large **Taleju Temple**, said to date from the 15th century, when Nuwakot was ruled by its own royal family. Nearby is the town's **Durbar Square** (now occupied by the army) and the two-tiered **Bhairabi Temple**, used for animal sacrifices. Nuwakot also has a small **museum** (entry Rs 25; ☉ hours vary) devoted to local history and culture.

Those enterprising chaps at **Himalayan Encounters** (☎ 01-4700426; www.himalayanencounters.com; Kathmandu Guest House, Thamel, Kathmandu; r per person with meals US$35) have recently established a charming lodge in a pair of old village houses. The 'Famous Farm' offers rooms with lots of local details set around a serene and peaceful garden. Many guests visit as part of a trekking trip to Langtang, and a new trekking route is now being developed to Gosainkund. For more on Himalayan Encounters see p102.

Getting to Nuwakot can be a little awkward as there is only one direct bus a day from Kathmandu's New Bus Park (Rs 130, four hours), but you can get here via a 1½ hour hike from Bidur on the bus route to Trisuli Bazaar. A taxi costs a steep Rs 6000. Pick up Nepa Maps' 1:125,000 *A Short Walk to Nuwakot* for walks in the area.

Dhunche

☎ 010 / elev 1950m

If you are going to Langtang you will pass through Dhunche (pronounced 'doon-chay'), 117km from Kathmandu. It's a fairly pleasant Tamang bazaar, but most people head straight for the trailhead at Syabrubesi – see p347. Just before you reach Dhunche, you must pay the Rs 1000 entry fee to Langtang National Park.

If by some miracle your bus arrived early and you have time to kill, check out the small Tamang Museum (admission Rs 100), below the road and accessed via the steps beside the Annapurna Hotel.

SLEEPING & EATING

Hotel Langtang View (☎ 540141, Kathmandu 01-4355481; s/d Rs 300/400, without bathroom Rs 100/200) The most popular place to stay, with a good restaurant and rooftop seating that boasts views into Tibet. Staff can arrange porters and 4WD transport back to Kathmandu.

Himalaya Legend (☎ 540112; r with/without bathroom Rs 200/150) Another good choice, with a cosy dining hall on the top floor and a small bakery.

GETTING THERE & AWAY

Although it is only 117km from Kathmandu to Dhunche, the journey takes forever. Buses to Dhunche (Rs 180, nine hours) leave at 6.30am, 7.30am and 8.30am from the Machha Pokhari (Fish Pond) junction, just north of the Kathmandu Ring Rd, and also from the nearby Gongabu bus station. One bus continues to Syabrubesi. The direct return bus to Kathmandu leaves Dhunche at 7.15am (reserve a seat the night before).

The Hotel Langtang View can arrange a 4WD to/from Kathmandu for Rs 8000 each way for four passengers.

Kathmandu to Pokhara

Before you sprint from Kathmandu to Pokhara, consider the 206km of classic Middle Hills countryside that you will pass through en route. The hills that flank the Prithvi Hwy are dotted with historic villages and ancient temples, but visitors often see nothing of this area apart from the views flashing by outside the bus windows. We strongly recommend taking at least two days for the journey between Kathmandu and Pokhara to see more of this interesting and unspoiled region.

Heading west from Kathmandu, the first interesting stop is the Manakamana Temple, steeped in history and reached by an exhilarating cable car ride from the bottom of the valley. Further west a road leads north to historic Gorkha, the birthplace of the founder of the Shah dynasty. Both Gorkha and Manakamana once lay on the trekking approach route to Pokhara and the Annapurnas.

West of Gorkha, another side road winds up into the hills from Dumre to Bandipur, a living museum of Newari architecture, set in gorgeous walking country well off the beaten tourist track. Dumre is also the gateway to Besi Sahar and the eastern arm of the Annapurna Circuit. Dotted between these settlements are numerous junction towns and roadhouses where buses stop for snacks and toilet breaks.

Even if you don't stop between Kathmandu and Pokhara, the scenery along the road is dramatic. The highway dives along a series of deep river valleys, passing cascading rice terraces, rocky gorges and the roaring rapids that offer the closest white-water rafting to Kathmandu. On clear days, there are views of Machhapuchhare and the Annapurna massif most of the way to Pokhara.

HIGHLIGHTS

- Fly like a yogi on the exhilarating **Manakamana cable car** (p237)
- Walk in the footsteps of royalty at Gorkha's magnificent hilltop **Gorkha Durbar** (p239)
- Stop for a lunchtime swim at the idyllic **River Side Springs Resort** (p238) in Kurintar
- Step back in time among the Newari houses of **Bandipur** (p241), on the ancient trade route to India
- Walk to caves, viewpoints, villages and mountain shrines in the **Bandipur hills** (p243)

KATHMANDU TO POKHARA

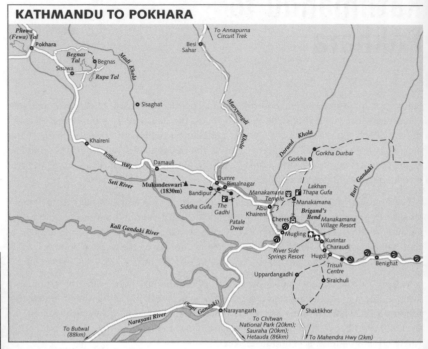

DANGERS & ANNOYANCES

Since the 2008 elections, there have been no major problems along the Prithvi Hwy. However, bandhs (strikes) can close the road for short periods. If this happens and you need to get back to Kathmandu in a hurry, flying back in from Pokhara may be your only option.

GETTING THERE & AWAY

Except on strike days, several dozen public and tourist buses and minivans run daily between Kathmandu and Pokhara, linking most of the important towns en route. The winding journey takes at least seven hours, and longer if the bus has to stop for army checkpoints.

For details of the mountain bike ride between Kathmandu and Pokhara see p98.

KATHMANDU TO MUGLING

The Kathmandu Valley is enclosed by a towering wall of hills and escaping in any direction takes time. The main thoroughfare to Pokhara is the Prithvi Hwy, which runs

west along the gorge of the Trisuli River, passing the turn-off for Narayangarh and the Terai. For information on rafting the Trisuli, see opposite.

At **Naubise**, 29km from Kathmandu, the little-used Tribhuvan Hwy (sometimes referred to as Rajpath) branches south and makes a dramatic passage across the hills of the Mahabharat Range to the plains town of Hetauda (p306). For details of mountain biking along this route, see p97.

From Naubise, the Prithvi Hwy follows the valley of the Mahesh Khola to meet the twisting, contorting Trisuli River. Many whitewater rafting companies set off from the small village of **Bhaireni**. The next big settlement is **Malekhu**, famous for its smoked river fish, which are sold from long wooden rakes on the roadside.

About 3km before Malekhu, a side road leads north to **Dhading**, a tiny cluster of stone houses on a terraced ridge overlooking the Ganesh Himalaya. The **Shreeban Nature Camp** (☎ 01-4258427; www.shreeban.com.np; outside Dhading; B&B per person per day US$25; ☷ closed winter) offers

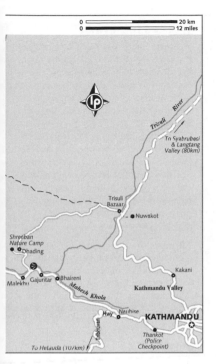

rock climbing, hang-gliding, mountain biking and trekking in the hills around Dhading but this is a more low-key operation than Borderlands Resort (p231) or the Last Resort (p232) – two big adventure outfits near the Tibetan border.

Arrange visits in advance from Kathmandu and contact them to check the rates.

Following the highway west from Malekhu, the next village is **Benighat**, where the roaring Buri Gandaki River merges with the Trisuli. The increased bore of the river creates some impressive rapids and rafting companies break for the night between Benighat and Charaudi, about 20km downstream.

About halfway between Benighat and Mugling, the tiny village of **Hugdi** is a possible starting point for treks to Chitwan National Park – see the boxed text, p238.

MANAKAMANA

From the tiny hamlet of Cheres (6km before Mugling), an Austrian-engineered cable car soars up an almost impossibly steep hillside to the ancient **Manakamana Temple** (☾ daylight), one of the most important temples in the Middle Hills. Hindus believe that the goddess Bhagwati, an incarnation of Parvati, has the power to grant wishes, and newlyweds flock here to pray for male children.

But this good fortune comes at a price – pilgrims seal the deal by sacrificing a goat, chicken or pigeon in a gory pavilion behind the temple. There's even a dedicated carriage on the cable car for sacrificial goats.

Built in the tiered pagoda style, the temple dates back to the 17th century. On Saturdays and other feast days, Manakamana almost vanishes under a sea of pilgrims and the paving stones run red with sacrificial blood.

For views of the Himalaya, walk uphill for about 3km past a small Shiva temple to

---

RAFTING ON THE TRISULI

After diving into the valley west of Kathmandu, the Prithvi Hwy follows the Trisuli River, the most popular destination for short rafting trips from Kathmandu. Most of the rapids along this route are grade 2 to grade 3, but the water can build up to grade 4 in the monsoon. Most companies put in near Bhaireni and take out for the first night near Benighat or Charaudi. Some groups camp on river beaches, but **Himalayan Encounters** (☎ 01-4700426; www.himalayanencounters.com) breaks the journey at its appealing Trisuli Centre, a delightful lodge and rafting centre in a converted village house at Big Fig beach. The **Royal Beach Camp** (☎ 01-4700531; www.royalbeachnepal .com) stops at its adventure camp near Charaudi and offers a thrilling variety of ways to get wet, from kayaking courses to rafting and canyoning. Rafting day trips cost Rs 1600, and three-night adventure packages cost Rs 9000.

Multiday trips continue downriver towards Narayangarh and Chitwan National Park, but the rapids below Kurintar are much more gentle. For a more dramatic descent, consider joining an eight-day rafting trip from Trisuli Bazaar. See p106 for more information.

Lakhan Thapa Gufa, a sacred cave offering uninterrupted views of the mountains.

If you feel like taking the scenic route to Pokhara, you can continue northwest along the ridge to Gorkha in around four hours, or follow the path downhill from Manakamana to Abu Khaireni in around five hours.

Sleeping & Eating

There are dozens of pilgrim hotels in the village surrounding the temple. Probably the best is **Sunrise Home** (☎ 064-460055; r with bathroom from Rs 300); the spotless, spacious rooms have fans and TVs and the restaurant downstairs serves delicious vegetarian and nonvegetarian curries, and cold beers (a rarity in these parts).

Numerous pilgrim restaurants along the path that goes to the cable-car station serve 'local chicken' and 'local mutton' – the meat is sourced from the animal sacrifices at the temple.

KURINTAR

There are a couple of upmarket options down in the valley at Kurintar, about 3km east of the cable-car station.

Manakamana Village Resort (☎ 056-540150; om@hons.com.np; r with bathroom from Rs 900, r with air-con from Rs 1200; 🗶) A modest but peaceful, tin-roofed resort, set in a small, flower-filled garden. All the rooms are the same; you pay more if you use the air-con.

ourpick **River Side Springs Resort** (☎ 056-540129; nangint@ccsl.com.np; permanent tents from US$20, s/d from US$40/50; 🗶 🗮) This sophisticated, colonial-style resort occupies a prime piece of real estate on the banks of the Trisuli. Accommodation is in classy cabins or luxury tents and there's an excellent restaurant and a glorious ring-shaped swimming pool (open to nonguests for Rs 275).

Getting There & Away

The awesome **Manakamana cable car** (adult US$12, luggage per kilo Rs 8; 🕑 9am-noon & 1.30-5pm, from 8am Sat) rises more than 1000m as it covers the 2.8km from the Prithvi Hwy to the Manakamana ridge. The price for goats is Rs 130 but they only get a one-way ticket...

> **TREKKING TO CHITWAN**
>
> From tiny Hugdi, you can trek south into the homeland of the Chepang tribe, reaching Sauraha (p290) on the edge of Chitwan National Park in five days. Trekkers stay in rustic teahouses and homestays in the villages of Hattibang, Jyandala, Gadi and Shaktikhor.
>
> On the way, you can visit forts and mountain viewpoints, go birdwatching and get involved in a variety of cultural activities. See www.mountainleaders.com/trekking/chitwan_chepang_heritage_trail.php for a detailed description of the route and the sights and activities along the way.

All buses that run between Kathmandu and Pokhara or Narayangarh pass the turn-off to the Manakamana cable car (look for the red-brick archway). If you want to walk to Manakamana, the trail starts at the village of Abu Khaireni, about 8km west of Mugling.

MUGLING
☎ 056

Mugling marks the junction between the Prithvi Hwy and the highway to the plains, but all you'll find here are roadhouses and dusty truck stops and there's no real reason to visit except to change buses.

Many of Mugling's gloomy hotels are actually fronts for prostitution, but the **Machhapuchhare Hotel & Lodge** (☎ 540029; r with bathroom Rs 250) is a legitimate hotel that provides lodging for the occasional stranded backpacker.

For food, there are dozens of local hotels along the main road.

ABU KHAIRENI

Another dusty junction town, Abu Khaireni marks the junction with the rutted road to Gorkha; buses and minibuses around the junction offer transfers to Gorkha for Rs 50. Abu Khaireni is also the starting point for the four- to five-hour climb to the Manakamana Temple (see p237).

To reach the temple, turn onto the road to Gorkha and turn right by the Manakamana

Hotel, then cross the suspension bridge and climb through terraced fields and small villages to the ridge.

Any bus going from Kathmandu to Pokhara can drop you at Abu Khaireni.

GORKHA

☎ 064

About 24km north of Abu Khaireni, Gorkha is famous as the birthplace of Prithvi Narayan Shah, who unified the rival kingdoms of Nepal into a single cohesive nation in 1769, but the Shah dynasty ended with the ignominious 'retirement' of Gyanendra Shah in 2008.

Nevertheless, Gorkha is still an important pilgrimage destination for Newars, who regard the Shahs as living incarnations of Vishnu.

The main attraction is the Gorkha Durbar, the former palace of the Shahs, which lords over Gorkha from a precarious ridge, but there are historic temples dotted all over town.

Sights

GORKHA DURBAR

Regarded by many as the crowning glory of Newari architecture, **Gorkha Durbar** (admission free; ⏱ 6am-6pm) is a fort, a palace and a temple all in one. This magnificent architectural confection is perched high above Gorkha on a knife-edge ridge, with superb views over the Trisuli Valley and glimpses north to the soaring peaks of the Annapurna and Ganesh Himalaya.

As the birthplace of Prithvi Narayan Shah, the Durbar has huge significance for Nepalis. The great Shah was born here in around 1723, when Gorkha was a minor feudal kingdom. Upon gaining the throne, Prithvi Narayan worked his way around the Kathmandu Valley, subduing rival kingdoms and creating an empire that extended far into India and Tibet.

Most pilgrims enter through the western gate, emerging on an open terrace in front of the exquisite **Kalika Temple**, a psychedelic 17th-century fantasy of carved peacocks, demons

KATHMANDU TO POKHARA

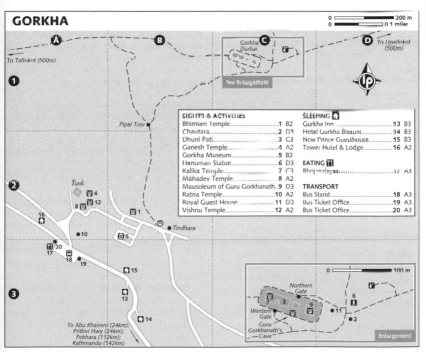

GORKHA

| 0 | 200 m |
| 0 | 0.1 miles |

To Tallokot (500m)

To Upallokot (500m)

Gorkha Durbar

New Enlargement

Pipal Tree

Tank

Tindhara

SIGHTS & ACTIVITIES	
Bhimsen Temple	1 B2
Chautara	2 D3
Dhuni Pati	3 C3
Ganesh Temple	4 A2
Gorkha Museum	5 B2
Hanuman Statue	6 D3
Kalika Temple	7 C3
Mahadev Temple	8 A2
Mausoleum of Guru Gorkhanath	9 D3
Ratna Temple	10 A2
Royal Guest House	11 D3
Vishnu Temple	12 A2

SLEEPING	
Gurkha Inn	13 B3
Hotel Gurkha Bisauni	14 B3
New Prince Guesthouse	15 B3
Tower Hotel & Lodge	16 A2

EATING	
Bhojanalaya	17 A3

TRANSPORT	
Bus Stand	18 A3
Bus Ticket Office	19 A3
Bus Ticket Office	20 A3

To Abu Khaireni (24km);
Prithvi Hwy (24km);
Pokhara (112km);
Kathmandu (142km)

Northern Gate

Western Gate

Guru Gorkhanath's Cave

| 0 | 100 m |

Enlargement

and serpents, carved onto every available inch of timber.

On *astami* (the half-moon day of the lunar calendar) and other important dates, dozens of goats, chickens, doves and buffaloes are dispatched to honour the goddess Kali, the destructive incarnation of Shiva's consort, Parvati.

Only Brahmin priests and the king can enter the temple, but non-Hindus are permitted to observe sacrifices from the terrace.

The east wing of the palace complex contains the **Dhuni Pati**, the former palace of Prithvi Narayan Shah. Like the temple, the palace is covered in elaborate woodcarvings, including a magnificent window in the shape of Garuda (the man-bird vehicle of Vishnu).

Only Hindus can ascend to the upper level that contains the throne room and the birth chamber where Prithvi Narayan Shah was born.

At the east end of the palace, but off limits to non-Hindus, is the mausoleum of **Guru Gorkhanath**, the reclusive saint who acted as a spiritual guide for the young Prithvi Narayan.

If you leave via the northern gate, you'll pass the former **Royal Guest House** – note the erotic roof struts and the crocodile carvings on the window frames – and a vividly painted **Hanuman statue**, surrounded by worn stone steles. A path leads east from here past a large **chautara** (stone resting platform) to an exposed rocky bluff with awesome views of the mountains and a set of carved stone footprints, attributed variously to Sita, Rama, Gorkhanath and Guru Padmasambhava.

The durbar is an important religious site. Shoes should be removed, photography is prohibited and leather (including belts) is banned inside the Gorkha Durbar complex. This is strictly enforced so use the lockers at the shoe stand near the western gate (bring your own padlock) or leave your camera at the guard house.

To reach the Durbar, go north from the bus stand and follow the main cobbled street through the bazaar.

You must then climb an exhausting stairway of 1500 stone steps, snaking up the hillside.

The stairway begins just before the post office – if you reach the public washing area, you've gone too far. As you climb, look out for the huge tin steamers used to strip the feathers off sacrificial chickens to prepare them for the cookpot.

From the durbar you can continue along the ridge east or west to reach the remains of two ancient forts, **Tallokot** and **Upallokot**. Both are occupied by the Nepali army, but the walk through the forest is quiet and peaceful.

OTHER MONUMENTS

There are more historic monuments in the old part of Gorkha. Immediately above the bus stand is the fortified **Ratna Temple**, the former Gorkha residence of King Gyanendra, now unoccupied. If you follow the road uphill, you'll reach a small compound that contains a collection of pretty Hindu temples. The two-tiered temple is dedicated to **Vishnu**, the squat white temple with the Nandi statue is dedicated to **Mahadev** (Shiva) and the small white shikhara (temple tower) by the tank is sacred to **Ganesh**.

A little further along, the road opens onto a large square with a miniature pagoda temple dedicated to **Bhimsen**, the Newari god of commerce.

A monumental gateway leads off this square to the **Gorkha Museum** (admission foreigner/ SAARC Rs 50/20, camera fee Rs 200/100; ⏰ 10.30am-5pm, to 4pm winter), housed inside the Tallo Durbar, a Newari-style palace built in 1835. Exhibits are limited, but it's interesting to see the finely carved timbers up close. The camera fee, on the other hand, is daylight robbery.

Sleeping & Eating

The hotels in Gorkha are strung out along the road that runs up to the bus stand.

New Prince Guesthouse (☎ 420030; r with bathroom Rs 250-400, without bathroom Rs 100-200) You get what you pay for at the New Prince. The paint is peeling but it's handy for the bus stand and you can't fault the price.

Tower Hotel & Lodge (☎ 420335; r without bathroom Rs 150) On the other side of the bus stand, this small hotel is stacked on top of some shops. It's basic but clean and the shopkeeper-owners provide a warm welcome.

Hotel Gorkha Bisauni (☎ 420107; gh_bisauni@hot mail.com; r with bathroom from Rs 800, r without bathroom from Rs 300) Set in landscaped grounds about 200m downhill from Gurkha Inn, this agreeable midrange place attracts local pilgrimage tours and business travellers. Rooms have carpets, TV and private or shared bathrooms with hot showers, and the restaurant serves a little bit of everything.

our pick **Gurkha Inn** (☎ 420206; s/d US$20/35) We like the Gurkha Inn; this probably has something to do with the lovely stepped garden facing the valley, the cosy patio restaurant and the bright, airy rooms.

The best restaurants are at the Hotel Gorkha Bisauni and Gurkha Inn, but there are numerous cheap bhojanalayas (snack restaurants) near the bus stand.

Getting There & Away
The bus stand is right in the middle of town and there are ticket offices at either end of the stand.

There are three daily buses to Pokhara (Rs 140, five hours) and 10 daily buses to Kathmandu (Rs 150 to Rs 180, five hours), or you can ride a local bus to Abu Khaireni (Rs 50, 30 minutes) and change there. A single minibus leaves Gorkha at 7am for Bhairawa (Rs 300, six hours) or there are regular buses to Narayangarh (Rs 110, three hours) until midday.

DUMRE
About 17km west of Abu Khaireni, Dumre is yet another dusty junction town. Roads lead north from here to Besi Sahar (the starting point for the Annapurna Circuit Trek – p353) and south to the delightful village of Bandipur, but few people stop overnight.

If you do find yourself stuck here, **Hotel Mustang Lodge** (☎ 065-690786; r without bathroom Rs 150) is friendlier than most. The owners speak English and can point you in the right direction for the walk to Siddha Gufa, said to be the largest cave in Nepal (see p243 for information on this walk and others).

Any bus travelling between Kathmandu and Pokhara can drop you on the highway in Dumre.

From the main junction, local buses and minivans run regularly to Besi Sahar (Rs 80 by bus, Rs 100 by minivan, three hours), but watch out for fare hikes on this route. Jeeps

to Bandipur (Rs 20 per person, Rs 300 for the whole jeep, one hour) loiter around on the highway about 200m west of the Besi Sahar junction.

BANDIPUR
☎ 065
Draped like a scarf along a high ridge above Dumre, Bandipur is a living museum of Newari culture. Its winding lanes are lined with tall Newari houses and people here seem to live centuries before the rest of the country. It's hard to believe that somewhere so delightful has managed to escape the ravages of tourist development.

The Bandipur Social Development Committee has opened Bandipur up to tourism. With help from the owners of the adventure company Himalayan Encounters (see p102), derelict buildings have been reborn as cafes and lodges, and temples and civic buildings have been pulled back from the edge of ruin. Yet Bandipur remains very much a living community, full of farmers and traders going about their business.

Bandipur was originally part of the Magar kingdom of Tanahun, ruled from nearby Palpa (Tansen), but Newari traders flooded in after the conquest of the valley by Prithvi Narayan Shah.

The town became an important stop on the India–Tibet trade route until it was bypassed by the Prithvi Hwy in the 1960s. The village saw a few problems during the Maoist uprising, but things have been quiet as a millpond since the elections in 2008.

Information
For advice on things to see and do around Bandipur, visit the EU-funded **Bandipur Tourist Information Counter** (www.bandipurtourism.com; ☯ 7am-6pm) near the main square. Guides can be arranged for around Rs 400 for a half-day.

The Bandipur Café (see p244) offers internet access for Rs 100 per hour.

Sights
With its glorious 18th-century architecture and medieval ambience, all of Bandipur is a sight. You could spend days wandering around the town and making short hikes to villages, temples, viewpoints and mysterious caves. See the boxed text, p243 for details.

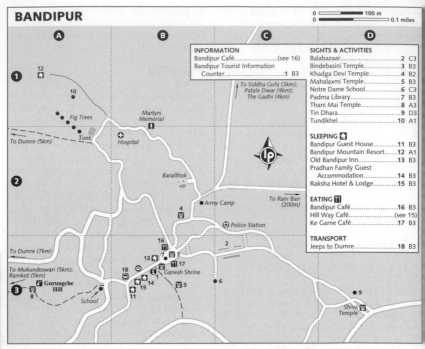

TUNDIKHEL

In centuries past, traders would gather on this flat-topped ridge to haggle for goods from India and Tibet before starting the long trek to Lhasa or the Indian plains. At dawn and sunset, the clouds peel back to reveal a stunning panorama of Himalayan peaks that include Dhaulagiri (8167m), Machhapuchhare (6997m), Langtang Lirung (7246m), Manaslu (8162m) and Ganesh Himal (7406m).

At the start of the Tundikhel are five enormous fig trees. In Nepali mythology, the different types of fig are symbols for different Hindu gods, and Vishnu, Brahma and Hanuman are all represented here.

TEMPLES

At the northeast end of the bazaar, which is the main shopping strip, the ornate, two-tiered **Bindebasini Temple** is dedicated to Durga. Its ancient walls are covered in carvings and an elderly priest opens the doors each evening. Facing the temple across the square is the **Padma library**, a striking 18th-century building with carved windows and beams. Nearby, a set of stone steps runs east to the small **Mahalaxmi Temple**, another centuries-old Newari-style temple.

Behind the Bindebasini Temple, a wide flight of stone steps leads up the hillside to the barn-like **Khadga Devi Temple**, which enshrines the sword of Mukunda Sen, the 16th-century king of Palpa (Tansen). Allegedly a gift from Shiva, the blade is revered as a symbol of shakti (consort or female energy) and once a year during Dasain it gets a taste of sacrificial blood.

OTHER SIGHTS

If you take the path leading east from the Bindebasini Temple, you'll pass the famous **Notre Dame School**, established by Catholic nuns from Japan in 1985. Just east of the school is **Balabazaar**, a striking arcade of old shop-houses formerly occupied by Newari cloth merchants. Turn right where the road forks and you'll reach the public washing area known as **Tin Dhara** (Three Spouts) where clean, cool spring water emerges from beneath the **Rani Ban** (Queen's Forest).

Sleeping

Bandipur Guest House (☎ 690634; r without bathroom Rs 250) Housed in a majestic, crumbling old shop-house at the start of the bazaar, the welcoming Bandipur Guest House offers simple wooden rooms with tiny balconies overlooking the Newari-style village. The attached restaurant serves some good meals (of the daal bhaat variety) and quite tasty ice cream as well.

ourpick **Old Bandipur Inn** (☎ 520110; r per person with meals US$20) Run by the highly professional team behind Himalayan Encounters (see p102 for more information), this beautifully restored mansion offers atmospheric rooms full of Buddhist and Newari art, set around a terracotta terrace facing the mountains. Many guests visit as part of rafting and trekking tours and rates include meals and guides for local walks.

Bandipur Mountain Resort (☎ 520125, in Kathmandu 01-4220162; www.islandjungleresort.com/bandipur; s/d with meals US$30/40; 💵) A calm midrange resort that benefits from a lovely setting, surrounded by swishing pines at the west end of Tundikhel. Rooms are a little dated but they're not bad for the price. Advance reservations are essential.

Simple rooms for around Rs 250 are also available along the bazaar at **Raksha Hotel & Lodge** (☎ 620161) and **Pradhan Family Guest Accommodation** (☎ 520106).

Eating

As well as the lodges, there are several restaurants along the main square that are open 7am to 9pm.

Ke Garne Café (snacks from Rs 50) The name of this cosy cafe means 'what to do?' so here are some suggestions for you: sip tea, munch

---

WALKS AROUND BANDIPUR

It's easy to pass several peaceful days exploring the hills around Bandipur. There are gobsmacking Himalayan views and the countryside is a gorgeous patchwork of terraced rice and mustard fields and small orchards. Most guest houses can arrange walking guides for around Rs 400.

One of the easiest walks is the 30-minute ascent to the **Thani Mai temple**, just west of the village at the top of Gurungche Hill. The trail starts near the school at the southwest end of the bazaar. The views are stunning and local children may make flying gestures as you pass (paragliders have launched from here in the past).

With more time on your hands, you can walk down to the famous **Siddha Gufa**, said to be the largest cave in Nepal. This cathedral-like chasm is full of twisted stalactites and stalagmites and hundreds of bats chirp and whistle overhead. Local youths are on hand to act as guides for Rs 200 (bring a torch).

The 1½-hour trek to Siddha Gufa starts near the abandoned army camp at the north end of the village. Follow the dirt path running north over the edge of the ridge, then turn right at the obvious junction. The track drops to a star-shaped stupa and then dives down through the forest to the cave. From here, you can continue downhill to Bimalnagar on the Prithvi Hwy (2km from Dumre) in around 20 minutes.

A two-hour walk east from Siddha Gufa is **Patale Dwar** (literally 'Gateway to the Underworld'), another cavern full of eye-catching geological formations. The chamber floods in the monsoon and the cave is only safe to visit in winter – ask the guides at Siddha Gufa for directions.

An hour's walk southeast of Bandipur (via a path running north from Bandipur, then southeast along a ridge) is the hilltop viewpoint known as the **Gadhi**, topped by the ruins of an ancient kot (fort). The view is sublime; from here you can trace the path of the Marsyangdi River north between the Annapurna and Manaslu massifs and most of the way to Manang.

Another interesting walk is the two-hour trek to **Mukundeswari** (1830m); there is a Magar shrine atop the distinctive twin-peaked hill northwest of Bandipur. Locals believe that this was the forest retreat of Mukunda Sen and the hilltop is adorned with an armoury of tridents, knives and swords left by devotees. On the same trip, you can drop into the Magar village of **Ramkot** with its striking round houses.

on Nepali snacks or play giant chess on the cafe's terrace.

Bandipur Café (meals from Rs 60; 🖳) A typical local restaurant on the square, serving a decent selection of Indian, Nepali and continental standards. You can check email for Rs 100 per hour.

Hill Way Café (meals from Rs 60) Every evening, Hill Way Café attracts couples keen to sit at the cloth-covered tables set out on the village square.

Getting There & Away

The road to Bandipur branches off the Prithvi Hwy about 2km west of Dumre; jeeps hang around by the junction charging Rs 20 per person or Rs 300 for the whole jeep.

You can also walk up from Dumre – pick up the trail on the highway about 500m west of the last house in Dumre and climb steeply to the southwest end of the Tundikhel. Allow three hours on the way up or 1½ hours on the way down.

EXPERIENCE NEPAL

Cresting the heights of the Himalaya, Nepal looms large in travellers' imaginations. And why not? Its well-developed tourist infrastructure and range of attractions mean that travellers can scramble up mountains, wander through rhododendron forests, seek spiritual solitude or get lost in vibrant festivals. Nepal offers a travel experience that can be challenging, calming, or strenuous, depending on your whim. But whatever you choose to do, Nepal is never anything less than invigorating.

Rocky Mountain Highs

Nepal may be home to mighty Everest, but you don't need the lungs of a Sherpa to tackle a trek in the Nepal Himalaya. With a range of trails at every conceivable degree of difficulty and distance, there is an opportunity for just about everyone to lace up their boots and experience the country as the Nepalis do: on foot.

① Everest Base Camp Trek
Appropriately enough, the trek (p340) to the base camp on the highest mountain on earth is a challenging trail taking you from the lowlands into the mighty Himalaya.

② Short Treks from Pokhara
Trekking needn't be a major undertaking. From Pokhara there are short treks (p275) to Ghachok, Chisopani and other spots.

③ Teahouse Trekking
Whether you are huddled by a cosy lodge stove or soaking up the afternoon sun on a spectacular terrace, it's the warm hospitable environment of Nepal's lodges that sets apart trekking in Nepal.

④ Annapurna Sanctuary Trek
A relatively short trek (p358) that packs a powerful punch as it takes in a breathtaking mountain amphitheatre of peaks and glaciers.

⑤ Helambu Trek
Easily accessible from Kathmandu, and taking no more than eight days, the Helambu trek (p351) offers a great introduction to trekking in Nepal and is a good winter choice.

⑥ Annapurna Circuit
The spellbinding valleys around Manang and Jomsom create a breathtaking backdrop on this ever-changing trek (p352) – one of the world's classic walks.

Wet & Wild

There's more to do in Nepal's rugged mountainscapes and wide open spaces than just trekking. Hardcore adrenaline junkies, or anyone seeking adventure, can throw themselves into those fantastic plunging valleys, endless vistas and racing rivers, and the forests of the Terai offer a chance to spot a tiger or a one-horned rhinoceros.

❶ Rafting & Kayaking

There's a lot of water working its way down from Nepal's peaks, enough to keep keen rafters and kayakers occupied – and breathless with white-water exertion (p100).

❷ Chitwan National Park

The vast expanse of Chitwan is home to Nepal's signature species – rhinos, tigers, sloth bears and elephants – and is just the place to do an elephant-top safari (p287).

❸ Bungee Jumping

There's nothing quite like gritting your teeth and throwing yourself headlong into a Himalayan gorge, but bungee aficionados will find one of Asia's deepest drops; see p87.

❹ Canyoning

The ultimate in water sports, canyoning (p88) among mighty boulders, waterfalls and natural water slides will set your pulse racing.

❺ Paragliding

Paragliding (p88) offers you an opportunity to soar silently like the majestic griffon over the valleys around Pokhara.

❻ Mountain Biking

A mountain bike is a terrific way of getting off the beaten track and reaching remote and untouched corners of the country under your own steam; see p91.

Temples

If the high altitude and gentle rhythms of the trek don't bring on a contemplative mood, then the spiritual life of Nepal surely will. Nepal boasts centuries of Buddhist and Hindu history, and a plethora of temples, stupas and religious traditions to match.

1 Lumbini

The birthplace of the Buddha, Lumbini (p296) is a pilgrimage site like no other, a place where the faithful come in respectful silence.

2 Kathmandu's Durbar Square

Wander Kathmandu's labyrinthine old town, then take a perch on one of the tiered temples of Durbar Sq (p119) to watch traditional city life pass beneath you.

3 Bodhnath Stupa

Join the throng of pilgrims as they chant, pray and circle mighty Bodhnath stupa (p174), one of the world's largest stupas and the religious centre for Nepal's exiled Tibetan community.

4 Butter Lamps

Light a butter lamp and enjoy a moment's contemplation among the other devotees and pilgrims.

5 Bhaktapur

The cobblestone streets of Bhaktapur (p194) link a string of temples, courtyards and monumental squares; the side streets are peppered with shrines, wells and water tanks.

6 Patan

In Patan's Durbar Sq (p181), you can indulge your fascination for temple architecture, then wander aimlessly through backstreets to discover more than 600 stupas and 185 bahals (courtyards).

7 Swayambhunath

Take in the views of Kathmandu from the hilltop setting of Swayambhunath (p163), the 'Monkey Temple'.

Festivals

Nothing better reveals the cultural richness of Nepal than its festivals. Masked dances, chariot races and tugs of war attract large crowds and enthusiastic participants. Visiting a festival, you will see the Nepalis at their colourful, energetic best.

❶ Losar

Triggered by the new moon in February, Losar (p23) marks the Tibetan New Year and involves 15 days of celebrations for Tibetan communities across the Himalaya.

❷ Bisket Jatra

The Nepalis celebrate their New Year with the festival of Bisket Jatra (p23), which features huge crowds dragging tottering chariots through the winding backstreets of the Kathmandu Valley.

❸ Holi

Known as the Festival of Colour, Holi (p23) must be the most riotous celebration on the Nepali calendar.

❹ Dasain

Celebrating the victory of the goddess Durga over the forces of evil, Dasain (p25) is the most important festival across Nepal.

Pokhara

If the Himalaya are the rooftop to the world, then Pokhara has prime position on its front porch, from where it rocks away contentedly beneath the serene guard of the Annapurna mountain range. Like a chilled-out version of Thamel, Pokhara prefers to kick back in the fresh mountain air than choke on traffic fumes. Though there's more to it than a laid-back charm. It's also the gateway to the world-famous Annapurna trek. Throw in a booming adventure-sports scene, and you can see how Pokhara puts in a strong claim to the title of Nepal's premier tourist town.

In reality there are two Pokharas. First there is Lakeside, settled along the calm waters of stunning Phewa Tal. Unashamedly touristy, Lakeside has provided a sanctuary for many a weary traveller. Whether you've just returned from a three-week trek or endured a bus trip from hell, Lakeside has you in mind. It's the perfect place to recharge the batteries, with juicy steaks, lively bars and internet cafes. Secondly, there's Old Pokhara, where you'll find how life was before the hippy trail stumbled upon its pristine surrounds. With pockets of charming Newari architecture and a bustling Nepali vitality, too few tourists make the trek out here.

When you're done lazing by the lake, find the time to actually get out there with a leisurely row on its sparkling waters. Or if you feel you're becoming too relaxed, get the heart pumping with the undisputed best views in town via a tandem paraglide flight. White-water rafting, microlight flights, or roaring through the countryside on a classic Enfield motorbike – there's plenty here to keep you busy.

HIGHLIGHTS

- Witness nature's ethereal lightshow as the sun rises over the Annapurna range from **Sarangkot** (p272) turning its peaks from pink to gold
- Row out to the middle of peaceful **Phewa Tal** (p257) to experience an unbelievable calm
- Literally soar like a bird of prey, as you follow your aviator guides into the thermals while **parahawking** (p261)
- Escape the tourist trap of Lakeside to see what's going on in the real Nepal at **Old Pokhara** (p257)
- Celebrate your trekking triumph with a huge steak and a cold beer at one of Lakeside's multicultural **restaurants** (p267)
- Be mesmerised by the sounds of chanting Tibetan monks in the atmospheric **Jangchub Choeling Gompa** (p259)

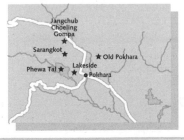

| ■ TELEPHONE CODE: 061 | ■ POPULATION: 200,000 | ■ ELEVATION: 884M |

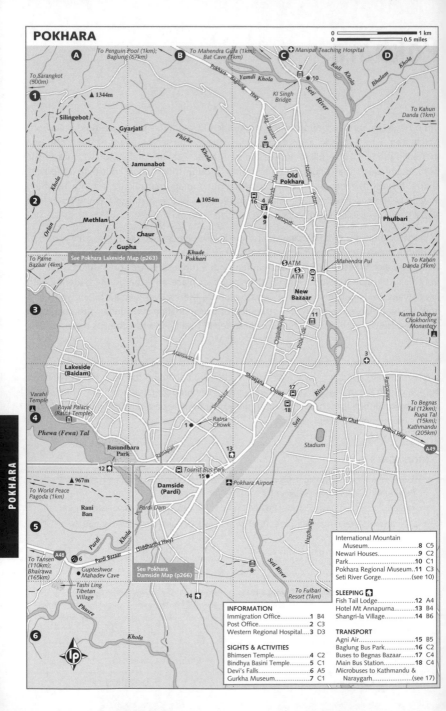

POKHARA

INFORMATION
Immigration Office..............1 B4
Post Office.........................2 C3
Western Regional Hospital....3 D3

SIGHTS & ACTIVITIES
Bhimsen Temple.................4 C2
Bindhya Basini Temple.........5 C1
Devi's Falls........................6 A5
Gurkha Museum..................7 C1
International Mountain
  Museum..........................8 C5
Newari Houses...................9 C2
Park................................10 C1
Pokhara Regional Museum..11 C3
Seti River Gorge................(see 10)

SLEEPING
Fish Tail Lodge..................12 A4
Hotel Mt Annapurna..........13 B4
Shangri-la Village..............14 B6

TRANSPORT
Agni Air...........................15 B5
Baglung Bus Park..............16 C2
Buses to Begnas Bazaar.....17 C4
Main Bus Station...............18 C4
Microbuses to Kathmandu &
  Narayagarh...................(see 17)

HISTORY

Before the construction of the Prithvi Hwy, getting to Pokhara involved a 10-day pony trek, with numerous deadly river crossings along the way. When Swiss explorer Toni Hagen visited in 1952, he found ambling buffalo carts and streets lined with brick Newari houses. Hints of this time can still be seen in Old Pokhara, just north of the Mahendra Pul bazaar.

Aside from the odd explorer, the first Westerners to reach Pokhara were hippies in the 1970s. With its lakeshore setting, laid-back pace and plentiful supply of marijuana, Pokhara made a perfect endpoint for the south Asian overland trail. From these barefoot beginnings it developed rapidly. By the 1980s Pokhara had transformed into a modern mountain resort, with hundreds of hotels, shops, bars and restaurants.

In the late 1990s busloads of tourists arrived in Pokhara until the Maoist conflict deterred many from visiting – resulting in a decade-long tourist slump. However, the good news is that things are back to normal and Pokhara's officially reopened for business.

CLIMATE

Pokhara sits about 400m lower than Kathmandu so the autumn and winter temperatures are generally much more comfortable. Even in the height of winter you can get away with a T-shirt during the daytime and you'll only need a sweater or jacket for evenings and early morning starts. From June to September the skies open and the mountain views vanish behind blankets of grey cloud; bring a brolly and be prepared to wade when the streets are flooded.

ORIENTATION

Famed as the city by the lake, Pokhara sprawls along the eastern shore of gorgeous Phewa Tal (Fewa Tal). Most travellers stay on the lakeshore in Lakeside, a seemingly endless string of budget hotels, restaurants, bars, internet cafes and souvenir shops, extending right around the lake from Basundhara Park to the northern shore.

More budget accommodation is available near the Phewa dam in Damside, which also has the tourist office and the Annapurna Conservation Area Project (ACAP) office.

Inland from Lakeside, you'll find the airport and the bus stand for tourist buses to Kathmandu (also known as the Mustang bus stand). The main public bus stand is at the north end of the Pokhara airstrip, while local buses to Baglung (for treks to the Annapurna Range) leave from the highway north of town.

The main shopping area for locals is Mahendra Pul, running north from the public bus stand. Just north of here is Pokhara's old town, bound by the Baglung Hwy and the Seti River gorge.

For convenience, we've divided the lakeshore into several sections. Starting from the Seti River dam, you'll pass through Damside, then Lakeside East (from Basundhara Park

---

POKHARA IN...

Two Days

Start your day browsing through the souvenir shops of **Lakeside** (p270) then rent a boat for a leisurely row on **Phewa Tal** (p257). Lunch on the strip then head inland for a wander round **Old Pokhara** (p257). On day two get up early to watch the sunrise over the Himalaya at **Sarangkot** (p272). Have breakfast on the **lake** (p267) before a visit to the **Gurkha Museum** (p258). In the afternoon, climb up to the sublime **World Peace Pagoda** (p258) for more incredible views.

Four Days

Take a walk north around the lake, before visiting one of the **Tibetan settlements** (p259) around Pokhara. Muster the courage to try **paragliding** (p261) with a Himalayan backdrop. Vary it up by wriggling through the **Bat Cave** (p273) and getting a taste for your trek at the **International Mountain Museum** (p258).

One Week

Consider the walk to **Poon Hill** (p276) or the four-day **Annapurna Skyline Trek** (p276). Hire a bike or motorcycle to explore **Begnas Tal** (p274) and the villages on the northern lakeshore.

to the Royal Palace), then Central Lakeside (from the palace to the junction known as Camping Chowk), then Lakeside North (from Camping Chowk to the northern shore). All these places have Nepali names, but most people use 'Lakeside' for the whole strip.

INFORMATION
Bookshops
There are dozens of bookshops along the strip at Lakeside. All sell secondhand novels, maps and postcards.

Emergency
The direct phone number for the police is ☎ 100. For medical emergencies, see Medical Services, right. The **tourist police** (Map p266; ☎ 462761) are located in Damside at the same site as the tourist office.

Immigration Office
The **immigration office** (Map p254; ☎ 465167; ⊗ visa extensions 10.30am-1pm Sun-Thu, 10am-noon Fri, office hours 10am-5pm Sun-Thu, to 3pm Fri) has a new location at Ratna Chowk, 1km east of Damside. Visa extensions cost US$30 for 15 days, and US$2 per extra day (up to 15 extra days), while a 60-day extension is US$120 – bring your passport and two photos, plus the visa fee in Nepali rupees. For more on visa extensions see p377.

Internet Access
Due to the high cost of rent, the price of internet access in Lakeside is the most expensive in all Nepal. All cafes charge the same rate – Rs 80 per hour, minimum Rs 15 charge. Once outside Lakeside you'll find the prices plummet to around Rs 25 per hour.

Internet Resources
For online information on Pokhara, visit www.pokharacity.com.

Laundry
Hotels can arrange same-day laundry services if you drop your clothes off first thing in the morning, or there are plenty of small laundry shops along the strip in Lakeside. Most charge Rs 80 per kilogram, with washing machines the preferred option to save your clothes being thrashed against rocks.

Medical Services
There are several pharmacies in Lakeside selling everyday medicines.

For anything serious, head to **Western Regional Hospital** (Map p254; ☎ 520066) on the east bank of the Seti River.

Money
There are plenty of foreign-exchange offices in Lakeside that change cash and travellers cheques in major currencies. All are open daily but rates are better at the **Standard Chartered Bank** (Map p263; ☎ 462102; ⊗ 9.45am-4.15pm Sun-Thu, to 1.15pm Fri), near Camping Chowk. There are several ATMs along the main strip in Lakeside that all accept foreign cards.

Post
The main **post office** (Map p254; ⊗ 10am-5pm Sun-Thu, to 3pm Fri) is a hike from Lakeside at Mahendra Pul. There's a much smaller branch in east Lakeside (Map p263), though alternatively most bookstores in Lakeside sell stamps and have a post box for letters and postcards.

CLOSE SHAVE AT A NEPALI BARBER

One of the delights of a trip to the subcontinent is a visit to the barber. If you've been out trekking for a few weeks, there's a good chance you'll return to Pokhara resembling a yeti, making it the perfect place to part with your trekking beard. All over Lakeside you'll see barbers set up in small shops, announcing themselves as you walk by with calls of 'Hello sir, you want shave?' For just over US$1 you'll get pampered with a precision shave and head massage. New blades are always used, though it's good to ensure this is the case by watching them take it out of the packet. Once your face has been thoroughly lathered up the barber will set about expertly shaving your whiskers using a straight razor, collecting the wads of shaving cream in the base of his palm. After two shaves your face is then rubbed with a rock of cooling alum balm, before the barber finishes up by cracking his knuckles over your head and performing a vigorous head and face massage – eyeballs included. The inevitable offer for a neck and shoulder massage will cost an additional few hundred rupees. For the ladies, there are plenty of Nepali beauty salons in Pokhara in which to indulge.

If you want to send anything valuable, **UPS** (Map p263; ☎ 462585) in Lakeside is costly but reliable.

Telephone

Internet cafes in Lakeside offer phone calls to Europe and most other places for around Rs 40 per minute.

Tourist Information

Nepal Tourism runs a helpful **tourist office** (Map p266; ☎ 465292; ☺ 10am-1pm & 2-5pm Sun-Fri) in Damside, sharing a building with the Annapurna Conservation Area Project.

Travel Agencies

Most of the travel agents in Lakeside can book tours, flights and bus tickets. The following travel agents are reputable.

Adam Tours & Travels (Map p263; ☎ 461806; www .adamnepal.com) IATA accredited agency for international flights.

Blue Sky Travel (Map p263; www.blue-sky-tours.com)

Wayfarers (Map p263; ☎ 463774; www.wayfarers.com .np) See p118 for details.

DANGERS & ANNOYANCES

Being a tourist town there's always going to be a degree of hassle from prospecting taxi drivers or barbers spotting your three-day growth, though most notorious are the bus-park hotel touts and Tibetan women hawking jewellery. But these annoyances should not affect your stay in Pokhara.

There's been the occasional mugging on treks up to the World Peace Pagoda and around Sarangkot, and hence it is recommended to do these walks in the safety of numbers.

SIGHTS
Phewa Tal

Nowhere better exemplifies Pokhara's amazing beauty and nature than the majestic Phewa Tal (Map p263) – Nepal's second largest lake. On calm days, the mountains of the Annapurna Range are perfectly reflected in the mirrored surface of the tal, which makes it the perfect spot to paddle its tranquil waters in a rowboat or kayak (see p260).

Many people walk or cycle around the lakeshore – the trek up to the World Peace Pagoda (see the boxed text, p258, for details) affords breathtaking views over the tal and the mountains beyond.

Mountains

Forming a spectacular backdrop to Pokhara is the dramatic Annapurna Massif, a chain of 2133m snowcapped mountains of the Himalaya range. Most prominent is the emblematic Mt Machhapuchhare ('Fish Tail' in Nepali), whose ghost-white triangular peak looms over the town, and remains the only virgin mountain in Nepal set aside as forbidden to be climbed.

From west to east, the peaks are Hiunchuli (6441m), Annapurna I (8091m), Machhapuchhare (6997m), Annapurna III (7555m), Annapurna IV (7525m) and Annapurna II (7937m).

A word of warning: the mountains can occasionally completely disappear behind cloud, particularly during the monsoon.

Old Pokhara

For a taste of what Pokhara was like before the trekking agencies and tourist restaurants set up shop, head out to the old town (Map p254), north of the bustling Mahendra Pul. The best way to explore is on foot or by bike.

From the Nepal Telecoms building at Mahendra Pul, head north along Tersapati, passing a number of small **religious shops** selling Hindu and Buddhist paraphernalia. At the intersection with Nala Mukh, check out the **Newari houses** with decorative brickwork and ornately carved wooden windows.

TREKKING PERMITS

If you plan to trek anywhere inside the Annapurna Conservation Area, you'll need a permit from the **Annapurna Conservation Area Project** (ACAP; Map p266; ☎ 061-463376; ☺ 10am-5pm Sun-Fri, to 3.30pm Sat) in Damside. It closes at 4pm in winter. The admission fee to the conservation area is Rs 2000/200 (foreigner/SAARC) and permits are issued on the spot (bring two passport-sized photos). There are ACAP checkpoints throughout the reserve and if you get caught without a permit, the fee rises to Rs 4000/400 (foreigner/SAARC). Independent trekkers without a guide will need to register with TIMS (Trekkers Information Management System; www.timsnepal.com), located in the same office.

WALKING TO THE WORLD PEACE PAGODA

Balanced on a narrow ridge high above Phewa Tal, the brilliant-white World Peace Pagoda (Map p273) was constructed by Buddhist monks from the Japanese Nipponzan Myohoji organisation to promote world peace. There are three paths up to the pagoda and several small cafes for snacks and drinks once you arrive.

The Direct Route (One Hour)

The most obvious route up to the pagoda begins on the south bank of Phewa Tal, behind the Fewa Resort. Boatmen charge around Rs 250 to the trailhead from Lakeside and the path leads straight up the hillside on cut stone steps. Ignore the right-hand fork by the small temple and continue uphill through woodland to reach the ridge just west of the pagoda. You can either continue on to Pokhara via the scenic route (described below) or go back the way you came.

The Scenic Route (Two Hours)

A more interesting route to the pagoda begins near the footbridge over the Pardi Khola, just south of the Phewa dam. After crossing the bridge, the trail skirts the edge of paddy fields before turning uphill into the forest near a small brick temple. From here the trail climbs for about 2km through gorgeous open sal forest and follows the ridge west. When you reach a clearing with several ruined stone houses, turn left and climb straight uphill to reach the flat, open area in front of the pagoda. An alternative starting point for this route is Devi's Falls – a small but obvious trail crosses the paddy fields behind the falls and runs up to meet the main path at the bottom of the forest.

The Easy Route (20 Minutes)

For views without the fuss, take a local bus from the public bus stand to Kalimati on the road to Butwal for Rs 5. Several small trails lead up from the road to the school in Kalimati village and on to the entrance to the pagoda.

Continue north on Bhairab Tole to reach the small two-tiered **Bhimsen Temple**, a 200-year-old shrine to the Newari god of trade and commerce, decorated with erotic carvings. The surrounding square is full of shops selling baskets and ceramics.

About 200m further north is a small hill, topped by the ancient **Bindhya Basini Temple**. Founded in the 17th century, the temple is sacred to Durga, the warlike incarnation of Parvati, worshipped here in the form of a saligram.

Varahi Mandir

Pokhara's most famous Hindu temple, the two-tiered pagoda-style **Varahi Mandir** (Map p263), stands on a small island near the Ratna Mandir (Royal Palace). Founded in the 18th century, the temple is dedicated to Vishnu in his boar incarnation, but it's been extensively renovated over the years and is inhabited by a loft of cooing pigeons. Rowboats to the temple (Rs 25 return) leave from near the city bus stand in Lakeside.

Museums

GURKHA MUSEUM

Situated just north of Mahendra Pul, near the KI Singh Bridge, this well-curated **museum** (Map p254; ☎ 541966; admission foreigner/SAARC Rs 150/80, camera Rs 20; ⏰ 8am-4.30pm) displays the achievements of the famous Gurkha regiment. Accompanied by sound effects of machine-gun fire, it covers Gurkha history from the 19th-century Indian Mutiny, through two World Wars to current-day Afghanistan. There is a fascinating display outlining the stories of the 13 Gurkhas who've been awarded the Victoria Cross medal. See the boxed text, opposite, for more information on the Gurkhas.

INTERNATIONAL MOUNTAIN MUSEUM

This **museum** (Map p254; ☎ 460742; www.mountainmuseum.org; foreigner/SAARC Rs 300/100; ⏰ 9am-5pm) is devoted to the mountains of Nepal and the mountaineers who climbed them. Inside you can see original gear from many of the first Himalayan ascents, as well as displays on the history, culture, geology, and flora and fauna of the Himalaya.

Now you've been inspired, outside there's a 21m climbing wall and a 9.5m-high climbable model of Mt Manaslu. A taxi here from Lakeside will cost you around Rs 400 return.

POKHARA REGIONAL MUSEUM

North of the bus station on the road to Mahendra Pul, this interesting little **museum** (Map p254; ☎ 520413; foreigner/SAARC Rs 10/5; ☯ 10am-5pm, to 3pm Mon, to 4pm in winter, closed Tue) is devoted to the history and culture of the Pokhara Valley, including the mystical shamanic beliefs followed by the original inhabitants of the valley.

Seti River Gorge

The roaring Seti River passes right through Pokhara, but you won't see it unless you go looking.

The river has carved a deep, narrow gorge through the middle of town, turning the water milky white in the process. The best place to catch a glimpse of the Seti River is the **park** (Map p254; adult Rs 10; ☯ 7am-6pm) just north of Old Pokhara near the Gurkha Museum.

Devi's Falls

Also known as Patale Chhango, this **waterfall** (Map p254; adult Rs 20; ☯ 6am-6pm) marks the point where the Pardi Khola stream vanishes underground. When the stream is at full bore, the sound of the water plunging over the falls is deafening, but the concrete walkways don't add much to the atmosphere.

According to locals, the name is a corruption of David's Falls, a reference to a Swiss visitor who tumbled into the sinkhole and drowned, taking his girlfriend with him! The falls are about 2km southwest of the airport on the road to Butwal, just before the Tashi Ling Tibetan Village.

Tibetan Settlements

Most of the Tibetan refugees who hawk souvenirs in Lakeside live in the Tibetan refugee settlements north and south of Pokhara.

The largest settlement is **Tashi Palkhel** (Map p273), a few kilometres north of Pokhara on the road to Baglung. With prayer flags flapping in the breeze in the rocky valley, it genuinely feels like you're in Tibet. The colourful **Jangchub Choeling Gompa** in the middle of the village is home to around 100 monks. Try to time your visit in the afternoon to

---

SIMPLY THE BEST

It might seem like an odd leftover from the days of empire, but the British army maintains a recruiting centre on the outskirts of Pokhara. Every year hundreds of young men from across Nepal come to Pokhara to put themselves through the rigorous selection process to become a Gurkha soldier.

Prospective recruits must perform a series of backbreaking physical tasks, including a 5km uphill run carrying 25kg of rocks in a traditional doko basket. Only the most physically fit and mentally dedicated individuals make it through – it is not unheard of for recruits to keep on running with broken bones in their determination to get selected.

Identified by their curved khukuri knives, Gurkhas are still considered one of the toughest fighting forces in the world. British Gurkhas have carried out peacekeeping missions in Afghanistan, Bosnia and Sierra Leone and Gurkha soldiers also form elite units of the Indian Army, the Singapore Police Force and the personal bodyguard of the sultan of Brunei.

The primary motivation for most recruits is money. The average daily wage in Nepal is less than one British pound (Rs 120), but Gurkha soldiers earn upwards of UK£1000 per month, with a commission lasting up to 16 years and a British Army pension for life, plus the option of becoming a British citizen on retirement. At the time of research the Maoist government had held talks on ending this alliance that enables Britain to recruit Nepal's crack soldiers.

Thakur Bahadur Rana, former Gurkha of 20 years and now a staff member at the museum, believes the Gurkhas' success is put down to 'we simply do the job we're given. But we train hard, and coming from Nepal gives us an advantage of being able to adapt to any terrain, any climate – mountainous, flat, hot or cold'.

POKHARA

experience the rumbling of monks chanting and horns blowing during the prayer session (held 3.30pm to 5pm).

Masked dances are held here in January/ February as part of the annual Losar (Tibetan New Year) celebrations.

To reach the gompa you have to run the gauntlet past an arcade of persistent handicraft vendors. Nearby is a chörten piled with carved mani stones bearing Buddhist mantras and a carpet-weaving centre, where you can see all stages of the process and buy the finished article. If you'd like to spend the night, **Friend's Garden** (r without bathroom Rs 250) has spartan rooms and a restaurant serving Tibetan food. You can reach here by bike, bus, taxi or foot.

Heading southwest from Pokhara on the road to Butwal, you'll come to the smaller **Tashi Ling Tibetan Village** (Map p254).

ACTIVITIES

See p363 for information on courses and p71 for volunteering opportunities in Pokhara. For trekking around Pokhara, see p272 and the Trekking chapter, p328.

Boating

Heading out onto the calm waters of Phewa Tal is the perfect tonic for when Lakeside's commercial set-up begins to get on your nerves. Colourful wooden *doongas* (rowboats) are available for rent at several boat stations, including near the city bus stand and next to the Fewa Hotel. Rates start at Rs 250 per hour with a boatman, or Rs 200/500 per hour/day if you row yourself. You can also rent plastic pedalos (Rs 300 per hour) and sailboats (Rs 300 per hour, or Rs 350 per hour for lessons).

Cycling & Mountain Biking

Pokhara is fairly flat and the traffic is quite light once you get away from the main highway – perfect for cycling. Indian mountain bikes are available from dozens of places on the strip in Lakeside for Rs 20/150 per hour/day. For better-quality mountain bikes try **Himalayan Frontiers** (Map p263; ☎ 461706; www .himalayanfrontiers.co.uk), which rents out bikes for Rs 1000 per day.

For a description of the bike trip out to Sarangkot and Naudanda see p99. Contact any of the Lakeside travel agents for details of mountain-biking trips in the hills around Pokhara.

Golf

Golfers can have a hit at **Himalayan Golf** (Map p273; ☎ 432314; green fees 9/18 holes US$35/45), about 7km east of Pokhara, or at the nine-hole golf course at the luxurious Fulbari Resort – see p267.

Gyms

Fitness freaks wanting more exercise than walking up and down mountains can head to **Lake Breeze Gym** (Map p263; ☎ 9804133573; Rs 50; ☺ 6-9am & 3-6pm) near the lake.

Horse Riding

Travel agents in Pokhara offer pony treks to various viewpoints around town, including Sarangkot, Kahun Danda and the World Peace Pagoda. Half-day trips (US$13) stick to the lakeshore; you'll need a full day (US$20) to reach the viewpoints.

Kayaking & Rafting

Another popular way to explore Phewa Tal is by kayak. **Ganesh Kayak Shop** (Map p263; ☎ 462657; www.ganeshkayak.com; ☺ 8am-9pm) rents out decent plastic kayaks for Rs 200/500/650 per hour/half-day/day and arranges fourday kayaking camping safaris (US$220) around Nepal.

Pokhara is a good place to organise rafting trips, particularly trips down the Kali Gandaki and Seti Rivers, and also kayak clinics on the Seti River and the scenic drift down the Narayani River to Chitwan National Park. See p100 for more information. Reliable rafting operators include the following:

Paddle Nepal (Map p263; ☎ 207077; www.paddle nepal.com; half-day US$45-50, 1 day US$45-60, 3 days from US$115)

Ultimate Descents/Adventure Centre Asia (Map p263; ☎ 463240; www.udnepal.com/index.html)

Massage

Trekkers with aching muscles can get traditional Ayurvedic massage at several places in Lakeside.

Seeing Hands Nepal (Map p263; ☎ 464478; www .seeinghandsnepal.org; 45min/1hr massage Rs 650/1000) has professionally trained blind Nepali therapists, who with a heightened sense of perception and touch provide excellent Swedish-style massages. Run by volunteers, Seeing Hands does excellent work in supporting Nepali blind people in a society where they're often marginalised.

PARAHAWKING

Invented by British falconer Scott Mason, **parahawking** (www.parahawking.com; tandem flights €100) is 100% unique to Pokhara and a must for thrill seekers and bird-lovers. Parahawking involves a combination of falconry and paragliding where birds of prey are trained to lead gliders to the best thermal currents (see p88 for more details). As a reward for their guidance, a whistle is blown to call in the bird to land on your outstretched gloved arm for you to feed it 2000ft in the air! All the parahawking birds (Egyptian vultures, kites and eagles) are taken in as injured or orphaned birds unable to survive in the wild, and you can see them at their roost at the Himalayan Raptor Centre at Maya Devi Village (see p270). Tandem parahawking trips are organised through Frontiers Paragliding (see p88).

Meditation & Yoga

Pokhara is the perfect spot to contemplate the nature of the universe and several centres around the lake offer meditation and yoga training.

Ganden Yiga Chopen Meditation Centre (Pokhara Buddhist Meditation Centre; Map p263; www.pokhara buddhistcentre.com) This calm place holds three-day meditation and yoga courses (Rs 3300 including lodging and meals) as well as daily sessions at 10am (Rs 200) and 5pm (Rs 150). The meditation and yoga room with a Tibetan altar and thangkas looks out to the lake.

Sadhana Yoga (Map p273; ☎ 464601, 9846078117; www.sadhana-asanga-yoga.com) This friendly and secluded retreat is hidden away in the village of Sedi Bagar, overlooking Phewa Tal, 2.5km northwest of Lakeside. One- to 21-day courses in Hatha yoga for Rs 1800 per day, including tuition, steam and mud baths, accommodation and meals. Enquire about yoga treks.

Microlight Flights

Avia Club Nepal (Map p263; ☎ 465944, www.aviaclub nepal.com) offers exhilarating microlight flights around the Pokhara Valley. In 15 minutes (€57) you can buzz around the World Peace Pagoda and lakeshore, but you'll need 30 minutes (€90) or one hour (€167) to get up above Sarangkot for the full Himalayan panorama. If you bring your own equipment, it can also arrange sky dives and base jumps.

Motorcycling

Ever felt envious at the sight of some dude zipping along winding roads on the back of a motorbike, but always lacked the nerve to give it a go yourself? Then **Hearts and Tears** (Map p263; ☎ 9846020293; www.heartsandtears.com) is the place to overcome your inhibitions. Tucked away in the entrance to Busy Bee (you can't miss the cool retro bikes), you can choose from customised Royal Enfields in a range of classic designs, and with an emphasis on safety, it's a great place to learn to ride (lessons from Rs 3500). It also offers motorcycle tours around Nepal, and rents bikes from Rs 600 per day.

Paragliding

Soaring through the air at 2500ft among gliding Himalayan raptors against a backdrop of the snowcapped Annapurna is a bona fide once-in-a-lifetime experience.

Frontiers Paragliding (Map p263; ☎ 461706, 9804125096; www.himalayan-paragliding.com; ⏱ 7.30am-10pm) is a British company offering three tandem flights: the Cloud Buster explores the thermals above Sarangkot (€70); one-hour cross country jumps across the valley north towards Annapurna (€100); and 20-minute acrobatic flights (€70) for thrill seekers.

See the boxed text, above, for info on parahawking, which is arranged through Frontiers Paragliding.

Other operators include the paragliding pioneers **Sunrise Paragliding** (Map p263; ☎ 463174; www.sunrise-paragliding.com; ⏱ 8am-9pm), offering identical flights and prices to Frontiers. The Swiss-Nepali owned **Blue Sky Paragliding** (☎ 463747; www.paragliding-nepal.com) is the other big operator. See p88 for more details. Paragliding only operates during fine weather, and the season closes during monsoon.

Swimming

The cool waters of Phewa Tal may seem perfect for a dip but there's a fair bit of pollution, so if you do swim it's advisable to hire a boatman to take you out to the centre of the lake. Watch out for currents and don't get too close to the dam in Damside.

Several upmarket hotels let nonguests swim in their pool for a fee. In Lakeside, Hotel Barahi (p264) charges Rs 226; Fish Tail Lodge (p265) costs Rs 300; and Castle Resort (p266) is a great place for a swim (Rs 50) after the sweaty climb up there.

Walking

Even if you don't have the energy or perhaps the inclination to attempt the Annapurna Circuit, there are plenty of short walks in the hills around Pokhara. If you just want to stretch your legs and escape the crowds, stroll along the north shore of Phewa Tal. A paved walkway runs west along the shoreline to the village of Pame Bazaar, where you can pick up a bus back to Pokhara.

Another hike is the three-hour trip to the viewpoint at **Kahun Danda** (1560m) on the east side of the Seti River. There's a viewing tower on the crest of the hill, built over the ruins of an 18th-century kot. The easiest trail to follow begins near the Manipal Teaching Hospital in Phulbari – ask for directions at the base of the hill.

One of the most popular walks around Pokhara is the trip to the World Peace Pagoda (see the boxed text, p258). For longer walks in the Pokhara area see p275.

TOURS

Travel agents in Pokhara can arrange local tours and activities, but it's just as easy to rent a bike and do things under your own steam.

FESTIVALS & EVENTS

Lakeside comes alive with a festive spirit during the annual **street festival** (28 December to 1 January), when the main strip closes to traffic as restaurants and bars set up tables on the road. As many as 500,000 visitors cram the streets to enjoy food, parades, street performances and carnival rides.

Every August, Pokhara's Newari community celebrates **Bagh Jatra**, which recalls the slaying of a deadly marauding tiger. Gurungs celebrate **Tamu Dhee** (Trahonte) at around the same time, beating drums to drive away evil spirits. August is also time for **Gai Jatra**, when cows are decorated with paint and garlands, and villagers perform dances to bring peace to the souls of the departed. See p23 for more.

Tibetan Buddhists hold celebrations and masked dances at gompas around Pokhara to celebrate **Losar** (Tibetan New Year) in January/February and **Buddha Jayanti** (the Buddha's birthday) in April/May.

SLEEPING

Most people stay near the lake in Lakeside, a nonstop strip of hotels, budget guest houses, travel agents, restaurants and souvenir shops. People looking for peace and quiet tend to head to the north end of the strip or skip Lakeside altogether in favour of Pokhara's peaceful surrounds. All hotels will hold your luggage if you plan on doing some trekking.

It's always worth asking for a discount, particularly during low season when most places offer discounts of between 20% and 40%.

Lakeside

As the main traveller centre in Pokhara, Lakeside is packed with hotels. You can set up your tent for free in the scrappy camping ground, next to the lake at Camping Chowk. However, there are no facilities, and the nearest toilets are at neighbouring restaurants.

CENTRAL LAKESIDE

This is the heart of the action at Lakeside, where you are never more than 20m away from a budget hotel, traveller restaurant or internet cafe.

Budget

Butterfly Lodge (Map p263; ☎ 461892; www.butterfly -lodge.org; dm Rs 150, r without bathroom Rs 300, s Rs 500-800, d Rs 600-1000) Spread over four villas, Butterfly Lodge has clean, big rooms, and a lovely lawn with banana lounges. Staff are very friendly and provide good information on the area. Some of the money goes to the Butterfly Foundation supporting local children.

Amrit Guesthouse (Map p263; ☎ 206226, 464240; www.amritnepal.com; dm Rs 150, s/d Rs 400/500, without bathroom Rs 200/300, ste Rs 1200) Arranged around a garden courtyard, Amrit's motel-like facade may lack character, but its rooms are comfortable and reasonably priced. If your budget allows it, the quaintly decorated suite makes for a fine choice. There's also a rooftop restaurant with a fireplace and lake views. Its recycling bins and refillable water (Rs 10 per bottle) set an excellent example.

Hotel Peace Plaza (Map p263; ☎ 461505; www .hotelpeaceplaza.com; s with/without bathroom Rs 500/300, d Rs 700-1200) This modern, white four-storey building is fitted out with spotless rooms (many with lake views) with soft beds, a desk, a bar fridge and satellite TV. Some also have a bath tub. Ask for discount internet in the cafe downstairs.

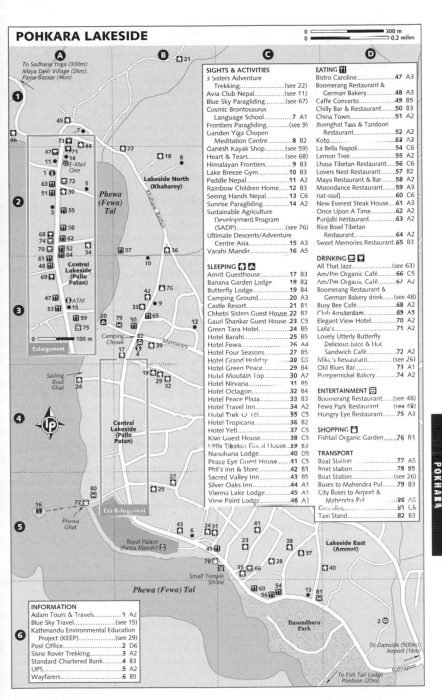

POKHARA LAKESIDE

0 — 300 m
0 — 0.2 miles

To Sadhana Yoga (300m);
Maya Devi Village (2km);
Pame Bazaar (4km)

Lakeside North
(Khaharey)

Phewa (Fewa) Tal

Central Lakeside
(Pallo Patan)

Central Lakeside
(Pallo Patan)

Camping Chowk

Manswara

Sailing Boat Ghat

Phewa Ghat

Royal Palace
(Ratna Mandir)

Small Temple Shrine

Lakeside East
(Ammat)

Basundhara Park

Phewa (Fewa) Tal

To Damside (500m);
Airport (1km)

To Fish Tail Lodge
Pontoon (20m)

Ratnapuri

SIGHTS & ACTIVITIES

3 Sisters Adventure
Trekking.....................(see 22)
Avia Club Nepal.................(see 11)
Blue Sky Paragliding...........(see 67)
Cosmic Brontosaurus
Language School................7 A1
Frontiers Paragliding............(see 9)
Ganden Yiga Chopen
Meditation Centre............8 B2
Ganesh Kayak Shop.........(see 59)
Heart & Tears................(see 68)
Himalayan Frontiers.............9 B3
Lake Breeze Gym..............10 B3
Paddle Nepal...................11 A2
Rainbow Children Home.....12 B3
Seeing Hands Nepal..........13 C6
Sunrise Paragliding...........14 A2
Sustainable Agriculture
Development Program
(SADP)......................(see 76)
Ultimate Descents/Adventure
Centre Asia...................15 A3
Varahi Mandir..................16 A5

SLEEPING

Amrit Guesthouse.............17 B3
Banana Garden Lodge........18 B2
Butterfly Lodge................19 B4
Camping Ground..............20 A3
Castle Resort...................21 B1
Chhetri Sisters Guest House..22 B2
Gauri Shankar Guest House..23 C5
Green Tara Hotel..............24 B5
Hotel Barahi...................25 B5
Hotel Fewa.....................26 A4
Hotel Four Seasons...........27 B5
Hotel Grand Holiday.........28 C5
Hotel Green Peace............29 B4
Hotel Moutain Top...........30 A2
Hotel Nirvana.................31 B5
Hotel Octagon.................32 B4
Hotel Peace Plaza.............33 B3
Hotel Travel Inn...............34 A2
Hotel Trek-O-Tel.............35 C5
Hotel Tropicana...............36 B2
Hotel Yeti.....................37 C5
Kiwi Guest House.............38 C5
Little Tibetan Guest House...39 B3
Nanohana Lodge..............40 D5
Peace Eye Guest House.......41 C5
Phil's Inn & Store.............42 B3
Sacred Valley Inn.............43 B5
Silver Oaks Inn................44 A1
Vienna Lake Lodge............45 A1
View Point Lodge.............46 A1

EATING

Bistro Caroline................47 A3
Boomerang Restaurant &
German Bakery..............48 A3
Caffe Concerto................49 B5
Chilly Bar & Restaurant......50 B3
China Town....................51 A2
Jhamghat Tass & Tandoori
Restaurant..................52 A2
Koto............................53 A3
La Bella Napoli................54 C6
Lemon Tree...................55 A2
Lhasa Tibetan Restaurant....56 C6
Lovers Nest Restaurant.......57 B2
Maya Restaurant & Bar.......58 A2
Moondance Restaurant.......59 A3
nat-ssul.......................60 C6
New Everest Steak House.....61 A3
Once Upon A Time............62 A2
Punjabi Restaurant............63 A2
Rice Bowl Tibetan
Restaurant..................64 A2
Sweet Memories Restaurant..65 B3

DRINKING

All That Jazz...................(see 63)
Am/Pm Organic Café.........66 C5
Am/Pm Organic Café.........67 A2
Boomerang Restaurant &
German Bakery drink....(see 48)
Busy Bee Café.................68 B3
Club Amsterdam...............69 A3
Elegant Venue Hotel..........70 A2
Laila's.........................71 A2
Lovely Utterly Butterfly
Delicious Juice & Hot
Sandwich Café..............72 A2
Mike's Restaurant............(see 26)
Old Blues Bar..................73 A1
Pumpernickel Bakery.........74 A2

ENTERTAINMENT

Boomerang Restaurant.....(see 48)
Fewa Park Restaurant........(see 19)
Hungry Eye Restaurant.......75 A3

SHOPPING

Fishtail Organic Garden.......76 B3

TRANSPORT

Boat Station...................77 A5
Boat Station...................78 B5
Boat Station...................(see 26)
Buses to Mahendra Pul......79 B3
City Buses to Airport &
Mahendra Pul..............80 A5
Greenline......................81 C6
Taxi Stand.....................82 B3

INFORMATION

Adam Tours & Travels...........1 A2
Blue Sky Travel................(see 15)
Kathmandu Environmental Education
Project (KEEP)...............(see 29)
Post Office.......................2 D6
Sisne Rover Trekking............3 A2
Standard Chartered Bank........4 B3
UPS..............................5 A2
Wayfarers........................6 B5

POKHARA

Hotel Mountain Top (Map p263; ☎ 461779; www
.mttop.com.np; s Rs 500-700, d Rs 600-800; ⌖) Take your
pick for lake or mountain views, or in the
case of room 426 – both! Rooms are tidy and
good value.

Little Tibetan Guest House (Map p263; ☎ 531898;
littletibgh@yahoo.com; s/d/tr Rs 500/650/850) This
Tibetan-run lodge is a favourite with many
for its calm and relaxed atmosphere. Rooms
are spacious with sparkling bathrooms,
and elegantly decorated with Tibetan wall
hangings and bedspreads. Balconies look
over a serene garden draped with prayer
flags.

Hotel Octagon (Map p263; ☎ 462878; hotelocta
gon@hotmail.com; s/d US$10/15, without bathroom
US$8/10) This unique octagonal building was
designed by the laid-back owner, and has
spotless rooms and is carpeted throughout
(shoes should be left outside).

Midrange

our pick Hotel Travel Inn (Map p263; ☎ 462631; www
.hoteltravelin.com; s US$5-15, d/f/ste US$30/40/50; ⌖) The
owner here claims tourists want three things:
clean, quiet and friendly, and this modern
hotel delivers on all fronts. Catering for all
budgets, rooms are spotless and their beds
imported from Germany will ensure a good
night's sleep. Deluxe rooms have all the mod
cons, while the honeymoon suite is suitably
mirrored up. It's the UN's choice of hotel
when they're in town.

Silver Oaks Inn (Map p263; ☎ 462147; www.hotel
pokhara.com; s/d US$10/15) Big rooms, bathtubs and
balconies with some of the best mountain
views in Lakeside make this one of the best
choices in town. In a quiet side-street location, rooms are reasonably priced, with soft
beds and furniture. Room 203 makes for a
great choice.

Hotel Four Seasons (Map p263; ☎ 465777; hotel
fourseasons@rocketmail.com; s/d US$20/30; ⌖) In no
way affiliated with the chain, this modern
hotel has pristine rooms with *the* most comfortable beds in Lakeside. Several rooms
have brilliant views of Mt Machhapuchhare,
with room 501 the pick with balcony
and bathtub.

Hotel Fewa (Map p263; ☎ 463151; www.hotelfewa
.com; s/d US$20/30, s/d/f cottage US$25/35/45) In a town
with little variation between lodgings, Hotel
Fewa gets full marks for its rustic mud/stone
cottages set right on the lake. A long-time
favourite, the cottages with loft make for

a memorable stay, and include a fireplace
and Buddhist motifs. The rooms in the back
building are overpriced and lack the same
charm.

Hotel Barahi (Map p263; ☎ 460617; www.barahi
.com; s/d US$32/41, deluxe US$65/81; ⌖ ⌖) The lovely
Hotel Barahi has a sparkling lap pool and
smart air-con rooms with small balconies.
The stone-clad buildings make it look a bit
like a Swiss ski chalet and there's free wi-fi in
rooms, 24-hour room service and a nightly
cultural show. Many rooms feature incredible
mountain vistas.

LAKESIDE EAST

Lakeside East is separated from Central
Lakeside by the Royal Palace, but it doesn't
take long to walk between the two.

Budget

our pick Peace Eye Guest House (Map p263; ☎ 461699;
www.peaceeye.co.uk; s/d Rs 350/450, without bathroom
Rs 150/250) Established in 1977, the chilled-
out Peace Eye retains all the qualities that
attracted the original visitors to Pokhara 30
years ago. Cheap, laid-back and friendly, its
brightly decorated rooms are spacious and
clean, and its guestbook glows with praise.
It also has a vegetarian restaurant and small
German bakery.

Gauri Shankar Guest House (Map p263; ☎ 462422;
gaurishankargh@hotmail.com; s Rs 250-400, d Rs 300-600)
Calm, quiet and reasonably priced, Gauri
Shankar has small, simple rooms set in a
secluded garden of pebbles and bushes. Its
atmosphere is social and friendly.

Kiwi Guest House (Map p263; ☎ 463652; bindu_adk@
hotmail.com; s/d Rs 300/400) This family-run place
of 25 years provides great value for money,
though some rooms are shabbier than others,
so have a look at a few. Room 202 is the pick
with mountain views.

Hotel Yeti (Map p263; ☎ 462768; www.hotelyeti.com
.np; s/d Rs 350/400) Draped in vines and bright
red flowers, Hotel Yeti's striking facade makes
for an excellent first impression. Rooms are
cheap, and though beds aren't overly soft and
walls are in need of a fresh coat of paint, it's
otherwise a fine choice.

Nanohana Lodge (Map p263; ☎ 464478; www.geo
cities.com/nanohanalodge; r Rs 400, s/d US$12/15) This
good-value banana-yellow hotel is popular
with Japanese and Korean travellers. Each
level has a balcony with table and chairs and
some rooms have cracking Annapurna views.

Before you get too excited about the giant hemp tree in the garden, it's a male.

Hotel Grand Holiday (Map p263; ☎ 462967; www .hotelgrandholiday.com; s/d Rs 500/600, with air-con US$20/25; ⊠) This newish hotel comes recommended by many, and with its mountain views it's not hard to see why. Its comfortable rooms get plenty of sun, and some have bathtubs. Also has an excellent rooftop sitting area and restaurant.

Hotel Nirvana (Map p263; ☎ 463332; hotelnirvana@ hotmail.com; r US$8-20, s without bathroom Rs 375; ⊠) Almost invisible behind a giant bougainvillea hedge, Hotel Nirvana is a much-loved place with a prim garden and spacious rooms with colourful ethnic bedspreads and curtains.

Sacred Valley Inn (Map p263; ☎ 461792; www.sacred valleyinn.com; r with/without bathroom Rs 600/400, upstairs US$15-20) Set in a shady garden across from the Royal Palace, Sacred Valley is a long-established traveller favourite. All the rooms are well maintained and those upstairs have gleaming marble floors and windows on two sides, allowing in plenty of light.

Midrange

Green Tara Hotel (Map p263; ☎ 462698; hgreentara@ hotmail.com; s US$10-25, d US$15-35; ⊠) Tucked down a quiet side street, Green Tara's rooms are smart, modern and clean; some boast excellent mountain views. Rooms 007 and 008 are the best picks.

Hotel Trek-o-Tel (Map p263; ☎ 464996; www.nepals hotel.com; s/d incl breakfast US$40/50; ⊠) Subtlety is the watchword at this smart modern hotel located in Lakeside East. Everything is tasteful and understated and rooms are housed in octagonal stone blocks in a pretty garden. Many guests are workers for international NGOs – a good marker of quality.

Top End

Fish Tail Lodge (Map p254; ☎ 465201; www.fishtail -lodge.com.np; s US$140-160, d US$150-170; ⊠ ▢ ▣) Reached by a rope-drawn pontoon from Basundhara Park, Fish Tail is charmingly understated and rooms are housed in low slate-roofed bungalows in a lush tropical garden. Rooms 16, 17 and 18 have excellent lake and mountain views but you'll need to book well in advance. Profits here are donated to a trust that helps cardiac patients in Nepal.

LAKESIDE NORTH

Things become simpler, quieter, cheaper as you head northwest from Camping Chowk. It's a perfect location for anyone seeking an added calmness, while being close enough to walk to the action of Central Lakeside.

Budget

Banana Garden Lodge (Map p263; ☎ 464901; s/d without bathroom Rs 100/150) The best and brightest of the budget guest houses, Banana Garden benefits from genial owners and a lovingly maintained garden. There are two shared solar-heated showers and the owners provide home-style Nepali meals.

View Point Lodge (Map p263; ☎ 462218; r with/without bathroom Rs 350/200) Perched above the lakeshore on a small bluff, this charming guest house has only three basic rooms, but they are clean and have unbeatable gorgeous lake views. Call before heading out to see if rooms are available.

Phil's Inn & Store (Map p263; ☎ 462009; phils@ fewanet.com.np; s/d Rs 500/1000, s without bathroom Rs 300) With welcoming staff, tidy and comfortable rooms, and killer lake views (room 2 is the pick), Phil's makes for an excellent choice. If you don't get a view from your room, the rooftop views make up for it. Bathrooms are large and clean.

Vienna Lake Lodge (Map p263; ☎ 464228; r Rs 350-750) Up a small track at the north end of the lakeshore development, this spick-and-span guest house has small, bright rooms and balconies full of pot plants looking out over the lake.

Midrange

Hotel Tropicana (Map p263; ☎ 462118; info@hotelthe tropicana.com; r US$10-30) This long-standing hotel of 20 years has large, spotless rooms with great lake and mountain views. Rooms on the 3rd floor (US$20) are the best value. The swing chair upstairs is a lovely spot to read a book looking out to the lake.

Chhetri Sisters Guest House (Map p263; ☎ 462066, 462912; www.3sistersadventure.com/Accomodation; s/d US$15/20, without bathroom US$12/15) Much smarter than the surrounding hotels, this tidy pink brick guest house is owned by the same people as Chhetri Sisters Trekking (see p331). Rooms are a tad overpriced (however breakfast is included), but are tastefully decorated and the location is peaceful.

Castle Resort (Map p263; ☎ 461926, 9856020784; www.pokharacastle.com; s/d €20/30; ✖ ☐ ☎) The perfect spot to build a castle (even if it is for tourists), perched high on the hill overlooking Lakeside, the secluded Castle Resort has a feel of exclusivity at reasonable prices. It has a solar-heated pool, lovely gardens, Irish pub, table tennis and wi-fi. It's a steep 20-minute trek up here, though you can prearrange a free porter service to meet you at the bottom.

Damside

This was one of the first areas to be developed for tourists but it feels very quiet these days. The big advantage here over Lakeside is its incredible mountain views that reveal themselves in their true glory. It's worth investing in a rental bike to get between here and Lakeside.

Dragon Hotel (Map p266; ☎ 460391; hdragon@wlink .com.np; s US$9-25, d US$11-30; ✖) A huge building reached through a private courtyard, Dragon Hotel is a Pokhara survivor of 35 years. A timely renovation has raised standards to their old levels and the foyer is full of Tibetan knick-knacks.

Hotel Mona Lisa (Map p266; ☎ 463863; r US$12-15, deluxe s/d US$20/30) The best and brightest of several similar places in this area, Mona Lisa tempts Japanese visitors with brightly coloured rooms and lounges with low *kokatsu* tables and cushions, and rooms have mountain or lake views.

Tibet Resort (Map p266; ☎ 460853; www.tibetresort .com.np; s/d US$23/34; ✖) Set back from the road in a huge garden full of marigolds, Tibet Resort has mountain views (go for room 208) and an air of peace and seclusion. Rooms are homely and there's a restaurant upstairs.

Elsewhere

You don't have to stay by the lake. There are several hotels and luxury places outside the centre by the Seti River or high in the hills above town.

ANADU

If you want to escape the tourist bustle of Lakeside, there are several peaceful getaways across the lake in the Anadu.

Park Anadu Restaurant & Lodge (Map p273; ☎ 984625557; r without bathroom Rs 300) Perched on Phewa Tal's western shore, the secluded Park Anadu has unbeatable views with rooms opening up to a perfect lake vista framed by a Himalayan backdrop. Situated a 20-minute boat trip from Lakeside (free transit back and forth), rooms are basic and have common bathroom with bucket hot water.

AIRPORT AREA

There are a few midrange and top-end places near the airport, though it's far from the most attractive part of town and not overly recommended.

Hotel Mt Annapurna (Map p254; ☎ 520037; mt annapurna@fewanet.com; s US$18-25, d US$25-35, ste US$45; ✖) Tibetan-owned and decked out with Tibetan knick-knacks, this '60s-style place is faded but friendly and it's very convenient for the airport. Rooms are plain but well appointed, and deluxe rooms offer the best value for money.

Shangri-la Village (Map p254; ☎ 462222; www.hotel shangrila.com; r US$250; ✖ ☐ ☎) This four-star hotel is a peaceful haven with a wonderful secluded swimming pool and tasteful rooms contained in imaginatively designed stone buildings. There are glorious mountain views

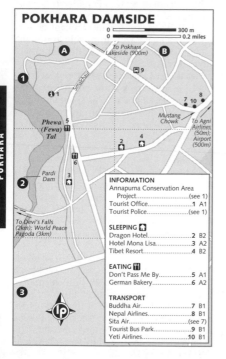

POKHARA DAMSIDE

0 — 300 m
0 — 0.2 miles

To Pokhara
Lakeside (900m)

Smrritrail

Phewa
(Fewa)
Tal

Mustang
Chowk

To Agni
Airlines
(50m);
Airport
(500m)

Pardi
Dam

To Devi's Falls
(2km); World Peace
Pagoda (3km)

from the gardens. Other facilities include a salon, sauna, spa and wi-fi.

OUTSKIRTS

If money is no object, there are several luxury resorts hidden away in the hills around Pokhara.

Tiger Mountain Pokhara Lodge (Map p273; ☎ in Kathmandu 01-4361500; www.tigermountain.com; cottages per person US$150; 🖭 🖵 🏊) Set on a lofty ridge, Tiger Mountain is about 10km east of town and the owners have made a real effort to make the place blend into the surroundings. Rooms are contained in stylish stone bungalows and there's an amazing mountain-view swimming pool. Rates include meals and transfers to/from Pokhara. Tiger Mountain prides itself on its sustainable tourism, such as growing its own produce and minimising imported goods.

Fulbari Resort (Map p273; ☎ 523451; www.fulbari .com; r from US$175; 🖭 🖵 🏊) South of Pokhara on the east bank of the Seti River, the Fulbari is a vast, five-star resort hotel. It's far enough from town for uninterrupted mountain views and inside you'll find every conceivable luxury, including a huge pool, health spa and golf club. Also has a honeymoon suite.

EATING

Pokhara has many restaurants and cafes serving up Western, Nepali, Indian and Chinese food to hungry travellers and trekkers. Restaurants are open from 6am to 10pm.

As well as the following restaurants, there are dozens of ultracheap local canteens offering momos, daal bhaat and fresh fruit juices (insist on purified water).

Lakeside

CENTRAL LAKESIDE

Punjabi Restaurant (Map p263; curries Rs 80-275) An authentic, Punjabi-run place churning out tasty vegetarian curries and tandoori breads. The front section has an inviting atmosphere with wicker lanterns and candles. The paneer curries and *masala dosas* are sensational.

China Town (Map p263; dishes Rs 90-320) An authentic Cantonese restaurant complete with Chinese chef, this place has a delicious selection of duck dishes, sweet-and-sour ribs, and spring rolls.

ourpick Moondance Restaurant (Map p263; dishes Rs 100-400) The much-loved Moondance is a Lakeside institution. Quality food, good

service and a roaring open fire all contribute to the popularity of this tastefully decorated restaurant. Its menu features salads, pizzas, steaks and decent Indian and Thai curries. For dessert, the lemon meringue pie is legendary. Wi-fi is available.

Once Upon a Time (Map p263; mains Rs 150-350) Another laid-back tourist restaurant, this place has a good combo of suave European cafe vibe up front, and traditional Nepali out back. The food is much the same as others, and features a 'patient menu' for those struck down by Delhi belly and special dietary requirements.

Lemon Tree (Map p263; meals Rs 160-290) With a bamboo porch draped in flower pots, and attractive Newari design within, the smart and sophisticated Lemon Tree is best known for its fish caught fresh from Phewa Tal. Meals are reasonably priced, and the service is friendly and attentive.

New Everest Steak House (Map p263; steaks Rs 280-1700) Carnivores flock to this old-fashioned steakhouse for 5cm-thick hunks of freshly grilled beef. Take your pick from an impressive selection of 34 types of steaks, with more novel choices including the 'Swiss style Pizza' and the 'Really red wine sauce' steak.

Boomerang Restaurant & German Bakery (Map p263; main dishes Rs 170-400) The best of the 'garden and dinner show' places, Boomerang has a large, shady garden with fresh flowers on each table. The food is good, as is its lake setting. There's a cultural show nightly from 7pm. The roadside bakery is also popular.

Maya Restaurant & Bar (Map p263; mains Rs 175-300) Serving up travellers' fare since 1989, the atmospheric Maya is still going strong. The walls are decorated with colourful images of Hindu deities, and its comfortable wicker furniture makes a great spot to people-watch with a pizza and a cold beer.

Rice Bowl Tibetan Restaurant (Map p263; momos Rs 100-205, mains Rs 175-300) This wildly popular restaurant has a laid-back atmosphere with cushion seating tables inside and sunny outdoor terrace. It serves up a typical Lakeside menu, and also decent Tibetan staples like momos and *thukpa* (noodle soup).

Koto (Map p263; mains Rs 180-460; ⏰ 11.30am-3pm & 6-9pm) Though it never seems busy, the authentic Japanese food here is faultless. The barbecued teriyaki beef is highly recommended.

Jhamghat Tass & Tandoori Restaurant (Map p263; tandoori mains Rs 195-310; ⏰ tandoori from 4pm) Popular with locals digging into daal bhaat, there's nothing fancy about this bamboo shack restaurant; rather, it's all about the quality tandoori dishes. The chicken and fish tikka dishes are spectacular.

Bistro Caroline (Map p263; mains Rs 350-600) This classy affair is more a place for a quiet romantic dinner than a noisy evening in the company of strangers. The European, Indian and Nepali food is first-rate and there's a good international wine list.

LAKESIDE EAST

La Bella Napoli (Map p263; pasta Rs 160-300) Another stalwart on the strip, this traveller restaurant specialises in tasty homemade pasta, though tries its hand at everything.

Lhasa Tibetan Restaurant (Map p263; meals Rs 175-375) Soothing temple music and Tibetan flags on the ceiling add a relaxed atmosphere to this big Tibetan eatery. Going strong since 1982, the menu has an excellent range of Tibetan dishes and you can warm up after dinner with a tankard of *tongba* (warm millet beer).

Caffe Concerto (Map p263; pizzas Rs 270-360) Potted marigolds and jazz on the stereo add to the bistro atmosphere at this cosy Italian place. The thin-crust pizzas are the best in town, wine is available by the glass and the gelato is delicious. Wi-fi is available.

[nat-ssul] (Map p263; mains Rs 280-500) This grassy outdoor restaurant opposite the lake serves up lip-smacking Korean barbecue. The sliced roast pork and grilled yak cheese makes for a good choice, while vegetarians can feast on *bibimbap* (bowl of rice coated in sesame oil with mixed vegetables and fried egg) served with an astounding assortment of dishes. Run by friendly owners, Mr October and Mrs April, there's also an inviting fire pit.

LAKESIDE NORTH

Things get decidedly quieter as you go north of Camping Chowk, but there are plenty of rustic shack restaurants with a sleepy charm.

Lovers Nest Restaurant (Map p263; meals Rs 90-300; 9am-9pm) Secluded and tranquil, this place is a real gem. Dine in thatched huts while watching the fishermen on the lake. The slow service in this case is a blessing, allowing you to take in the serenity.

Sweet Memories Restaurant (Map p263; meals Rs 160-360) An exceptionally friendly family-run restaurant serving all the usual fare, with standouts including sizzlers and eggplant lasagne.

The swanky new Chilly Bar & Restaurant (Map p263) overlooking the lake makes an excellent choice for pub food and a cold beer at sunset. There are some great chill-out areas, and the creepy photo of Heath Ledger as the Joker is class.

Damside

There's a branch of the German Bakery chain (Map p266) for cheesecake (Rs 85) and Danish pastries (Rs 35) and a few traveller restaurants on the road to Birauta Chowk. The highlight is **Don't Pass Me By** (Map p266; mains Rs 80-220), a cosy little restaurant that sits on the edge of the lake. With good travellers' fare, the outdoor seating among colourful flowers is delightful.

DRINKING
Bars

Pokhara nightlife generally winds down around 11pm, but a handful of bars flaunt the rules and rock till around midnight. Local bands play covers of Western rock hits. There are also the Nepali nightclubs, which can be fun, though these days have a seedy undercurrent.

Old Blues Bar (Map p263; 4-11.30pm) A relaxed option, the Blues Bar is popular with stoners, and large banners of Jimi Hendrix and John Lennon add to its appeal.

All That Jazz (Map p263; live music 7-10.30pm) Dark, smoky and intimate, it's everything a jazz bar should be. Live jazz musicians swing to an appreciative audience who sit at small tables below the stage. It's located above Punjabi Restaurant.

Other options include Laila's (Map p263), a small upstairs bar with graffiti on the walls and a pool table that's usually engulfed in a cloud of hash smoke. You can request CDs from Laila's large range, from John Lee Hooker to the Beatles.

The boisterous and loud Club Amsterdam (Map p263) is an old favourite on the strip. With live music, pool tables and football on the TV, it has got it all covered.

The liveliest bar in town and our pick of the bunch is Busy Bee Café (Map p263), which has live bands rocking to headbanging locals and a courtyard with a fire pit, which is a great spot to meet other travellers. There's also a smoky pool room down in the den. Look out for Busy Bee's furry resident mascot on the bar.

POKHARA

THE DAMAGE GLITTER BAND

Sailendra (vocals, 23); Bishnu (lead guitar, 23); Anil (rhythm guitar, 24); Bimal (drums, 18); Arjun (bassist, 24). The band mainly play covers and have been together for three years.

How would you describe your band? [Bishnu]: We play hard rock and alternative music. [Bimal]: Our main influences are Rage Against the Machine, AC/DC, Deep Purple and Jimi Hendrix.

How would you describe Pokhara's music scene? [Bishnu]: We have a lot of people who want to be good musicians here, but there are few opportunities. We are supported by some good fans, but generally people don't understand our music. [Arjun]: People are into *Indian Idol*! *[The band groan collectively, and laugh with disdain]* [Bimal]: People here do not have good education for music. It's hard to find good music, apart from Damage Glitter! [Arjun]: The revolution of Damage Glitter is to introduce good music to Nepal.

What are your current opinions of Nepal's political situation? [Anil]: It's bullshit! Every time the people choose a politician they promise they will do good, but every time they go against the people. They say they will make changes but they still don't fix things! [Bishnu]: Problems include 16-hour power cuts, bandhs (transport strikes), bars closing at 11pm and inflation, and petrol is not easily available.

What do you love about Pokhara/Nepal? [Bishnu]: I love the people, the culture and the tradition. Though I think the real Pokhara is in the city centre. However Lakeside is beautiful and is great to hang out with tourists.

Is there anything you dislike about Pokhara/Nepal? [Bishnu]: For us locals there is a problem with police here. Though there is no problem whatsoever for tourists. [Bimal]: Being a live band we really like to party and play music, and we wanna hang out late at night, but they say no music after 11pm! [Arjun]: The system sucks! [Sailendra]: They kick our arses. [Vishnu]: Many times we get locked up in police station. *[They all laugh]* [Bimal]: They are very narrow-minded, they don't want to understand us, or the happiness music brings to people.

Where do you see the future of Nepal heading? [Bishnu]: *[Shakes head]* Going down day by day. [Sallendra]: Corrupt cops, no human rights. [Anil]: There's no hope with the new government. They (the Maoists) demanded a new Nepal and made us believe it would be all good. Yet still the same bullshit. So our hope is not good. [Bimal]: Politicians have no respect for the future of Nepal. [Bishnu]: Though it's only been six months (since new government), the future of Nepal is unknown.

How do you see the difference between Kathmandu and Pokhara? [Anil]: Pokhara is much better! Less pollution, and it's much more beautiful. [Bishnu]: Kathmandu's musicians are technically very good and better than Pokhara's, though they play with no feeling or energy. When playing music with no energy, it lacks enjoyment. Here, we play with passion. People dance and rock out to our music. There that doesn't happens much. *[Arjun sticks finger down throat to describe Kathmandu and its music]*. [Bimal]: In Kathmandu they criticise too much, here we are all about having fun. [Sailendra]: Pokhara girls are much, much better *[Table erupts in excitable laughter]*. [Bimal]: Kathmandu girls are party girls with lots of make-up. In Pokhara we have natural girls who are much more beautiful. In Kathmandu, their clothes are open, though their minds are closed.

Cafes

The following cafes open at around 7am.

Lovely Utterly Butterfly Delicious Juice & Hot Sandwich Café (Map p263; lassis from Rs 100, sandwiches Rs 150) This tiny Lakeside shack is brimming with tropical fruits, and its name sums it up beautifully.

Am/Pm Organic Café (Map p263; cappuccino Rs 90) This shack run by a Nepali trained as a barista in London has organic Himalayan coffee from Palpa and tasty pastries from its German Bakery. There's a second branch in Lakeside.

our pick Elegant View Hotel (Map p263 ; breakfast Rs 150, organic coffee Rs 90) Basking on the lakeshore, this aptly named restaurant is an excellent choice for a lazy breakfast and strong filtered coffee. The beautifully manicured garden is set up with rather quaint furniture and decorated with prayer flags. If you feel like something sweet try 'Hello to the Queen'.

Mike's Restaurant (Map p263; breakfast Rs 245, sandwiches from Rs 180) An enterprise from the late Mike, of Mike's Breakfast fame in Kathmandu, the lakeside setting makes it a delightful spot for breakfast, a cup of tea or a fresh sandwich to the accompaniment of classical music.

Maya Devi Village (p273; ☎ 463650; ⏱ 9.30am-5pm) Run by the guys from Frontiers Paragliding, this relaxed spot north of the lake is on the road to Pame Bazaar. It is best known for its BLT sandwiches (Rs 195) and social Sunday afternoon barbecues (Rs 500 for all you can eat).

ENTERTAINMENT

Several restaurants along the strip have nightly Nepali cultural song-and-dance shows that are enthusiastic, if not entirely authentic. There's no additional charge and most shows start at 6.30pm or 7pm – try Fewa Park Restaurant, Boomerang Restaurant or Hungry Eye Restaurant. Hotel Barahi (p264) has a buffet dinner and cultural show from 6.30pm (US$10). If you reserve a table early, you can use the pool for free during the day.

Every month full-moon raves are held at Pame Bazaar, which, while far from the scale of Goa or Ko Pha Ngan, are worth checking out if trance music is your thing.

SHOPPING

If you've been to Thamel in Kathmandu, you know what to expect. Dozens of traveller boutiques in Lakeside sell pirate CDs, Buddhist masks, prayer flags, counterfeit trekking gear, wall hangings, Nepali khukuri knives and antiques of dubious antiquity. Pokhara is also a good place to pick up saligrams, but these are often overpriced.

As well as the shops in Lakeside, legions of Tibetan refugee women wander from restaurant to restaurant offering Tibetan knick-knacks for sale. For a better selection of Tibetan arts and crafts, including handmade carpets, head to the Tashi Palkhel and Tashi Ling Tibetan communities north and south of Pokhara – see p259.

Fishtail Organic Garden (Map p263; ☎ 9841523603; www.sadpnepal.org; ⏱ 7.30am-8pm) is run by the NGO Sustainable Agriculture Development Program (SADP) and sells organic products from yak milk soaps, wild honey, organic coffees and Ilam tea. SADP can organise volunteer placements.

There are numerous supermarkets in Lakeside where you can stock up on chocolate, biscuits, toiletries and other goods before heading out on your trek.

GETTING THERE & AWAY
Air

There are flights to Kathmandu (25 minutes) several times a day, with **Yeti Airlines** (Map p266; ☎ 464888, airport 465888; www.yetiairlines.com), **Buddha Air** (Map p266; ☎ 465998; www.buddhaair.com), **Nepal Airlines** (Map p266; ☎ 465021, airport 465040; www.royal nepal-airlines.com), **Sita Air** (Map p266; ☎ 465364; www .sitaair.com.np) and **Agni Air** (Map p254; ☎ 462968; www .agniair.com) sharing the load.

Nepal Airlines, Sita Air and Agni Air also have daily flights to Jomsom (20 minutes). There are great Himalayan views if you sit on the right-hand side of the plane heading into Pokhara (or the left on the way to Kathmandu). Nepal Airlines also flies to Manang (25 minutes) on Monday, Wednesday and Friday.

All the airlines have offices opposite the airport near Mustang Chowk but it's easier to get one of the travel agents in Lakeside to do the running around for a ticket.

The domestic departure tax from Pokhara is Rs 170.

Bus

There are three bus stations in Pokhara. Tourist buses that go to Kathmandu and Royal Chitwan National Park leave from the tourist bus park (Map p266) at Mustang Chowk. The dusty and chaotic main public bus stand (Map p254) at the northeast end of the Pokhara airstrip has buses to Kathmandu and towns in the Terai. You will find the main ticket office at the back and the night ticket office at the top of the steps near the main highway. Buses going to the trailheads for the Annapurna Conservation Area leave from the Baglung bus park (Map p254), about 2km north of the centre on the main highway.

Day buses run from about 5am to noon; night buses leave between 4pm and 6pm.

TO/FROM KATHMANDU

The bus trip between Kathmandu and Pokhara takes six to eight hours, depending on the condition of the road.

Tourist buses (Rs 400 to Rs 450) are the most hassle-free option and leave from the tourist bus park at 7.30am.

Taxis meet the tourist buses on arrival but brace yourself for Pokhara's notorious hotel touts.

Greenline (Map p263; ☎ 464472; www.greenline .com.np) has a daily air-con bus to Thamel (US$18 with lunch, six to seven hours) at 8am from its east Lakeside office. **Golden Travels** (☎ 462713) has a similar service to Durbar Marg (US$15 with lunch) in central Kathmandu, leaving from the tourist bus park.

Public buses to Kathmandu (day/night Rs 300/330) leave from the main public bus station. Faster microbuses run to Kathmandu (Kalanki) for Rs 450, leaving from the highway in front of the public bus stand.

Stops along the road to Kathmandu include Dumre (Rs 85, two hours), Abu Khaireni (Rs 115, three hours) and Mugling/Manakamana (Rs 120, four hours).

There are also four daily direct buses going to Gorkha (Rs 140, five hours). See the Kathmandu to Pokhara chapter, p235, for more information on sights and stopovers along the way.

TO/FROM CHITWAN NATIONAL PARK

The best way to get to Chitwan is by 'tourist' bus. Buses leave the tourist bus park daily at 7.30am for Sauraha (Rs 400 to Rs 450, seven hours), arriving at Bechauli, a 15-minute walk from town, or there are jeeps waiting to transfer travellers to their hotel – see p281 for details.

Greenline (above) has a daily deluxe air-con bus to Sauraha (US$15 including lunch, 5½ hours) at 8am from its east Lakeside office.

TO/FROM THE INDIAN BORDER

The closest border crossing to Pokhara is Sunauli, which is just south of the town of Bhairawa. See the individual towns in the Terai chapter for more details on transport to India.

Travel agents might try to tempt you with the offer of tourist buses to the border and direct buses to towns in India. Don't be fooled – there are no tourist buses to Sunauli and no through-buses to India; without exception, you must change at the border.

There are two buses to Sunauli (Rs 450, seven to nine hours), via Narayangarh (departing 7.15am) or the Siddhartha Hwy (the speedier option, departing at 6.30am), from the tourist bus park. From the main public bus

stand there are nearly 20 day and night buses daily for Bhairawa (Rs 380/445 day/night, eight hours), where you can pick up a local bus to the border post at Sunauli.

There are also day/night buses heading to Birganj (Rs 350/425, nine hours), Nepalganj (Rs 715/810, 12 hours), Mahendranagar (Rs 1015, 16 hours) and Kakarbhitta (Rs 1500, 17 hours).

TO/FROM THE TERAI

As well as the buses to the Indian border, there are regular day/night services to Narayangarh (Rs 250, five hours), where you can change to buses heading east and west along the Mahendra Hwy. A few buses go to Biratnagar (Rs 760/885 day/night, 12 hours) and Janakpur (Rs 515, 10 hours). All buses leave from the main bus stand.

Most buses go via Mugling, but there are also buses along the dramatic Siddhartha Hwy to Butwal (Rs 390, six hours) and Tansen (Rs 280, five hours).

TO/FROM TREKKING ROUTES

Buses to the trailheads for most treks in the Annapurna Conservation Area leave from the Baglung bus park. One important exception is the Annapurna Circuit Trek, which normally starts at Besi Sahar. See p339 and p275 for more information on these trekking routes.

The following stops are all on the bus route from Pokhara to Beni:

Stop	Fare (Rs)	Duration (hr)	Trek
Hyangja	25	1	Ghachok trek
Phedi	50	1½	Annapurna Sanctuary trek
Naya Pul	100	2	Ghorepani (Poon Hill) to Ghandruk trek, Annapurna Sanctuary trek, Annapurna Circuit Trek
Baglung	135	3	Annapurna Circuit trek
Beni	250	4	Annapurna Circuit trek

Buses leave about every half-hour from 5.30am to 3.30pm. Cranky old Toyota taxis leave from the same bus stand – the fare is Rs 700 to Phedi and Rs 1500 to Naya Pul, Rs 1250 to Baglung

POKHARA

and Rs 3000 to Beni (from where you can now get a jeep to Jomsom for Rs 500).

For Besi Sahar (Rs 200, five hours), there are two early morning and two lunchtime buses from the main public bus stand and Mustang (tourist) bus stand (Rs 230), or you can take any bus bound for Kathmandu and change at Dumre.

GETTING AROUND
Bicycle
There are lots of bicycle rental places at Lakeside – see p260 for hire prices.

Bus
Small local buses shuttle between Lakeside, the airport, the public bus stand and Mahendra Pul but routes are erratic and there isn't much space for baggage. Fares start at Rs 15.

Local buses to Pame Bazaar (Rs 15) and other places on the north shore of Phewa Tal leave Camping Chowk every hour or so until mid-afternoon. Buses to Begnas Tal (Rs 40) leave from the main bus stand.

Motorcycle
Several places in Lakeside rent out motorcycles and scooters for around Rs 300 per day. Check the bikes out first to make sure they start up easily, brake smoothly and the lights work. See p261 for motorcycle rental and tour information.

Taxi
Taxis meet tourist buses at the tourist bus stand (Mustang Chowk), but you can expect a hotel tout to come along for the ride. The fare to Lakeside is Rs 80 whether you take the tout's advice or not, so insist on being taken where you want to go. Heading out from Lakeside, you'll pay Rs 100 to the public bus stand, the Baglung bus stand or the airport. Taxis from the airport charge Rs 200 to Lakeside (and around Rs 100 to get to the airport from Lakeside).

AROUND POKHARA

Trekking in the Annapurna Conservation Area Project is easily the biggest attraction around Pokhara (see p352 for details) but you don't have to be a seasoned trekker to appreciate the glory of the peaks. There are

several dramatic viewpoints on the rim of the Pokhara Valley that can be reached by taxi, mountain bike or rented motorcycle from Pokhara, and gorgeous Begnas Tal and Rupa Tal offer similar lake and mountain vistas to Phewa Tal, but without the crowds.

SARANGKOT
The view of the Annapurna Himalaya from Sarangkot (adult Rs 25) is almost a religious experience. From here, you can see a panoramic sweep of Himalayan peaks, from Dhaulagiri (8167m) in the west to the perfect pyramid that is Machhapuchhare (6997m) and the rounded peak of Annapurna II (7937m) in the east. Most people come here at dawn or dusk, when the sun picks out the peaks, transforming them from a purple-pink to a celestial gold. If you feel noisy teenagers are ruining the peace at the viewing tower, try walking further along to the secluded grassy helicopter pad (though there are no seats here).

The main village is just below the ridge, but a set of steps leads uphill to a dramatic viewpoint in the ruins of an ancient kot. It's currently occupied by the army, but photography is fine, as long as you don't take pictures of the soldiers.

There's a ruined fort at **Kaskikot** (1788m), a one-hour walk west of Sarangkot along the ridge road, with similarly jaw-dropping views.

Sleeping & Eating
There are several places to stay and eat in Sarangkot. The cheapest options are along the concrete steps to the fort.

Mountain View Lodge (☎ 9804180714; s/d Rs 300/450, without bathroom Rs 250/350) The Mountain View doesn't actually have mountain views, but rather it looks out to the soaring Pokhara valley. Most importantly, it's comfortable, quiet and welcoming.

our pick **Sherpa Resort** (☎ 9841456639, in Kathmandu 01-4820201; www.sherparesort.com; r with/without bathroom Rs 600/500) If you've come to Nepal for views of the Himalaya, this is your place. Basic rooms and hard beds are a small sacrifice to wake up with the Himalaya peering right into your window. Rooms 201 and 202 are the best picks.

Getting There & Away
Taxi drivers in Lakeside offer dawn rides up to the ridge to catch the morning sunrise

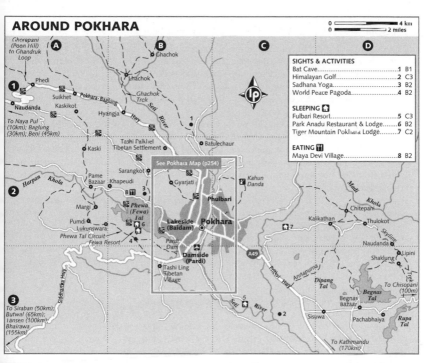

AROUND POKHARA

SIGHTS & ACTIVITIES	
Bat Cave	1 B1
Himalayan Golf	2 C3
Sadhana Yoga	3 B2
World Peace Pagoda	4 B2

SLEEPING	
Fulbari Resort	5 C3
Park Anadu Restaurant & Lodge	6 B2
Tiger Mountain Pokhara Lodge	7 C2

EATING	
Maya Devi Village	8 B2

for around Rs 600. The taxi fare is the same whether the driver waits to drive you back or you walk down. Be prepared for a guide to jump in your taxi who'll do his best to convince of his services, though a guide is unnecessary as it is easy to get to the top via the path.

By motorcycle or mountain bike, follow the road that branches off the Baglung Hwy near the Bindhya Basini Temple. When the road levels out below the ridge, look for the Sarangkot turning on the right, opposite a large group of tin-roofed school buildings. For details of the ride out to Sarangkot and on to Naudanda see p99.

A more challenging option is the three-to four-hour walk from Pokhara. The most popular path begins on the highway opposite the Baglung bus park.

The obvious trail runs west across the fields and up the side of Gyarjati Hill, meeting the dirt road at Silangabot, about 1km east of the Sarangkot turning.

There's also a scenic route from Phewa Tal but the trail is hard to follow and there have been muggings along this path. The trail begins near the village of Khapeudi on the road to Pame Bazaar (look for the signpost about 50m after the Green Peace Lodge), meeting the road just west of the turn-off to Sarangkot. It's usually easier to follow this trail on the way down.

BAT CAVE

You won't find Adam West or Christian Bale lurking in the dark and spooky **Bat Cave** (Map p273; Chameri Gufa; adult Rs 10; 6am-6pm), but instead thousands of live horseshoe bats, clinging to the ceiling of a damp and slippery chamber and occasionally chirruping into the darkness – claustrophobics beware. Daredevils can continue to the back of the vault and wriggle out through a tiny chute to the surface.

Torches can be hired for Rs 20, and guides (no fixed rate) can show you the narrow exit tunnel. Ask about tours to other newly discovered caves. It's easily visited from Pokhara on foot, by bike or by taxi (Rs 500).

POKHARA

JOMSOM

With the upgrading of the path to Jomsom (Dzongsam) into a proper road, growing numbers of travellers are heading north to this once remote village and making shorter treks from there. Although the village itself is a fairly scruffy administrative centre, flying or taking the bus here will allow you to get much closer to the peaks. With a few days to spare, you could walk south to Marpha or go east to Kagbeni and Muktinath (see p352). Hotels and shops can arrange porters for around Rs 700 per day.

To visit, you must pay the Rs 2000 fee for the Annapurna Conservation Area Project (ACAP) and present your receipt and Trekking Information Management System (TIMS) permit at the police checkpoint by the ACAP visitor centre. The nearby **Machhapuchhare Bank** (☽ 9am-2.30pm Sun-Thu, 9am-12.30pm Fri) changes cash and travellers cheques and even boasts an ATM, whenever there's electricity! The **Rural Information Center** (Rs 5-8 per min; ☽ 8am-6.30pm) offers pretty fast internet access.

At the south end of town a concrete stairway leads to the **Mustang Eco Museum** (admission Rs 50; ☽ 10am-5pm Tue-Sun, to 3pm Fri, to 4pm in winter), which is worth a visit for its displays on herbal medicine and its recreated Buddhist chapel. Just north of here is the airport, where you'll find the main hotels, restaurants, shops and airline offices.

Xanadu Guesthouse (☎ 069-440060; chandramohangauchan@yahoo.com; s/d Rs 350/500, r without bathroom Rs 100) is popular for its clean rooms, excellent restaurant (yak steaks and hot chocolate apple pie!) and laundry service. The downstairs shop sells good nak cheese.

Other good places on the main drag include the Trekkers Inn, Majesty, Moonlight and Tilicho hotels, all with rooms between Rs 250 and Rs 500, as well as Rs 100 to Rs 150 for box rooms without bathroom.

More upmarket options include rambling **Om's Home** (☎ 069-440042; omshome@wlink.com.np; s/d Rs 400/500, deluxe Rs 700/800), with private tiled hot-water bathrooms, a sunny courtyard and a table tennis table, and the **Alka Marco Polo** (☎ 069-440007; s/d Rs 300/500), which accepts credit cards and boasts a sauna (Rs 500) and internet access.

Sita Air, Agni Air and Nepal Airlines operate flights between Pokhara and Jomsom (US$78 to US$82, 50 minutes) and have offices where you can book and reconfirm tickets.

All flights depart between 7am and 9am. Jeeps operate on the new road to/from Beni (Rs 500, nine hours), 45km west of Pokhara, where you can board another bus to Pokhara (Rs 250, four hours). For jeeps east to Muktinath (Rs 500, three hours) see the office at the northern edge of Old Jomsom.

BEGNAS TAL & RUPA TAL

About 10km southeast of Pokhara, a road leaves the Prithvi Hwy for Begnas Tal and Rupa Tal, two gloriously serene lakes that see few foreign visitors, despite their proximity to Pokhara.

It's a peaceful spot and the mountains of the Annapurna Range are brilliantly reflected in the rippling waters. Boats can be rented for a leisurely paddle on the lake for Rs 200 per hour.

Rupa Tal is via a 3km hike along the trail that winds uphill from the bus stand in Begnas Bazaar. It's much more isolated than Begnas Tal but the surrounding countryside is delightful and you can stay at several laid-back teahouses on the ridge overlooking the lake.

Sleeping & Eating

Hotel Day Break & Restaurant (☎ 560011; s Rs 150-200, d Rs 300-500) Located at the start of the walking trail in Begnas Bazaar, this friendly place has bright rooms with Formica floors, hot showers and mountain views from the roof.

Rupa View Point (☎ 622098; d old/new building Rs 300/750) A lovely family-run place above the village of Pachabhaiya, overlooking Rupa Tal. There are two basic rooms, plus a new building with new rooms and solar hot water. In the evening meals are prepared by the farmer's wife using vegetables from their garden. To get here, follow the signposted path off the main trail, then take the steps on the left, then the path on the right.

Reached via the path across the Begnas Tal dam, followed by a steep climb, are **Annapurna Lake View** (r without bathroom Rs 200) and **Hilltop Restaurant & Rest House** (☎ 9846048082; r without bathroom Rs 350), two rustic ridge-top guest houses. Both have two rudimentary rooms and a small restaurant looking out over the lake. Here you'll feel very much off the beaten track.

Getting There & Away

Buses to Begnas Tal (Rs 21, one hour) stop on the highway opposite the main public bus stand in Pokhara. By bike or motorcycle, take the Prithvi Hwy towards Mugling and turn left at the obvious junction in Tal Chowk.

SIRUBARI

Situated 56km south of Pokhara, the remote Gurung village of Sirubari has been developed as a destination for cultural tourism by the Nepal Tourism Board. Far from being a tacky tourist experience, this is more like a rural homestay – accommodation and meals are provided by local farmers and the only way to get there is on foot via a four-hour trek from the village of Arjunchaupari near Syangja on the Siddhartha Hwy.

The village is full of traditional stone buildings, including a charming gompa (Buddhist monastery), and there's a rugged viewpoint nearby at **Thumro** (2300m) overlooking the full sweep of the Himalayan peaks.

However, few people in Sirubari speak English and you may have problems if you drop in unannounced. The easiest way to visit is to make advance arrangements with a travel agent in Kathmandu or Pokhara – they'll arrange your accommodation and a guide, and put you on the right bus to the trailhead. Otherwise contact Jum Gurung (☎ 061-692496, 980412642), the tourism officer for the village. Two-day tours cost Rs 2500.

SHORT TREKS AROUND POKHARA

Without the Himalaya, there would be no Pokhara, at least in tourist terms. You'll need at least a week to reach the snowline on the Annapurna Sanctuary trek (see p358 for details), but there are some fascinating short treks in the lower foothills with epic views of the Annapurna Himalaya.

Most villages in the area have basic teahouses where you can find a meal (almost invariably daal bhaat or chow mein) and a bed for the night, and the only gear required is a sleeping bag and a warm jacket for the evenings. Nevertheless, the usual precautions for safe and responsible trekking apply (see p335).

You should equip yourself with a suitable map, particularly if you fancy branching off the established tourist route. Lonely Planet's *Trekking in the Nepal Himalaya* has more detail on trekking options around Pokhara.

Phewa Tal Circuit (One Day)

If you get an early start, it's possible to walk right around the shore of Phewa Tal, beginning on the path to the Peace Pagoda. Starting from the World Peace Pagoda, continue along the ridge to the village of Lukunswara and take the right fork where the path divides. Once you reach Pumdi, ask around for the path down to Margi on the edge of the lake. From Margi, you can either cut across the marshes over a series of log bridges or continue around the edge of the valley to the suspension bridge at Pame Bazaar, where a dirt road continues along the northern shore to Pokhara. If you run out of

---

BEATING THE BOTTLE

Abandoned plastic drinking water bottles are one of the plagues of the Himalaya. Some trekking routes are vanishing under a tide of plastic rubbish that will take thousands of years to decay. You can do your bit to keep the Himalaya beautiful by purifying your own water – there are springs and wells in most villages and water can easily be purified using water purification tablets or a water filter. Some lodges in the Annapurna Conservation Area now offer refills of purified water for a nominal charge – part of a joint initiative by the Annapurna Conservation Area Project and the New Zealand government. Start off on the right foot by visiting the **Kathmandu Environmental Education Project** (KEEP; Map p263), based in Hotel Green Peace in Lakeside. KEEP provides all sorts of information on environmental pollution in the hills and offers a canteen refilling service for Rs 10.

energy, local buses pass by every hour or so. See Map p273 for details of the circuit.

Ghachok Trek (Two Days)

This interesting two-day trek goes north from Pokhara to the traditional Gurung villages around Ghachok. It starts from Hyangja, near the Tashi Palkhel Tibetan settlement, and crosses the Mardi Khola to Lhachok before ascending to the stone-walled village of Ghachok, where you can stop overnight before turning south and returning to Pokhara via Batulechaur. With more time, you can extend this walk to visit some even more remote villages in the valley leading north from Ghachok. See Map p273 for an outline of the route.

Ghorepani (Poon Hill) to Ghandruk Loop (Six Days)

In an area packed with mountain viewpoints, Poon Hill (3210m) stands out. A steep 1.5km walk above Ghorepani, this exposed bluff looks out over an incredible vista of snowy peaks, including Annapurna South (7273m) and Machhapuchhare (6997m). Some people include Poon Hill as a detour on the Annapurna Circuit, but it's also a popular trekking destination in its own right.

Most people include Poon Hill as part of the popular six-day Ghorepani to Ghandruk loop, which also includes a stop at the Gurung village of Ghandruk.

The trail starts at Naya Pul, on the road from Pokhara to Baglung, and follows the Annapurna Circuit trail for the first two days, with overnight stops in Tikedhunga and Ghorepani. On day three, most people leave before dawn for the hike to Poon Hill and relax in Ghorepani for the rest of the day.

Day four involves a gentle descent to Tadapani, and day five continues downhill to Ghandruk, a scenic village of stone and slate houses with a colourful Buddhist

monastery. The final day is an easy descent back to Naya Pul, where you can pick up buses back to Pokhara. Alternatively, head east across the valley to Landruk and stop overnight at Tolka, before continuing to Phedi on the Baglung Hwy. See Map pp354–5 for an outline of the route.

Annapurna Skyline Trek (Royal Trek) (Four Days)

Following a low ridge east of Pokhara, with spine-tingling views of the Annapurna peaks, the four-day Annapurna Skyline Trek (or Royal Trek) was famously walked by Prince Charles in 1980. The path is wide and easy to follow; however, because it lies off the main tourist circuit there's no teahouse accommodation en route, except at Begnas Tal. Most people bring a stove and camp at basic campsites along the route.

The trail starts near the army camp on the Prithvi Hwy, just east of the Bijayapur Khola, and crosses a flat area of rice fields before climbing the ridge to the village of Kalikathan (1370m), which has two basic campsites with fine views.

On day two the trail follows the forested ridge through Thulokot to Mati Thana, where you can take a tea-shop lunch, before climbing to Naudanda, Lipini and finally Shaklung (1730m) with another simple camping ground.

On day three the trail descends to the valley floor, then rises to the attractive Gurung village of Chisopani (1629m) – the campsite is a short walk beyond the village near a ridge-top temple and the views are sublime. The final day involves a leisurely stroll along the ridge that separates Rupa Tal and Begnas Tal, emerging on the valley floor at Begnas Bazaar (see p274), where buses leave regularly for Pokhara. See Map pp354–5 for details of this route.

The Terai & Mahabharat Range

For the flat, southern half of Nepal, competing against the might of the Himalaya as the star attraction is always going to be a tall order. Despite the mismatch the Terai region manages to pull some spirited punches with its lure of wildlife parks and some fascinating cultural offerings. With prime areas reopening for business since the end of the Maoist insurgency, the region awaits visitors on a greater scale than that previously limited to the more intrepid traveller.

Of course Chitwan is an exception to the rule. Famous as one of the best places to stalk wildlife in Asia, Chitwan National Park is justifiably one of Nepal's main attractions. Spying one-horned rhinos and the elusive tiger from an elephant-top vantage point is an experience that makes Chitwan an essential stop along the Pokhara–Kathmandu 'tourist triangle'. There's also Bardia National Park, which has managed to escape mass tourism through the tyranny of distance: blessed with rich wildlife, it beckons the more adventurous and is a less exploited alternative.

Home to over half Nepal's population, the Terai's colourful mix of ethnicities is showcased through the thatched mud-hut villages of the Tharu people and the vibrant art of Mithila women. As the birthplace of the Buddha, Lumbini is an immensely sacred site that attracts Buddhists from around the world. Janakpur likewise is an important Hindu pilgrimage town that pulsates with religious fervour. With the laid back Newari hill town of Tansen, tea plantations at Ilam and a launching point for treks into northwest Nepal, the Terai boasts some genuine highlights worth going out of your way to explore.

HIGHLIGHTS

- Exploring the cobblestone streets of medieval **Tansen** (p302) before hiking down to the spooky abandoned palace at **Ranighat** (p303)
- Being brought back to even pegging within the animal hierarchy as you walk on foot in **Bardia National Park** (p309)
- Taking an all-terrain pachyderm vehicle to track one-horned rhinos in **Chitwan National Park** (p281)
- Cycling through **Lumbini's** (p296) peaceful landscaped grounds of Buddhist temples
- Strolling through **Ilam's** (p324) teafields – arguably the most peaceful spot in the Mahabharat Range
- Popping in to visit Mithila women artists at work in **Janakpur** (p316); try to coincide your visit with one of its big festivals

HISTORY

Travelling through the Terai today, it's hard to believe that this was once one of the most important places in the subcontinent. In 563 BC, the queen of the tiny kingdom of Kapilavastu gave birth to a son named Siddhartha Gautama and, 35 years later under a Bodhi tree (pipal tree) at Bodhgaya in India, Buddhism was born. The Indian Buddhist emperor Ashoka made a famous pilgrimage here in 249 BC, leaving a commemorative pillar at the site of the Buddha's birth in Lumbini.

Nepal also played a pivotal role in the development of Hinduism. Sita, the wife of Rama and heroine of the Ramayana, was the daughter of the historical king Janak, who ruled large parts of the plains from his capital at Janakpur. Janak founded the Mithila Kingdom, which flourished until the 3rd century AD, when its lands were seized by the Gutpas from Patna in northern India.

The depopulation of the Terai began in earnest in the 14th century, when the Mughals swept across the plains of northern India. Hundreds of thousands of Hindu and Buddhist refugees fled into the hills, many settling in the Kathmandu Valley, which later rose to prominence as the capital of the Shah dynasty. Aided by legions of fearsome Gurkha warriors, the Shahs reclaimed the plains, expanding the borders of Nepal to twice their modern size.

Although the British never conquered Nepal, they had regular skirmishes with the Shahs. A treaty was signed in 1816 that trimmed the kingdom to roughly its current borders. Nepal later regained some additional land (including the city of Nepalganj) as a reward for assisting the British in the 1857 Indian Uprising.

The Terai was covered by swathes of jungle well into the 1950s. The indigenous people of the plains, the Tharu, lived an almost stone-age existence until 1954, when DDT was used to drive malaria from the plains and thousands of land-hungry farmers flocked into the Terai from India and the Nepali hills.

Today, the Tharu are one of the most disadvantaged groups in Nepal, and huge areas of the forest have been sacrificed for farmland and industrial development. Nevertheless, some large patches of wilderness remain, preserved in a series of excellent national parks, and the massive industrial and agricultural development in the plains is slowly raising the quality of life for the nation, at least in economic terms.

CLIMATE

The Terai has a similar climate to the northern plains of India – hot as a furnace from May to October and drenched by monsoon rains from June to September. Try to visit in winter (November to February) when skies are clear and temperatures are moderate.

DANGERS & ANNOYANCES

The annual monsoon rains can severely affect transport in the region – dirt roads turn to mud, dry stream beds become raging torrents and roads and bridges are routinely washed away. Allow extra time for any long-distance journeys and be prepared to fly if necessary to get around these obstacles.

Road safety is another concern in the Terai, with hundreds of Nepalis killed every year in bus crashes. Night buses are by far the worst offenders. To maximise safety travel in daylight hours and avoid the front seats. Many expats and NGO workers prefer to fly rather than gamble on the buses.

Much to everyone's chagrin, bandhs (public transport strikes) are notorious for making transport grind to a halt, and with little warning can leave you stranded in a town for anywhere from a few hours to several days (see also p366).

Despite the end of the Maoist insurgency, the Terai is still not entirely free of political instability. The region has seen the emergence of numerous Madhesi insurgent groups who have launched an often-violent campaign for greater equality, and there have been several bombings in the southeast of Nepal. It's advisable to stay informed of the situation if travelling in the region.

GETTING THERE & AWAY

The Terai is easily accessible from Kathmandu and Pokhara in Nepal and from West Bengal, Bihar and Uttar Pradesh in India. The Indian rail network passes close to several of the most important border crossings and there are frequent bus and air connections from the Terai to towns and villages across Nepal.

Air

Budda Air (www.buddhaair.com) and **Yeti Airlines** (www.yetiairlines.com) are the main airlines offering flights around the Terai. Currently,

You can fly from Kathmandu or Pokhara to Nepalganj, Biratnagar, Bharatpur, Bhairawa, Janakpur, Simara (for Birganj) and Bhadrapur (for Kakarbhitta) – see these individual towns for details.

Land

All of Nepal's land border crossings are in the Terai. Heading from east to west, you can cross between India and Nepal at the following points:

Border crossing (Nepal to India)	Page
Mahendranagar to Banbassa for Delhi & hill towns in Uttaranchal	p313
Nepalganj to Jamunaha for Lucknow	p309
Sunauli for Varanasi, Agra & Delhi	p296
Birganj to Raxaul Bazaar for Patna & Kolkata	p317
Kakarbhitta to Panitanki for Darjeeling, Sikkim & Kolkata	p326

The Sunauli crossing is by far the most popular route between the two countries, but immigration staff are used to seeing foreign tourists at all the crossings. Nepali visas are available on arrival: you'll need one passport photo and US dollars cash for the visa fee (US$25 with multiple entry for 15 days, US$40 for 30 days and US$100 for 90 days).

Details of border opening times and onwards travel into India are included in the 'Crossing the Border' boxed texts under Sunauli, Nepalganj, Birganj, Mahendranagar and Kakarbhitta. For more on crossing between Nepal and India, see p383

GETTING AROUND

Bicycle

On the face of it, the Terai is perfectly suited for cycling – the terrain is pool-table flat, there are villages every few kilometres and traffic is relatively sparse. However, the condition of the roads leaves a lot to be desired so a sturdy mountain bike is strongly recommended. If you run out of steam along the way, you can usually put your bike on the roof of a bus. See p94 for details of biking routes from Kathmandu to Hetauda and Hetauda to Mugling, as well as general biking information.

Bus

Buses and minibuses are the main form of transport around the Terai. However, road safety can be an issue, particularly for night travel – see opposite for more information.

Roof riding is prohibited in the Kathmandu Valley but there is no such restriction in the Terai, and riding on the luggage rack with the wind in your hair can be an exhilarating experience. See p387 for more details on bus travel.

Car

To avoid the hassle of local bus services you can hire a car and driver in most Terai towns. Most hotels and travel agencies can make arrangements and the going rate for a decent car and driver is around Rs 4000 per day.

CENTRAL TERAI

As the most popular border crossing for those travelling to/from India via Sunauli, the central Terai sees the most tourist traffic in the region by a long shot. Its chief attraction is Chitwan National Park, which rightfully remains high on most visitors' to-do lists. Lumbini, the historical birthplace of the Buddha, is an increasingly common stopover point while Tansen, likewise, no longer remains a secret.

NARAYANGARH & BHARATPUR

☎ 056

Narayangarh sits at the junction of the Mugling Hwy and the Mahendra Hwy, which runs the length of Nepal from Mahendranagar to Kakarbhitta. It's the first major town you come to once you leave the hills and it's an important transport hub. Visitors here are either on their way to or from Chitwan National Park, whether catching a flight from Bharatpur or jumping on a bus in Narayangarh.

Nabil Bank (🕑 10am-5pm Sun-Thu, 10am-3pm Fri) has both foreign exchange and an ATM accepting foreign cards. You can check your email at **Pulchowk Cyber Cafe** (☎ 523953; per hr Rs 25; 🕑 7.30am-8.30pm) opposite the bus stand.

Sleeping & Eating

There are a couple of upmarket choices in Bharatpur, which are handy for the airport.

Royal Rest House (☎ 522898; Pulchowk; s/d with bathroom from Rs 500/700, s/d with air-con from Rs 1000/1200; 🗷) Right on the highway at Pulchowk, the Royal has a tandoori restaurant downstairs and good rooms with hot showers upstairs.

THE TERAI & MAHABHARAT RANGE

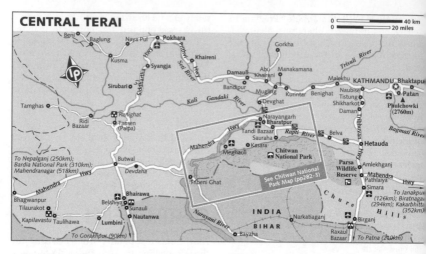

Hotel Global (☎ 525513; www.hotel-global.com.np; Bharatpur; s US$20-40, d US$25-50; ✦ ☻) This rather luxurious hotel has well-kept gardens and a palm-fringed swimming pool. Standard rooms are a little boxy, while more deluxe options are far better value with all the mod cons.

Kitchen Cafe (☎ 520453; mains Rs 60-200; ⏱ 8am-8.30pm) Just before the bridge over the Narayani, this baroque colonial garden restaurant serves the best food in town. The spicy Chinese dishes are recommended.

Getting There & Away

Bharatpur (2km south of Narayangarh) is the closest airport to Chitwan National Park. There are daily flights to/from Kathmandu (US$86, 30 minutes) with **Buddha Air** (☎ 528790) and **Yeti Airlines** (☎ 523136).

The main bus station, known as the Pokhara bus stand, is at the east end of town on the road to Mugling. Minivans run regularly to Pokhara (Rs 250, five hours) and Kathmandu (Rs 250, five hours). A few buses also run north to Gorkha (Rs 110, three hours).

There are also regular buses to Butwal (Rs 195, three hours), Sunauli/Bhairawa (Rs 230, three hours), Birganj (Rs 250, three hours), Janakpur (Rs 280, six hours), Biratnagar (Rs 730, nine hours), Nepalganj (Rs 650, 10 hours), Kakarbhitta (Rs 850, 12 hours) and Mahendranagar (Rs 1000, 12 hours).

For Chitwan you could take a local bus to Tandi Bazaar/Sauraha Chowk (Rs 30, 20 minutes) and then either a rickshaw (Rs 50), pony cart (Rs 50) or jeep (Rs 300) to Sauraha, but it's usually better to take a taxi all the way from Pulchowk (Rs 700).

AROUND NARAYANGARH
Devghat

Hidden away in the forest 6km northeast of Narayangarh, Devghat marks the sacred confluence of the Kali Gandaki and Trisuli Rivers, two important tributaries of the River Ganges. Hindus regard the point where the rivers meet as especially sacred and many elderly high-caste Nepalis come here to live out their final years and eventually die in the sight of god on the banks of the holy river. Far from being gloomy, it's an uplifting place and the calm, contemplative atmosphere is wonderfully soothing after the hectic pace of the plains. The sounds of clashing cymbals and chanting emanating from the small temples can be mesmerising.

The best way to see Devghat is to wander around and discover. The well-maintained village is reached by a suspension bridge over the rushing waters of the Trisuli and the streets are lined with ashrams and temples and shops selling saligrams (fossil ammonites, revered as a symbol of Vishnu). On the first day of the Nepali month of Magh (mid-January), thousands of pilgrims flock to Devghat to immerse themselves in the river to celebrate the Hindu festival of Magh Sankranti (see p23).

Local buses to Devghat (Rs 60, 20 minutes) leave from the Pokhara bus stand in Narayangarh.

THE TERAI & MAHABHARAT RANGE

CHITWAN NATIONAL PARK
☏ 056

The World Heritage–listed Chitwan National Park is one of the big tourist drawcards in Nepal. The reserve protects over 932 sq km of sal forest, water marshes and rippling elephant grassland and, with the snowcapped Himalaya in the distance, it's little wonder this place is so popular. Meaning 'Heart of the Jungle', Chitwan is famous as one of the premier wildlife-viewing national parks in Asia, and you'll have an excellent chance of spotting one-horned rhinos, deer, monkeys and 450 species of bird. If you're extremely lucky you'll see leopards, wild elephants or sloth bears, though, of course, people are attracted in their droves for the once-in-a-lifetime chance to spot the majestic royal Bengal tiger.

Two whole days in the park is really the minimum for wildlife spotting. The nature of dense scrub, high grasslands and the nocturnal hours kept by many animals are all factors that make spotting the big animals far from guaranteed. A good approach is to treat wildlife viewing as one would the pastime of fishing: some days you'll get plenty of bites, others not a nibble; irrespective, it's all about being out in nature and the thrill of the chase, knowing you're deep in tiger and rhino country.

Sadly, Chitwan lost many animals during the decade-long Maoist insurgency, when the Nepali army were too preoccupied with the conflict to provide adequate protection from poachers. However, while numbers are depressingly lower compared to a decade ago, the good news is that figures from the 2008 census show an increase in rhinos since the 2005 count. The tiger count was under way at the time of research. While the recent installation of electric fences has been an undoubted success in preventing pachyderms stomping through villages (especially those with a taste for home-brewed liquor) and destroying crops, it's also put an end to the sightings of animals quenching their thirst along the banks of the Rapti River in Sauraha.

Depending on your choice of accommodation, Chitwan will offer you two distinct experiences. The best option, if your budget will allow it, is to stay in one of the luxury lodges located deep inside the park. Being surrounded by the sounds of the jungle bestows visitors with the kind experience you'd expect from visiting a national park. Most budget travellers opt for the more affordable lodging in Sauraha, a small village settled on the edge of the park. It has a thriving backpacker scene straight out of the Thamel mould. While many enjoy its social nature, and it is a great place to have a beer watching the sunset over the river, others are let down by its commercial set-up.

History

Chitwan National Park was created in 1973, but the area has been protected since at least the 19th century as a hunting reserve for Nepali and foreign aristocrats. Britain's King George V and his son, the young Edward VIII, managed to slaughter a staggering 39 tigers and 18 rhinos during just one blood-soaked safari to Chitwan in 1911.

Until the late 1950s, the only inhabitants of the Chitwan Valley were small communities of Tharu villagers, who were blessed with a natural resistance to malaria. After a massive malaria eradication program in 1954, land-hungry peasants from the hills swarmed into the region and huge tracts of the forest were cleared to make space for farmland.

As their habitat disappeared, so did the tigers and rhinos. By the mid-1960s there were fewer than 100 rhinos and 20 tigers. News of the dramatic decline reached the ears of King Mahendra and the area was declared a royal reserve, becoming a national park in 1973. Some 22,000 peasants were removed from within the park boundaries, but it was only when army patrols were introduced to stop poaching that animal numbers really started to rebound. Chitwan was added to the Unesco World Heritage list in 1984.

While things have improved markedly since then, there was an alarming drop in numbers during the Maoist rebellion. Poachers have reduced rhino and tiger numbers by a quarter, selling animal parts on to middlemen in China and Tibet. To make things worse, many animals perished in the monsoon floods of 2002.

Geography

Chitwan National Park covers an impressive 932 sq km. A further 499 sq km is set aside as the Parsa Wildlife Reserve and new conservation areas have been created in the community forests at Baghmara and Kumrose, which have been replanted with fast-growing trees to provide villages with an alternative source of firewood and fodder. Because of the topography,

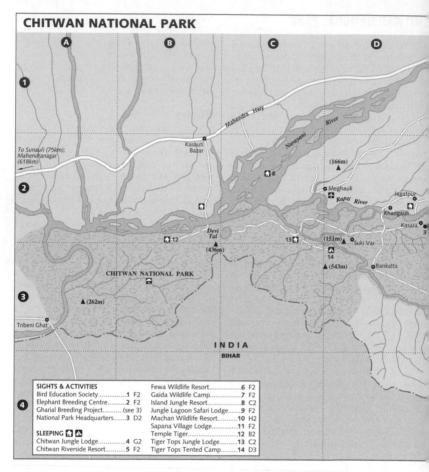

CHITWAN NATIONAL PARK

SIGHTS & ACTIVITIES
Bird Education Society.................1 F2
Elephant Breeding Centre.........2 F2
Gharial Breeding Project............(see 3)
National Park Headquarters......3 D2

SLEEPING
Chitwan Jungle Lodge..............4 G2
Chitwan Riverside Resort..........5 F2

Fewa Wildlife Resort.................6 F2
Gaida Wildlife Camp.................7 F2
Island Jungle Resort.................8 C2
Jungle Lagoon Safari Lodge......9 F2
Machan Wildlife Resort..........10 H2
Sapana Village Lodge.............11 F2
Temple Tiger..........................12 B2
Tiger Tops Jungle Lodge.........13 C2
Tiger Tops Tented Camp........14 D3

most tourist activities are restricted to the floodplain of the Rapti River.

As well as the river, there are numerous tal (small lakes) dotted around the forest. The most interesting of these, particularly for viewing birds, are **Devi Tal** near Tiger Tops Jungle Lodge and **Lami Tal** near Kasara. In March it looks spectacular as pink lotus flowers bloom on the lake. There's another group of lakes and pools just outside the park boundary, known collectively as **Bis Hajaar Tal** (literally '20,000 lakes').

Plants

Around 70% of the national park is covered in sal forest, but there are also large areas of *phanta* (grassland), particularly along the banks of the Rapti and Narayani Rivers. Growing up to 8m in height, the local elephant grass provides excellent cover for rhinos and tigers. In the forest, you'll find shisham, kapok, palash, pipal and strangler fig, and scarlet-flowered kusum trees, as well as the ubiquitous sal, the principal hardwood species in the Terai.

Animals

Chitwan boasts more than 50 different species of mammals, including rhinos, tigers, deer, monkey, elephants, leopards, sloth bears, wild boar and hyenas. Birdwatchers can tick off 450 different species of birds and butterfly-spotters have identified at least 67 species of butterfly, some as large as your hand.

THE TERAI & MAHABHARAT RANGE

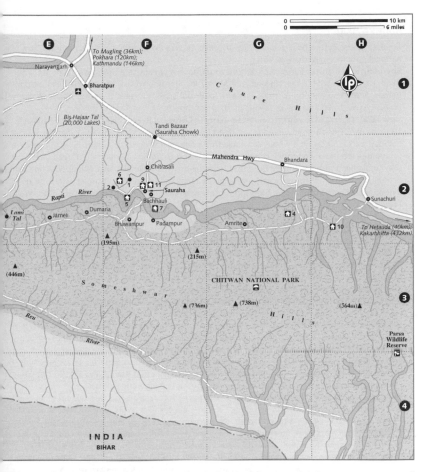

The one-horned Indian rhinoceros is the most famous animal at Chitwan and you stand a good chance of seeing one on an elephant safari, despite the impact of poaching.

Chitwan also has significant populations of gharial crocodiles – see the boxed text, p286, for more on Chitwan's signature species.

As well as these high-profile animals, you may spot barking deer, spotted deer, hog deer, sambar and massive gaurs (Indian wild oxen) skulking in the bushes. The most commonly seen monkey at Chitwan is the stocky rhesus macaque, but you also stand a good chance of spotting the larger and more elegant langur. These agile grey apes were the basis for the monkeys in Disney's cartoon of the *Jungle Book* (apart from King

Louie, who was plainly an orang-utan and about 3000km from his native home in Sumatra!). Spotted deer often follow the langurs around, taking advantage of their profligate feeding habits. They also cooperate to alert each other when predators are in the area: the hoots of monkey or deer serve as a good indicator to keep your eyes peeled for an animal sighting.

Birds seen in Chitwan include bulbuls, mynahs, egrets, parakeets, jungle fowl, peacocks, kingfishers, orioles and various species of drongos. Birders should bring a pair of binoculars and keep an eye out for rarer species, such as ruby-cheeked sunbirds, emerald doves, jungle owlets and crested hornbills.

THE TERAI & MAHABHARAT RANGE

RUCHRA HARI

Aged 46 years, Ruchra has lived in Chitwan since he was five, and has been a naturalist in the national park for more than 20 years.

Spending so much time in the park, you must have a favourite animal? My favourite is the rhino. It's very beautiful; the big one, you know? It's amazing to see, though they can be dangerous. Sometime they try to charge: I've helped tourists climb trees to escape them so many times! I haven't had any real problems in 20 years though.

How about tigers, have you encountered many in Chitwan? In 20 years I have seen them maybe 10 times. Why? Because you need to go deep into the sal forest, and you can't reach it from a half-day walk. You can in a whole-day walk; this is the best way to see a tiger. If we're lucky we sometimes see them when they come to the grassland to drink water and hunt deer. One time I saw movement in the elephant grass so I went to see what animal it was. I climbed a tree but I couldn't see anything, then I saw moving grass again and heard a giant growl [which he does a good job of demonstrating], a big sound! I saw it: a really big royal tiger with two cubs. When I ran to the jeep the tourists laughed at me and asked why I was running. I told them a tiger was chasing me: they stopped laughing when they saw it. Afterwards I asked them why they hadn't taken photos: they say they were too scared and couldn't move their fingers to use their cameras! They said they took the picture in their minds, you know?

Is there any one animal you're most afraid of? I am afraid of tigers. Many people say sloth bears, but with tigers you can't do anything to fight back. They are very strong; really big! You can't do a thing. Tigers are shy so don't usually come to people but, if they do…

You mentioned that the sloth bear is dangerous; why is that? They don't like human faces; they don't like our eyes. When they attack, they attack the face so that you can't see; you can't do anything. If you climb a tree to escape, they climb too. If you run, they run too, and it's enough fast for us! If I see one I tell tourists not to run: you must stay still in a group. One time we hid in a hole and I realised a baby sloth bear was there! We left very slowly, then the mother suddenly came at me through the grass. I made a noise like a dog and banged my stick on the ground and, luckily, the bear went away. I looked for the tourists and they were far away, laughing. I asked them why they had run when I said not to: they were too scared and had to run. They were laughing because we had survived one of the most dangerous animals.

What do you think of the current state of the park? It makes me sad because there are very few animals now. When I begin as guide I would walk for four hours and see lots of animals. Now it's hard to even see a herd of deer. One reason is that many animals were washed away in floods a few years back. Many died in the mud: they couldn't move so they couldn't eat or drink. Rhinos, sloth bear and leopards were washed up dead at the Indian border. There are fewer animals because of poaching during the Maoist uprising also. There were five army posts but, during that time, there was only one because they were fighting the Maoists, so it was easy for poachers to get into the park. Another problem is the vines that appeared after flooding, which kill native plants by strangling them. If it stays like that, in a few years the animals will lose their habitat.

Now the Maoist conflict is over and the army is back patrolling the park, do you think animal populations will increase? Yeah, yeah [nodding head resolutely]. I think the problem has gone away now.

Information

Sauraha's **park office** (☎ 521932; foreigner/SAARC/child under 10 per day Rs 500/200/free; ☺ ticket office 6-9am & noon-4.30pm) handles admission fees to the park, although this is usually bundled into the overall charge when booking a tour either independently or as a package. At the time of research there was talk of increasing admission fees, so don't be surprised if prices are slightly higher than quoted here. You can also book an elephant safari here; see p287.

There's also the small **National Park Visitors Centre** (☺ 6am-4pm) that displays information on wildlife and dioramas on the Chitwan food chain.

There's no bank in Sauraha, but several private moneychangers accept foreign currency and travellers cheques at reasonable rates.

Chitwan Money Changer (⊗ 7am-8pm) does credit card cash advances. There are a number of STD/ISD phone services in Sauraha, as well as internet cafes with slow connection, including Sauraha Cyber Cafe (per hr Rs 100; ⊗ 7.30am-11pm).

When to Visit

The ideal time to visit Chitwan is from October to March, when skies are clear and the average daily temperature is a balmy 25°C. The best time to see animals is late January to March when the towering *phanta* grass is slashed by villagers, improving visibility considerably. At other times the grass can grow as high as 8m tall, making it difficult to spot animals that may be as close as a few feet away. Jeep safaris are difficult during the monsoon (June to September) when tracks through the park become impassable.

Dangers & Annoyances

Tigers, leopards and rhinos are all quite capable of killing humans, and there have been some serious attacks on tourists. Most people have a good experience on jungle walks, but you should be aware that there's a small but significant risk – being chased by a rhino seems a lot less funny when you consider the phrase 'trampled to death' (see the boxed text, p289).

Insects are another unwelcome aspect of life in the jungle. Mosquitoes are an inescapable fact of life in Chitwan and are present in large numbers year-round. Malaria may be present in some areas of the park, so remember to bring insect repellent. During the monsoon the forest comes alive with *jukha* (leeches). See p397 for tips on how to deal with these pests.

Sights

NATIONAL PARK HEADQUARTERS

The National Park Headquarters (☎ 521932) are inside the park at Kasara, about 13km west of Sauraha on the south bank of the Rapti River. Most people visit as part of an organised jungle safari and there's a small visitor centre with displays on wildlife. At the gharial breeding project (admission Rs 100) you can see both gharial and marsh mugger crocodiles up close; the program has been a great success in releasing both endangered species back into the wild.

Sadly, the tiger you're most likely to see in Chitwan is the encaged tigress at the park headquarters. Orphaned when its mother was killed after mauling four people in 60 days, it was rescued as a cub while chasing a goat in a village. Its only chance of survival was to live in captivity.

ELEPHANT BREEDING CENTRE

About 3km west of Sauraha on the far side of the small Bhude Rapti River, the elephant breeding centre (☎ 580154; foreigner/SAARC Rs 50/25; ⊗ 6am-6pm) is a must-see sight in Chitwan. Providing most of the elephants for elephant safaris at Chitwan, it's fascinating watching the interaction between mother and baby elephants, as well as the multi-task use of their trunk (which has a staggering 40,000 muscles), such as covering themselves in dust to ward off mosquitoes or scratching their backside with a bamboo stick.

The elephants spend much of the day grazing in the jungle so come before 10.30am or after 3.30pm if you want to see the cute baby elephants. As adorable and harmless as they may seem, treat baby elephants with caution as most have a naughty streak and are surprisingly powerful units. Much to the delight of locals, twin male calves were born here in late 2008.

Morning is a good time to visit as, not only are there less tourists, you get to watch on as the *mahouts* (elephant riders) prepare *kuchiis* – elephant sweets made from molasses, salt and rice wrapped in grass (which actually looks rather appetising). The breeding centre is an easy walk or cycle along the road past Jungle Lagoon Safari Lodge.

ELEPHANT POLO

About 25km southwest of Narayangarh, the Tharu village of Meghauli is a sleepy place full of thatched huts and wandering chickens. However, the town wakes up every December for the annual Elephant Polo Championships, a jumbo-sized sporting spectacular held on the Meghauli airstrip. The event attracts teams from around the world, including several countries that don't have native elephants (Scotland won in 2007). Few travellers visit at other times, but you can get here by bike from Sauraha or by local bus from Narayangarh.

BIRD EDUCATION SOCIETY

Run by local volunteers, the friendly Bird Education Society (☎ 580113, 9745003399; ⊗ 7am-5.50pm) should be the first port of call for twitchers. In a new location on the road to

SIGNATURE SPECIES

Chitwan has some high-profile species that everyone wants to see, including the following:

One-Horned Indian Rhino

Chitwan is one of the last refuges of the rare one-horned Indian rhinoceros; they are one of the most commonly seen animals on elephant safaris in the park. Only about 2500 survive worldwide, most of them in Chitwan and Kaziranga National Park in Assam, India. Sadly, poaching has increased significantly since the start of the Maoist insurgency. In 2000, there were 544 rhinos in the park; 372 animals were found in the 2005 census. Though the good news is the 2008 counts yielded a slight increase to 408 rhinos.

Asian Elephant

The Asian elephant is the world's second-largest land mammal behind its African counterpart. The only elephants you're likely to see in Chitwan are domestic elephants that ferry visitors around the park on wildlife-spotting safaris, though there's a small population of approximately 25 to 30 wild elephants in the Parsa Wildlife Reserve adjoining Chitwan National Park.

Royal Bengal Tiger

This lean, mean, killing machine is the top predator in the jungles of Nepal and the cunning, intelligence and savage power of the royal Bengal tiger make it one of the most-feared animals in the subcontinent. Both locals and foreigners have been attacked by tigers at Chitwan – something to think about before joining a guided walk. There are currently around 150 tigers in Chitwan – sightings are rare as tigers lay low during daylight hours, but keep your eyes peeled. It's said that tigers are a hundred times more likely to spot you, than you them.

Gharials

A distant relative of the Australian salt crocodile, the gharial is a bizarre-looking beast, with a slender, elongated snout crammed with ill-fitting teeth and a bulbous protuberance at the end of its snout, resembling a *ghara* (local pot) from which it gets its name. In fact, the gharial is perfectly evolved for its diet of river fish – 110-million-year-old fossils have been found with exactly the same body plan. Gharials are endangered but there are breeding programs at Chitwan and other national parks, and young gharials have been released into many rivers in the Terai.

Sloth Bear

These shaggy black bears, the size of a large dog, have a reputation as the most-feared animal (tiger included) among locals. Getting their name from being confused with sloths in the 19th century, due to their long claws and excellent tree-climbing abilities, sloth bears otherwise bear no resemblance to sloths whatsoever. The bears' diet is mainly termites and ants – they use their protruding muzzles to vacuum them up through a gap between their teeth, a sound that can be heard up to 100m away.

the elephant breeding centre, the society has a library of bird books and a binocular rental service (Rs 50/100 per hour/day) and also has guided birdwatching excursions every Saturday from 7am to 11am. There's no charge but donations help fund the activities.

THARU CULTURAL SHOW

Most of the big park lodges put on shows of traditional Tharu songs and dances for guests, including the popular stick dance, where a great circle of men whack their sticks together

in time – it's the Nepali equivalent of Morris dancing! It's very much a tourist experience, but the shows are fun and they provide employment for local people. In Sauraha there's a nightly performance at the **Tharu Culture Program** (tickets Rs 60; ☾ 7.30pm).

THARU VILLAGES

Sauraha is surrounded by small Tharu villages, which you can explore by bike or on foot. Resist the urge to hand out sweets, pens and money; instead, if you want to help local people, shop n the village shops or eat in village bhojana-ayas (basic restaurants). Farming is the main industry and many people still decorate their houses with Mithila paintings and adobe bas-reliefs of animals. The nearest Tharu village is **Bachhauli**, a pleasant cycle or 20-minute walk out through the mustard fields of bright yellow flowers. Here you will find the informative **Tharu Cultural Museum & Research Center** (admission Rs 20; ☯ 6am-4pm) with colourful murals and exhibits on artefacts and local dress. It's a must-see for those interested in Tharu culture, and worth visiting before venturing into the villages to get some background info.

Harnari is one of the best villages to get a taste of Tharu culture. Bordering the community forest, it's less visited than Bachhauli and has a more authentic feel with its unpaved roads. There's a tiny **Tharu Cultural Museum** (admission by donation) here with displays of ornaments and a *rakshi* distillery pot. If it's closed, ask around and someone will open it up. There are plans to set up a homestay in a Tharu mud hut next to the museum. It's a 20-minute bike ride to get here.

Sapana Village Lodge (see p292) runs excellent tours of Tharu villages and organises activities from walking tours and planting rice in the fields with villagers to fishing trips, cooking and art classes.

WILDLIFE DISPLAY & INFORMATION CENTRE

The new **Wildlife Display & Information Centre** (admission Rs 25; ☯ 7am-5pm) in Sauraha has educational displays on wildlife, including a rather macabre collection of animal foetuses in jars, skulls, plaster-cast footprints and a collection of animal poo, while the various animal reproductive organs preserved in formaldehyde make for a novel exhibit.

Activities

You'll need to add a further Rs 500 for the cost of the park permit per day on all prices quoted for the following activities.

ELEPHANT RIDES

For many visitors, lumbering through the jungle on the back of a five-tonne jumbo spotting wildlife is the defining Chitwan experience. It's the best way to see wildlife in the park, offering a fantastic vantage point high above the tall grasses of the *phanta*. The wildlife is much more tolerant of elephants than of noisy jeeps or walkers, and they also effectively mask the scent of humans.

Riding an elephant is thrilling rather than comfortable. Elephants move with a heavy, rolling gait, and three or four passengers are crammed into each wooden howdah (riding platform). Each elephant is controlled by a *mahout*, who works with the same elephant throughout its life.

Many visitors are upset by the sight of shackled elephants at the breeding centre, as well as their treatment by *mahout*s, who whack their skulls with sticks and metal hooks to prevent them straying off course. It's one of the unfortunate drawbacks to transforming elephants into domestic animals. Elephants play an important role in the park on patrols, looking for poachers and injured animals; the elephants are otherwise treated well and spend a good five hours each day grazing in the park. The WWF has launched an initiative to introduce less severe training methods that involve psychological techniques, compared to the more distressing traditional methods employed by *mahout*s.

Government-Owned Elephants

The national park has its own herd of domesticated elephants; **jungle safaris** (foreigner/SAARC Rs 1000/400) leave the visitor centre at Sauraha at 8am and 4pm daily, and 7am and 5pm during summer. Children are half price. There are no advance bookings so the first thing you should do on arrival is buy a ticket from the National Park Visitors Centre, or organise it through your hotel. Safaris last one to two hours and

---

ELEPHANT BATHTIME

There are few experiences that create such a feeling of childlike wonder as helping to bath an elephant. Every day from 11am to noon, the elephants in Sauraha march down to the river near the Hotel River Side for their morning scrub, and everyone turns out to watch the spectacle. If you bring your swimming costume, you can join in the fun. There's no better way of cooling off on a hot day than sitting on the back of a submerged elephant and shouting *chhop!* – if you get the accent right you'll be rewarded with a refreshing trunkful of cold water! Lodges with their own elephants offer similar elephant bathtimes.

run through the dense *phanta* along the Rapti River, a favourite feeding ground for deer and rhinos.

Privately Owned Elephants

Most of the lodges inside the park have their own elephants and elephant safaris are included in most package tours. In Sauraha you can arrange inexpensive elephant safaris through **Unique** (☎ 580080) and **United** (☎ 580219; rameshmalpur@yahoo.com). Safaris last 1½ hours and cost Rs 800, plus the park fees.

Both companies run morning and afternoon safaris in the Baghmara Community Forest, a buffer zone on the western edge of the park with decent wildlife populations. From September to January, spotting wildlife in the community forest is often better than inside the park, where long grass makes visibility difficult.

JUNGLE WALKS

Exploring the park on foot when accompanied by a guide is a fantastic way to get close to the wildlife. Be aware, though, that you enter the park with the real risk of encountering bad-tempered mother rhinos, tigers and sloth bears protecting their young. Generally, the bigger the group, the safer the walk, but the experience of your guide counts for a lot. Levels of experience vary and some of the guides have a worryingly devil-may-care attitude to creeping up on rhinos. Therefore, jungle walks are not recommended for the faint-hearted; see the boxed text, opposite.

Walks can be arranged through any of the lodges or travel agents in Sauraha. The going rate is Rs 650 for a half-day and Rs 800 for a full day. **United Jungle Guide Service** (☎ 580034) is a co-operative of 30 local guides, who provide good options for jungle walks. If you have the time, try a whole-day jungle walk, rather than the half-day, which will take you deeper into the park and maximise wildlife-viewing opportunities.

Another alternative is to trek through the Chepang hills to the Kathmandu–Pokhara (Prithvi) Hwy – see p238.

CANOEING

An altogether more relaxing way to explore the park is on a canoeing trip on the Rapti or Narayani Rivers. You have a good chance of spotting water birds and crocodiles. Canoe trips from Sauraha cost Rs 350 to Rs 1000 per person, which includes a one-hour trip downriver followed by a two-hour guided walk back to Sauraha, with a stop at the elephant breeding centre. Canoe trips can be arranged either through your hotel or one of the many booking agencies in Sauraha.

4WD SAFARIS

It may not have quite the same romance as riding through the jungle on the back of an elephant, but jeep safaris are another popular way to explore the park. Animals are less fazed by the rumble of jeep engines than you might suspect and you'll have the opportunity to get much deeper into the jungle. Half-day safaris start at Rs 1000 per person. Safaris can be booked either through your hotel or an agency in Sauraha.

CYCLING

You can't cycle inside the park itself but the surrounding countryside is ideal for bicycle touring, with dozens of small Tharu farming communities to visit. Another possible destination is **Bis Hajaar Tal**, a collection of bird-filled lakes and ponds about 1½ hours northwest of Sauraha, accessible via the Mahendra Hwy.

Mountain bikes can be rented from various shops in Sauraha for around Rs 100 per half-day and Rs 170 per full day.

For information on a mountain bike trip that passes Chitwan see p98.

Festivals

The **Chitwan Festival**, most famous for its elephant race, is held in late December; it also has food stalls and cultural performances.

Sleeping

You can stay either inside the park or at Sauraha, the small traveller centre on the north shore of the Rapti River.

Many people visit Chitwan on package tours arranged through travel agents in Kathmandu, Pokhara or overseas. This is by far the easiest approach if you plan to stay at one of the upmarket lodges in the park. If you're planning to stay in Sauraha, packages are unnecessary and expensive, and it's easy enough to arrange accommodation and activities independently. Discounts of 20% to 50% are available in the low season, particularly from May to September.

You can also arrange overnight trips to both Kumrose and Baghmara community forests for Rs 2250 per person. Transport,

JUNGLE SURVIVAL

Chitwan and Bardia are two of the few wildlife parks in the world that you can explore on foot when accompanied by a guide. It's both an exhilarating and humbling experience being brought back to an even playing field within the animal hierarchy, with the only protection between man and beast being the bamboo stick carried by your guide (which can be surprisingly effective in beating off advancing animals). The sound of a twig snapping in the forest, or the warning cry of deer and monkey alerting each other of nearby predators will make your heart race.

However, that said, jungle walks are a risk. While dangerous run-ins are not overly common, you'll hear enough stories of tourists experiencing terrifying encounters with animals to make you want to devise a plan of attack as an angry rhino charges 40km/h in your direction. Nearly all incidents involve protective mothers in the company of their young. The most crucial piece of advice is to never venture into the park without a guide, nor outside the park visiting hours.

Rhinos

Being charged by rhinos is the most common dangerous encounter tourists have in the park. With poor eyesight, rhinos rely on a keen sense of smell that enables them to sniff out threats, which includes humans. If you are charged, the best evasive action according to Eak Krishna Shrestha, naturalist of 23 years, is 'to climb the nearest big tree', which are usually easy enough to climb. Alternatively, hiding behind a tree can be effective, though be prepared for several repeated charges from the rhino. Failing trees, Eak suggests 'running zigzag before dropping an item of clothing or your camera as a decoy' as another effective strategy.

Sloth Bears

Due to their unpredictable temperament, sloth bears have the reputation as the most-feared animal in Chitwan. Their nocturnal hours make sightings rare, though mothers and cubs sometimes move during the day, which makes encounters fraught with danger. Eak, who bears the scars of a sloth bear attack, warns that 'males go for the face; however, females go for down there!' [pointing to his nether region]. 'If in danger, it's best not to run; rather, stay perfectly still and huddle in a group to make you look more threatening, while your guide bangs a stick on the ground to scare it away.'

Tigers

In the unlikely event you cross paths with a tiger, which are known to be extremely shy, the best advice according to Santa Chaudhari, a naturalist from Bardia National Park, is 'not to run; maintain eye contact and back away slowly'. Certainly easier said than done.

Elephants

Due to numerous deaths of villagers each year, wild elephants are rightfully feared by locals. If you are in a threatening situation, the most effective means of escape is to simply run for your dear life!

guide, meals, sleeping bag and permit are all included in the price.

INSIDE THE NATIONAL PARK

By far the most atmospheric way to visit Chitwan is to stay at one of the upmarket resorts inside the park. The resorts are expensive, but it's hard to put a price on the experience of staying deep in the forest, surrounded by the sounds of the jungle. Most of the lodges offer a choice of Tharu-style jungle cottages or comfortable safari tents, all with private bathrooms and hot showers. The lodges all have bars and restaurants but there are few other mod cons, reflecting the 'getting back to nature' ethos. All prices listed include lodging, meals and jungle activities. Transport to the lodges costs extra.

At the time of research, there was talk of the lodges within the national park being forced to relocate outside the park's perimeter when their leases expire at the end of 2009. While it's unlikely that this will happen, it's worth double-checking the situation before booking.

Gaida Wildlife Camp (☎ in Kathmandu 01-4215409; www.gaidawildlife.com; s/d US$88/176) The bungalow rooms at Gaida are nothing spectacular: it's all about the location. It's the closest lodge to Sauraha, so by far the easiest to access, and the only park accommodation on the north bank of the Rapti River. Wildlife is not particularly prolific at the main camp though you never know your luck. There are also cultural dances, a separate restaurant and classy bar.

Machan Wildlife Resort (☎ in Kathmandu 01-4225001; www.nepalinformation.com/machan; 1-/2-night package US$135/285, additional nights US$110; 🗪) At the eastern end of the park, this attractive place has recently been renovated and is the closest resort to the Parsa Wildlife Reserve. Guests stay in well-designed, timber-frame bungalows set among the trees and there's a delightful natural swimming pool, a bar and restaurant and a video library of wildlife films. Children aged three to 12 are half price.

Chitwan Jungle Lodge (☎ in Kathmandu 01-4442240; www.chitwanjunglelodge.com; 3-day/2-night package US$220, additional nights US$100) Set near the south bank of the Rapti River amid sal forest in the eastern part of Chitwan, this sensitively themed resort makes extensive use of thatch and natural materials. There's a very inviting open-air bar and restaurant, and the spacious rooms are lined with reed matting. Rates include park fees and children between four and 10 years of age pay half rates. The resort is closed from June to August.

our pick **Island Jungle Resort** (☎ in Kathmandu 01-4220162; www.islandjungleresort.com; 3-day/2-night package US$230, additional night per person US$90) One of the more popular places, it has a superb location on a large island in the middle of the Narayani River at the western end of the park. The cottages at the main resort are simple but tasteful and decorated with animal paintings. There's a lovely riverside breakfast terrace, plus the obligatory Tharu-style restaurant and bar. Children aged three to 10 pay half price.

Temple Tiger (☎ in Kathmandu 01-4221637; www .catmando.com/temple-tiger; packages per person per night US$250) Surrounded by dense jungle on the south bank of the Narayani River in the west of the park, Temple Tiger offers raised wooden cabins with thatched roofs, each with a private viewing platform looking over the *phanta*. Children under 12 are half price.

Tiger Tops Tented Camp (☎ in Kathmandu 01-4361500; www.tigermountain.com; packages per person per night US$300) Three kilometres southeast of

the Tiger Tops Jungle Lodge in the serene Surung Valley, this feels much more like a traditional jungle safari: it's easy to imagine what life must have been like for the *pukkah sahibs* (colonial gentlemen) who came here to hunt at this lodge in the early 20th century. The comfortable safari tents have twin beds, modern bathrooms and small balconies, and there's a delightful raised bar and restaurant.

Tiger Tops Jungle Lodge (☎ in Kathmandu 01-4361500; www.tigermountain.com; packages per person per night US$400) The original tree-top guest house that forged the Tiger Tops brand, its rooms in stilt houses are still some of the most characterful accommodation anywhere in Nepal everything is constructed from local materials. The lodge sits beside the small Reu Khola at the western end of the park and the spacious rooms have solar-powered lights and fans. There are always elephants wandering about the place, adding to the jungle atmosphere.

SAURAHA

Most independent travellers to Chitwan stay in the village of Sauraha on the northern fringes of the park. There are dozens of lodges and hotels here, from upmarket package accommodation to simple cottage resorts run by local villagers. Almost all have mosquito nets and solar-powered showers that only run hot after a few hours of morning sunshine.

Budget

All the budget options are very similar, so choosing between them is often a decision of whether to stay along the main strip or in its more peaceful surrounds.

Chilax House (☎ 580260; chilaxhouse@yahoo.com, s/d without bathroom Rs 100/150, s/d with bathroom Rs 200/300) Geared for travellers on the cheap, this family-run guest house is one of Chitwan's best budget options. Rooms in the small cottages are clean, and it has a homely dining room with an open kitchen and organic vegetable garden.

Hotel Royal Kasturi (☎ 9845075361; royalkasturi@ hotmail.com; r without bathroom Rs 200) Situated in Bairiya Village, 2.5km east of Sauraha, this is the perfect spot to get some peace and quiet. Rooms are basic, but you'll feel well off the tourist path. The garden has an assortment of fruit trees, and there's a small trout farm where you can catch your dinner. Call in advance to be picked up from the bus station.

Chitwan Rest House (☎ 561162, in Kathmandu 01-
266064; kisna107@yahoo.com; r without bathroom Rs 200,
with bathroom Rs 250-500) Located 500m north of
the centre, this is a friendly budget option
with basic rooms set in neat mud cottages
with a small garden and a cheap restaurant.

Chitwan Gaida Lodge (☎ 580083, in Kathmandu 01-
081258; www.gaidalodge.com; r Rs 300-500) Run by one
of Nepal's leading ornithologists, Gaida Lodge
has green leafy surrounds with hammocks to
lounge in. Rooms are large and spotless, with
clean, tiled bathrooms. There's a telescope for
guests' use in the park.

Eden Jungle Resort (☎ 580071, in Kathmandu 01-
700481; www.edenresort.com.np; r Rs 400) In a secluded
part of town, this relaxed place has a shady
garden with a well-maintained lawn. Rooms

in its cottages offer far better value than those
in the modern pink building.

Chitwan Riverside Resort (☎ 580297, in Kathmandu
01-4112107; www.chitwanriverside.com; r Rs 500) Here it's
all about the idyllic riverside location away
from Sauraha. There's a choice between lovely
cottages without views or rooms in the newer
building with excellent river views. The shady
thatched hut on the river bank is a magnificent
spot to sit back during sunset and, if you're
lucky, you'll spot some thirsty wildlife.

Chitwan Tiger Camp (☎ 580060, in Kathmandu
01-2110299; www.chitwantigercamp.com; r Rs 500-800) A
popular choice, Tiger Camp has welcom-
ing staff and experienced jungle guides.
Downstairs rooms are fairly standard, while
rooms upstairs are much more attractive with

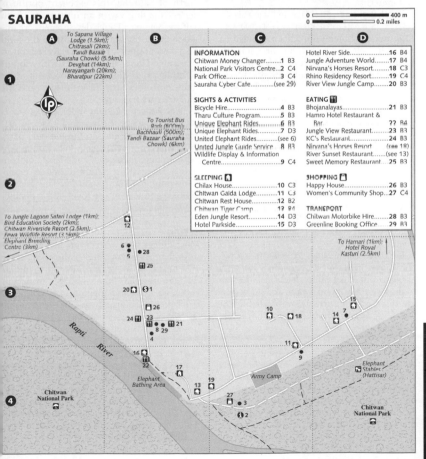

SAURAHA

0 — 400 m
0 — 0.2 miles

INFORMATION
Chitwan Money Changer........1 B3
National Park Visitors Centre..2 C4
Park Office.............................3 C4
Sauraha Cyber Cafe............(see 29)

SIGHTS & ACTIVITIES
Bicycle Hire...........................4 B3
Tharu Culture Program..........5 B3
Unique Elephant Rides...........6 B3
Unique Elephant Rides...........7 D3
United Elephant Rides.........(see 6)
United Jungle Guide Service...8 B3
Wildlife Display & Information
Centre...............................9 C4

SLEEPING
Chilax House.......................10 C3
Chitwan Gaida Lodge...........11 C3
Chitwan Rest House.............12 B2
Chitwan Tiger Camp............13 B4
Eden Jungle Resort..............14 D3
Hotel Parkside.....................15 D3

Hotel River Side...................16 B4
Jungle Adventure World........17 B4
Nirvana's Horses Resort........18 C3
Rhino Residency Resort........19 C4
River View Jungle Camp........20 B3

EATING
Bhojanalayas.......................21 B3
Hamro Hotel Restaurant &
Bar..................................22 B4
Jungle View Restaurant........23 B3
KC's Restaurant...................24 B3
Nirvana's Horses Resort.....(see 18)
River Sunset Restaurant.....(see 13)
Sweet Memory Restaurant....25 B3

SHOPPING
Happy House.......................26 B3
Women's Community Shop...27 C4

TRANSPORT
Chitwan Motorbike Hire........28 B3
Greenline Booking Office.......29 B3

To Sapana Village
Lodge (1.5km);
Chitrasali (2km);
Tandi Bazaar
(Sauraha Chowk) (5.5km);
Devghat (14km);
Narayangarh (20km);
Bharatpur (22km)

To Tourist Bus
Park (600m);
Bachhauli (500m);
Tandi Bazaar (Sauraha
Chowk) (6km)

To Jungle Lagoon Safari Lodge (1km);
Bird Education Society (2km);
Chitwan Riverside Resort (2.5km);
Fewa Wildlife Resort (3.5km);
Elephant Breeding
Centre (3km)

Rapti River

Chitwan
National Park

Elephant
Bathing Area

Army Camp

To Harnari (1km);
Hotel Royal
Kasturi (2.5km)

Elephant
Stables
(Hattisar)

Chitwan
National Park

THE TERAI & MAHABHARAT RANGE

a bamboo design and worth the extra rupee. Reservations are recommended.

Hotel River Side (☎ 580009; www.wildlifechitwan .com; r Rs 500-1500) Take your choice between delightful thatched huts or the less atmospheric modern rooms with a balcony delivering unbeatable river views. The cheapest rooms on the bottom floor are unremarkable but decent. There's a riverside restaurant, helpful staff and a garden full of hammocks.

Nirvana's Horses Resort (☎ 580453; www.nirvana horsesresort.com; r Rs 650) Under French/Spanish/ Nepali management, this place is a must for horse lovers. Brightly painted stables are home to healthy looking thoroughbreds, while the rooms for humans are fantastically decorated with Buddhist and Tharu wall hangings and lanterns.

Hotel Parkside (☎ 580159, in Kathmandu 01-4232953; www.hotelparkside.com; r Rs 600-1000; 🔀) This modern hotel is not what most visitors expect in a place like Chitwan, though it gets a big thumbs up for comfortable, spacious rooms with plenty of natural light. It features some beautiful artwork in the hallways and an impressive giant mural on its outside wall. Its location, well removed from the tourist trap area of Sauraha, is appealing for many too.

our pick Jungle Adventure World (☎ 580301, 9845043542; sharad2029@yahoo.com; r Rs 700) This attractive lodge has a Tibetan Buddhist theme, and is adorned with prayer flags, wall hangings and flags draped over each door. The bungalows are inviting with lanterns on each private porch, and it has a shady garden that makes for a great place to escape the heat.

River View Jungle Camp (☎ 580096; rvjcsauraha@ hotmail.com; cottages US$10) Its pink brick cottages are set along a long garden leading all the way to the river. The mood is calm and the rooms are tidy and comfortable, with reliable hot water. It's a good central choice with friendly staff and expert guides.

Midrange

Jungle Lagoon Safari Lodge (☎ 580126, in Kathmandu 01-4258427; www.lagoon.com.np; r Rs 1000) On the road to the elephant breeding centre, Jungle Lagoon has a lovely spot on the river bank. Priding itself as a 'birdwatching paradise', there are plenty of exotic birds to spot on the river as well as feeding on the lodge's fruit trees – some of which are home to fruit bats.

Rooms are spacious and clean with carpet like Astroturf. 'Sunset point' is a wonderful spot to sit by the lake, though its chairs are in serious need of maintenance.

Fewa Wildlife Resort (☎ 580150, in Kathmandu 01-4263185; www.fewawliferesort.com; s/d US$20/25 s/d with air-con US$30/35; 🔀) Tucked right on the border of the community forest, this is the closest place you'll get to the park without being inside. Popular with package tourists, rooms are fairly standard but its gardens make for a great place to read a book to the accompaniment of chirping birds. There's also a rickety wildlife watchtower and plans for a swimming pool.

Sapana Village Lodge (☎ 580308; www.sapanalodge .com; s/d/tr incl breakfast US$20/28/35) Situated 1.5km north of Sauraha, this excellent option is perfect for those with an interest in Tharu culture. Set up by Dutch development organisations with the aim of supporting the local Tharu community, rooms are decked out in charming Tharu-style designs with vibrant paintings, rugs and wicker stools. Its smart restaurant does tasty Tharu dishes, and the staff are very friendly.

Rhino Residency Resort (☎ 580095, in Kathmandu 01-420431; www.rhino-residency.com; r US$40; 🔀 🖳) Right by the entrance to the national park, this elegant resort's styling falls somewhere between English Regency and Malay Colonial. It has an inviting nature-designed swimming pool, bar and restaurant. The displays of snakes in jars in the foyer add a distinct national park feel.

Eating

Most lodges have restaurants and there are several independent places in the main bazaar at Sauraha. All serve cocktails and a familiar menu of travellers fare. Most open from 6am and close at around 10pm to 11pm.

Jungle View Restaurant (mains Rs 85-310) Probably the best of the terrace restaurants, Jungle View has all your traveller favourites, as well as a beer garden and views looking over the main strip.

Sweet Memory Restaurant (mains Rs 90-200) An attractive family-run shack restaurant with plenty of flowers and pot plants, Sweet Memory prides itself on its home-style cooking. The roast chicken is recommended, and it also serves up good filtered coffee.

our pick KC's Restaurant (mains Rs 215-315) The most popular choice in Sauraha, KC's is set in a Spanish-style hacienda with an open terrace and a fire pit at the back. The chefs here cook up a feast and the menu runs from Nepali and Indian curries to pizzas and pasta.

There's another cluster of laid-back traveller restaurants on the sandy banks of the river that are most popular during elephant bathtime and Sauraha's famous sunset. **River Sunset Restaurant** (meals Rs 95-450, BBQ Rs 450-1350) is the most popular of these and does a mouth-watering evening barbecue of duck, pork, chicken and buffalo over an open fire. **Hamro Hotel Restaurant & Bar** (mains Rs 90-350) makes for a delightful spot to breakfast on the banks of the Rapti.

In a town where menus are almost identical, an excellent alternative is the tastefully decorated **Nirvana's Horses Resort** (☎ 580453; crepes Rs 95, mains Rs 250-375) featuring a dazzling menu of French, Spanish and Tharu cuisine.

For real bargain-basement meals, there are a few rustic bhojanalayas in the bazaar.

Shopping

Souvenir shops in Sauraha sell the usual range of Tibetan, Kashmiri and Nepali arts and crafts. Local specialities include tiger pugmark ashtrays and wood carvings of elephants and rhinos, including dubious mating scenes. For something a bit more upmarket head to **Happy House** (☎ 580026; ☼ 7am-9pm) near the Jungle View Restaurant. This small, family-run business produces its own honey (in various delectable varieties) and sells gorgeous Mithila paintings produced by women's craft cooperatives near Janakpur.

The small **women's community shop** (☼ 7am-5pm), opposite the visitors centre, sells souvenirs with all proceeds going to developing local women's community groups.

Getting There & Away

AIR

When there is sufficient tourist demand, Yeti Airlines has flights from Kathmandu to the tiny runway at Meghauli for US$106 (30 minutes), but you'll need to make advance arrangements with your lodge for a pick-up as there is not much going on in Meghauli. If you're bound for Sauraha, it's better to fly into Bharatpur near Narayangarh and take a taxi (Rs 700). Both Buddha and Yeti Air offer daily flights to Bharatpur from Kathmandu (US$86, 30 minutes). Travel agents and hotels can make bookings.

BUS

By far the easiest way to reach Chitwan is by tourist bus from Kathmandu (Rs 400 to Rs 450, five to seven hours) or Pokhara (Rs 400 to Rs 450, five to seven hours). Buses leave from the tourist bus stand in Pokhara and the Thamel end of Kantipath in Kathmandu at around 7am. The final stop is Bachhauli tourist bus park, a 15 minute walk from Sauraha. Jeeps, and the dreaded hotel touts, await to transfer new arrivals to hotels for Rs 50. There's no obligation to commit to staying at any particular resort, regardless of what the touts say. In the opposite direction, buses leave Bachhauli at 9.30am. Any hotel or travel agent can make bookings.

A more comfortable option is the daily air-con bus operated by **Greenline** (☎ 560126; www .greenline.com.np), which runs to Kathmandu or Pokhara for US$15 including brunch. From Kathmandu or Pokhara it leaves at 7.30am; from Bachhauli, it leaves at 9.30am.

You can pick up public buses at Tandi Bazaar (also known as Sauraha Chowk) on the Mahendra Hwy, about 6km north of Sauraha, or less frequently at Chitrasali, 2km north of Sauraha. Destinations include Kathmandu, Pokhara and Bhairawa/Sunauli (Rs 300, five to six hours), which all depart at 9.30am, as well as other destinations in the Terai. For the airport in Bharatpur you can get a bus from Tandi Bazaar to Narayangarh (Rs 30).

CAR

Travel agents and upmarket lodges can arrange transfers to Chitwan by private car. The going rate for a car and driver is around US$100 and the journey from Pokhara or Kathmandu takes about five hours. Cars usually drop guests off at the turn-offs to the resorts; you must complete the journey by lodge 4WD or elephant!

RAFT

A more interesting way to arrive at Chitwan is by river raft. Most of the big Kathmandu rafting operators offer trips down the Trisuli and Narayani Rivers, culminating at the national park, usually as part of a package tour. The rafting experience is more of a leisurely drift – but there are some fine views and the sandy beaches along the riverside offer great camping spots.

Mugling is the main embarkation point on the Prithvi Hwy, about halfway between

THE TERAI & MAHABHARAT RANGE

Kathmandu and Pokhara. It takes two or three days to raft down to Chitwan. Most people combine rafting with a safari package in the national park – expect to pay around US$80 per person for the rafting section of the trip. Most rafting companies (see p100) can make arrangements.

Getting Around

BICYCLE & MOTORCYCLE

Several shops in Sauraha rent out bicycles for exploring the surrounding villages; the going rate is Rs 170 per day. **Chitwan Motorbike Hire** (☎ 580208) rents out motorbikes (half/whole day Rs 300/600).

JEEP

From Sauraha, shared jeeps to Chitrasali cost Rs 50. A reserve jeep will cost Rs 300 to Chitrasali, Rs 400 to Tandi Bazaar and Rs 700 to the airport at Bharatpur. You can pick up a public bus at Chitrasali or Tandi Bazaar.

PONY CART

You can get a pony cart from Tandi Bazaar to Sauraha for Rs 50.

RICKSHAW

A rickshaw from Tandi Bazaar to Sauraha will cost around Rs 70, but allow 40 minutes for the journey.

SUNAULI & BHAIRAWA
☎ 071

Sunauli is easily the most popular tourist border crossing between Nepal and India, seeing people on their way south to Varanasi or Delhi, or northwards to Lumbini, Pokhara or Kathmandu. Typical of many border towns, it's a dusty hell hole that you won't want to hang around for any length of time. Most people just get their passports stamped and continue on their way. If you do choose to spend a night here there are several decent hotels along the unattractive strip, but it makes much more sense to escape its gridlock of honking trucks and stay in the more relaxed town of Bhairawa 4km north. Better yet, head to Lumbini a further hour's journey by bus.

If you've got time to kill in Bhairawa, you can visit the **Mosaic Art Workshop** (☎ 9847038877; nepalchild_btw@wlink.com.np; ⏰ 10am-3.30pm Mon-Fri) which trains deaf Nepali people and girls rescued from circuses in India in mosaics and other crafts.

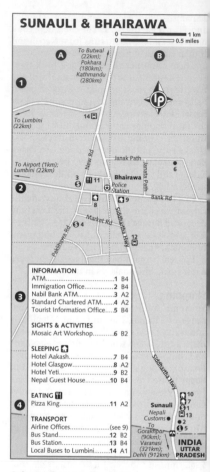

SUNAULI & BHAIRAWA

INFORMATION	
ATM	1 B4
Immigration Office	2 B4
Nabil Bank ATM	3 A2
Standard Chartered ATM	4 A2
Tourist Information Office	5 B4

SIGHTS & ACTIVITIES	
Mosaic Art Workshop	6 B2

SLEEPING 🏠	
Hotel Aakash	7 B4
Hotel Glasgow	8 A2
Hotel Yeti	9 B2
Nepal Guest House	10 B4

EATING 🍴	
Pizza King	11 A2

TRANSPORT	
Airline Offices	(see 9)
Bus Stand	12 B2
Bus Station	13 B4
Local Buses to Lumbini	14 A1

Orientation & Information

Most people refer to both sides of the border as Sunauli, though officially the Nepali border town is called Belahiya. Buses run directly from the border to most major towns in Nepal so, unless you plan to stay overnight, there's no need to go into Bhairawa. To further confuse things, Bhairawa is also known as Siddharthanagar but you can get away with Bhairawa for the town and Sunauli for the border.

The government of Nepal runs a small **tourist information office** (☎ 520304; ⏰ 10am-5pm Sun-Fri) on the Nepal side of the border. Bhairawa has several banks but it's usually easier to change money at the border. The ATM in Sunauli accepts only credit cards, while Nabil Bank and Standard Chartered Bank in Bhairawa both have ATMs that accept foreign cards. There are several net cafes around the junction of Bank Rd and New Rd in Bhairawa, charging Rs 25 per hour. Net cafes in Sunauli are slower and more expensive.

Sleeping
SUNAULI
Nepal Guest House (☎ 520876; 4-bed dm Rs 50, r Rs 160) Travellers on a tight budget need look no further. Rooms here are pretty basic but good for the money, and there's also a decent restaurant.

Hotel Aakash (☎ 524371; s/d Rs 600/700, s/d with air-con Rs 1200/1400; ❄) Rather posh for this locale, this business-class hotel has huge comfortable rooms with TV. It's popular with Indian travellers and has an excellent restaurant.

BHAIRAWA
Hotel Glasgow (☎ 523737; hotelglasgow@gmail.com; Bank Rd; s/d Rs 700/900, s/d with air-con Rs 1200/1500; ❄) The best place in town, Hotel Glasgow has comfy, spacious rooms, piping-hot showers, attentive staff and an excellent restaurant.

Hotel Yeti (☎ 520551; hotelyeti@ntc.com; cnr Bank Rd & Siddhartha Hwy; s/d US$30/35, s/d with air con US$35/45; ❄) This is the preferred choice of upmarket tour groups and it's very modern and comfortable. All rooms have TVs, phones and reliably hot showers.

Eating
All the hotels have restaurants serving the usual range of Nepali, Indian and continental dishes. In Sunauli there are a few small restaurants near the bus station.

The best option in town is **Pizza King** (mains Rs 70-135), a garden oasis of low tables, cushions and atmospheric lighting. The food is cheap, and the spring rolls and garlic chicken are recommended.

Getting There & Away
AIR
Both **Buddha Air** (☎ 526893) and **Yeti Airlines** (☎ 527527) offer flights between Kathmandu and Bhairawa (US$114, 40 minutes). Bhairawa airport is about 1km west of town, easily accessible by rickshaw. Most airline offices are around the junction of Bank Rd and the Siddhartha Hwy.

BUS
Buses for Kathmandu and Pokhara leave regularly from both Sunauli and Bhairawa. For other destinations, you're best off going to Bhairawa. Be suspicious of travel agents in India or Nepal who claim to offer 'through tickets' between the two countries: everyone has to change buses at the border. For more on this see p384.

There are regular day and night buses to Pokhara (day/night Rs 450, seven to nine hours) and Kathmandu (Rs 425, eight hours) via Narayangarh (Rs 230, three hours). There are also buses to Pokhara via Tansen (Rs 115, five hours). Minivans to Pokhara/Kathmandu cost Rs 445/475.

A slightly more comfortable option is the daily **Golden Travels** (☎ 520194) air-con bus to

---

CROSSING THE BORDER

Border Hours
The immigration office on the Nepali side of the border is open 24 hours, but the Indian border post is only staffed from 6am to 10pm. After 7pm and before 7am, you may need to go searching for the immigration officials on either side.

Foreign Exchange
Several moneychangers on the Nepali side of the border exchange Nepali and Indian rupees, as well as cash and travellers cheques in US dollars, UK pounds and euros. Shops and hotels on both sides of the border accept Indian and Nepali rupees at a fixed rate of 1.6 Nepali rupees to one Indian rupee.

Onward to India
All travellers bound for India must change buses at the border. From the bus station on the Indian side of the border, there are direct morning buses to Varanasi (with/without air-con INRs 215/172, 10 hours). There are also buses to Gorakhpur (INRs 56, three hours) where you can connect with the Indian broad-gauge railway.

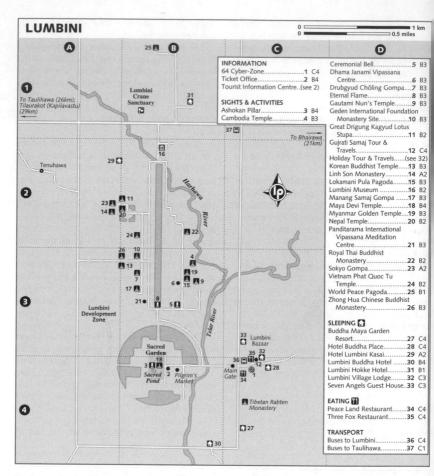

LUMBINI

0	1 km
0	0.5 miles

INFORMATION
64 Cyber-Zone....................1 C4
Ticket Office........................2 B4
Tourist Information Centre..(see 2)

SIGHTS & ACTIVITIES
Ashokan Pillar.......................3 B4
Cambodia Temple..................4 B3

Ceremonial Bell....................5 B3
Dhama Janami Vipassana
  Centre................................6 B3
Drubgyud Chöling Gompa....7 B3
Eternal Flame.......................8 B3
Gautami Nun's Temple.........9 B3
Geden International Foundation
  Monastery Site..................10 B3
Great Drigung Kagyud Lotus
  Stupa................................11 B2
Gujrati Samaj Tour &
  Travels..............................12 C4
Holiday Tour & Travels......(see 32)
Korean Buddhist Temple......13 B3
Linh Son Monastery............14 A2
Lokamani Pula Pagoda.........15 B3
Lumbini Museum..................16 B2
Manang Samaj Gompa.........17 B3
Maya Devi Temple...............18 B4
Myanmar Golden Temple......19 B3
Nepal Temple......................20 B2
Panditarama International
  Vipassana Meditation
  Centre..............................21 B3
Royal Thai Buddhist
  Monastery..........................22 B2
Sokyo Gompa......................23 A2
Vietnam Phat Quoc Tu
  Temple..............................24 B2
World Peace Pagoda............25 B1
Zhong Hua Chinese Buddhist
  Monastery..........................26 B3

SLEEPING
Buddha Maya Garden
  Resort...............................27 C4
Hotel Buddha Place..............28 C4
Hotel Lumbini Kasai.............29 A2
Lumbini Buddha Hotel 30 B4
Lumbini Hokke Hotel............31 B1
Lumbini Village Lodge..........32 C3
Seven Angels Guest House....33 C3

EATING
Peace Land Restaurant.........34 C4
Three Fox Restaurant...........35 C4

TRANSPORT
Buses to Lumbini..................36 C4
Buses to Taulihawa...............37 C1

Kathmandu (US$14, six to seven hours); it leaves Kathmandu at 6.30am and Sunauli at 7am.

From the bus stand in Bhairawa, buses leave every 15 minutes to Butwal (Rs 35, 45 minutes) where you can change for Nepalganj (Rs 415, seven hours) as well as other destinations in the western Terai region. Heading east, there are buses to Janakpur leaving at 6.10am and 4.30pm (day/night Rs 475/595, eight hours) and to Kakarbhitta (day/night Rs 826/961, 12 hours). Buses heading for Gorkha (Rs 300, six hours) leave early in the morning: it's best to ask locally for the current departure times.

Local buses for Lumbini (Rs 40, one hour) and Taulihawa (Rs 65, three hours) leave

from the junction of the Siddhartha Hwy and the road to Lumbini, about 1km north of Bank Rd.

Getting Around
Regular jeeps and local buses shuttle between the border and Bhairawa for Rs 10. A rickshaw will cost Rs 40.

LUMBINI
☎ 071

It was here in Lumbini, in the year 563 BC, that one of history's greatest and most revered figures, Siddhartha Gautama, better known as the Buddha, was born. It's no great surprise then to learn that the World Heritage–listed Lumbini is of huge religious significance and attracts Buddhist pilgrims from around the world.

The spiritual heart of Lumbini is Maya Devi Temple, which marks the exact spot where the Buddha was given birth to under a Bodhi tree. In the adjoining sacred garden you'll find a sea of maroon- and saffron-robed monks congregating under a sprawling Bodhi tree decorated with prayer flags paying homage to the Lord Buddha. Maya Devi is set in the middle of the large 4km by 2.5km park grounds, known as the Lumbini Development Zone. Designed by Japanese architect Kenzo Tange in 1978, it's a work in progress that steadily follows the design of the 'master plan' as donations trickle in. It comprises landscaped lakes and monasteries that have been constructed by Buddhist communities from around the world, with a vision for the sacred garden to be entirely surrounded by water and only navigable by boat.

Located 26km west of Sunauli, most people rush through Lumbini only allowing a few hours. The trick to appreciating Lumbini is to spend a night here, so you can take in its peaceful atmosphere early in the morning or late afternoon. Outside the Development Zone, the calm feel of a Buddhist sanctum quickly vanishes into a cloud of dust at Lumbini Bazaar, a typical small rural Terai town.

History

After years of work at Lumbini, archaeologists are now fairly certain that Siddhartha Gautama, the historical Buddha, was indeed born here in 563 BC. A huge complex of monasteries and stupas were erected on the site by his followers, and the Indian emperor Ashoka made a pilgrimage here in 249 BC, erecting one of his famous pillars.

Shortly after this, an unknown cataclysm affected Lumbini. When the Chinese pilgrim Fa Hsien (Fa Xian) visited in AD 403, he found the monasteries abandoned and the city of Kapilavastu in ruins. Two hundred years later Hsuan Tang (Xuan Zang), another Chinese pilgrim, described 1000 derelict monasteries and Ashoka's pillar shattered by lightning and lying on the ground. However, the site was not entirely forgotten. The Nepali king Ripu Malla made a pilgrimage here in 1312, possibly leaving the nativity statue that is still worshipped in the Maya Devi Temple.

Mughal invaders arrived in the region at the end of the 14th century and destroyed the remaining 'pagan' monuments at both Kapilavastu and Lumbini. The whole region then returned to wilderness and the sites were lost to humanity, until the governor of Palpa, Khadga Shumsher Rana, began the excavation of Ashoka's pillar in late 1896.

Lumbini is now creating a new archaeology for itself in the Lumbini Development Zone – if explorers rediscover the site in a thousand years, they'll find the ruins of dozens of vast 21st-century monasteries, reflecting Buddhist cultures from across the globe.

Information

There's a small **tourist information centre** (6am-6pm) at the ticket office that displays the master plan of the complex. For moneychangers, the upmarket hotels along the eastern perimeter of the grounds are the best bet. **64 Cyber-Zone** (per hr Rs 60; 8am-8pm) in Lumbini Bazaar has slowish internet connection.

Sights

MAYA DEVI TEMPLE

The **Maya Devi Temple** (foreigner/SAARC Rs 50/10, camera Rs 70; 6am-6pm) sits on the exact site of the birth of the Buddha, according to Buddhist scholars. It's reputed that it was here where the heavily pregnant Maya Devi came upon a pond of extraordinary beauty amid the thick jungle, and gave birth to Siddhartha Gautama under the auspicious Bodhi tree.

Excavations carried out in 1992 have revealed a succession of ruins on the site dating back at least 2200 years, including a commemorative stone on a brick plinth, matching the description of a stone laid down by Emperor Ashoka in the 3rd century BC. There are plans to raise a grand monument on the site but, for now, the ruins are protected by a plain brick pavilion.

If you remove your shoes, you can walk around the ruins on a raised boardwalk. The focal point for pilgrims is a famous sandstone carving of the birth of the Buddha, reputedly left here by the Malla king, Ripu Malla, in the 14th century, when Maya Devi was worshipped as an incarnation of the Hindu mother goddess. The carving has been worn almost flat by centuries of veneration, but you can just discern the shape of Maya Devi grasping a sal branch and giving birth to the Buddha, with Indra and Brahma looking on. Directly beneath this is

THE BIRTH OF THE BUDDHA

The historical Buddha, Siddhartha Gautama, was the son of Suddhodana, ruler of Kapilavastu, and Maya Devi, a princess from the neighbouring kingdom of Devdaha. According to legend, the pregnant Maya Devi was travelling between the two states when she came upon a tranquil pond surrounded by flowering sal trees. After bathing in the cool water, she suddenly went into labour, and just had enough time to walk 25 steps and grab the branch of a tree for support before the baby was born. The year was 563 BC and the location has been positively identified as Lumbini.

After the birth, a seer predicted that the boy would become a great teacher or a great king. Eager to ensure the later, King Suddhodana shielded him from all knowledge of the world outside the palace. At the age of 29, Siddhartha left the city for the first time and came face to face with an old man, a sick man, a hermit and a corpse. Shocked by this sudden exposure to human suffering, the prince abandoned his luxurious life to become a mendicant holy man, fasting and meditating on the nature of existence. After some severe austerities, the former prince realised that life as a starving pauper was no more conducive to wisdom than life as a pampered prince. Thus was born the Middle Way.

Finally, after 49 days meditating under a Bodhi tree on the site of modern-day Bodhgaya in India, Siddhartha attained enlightenment – a fundamental grasp of the nature of human existence. He travelled to Sarnath, near Varanasi, to preach his first sermon and Buddhism was born. Renamed Buddha ('the enlightened one'), Siddhartha spent the next 46 years teaching the 'Middle Way' – a path of moderation and self-knowledge through which human beings could escape the cycle of birth and rebirth and achieve nirvana, a state of eternal bliss.

The Buddha died at the age of 80 at Kushinagar, near Gorakhpur in India. Despite the Buddha's rejection of divinity and materialism, all the sites associated with his life have become centres for pilgrimage and the Buddha is worshipped as a deity across the Buddhist world. The ruins of Kapilavastu were unearthed close to Lumbini at Tilaurakot (see p300), and devotees still cross continents to visit Bodhgaya, Sarnath and Kushinagar in India. More recently, the site of Devdaha, the home of Maya Devi, was identified on the outskirts of the Nepali town of Butwal.

a markerstone encased within bulletproof glass, which pinpoints the exact spot where the Buddha was born.

The **sacred pond** beside the temple is believed to be where Maya Devi bathed before giving birth to the Buddha. Dotted around the grounds are the ruined foundations of a number of brick stupas and monasteries dating from the 2nd century BC to the 9th century AD.

ASHOKAN PILLAR

The Indian emperor Ashoka visited Lumbini in 249 BC, leaving behind an inscribed sandstone pillar to commemorate the occasion. After being lost for centuries, Ashoka's pillar was rediscovered by the governor of Palpa, Khadga Shumsher Rana, in 1896. The 6m-high pink sandstone pillar has now been returned to its original site in front of the Maya Devi Temple – the pillar isn't much to look at, but it is highly revered by Nepali Buddhists.

BUDDHIST MONASTERIES

Since the Lumbini Development Zone was founded in 1978, Buddhist nations from around the world have constructed extravagant monasteries around the birthplace of the Buddha. Separated by a long canal, the monastic zone is divided into Mahayana and Theravada sects. Each reflects the unique interpretation of Buddhism of its home nation and together the monasteries create a fascinating map of world Buddhist philosophy.

The site is *extremely* spread out, so hire a bicycle in Lumbini Bazaar or rent one of the waiting rickshaws at the entrance to the archaeological zone. Unless otherwise stated, all the monasteries are open daily during daylight hours.

West Monastic Zone

The West Monastic Zone is set aside for monasteries from the Mahayana school, which is distinguished by monks in maroon robes and a more clamorous style of prayer involving blowing horns and clashing cymbals. Starting at the **Eternal Flame** (just north of the Maya Devi Temple), follow the dirt road along the west bank of the pond to the **Panditarama International Vipassana Meditation Centre** (☎ 580118; www.panditarama-lumbini.info), where serious practitioners of meditation can study for a nominal donation.

Heading north, a track turns west to the **Drubgyud Chöling Gompa**, a classic Tibetan-style gompa built in 2001 by Buddhists from Singapore and Nepal. The mural work inside is quite refined and a gigantic stupa is under construction next door. A small track veers south to the tasteful **Manang Samaj Gompa**, a giant chörten (Tibetan reliquary stupa) constructed by Buddhists from Manang in northern Nepal.

Further west is the elegant **Zhong Hua Chinese Buddhist Monastery**, one of the most impressive structures at Lumbini. Reached through a gateway flanked by Confucian deities, this elegant pagoda-style monastery looks like something from the Forbidden City. Not to be outdone, the government of South Korea is building a huge **Korean Buddhist Temple** on the other side of the road.

Just north of the Chinese temple is the charming **Vietnam Phat Quoc Tu Temple**, due to be completed in 2010. The pagoda-style monastery is beautifully landscaped and the dragon-tiled roof is delightful. Nearby is a new complex of stupas and monastery buildings being constructed by the Austrian **Geden International Foundation**. New monasteries are also planned by the governments of Mongolia and Bhutan.

Further north is a second group of Mahayana monasteries, set around an L-shaped pond. The truly extravagant **Great Drigung Kagyud Lotus Stupa** (8am-noon & 1-5pm) is one of the most beautiful temples here and was constructed by the German Tara Foundation. The domed ceiling of the main prayer room is covered in some inspired Buddhist murals.

Across from the German monastery is a domed-roof **Nepal temple** that was still being constructed at the time of research.

Behind the German monastery is the **Sokyo Gompa**, a traditional Tibetan-style gompa built by the Japanese Sokyo Foundation. The new **Linh Son Monastery** is being constructed by French Buddhists next door.

East Monastic Zone

The East Monastic Zone is set aside for monasteries from the Theravada school, common throughout Southeast Asia and Sri Lanka and recognisable by their saffron-coloured robes.

Close to the north end of the pond, the stunning **Royal Thai Buddhist Monastery** (8am-noon & 1-5pm) is an imposing *wat* (Thai-style monastery) built from gleaming white marble that gives it the appearance of having been carved from ivory.

A short cycle ride south is the **Myanmar Golden Temple**, one of the oldest structures in the compound. There are three prayer halls here – the most impressive is topped by a corncob-shaped shikhara (tower), styled after the temples of Bagan. Nearby is the **Lokamani Pula Pagoda**, a huge gilded stupa in the southern Burmese style, inspired by the Shwedagon Paya in Yangon. Further north is a Cambodian temple scheduled for completion in 2011.

Behind the stupa is the modest **Gautami Nun's Temple**, the only monastery in the compound built for female devotees. Across the road is the small **Dhama Janami Vipassana Centre**, where followers of the Theravada school can practice meditation.

Further south, a track leads down to the new **Sri Lankan Monastery** that's very slowly being built. A short walk south from here takes you back to the Eternal Flame, passing a huge **ceremonial bell** inscribed with Tibetan characters.

LUMBINI MUSEUM

Tucked away at the back of the compound at the north end of the pond, this **museum** (☎ 580318; foreigner/SAARC Rs 50/10; 10am-4pm Wed-Mon) is devoted to the life of the Buddha, with artefacts and photos from Buddhist sites around the world, from Kathmandu to Kandy. The building is an interesting contemporary design, with a series of brick cylindrical blocks fitted with large round windows.

WORLD PEACE PAGODA & LUMBINI CRANE SANCTUARY

Outside the main compound, but easily accessible by bike, the impressive gleaming white **World Peace Pagoda** (daylight) was constructed by Japanese Buddhists at a cost of US$1 million. The shining golden statue depicts the Buddha in the posture he assumed when he was born. Near the base of the stupa is the grave of a Japanese monk murdered by anti-Buddhist extremists during the construction of the monument.

The surrounding wetlands are protected as part of the **Lumbini Crane Sanctuary** and you stand a good chance of seeing rare sarus cranes stalking through the water meadows. There's no formal entrance to the sanctuary and no admission fee – just stroll into the damp meadows behind the pagoda. Otherwise, the Vietnam Phat Quoc Tu Temple has resident sarus cranes that feed in its grounds.

AROUND LUMBINI
Tilaurakot

About 29km west of Lumbini, Tilaurakot has been identified as the historical site of **Kapilavastu**, where Siddhartha Gautama spent the first 29 years of his life. The site sits in a peaceful meadow, about 3km from Taulihawa. Although you can still see the foundations of a large residential compound, it takes a certain amount of imagination to visualise the city of extravagant luxury that drove the Buddha to question the nature of existence. The surrounding farmland looks much the same today as it did in the time of Siddhartha Gautama. It isn't hard to imagine Siddhartha walking out through the imposing city gateway for the first time and seeing an old man, a sick man, a hermit and a corpse.

There's a small **museum** (☎ 076-560128; admission Rs 50; ☼ 10am-4pm Wed-Mon) that displays some of the artefacts found at the site.

To get here from Lumbini catch a local bus from the Lumbini Bus Stand to the junction (Rs 5, 10 minutes) and change to a bus bound for Tilaurakot (Rs 50, 1½ hours), 3km north of Taulihawa. You can take a rickshaw to the site from Tilaurakot for Rs 100/175 one way/ return. Otherwise a taxi can make the return trip from Lumbini for around Rs 1600.

The best way to get here is through Lumbini Village Lodge (see right), which can organise a van for Rs 500 with a day's notice.

Tours

Hiring a guide to explain the various sights within the Development Zone is a good way to learn about the Buddhist sites in Lumbini. Otherwise most travel agents rent out bicycles for Rs 100 per day.

Holiday Tour & Travels (☎ 580432), attached to Lumbini Village Lodge, arranges interesting

tours that really get under the surface of life in the Terai. Guides are available for Rs 500 per day, or you can get a map (Rs 20) and make your own way by bike. Next door, **Gujrati Samaj Tour & Travels** (☎ 580210) has knowledgeable guides for the Development Zone, and also offers birdwatching.

Festivals & Events

The most important Buddhist celebration at Lumbini is the annual **Buddha Jayanti** festival in April or May, when busloads of Buddhists from India and Nepal come here to celebrate the birth of the Buddha. Pilgrims also come here to worship each **purnima** (the night of the full moon) and **astami** (the eighth night after the full moon).

Many Hindus regard the Buddha as an incarnation of Vishnu and thousands of Hindu pilgrims come here on the full moon of the Nepali month of Baisakh (April–May) to worship Maya Devi as **Rupa Devi**, the mother goddess of Lumbini.

Sleeping
BUDGET

Most of the budget options are in Lumbini Bazaar, the small village opposite the entrance to the Lumbini Development Zone.

ourpick **Lumbini Village Lodge** (☎ 580432; lumbini villagelodge@yahoo.com; dm Rs 100, s Rs 250-450, d Rs 350-750) This inviting lodge has a central courtyard shaded by a mango tree and big, clean rooms with fans and window nets. There's a peaceful rooftop setting and views looking over mustard fields.

Hotel Buddha Place (☎ 9847135543; r Rs 400-500) The walls may be in desperate need of fresh paint, but the rooms are otherwise pleasant and the bathrooms spotless.

Seven Angels Guest House (☎ 580338; tenzeesherpa@ yahoo.com; r Rs 800-1000) On the main road, this peaceful guest house has bright, sunny rooms looking out to mustard fields. There's an excellent gallery next door run by the same owner, with fantastic traditional and modern paintings for sale.

MIDRANGE & TOP END

Most of the upmarket hotels are on the main road around the eastern side of the Development Zone. Unless otherwise stated, rooms at all the following hotels have all mod cons.

Lumbini Buddha Hotel (☎ 580114; ibuddha@mos .com.np; r US$6-15; ☒) In a small area of woodland at the south end of the Development Zone, this calm, institutional hotel is a bit removed from everything, and it's overpriced, but the rooms in safari-style buildings are decent enough.

Buddha Maya Garden Hotel (☎ 580220, in Kathmandu 01-4700800; www.ktmgh.com/buddha; s/d from US$60/70; 🗶) Set in large grounds about 500m southeast of the site, this upmarket resort offers very comfortable rooms in calm surroundings. There's a good restaurant too. Ask about discounts.

Lumbini Hokke Hotel (☎ 580136; www.theroyal residency.net/lumbini/index.htm; s/d/tr US$100/120/140; 🗶) Built with real style, the Hokke looks a bit like a traditional Japanese village; rooms are Western-style or Japanese-style, with tatami floors, paper partitions and Japanese furniture. The restaurant serves top-notch Japanese set meals.

At the time of research the midrange Lumbini Hotel Kasai was being built, which makes it the only lodging within the Development Zone.

Eating

Peace Land Restaurant (mains Rs 60-220) Popular with locals, this lime-green restaurant has tasty chicken chow mein, curries and cold beer.

our pick **Three Fox Restaurant** (mains Rs 110-200) This upstairs restaurant is beautifully decorated with colourful Buddhist curtains and paintings on the wall. There's a range of Tibetan, Indian and Western food, and outdoor seating looking over the bazaar.

Getting There & Away

Local buses run regularly between Lumbini and the local bus stand in Bhairawa (Rs 40, one hour). The road to Lumbini is lined with traditional farms and tall mango trees – a perfect setting for a bit of roof riding.

To reach Taulihawa from Lumbini, take a local bus to the junction with the Bhairawa road (Rs 5) and change to a bus bound for Taulihawa (Rs 110, 1½ hours).

If you need to be in Bhairawa in a hurry, taxis in Lumbini Bazaar charge Rs 800 to the main Bhairawa bus stand and Rs 900 to the border at Belahiya (Sunauli).

Getting Around

The best way to get around the compound is by bicycle – Lumbini Village Lodge in Lumbini Bazaar charges Rs 100 per day for fairly reliable Chinese Hero-brand bikes.

Hiring a rickshaw is a good alternative. Loads of rickshaw-wallahs loiter near the entrance to the Development Zone, charging around Rs 150 per hour.

THE SIDDHARTHA HIGHWAY

The often dramatic Siddhartha Hwy winds through a series of landslide-scarred valleys between Butwal and Pokhara with spectacular Himalayan views. Buses run fairly regularly on this route, and it is also regarded as one of the finest and most scenic motorcycle journeys in Nepal. The road is often blocked by landslides and floods during the monsoon.

Butwal

☎ 071

Flat, dry and dusty, Butwal has all the hallmarks of your typical Terai town. Its wide streets are dominated by a cacophony of bell-ringing rickshaws and an atmosphere of bustling activity. An important trade and transport hub, Butwal offers no sights of interest for visitors, and hence most people choose to pass right through. However, if you're one for chaotic cities and getting off the beaten track, it's worth spending a night here.

If you've got time in Butwal you can follow the Siddhartha Hwy north into the spooky-looking Tinau Gorge, where you'll come to a series of dramatic **waterfalls**, accessible by a mini-suspension bridge. There are also some pleasant walks east of Hospital Chowk in the forested hills surrounding Butwal.

Archaeologists have recently identified a village 15km east of Butwal as the site of the kingdom of **Devdaha**, home to the mother of Siddhartha Gautama (the Buddha). Only limited excavations have been carried out so far but there's a small memorial park on the site, signposted off the Mahendra Hwy towards Narayangarh.

The region is also known as the site where fossils of the humanoid *Ramapithecus* were discovered; the humanoid inhabited the region more than 10 million years ago.

INFORMATION

Numerous internet centres on the main road near Traffic Chowk offer cheap internet access for Rs 15 per hour. There's an ATM on Traffic Chowk, opposite Hotel Royal, that takes international cards.

SLEEPING & EATING

Hotel Kandara (☎ 540175; s Rs 350-1000, d Rs 450-1200; ⊠) Situated on the busy strip, Kandara is a good choice where you can take your pick between simple, comfortable rooms to deluxe rooms with bathtubs and air-con.

Hotel Greenland Restaurant & Bar (☎ 543411; hotelgreenland@hotmail; s/d without air-con US$15/20, s/d with air-con US$25/35; ⊠) Greenland is a quiet, clean and modern hotel well removed from the madness of Traffic Chowk. Ask for a discount. It also has a quality restaurant and bar decorated with retro orange couches.

Nanglo West (☎ 544455; mains Rs 80-260; ⏲ 10.30am-8.30pm) Hidden away in the old town on the west bank of the river, this Kathmandu chain restaurant is by far the best in town, featuring interesting Newari dishes and pleasant outdoor garden seating.

GETTING THERE & AWAY

All long-distance buses leave from the main bus park just south of Traffic Chowk. There are buses every half hour or so to Kathmandu (Rs 415, seven hours) and Pokhara (Rs 400, eight hours) via Mugling and the Prithvi Hwy. There are also several daily buses on the scenic route to Pokhara (Rs 390, six hours) via Tansen (Rs 80, 2½ hours). Local buses leave for Sunauli/Bhairawa (Rs 35, 45 minutes) every 10 minutes.

Along the Mahendra Hwy, there are regular buses to Narayangarh (Rs 150, three

hours), Nepalganj (Rs 430, 12 hours) and Mahendranagar (Rs 790, nine hours).

Tansen (Palpa)
☎ 075 / elev 1372m

Only rarely will you hear a bad word spoken about Tansen. Instead you'll hear how rewarding it is to experience a Nepali town not geared up for tourists and the refreshing lack of hassle that comes with this. Wandering about in Tansen's fresh climate along its steep cobblestone streets, the only 'namaste' you'll get here is from friendly locals who aren't intent on trying to sell you something. On winter mornings a sheet of mist is cast over the valley, earning it the moniker 'White Lake'.

Located 119km south of Pokhara, Tansen's main attraction is both its Newari charm and distinct medieval feel. Wooden Newari houses with intricately carved windows are found throughout the centre of town, from where the clacking of looms can be heard within. Chatting to locals you'll find they're fiercely proud of their hometown, which no doubt stems from its rich history during the glory years as the capital of the Magar kingdom of Tanahun. Until the rise of the Shahs, Tanahun was one of the most powerful kingdoms in Nepal. Troops from Palpa even came close to conquering Kathmandu in the 16th century under the leadership of King Mukunda Sen. The power of the Magars waned in the 18th century and Tansen was reinvented as a Newari trading post on the trade route between India and Tibet.

Today, Tansen remains the administrative headquarters of Palpa district, and many Nepalis still refer to the town as Palpa.

ORIENTATION

Tansen is veritable maze of narrow alleys, but getting lost is part of the pleasure. The main road snakes around the western edge of town, but most places of interest are tucked away on the cobbled streets of the old town. The most important landmark is the octagonal pavilion in the middle of Sitalpati, the main market square. The main shopping street is Bank Rd (Makhan Tole), running south from Sitalpati; the bus station is at the bottom of town about 500m south of the centre on the main road.

MISTHAN BHANDARS

An unlikely blend of sweet shop and vegetarian restaurant, misthan bhandars offer the full range of Indian sweetmeats, from *gulab jamun* (dough balls in sweet syrup) to *barfi* (milk and nut fudge) and *halwa* (soft fruit slices). Alongside these sweet treats, you'll find the spicy vegetarian flavours of South Indian cuisine – *dosas* (lentil-flour pancakes), *idly* (steamed rice cakes) and *vadai* (gram-flour doughnuts), all served with coconut chutney and *sambar* (a spicy dipping sauce with cinnamon and tamarind). If you travel for any length of time in the Terai, you'll find yourself visiting misthan bhandars quite regularly for a break from the daal bhaat, chow mein and chilli chicken.

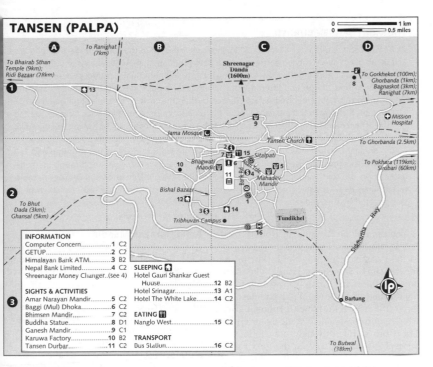

TANSEN (PALPA)

INFORMATION

The first port of call should be **GETUP** (Group for Environmental & Tourism Upgrading Palpa; ☎ 520563, 9847028885; www.tansenpalpa.net/getup_palpa/index.htm; ⏰ 2-5pm Sun-Fri), one of the most helpful tourist information centres in the country. Led by the irrepressible Man Mohan, this NGO was set up by enterprising locals passionate about promoting Tansen as a tourist destination. They sell excellent trekking maps (Rs 20) for short treks around Tansen, including the classic loop to Ranighat – see right and the boxed text, p305, for more information.

Staff can also arrange homestay accommodation and guided trips to metalworking centres, fabric workshops and organic coffee plantations, which Tansen is renowned for.

A good online resource for more information on Tansen can be found at www.tansenpalpa.net.

Himalayan Bank has an ATM that accepts foreign cards. For foreign exchange the best option is **Shreenagar Money Changer** (⏰ 7.30am-6pm), and for travellers cheques go to **Nepal Bank Limited** (⏰ 10am-3pm Sun-Fri), both on Bank Rd just east of Sitalpati. Hotel Srinagar can change travellers cheques, dollars and euros.

There are several internet cafes; **Computer Concern** (per hr Rs 25; ⏰ 7am-8pm) has a reliable connection.

SIGHTS
Ranighat Durbar

The most famous sight near Tansen is the eerie ruins of the grand Ranighat Durbar on the east bank of the Kali Gandaki. Fancifully referred to as Nepal's Taj Mahal, this crumbling baroque palace was built in 1896 by Khadga Shamsher Rana in memory of his beloved wife, Tej Kumari. Khadga was an ambitious politician who was exiled from Kathmandu for plotting against the prime minister, which he followed up with another abortive attempt to seize power in 1921 and was exiled again, this time to India. After his departure, the Durbar was stripped of most of its valuable fittings, but the building still stands, slowly fading on the banks of the Kali Gandaki. It's worth bringing your swimmers for a dip in the river.

THE NIGHT TANSEN BURNED

At 10.45pm on the night of 31 January 2006, locals were woken to the sound of machine gun fire and bomb blasts as a terrifying battle unfolded between more than 4000 Maoists and the Nepali security forces. Continuing through to dawn, when the fighting finally ended, people emerged cautiously to find the ground littered with bullet shells, bloodstains, 30 dead bodies and the smouldering ruins of its beloved palace, Tansen Durbar, the town's most beautiful building.

At the time of research the palace was in the process of being rebuilt, brick by brick, by the Ministry of Peace and Reconstruction, a project which is ironically overseen by a Maoist ex-guerrilla. Due for completion in 2010, the Rs 50 million project has been set aside to house a museum.

The original building was built for the provincial governor in 1927. A fan of pomp and circumstance, the governor used to ride out to greet his subjects on an elephant through the huge gateway on the south side of Sitalpati (known locally as Baggi Dhoka or Mul Dhoka). In more recent times its 64 rooms served as the district administrative buildings, which explains why it was targeted by the Maoists.

You can walk to Ranighat in around three hours (return trip seven hours) along an easy-to-follow trail, beginning in Gorkhekot at the east end of Shreenagar Danda. The route down to the river is mainly downhill, passing through some peaceful rice paddies and forest from which the majestic ruined palace with a grand colonnaded facade materialises. The return leg is fairly tough going, following a steeply ascending trail on the next ridge, emerging near Hotel Srinagar. It's not possible to walk here during monsoon season due to the slippery conditions. There's some basic accommodation in Ranighat if you choose to stay the night.

GETUP sells an excellent route guide and map (Rs 10). Rafting trips on the Kali Gandaki sometimes make it as far as the palace – see p108.

Sitalpati

The main market square in Tansen is dominated by a curious octagonal pavilion, used for public functions in the days when Tansen was ruled by the governors of the Shah regime. Today it's a popular meeting spot for locals to have a chat. At the northwest corner of the square, the small, two-tiered **Bhimsen Mandir** is sacred to the Newari god of trade and commerce. Several shops on the square, and along nearby Bank Rd, sell dhaka, the fabric used for traditional Nepali jackets and *topis* (cloth hats). **Karuwa Factory** (admission free) can make for an interesting visit to see the brass jugs that Tansen is famous for being made.

Amar Narayan Mandir

At the bottom of Asan Tole (the steep road running east from Sitalpati), the Amar Narayan Mandir is a classic three-tiered, pagoda-style wooden temple. The mandir was built in 1807 by Amar Singh Thapa, the first governor of Tansen, and it's considered to be one of the most beautiful temples outside the Kathmandu Valley. The carved wooden deities are quite exquisite; note the erotic scenes on the roof struts and the alternating skulls and animal heads on the lintel. Devotees come here every evening to light butter lamps in honour of the patron deity, Lord Vishnu.

SLEEPING & EATING

Hotel Gauri Shankar Guest House (☎ 520150; s/d without bathroom Rs 250/350, s with bathroom Rs 350-550, d with bathroom Rs 400-600) Not a bad option with spacious rooms, TV and Western toilets. Go for rooms on the 2nd level away from the noisy street. To get here take the stairs down from Hotel Gautam Siddhartha.

Hotel The White Lake (☎ 520291; s/d without bathroom Rs 300/450, s/d with bathroom US$12/15, deluxe s/d US$15/20) The second-best hotel in town, its deluxe rooms are comfortable but overpriced, and the cheaper rooms are run-of-the-mill.

Hotel Srinagar (☎ 520045; www.hotelsrinagar.com; s/d with bathroom US$24/32; 🞕) The most luxurious option, about 2km away on the ridge above town, a 20-minute walk west of the summit of Shreenagar Danda. Although rather isolated, rooms are sumptuous, and the views are sensational. There's a good restaurant staffed by its charismatic waiter, Rambo, who's a good source on everything Tansen.

GETUP (p303) can also arrange homestay accommodation in Tansen or in the surrounding villages from Rs 250.

You can't go without sampling the Nepali delights at **Nanglo West** (☎ 520184; mains Rs 80-260; ☺ 10.30am-8.30pm). This Kathmandu chain is a class act, serving local Newari dishes like *choyla* (dried buffalo or duck meat with chilli and ginger), served with *chura* (flattened rice) and spiced potatoes in curd. There's also a decent bakery out front.

GETTING THERE & AWAY

The bus station is at the bottom of town at the southern entrance to Tansen and the ticket office is at the east end of the stand. Buses to Pokhara (Rs 280, five hours) leave at 6am and 10am; there are also buses to Kathmandu (Rs 475 to Rs 500, 10 to 12 hours).

There are regular services south to Butwal (Rs 80, 2½ hours) from 6.30am to 5pm. Local buses for Ridi Bazaar (Rs 80, two hours) leave fairly regularly during the same hours – get an early morning start if you want to be back the same day.

Around Tansen

As well as the popular walks around Tansen (see the boxed text, below), there are a few interesting villages that you can reach on foot or by bus.

RIDI BAZAAR

About 28km northwest of Tansen by road (or 13km on foot), the Newari village of Ridi Bazaar sits at the sacred confluence of the Kali Gandaki and Ridi Khola Rivers. Ridi is a popular destination for pilgrimages, and the site is further sanctified by the presence of saligrams – the spiral fossils of ancient sea creatures, distantly related to the modern nautilus – revered as symbols of Vishnu.

The principal religious monument in Ridi is the **Rishikesh Mandir**, which was founded by Mukunda Sen in the 16th century. According to legend, the Vishnu idol inside was discovered fully formed in the river and has miraculously aged from boy to man. The temple is on the south bank of the Ridi Khola, near the bus stand.

To reach Ridi on foot, take the trail leading northwest from the Tansen–Tamghas road near Hotel Srinagar. Buses to Ridi (Rs 80, two hours) leave from the public bus stand in Tansen.

WALKS AROUND TANSEN

Tansen is set in the middle of fantastic walking country and the tourist office GETUP (p303) can recommend some excellent walks in the surrounding hills.

One of the nicest short walks is the one-hour stroll up **Shreenagar Danda**, the 1600m-high hill directly north of town. The trail starts near the small **Ganesh Mandir** (temple) above Tansen and climbs steeply through open woodland to the crest of the hill. When you reach the ridge, turn right; a 20-minute stroll will take you to a modern **Buddha statue** and a viewpoint with fabulous views over the gorge of the Kali Gandaki River and the Himalaya.

Another short and easy walk is the two-hour stroll to the **Bhairab Sthan Temple**, 9km west of Tansen. The courtyard in front of the temple contains a gigantic brass trident and inside is a silver mask of Bhairab, allegedly plundered from Kathmandu by Mukunda Sen. The walk follows the road from Tansen to Ridi Bazaar.

If you fancy something more challenging, the three-hour walk to the village of **Ghansal** passes several hilltop viewpoints, emerging on the highway about 3km south of Tansen. The walk is mainly downhill and there are spectacular valley views from Bhut Dada, about halfway along the route. GETUP sells a map (Rs 20) with a detailed description of the trail.

Other possible destinations for walks include **Ghorbanda**, a small village northeast of Tansen on the way to Pokhara, and **Bagnaskot**, on the ridge east of Gorkhekot, which has a small Devi temple and a wonderfully exposed hilltop viewpoint. You can also follow the old **trade route** from Tansen to Butwal – GETUP has a map (Rs 10) with a detailed description of the trail. All three walks can be completed in a day if you get an early start, or there's simple lodging along the way if you're not in a hurry.

THE TRIBHUVAN HIGHWAY

From Birganj, the easiest and fastest route to Kathmandu or Pokhara is along the Mahendra Hwy to Narayangarh and then north to Mugling, but when were the best travel experiences ever easy? It's much more fun to take the winding and dramatic Tribhuvan Hwy, which leaves the Mahendra Hwy at Hetauda, just east of Chitwan. The road is sometimes blocked by floodwaters and landslides after the monsoon, but the scenery is breathtaking and you can stop on the way at Daman for some of the best Himalayan views in Nepal. For details of the mountain bike ride along this route see p97.

Hetauda

☎ 057

The bustling town of Hetauda marks the junction between the flat Mahendra Hwy and the steep, spectacular Tribhuvan Hwy. There isn't any great reason to stop here except to change buses.

Nabil Bank has an ATM, and there are several internet cafes on the main road offering internet access for Rs 25 per hour.

The best place to stay is **Motel Avocado & Orchid Resort** (☎ 520429; www.orchidresort.com; Tribhuvan Hwy; Nissan hut s/d Rs 400/600, hotel s/d from Rs 800/1000, deluxe s/d from Rs 1500/2000; 🔀), a quirky resort set in a peaceful garden of rhododendron and avocado trees, which are ripe August to January.

GETTING THERE & AROUND

The main bus stand is just west of Mahendra Chowk. There are regular morning and afternoon buses to Pokhara (Rs 400/500, six hours) and Kathmandu (day/night Rs 400/500, six hours) via Narayangarh (Rs 150, one hour). You can also pick up services to destinations east and west along the Mahendra Hwy. Local buses and minibuses run regularly to Birganj (Rs 100, two hours).

Buses along the Tribhuvan Hwy leave from a smaller bus stand, just north of Motel Avocado. There are buses every hour or so to Kathmandu (Rs 400, eight hours) via Daman (Rs 250, four hours) until around 2pm. Rickshaws and autorickshaws can ferry you from town to the bus stand for Rs 30.

Daman

☎ 057

Perched 2322m above sea level, with clear views to the north, east and west, Daman boasts what is arguably *the* most spectacular outlook on the Himalaya in the whole of Nepal. There are unimpeded views of the entire range from Dhaulagiri to Mt Everest from the concrete **viewing tower** (adult Rs 20) inside the Daman Mountain Resort. The **Mountain Botanical Gardens** (⏱ 10am-5pm) spans over 193 acres of forest full of interesting plant species. February to March is the best time to visit, when the rhododendrons (the national flower of Nepal) are in full bloom, providing a stunning scenery with the Himalaya backdrop.

About 1km south of the village, a trail leads west through the forest to the tiny **Shree Rikheshwar Mahadev Mandir**, sacred to Shiva. On the way, you can drop into a gorgeous little **gompa** in a glade of trees draped with thousands of prayer flags.

SLEEPING & EATING

There are three rustic guest houses in the middle of the village owned by local families that have simple rooms (single/double Rs 200/400) and daal bhaat for Rs 60.

Hotel Sherpa Hillside & Lodge (☎ 690057; s/d/tr Rs 100/200/300) Located opposite the botanical gardens, this run-down country house is the best budget choice. It's a rickety old wooden structure that sits secluded from the rest of the town, and while it's a tad spooky, that's also very much part of its appeal.

Daman Mountain Resort (☎ 9845070514; cottage tents without bathroom s/d Rs 520/900, s/d with bathroom Rs 750/1550) This ageing resort at the start of the village is a more comfortable option. It's not the Savoy, but rooms are clean and cosy, and the viewing tower has the best views in Daman. The tents with thatched roofs are best avoided in winter.

WALKS AROUND DAMAN

The Palung Valley is a fascinating base for walks and mountain biking trips. Most towns in the area have basic lodges and bhojanalayas (snack restaurants). Just equip yourself with a decent topographical map and go exploring. Probably the best starting point for walks is **Shikharkot**, about 10km north of Daman. There are several rustic lodges on the main road and buses between Kathmandu and Daman pass through several times a day.

ourpick **Everest Panorama Resort** (☎ 621480, in Kathmandu 01-4428500; s/d US$80/100; ❄) Easily the most charming place to stay in Daman, this upmarket mountain resort offers tasteful cottages with sun decks scattered across a sunny hillside facing the Himalaya. All the rooms have heaters, TVs, hot showers and mountain views. Reception is a 200m walk from the highway along a winding boardwalk.

GETTING THERE & AWAY

There are two daily buses to Kathmandu (Rs 150, four hours) leaving at 10.30am and 11.30am, and there are also buses to Hetauda (Rs 250, four hours). Alternatively, this is one of the most spectacular (and gruelling) mountain-bike routes in Nepal (see p97 for details).

WESTERN TERAI

The Mahendra Hwy runs west from Butwal to meet the Indian border at Mahendranagar, passing through one of the least developed parts of Nepal. Few travellers pass through the area and fewer still stop to investigate its little-visited national parks.

NEPALGANJ

☎ 081

With the exception of its glowing red sunsets, attractive is the last word you'd use to describe Nepalganj. Rather, it's a gritty border town with a hectic Indian flavour. As the unofficial capital of western Nepal, Nepalganj is an important transport hub that sees visitors waiting around for flights to Kathmandu or Jumla, stopping over en route to Bardia National Park and, less frequently, coming to/from Lucknow in India. With its oppressive heat and lack of shade, many see it as a necessary evil to get elsewhere, though it has a spirited character and is a good place to gauge a perspective of life in the Terai. It's also culturally rich, and you'll hear more Hindi spoken than Nepali; it's also home to Nepal's largest Muslim community, as well as having a sizeable expat community of foreign-aid workers.

If you find yourself spending time in Nepalganj, take a stroll through the old **bazaar**. You'll find some attractive silver Tharu

jewellery and shop windows crammed with smuggled goods. There are half a dozen small temples strung out along the main road through the bazaar, with the garish **Bageshwari Mandir**, devoted to Kali, probably the most interesting.

Orientation & Information

Nepalganj is 16km south of the Mahendra Hwy and 6km north of the Indian border. It's about 1km from the Nepali border post at Jamunaha to the Indian border post at Rupaidha Bazaar – walkable, but easier by rickshaw.

Nabil Bank (⌚ 10am-4.30pm Sun-Thu, 10am-2.30pm Fri) has both foreign-exchange services and a 24-hour ATM.

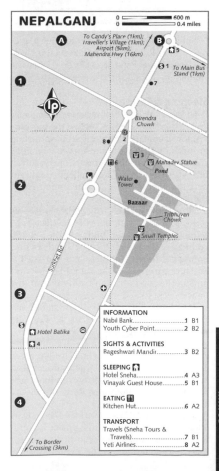

INFORMATION	
Nabil Bank	1 B1
Youth Cyber Point	2 B2
SIGHTS & ACTIVITIES	
Bageshwari Mandir	3 B2
SLEEPING	
Hotel Sneha	4 A3
Vinayak Guest House	5 B1
EATING	
Kitchen Hut	6 A2
TRANSPORT	
Travels (Sneha Tours & Travels)	7 B1
Yeti Airlines	8 A2

THE TERAI & MAHABHARAT RANGE

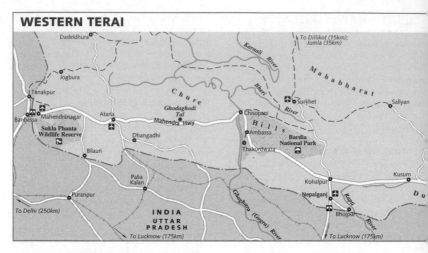

Subject to power cuts, a couple of places on Surkhet Rd offer internet access, including **Youth Cyber Point** (per hr Rs 25; ☯ 8am-6pm Sun-Fri).

Sleeping & Eating

Hotel Sneha (☎ 520119; hotel@sneha.wlink.com.np; dm Rs 200, s/d with air-con US$30/37; ☒) This big old-fashioned conference hotel is set in sprawling grounds on the way to the border. The huge rooms are set around a grassy courtyard full of royal palms. It has an excellent restaurant here too. If booked out, try the similar Hotel Batika up the road.

Vinayak Guest House (☎ 522138; s Rs 200-450, d Rs 250-550, s/d with air-con Rs 900/1000; ☒) Vinayak caters to all budgets; the Rs 450 rooms are the best choice, being clean and comfortable with homely armchairs, TV and nice bathrooms. The obtrusive air-coolants in the corridors don't add much to the charm.

Traveller's Village (☎ 550329; travil@wlink .com.np; r incl breakfast Rs 700-1550; ☒ ▯) The choice of hotel for UN and NGO workers, Traveller's Village is run by a welcoming American lady (Candy) who's lived here for 16 years. Its rooms are large, modern and spotless, and the bathrooms even have fans for the steaming-hot water. Reservations are essential.

Kitchen Hut (☎ 524349; mains Rs 50-170; ☯ 10am-9.30pm) This bright and bustling place is popular with young students who flock here for tasty and cheap food. The menu runs the gamut from *dosas* (fried lentil-flour pancakes) and momos (dumplings) to pizza.

Candy's Place (☎ 550329; mains Rs 75-375) Located upstairs at Traveller's Village, Candy's Place is like an oasis in Nepalganj. If you've OD'd on daal bhaat, Candy serves up juicy cheese-and-bacon burgers or medium-rare tenderloin steak washed down with Australian red wine. Homemade lemon meringue pie or butterscotch ice cream are served for dessert.

Getting There & Away

AIR

Nepalganj is the main air hub for western Nepal. There are daily flights to Kathmandu through **Yeti Airlines** (☎ 526556) and **Buddha Air** (☎ 525745). Sita Air has morning flights to Jumla (45 minutes) for US$89, though delays and cancellations are common due to poor weather. Yeti Airlines also offers occasional flights to Dolpo for US$114. Nepal Airlines has flights to Simikot (US$105) on Tuesday and Thursday.

If the airline offices are closed, try **Sneha Tours & Travels** (☎ 522507) on the main road.

BUS

The well-organised bus stand is about 1km northeast of Birendra Chowk. Buses to Kathmandu (Rs 857, 12 hours) and Pokhara (Rs 825, 12 hours) leave early in the morning or early in the afternoon; all buses run via Narayanghat (Rs 650, 10 hours). Buses for Mahendranagar (Rs 360, five hours) leave

hourly from 5.30am until 1pm. Buses to Butwal (Rs 430, seven hours) leave hourly.

Local buses to Thakurdwara (for Bardia National Park) leave at 11.20am and 1.30pm (Rs 200, three hours).

Getting Around

Shared tempos (three wheelers) and *tongas* (horse carriages) run between the bus stand and the border for Rs 15. A cycle-rickshaw costs Rs 80 to the airport and Rs 80 all the way to Rupaidha Bazaar in India. A taxi to the airport costs Rs 400.

BARDIA NATIONAL PARK
☎ 084

Situated between Butwal and Mahendranagar, Bardia National Park is often described as what Chitwan was like 30 years ago, before being overrun by mass tourism. Bardia is the largest and most pristine national park in the Terai and has excellent wildlife-watching opportunities. It's known as one of the best places in the world to spot a tiger – though you'll still need exceptionally good luck to see one. There are also healthy populations of wild elephants and one-horned rhinos among the 30 species of mammals living in Bardia's 1550 sq km of sal forest and rippling grassland.

If there's one place in Nepal that's been most affected by the tourist slump during the Maoist insurgency, Bardia is surely it. Located in a hotbed of Maoist activity, the past decade has deprived it of many visitors. Furthermore, it's been hit hard by poaching due to inadequate protection in the park, with its tiger population halved in the past 10 years. The good news is that things are finally back to normal and, while it's a long, arduous journey out here, it's well worth the effort.

Orientation & Information

Park fees should be paid at the **park headquarters** (☎ 429/19; permits foreigner/SAARC/child under 10 Rs 500/200/free; ☼ sunrise-sunset Sun-Fri) located about 13km south of the Mahendra Hwy in the village of Thakurdwara. The bumpy access road leaves the highway at Ambassa, about 500m before the Amreni army checkpost.

The park headquarters has a small **visitor information centre** (admission free; ☼ 10am-4pm Sun-Fri), which features informative displays of wildlife in Bardia. The best source of information is through your lodge.

Most of the safari lodges are close to Thakurdwara but, because of the poor condition of the roads, visitors usually arrange to be transferred to the lodges by 4WD. Note

---

CROSSING THE BORDER

Border Hours

Both sides of the border are open from 5am to 10pm, but you may be able to cross later if you can find the immigration officials. The immigration office is about 1km from the border.

Foreign Exchange

There are several moneychangers on the Nepali side of the border, but they only exchange Indian and Nepali rupees. The Nabil Bank in Nepalganj may be able to exchange other currencies.

Onward to India

For Rs 80 you can take a rickshaw from the Nepalganj bus stand to the border at Jamunaha and on to the bus stand in Rupaidha Bazaar. From here, buses and share taxis run regularly to Lucknow (seven hours). The nearest point on the Indian rail network is Nanpara, 17km from the border.

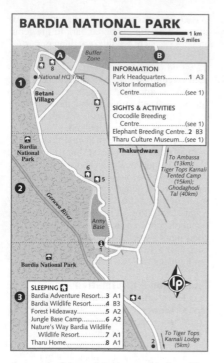

BARDIA NATIONAL PARK

0 ————————— 1 km
0 ————————— 0.5 miles

INFORMATION
Park Headquarters............1 A3
Visitor Information
   Centre........................(see 1)

SIGHTS & ACTIVITIES
Crocodile Breeding
   Centre........................(see 1)
Elephant Breeding Centre..2 B3
Tharu Culture Museum...(see 1)

SLEEPING
Bardia Adventure Resort...3 A1
Bardia Wildlife Resort........4 B3
Forest Hideaway.................5 A2
Jungle Base Camp.............6 A2
Nature's Way Bardia Wildlife
   Wildlife Resort................7 A1
Tharu Home....................8 A1

To Ambassa
(13km);
Tiger Tops Karnali
Tented Camp
(15km);
Ghodaghodi
Tal (40km)

To Tiger Tops
Karnali Lodge
(5km)

that much of the park is inaccessible from May to September because of flooding.

Money exchange and slow internet access are available at Forest Hideaway.

Animals

There are estimated to be around 100 royal Bengal tigers, 75 wild elephants and, according to the March 2008 count, 22 one-horned rhinos at Bardia, but these animals are elusive and sightings are rare. Other mammals in the park include grey langurs, rhesus macaques, leopards, civets, hyenas, sloth bears and barking, spotted, sambar and hog deer. Bardia also has more than 250 species of birds, including the endangered Bengal florican and sarus crane. Gharial and marsh mugger crocodiles and Gangetic dolphins are occasionally spotted on rafting and canoe trips along the Geruwa River.

Sights & Activities

Most people visit Bardia on an **elephant safari**, which is best done early in the morning or late afternoon. Rides on the park elephants (foreigner/SAARC Rs 1000/400) should be

booked in advance at the park headquarters. Jeep safaris can be arranged directly through the lodges (half/whole day Rs 2500/3500 per person).

The best way to spot wildlife in the park, and certainly the most thrilling, is on a **guided walk** (half/whole day Rs 350/600). Venturing into the park on foot with your guide, however, is obviously a risk you take into your own hands (see p289).

Raft trips (per person Rs 2500) along the Geruwa River in inflatable rafts are a relaxing way of seeing the park, as well as giving you a good chance of spotting animals along the river bank. Stopping for lunch, you'll get to walk around the sandy bank where you'll observe the heavy traffic of animal footprints; crater marks of elephants and rhinos are crisscrossed with perfectly imprinted tiger pug marks, the scraping claws of sloth bears and delicate monkey prints. Even if you don't see the big animals, this provides perfect proof of just how much wildlife there is in Bardia.

In the park headquarters there's a rather grim **breeding centre** for turtles, and marsh mugger and gharial crocodiles. Around the grounds you'll likely spot Shivaram, the **resident rhino**, wandering about. Injured as a baby in Chitwan, and blind in one eye, it's important you keep a safe distance: while he's semi-domesticated he still has potential to be dangerous, as the locals will tell you.

Also located here is the intriguing **Tharu Cultural Museum** (adult Rs 50; ☺ noon-3pm Sun-Fri), which explores the customs and rituals of the Tharu people. You can also arrange cultural tours of the villages through most hotels, otherwise rent a bike and explore by yourself.

The **elephant breeding centre** (adult Rs 50; ☺ 10am-4pm) south of the park headquarters is worth a visit in the afternoon for feeding time when the elephants have returned from grazing in the park.

The Karnali River is also famous for *mahaseer,* the giant South Asian river carp, which can reach 80kg in weight. Anglers can obtain **fishing permits** (foreigner/SAARC Rs 500/200) at the park headquarters. Due to their endangered status, any fish you catch will need to be released back into the water.

The picturesque **Ghodaghodi Tal** is known for its fabulous birdwatching. Located 40km from Bardia, the scene is straight out of an Impressionist painting, with its lotus flowers, water lilies and soft pastel colours and is home to 142 different species of bird including the grey-headed fishing eagle. You can organise a jeep and guide for Rs 5000, or catch a bus (Rs 600).

Sleeping & Eating

Hotels are located in close vicinity of each other on the border of the buffer zone. The only eating option is the hotels, which each have their own restaurants.

Bardia Wildlife Resort (☎ 692083; bardia_tiger@ yahoo.com.au; s without bathroom Rs 150, r with bathroom Rs 300-500) Located south of park headquarters, its peaceful spot along the river bank gives it a true national park feel. The cottages have large rooms with hot-water showers (using a bucket of water), and there's a campfire and lovely garden with flowers and papaya trees.

Jungle Base Camp (☎ 690487; junglehukum@gmail .com; s Rs 200, d Rs 500-700) The delightful Jungle Base Camp has rustic mudbrick huts with lantern lighting that exude an exotic jungle charm. Rooms are cheap, clean and feature a private verandah with hammock, and carved designs of animals on their mud walls.

Bardia Adventure Resort (☎ 429721, in Kathmandu 01-4413361; www.bardia-adventure.com; s/d without bathroom Rs 300/400, r with bathroom Rs 600) With its prime location looking out to the buffer zone, this resort has simple thatched mud huts and a large rustic dining hall. The highlight here is the resort's own animal watchtower, where you can enjoy a cold beer while keeping your eyes peeled for a leopard lurking on the park's perimeters.

our pick **Forest Hideaway** (☎ 620237, in Kathmandu 01-4225973; www.foresthideaway.com; r without bathroom Rs 300-400, r with bathroom Rs 600-800; ▣) About 1km north of the park headquarters, this cosy Tharu-style resort is one of the best choices at Bardia. The grass-roofed cottages have solar power and are set around a pleasant garden, some of which look onto villager's fields. It has expert guides and friendly, welcoming staff.

Tharu Home (☎ 429722; tharuhome@ntc.net.np; r Rs 300-500) With a roaring campfire and youthful owners who've been working as guides since they were 11, this is the most social place in town. The Rs 500 rooms are rather regal looking with their quaint curtains, bed covers and thick rugs.

Nature's Way Bardia Wildlife Resort (☎ 690682; r Rs 350) Though at the time of research this new lodge was very much a work in progress, its rooms are cheap and there's a real focus on growing their own produce.

Tiger Tops Karnali Lodge (☎ in Kathmandu 01-4361500; www.tigermountain.com; package per night US$350) Run by the same team as Tiger Tops in Chitwan, this recommended top-end lodge is set on the southern edge of the buffer zone. Accommodation is in stylish Tharu-style cottages near Thakurdwara. Package rates include meals and all activities (park fees and local transfers are extra).

Tiger Tops Karnali Tented Camp (☎ in Kathmandu 01-4361500; www.tigermountain.com; package per night US$350) Sitting on the banks of the Geruwa River, this safari-style tented camp is the only lodging in Bardia within the park. Tents are spacious and have bamboo-fitted en suite bathrooms. It's located in the northwest of the park, not far from Chisopani. It closes during the monsoon season.

Getting There & Away

If you intend to make your own way to the park, call ahead to make sure the resorts are open and arrange a pick-up from Ambassa. The nearest airport is at Nepalganj (see p308).

To reach Bardia by public transport, buses leave Pokhara (Rs 950, 14 hours) at 1pm and Kathmandu (Rs 950, 14 hours) at 1.30pm. There's also a bus from Kathmandu leaving at midday that includes dinner (Rs 1150, 14 hours). There are two buses leaving from Chitwan to Bardia (Rs 575, nine hours) at midnight and 4pm.

Change at Ambassa for buses to Mahendranagar (Rs 300, four hours).

JUMLA
☎ 087 / elev 2730m

Hidden away in the foothills of the Sisne Himalaya, the remote village of Jumla is the gateway to the wild northwest – the least developed and most inaccessible region of Nepal. On arrival you'll get the distinct feeling that life goes on here much as it did 1000 years ago. The lack of motorised traffic, broken slate–paved streets and ramshackle wooden shacks all lend to an outpost feel. It's not an overly pretty town, and unmistakably one of the most desperately poor regions of Nepal, attributed to its isolation, harsh climate and lack of basic health care.

YARSAGUMBA – THE NEW GOLD RUSH

Translating from a Tibetan word meaning 'summer plant, winter insect', Yarsagumba is a fascinating and lucrative species of fungus that undergoes an astounding metamorphosis from insect to plant. Found in western Nepal in subalpine pastures at altitudes higher than 3500m, Yarsagumba grows when the fungus Cordyceps consumes the underground larvae of the Thitarodes caterpillar, resulting in the mushroom growing out from the larvae above the ground. It has numerous medicinal qualities but is most famous for its use as a Himalayan Viagra.

The market price of the fungus is around US$3000 per kilo for the lowest quality to over US$15,000 for the top-notch stuff, and it's estimated that one collector can earn up to Rs 2500 (approximately US$35) a day, which is more than a month's salary in most Nepali households. Hence, every summer villagers from remote areas and from across the border in India come to the region in their thousands to collect Yarsagumba. During the 'Yarsagumba rush' it's not uncommon for schools to close as teachers and students alike take unofficial holidays to go prospecting for Yarsagumba. In doing so they risk their lives, with each year bringing deaths and severe illness due to inadequate lodging and protection from blizzards.

The Thakuri are the most prominent ethnic group in the region. Their weathered faces have immense character and are often ornamented with beautiful silver nose piercings. Apart from the odd foreign-aid worker, the few visitors to Jumla are here for trekking in the remote Karnali region. Most popular is the three- to four-day trek to **Rara National Park** (foreigner/SAARC Rs 1000/100) with its famous sky-blue lake, the largest in Nepal.

Rural Community Development Service (RCDS; ☎ 520227) does some excellent work in improving local living standards as well as promoting tourism. If you arrive without a trekking group, the RCDS will be able to find you a guide and porters. One of the best trekking companies for the region is **3 Sisters Adventure Trekking** (☎ 61-462066; www.3sistersadventure.com) based in Pokhara.

There's also an **NGO souvenir shop** at the chamber of commerce that sells local products such as apple brandy and hand-woven carpets.

Sleeping & Eating

Hotel Snowland (☎ 520188; r without bathroom Rs 500) The best choice in the bazaar, this rustic and rickety wooden lodge is set over three levels. It gets chilly at night so you'll need to rug up, but otherwise its small rooms are perfectly fine. Staff speak little English, but are friendly and welcoming. It's a 15-minute walk from the airport. Look out for the sign in the bazaar directing you down a small side street.

Hotel Kaliash (☎ 520131; r from Rs 500-700) Despite its inconvenient location far removed from the bazaar, Kaliash is the nicest hotel in Jumla. If you plan on staying it's worth calling ahead so they can meet you at the airport.

Getting There & Away

The only realistic way to reach Jumla is by flying. Sita Air offers daily flights between Jumla and Nepalganj (US$89, 45 minutes) – weather permitting.

SUKLA PHANTA WILDLIFE RESERVE

Tucked against the Indian border, **Sukla Phanta Wildlife Reserve** (☎ 099-521309; foreigner/SAARC per day Rs 500/200) covers 305 sq km of sal forest and *phanta* along the banks of the Bahini River. The terrain is similar to Bardia National Park and the reserve has tigers, rhinos, crocodiles, wild elephants and Nepal's largest population of swamp deer (currently numbering around 2000) as well as large numbers of migratory birds. Like other national parks in Nepal, Sukla Phanta has been badly affected by poaching and human encroachment.

Visiting Sukla Phanta has always been difficult, and camping is the only way to stay overnight. The few visitors who make it to the park generally come on day trips from Mahendranagar with a hired car and driver (per jeep Rs 4500). **Elephant rides** (foreigner/SAARC Rs 1000/500) can be booked at the park headquarters, but call ahead to make sure somebody will be around. **Safari Guide Office** (☎ 9748004073; camping 1/2 nights Rs 2500/4500) located at the Mahendranagar border is a good place to arrange camping trips, guides and jungle walks. Otherwise ask for **Eshwar Raj Pant** (☎ 995247303; shuklaphanta@rediff mail.com) near the park headquarters, who can provide service as a guide and is an excellent source of information on the park.

The best time to visit is November to January; the main vehicle track within the park is impassable from June to September because of monsoon flooding.

MAHENDRANAGAR
☎ 099

One of Nepal's more relaxed border crossings, those arriving to Mahendranagar from India will feel an instant sense of relief. While it's not somewhere you'll want to spend any length of time (ie until your bus is ready to depart), its lack of hassle and chaos makes it a delight compared to other border towns. As the most westerly border crossing between Nepal and India, Mahendranagar offers an interesting back route to Delhi and the hill towns of Uttaranchal. If you have time here, Mahendranagar provides an excellent base to visit Sukla Phanta Wildlife Reserve or the surrounding Tharu villages.

Orientation & Information

Mahendranagar is just south of the Mahendra Hwy, about 5km east of the Indian border. From the Nepali border post at Gaddachauki, it's about 1km to the Indian border post at Banbassa – a rickshaw is probably the way to go.

The bus stand is right on the Mahendra Hwy so there's no need to come into the centre unless you plan to stay the night.

The Nepal Tourism Board runs a small **tourist information centre** (☎ 523773; ◷ 9.30am-5pm Sun-Fri) on the Nepal side of the border. If you need to check email, there are several places with fast net access for Rs 25 per hour.

A 15-minute autorickshaw ride (Rs 15) from the border, **Nabil Bank** (☎ 525450; ◷ 10am-5pm Sun-Thu, to 3pm Fri) has a foreign exchange service and an ATM.

Sleeping & Eating

Hotel Sweet Dream (☎ 522313; Mahendra Hwy; s/d from Rs 400/450, s/d with air-con Rs 1000/1200; ✷) On the highway about 100m east of the bus station, this friendly midrange place has comfortable rooms and a decent restaurant. The colour scheme is a bit overpowering but the welcome is warm.

Hotel New Anand (☎ 521693; Line 3; r with/without bathroom Rs 600/800, r with air-con Rs 1200; ✷) The anything but new Anand has a central location with simple rooms with a geyser, TV and a comfy chair to watch it from.

Hotel Opera (☎ 522101; www.hoteloperanepal.com; r Rs 600, deluxe r Rs 800-1200, ste Rs 2500; ✷) The most luxurious hotel in town. Not only are the rooms spacious and immaculate, but its quiet location may be just the thing you need. It also has the best restaurant in town, serving delicious Nepali and Indian dishes as well as 'Macdonalo' burgers!

Getting There & Away

There are no longer flights departing from Mahendranagar airport. The closest airport is at Dhangadhi, 50km east of Mahendranagar, which has three daily Buddha Air flights to Kathmandu (US$182, one hour) and two

---

CROSSING THE BORDER

Border Hours

The Nepali side of the border is open to tourists 24 hours but, before 5am and after 8.30pm, you may need to go searching for the Nepali officials. The Indian side of the border is only open to vehicles from 5am to 6am, noon to 1pm and 5pm to 6pm. In winter (November to January) the Indian side of the border opens later, from 6.30am to 7.30am, with all other hours the same.

Foreign Exchange

There's a small bank counter near the Nepali customs post but it only exchanges Indian and Nepali rupees. In the main town, Nabil Bank has foreign exchange and an ATM. An autorickshaw into town costs around Rs 15.

Onward to India

From the Indian border post, it's an INRs 10 rickshaw ride to the bus station in Banbassa, where you can pick up long-distance buses to Delhi (INRs 184, 10 hours). Local buses and shared jeeps serve Almora, Nainital and other towns in Uttaranchal. There's also a slow metre-gauge train to Bareilly, where you can pick up trains to other destinations in India.

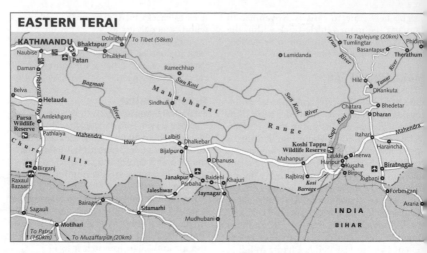

daily to Nepalganj. Buses to Dhangadhi (Rs 80) leave every 30 minutes from the main bus station.

The bus station is about 1km from the centre on the Mahendra Hwy. Long-haul buses leave for Kathmandu (Rs 1010, 15 hours) at 2pm, 3pm, 4pm and 4.30pm. There's also a single Pokhara service (Rs 1015, 16 hours) at 2.25pm. Local buses run every 30 minutes to Nepalganj (Rs 360, five hours), passing the turn-off to Bardia National Park at Ambassa (Rs 300, four hours).

THARU HOMES

The indigenous Tharu people of the western Terai are masters of improvisation. Villagers make almost everything they need using the natural materials around them. Even houses are built up from woven twigs and grass coated in thick layers of river mud. As well as being extremely environmentally friendly, the mud acts as a natural heat shield, keeping the homes surprisingly cool, even in summer. The same technique is used to produce most of the furniture inside, from cupboards and bedsteads to the water cooler and wood-fired kitchen range. However, fresh layers of mud must be applied throughout the year to fill in cracks and replace material washed away by the monsoon rains.

Getting Around

Buses, tempos and *tongas* run regularly between the bus station and the border for Rs 15. From the border into the main town a rickshaw costs around Rs 80.

Taxis can be hired for trips to Sukla Phanta Wildlife Reserve for Rs 4500 per day (plus Rs 500 per additional person).

EASTERN TERAI

Bound by the Indian states of Bihar, Sikkim and West Bengal, the eastern Terai is broadly a mirror image of the west. The rolling hills of the Mahabharat Range are squeezed between the dry eastern plains and the Himalaya. The Mahendra Hwy cuts east to meet the Indian border at Kakarbhitta, providing easy access to Sikkim and Darjeeling.

BIRGANJ
☎ 051
There's very little in the hectic border town of Birganj to suggest you're not in India. As the main transit point for freight between India and Nepal, the town is mobbed by trucks, deafened by car horns and jostled by rickshaws. Most of Nepal's exports leave the country via the hectic border crossing at Raxaul Bazaar.

This crossing is the best for travellers heading to/from Kolkata in India.

If you can get over the heat and noise, there are some interesting buildings dotted

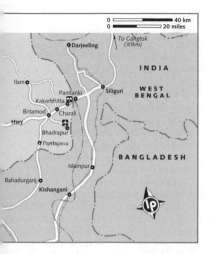

round town. The fanciful **clock tower** to the north of the town centre is covered in Buddhist and Hindu iconography, and just southwest is the popular **Gahawa Maysan Mandir**, sacred to Durga.

Orientation & Information

Birganj follows a simple grid system. Main Rd runs through the middle of town to the Indian border and most of the hotels are on the streets running west. The bus stand is at the end of Ghantaghar Rd (New Rd), which runs east from the clock tower at the north end of town.

Standard Chartered Bank (9.45am-3.30pm Sun-Thu, to 12.30pm Fri) is the best place to change money and travellers cheques, while Machhapuchchhre Bank has an ATM.

Fast internet access is available from **Shree Shyam Cyber Cafe** (per hr Rs 30; 6.30am-8.30pm), around the corner from Hotel Kailas.

Sleeping

There are a number of noisy budget places near the main bus stand, and a handful of more upmarket choices in the centre.

Hotel Welcome Nepal (524057; Ghantaghar Rd; s/d without bathroom Rs 150/250, d with bathroom Rs 350) The most salubrious choice in this area, Hotel Welcome Nepal gets slightly less traffic noise than the places right next to the bus stand.

Hotel Makalu (523054; hmakalu@wlink.com.np; cnr Campus & Main Rds; r with/without air-con Rs 1200/800;) This recommended business-class hotel is very calm and relaxed – just what you need in hectic Birganj. Rooms have TVs, carpets and 24-hour hot showers, and there's a very good restaurant.

Eating

All the hotels have restaurants, or try the following places in the town centre.

Star Hotel (meals Rs 40-75; 9am-3pm & 7-10pm) This simple tandoori canteen serves cheap and tasty *thalis* (Indian plate meals) and tandoori chicken.

Two reliable misthan bhandar (sweet shop and vegetarian restaurant) are **Himanchal Cabin** (Main Rd; mains Rs 35-80; 7am-9pm), close to the clock tower, and **Pooja Sweets** (mains Rs 40-85; 8am-9pm).

Getting There & Away

Yeti Airlines (525389; Campus Rd) and other private carriers fly daily between Simara (the airport for Birganj; a 20-minute drive) and Kathmandu (US$79, 20 minutes).

THE BUDDHA OF BARA

At the start of 2005, nobody had heard of Ram Bahadur Banjan. By the end of the year, thousands of Nepali Buddhists were hailing the long-haired 16-year-old Tamang boy as the second incarnation of the Buddha. Followers of the teenage lama (monk) claim that Banjan has been meditating without food or water in the forest east of Birganj for nearly 10 months. Although that sounds unlikely, the Nepali government asked the Nepal Academy of Science and Technology to investigate the claim and, if necessary, declare a miracle. Before any conclusions could be reached, Banjan mysteriously disappeared. After reappearing on three brief occasions since, in late 2008 he re-emerged from the jungle in Ratanpuri 150km southeast of Kathmandu to worldwide media attention. Devotees came in their hundreds to see him, with many suspecting he had attained enlightenment in Bodhgaya, just like the historical Buddha did in 592 BC. It's unlikely to be the end of the story; you can check www.paldendorje.com for the latest updates.

BIRGANJ

0 — 500 m
0 — 0.3 miles

To Kathmandu (185km)

Ghantaghar (New) Rd

To Hotel Welcome Nepal (250m); Bus Stand (300m)

Tank

Ghariarwa Pokhari

Bal Mandir

Market

ATM

Adarshnagar

Main Rd

Shiv Temple

Campus Rd

To Indian Border (4km); Patna (210km)

INFORMATION
Machhapuchhhre Bank ATM.1 B2
Shree Shyam Cyber Cafe......2 B2
Standard Chartered Bank......3 A2

SIGHTS & ACTIVITIES
Clock Tower......................4 B1
Gahawa Maysan Mandir.......5 B2

SLEEPING
Hotel Makalu......................6 B3

EATING
Himanchal Cabin..................7 B1
Pooja Sweets.......................8 B2
Star Hotel..........................9 B2

TRANSPORT
Yeti Airlines........................10 B3

Buses leave from the large and hectic bus stand at the end of Ghantaghar Rd. There are plenty of day and night buses to Kathmandu (day/night Rs 350/400, nine hours), and Pokhara (day/night Rs 350/425, nine hours) via Narayangarh (Rs 250, three hours). There are also regular buses to Janakpur (Rs 200, five hours) and Hetauda (Rs 100, two hours).

Getting Around

Rickshaws charge Rs 50 to Rs 100 to go from town to the Nepali border post and on to Raxaul Bazaar. Alternatively, you can take a tempo or *tonga* from the bus station to the Nepali border post for Rs 10 and then walk to the Indian side.

JANAKPUR

☎ 041

Like the other border towns in the Terai, Janakpur's way of life is unmistakably Indian, though there's a lot more going on here than rickshaws and bustling bazaars. What makes Janakpur one of the most fascinating towns in the Terai is its electric religious atmosphere mixed with a rich historical and cultural heritage. Even though there's no architecture pre-dating 1880, it manages to evoke an aura of grandeur not found elsewhere in the Terai.

It's known foremostly as an important pilgrimage site for Hindus all over Nepal and India, who come to pay homage to Janakpur's connection with the Hindu epic the Ramayana. Legend has it that it's the site where Sita was born, and where she was married to Rama. At the heart of Janakpur lies the exquisite marble Janaki Mandir, one of the finest pieces of architecture in Nepal. Dedicated to Sita, it marks the spot where she was believed to be found as a baby by King Janak. Today you'll find devout pilgrims chanting 'Sita Ram, Sita Ram' and sadhus (holy men) sprawled out while priests perform rituals in an atmosphere thick with burning incense.

The other lure in Janakpur is its Mithila culture. Janakpur was once the capital of the ancient kingdom of Mithila, a territory now divided between Nepal and India – more than two million people in the area still speak Maithili as their native tongue. The people of Mithila are famous for their wildly colourful paintings – see the boxed text, p319.

Janakpur is actually the third city on this site. The city mythologised in the Ramayana existed around 700 BC, but it was later abandoned and sank back into the forest. Simaraungarh grew up in its place, but this city was also destroyed, this time by Muslim invaders in the 14th century.

Orientation

About 20km south of the Mahendra Hwy, Janakpur is a maze of narrow, winding streets. The official centre of town is the Janaki Temple in the middle of the bazaar, but most of the hotels are further east on the road running up to Bhanu Chowk and the train station.

If you come in on the highway, you'll arrive at Ramanand Chowk, topped by a giant metal culture of crossed elephant tusks. The town centre is east of the junction while the bus tand is due south at Zero Mile Chowk.

Information

There's a small **tourist office** (☎ 520755; ⏲ 10am-
5pm Sun-Thu, 10am-3pm Fri) upstairs in an arcade on the main road close to Bhanu Chowk. At time of research they were scouting for a new location, so it's best to check before setting out here.

Everest Bank has an ATM tucked away inside the eastern entry of the Janaki Mandir.

There are several internet cafes in town, with **A to Z Cyber House** (per hr Rs 15; ⏲ 8am-8pm) being the cheapest, fastest and most reliable.

Sights

JANAKI MANDIR

Janakpur's most important temple is dedicated to Sita, the wife of Rama and heroine of the Ramayana. Built in extravagant baroque Mughal style, the Janaki Mandir is believed to stand on the exact spot where King Janak found the infant Sita lying in the furrow of a ploughed field. The temple only dates from 1912, but it feels much older with its white marble arches, domes, turrets and screens. It looks a little like a glorious wedding cake, designed for a maharajah.

According to the ancient text, Sita was kidnapped by Ravana, the demon-king of Lanka, and her husband sped south to save her aided by the loyal monkey god Hanuman. Although Rama and Sita were historical figures, Hindus regard Rama as an incarnation of Vishnu and Sita as an incarnation of Lakshmi.

A steady stream of pilgrims file in through the gatehouse to worship the Sita statue in the **inner sanctum** (⏲ 5-7am & 6-8pm). The temple is particularly popular with women, who wear their best and most colourful saris for the occasion. Early evening is the most atmospheric time to visit, as the temple is draped with colourful lights and pilgrims arrive in their masses.

RAM SITA BIBAHA MANDIR

Almost next door to the Janaki Mandir, this rather bizarre **temple** (admission Rs 2, camera Rs 5, video Rs 21; ⏲ 5am-9pm) marks the spot where Rama and Sita were married. The temple is topped by a modernist interpretation of a tiered pagoda roof and the walls are glass so you can peer in at the kitsch life-sized models of Sita and Rama.

RAM MANDIR & DANUSH SAGAR

Hidden away in a stone courtyard southeast of the Janaki Mandir, the **Ram Mandir** is the oldest temple in Janakpur (constructed in 1882), built in the classic tiered pagoda style of the hills. The main temple is sacred to Rama but there are several smaller shrines to Shiva, Hanuman and Durga dotted around the compound. It's busiest in the early evening, when

---

CROSSING THE BORDER

Border Hours
The Nepali side of the border is open 24 hours (if no one is here you may have to ask around) but the Indian side is usually only staffed from 4am to 10pm, though you may be able to find someone to stamp you through outside these times. Nepali visas are available on arrival from the Nepal immigration office but payment must be in US dollars.

Foreign Exchange
There are no facilities at the border, but there are banks and moneychangers in Birganj.

Onwards to India
The border is 5km south of Birganj, and it's about 500m from the Nepali border post to the bus station in Raxaul Bazaar. Most people take a rickshaw straight through from Birganj (Rs 50). From Raxaul, there are regular buses to Patna (INRs 110, five hours) or you can take the daily *Mithila Express* train to Kolkata's Howrah train station – it leaves Raxaul at 10.20am, arriving into Howrah at 5am the next morning. Seats cost INRs 210/591/821 for sleeper class/three-tier/two-tier (sleeper and two-tier class prices include air-con) and the trip takes 18 hours.

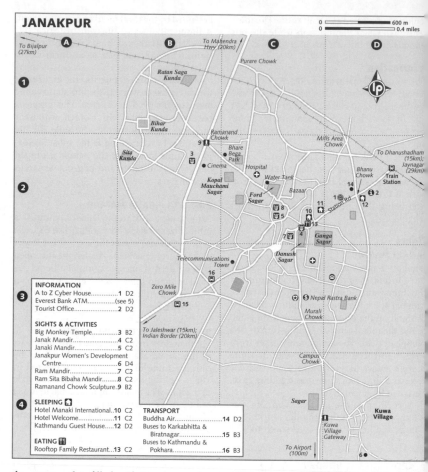

JANAKPUR

INFORMATION
A to Z Cyber House..............1 D2
Everest Bank ATM..............(see 5)
Tourist Office......................2 D2

SIGHTS & ACTIVITIES
Big Monkey Temple.............3 B2
Janak Mandir.......................4 C2
Janaki Mandir......................5 C2
Janakpur Women's Development
    Centre..............................6 D4
Ram Mandir..........................7 C2
Ram Sita Bibaha Mandir........8 C2
Ramanand Chowk Sculpture.9 B2

SLEEPING
Hotel Manaki International..10 C2
Hotel Welcome...................11 C2
Kathmandu Guest House.....12 D2

EATING
Rooftop Family Restaurant...13 C2

TRANSPORT
Buddha Air.........................14 D2
Buses to Karkabhitta &
    Biratnagar.....................15 B3
Buses to Kathmandu &
    Pokhara.........................16 B3

the courtyard is filled with incense smoke and music.

Opposite the entrance are a series of ghats (steps for ritual bathing) leading down into the **Danush Sagar**, the largest ceremonial tank at Janakpur. There are small shrines all around the perimeter and vendors in front sell flower garlands, *tika* powder, sacred threads and other ritual objects for pujas (prayers).

Nearby is the small **Janak Mandir**, sacred to the father of Sita.

OTHER TEMPLES & PONDS

There are numerous other temples and sacred ponds scattered around the outskirts of town, accessible on foot or by rickshaw.

Over on the other side of town, Hanuman is worshipped in the form of a live rhesus macaque at the tiny **Big Monkey Temple**. The monkey is morbidly obese due to its small cage and over-feeding through pilgrims' offerings of bananas and sweets. Its predecessor grew to a massive 60kg before it died. It's easy to miss the temple – the gateway is almost opposite the cinema, about 100m south of Ramanand Chowk.

If you head west from Ramanand Chowk, you'll reach two more ceremonial tanks – **Bihar Kunda** and **Ratan Saga Kunda**.

TRADITIONAL VILLAGES

The sugar cane fields and Mithila villages around Janakpur form a lush and magical mosaic. Many of the villages are built in the

THE TERAI & MAHABHARAT RANGE

raditional Mithila style, with mud walls deco-ated with colourful paintings of people and animals.

The easiest village to reach from Janakpur s **Kuwa**, about 1km south of Murali Chowk. People are very friendly, as long as you aren't too intrusive with your camera, and you can drop in on the **Janakpur Women's Development Centre** – see the boxed text, below. If you feel like roaming further afield, **Dhanushadham**, 15km northeast of Janakpur, marks the spot where Rama allegedly drew Shiva's magic bow.

estivals & Events

By far the most interesting time to visit Janakpur is during **Sita Bibaha Panchami** (Vivaha Panchami) on the fifth day of the waxing moon in November/December. Tens of thousands of pilgrims descend on the town to celebrate the re-enactment of Sita's marriage to Rama. There are processions and performances of scenes from the Ramayana in the streets.

Rama Navami (March/April), celebrating Rama's birthday, is also accompanied by a huge procession. If you're about for these festivals be sure to visit Bhare Bega Park, which is transformed into a colourful amusement park that is sure to bring a smile to your face.

Chhath is a major four-day Hindu festival celebrated by Mithila people twice a year (usually around May and November) in honour of the sun god. Thousands of devotees gather around Janakpur's Ganga Sagar and other lakes and ponds to worship the rising and setting sun.

In March, Janakpur gets boisterous during **Holi**, but be warned: foreigners are not exempt from a ritual splattering with coloured powder and water. If you visit during **Tihar** (Deepawali) in October/November, you'll

MITHILA ART

The vibrant artwork of the Mithila women can be traced back as far as the 7th century and is a tradition that has been passed through the centuries, generation to generation. As the former capital of the kingdom of Mithila, it is appropriate that Janakpur has emerged as the centre for both preserving and promoting the ancient art of Mithila painting.

Mithila painting is part decoration, part social commentary, recording the lives of rural women in a society where reading and writing are reserved for high-caste men. Scenes in Mithila paintings colourfully record the female experience of life in the Terai – work, childbirth, marriage and the social network among village women. Today you will also see more modern subject matter, such as aeroplanes and buses, blended with traditional themes like Hindu mythology and village life.

Traditionally, Mithila paintings were used as a transient form of decoration during festivals when the mud walls of village huts were painted in white and ochre with abstract patterns or complex scenes of everyday village life. You can still see houses in the villages surrounding Janakpur with painted walls. More recently, Mithila painting has taken off as a more contemporary and collectable art form, with the women painting on canvasses of rough handmade paper that is similar in texture to the mud hut walls. Not only are Mithila paintings now exhibited in galleries across the world, but more importantly the art has opened up a whole new industry for women in impoverished rural communities.

One of the best-known social projects is the **Janakpur Women's Development Centre** (JWDC; Nare Bekas Kendra; ☎ 521080; ☼ 10.30am-5pm Sun-Fri, 10.30am-4pm Nov-Feb), just outside Janakpur in the village of Kuwa. Around 40 Mithila women are employed at the centre, producing paper paintings, papier-mâché boxes and mirrors, screen-printed fabrics and hand-thrown ceramics. The bright colours and animated imagery are both unique and delightful, and the money raised goes directly towards improving the lives of rural women. You can meet the artisans and buy directly from the centre. It's also worth picking up a copy of the *Master Artists of Janakpur*, which provides an excellent insight into the lives of several of the artists and how they've benefited from the JWDC. A rickshaw from Janakpur to the centre will cost around Rs 80.

SAPT KOSI FLOODS

On 17 August 2008, the Sapt Kosi (Koshi) River broke its banks and turned the region into a disaster zone, with significant damage to livelihoods and infrastructure. Bihar in India bore the brunt of the catastrophe, but in Nepal more than 50,000 people were left homeless. What were once fields and villages were submerged in a torrent of water, which then dried out to create a barren desert of white silt littered with rubbish and fallen powerlines. For miles the road was lined with tarpaulin shelters housing the thousands who'd lost their homes.

The floods also effectively cut off the eastern Terai from the rest of the country, including Nepal's second-largest and main industry town, Biratnagar. Drinking water and electricity supplies were cut off, schools and public buildings were destroyed and many houses and domestic animals were swept away. Koshi Tappu Wildlife Reserve was also badly affected, particularly in the eastern buffer zone, where the habitat for rare birds and animals was damaged.

At the time of research, travellers were forced to disembark at the collapsed bridge and catch a ferry across the river (Rs 50), before transferring to another bus. Until the new bridge is built (expected in 2009), expect at least an hour to be added onto the journey times quoted in this book when travelling to or from eastern Nepal.

---

see Mithila women repainting the murals on their houses.

Sleeping & Eating

Kathmandu Guest House (☎ 521753; Bhanu Chowk; s/d without bathroom Rs 150/200, s/d with bathroom Rs 200/250) A very simple but otherwise reliable cheapie. Rooms have fans, mosquito nets and clean bathrooms with squat toilets.

Hotel Welcome (☎ 520646; Station Rd; s/d with bathroom Rs 300/500, s & d with air-con Rs 2000; 🅱) The hotel 'where welcome never end', this place is slightly run-down but reasonably good value. The location is convenient and some rooms have cheerful Mithila-inspired paintings on the walls. Go for the rooms off the main street. There's also a decent vegetarian restaurant.

Hotel Manaki International (☎ 521540; hotel manaki@hotmail.com; Shiv Chowk; s/d with bathroom Rs 1200/1400, s/d with air-con Rs 2000/2500; 🅱) The only really upmarket choice in Janakpur, the Manaki International has cavernous deluxe rooms with all mod cons, and more modest standard rooms.

Rooftop Family Restaurant (Station Rd; mains Rs 50-200; 🕙 9.30am-9.30pm) Facing the small Janak Mandir, this upmarket place claims to be 'the only choice of smart people' in Janakpur, and we're inclined to agree. There's an excellent selection of vegetarian curries and the Chinese food is pretty good too.

Getting There & Around

Buddha Air (☎ 525022) has three daily flights between Janakpur and Kathmandu (US$95,

20 minutes). The airport is a Rs 100 rickshaw ride south of the centre. If arriving at Janakpur airport, rickshaws are considerably cheaper when you make the short walk outside the airport.

There are daily day and night buses north to Kathmandu (day/night Rs 450/500, 10 hours) via Narayangarh (Rs 280, six hours) and to Pokhara (day/night Rs 500/600, 10 hours). The bus stand is a Rs 50 rickshaw ride from central Janakpur.

Buses heading east to Kakarbhitta (Rs 450, seven hours) are at the dusty bus park near Zero Mile Chowk, where you'll also find several morning buses for Biratnagar (Rs 400, four hours). Local buses run hourly to Birganj (Rs 200, five hours) until about 3pm.

The train station at the north end of Station Rd is the starting point for the slow metre-gauge train that runs east across the Indian border to the dusty plains town of Jaynagar. Only Indians and Nepalis can actually cross the border, but the train ride provides a delicious taste of the subcontinent. This must be one of the last trains in Asia where people routinely ride on the roof. It's a breezy ride up top, but the train passes through some wonderfully unspoiled countryside, stopping at a series of small Terai villages. Foreigners can travel as far as Khajuri (2nd-/1st-class Rs 20/34, three hours), about 21km southeast of Janakpur. Trains leave Janakpur at 6.45am, 11.30am and 3.20pm, returning from Khajuri at around noon and 3pm.

THE TERAI & MAHABHARAT RANGE

KOSHI TAPPU WILDLIFE RESERVE
☎ 025

The smallest of the Terai's national parks, **Koshi Tappu Wildlife Reserve** (☎ 530897; foreigner/ SAARC per day Rs 500/200) is a birdwatcher's paradise. Consisting of 175 sq km of wet and grassland habitat Koshi Tappu is home to at least 439 species of birds, as well as being the last habitat of the endangered *arna* (wild water buffalo). It was founded in 1976 to protect a small triangle of *phanta* and tappu (small islands) in the floodplain of the Sapt Kosi River.

It's a wonderfully serene spot and most travellers who visit are birdwatchers in search of rare species such as the Bengal florican and sarus crane. Migratory species from Siberia and Tibet take up residence from November to February. *Arna* tend to hang out on the tappu and you may also spot deer, wild boars, pythons and crocodiles. There are thought to be a handful of Gangetic dolphins in the Sapt Kosi but they are very rarely seen.

Most visitors come on organised tours from Kathmandu or Pokhara, which include birdwatching walks, elephant rides, boat trips, accommodation and meals at the tented camps inside the park and transfers from Biratnagar airport. There are few facilities for independent travellers.

Information
The **reserve headquarters** (☎ 530897; ☺ 10am-5pm) at Kusaha has an interesting information centre and museum, with elephant, deer and guar skulls, and a desiccated gharial. This is where visitors pay the daily park admission fees.

Sights & Activities
As with other national parks in the Terai, the most popular way to explore is by elephant. **Elephant safaris** (foreigner/SAARC Rs 1000/400) can be arranged at the park headquarters. All the lodges can arrange tours of the tappu by canoe or *dunga* (wooden boat) – the going rate for a boat and driver is about Rs 1500, covering up to five passengers.

Every lodge has a resident ornithologist who leads bird-spotting walks around the park, usually included in the package rates. If you come here independently, ask about hiring a guide at the park headquarters.

Sleeping
There are several lodges, but call ahead to make sure they're open before turning up at the front door, especially during the monsoon. As well as the package rates you'll have to pay the park admission fee, the park camping fee (Rs 300 per person) and 13% tax.

Koshi Tappu Wildlife Camp (☎ 9851022162, in Kathmandu 01-4226130; www.koshitappu.com; package per person US$150) This peaceful jungle camp sits out on the northeastern edge of the reserve. Guests stay in simple safari tents but the jungle atmosphere is very appealing. A small water course flows through the grounds so you can watch birds from the comfort of the bar.

Koshi Camp (☎ in Kathmandu 01-4429609; www .kosicamp.com; 3-day/2-night package US$189) A popular choice for birders, Koshi Camp is located on the western edge of the park, near several waterholes. It's refreshingly small and low-key; accommodation is in comfortable safari tents.

Aqua Birds Unlimited Camp (☎ in Kathmandu 01-4434705; www.aquabirds.com; 3-day/2-night package US$190) Again, the focus here is on our feathered friends. The resident birdwatching guides are very experienced and accommodation is in big safari tents with solar-powered hot showers.

Getting There & Away
Almost everyone comes here on a package tour with a pre-arranged pick-up from Biratnagar airport. Visiting independently is inconvenient transport-wise, but can be done. The best way to get here is to fly from Kathmandu to Biratnagar then take a private car (two hours) to Koshi Tappu.

You can also catch a bus here from Kathmandu (Rs 750, 12 to 14 hours). If coming from the east, buses head along the Mahendra Hwy. From Itahari (22km north of Biratnagar) catch the bus to Haripur (Rs 63, two to three hours). You'll then need to walk the remaining 2.5km to the park headquarters south of the Mahendra Hwy.

ITAHARI
Itahari is an undistinguished town at the junction of the Mahendra Hwy and the roads to Biratnagar and Hile. All long-distance buses along the Mahendra Hwy pull into the well-organised bus stand and there are fast and frequent local services

THE TERAI & MAHABHARAT RANGE

to Biratnagar and places along the road to Hile.

If you get stuck overnight, the **Jay Nepal Hotel** (☎ 021-580113; s/d Rs 350/450, r with air-con Rs 1000; 🕃) has reasonable rooms; it is situated by the roundabout at the turn-off to Dharan.

BIRATNAGAR
☎ 021
For what is Nepal's major industrial centre and second most-populated city (approximately 170,000 people), Biratnagar is surprisingly low-key. Sure, you'll have to dodge a rickshaw here or there in the town's centre, but it's neither polluted nor swarming with bustling activity. Instead

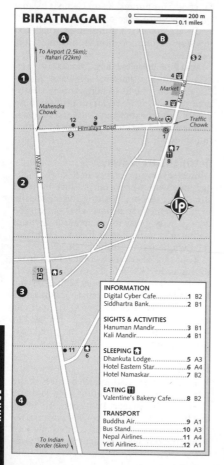

most of its heavy industry is located in its sprawling surrounds on the road to Itahari.

Hidden away in the southeastern corner of Nepal, there is nothing of great interest here. What few visitors there are in Biratnagar are on their way to/from Koshi Tappu Wildlife Reserve or to catch a flight to Taplejung, the main trailhead for treks in the eastern hills. Most foreigners you see here are likely to be foreign-aid workers. The centre of town has a more progressive feel than your average Terai town, and you'll notice plenty of uni students wearing trendy Western clothing. If you find yourself killing time here, there are several Hindu temples you can visit, including the gaily painted **Hanuman Mandir** and **Kali Mandir** near the market.

Information & Orientation
Biratnagar is about 22km south of the Mahendra Hwy. The official centre of town is Traffic Chowk and the municipal market is just north on Main Rd. Most of the hotels are further west on Malaya Rd, which runs south to the border.

Siddhartra Bank (☎ 532901; Main Rd; 🕘 10am-3pm Sun-Thu, to 1pm Fri, 11am-2pm Sat) has an ATM down a small side street off Main Rd, and foreign exchange. Several internet cafes at Traffic Chowk offer fast connections for Rs 20 per hour, with **Digital Cyber Cafe** (🕘 7.30am-9pm) being a reliable choice.

Sleeping & Eating
Dhankuta Lodge (☎ 522925; s/d/tr Rs 200/250/300) Don't expect frills at this rudimentary place opposite the bus station. Rooms are dingy but tolerable; try to get one at the back, away from the traffic noise. There's no hot water available here.

Hotel Namaskar (☎ 521199; hotelnamaskar@wlink .com.np; Main Rd; r Rs 800-900, r with air-con Rs 1300-1600; 🕃) With an excellent central location, the rooms with air-con are large and inviting, while rooms without are smallish and overpriced. It's run by devotees of Sai Baba (with his posters hung about to prove it), and its restaurant is one of the best in town – serving quality Indian and Western food.

Hotel Eastern Star (☎ 530626; easternstar_brt@wlink .com.np; s/d Rs 900/1100, s/d with air-con from Rs 1500/1700; 🕃) It may not be as fancy as the expensive Hotel Xenial (a popular stop for foreigners),

Map: BIRATNAGAR

0 ——— 200 m
0 ——— 0.1 miles

To Airport (2.5km); Itahari (22km)

Mahendra Chowk

Himalaya Road

Market

Police

Traffic Chowk

Malaya Rd

To Indian Border (6km)

INFORMATION
Digital Cyber Cafe...............1 B2
Siddhartra Bank...................2 B1

SIGHTS & ACTIVITIES
Hanuman Mandir..................3 B1
Kali Mandir...........................4 B1

SLEEPING 🏠
Dhankuta Lodge...................5 A3
Hotel Eastern Star................6 A4
Hotel Namaskar....................7 B2

EATING 🍴
Valentine's Bakery Cafe........8 B2

TRANSPORT
Buddha Air...........................9 A1
Bus Stand...........................10 A3
Nepal Airlines.....................11 A4
Yeti Airlines........................12 A1

THE TERAI & MAHABHARAT RANGE

out Eastern Star is definitely the best value. It has massive, well-furnished rooms with comfortable beds and clean tiled bathrooms (some with bathtubs). Staff are friendly and professional, and it has a classy restaurant with excellent Indian dishes.

Valentine's Bakery Cafe (🕑 10am-8.30pm) This friendly, clean and modern little cafe specialises in lassies, cakes and momos. It's popular with students, and one of the few places in the Terai that's nonsmoking.

Getting There & Away

Buddha Air (☎ 526901) and **Yeti Airlines** (☎ 536612) both have numerous daily flights between Biratnagar and Kathmandu (US$122, 40 minutes). **Nepal Airlines** (www.royalnepal-airlines.com) flies three times a week to Suketar/Taplejung (US$62, 30 minutes). Travel agents around Traffic Chowk can make bookings. A rickshaw to the airport will cost around Rs 100.

The bus stand is a Rs 20 rickshaw ride southwest from Traffic Chowk. There are buses to Kathmandu (Rs 1000, 14 hours) via Narayangarh (Rs 730, nine hours), and several buses leave every morning for Janakpur (Rs 400, four hours). There are also regular services along the Mahendra Hwy to Kakarbhitta (Rs 300, 3½ hours).

Local buses run regularly to Dharan (Rs 50, one hour) throughout the day. There are also early morning buses to Dhankuta (Rs 170, three hours) and Hile (Rs 180, 3½ hours).

Those heading to Koshi Tappu can catch a bus to Haripur (Rs 63, three hours), and then walk 2.5km to the park headquarters.

DHARAN TO HILE

About 17km north of Itahari, Dharan marks the start of yet another dramatic route into the hills. From here, a decent tarmac road runs north into the foothills of the Himalaya, providing access to a series of attractive hill towns and trekking trailheads.

Dharan

☎ 025

Dharan is a prosperous market town with a pleasant, sleepy feel. The sprawling town has three distinct characters. On the western perimeter you'll find an affluent, almost middle-class suburbia feel, with quiet streets lined with well-maintained bungalows, neatly paved sidewalks, rubbish bins and a country club with a golf course. Up until

1990 Dharan was the Gurkha recruiting area (before relocating to Pokhara), and its wealth can be largely attributed to money brought in by these world-famous Nepali-British soldiers. The eastern side has steep streets and a relaxed hill town feel resembling Southeast Asia with its banana plants, bamboo-forested hills and rustic shacks. You're also likely to encounter tribal Kiranti women wearing gold jewellery. Dividing the two areas, in the centre is the lively Dharan Bazaar, which has a more typical Terai flavour, with its flat and dusty market.

Dharan is also one of the *shakti peeths*, marking the spot where part of the body of Shiva's first wife, Sati, fell after she was consumed by flames. There are several important Shaivite temples northeast of the centre in the village of **Bijayapur**, which is a peaceful spot well worth a visit. Set among dense bamboo thickets down the path beside the four-tiered concrete tower, **Budha Subba Mandir** contains a curious collection of rocks covered in mud, which are said to represent the reclining body of Mahadev (Shiva). On Saturdays you'll encounter chickens being sacrificed and, with a pool of blood and headless chooks flapping about (to both the horror and amusement of locals), it's not for queasy stomachs. To reach Bijayapur, take the steps leading uphill near the Panas Hotel, or charter an autorickshaw (return Rs 200).

Several net cafes around Bhanu Chowk (the square with the bus stand and the clock tower across the road) offer fast net access for Rs 20 per hour. Both Nabil Bank and Himalyan Bank have 24-hour ATMs that accept foreign cards.

Keen golfers will want to head to **Nirvana Country Club** (☎ 526801; green fee Rs 500, club hire Rs 500) with 18 holes on a well-maintained course, though you'll probably be putting on 'browns' rather than greens.

SLEEPING & EATING

Hotel Naya Yug (☎ 524797; r without bathroom Rs 300, r with bathroom Rs 400-500) Don't be put off by the red lights in the windows – this is actually a fairly respectable cheapie. It's a little decrepit but the simple rooms have spongy beds and Western toilet. Bucket hot water is Rs 30. Its small restaurant does an excellent paneer mushroom curry (Rs 120).

New Dreamland Hotel & Lodge (☎ 525024; r with/ without bathroom Rs 800/500, r with air-con Rs 1200; ✿)

This nice midrange hotel is located in a peaceful, well-to-do part of town, and has large rooms that look bare without any furniture except a bed.

Dharan Kitchen (mains Rs 50-200; ⊗ 9am-10pm) Located upstairs from the taxi stand (opposite the clock tower), this restaurant has an excellent ambience with bamboo walls and Buddhist motifs. It serves quality Indian and Western food and cheap, cold beer. Our favourite is the local take on stroganoff – the 'Chicken Strong On/Off'. It also has decent rooms with shared bathroom for Rs 500.

GETTING THERE & AROUND

Afternoon buses leave from Bhanu Chowk at 1pm and 1.30pm for Kathmandu (Rs 1000, 15 hours) and Biratnagar (Rs 50, one hour). Heading north, local buses run regularly from 4am to 4pm to Bhedetar (Rs 45, one hour), Dhankuta (Rs 160, two hours) and Hile (Rs 170, 2½ hours). Early morning buses continue from Hile to Basantapur and Therathum. See p110 for details of treks from Basantapur and rafting on the Tamur River.

Bhedetar

Tiny and laid-back Bhedetar comprises no more than a cluster of wooden shacks on the road to Dhankuta, but the location – perched at 1420m with soaring views over Everest and Makalu – is spectacular on a clear day. There are giddying views over the Terai and mountains from the 20m-high viewing tower at **Bhedetar Charles Point** (foreigner/SAARC Rs 50/10; ⊗ daylight), named after Prince Charles, who visited Bhedetar during the 1980s.

Hotel Aruu Valley Hilltop Restaurant (☎ 9842055086; tent Rs 500, r Rs 800) makes for a pleasant place to spend the night. Set among a garden of bright flowers, its rooms are delightfully decorated and have thick carpets, wicker furniture and comfortable beds with warm blankets.

There are also several tin-roofed bhojanalayas serving simple, filling meals, *tongba* (millet beer) and *raksi*.

There's a small **festival** in the first week of December with a carnival atmosphere and food stalls.

Hile

☎ 026

Hile was once the starting point for the camping trek to Makalu and the end point for the lodge trek from Lukla, but the road has advanced along the valley, reaching almost as far as Tumlingtar and Khandbari. As a result, Hile is no longer the busy trekking hub it once was. Nevertheless, the village has a bustling bazaar feel, particularly during the weekly Thursday market, and there's a good mountain viewpoint about 30 minutes' walk above town (follow the Basantapur road to the army post, then turn north along the trail to Hattikharka).

Many local inhabitants are Tibetans who resettled here after fleeing the Chinese occupation of Tibet in 1959, founding several gompas in the middle of the village. Just south of Hile on the road to Dhankuta are the organic tea gardens of the **Guranse Tea Estate** (☎ in Kathmandu 01-4478301) – tours can be arranged if you phone ahead. Unless you reach Hile by lunchtime, there's a good chance that you'll have to stay overnight, but that's not all bad news – the village hotels serve filling Tibetan food and warming wooden pots of *tongba*.

SLEEPING & EATING

There are a handful of simple lodges along the main road through the village. A jumble of pot plants lends a cosy feel to the **Hotel Himali** (☎ 540140; d/tr Rs 150/250), which also has a *Raiders of the Lost Ark*-style bar at the back. Across the road, the similar **Gumba Hotel** (☎ 540173; r Rs 150) is appropriately named – it's right next to the main village gompa.

GETTING THERE & AWAY

Frequent local buses run from Dharan to Hile (Rs 150 to Rs 180, three hours) and a few continue up the Arun Valley as far as Leguwa (Rs 280 from Dharan, five hours). Some buses from Dharan continue to Basantapur (Rs 70 from Hile, 1½ hours). Jeeps leave when full for the bumpy ride to Tumlingtar, stopping just before Kotlay Bhanjyang (Rs 500, five hours).

ILAM

☎ 027

Like its neighbour Darjeeling across the border, Ilam (pronounced 'ee-lam') is synonymous with only one thing – tea. The two share an almost identical climate and topography and, while Darjeeling is a household name, Ilam quietly sets about its business in making a name for itself internationally through its quality tea.

Situated in the far east of Nepal, 90km from the border at Kakarbhitta, the small clusters of green tea plants that carpet the hills from a distance look like miniature model plastic trees in a diorama set, and a walk here will take you to one of the most tranquil spots in the Terai.

Ilam itself is focused along one long strip of shops, small restaurants and wooden houses. Ilam Bazaar is the main square where locals congregate to chat over a cup of tea.

There's a helpful **tourist information centre** (☎ 521692, 9842662200; ilam_2010@yahoo.com; ⏲ 9am-6pm Sun-Fri) situated by the bus stand that has some good information on what to see in the region. It's closed on Saturdays, but it's worth giving the mobile a call to see if anyone is nearby.

There's no ATM in Ilam but **Bank of Asia** (☎ 521702; ⏲ 9.30am-4pm Sun-Thu, to 1pm Fri) can exchange foreign currency. A few internet cafes offer painfully slow connection for Rs 30 per hour.

Koseli Gham (⏲ 7am-7pm Sun-Fri, 10am-4pm Sat) is a small cooperative that sells Ilam tea, honey and sweets, with proceeds going to the local community. It is located on the main strip near the bus stand.

Sleeping & Eating

All of the sleeping options Ilam has to offer are very basic with hard beds and few have hot water available. Most also have attached restaurants that serve up daal bhaat and chow mein.

Sungava Guest House (☎ 521701; s/d without bathroom Rs 150/200, r with bathroom Rs 500) In a quiet location just off the main square, Sungava is a new hotel with clean rooms, satellite TV and large, clean bathrooms with Western toilets. At the time of research there was no hot water, but there are plans for bucket hot water to be provided.

Danfe Guest House (☎ 520048; r Rs 150-200) Immersed within the tea plantation, this rustic blue-and-white cottage decorated with prayer flags has very basic but otherwise fine rooms.

Green View Guest House (☎ 520103; s/d without bathroom Rs 250/400, r with bathroom Rs 550) The best option in town, Green View has a prime location at the edge of a tea garden, and several rooms do indeed have a green view – of tea plantations. Rooms are rather simple and have TV and hot water.

Chyangba Hotel (daal bhaat Rs 50, tongba Rs 30; ⏲ 9am-8pm) This popular restaurant on the main strip is set out in a back room full of brass pots and drying chillis. It's an excellent spot to enjoy a cup of *tongba*, served in a large wooden tankard; it does good momos and chow mein.

Getting There & Away

The dusty bus station is to the west of town, while the jeep and taxi stand is just off the main square.

The road to Ilam branches off the Mahendra Hwy at Charali (Rs 200, two hours) but buses and jeeps to Ilam originate in the nondescript highway town of Birtamod. On the Mahendra Hwy any bus heading to Kakarbhitta can drop you off at Birtamod. Buses to Ilam (Rs 150, four hours) leave from the highway, just east of the main roundabout. Jeeps do the same journey in three hours (Rs 200). You can follow the same road north to Taplejung, the starting point for group treks to the base of Kanchenjunga.

The four-hour scenic journey up to Ilam can be a little frightening. The tight, twisting roads with plunging cliffs appear far too narrow for buses, and the sight of bus wrecks on the side of the road doesn't do much for the nerves. It's advisable to catch a jeep up here, which is also a much quicker option.

AROUND ILAM

Other than strolling through its tea fields, there's not much else to do in Ilam, but there are some worthwhile areas you can visit in its surrounds.

A pleasant half-day trip from Ilam is the attractive lake at **Mai Pokhari**. The 1½-hour jeep trip along a rocky track leads you to this incredibly peaceful spot, which was declared a Ramsar site in late 2008. An important pilgrimage site for Hindus and Buddhists, the lake is a striking emerald colour and is covered in water lilies and swimming with goldfish. Surrounded by cone trees and rhododendrons (which bloom in March) it makes for a beautiful stroll.

The lake is home to 300 species of birds, tree frogs, leopards and jackals; the area is also known for its medicinal plants, which are claimed to cure everything from hysteria to cancer. If you've got time on your side, it makes for an excellent eight-hour round-trip walk.

THE TERAI & MAHABHARAT RANGE

CROSSING THE BORDER

Border Hours

Both sides of the border are staffed between 6am and around 9pm to 10pm. You may still be able to cross outside these times but you'll need to go searching for the immigration officials.

Foreign Exchange

Nepal Bank operates a foreign exchange desk (⊙ 7am to 5pm) close to the border. You can change cash and travellers cheques in US dollars, UK pounds and euros, as well as Indian and Nepali rupees.

Onwards to India

It's about 100m from the Kakarbhitta bus stand to the border, and another 100m to the Indian border post at Panitanki. Rickshaws charge Rs 20 from Kakarbhitta all the way through to the bus stand at Panitanki, which has regular services to Siliguri (INRs 20, one hour) where you can pick up buses to Darjeeling (INRs 60, three hours). Jeeps to the same destinations, and Gangtok (INRs 160, 4½ hours) in Sikkim line up just beyond the Indian visa post. Siliguri lies on the main train line from Kolkata to northeast India.

Some other trips possible from Ilam include the **Kanyam Tea Gardens** (46km from Ilam), where you can visit the tea factory. Here you'll also find a **picnic spot** popular with groups of merry Nepali teenagers. Another excellent option is a visit to **Sandakpur**, on the border with Darjeeling, where you can watch an incredible sunrise over four of the world's five highest peaks, and a habitat for **red pandas**. However, it's not the easiest place to get to: it involves getting a taxi from Ilam Bazaar to Biblate (Rs 15), then another taxi for 2½ hours to Khirsabutor (Rs 300), and finally a six-hour walk. There are several basic lodges in Sandakpur, and you'll need to ensure you bring warm clothing.

Ilam is also a good launching point for treks in the foothills of Mt Kanchenjunga (8598m), the world's third-highest peak. The main trailhead for mountain treks is Taplejung, accessible by plane from Biratnagar and bus from Birtamod.

KAKARBHITTA

☎ 023

Kakarbhitta (Kakarvitta) is the easternmost crossing between India and Nepal, and it's just a few hours' drive from Siliguri and Darjeeling in West Bengal and Gangtok in Sikkim. This is one of the easiest border crossings and the bazaar by the bus stand is packed with vendors selling Indian spices, Nepali khukuris (Gurkha knives), Chinese radios and other black-market goods. Like Nepal's other border towns, Kakarbhitta is hot, dusty and stressful, and there isn't any great reason to linger here other than to break up your journey. However, 10 minutes' walk south is the **Satighata tea plantation**, which can be a nice way to spend time here, and is a taste of things to come on the Darjeeling side of the border.

Information & Orientation

The Nepali border post at Kakarbhitta and the Indian border post at Panitanki are just a few hundred metres apart, so you can cross the border easily on foot. In Kakarbhitta the bus stand is about 100m west of the border, on the north side of the highway. Most of the hotels are in the surrounding streets.

The government of Nepal runs a small **tourist information centre** (☎ 562035; ⊙ 10am-4pm Sun-Fri) on the Nepal side of the border. You can check your email at **Net Point Cyber Zone** (☎ 562040; per hr Rs 30; ⊙ 8am-8pm) on the north side of the bus station near Hotel Mechi.

Sleeping & Eating

Most of the hotels are crammed together in the narrow alleys leading west from the back of the bus stand. For meals, all the lodges have restaurants serving Indian, Nepali and Chinese fare.

Hotel Mechi (☎ 562040; dm Rs 120, s Rs 300-600, d Rs 400-1200, s/d with air-con US$10-20; ✉) On the northern edge of the bus station, Mechi has rooms to suit all budgets. Rooms are large and comfortable, and excellent value. It also has a restaurant with tasty Indian dishes.

Hotel Rajat (☎ 562033; r Rs 500-800, r with air-con Rs 1400; ❄) The welcome here is friendly while the rooms are simple but inviting. There's a bistrolike restaurant with gingham tablecloths downstairs, and the owner is a great source of advice for onward travel. It's located just up the road from Hotel Mechi.

Getting There & Away

AIR

The nearest airport is at Bhadrapur, 10km southeast of Birtamod, which in turn is 13km west of Kakarbhitta. **Yeti Airlines** (☎ 455232) has daily flights to Kathmandu (US$154, 50 minutes) – any of the travel agents around the bus stand can issue tickets. A taxi from Kakarbhitta bus stand to the airport costs Rs 600, or you can take a local bus to Birtamod, then a second bus to Bhadrapur followed by a rickshaw to the airport.

BUS

Travel agents in Kathmandu and Pokhara offer 'through-tickets' to Darjeeling, but you must change buses at Kakarbhitta, then again change at Siliguri – it is just as easy to do the trip in stages. The bus stand in Kakarbhitta is the usual chaotic affair. Be extra wary of luggage thieves if travelling after dark.

There are several daily services to Kathmandu (Rs 1500, 17 hours) and Pokhara (Rs 1500, 17 hours all travelling via Narayangarh (Rs 850, 12 hours). Consider the poor safety record of night buses in Nepal before committing to 17 hours on unlit roads.

Within the eastern part of the Terai, to get to Ilam there are plenty of buses to Birtamod (Rs 30, 25 minutes) from where you can get a bus or jeep. There are four or more daily buses to Janakpur (Rs 450, seven hours), Biratnagar (Rs 300, 3½ hours) and Birganj (Rs 800, eight hours). If for some reason you wanted to cross Nepal in one go, a single bus leaves at 12.40pm daily for Mahendranagar (Rs 1425, 24 hours) and other towns in the western Terai.

Trekking

The vast majority of the countryside in Nepal is still inaccessible by road, hidden behind endless ridges and valleys and criss-crossed by a network of trails trodden for centuries by porters, traders, pilgrims, mountaineers and locals travelling from village to town, plains to hills, Nepal to Tibet. Until you've hit this network of trails on foot you can't truly say you've experienced the essence of Nepal.

The backdrop to these trails is some of the most spectacular and beautiful scenery in the world. Nepal enjoys a near monopoly on the world's highest peaks – eight of the 10 highest are found here – and there is absolutely nothing like strolling from teahouse to teahouse under crystal-clear Himalayan skies as an 8000m peak towers over you.

Trekking in Nepal is not like hiking through an uninhabited national park. Local people are constantly passing by on the trails, usually carrying extraordinarily heavy loads. You'll meet Sherpas, Gurungs, Rai and Thakali people and pass by monasteries, temples and sacred lakes, some of which host spectacular religious festivals. Wherever you go, as a trekker you'll get to experience the friendliness, outgoing nature and good humour that characterises almost all Nepalis. Most trekkers comment that while they came to Nepal for the mountains, they will return because of the people.

This chapter outlines the basic requirements for safe trekking in Nepal's mountains and gives an overview of the major teahouse trekking routes – where you can be sure to find food and accommodation. For treks to more remote regions, you will require more detailed advice, maps and route descriptions; for this see Lonely Planet's *Trekking in the Nepal Himalaya*.

HIGHLIGHTS

- Walk into the heart of the world's highest mountains at **Everest Base Camp** (p340), following in the footsteps of famous mountaineers

- Watch the golden dawn inch down a panorama of fluted white peaks at **Annapurna Sanctuary** (p358)

- Visit Sherpa communities, ogle stunning Mt Ama Dablam and chow down on apple pie in the villages around **Namche Bazaar** (p343)

- Trek up the ever-changing Marsyangdi Valley to the glaciers, monasteries and awesome views of the Annapurna massif around **Manang** (p356)

- Hike past bamboo groves, rhododendron forests and yak pastures in the **Langtang Valley** (p346) before gazing at glaciers and 7000m peaks

BEFORE YOU GO

PLANNING

Nepal offers plenty of opportunity for walks lasting a day or less, though most are considerably longer. From Pokhara (p275) or around the Kathmandu Valley (p170) you can do a variety of two-, three- or four-day walks, but Nepal's main treks take at least a week. For the very popular Everest Base Camp and Annapurna Circuit treks you have to allow three weeks each. Don't take on one of these treks too lightly; the end of the first week is not the time to discover that you're not that keen on walking.

When to Trek

The best time to trek is the dry season from October to May; the worst time is the monsoon period from June to September. This generalisation does not allow for the peculiarities of individual treks. Some people even claim that the undeniable difficulties of trekking during the monsoon are outweighed by the virtual absence of Western trekkers.

The first two months of the dry season, October and November, offer the best weather for trekking and the main trails are heaving with trekkers at this time, for good reason. The air, freshly laundered by the monsoon rains, is crystal clear, the mountain scenery is superb and the weather is still comfortably warm.

December, January and February are still good months for trekking, but the cold can be bitter and dangerous at high altitudes. Getting up to the Everest Base Camp can be a real endurance test and the Thorung La on the Annapurna Circuit is often blocked by snow.

In March and April the weather has been dry for a long time and dust is starting to hang in the air, affecting visibility somewhat. The poorer quality of the Himalayan views is more than compensated for by fewer crowds, the warm weather and the spectacular rhododendron blooms.

By May it starts to get very hot, dusty and humid, and the monsoon is definitely just around the corner. From June to September the trails can be dangerously slippery due to the monsoon rains, and raging rivers often wash away bridges

and stretches of trail. Nepal's famous *jukha* (leeches) are an unpleasant feature of the wet season but, with care, trekking can still be possible and there are certainly fewer trekkers on the trail.

What Kind of Trek?

There are many different styles of trekking to suit your budget, fitness level and available time. Most independent trekkers plan to sleep and eat in lodges every night and forego the complications of camping. You can carry your own pack and rely on your own navigation skills and research. Or you might find it makes sense to hire a local porter to carry your heavy backpack so that you can walk with only a day pack. A good guide will certainly enhance the trekking experience, though most of the trails in this chapter are not hard to follow in good weather. To save time, many people organise a trek through a trekking agency, either in Kathmandu or in their home country. Such organised treks can be simple lodge-to-lodge affairs or magnificent expeditions with the full regalia of porters, guides, portable kitchens, dining tents and even toilet tents.

Trekking is physically demanding. Some preparation is recommended, even for shorter treks. You will need endurance and stamina to tackle the steep ascents and descents that come with trekking in the highest mountain range in the world.

On the trail you will begin to realise just how far you are from medical help and the simple comforts that you usually take for granted. For most people this is part of the appeal of trekking, but for some it is a shock to realise just how responsible you are for your own well-being. A simple stumble can have catastrophic results. Even a twisted ankle or sore knee can become a serious inconvenience if you are several days away from help and your companions need to keep moving.

Independent Trekking

Independent trekking does not mean solo trekking; in fact we advise trekkers not to walk alone. It simply means that you are not part of an organised tour. The trekking trails described in this chapter have accommodation and food along their entire length, often every hour or two, so there's no need to pack a tent, stove or mat.

THE HISTORY OF TREKKING

Nepal has always been a nation of traders and current-day trekking trails evolved from ancient trade routes. Today's trekkers walk in the countless footprints of porters, yak caravans, salt traders and seasonal herders, as well as generations of Nepalis who have walked from village to village for weddings, funerals, festivals, pilgrimages, work, school, and government or military business.

Because Nepal was closed to the outside world until the 1950s, the only foreigners who visited the hills of the country were illegal visitors, such as Japanese explorer Ekai Kawaguchi, and secret map-makers, called 'pundits', who were sent into Nepal by the Survey of India.

The first trekker in Nepal was Bill Tilman, who wrangled permission from the maharaja (king) in 1949 to make several treks, including around the Kali Gandaki, Helambu and Solu Khumbu regions, becoming the first foreigner to trek to Everest Base Camp in 1950. The first group of Westerners to trek up the Kali Gandaki Valley was a French expedition to Annapurna led by Maurice Herzog in 1950. The decade of the 1950s witnessed the golden age of Himalayan climbing (13 of the world's 14 peaks over 8000m were climbed for the first time between 1950 and 1960) and the reconnaissance work of these early expeditions opened up many of today's trek routes.

During King Tribhuvan's visits to India he met Boris Lissanevitch, a White Russian ballet dancer who was running a club in Calcutta. Boris convinced the king that people would like to visit Nepal and would even pay for the experience. Soon a few well-heeled ladies flew from Patna to Kathmandu in an Indian Airlines Dakota, where Boris accommodated them in his new establishment, the Royal Hotel. The women were charmed by Boris and the exotic kingdom of Nepal, and Nepal's tourism industry was born. The Royal Hotel and its Yak & Yeti bar became the meeting place for climbers from the 1950s until 1971, when the hotel closed.

Colonel James 'Jimmy' Roberts was the first person to realise that trekking might appeal to tourists. Roberts had spent years in Nepal attached to the British residency as a Gurkha recruiter and accompanied Tilman on his first trek, making first ascents of several peaks. In 1965 he took a group of ladies up the Kali Gandaki and founded Mountain Travel, the first of Nepal's trekking companies and the inspiration for the entire adventure-travel industry.

For experienced hikers, guides and porters are not necessary on the Annapurna or Everest treks. A good guide or porter will enhance your experience, but a bad one will just make life more complicated. See right for information on guides and porters.

There are many factors that influence how much you spend on an independent trek. In most places accommodation costs around Rs 100 to Rs 200, a simple meal of daal bhaat (rice and lentils) around Rs 150 to Rs 200. As you get further from the road on the Annapurna Circuit and in the Everest region, prices can more than double and you can easily double that again by splashing out on a cold beer or slice of apple pie at the end of a long hiking day. A reasonable daily budget in the Annapurna and Everest regions is US$15 to US$20 per day, which should cover the occasional luxury but not a guide or porter.

In almost all lodges prices are fixed and quite reasonable. Remember this – and the real value of the rupee – before you get carried away with bargaining.

Guides & Porters

If you can't (or don't want to) carry a large pack, if you have children or elderly people in your party, or if you plan to walk in regions where you have to carry in food, fuel and tents, you should consider hiring a porter to carry your heavy baggage.

If you make arrangements with one of the small trekking agencies in Kathmandu, expect to pay around US$10 to US$15 per day for a guide, and US$7 to US$10 for a porter. These prices generally include your guide/porter's food and lodging.

FINDING GUIDES & PORTERS

To hire a guide, look on bulletin boards, check out forums like such as www.lonely planet.com/thorntree or www.trekinfo.com, hire someone through a trekking agency, or check with the office of the **Kathmandu Environmental Education Project** (KEEP; Map p140; ☎ 01-4216775; www.keepnepal.org; Thamel; ✆ 10am-5pm Sun-Fri). It's not difficult to find guides and porters, but it is hard to be certain of their honesty and ability. A porter or guide found at a street corner can easily disappear along the trail with all your gear, even if they are carrying a slew of letters from past clients certifying their honesty.

There is a distinct difference between a guide and a porter. A guide should speak English, know the terrain and the trails, and supervise porters, but probably won't carry a load or do menial tasks such as cooking or putting up tents. Porters are generally only hired for load-carrying, although an increasing number speak some English and know the trails well enough to act as guides.

If during a trek you decide you need help, either because of illness, problems with altitude, blisters or weariness, it will generally be possible to find a porter. Most lodges can arrange a porter, particularly in large villages or near an airstrip or roadhead where there are often porters who have just finished working for a trekking party and are looking for another load to carry.

Chhetri Sisters Trekking (☎ 061-462066; www.3 sistersadventure.com) at Lakeside North, Pokhara, organises women porters and guides for women trekkers. Chhetri Sisters also runs a guest house in Pokhara; see p265 for more information.

OBLIGATIONS TO GUIDES & PORTERS

An important thing to consider when you decide to trek with a guide or porter is that you become an employer. This means that you may have to deal with personnel problems, including medical care, insurance, strikes, disagreements over trekking routes and pace, money negotiations and all the other aspects of being a boss. Be as thorough as you can when hiring people and make it clear from the beginning what the requirements and limitations are. After that, prepare yourself for some haggling – it's part of the process.

When hiring a porter you are responsible (morally if not legally) for the welfare of those you employ. Many porters die or are injured each year (see the boxed text, p332) and it's important that you don't contribute to the problem. If you hire a porter or guide through a trekking agency, the agency will naturally pocket a percentage of the fee but should provide insurance for the porter.

The following are the main points to bear in mind when hiring and trekking with a porter:

- Ensure that adequate clothing is provided for any staff you hire. Clothing needs to be suitable for the altitudes you intend to trek to and should protect against bad weather. Equipment should include adequate footwear, headwear, gloves, windproof jacket, trousers and sunglasses, and a blanket, a sleeping mat and tent if you are trekking to remote areas or high altitude.
- Ensure that whatever provision you have made for yourself for emergency medical treatment is available to porters working for you.
- Ensure that porters who fall ill are not simply paid off and left to fend for themselves (it happens!).
- Ensure that porters who fall ill, and are taken down and out in order to access medical treatment, are accompanied by someone who speaks the porter's language and also understands the medical problem.

Whether you're making the arrangements yourself or dealing with an agency, make sure you clearly establish your itinerary (write it down and go through it day by day), how long you will take, how much you are going to pay and what you will supply along the way. It's always easier to agree on a fixed daily rate for food rather than pay as you go. Arrangements where you pay for the guide or porter's accommodation and food can end up being surprisingly expensive. The amount of food a hungry Nepali guide can go through can be stunning. You will need to increase the allowance at higher elevations where food is more expensive.

When you provide equipment for porters, be sure to make it clear whether it is a loan or a gift. In reality it can be very hard to get back equipment that you have loaned unless you are very determined and thick-skinned. If you're hiring your own porters, contact Kathmandu's two porter clothing banks (see the boxed text, p332), a scheme that allows you to rent protective gear for your porter.

It's common practice to offer your guide and porter a decent tip at the end of the trek for a job well done. Figure on around one day's wages per week, or around 15% to 20% of the total fee. Always give the tip directly to your porters rather than the guide or trek company.

TREKKING

TREKKING WITH A PORTER

Porters are the backbone of the trekking industry in Nepal and yet every year there are incidents (all of them preventable) involving porters suffering from acute mountain sickness (AMS), snow blindness and frostbite. At times these illnesses have resulted in fatalities. There are some trekking companies in Nepal, especially at the budget end of the scale, who simply don't look after the porters they hire. This does not apply to all companies, but some seem to be more worried about their profits than the welfare of those they rely on to generate that profit.

Porters often come from the lowland valleys, are poor and poorly educated, and are sometimes unaware of the potential dangers of the areas they are being employed to work in. Stories abound of porters being left to fend for themselves, wearing thin cotton clothes and sandals when traversing high mountain passes in blizzard conditions. At the end of each winter a number of porters' bodies are discovered in the snowmelt – they become tired, ill or affected by altitude and simply sit down in the snow, get hypothermia and die. If you are hiring a porter independently, you have certain obligations to meet. If you are trekking with an organised group using porters, be sure to ask the company how they ensure the well-being of porters hired by them. You can learn a lot about the hardships of life as a porter by watching the excellent BBC documentary Carrying the Burden, shown daily at 2pm at KEEP (Map p140; ☎ 01-4216775; www.keepnepal .org; Thamel; ⏱ 10am-5pm Sun-Fri).

In order to prevent the abuse of porters, the International Porter Protection Group (IPPG; www.ippg.net) was established in 1997 to improve health and safety for porters at work, to reduce the incidence of avoidable illness, injury and death, and to educate trekkers and travel companies about porter welfare.

The Mountain Fund (www.mountainfund.org) runs a Langtang Porters Support program based in Syabrubesi and operates a clothing bank there, where porters can borrow warm gear, equipment and shoes. They accept donations of clothing at their office, the Mountain Volunteer (Map pp114-15; Milijuli Tol, House No 209) in Maharajganj, near the ring road, and will pick up from Thamel hotels. A youth organisation, the Himalayan Club, operates a similar clothing bank for porters in Lukla. If you've got gear left over at the end of your Everest trek, consider donating it there (it is well signed and just off the main drag in Lukla).

Organised Trekking

Organised treks can vary greatly in standards and costs. Treks arranged with international travel companies tend to be more expensive than trips arranged within Nepal.

INTERNATIONAL TREKKING AGENCIES

After reading the glossy brochure of an adventure-travel company, you pay for the trek and everything is organised before you leave home. The cost will probably include flights to and from Nepal, accommodation in Kathmandu before and after the trek, tours and other activities, as well as the trek itself. A fully organised trek provides virtually everything: tents, sleeping bags, food, porters, as well as an experienced English-speaking sirdar (trail boss), Sherpa guides and usually a Western trek leader. All you need worry about is a day pack and camera.

Companies organising trekking trips in Nepal include Mountain Travel-Sobek (www.mt

sobek.com), Wilderness Travel (www.wildernesstravel .com) and Above the Clouds (www.abovecloudS.com) in the US; World Expeditions (www.worldexpeditions .com.au) or Peregrine Adventures (www.peregrine adventures.com) in Australia; and Exodus (www .exodus.co.uk), Explore Worldwide (www.explore .co.uk) and KE Adventure (www.keadventure.com) in the UK. There are many, many more. Foreign-run companies that are based in Nepal include Project Himalaya (www.project -himalaya.com).

Although the trek leaders may be experienced Western walkers from the international company, the on-the-ground organisation in Nepal will most probably be carried out by a reputable local trekking company.

LOCAL TREKKING AGENCIES

It's quite possible (and it can save a lot of money) to arrange a fully organised trip when you get to Nepal, but if you have a large group it's best to make the arrangements well in advance. Many trekking companies in Nepal can put together a fully equipped trek if you give them a few days notice. With the best of these companies a trek may cost upwards of US$60 or US$70 per person per day and you'll trek in real comfort with tables, chairs, dining tents, toilet tents and other luxuries.

There are more than 300 trekking agencies in Nepal, ranging from those connected to international travel companies, down to small agencies that specialise in handling independent trekkers. These small agencies will often be able to fix you up with individual porters or guides. A group trek organised through one of these agencies might cost US$30 to US$50 per person per day. Group treks staying at village inns along the route can be cheaper still (around US$25 a day including a guide and food).

Some trekking agencies that have been recommended include the following (all are Kathmandu-based unless noted):

Adventure Treks Nepal (☎ 01-2266534; www .adventurenepaltreks.com)
Ama Dablam Trekking (☎ 01-4415372; www.ama dablamadventures.com)
Asian Trekking (☎ 01-4415506; www.astrek.com)
Crystal Mountain Treks (☎ 01-4428013; www .crystalmountaintreks.com)
Dharma Adventures (☎ 01-4430499; www.dharma adventures.com)
Earthbound Expeditions (☎ 01-4701051; www .enepaltrekking.com)
Explore Himalaya (☎ 01-4418100; www.explore himalaya.com)
Explore Nepal (☎ 01-4226130; www.explore-nepal -group.com.np)
Friends in High Places (☎ 01-5533258; www.fihp .com)
High Spirit Treks (☎ 01-4701084; www.allnepaltreks .com)
Himalaya Journey (☎ 01-4383184; www.himalaya journeys.com)
International Trekkers (☎ 01-4371397; www .intrekasia.com)
Journeys International (☎ 01-4414662; www .journeys-nepal.com)
Langtang Ri Trekking (☎ 01-4423586; www.langtang .com)
Malla Treks (☎ 01-4423143; www.mallatreks.com)
Mountain Travel Nepal (☎ 01-4361500; www.tiger mountain.com)
Multi-Adventure (☎ 01-4257791; www.multiadventure .com)

Sherpa Shangrila Treks (☎ 01-4810373; www.trek andclimb.com)
Sherpa Society (☎ 01-4470361; www.sherpasociety trekking.com)
Sherpa Trekking Service (☎ 01-4421551; www.sts .com.np)
Sisne Rover Trekking (☎ 061- 461893; www.sisne rover.com) In Pokhara.
Thamserku Trekking (☎ 01-4354491; www.thamserku trekking.com)
Three Sisters Adventure Trekking (☎ 061-462066; www.3sistersadventure.com) In Pokhara.
Trek Nepal International (☎ 01-4701001; www.trek nepal.com)
Yeti Mountaineering & Trekking (☎ 01-4425896; www.yetimountaineeringntrek.com)

Maps

Most trekkers are content to get one of the trekking route maps produced locally by Himalayan Map House, Nepa Maps or Shangri-La Maps. They are relatively inexpensive (Rs 400 to Rs 800) and are adequate for the popular trails, though not for off-route travel. They are readily found in map and bookshops in Thamel. Be aware that there is a great deal of repackaging going on; don't buy two maps with different covers and names assuming you are getting significantly different maps.

The best series of maps of Nepal is the 1:50,000 series produced by Erwin Schneider and now published by Nelles Verlag. They cover the Kathmandu Valley and the Everest region from Jiri to the Hongu Valley. There are also 1:100,000 Schneider maps of Annapurna and Langtang available.

National Geographic produces 1:125,000 trekking maps to the Khumbu, Everest Base Camp, Annapurna and Langtang areas, as part of its Trails Illustrated series.

All of these maps are available at bookshops in Kathmandu and some speciality map shops overseas stock a selection. Most are available online from **Stanfords** (www.stanfords.co.uk), **Omni Resources** (www.omnimap.com) or **Melbourne Map Centre** (www.melbmap.com.au).

What to Bring
CLOTHING & FOOTWEAR

The clothing you require depends on where and when you trek. If you're going to Everest Base Camp in the middle of winter you must be prepared for very cold weather and take down gear, mittens and thermals. If you're

HIRING VS BUYING EQUIPMENT

It's always best to have your own equipment since you will be familiar with it and know for certain that it works. If there is some equipment that you do not have, you can always buy or rent it from one of Nepal's many trekking shops. Much of the equipment available is of adequate quality (but check items carefully) and the rental charges are generally not excessive, but large deposits are often required (usually equal to a generous valuation of the equipment itself). Never leave your passport as a deposit.

Hire rates in Kathmandu vary depending on quality. You can hire a sleeping bag (four season) for Rs 60 or a down jacket for Rs 40 to Rs 50 without much trouble. Tents are harder to find; hire costs around Rs 250.

Thamel is the centre for equipment shopping in Nepal, though Pokhara and Namche Bazaar also have trekking-equipment outlets. There is almost nothing you can't pick up in Kathmandu these days and you can even purchase sundries like sunblock on the trek in places like Chame and Namche Bazaar.

Some trekking gear, including sleeping bags, down jackets, fleeces, duffel bags, backpacks, camera cases, ponchos and wind jackets, is manufactured in Kathmandu and sold in Thamel at very reasonable prices. Much of this locally produced gear is liberally decorated with well-known brand names, but don't be deceived into thinking you're getting top-quality merchandise at a bargain price. The backpacks won't quite fit comfortably, the seams on the Gore-Tex jackets will leak and stitching will start to fray eventually. Even so, most items are well made and will stand up to the rigours of at least one major trek. The best buys are probably down jackets, fleeces and jackets.

Kathmandu does have several pukka (authentic) equipment showrooms such as the North Face and Mountain Hard Wear on Tridevi Marg (Map p140), with prices similar to those in the US.

doing a short, low-altitude trek early or late in the season the weather is likely to be fine enough for T-shirts and a fleece to pull on in the evenings.

Apart from ensuring you have adequate clothing to keep warm, it's important that your feet are comfortable and will stay dry if it rains or snows. Uncomfortable shoes and blistered feet are the worst possible trekking discomforts. Make sure your shoes are broken in, fit well and are comfortable for long periods. Running shoes are adequate for low-altitude (below 3000m), warm-weather treks where you won't encounter snow, though they lack ankle support. Otherwise the minimum standard of footwear is lightweight trekking boots. You can buy Korean-made trek shoes in Kathmandu but in general the quality of trek shoes for sale in Nepal is low and a Himalayan trek is not the place to break in a new pair of shoes. Bring your own worn-in boots.

OTHER GEAR

In winter or at high altitudes a top-quality four-season sleeping bag will be necessary. If you are going on an organised trek check what equipment is supplied by the company you sign up with. If you need to hire a sleeping bag, it could be grubby; check for fleas or worse.

Rain is rare during most of the trekking season, though weather patterns in the Bay of Bengal can cause massive rainstorms during autumn and there are sure to be a few rainy days during spring. You should be prepared for rain by carrying waterproof gear, or at least a portable umbrella. The rainy season just before and after the monsoon months also brings leeches with it, and it's good to have some salt or matches to deal with them. Take a torch (flashlight) for those inevitable calls of nature on moonless nights.

At high altitudes the burning power of the sun is strong, so make sure you have a pair of good sunglasses, a hat and sunblock. If there is any likelihood that you'll be walking over snow, sunglasses are insufficient; you need mountaineering glasses with side-pieces. Ensure that your porters also have adequate eyewear.

Other essentials include lip balm, three pairs of good hiking socks, a blister kit with tape and scissors, water purification tablets or iodine, a fleece hat and a medical kit (see p391). Also useful are a quick-drying camp towel, a padlock (for lodges), spare batteries and antibacterial hand gel.

MONEY
You can change cash in Namche Bazaar, Chame and some trailheads, and access ATMs in Jomsom and Namche Bazaar but you should generally bring all the cash you need with you, plus a stash of US dollars in case you need to buy an emergency flight home.

DOCUMENTS & FEES
Trekking Permits
Trekking permits are not required for treks in the Everest, Annapurna and Langtang regions described in this book.

TIMS Card
All trekkers are required to register their trek by obtaining a Trekking Information Management System (TIMS; www.timsnepal .com) card. The best palce to get a TIMS card is from the **Tourist Service Centre** (Map p126; ☎ 01-4256909 ext 223, 24hr tourism hotline 01-4225709; www .welcomenepal.com; Bhrikuti Mandap, Kathmandu; ◷ 10am-1pm & 2-5pm Sun-Fri) because you can also pay fees to enter Annapurna and buy national park tickets in this building.

Alternatively you can obtain the TIMS card at the **Trekking Agencies' Association of Nepal** (TAAN; Map pp114-15; ☎ 01-4427473; www.taan.org.np; Maligaun, Ganeshthan, Kathmandu; ◷ 10am-4pm Sun-Fri). The card cost is Rs 1580 (US$20) for individual trekkers or Rs 790 (US$10) if you are part of a group. Bring a photocopy of your passport and two passport photos – the card is issued on the spot.

You need to show the TIMS card at the start of the Annapurna, Langtang and Everest treks.

National Park & Conservation Fees
If your trek enters a national park such as Langtang or Sagarmatha (Everest), you must pay a national park fee.

If you are trekking in the Annapurna region you must pay a conservation area fee to the **Annapurna Conservation Area Project** (ACAP; Map p126; ☎ 01-4222406; www.ntnc.org.np; Pradarshanti Marg; ◷ 9am-5pm Sun-Fri, to 2pm Sat) in the same building as the Tourist Service Centre, a 20-minute walk from Thamel in Kathmandu (the ACAP is on the eastern side of the building). Bring Rs 2000 and one photograph. The permit is issued on the spot and isn't a hassle unless there is a long queue. Note that if you arrive at an ACAP checkpoint without a permit you will be charged double for the permit. This is also the place to get a Manaslu area permit.

Entrance tickets for national parks are available at the next door **national parks office** (◷ 9am-2pm Sun-Fri). The fee is Rs 1000 (US$15) for each park and you can also pay the fee when you arrive at the park entrance station. No photo is required.

Conservation fees for the Annapurna area are also payable in Pokhara at the **ACAP** (Map p266; ☎ 061-463376; ◷ 10am-5pm Sun-Fri, to 3.30pm Sat, to 4pm winter), at Damside inside the Nepal Tourism Board's (NTB) office.

RESPONSIBLE TREKKING
Nepal faces several environmental problems as a result of, or at least compounded by, tourists' actions and expectations. These include the depletion of forests for firewood; the build-up of nonbiodegradable waste, especially plastic bottles; and the pollution of waterways. You can help by choosing an environmentally and socially responsible trekking company and heeding some of the following advice.

Trekking Gently in the Himalaya, a booklet by Wendy Brewer Lama, is an excellent resource that has essential tips for trekkers. It's available at the KEEP offices in Kathmandu (Map p140) and Pokhara (Map p263); go to www.keepnepal.org for more details. For general information on travelling sustainably in Nepal see p70.

Firewood & Forest Depletion
Minimise the use of firewood by staying in lodges that use kerosene or fuel-efficient wood stoves and solar-heated hot water. Avoid using large open fires for warmth – wear additional clothing instead. Keep showers to a minimum and spurn showers altogether if wood is burnt to produce the hot water.

Consolidate cooking time (and wood consumption) by ordering the same items at the same time as other trekkers. Daal bhaat (rice and lentils) is usually readily available for large numbers of people, does not require lengthy cooking time, and is nutritious and inexpensive. Remember that local meals are usually

DB GURUNG

DB Gurung, Director, Kathmandu Environmental Education Project (KEEP), spoke to us about how travellers and trekkers can minimise their environmental footprint in Nepal.

What are the most pressing threats facing the environment in Nepal?
Deforestation and vanishing wildlife in the hills, and the accumulation of nonbiodegradable garbage along trekking routes, polluting water sources and rivers.

What can travellers do to minimise their impact while travelling in Nepal?
While trekking, stay at lodges that use alternative fuels for cooking. Don't make campfires and only take showers if the water is solar heated. Leave all nonbiodegradable items at home and carry out anything you do bring in. Avoid drinks or foods in plastic wrappers, bottles and tins, and purify your own drinking water with iodine. Also, use biodegradable soaps for washing and take your batteries home for proper disposal.

What can travellers do to aid the welfare of porters while trekking?
Trekkers should provide porters with a fair wage. Do not overload your porters, and provide adequate clothing. If you join an organised trek, ensure that the company takes care of its porters and provides them with medical and life insurance.

Do you have any safety tips for trekkers?
Never trek alone. Trekking with a guide or porter is the safest way to go. For any trek, prepare in advance, bring all the things that you may need and register with your embassy in Kathmandu and at every check post on the trekking route. And stay in good health!

Has trekking changed since you first became involved in the industry?
Of course! When I first started trekking in 1978, we used to cook with firewood and make campfires every evening to keep our clients warm. Now, all the camping groups use kerosene or gas for cooking and we never make campfires. Here at KEEP, we conduct workshops and training courses on conservation issues so guides, kitchen crew and porters are aware of the environmental impact of trekking. Most trekkers are already aware of the environmental problems – after all, this is a global issue!

---

prepared between 10am and 11am, so eating then will usually not require lighting an additional fire. Treat your drinking water with iodine rather than boiling it.

Those travelling with organised groups should ensure kerosene is used for cooking, including by porters. In alpine areas ensure that all members are outfitted with enough clothing so that fires are not a necessity for warmth.

Garbage & Waste

You can do several things to reduce the amount of rubbish and pollution in the hills. Purifying your own water instead of buying mineral water in nonbiodegradable plastic bottles is the most important of these.

Bring a couple of spare stuff sacks and use them to compact litter that you find on mountain trails to be disposed of down in Kathmandu.

Independent trekkers should always carry their garbage out or dispose of it properly. You can burn it, but you should remember that the fireplace in a Nepali home is sacred

and throwing rubbish into it would be a great insult. Take away all your batteries, as they will eventually leak toxins. Don't bury your rubbish.

Toilet paper is a particularly unpleasant sight along trails; if you must use it, carry it in a plastic bag until you can burn it. If you are camping, carry a small plastic trowel to bury your faeces (at least 100m away from any streams). Those travelling with organised groups should ensure that toilet tents are properly organised, that everyone uses them (including porters) and that rubbish is carried out. Check on the company's policies before you sign up.

Water

Do your bit to minimise pollution and don't soap up your clothes and wash them in the streams. Instead, use a bowl or bucket and discard the dirty water away from watercourses.

On the Annapurna Circuit, the ACAP (with New Zealand government assistance) has introduced the Safe Drinking

Water Scheme – a chain of 16 outlets selling purified water to trekkers. Its aim is to minimise the estimated one million plastic bottles that are brought into the Annapurna Conservation Area each year, creating a serious litter problem. The outlets are found in Tal, Bagarchhap, Chame, Pisang, Hongde, Manang, Letdar, Thorung Phedi, Muktinath, Kagbeni, Jomsom, Marpha, Tukuche, Khobang, Lete and Ghasa and a litre of water costs between Rs 35 and Rs 60, which is a fraction of the cost of bottled water.

USEFUL ORGANISATIONS

The following two organisations in Kathmandu offer free, up-to-date information on trekking conditions, health risks and minimising your environmental impact. They are also excellent places to visit and advertise for trekking companions.

KEEP (Map p140; ☎ 01-4216775; www.keepnepal .org; Thamel; ☼ 10am-5pm Sun-Fri) has a library, some useful notebooks with up-to-date information from other trekkers, an excellent noticeboard and embassy registration forms for most countries. It also sells iodine tablets (Rs 500), biodegradable soap, trekking garbage bags and other environmentally friendly equipment.

Himalayan Rescue Association (HRA; Map p140; ☎ 01-4445505; www.himalayanrescue.org; Thamel; ☼ 10am-1pm & 2-5pm Sun-Fri) has information and videos about AMS, plus weather updates and embassy registration forms. It runs health posts at Pheriche, Machhermo and Manang and hopes to eventually run a post at Thorung Phedi on the Annapurna Circuit. Free lectures on altitude sickness are held at the Thamel office at 3pm Monday to Friday. There's a **Lazimpat branch** (Map p126; ☎ 01-4440292) of HRA in central Kathmandu.

The slide shows held in the Kathmandu Guest House (p142) by Chris Beall, a British freelance photographer, writer and trek leader, are another good source of up-to-date information in Kathmandu for independent trekking. The shows cost Rs 400 (including tea/coffee and biscuits) and you get plenty of time to ask questions at the end. You'll see posters up at the guest house.

Several organisations are attempting to deal with the environmental problems created by trekking. The ACAP (p76) has done a great deal to encourage sustainable development in the Annapurna region and has offices in Kathmandu, Patan and Pokhara.

HEALTH

AMS or altitude sickness is the major concern on all high-altitude treks – be ever-alert to the symptoms of AMS (p395). For the majority of trekkers health problems are likely to be minor, such as stomach upsets and blisters, and commonsense precautions are all that are required to avoid illness.

Take care that water is always safe to drink. The best method is to treat water with iodine, as this is safe and does not require the use of firewood or kerosene to boil water. Diarrhoea is a fairly minor problem but it can ruin a trek, so watch what you eat and ensure your medical kit contains antidiarrhoeal medicine such as Lomotil or Imodium (for emergencies only) and a broad-spectrum antibiotic like Azithromycin or Norfloxacin. You can buy these antibiotics without a prescription at pharmacies in Kathmandu and Pokhara. The food at a lodge or on an organised trek is unlikely to cause problems, but hygiene at local inns can be suspect.

Many people suffer from knee and ankle strains, particularly if they are carrying their own pack. If you have a predisposition to these injuries, carry elastic supports or bandages, as well as Ibuprofen tablets and analgesic cream to ease swelling. Lightweight, collapsible trekking poles are invaluable, providing extra support and stability, especially on those knee-pounding descents. You should also carry moleskin, plasters (Band-Aids) and tape in your day pack in case of blisters.

Make sure you are in good health before departing, as there is very little medical attention along the trails and rescue helicopters are not only very expensive but *must* be cleared for payment in advance. Your embassy can do this if you have registered with it. See p341 for more information on medical assistance on the Everest trek, and p347 for Langtang. In general, Himalayan hospitals can offer only very limited facilities and expertise.

See p390 for more detailed information on staying healthy while in Nepal.

TREKKING SAFELY

Usually, the further you get from heavily populated centres the less likely it is that your personal safety will be threatened.

Assaults in remote places are not unheard of, however. Several basic rules should be followed: don't trek alone, don't make ostentatious displays of valuable possessions and don't leave lodge doors unlocked or valuables unattended.

See p367 for more information on dangers while trekking.

Choosing Companions

You should never trek alone. You'll appreciate having someone around when you're lost, sick or suffering from altitude sickness. It's useful to have someone to occasionally watch your pack or valuables when you visit the bathroom or take a shower. Solo women travellers should choose trekking companions and guides particularly carefully.

If you do not already have a travelling companion, then you should find either a guide or another trekker in Kathmandu or Pokhara to trek with. If you're looking for a Western companion, check hotel bulletin boards or post a message on www.trekinfo.com, www.yetizone.com or www.lonelyplanet.com/thorntree, or just chat with travellers you meet and perhaps your schedules and ambitions will match. Unless you are an experienced trekker or have a friend to trek with, you should at least take a porter or guide.

Trail Conditions

Walking at high altitudes on rough trails can be dangerous. Watch your footing on narrow, slippery trails and never underestimate the changeability of the weather – at any time of the year. If you are crossing high passes where snow is a possibility, never walk with less than three people. Carry a supply of emergency rations, have a map and compass (and know how to use them), and have sufficient clothing and equipment to deal with cold, wet, blizzard conditions.

You will be sharing the trail with porters, mules and yaks, all usually carrying heavy loads, so give them the right of way. If a mule or yak train approaches, always move to the high side of the trail to avoid being knocked over the edge.

Register With Your Embassy

All embassies and consulates strongly recommend that their citizens register with them before they hit the trail. See the boxed text, p368.

RESTING – A NEPALI INSTITUTION

With the tortuous nature of the Nepali landscape, getting around on foot can be heavy going. To ease the burden on travellers, villagers across Nepal have created thousands of chautaras – stone platforms shaded by pipal or banyan trees – where walkers can rest their weary bones and comfortably set down their loads. Many chautaras stand on the site of ancient pre-Hindu shrines and are a focal point for village life – a place to meet and chat, or trade and carry out religious rituals. Even today, constructing a chautara is seen as a sure-fire way to improve karma (the Buddhist and Hindu law of cause and effect) for future existences.

Rescue Insurance

Check that your travel-insurance policy does not exclude mountaineering or 'alpinism'. Although you will not be engaging in these activities on a trek, you may have trouble convincing the insurance company of this fact. Check what insurance is available through your trekking company, if using one. Rescue insurance will need to cover an emergency helicopter evacuation or a charter flight from a remote airstrip, as well as international medical evacuation. A helicopter evacuation from 4000m near Mt Everest will cost you US$2500 to US$10,000.

You can purchase rescue insurance from most alpine clubs in Western countries, including the **British Mountaineering Council** (www.thebmc.co.uk). In Nepal, **Neco Insurance** (☎ 01-4427355; www.necoins.com.np; Hattisar, Kathmandu) offers trekking policies. Personal accident, medical and evacuation insurance for trekkers is around US$7 per day for the first 15 days of trekking and US$5 per day thereafter.

Altitude

Walking the trails of Nepal often entails a great deal of altitude gain and loss; even the base of the great mountains of the Himalaya can be very high. Most treks that go through populated areas stick to between 1000m and 3000m, although the Everest Base Camp Trek and the Annapurna Circuit Trek both reach over 5000m. On high treks like these ensure adequate acclimatisation, and the maxim of 'walking high, sleeping low' is good advice; your night halt should be at a lower level than the highest point reached in the day. Make a point to catch the free altitude lectures given by the **HRA** (Map p140; ☎ 01-4445505; www .himalayanrescue.org; ☺ 10am-1pm & 2-5pm Sun-Fri; Thamel) in Kathmandu, or at their Manang and Pheriche aid posts on the Annapurna and Everest treks respectively.

TREKS

ROUTES & CONDITIONS

Most trails are clear and easy to follow, though they are often steep and taxing, with long stretches of switchbacks or stone staircases. The old adage that 'the shortest path between two points is a straight line' appears to have been firmly drummed into Nepalis, irrespective of any mountains or valleys that may get in the way! Distances on a map quickly become irrelevant with the many ups and downs and twists and twists of Nepal's trails.

A typical day's walk lasts from between five to seven hours and rarely spends much time on level ground. On an organised camping trek the day is run to a remarkably tight schedule. A typical pattern would be: up at 6am, start walking at 7am, stop for lunch at 10am, start after lunch at noon, stop walking at 3pm. Nepalis rise early, eat very little for breakfast, eat a large lunch in the late morning and a second meal before dark, then retire early – you will be best off to try and follow a similar schedule.

A little rudimentary knowledge of the Nepali language will help to make your trek easier and more interesting, although finding your way is rarely difficult on the major trekking routes and English is fairly widely spoken. See p401 for some useful Nepali words and phrases.

Sleeping

Organised treks camp each night and all you have to do is eat and crawl into your tent. Even erecting the tent is handled by the trekking crew, who put it up for you at the site selected by your *sirdar* (group leader).

On the treks described in this chapter, trekkers can stay in lodges or teahouses that pop up alongside the trail every couple of hours. These lodges range from simple extensions of a traditional wooden family home to quite luxurious places with private rooms, multipage menus, and even attached toilets and showers. Most mattresses are foam (of varying thicknesses) and bedding is always supplied. Nevertheless, it's still a good idea to carry a sleeping bag, especially at higher elevations and during peak season.

Eating

On an organised trek your only concern with food is sitting down to eat it. The porters carry virtually all of the ingredients with them and there will be a cook with well-drilled assistants who can turn out meals with impressive ingenuity.

Independent trekkers will find numerous places to eat along the most popular trails, although it's wise to carry some emergency food supplies such as granola (muesli) bars, dried fruit or chocolate. On the Everest and Annapurna treks it's unlikely that you will walk more than an hour or two without coming across some sort of establishment that offers chow mein, fried potatoes, momos, fried rice and a half-dozen types of tea, by the cup or pot. The local staple of daal bhaat is nutritious, available everywhere, and requires minimum fuel for preparation. It's also the only meal that will truly fill you up after a day trekking. You'll lessen your impact on the environment and usually eat better if you adapt to the local diet.

The lodges around Jomsom and Namche Bazaar specialise in delicious apple pie, a trekkers' staple these days, along with local versions of pizza. It's surprising how many places even have cold beer available as well; before you complain about the price (as much as Rs 350 a bottle), consider that somebody had to carry that bottle of beer all the way up there and will probably have to carry the empty bottle back again!

CHOOSING A TREK

It is possible to do short treks in Nepal that do not reach demanding altitudes or need sophisticated equipment, years of experience or athletic stamina. A certain level of mental and physical fitness plus sensible planning and preparation will ensure that yours is an enjoyable experience. For a selection of short treks see p275 and p170.

Six popular treks are described in this chapter; between them they account for 90% of

TREKKING

THE LURE OF MT EVEREST

During the 1920s and '30s, reaching the top of Mt Everest came to dominate the Western imagination. Apart from the difficulties inherent in reaching such heights, the political constraints further upped the ante. Nepal continued to be totally isolated from outsiders, and all attempts on Everest had to be made from the Tibetan side.

British assaults were made in 1921, 1922 and 1924. The 1922 expedition used oxygen to reach 8326m, while the 1924 expedition fell just 300m short of the top, reaching 8572m without the use of oxygen. In addition to numerous climbers and support staff, the 1924 expedition utilised at least 350 porters. Such massive numbers of porters and staff set a pattern that was to continue until recent years.

The discovery in 1999 of the body of British climber George Mallory, frozen near the summit, was a new chapter in one of the enduring mysteries of mountaineering history. In 1924 Mallory and his climbing partner, Andrew Irvine, disappeared within sight of the top. Did they reach the summit? No one can be sure. However, Mallory did leave behind his famous explanation of mountaineering: when asked why he was climbing Mt Everest he said, 'Because it's there'.

In 1951 a climber who would soon become very famous took part in an exploratory expedition to the mountain – the climber was New Zealander Edmund Hillary. Another name, soon to be equally famous, appeared on the list of climbers on the Swiss Everest expedition of 1952 when Sherpa climber Tenzing Norgay reached 7500m. The conquest of Everest finally took place in 1953 when a British team led by John Hunt put those two climbers, Tenzing and Hillary, atop the world's highest peak.

---

all trek trips in Nepal. The two most popular the Everest Base Camp and Annapurna Circuit treks. Both offer spectacular scenery and cultural depth, as well as plenty of crowds. Everest has become insanely busy in recent years, while the Annapurna region has been affected by road building along the Jomsom side. The Annapurna Circuit has the advantage of being a loop route, while Everest is an out-and-back trek, returning to Lukla via the same route. The Annapurna Sanctuary is a relatively short trek that combines superb views of Machhapuchhare with close-up views of some huge Himalayan peaks. It's easily combined with the Annapurna Circuit to create a definitive month-long trek. Noticeably quieter are the Langtang and Gosainkund regions. Helambu is a good low-altitude choice in winter.

EVEREST BASE CAMP TREK
Duration 14 to 20 days
Maximum elevation 5545m
Best season October to December
Start Lukla
Finish Lukla

Everybody has heard of the world's highest mountain and that's the reason why the Everest Base Camp Trek is so popular.

The trek has a number of stunning attractions, not least of these is being able to say you've visited the highest mountain in the world. The trek gets you right into the high-altitude heart of the high Himalaya, more so than any other teahouse trek, there are some lovely villages and gompas (monasteries), and the friendly Sherpa people of the Solu Khumbu region make trekking through the area a joy.

A return trek to Everest Base Camp from the airstrip at Lukla takes at least 14 days but you are better off budgeting a further week to take in some of the stunning and less-visited side valleys. If you have the time, one way to beat the crowds is to walk in from Shivalaya or Jiri and fly out from Lukla. If you fly straight to Lukla, be sure to schedule acclimatisation days at Namche and Pheriche to avoid altitude sickness. A shorter week-long trek from Lukla could take you on a loop through Namche Bazaar, Thame, Khumjung and Tengboche Monastery.

The trek reaches a high point of 5545m at Kala Pattar, a small peak offering views of Mt Everest and the Khumbu Icefall. Ironically, the Everest views from base camp are actually quite unimpressive (in the words of mountain writer Ed Douglas, 'Everest is like a grossly fat man in a room full of beautiful women').

Far more stirring are the graceful lines of surrounding peaks, such as Ama Dablam, Pumori and Nuptse. Perhaps the best scenery of the trek is found in the neighbouring Gokyo Valley, off the main trail.

In the last decade the tourist crowds in the Khumbu region have swollen to record numbers, partly due to Nepal's Maoist rebellion (the Khumbu was not affected by the insurgency) and partly because of the 'Krakauer effect' – the surge in Everest-mania since the release of the bestselling Jon Krakauer book *Into Thin Air,* and the endless documentaries and publications that followed in its wake. The scenery is still breathtaking, but don't expect to have the place to yourself. This is one trek you might consider tackling outside of October, so you won't have to share the trails with 9000 or so other trekkers.

Facilities on the Everest trek are excellent. The upper reaches of the trek are through essentially uninhabited areas but lodges operate throughout the trekking season. These days trekking and mountaineering are the backbone of the Sherpa economy. More than half of the population in the region is now involved with tourism, and the bookstore, trek-gear shops, bakeries and internet cafes in Namche Bazaar make it look more like an alpine resort than a Sherpa village.

The walking on this trek is (surprisingly) not all that strenuous, mainly because new arrivals can only walk a few hours each day before they have to stop to acclimatise. If trekkers fail to reach their goal it is usually because they failed to devote enough time to acclimatisation. It may be tempting to keep walking at the end of a three-hour day, but it's essential to take it slowly on the first 10 days of this trek. For more on mountain sickness see p395.

Emergency Facilities

There are small hospitals in Jiri, Phaplu and Khunde (just north of Namche Bazaar); the Himalayan Rescue Association (HRA) has a medical facility in Pheriche.

Access

FLIGHTS FROM KATHMANDU TO LUKLA

Most Everest trekkers opt to fly to Lukla to maximise their time in the high mountains and up to 50 flights land here each day during the high season. In 2008 a Yeti Airlines plane crashed at Lukla in bad visibility,

killing 14 trekkers and four Nepalis. Backlogs of trekkers can build up during bad weather, so give yourself a buffer of a day or two, but these days there are enough flights to keep everyone happy.

SHIVALAYA TREK

While most people fly in and out of Lukla these days, it is possible to trek in or out from the trailhead at Shivalaya, just past Jiri. The trek from Shivalaya to Lukla is a hard slog and pretty sparse in the breathtaking-views department but you will at least shake the crowds. The trek doesn't follow valleys, it cuts across them, so day after day it is a tiring process of dropping down one side of a steep valley and climbing up the other. By the time you reach the base camp your ascents will total almost 9000m – the full height of Everest from sea level!

There is one bus a day at 6am from Kathmandu's Ratna Park (City) bus station to Shivalaya (Rs 550), as well as more frequent departures to Jiri (Rs 360, departures between 5.30am and 8.45am), from where you can catch local transport on to Shivalaya. Keep a close eye on your luggage.

The trek stages generally work out as follows; lodges are available at every night's stop:

Day 1: Shivalaya to Bhandar
Day 2: Bhandar to Sete
Day 3: Sete to Junbesi
Day 4: Junbesi to Nunthala
Day 5: Nunthala to Bupsa
Day 6: Bupsa to Lukla

The Trek

DAY ONE: LUKLA TO PHAKDING

After flying to Lukla, arranging your packs and maybe a porter, trek downhill to lodges at Cheplung (Chablung). From here the trail contours along the side of the Dudh Kosi Valley before ascending to Ghat (Lhawa; 2530m). The trail climbs again to Phakding, a collection of about 25 lodges at 2610m.

DAY TWO: PHAKDING TO NAMCHE BAZAAR

The trail crosses the river on a long, swaying bridge and then leads you along the river to climb to Benkar (2700m), a decent alternative overnight stop. A short distance beyond Benkar the trail crosses the Dudh Kosi to its east bank on a suspension bridge and climbs to Chumoa.

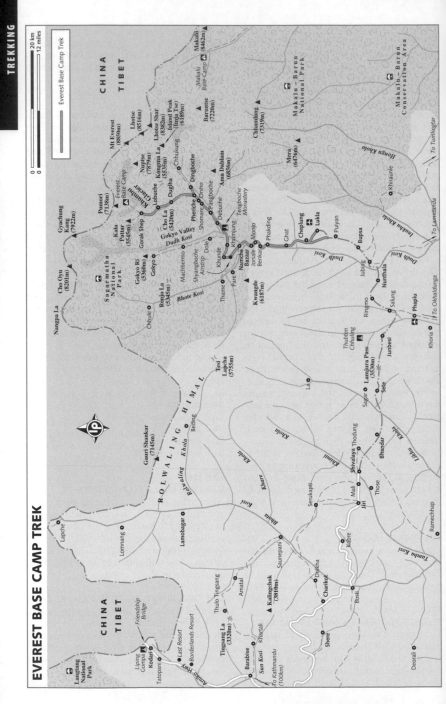

EVEREST BASE CAMP TREK

Everest Base Camp Trek

It's a short climb through forests to Monjo (2800m), where there are some good places to stay. Show your entrance ticket or buy one for Rs 1000 at the Sagarmatha National Park entrance station and register your TIMS card, then descend to cross the Dudh Kosi. On the other side it's a short distance to Jorsale (Thumbug; 2830m), the last settlement before Namche Bazaar, then the trail crosses back to the east side of the river before climbing to the high suspension bridge over the Dudh Kosi.

It's a steady two-hour climb from here to Namche Bazaar (3420m). As this is the first climb to an altitude where AMS may be a problem, take it easy and avoid rushing. There is another national park entrance station just below Namche where permits are again checked and fees collected.

DAY THREE: ACCLIMATISATION DAY IN NAMCHE BAZAAR

Namche Bazaar is the main trade and administrative centre for the entire Solu Khumbu region and has trek shops, restaurants, bakeries, pharmacies, hotels with hot showers, a pool hall, massage centre, post office, moneychanger, bank, ATM and even internet cafes. Pay a visit to the office of the **Sagarmatha Pollution Control Committee** (10am-5pm Mon-Fri) to find out about conservation efforts being made in the region and visit the excellent **Sagarmatha National Park Visitor Centre**

(admission free; 8am-4pm Sun-Fri) on the ridge above town.

Namche Bazaar and the surrounding villages have an ample supply of hydroelectricity, used for lighting and cooking as well as powering the video parlours. There is a colourful market each Saturday.

There is plenty to do around Namche Bazaar and you should spend a day here acclimatising. Remember that victims of AMS are often the fittest, healthiest people who foolishly overextend themselves. It's helpful to do a strenuous day walk to a higher altitude as part of your acclimatisation, coming back down to Namche to sleep. For this purpose, the six- to seven-hours-return day walk west to Thame is worthwhile.

DAY FOUR: NAMCHE BAZAAR TO TENGBOCHE

The slightly longer route from Namche Bazaar to Tengboche via Khumjung and Khunde is more interesting than the direct one. The route starts by climbing up to the Shyangboche airstrip. Above the airstrip is the Hotel Everest View, listed in the Guinness Book of Records as the highest hotel on earth.

From the hotel or the airstrip you climb to Khunde (3840m), then Khumjung (3790m) and then rejoin the direct trail to Tengboche. The trail descends to the Dudh Kosi (3250m) where there are several small lodges and a series of picturesque water-driven prayer

---

EVEREST NUTS *Bradley Mayhew*

The world's highest peak has attracted many commendable achievements: the first ascent without oxygen (1978), first summit with an artificial leg (1998), the first ski descent (2000), the first blind ascent (2001), most ascents (18), youngest ascent (aged 16), oldest ascent (78) and fastest ascent (eight hours). Sherpa Babu Chiru spent a particularly amazing 21 hours on top of Everest without oxygen in 1999.

But there have also been some admirably silly achievements.

Perhaps most ambitious was the Briton Maurice Wilson, who planned to crash his Gipsy Moth plane halfway up the mountain and then climb from there to the top, not letting his almost total lack of mountaineering or flying experience get in the way of an obviously silly plan. He eventually froze to death at Camp III dressed in a light sweater (and, it is rumoured, women's clothing).

Maybe it's something in the national psyche (this is after all the nation that gave us Monty Python), for it was also a team of Brits who trekked all the way to Everest Base Camp to play the 'world's highest game of rugby' at 5140m. They lost. Another British team staged a similarly high cricket match in 2009 at Gorak Shep.

My personal Everest heroes are the British (!) pair who carried an ironing board up Everest to 5440m to do some extreme ironing ('part domestic chore, part extreme sport'). For anyone contemplating a repeat expedition, the duo have revealed that expedition preparation can be limited to three important factors: 'a few beers, a drunken bet and a stolen ironing board'.

YETI!

Along with the equally slippery notion of Shangri La, the yeti is one of Nepal's most famous cultural exports, occupying a hotly debated biological niche somewhere between zoology and folk religion.

Before you throw your arms up in the air and storm out of the room, bear in mind that the pro-yeti camp has some serious proponents. In 1938 mountaineer Bill Tilman tracked yeti footprints for over a mile, later writing that their 'existence is surely no longer a matter for conjecture'. Eric Shipton photographed a yeti print on the Menling/Menlungtse glacier in 1951. Edmund Hillary led an expedition to Rolwaling in 1960 to track the yeti, as did Chris Bonington in 1986 and travel writer Bruce Chatwin. Reinhold Messner claimed to have seen a yeti in Tibet in 1986 and wrote a book about the subject called *My Quest for the Yeti*.

There are dozens of cases of local sightings. Villagers in the Rongbuk region of Tibet apparently discovered a drowned yeti corpse in 1958. In 1998 the official police report on the murder of a Sherpa woman near Dole on the Gokyo trek in Nepal cited 'yeti attack' as the cause of death! Japan's most celebrated yeti hunter is Yoshiteru Takahashi, who in 2003 claimed to have found a yeti cave on the slopes of Dhaulagiri (his camera froze before he could take a photo…).

The Rolwaling region seems to be the heartland of yeti sightings, followed closely by the Khumbu. Trekkers on the Everest Base Camp Trek can still see the yeti scalp at Khumjung Monastery (actually made from the skin of a serow – a type of goat/antelope), though the yeti hand of Pangboche, said to have been that of a mummified lama, has mysteriously disappeared. The region's 'yeti pelts' actually belong to the Himalayan blue bear.

The word 'yeti' comes from the Tibetan *yeh-teh*, or 'man of the rocky/snowy places'; the alternative Tibetan names are the *migyu* and *mehton kangmi*, or 'abominable snowman'. Reports from western Nepal talk of the *lamkarna*, or 'long-eared' monster. First-hand accounts of the yeti describe it as having reddish fur, a conical head, a high-pitched cry and strange body odour that smells of garlic, but a sign at Khumjung Monastery outlines the different types of yeti in more subtle and, more importantly, cultural terms. The apelike *dre-ma* and *tel-ma* are messengers of calamity, it says, while the *chu-ti* moves on all fours and preys on goats, sheep and yaks. Worst of all is the *mi-te*, a man-eater, 6ft to 8ft tall, with 'a very bad temperament'. Consider yourself warned.

wheels. A steep ascent brings you to Tengboche (3870m). The famous gompa, with its background of Ama Dablam, Everest and other peaks, was burnt down in 1989 but has since risen phoenixlike from the ashes. There's a camping area and several busy lodges. During the October/November full moon the colourful Mani Rimdu festival is held here with masked dancing and Tibetan opera in the monastery courtyard – accommodation becomes extremely difficult to find. See www.tengboche.org for upcoming dates; see p26 for more information.

DAY FIVE: TENGBOCHE TO PHERICHE

Beyond Tengboche the altitude really starts to show. The trail drops down to Debuche, crosses the Imja Khola and climbs through rhododendron forest past superb mani stones (carved with the Tibetan Buddhist mantra *om mani padme hum*) to Pangboche (3860m).

The gompa here is the oldest in the Khumbu and until 1991 it was said to hold the skull and hand of a yeti. The village is a good place for a lunch stop.

The trail then climbs past Shomare and Orsho to Pheriche (4240m), where there is an HRA trekkers' aid post and possible medical assistance. Pheriche has a dozen or so lodges, some of which offer exotic canned dishes left over from international mountaineering expeditions.

DAY SIX: ACCLIMATISATION DAY IN PHERICHE

Another acclimatisation day should be spent at Pheriche. As at Namche, a solid day walk to a higher altitude is better than just resting; the villages of Dingboche and Chhukung (4730m) are possible destinations and both offer good views. Nangkartshang Gompa, on the ridge north of Dingboche, offers good views east to Makalu (8462m), the world's fifth-highest mountain. Chhukung is a five- to six-hour return hike up the Imja Khola Valley that offers stunning views. There is food and accommodation at Chhukung.

DAY SEVEN: PHERICHE TO DUGLHA

The trail climbs to Phulang Kala (4340m) then Duglha (4620m). It's a two-hour trek to Duglha but the HRA doctors at Pheriche urge everyone to stay a night here to aid acclimatisation.

DAY EIGHT: DUGLHA TO LOBUCHE

From Duglha the trail goes directly up the gravely terminal moraine of the Khumbu Glacier for about one hour, then bears left to a group of memorials to lost climbers and Sherpas, including Scott Fischer who died in the 1996 Everest disaster. It's a short climb past views of Pumori to the summer village of Lobuche (4930m). The altitude, cold and crowded lodges combine to ensure a fitful night.

DAY NINE: LOBUCHE TO GORAK SHEP

The return trip from Lobuche to Gorak Shep (5160m) takes just a couple of hours, leaving enough time to continue to the peak of Kala Pattar (three hours return) – or you can overnight in Gorak Shep and reach Kala Pattar early the next morning for the best chance of good weather. At 5545m this small peak offers the best view you'll get of Everest in Nepal without climbing it.

Gorak Shep was the base camp for the 1952 Swiss expedition to Everest. There is accommodation here but it's cold and the altitude makes life uncomfortable. If the altitude is getting to you, descending to Lobuche or, better, Pheriche, makes a real difference.

DAY 10: GORAK SHEP TO LOBUCHE

If you want to visit Everest Base Camp (5360m), it's a six-hour round trip from Gorak Shep. EBC is dotted with tents in the April/May climbing season but in other months there's not a great deal to see except for views of the Khumbu Icefall. There are no views of Everest from base camp. If you only have the energy for one side trip, make it Kala Pattar.

The two-hour trek back down to Lobuche seems easy after all the climbing, and some trekkers continue for another three hours down to Dingboche or Pheriche the same day.

DAY 11: LOBUCHE TO DINGBOCHE

Staying the night at Dingboche (4410m) makes an interesting alternative to Pheriche. There are good lodges, Nepal's highest internet cafe and fine views of Island Peak (Imja Tse; 6189m) and Lhotse (8516m).

DAYS 12 TO 14: DINGBOCHE TO LUKLA

The next three days retrace your steps down to Lukla via Tengboche and Namche Bazaar. If you are flying out of Lukla, get to the airline office the day before to reconfirm your seat (the airline offices are usually open from 5pm to 6pm, but sometimes it's 6pm to 7pm). If the weather has been bad you might be vying for a flight with dozens of other trekkers, but generally you shouldn't have a problem.

Alternative Routes & Side Trips

The side trips off the Everest Base Camp Trek rank as some of the region's highlights so it makes sense to add on an extra week or so to explore the region more fully. A particularly scenic side trip is the six-day detour from Namche Bazaar to the **Gokyo Valley**, culminating in the spectacular glacier and lake views from 5360m Gokyo Ri. It's important to ascend the valley slowly, overnighting in Phortse Thenga, Dole, Machhermo and Gokyo to aid acclimatisation. From Gokyo you can rejoin the main EBC trail near Khumjung or Pangboche. You can even combine both the Gokyo Valley and Everest Base Camp by crossing the 5420m Cho La, but you need to take this route seriously and enquire about the conditions before setting out. Some months the pass is clear of snow, at other times you'll need crampons for this high crossing. A loop route taking in the Gokyo Valley and Everest Base Camp via Cho La takes around 17 days.

A shorter side trip is from Namche Bazaar to Thame, the gateway to the forbidden Nangpa La and Tibet. You can do a round trip to Thame in one very long day, but it's better to stay overnight to catch the morning views.

Another recommended side trip is up the Imja Khola Valley to Chhukung, for awesome mountain views. Chhukung is also the staging post for climbers heading to Island Peak (see p111) and the valley is well worth exploring.

TREKKING

PHURBA SHERPA

Based in the village of Chaurikharka near Lukla, Phurba Sherpa works as a trekking guide around the Everest region.

How old were you when you first worked as a porter or guide?

I was 15 years old when I first started working as a porter, hauling bags for trekkers. Yes, it was hard work, but I needed some education to become a guide and I was happy to carry the baggage and learn some English words.

What do you do when you are not guiding trekkers?

I have a farm near Lukla and I spend the rest of the year in the fields. In winter, we plough the land with oxen and put down leaves and dung as fertilizer, then we plant potatoes. In March, when the plants are about 4in high, we plant corn among the potatoes, then after the harvest in August and September we plant wheat which runs through till the next winter. My wife looks after the farm and our two daughters when I go trekking. I used to have several yaks and a dog, but I sold the yaks after one became sick and the dog disappeared – I think it was taken by a leopard.

How do you prepare for a trek?

As Buddhists, we Sherpas always offer a prayer for good luck before we go trekking, before we do any business and for everything else in life, including getting married! When I go trekking, I often talk to lamas at monasteries to learn new mantras that I can use at home.

What is life like in the Khumbu outside the tourist season?

During the monsoon, we take our yaks and naks to the high mountains to graze around places like the base camp for Mt Ama Dablam and the meadows above Pheriche and Dingboche. If I can afford it, I go to see my sister and parents in Kathmandu, but this depends on finding enough work as a porter and guide. Winters can be hard. We use this time to get everything ready for the next season – collecting wood and leaves for fodder, and gathering animal dung to use for cooking and heating the house through the winter.

As an alternative to flying back to Kathmandu you can escape the crowds on the nine-day teahouse trek southeast from Lukla to Tumlingtar, from where you can fly or bus back to Kathmandu. For full details see Lonely Planet's *Trekking in the Nepal Himalaya* guide.

LANGTANG TREK

Duration seven to eight days
Maximum elevation 3870m
Best season September to May
Start Syabrubesi
Finish Syabrubesi

The Langtang region is the third most popular trekking area in Nepal but receives only a fraction of the crowds that hit the Annapurna or Everest trails. Langtang has many things going for it: it's close to Kathmandu, there's a wide range of scenery, you get right into the mountains within a couple of days, there are fewer trekkers, the accommodation is good and there are lots of possible trek combinations.

The trek ascends the Langtang Valley from just 1470m at Syabrubesi to 3870m at Kyanjin Gompa, past ever-changing scenery and Tamang villages to a collection of high alpine pastures, glaciers and peaks on the border with Tibet. Although the trek passes through lightly populated and undeveloped areas, there are still plenty of lodges along the route. The trail offers exceptionally diverse scenery and culture. The superb day hikes from Kyanjin Gompa in particular offer spectacular close-up views of the surrounding peaks and glaciers of Langtang Lirung (7246m), Kimshung (6781m) and Langshisha Ri (6370m).

Potential add-ons to a Langtang trek include a trek along the Tamang Heritage Trail (see p233) or a visit to the Gosainkund lakes, after which you can either return to Dhunche (12 days total) or continue over the Laurebina La to Kathmandu (14 days total; p350).

If you want real adventure then enlist the aid of a trekking company, pack camping gear and some porters and link the Langtang and

Helambu treks over the 5106m Ganja La pass, a four-day expedition. Note that the Ganja La is one of the more difficult passes in Nepal and should not be attempted without a knowledgeable guide, adequate acclimatisation, good equipment and some mountaineering experience. See Lonely Planet's *Trekking in the Nepal Himalaya* for details.

The treks all enter the Langtang National Park and the army collects a Rs 1000 park entrance fee. Checkposts are at Dhunche and at Ghora Tabela. Video cameras are only allowed into the national park after paying a whopping US$1000 fee.

Emergency Facilities

There are national park radios at Ghora Tabela and Langtang, and there are telephones at Dhunche and Thulo Syabru. The Yeti Guest House in Kyanjin Gompa has a satellite phone that can be used to summon a helicopter in an emergency.

Access: Kathmandu to Syabrubesi

The bus ride from Kathmandu to Syabrubesi is probably the worst thing about the Langtang trek. Until you actually take the journey it's hard to imagine how any bus could take nine hours to cover 117km! Buses leave Kathmandu at 6.30am, 7.30am and 8.30am for Dhunche (Rs 180 to Rs 230, nine hours) and at least one continues to Syabrubesi (Rs 250 to Rs 290, 10 hours), 15km further. At Dhunche you must pay the entrance fee to Langtang National Park, though you can also buy the permit in Kathmandu before starting your trek. For more details on Dhunche, see p234.

Syabrubesi is a string of shops and lodges. A bus departs Syabrubesi for Kathmandu at 7.30am. You should book a seat in advance at the roadside ticket office.

The Trek

DAY ONE: SYABRUBESI TO LAMA HOTEL

The trail branches off Syabrubesi's main road opposite the Hotel Village View and descends to a camping area below the town. Walk northward past a police post (you'll need to register) to a suspension bridge over the Bhote Kosi, just north of the junction with the Langtang Khola. Turn right at the eastern end of the bridge and climb through the village of Old Syabru to cross a bridge to the south side of the Langtang Khola.

The trek becomes a pleasant walk through trees where langur monkeys frolic, passing a bridge, small waterfall and *bhatti*s (village inns) beside the stream at Doman (1680m). The trail then makes a steep climb over a rocky ridge to the easily missed junction where the route from Thulo Syabru joins from above. Over the rest of the day's walk and the following morning, you will pass few settlements, but the forest abounds with birds.

It's then a long climb in forest past the waterfalls and two lodges of Pairo (meaning 'landslide'; 1800m) to Bamboo, a cluster of three hotels (none made of bamboo) at 1930m. Beyond Bamboo the trail crosses the Dangdung Khola, then climbs to a steel suspension bridge over the Langtang Khola at 2000m.

On the north bank of the Langtang Khola the route climbs alongside a series of waterfalls formed by a jumble of house-sized boulders. Climb steeply to a landslide and two sets of lodges, 15 minutes apart, at Renche (2400m), and then gently to a collection of six lodges at Changtang, popularly known as Lama Hotel, at 2480m.

DAY TWO: LAMA HOTEL TO LANGTANG

The trail continues to follow the Langtang Khola, climbing steeply through a forest of hemlocks, maples and rhododendrons, past isolated lodges at Gumanchok (Riverside) and Ghunama to the popular lunchtime spot of Ghora Tabela (2970m). There are fine views of Langtang Lirung from here, which you can admire as the army checks your national park entry permit.

From Ghora Tabela the trail climbs more gradually through a U-shaped glacial valley to the villages of Thangshyap, Ghumba and finally Langtang (3430m). The national park headquarters is here, along with a cooperative bakery and a dozen lodges. Langtang and the villages around are in Tibetan style, with stone walls around the fields, and herds of yaks.

DAY THREE: LANGTANG TO KYANJIN GOMPA

It only takes the morning (passing through small villages) to climb to Kyanjin Gompa (3860m) where there is a monastery, several lodges and a cheese factory (May to December). It's worth spending two full days here to really appreciate the scenery.

TREKKING

LANGTANG, GOSAINKUND & HELAMBU TREKS

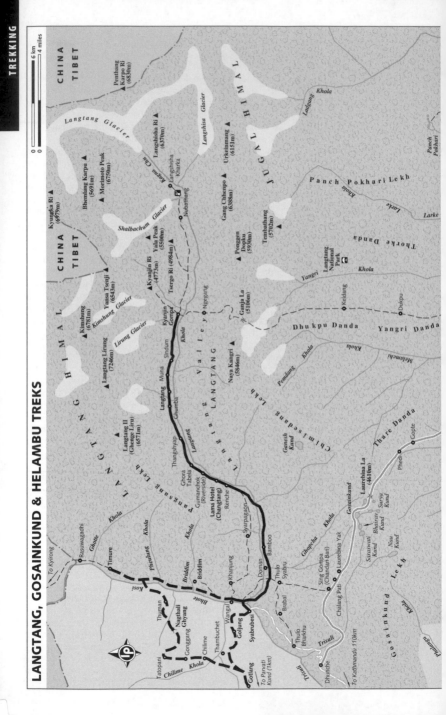

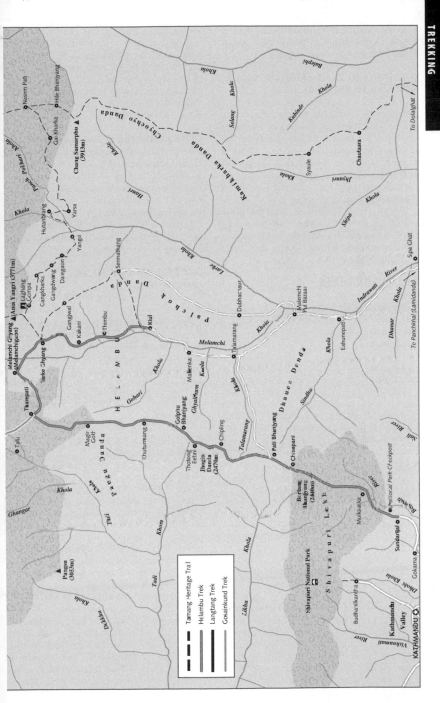

If you are intending to continue over the Ganja La to Helambu you should spend some time here acclimatising.

DAYS FOUR TO EIGHT: LANGTANG VALLEY & RETURN TO SYABRUBESI

From Kyanjin Gompa you can climb to a viewpoint at 4300m on the glacial moraine to the north for superb views of Langtang Lirung. The most popular hike is to the Kyanjin Ri viewpoint (4600m), while a tougher option is the climb to Tsergo Ri (4984m). Another popular day hike leads up the valley to the pastures around Langshisha Kharka for more spectacular views.

To return to Syabrubesi, take the same path back down the valley. To connect to the Gosainkund trek, take the left branch at the junction just before Doman and climb to Thulo Syabru.

GOSAINKUND TREK

Duration seven to eight days
Maximum elevation 4610m
Best season October to November, March to April
Start Dhunche, Syabrubesi or Thulo Syabru
Finish Sundarijal

In good weather you can link the Langtang and Helambu treks via a trek to the sacred, picturesque and high-altitude Gosainkund lakes. It's also possible to hike the route as a stand-alone trek or even as a return visit from Dhunche to the lakes (seven days), though the rate of ascent in these two cases can cause acclimatisation problems (if you've already done the Langtang trek, you'll be well acclimatised). Take particular care to acclimitise if attempting this trek in the opposite direction.

There are lodges along the route, so finding food and accommodation is not a problem in the trekking season. This route over the Laurebina La becomes impassable during winter.

It takes four days to walk from Dhunche, near the start of the Langtang trek, to Tharepati in the Helambu region. The trek can also be done by turning off the Langtang trek from Thulo Syabru, and it is an excellent choice as a return route to Kathmandu from the Langtang trek. Lodge facilities are good in Thulo Syabru, Sing Gompa and Tharepati, but rooms in Phedi and Gopte are basic.

Gosainkund is the site for a great Hindu pilgrimage each August, when thousands of sadhus (holy men) trek to the sacred lakes. This is the height of the monsoon, so it's not a pleasant time for trekking. The large rock in the centre of the lake is said to be the remains of a Shiva shrine and pilgrims believe that a channel carries water from the lake directly to the tank at the Kumbeshwar Temple in Patan, 60km to the south.

DAY ONE: DHUNCHE TO SING GOMPA

The first day is a strenuous one, climbing from Dhunche at 1950m to Sing Gompa (Chandan Bari) at 3330m, via Deorali. If you are coming from the Langtang trek, the route from Thulo Syabru to Sing Gompa, via Phobrang Danda, can be confusing so ask directions. It's also possible to get to Sing Gompa from Syabrubesi or the Langtang trek, via Thulo Syabru.

DAY TWO: SING GOMPA TO LAUREBINA YAK

The walk climbs steeply, quickly offering fine views of the Ganesh Himal range, to emerge onto a saddle at the teahouses of Chalang Pati (3550m). The trail continues to climb to Laurebina Yak and the excellent Mount Rest Hotel. The magnificent views include the Annapurnas, Manaslu (8156m), the four peaks of the Ganesh Himal and Langtang Lirung. You should overnight in Laurebina Yak to help acclimatisation. You are now above the tree line.

DAY THREE: LAUREBINA YAK TO GOSAINKUND LAKES

The trail climbs to a pass and then continues on an exposed trail, offering views of Saraswati Kund at 4100m, the first of the Gosainkund lakes. The second lake is Bhairav (or Bhairab) Kund and the third is Gosainkund itself, at an altitude of 4380m. There are half a dozen lodges, a shrine and numerous pilgrim shelters on the northwestern side of the lake. You can walk around the lake in an hour, or climb the ridge above the lodges for fine views.

DAY FOUR: GOSAINKUND LAKES TO GOPTE

The trail climbs from the Gosainkund lakes to four more lakes near the Laurebina La at 4610m. It then drops steeply past a very basic seasonal lodge at Bera Goth to simple lodges at Phedi (3740m). Nearby is the site where a Thai International Airbus crashed into a mountain in 1992. Continue over side valleys to ascend Kasturee Danda (Musk Deer Ridge) before dropping to two simple, seasonal lodges at Gopte (3440m). It was in the Gopte area that an Australian trekker got lost in 1991 and was found alive after 43 days.

DAY FIVE: GOPTE TO THAREPATI
The final day's walk descends to a stream and then climbs to Tharepati at 3640m, where this trail meets up with the Helambu trek.

DAYS SIX TO EIGHT: THAREPATI TO SUNDARIJAL
At Tharepati you're on the Helambu trek and can either take the direct route south to Khutumsang, Chisopani and Sundarijal (two to three days). Alternatively go east to Tarke Ghyang and Kiul (three days).

SUNDARIJAL OR KIUL TO KATHMANDU
You can bus back to Kathmandu from Sundarijal (see p347) or Kiul (see p352).

HELAMBU TREK
Duration six days
Maximum elevation 3640m
Best season October to April
Start Sundarijal
Finish Kiul

Although it's not as well known and popular as the other treks in this book, the week-long Helambu trek offers a number of distinct advantages. The trek is easily accessible from Kathmandu. Indeed, you could leave your hotel in Kathmandu and set foot on the Helambu trail within an hour. At less than a week long it's a good taster trek if you're unsure of committing to a longer, higher trek. And since it stays at relatively low altitudes it also does not require bulky cold-weather equipment and clothing.

The Helambu trek starts from Sundarijal at the eastern end of the Kathmandu Valley, making a half-loop through the Sherpa-populated Helambu region to the northeast of Kathmandu. There is not a lot of high mountain scenery but it is a culturally interesting region. The Sherpa people of the Helambu region are friendly and hospitable, just like their kinfolk of the Solu Khumbu region. There is plenty of accommodation along the route, but it's still a good idea to carry a sleeping bag.

Wherever you trek in the region, you will enter the Langtang National Park (admission Rs 1000). You can pay the entrance fee in advance at the national parks office in Kathmandu (see p335) or pay on the spot in Khutumsang or possibly Sermathang.

Access: Kathmandu to Sundarijal
Occasional buses leave from Kathmandu's Ratna Park bus station to Sundarijal (Rs 50, one hour), 15km from Kathmandu, or get a bus to Jorpati, just beyond Bodhnath, and catch a Sundarijal bus at the road junction. A taxi will cost Rs 800. At Sundarijal you enter the Shivapuri National Park (admission Rs 250; see p180).

The Trek
DAY ONE: SUNDARIJAL TO CHISOPANI
From Sundarijal the trail starts off up concrete steps beside the pipeline that brings drinking water down to the valley. Stop to pay the entry fee at the park checkpost. Eventually the trail leaves the pipeline from near the dam and reaches Mulkharka, sprawling up the ridge around 1800m, 400m above Sundarijal. There are superb views back over the valley and some teashops for rest and refreshment.

The trail continues to climb, but less steeply, to the Borlang Bhanjyang (bhanjyang means 'pass') at 2440m, before dropping to Chisopani (2140m). Chisopani is rather like a grubby little truck stop without the trucks, but the mountain views in the morning can be very fine. Take care of your possessions here; it's still rather close to the Kathmandu Valley. There are a number of lodges at Chisopani.

DAY TWO: CHISOPANI TO GOLPHU BHANJYANG
The trail heads down to Pati Bhanjyang (1860m), which has a number of lodges. The trail rises and falls through Chipling (2170m). From here the trail climbs again to reach a 2470m pass atop Jhogin Danda, before descending through rhododendron forests to Thodang Betini (2250m). Continuing along the forested ridge, the trail descends to a large white chörten (Tibetan-style stupa) overlooking the Tamang village of Golphu Bhanjyang (Gul Bhanjyang; 2140m). This is a classic hill village with a pleasant main street, several shops and a number of places to stay.

DAY THREE: GOLPHU BHANJYANG TO THAREPATI

This is the toughest and most dramatic day of the trek, ascending 1650m. The trail climbs the ridge from Golphu Bhanjyang to another pass at 2580m, then it's downhill to Khutumsang (2450m), which lies in a saddle atop the ridge. Show your park entry permit or pay the Rs 1000 at the Langtang National Park office at the far side of the village.

The trail follows the Yurin Danda ridgeline, with views of the Langtang and Gosainkund peaks, through sparsely populated forests to Magin Goth before climbing further to finally reach Tharepati (3640m). The trail to Gosainkund and the Langtang trek branches off northwest from here. Tharepati has half a dozen good lodges.

DAY FOUR: THAREPATI TO MELAMCHI GHYANG

From the pass the trail turns east and descends rapidly down a ravine, losing over 1000m to the large Sherpa village of Melamchi Ghyang (Malemchigaon; 2530m). There are plenty of lodges in the village, and a very brightly painted gompa.

DAY FIVE: MELAMCHI GHYANG TO TARKE GHYANG

From Melamchi Ghyang the trail continues to drop, crossing the Melamchi Khola by a bridge at 1920m and then making the long climb up the other side of the valley to Tarke Ghyang (2590m), the largest village in Helambu. There are a number of lodges including the pleasant Mount View Hotel on the Melamchi Ghyang side of the village. Tarke Ghyang is a good place for a rest day or you can take a gruelling half-day side trip 1200m up to the Ama Yangri (3771m), the chörten-topped peak overlooking the village. This is the end of the trekking route down from the Ganja La.

DAY SIX: TARKE GHYANG TO KIUL

The final day of the trek leaves Tarke Ghyang, passing the Tarkeyghyang Hotel and mani wall (walk to the left), then drops off the west side of the ridge in a rhododendron forest, along a broad, well-travelled path. Passing through the Sherpa villages of Kakani (2070m) and Thimbu (1580m), the trail enters the hot, rice-growing, banana-and-monkey country of the Melamchi and Indrawati Valleys.

The steep descent continues down to Kiul (1280m), strung out on terraces above the Melamchi Khola.

KIUL TO KATHMANDU

Four buses a day run between Kiul and Kathmandu's Ratna Park bus station (Rs 150, five to six hours) and you may even find buses running from Thimbu.

Alternative Route

A pleasant and little-trekked alternative route runs from Tarke Ghyang to Sermathang. The easy trail descends gently through a beautiful forest to Sermathang (2620m), the centre of an important apple-growing area. Sermathang is more spread out than the closely spaced houses of Tarke Ghyang; there are fine views of the valley of the Melamchi Khola to the south. There are a couple of lodges.

From Sermathang the trail branches off near the Karma Lodge and descends the spur to Kiul (two hours).

ANNAPURNA CIRCUIT TREK

Duration 12 to 19 days
Maximum elevation 5416m
Best season October to November
Start Besi Sahar
Finish Jomsom or Naya Pul

It takes nearly three weeks to walk the entire Annapurna Circuit. For scenery and cultural diversity this has long been considered the best trek in Nepal and one of the world's classic walks. It follows the Marsyangdi Valley to the north of the main Himalayan range and crosses a 5416m pass to descend into the dramatic desertlike Tibetan-style scenery of the upper Kali Gandaki Valley.

Since it opened to foreign trekkers in 1977, the trek around Annapurna has been the most popular in Nepal. It passes picturesque villages home to Gurungs, Manangis and Thakalis, offers spectacular mountain views of the numerous 7000m-plus Annapurna peaks and it boasts some of the best trekking lodges in Nepal.

Road construction is having an effect on the popularity of the Annapurna Circuit. The first half of the circuit in the Manang side is little affected but the former Jomsom trek through the Kali Gandaki Valley on the west side is now cut by a dirt road, plied by dusty jeep and motorbike traffic. Some trekkers now end their trek in Jomsom. All is not lost though; a series of new trails on the eastern side of the valley avoids the new road, the scenery is equally if not more spectacular, and the lodges are still excellent. The nature of the trail has changed from a long-distance trek to a series of day hikes from bases on the road, but in reality this trek was never a wilderness walk.

The circuit is usually walked counter clockwise because the climb to the Thorung La from the western side is too strenuous and has too much elevation gain to consider in one day. At 5416m the Thorung La is often closed due to snow from mid-December to mid-March, and bad weather can move in at any time. The trail to the pass can be hard to find in fresh snow and you should be prepared to turn back due to the weather and altitude. It's essential to take your time between Manang and the pass in order to acclimatise properly. All trekkers, including porters, must be adequately equipped for severe cold and snow.

Our best tip for this trek is to remember that the side trips and excursions from places like Manang, Muktinath and Jomsom rank as some of the highlights of the trek. It's worth adding a couple of days to your itinerary and exploring some of these trails. You'll be better acclimatised for the pass and you'll manage to shake some of the crowds. This is not scenery to rush through.

Access: Kathmandu or Pokhara to Besi Sahar

Buses run to Besi Sahar between 6.30am and noon from Kathmandu (Rs 350, six hours) and there are three buses in the morning and one in the afternoon from Pokhara (Rs 200 to Rs 230, five hours).

From Besi Sahar (800m) buses run every hour or two to Bhulbule (Rs 60, 30 minutes to one hour), though most drivers insist on charging foreigners three or four times the local price. It's such an uncomfortable ride that you're probably better off walking anyway. Cramped jeeps run as far as Syange (Rs 250), when the dirt road isn't blocked by monsoon landslides.

The Trek

DAY ONE: BESI SAHAR TO BHULBULE

If you arrive in Besi Sahar at lunchtime it's possible to take the bus or hike along the road to Bhulbule or even Ngadi that same day. The approach to Bhulbule (840m) offers fine views of Himalchuli (to the northeast) and Ngadi Chuli (aka Manaslu II or Peak 29). You enter the Annapurna Conservation Area in Bhulbule and should register at the ACAP checkpoint. If you did not get your ACAP permit in advance, you will have to pay double here.

DAY TWO: BHULBULE TO GHERMU

The trail leaves the road at Bhulbule and crosses to the east bank of the Marsyangdi, continuing to Ngadi (a good alternative first night) before reaching Bahundanda (1270m), 'Hill of the Brahmins', on a ridge. Bahundanda has several lodges, shops and restaurants.

From Bahundanda the trail drops steeply to Lili Bhir and then follows an exposed trail to Kanigaon and Ghermu (1140m), with its views of the high waterfall across the river.

DAY THREE: GHERMU TO TAL

Descend to Syange (1080m) and cross to the west bank of the Marsyangdi Khola on a suspension bridge. The trail then climbs steeply and crosses a cliff face to the stone village of Jagat, perched strategically in a steep-sided valley and looking for all the world like the toll station for the Tibetan salt trade that it was. The trail descends before climbing through forest to Chamje (1410m).

The rocky trail crosses the Marsyangdi Khola again, then follows the valley steadily uphill to Tal (1700m), a former lakebed. Here the valley has been filled by ancient landslides and the river meanders through the fertile flat land before disappearing under some huge boulders. Tal is the first village in the Manang district.

DAY FOUR: TAL TO CHAME

Today is a long day, so consider breaking your walk in Timang or Koto. The trail crosses the valley floor then climbs a stone stairway before dropping down to another crossing of the Marsyangdi. The trail continues past Khotro and Karte to Dharapani (1960m), which is marked by a stone-entrance chörten typical of the Tibetan-influenced villages from here northward.

Bagarchhap (2160m) is a good lunch spot. A landslide roared through the centre of this village in late 1995 and managed to wipe out much of it, including two lodges. There are more lunch spots at nearby Danaque.

ANNAPURNA TREKS

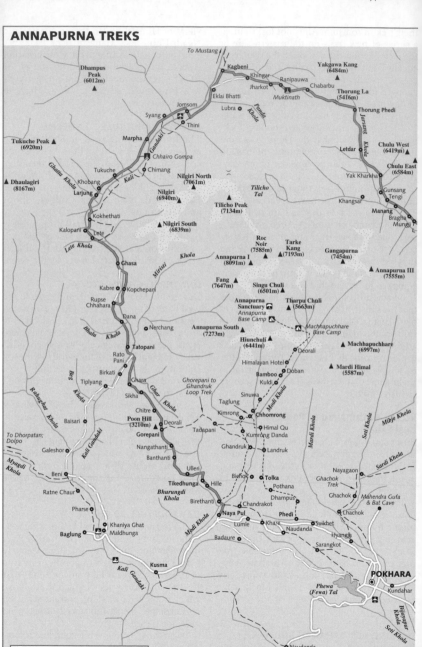

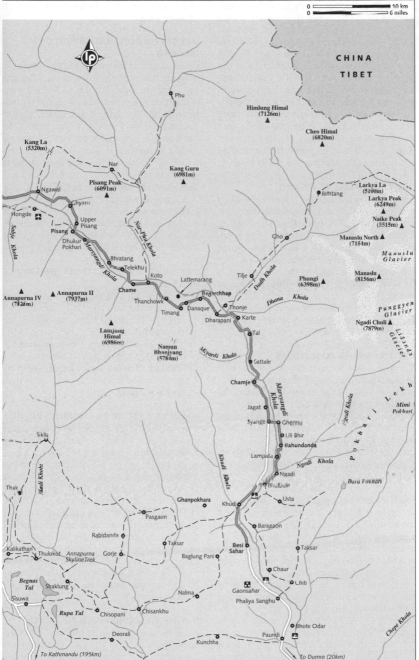

The trail climbs steeply from Danaque, gaining 500m to Timang and then continues through forest of pine and fir, past the traditional village of Thanchowk to Koto (2640m), at the junction of the Nar-Phu valley. Nearby Chame (2710m) is the headquarters of the Manang district and its buildings include lodges, internet cafes, trek-gear shops, a health post and a bank. At the entrance to the village you pass a large mani wall with many prayer wheels. Walk to the left of the wall as all Buddhists do. There are fine views of Annapurna II as you approach Chame. The route crosses the Marsyangdi Khola here.

DAY FIVE: CHAME TO PISANG
The trail runs through deep forest in a steep and narrow valley and recrosses to the south bank of the Marsyangdi Khola at 3080m. Views include the first sight of the soaring Paungda Danda rock face, an awesome testament to the power of glacial erosion. The trail continues to climb to the popular lunch spot at Dhukur Pokhari, before arriving at the lodges, cappuccinos and pizzas of Pisang (3240m). You'll get better views and simpler accommodation by staying at upper Pisang (3310m), just above town.

DAY SIX: PISANG TO MANANG
The walk is now through the drier upper part of Manang district, cut off from the full effect of the monsoon by the Annapurna Range. The people of the upper part of the Manang district herd yaks and raise crops for part of the year, but they also continue to enjoy special trading rights gained way back in 1784. Today they use these rights to buy electronic goods and other modern equipment in Bangkok and Hong Kong to resell in Nepal.

From Pisang there are two trails, north and south of the Marsyangdi Khola, which meet up again at Mungji. The southern route via the airstrip at Hongde (3420m) involves less climbing than the northern route, but the mountain views on the upper trail via Ghyaru and Ngawal (3660m) are infinitely better and will aid your acclimatisation.

The trail continues from Mungji (3500m) past the extraordinarily picturesque village and gompa of Bragha (3470m) to nearby Manang (3540m), where there are lots of lodges, shops, a museum and a HRA post (it's worth attending the free daily lecture on altitude sickness). Bragha also has good lodges

and is a quieter place to base yourself than Manang village.

DAY SEVEN: ACCLIMATISATION DAY IN MANANG
It's important to spend a day acclimatising in Manang before pushing on to the Thorung La. There are some fine day walks and magnificent views around the village, and it's best to gain altitude during the day, returning to Manang to sleep. The view of Gangapurna glacier is terrific, either from the viewpoint above the lake or from the Praken Gompa, an hour's walk above Manang. More strenuous day hikes include to Milarepa's Cave and the Ice Lake, high above the valley floor at 4600m.

Manang is a major trading centre and the canny shopowners know exactly what trekkers want. You can buy film, batteries, sunscreen, Snickers bars and just about anything else a trekker could break, lose or crave.

DAY EIGHT: MANANG TO YAK KHARKHA OR LETDAR
From Manang it's an ascent of nearly 2000m to the Thorung La. The trail climbs steadily through Tengi and Gunsang, leaving the Marsyangdi Valley and continuing along the Jarsang Khola Valley. The vegetation becomes shorter and sparser as you reach Yak Kharkha (4020m) and then Letdar (4230m). A night in Yak Kharkha or Letdar is important for acclimatisation.

DAY NINE: LETDAR TO THORUNG PHEDI
Cross the river at 4310m and then climb up through desolate scenery to Thorung Phedi (4540m). There are two lodges here – at the height of the season as many as 200 trekkers a day may cross over the Thorung La and beds can be in short supply. Some trekkers find themselves suffering from AMS at Phedi. If you are one of these you must retreat downhill; even the descent to Letdar can make a difference. Be sure to boil or treat water here; the sanitation in Letdar and Thorung Phedi is poor and giardiasis is rampant. There is a satellite phone in Thorung Phedi that you can use for US$5 per minute in an emergency.

DAY 10: THORUNG PHEDI TO MUKTINATH
Phedi means 'foot of the hill' and that's exactly where it is, at the foot of the 5416m Thorung La. The trail climbs steeply but

is well used and is easy to follow. The altitude will have you wheezing and snow can cause problems; when the pass is covered in fresh snow it is often impossible to cross. It takes about four to six hours to reach the pass, marked by chörtens and prayer flags, and en route you'll pass two teashops, plus one on the pass itself. The effort is worthwhile as the view from the top – from the Annapurnas, along the Great Barrier to the barren Kali Gandaki Valley – is magnificent. From the pass you have a knee-busting and sometimes slippery 1600m descent to Muktinath (3800m).

Some people start out for the pass at 3am but this is not only unnecessary but also potentially dangerous due to the risk of frostbite and accidents in the darkness. A better starting time is 5am to 6am.

Muktinath itself has no accommodation; for that you'll have to continue for 10 minutes to nearby Ranipauwa.

DAY 11: MUKTINATH TO KAGBENI
Muktinath is a pilgrimage site for Buddhists and Hindus alike. You'll see Tibetan traders here as well as sadhus from as far away as the south of India. The shrines, in a grove of trees, include a Buddhist gompa, a Vishnu temple and the Jwalamai (Goddess of Fire) Temple, which shelters a spring and natural gas jets that provide Muktinath's famous eternal flame. It's the combination of earth, water and fire in such proximity that accounts for Muktinath's great religious significance.

From Ranipauwa the road descends through a desertlike trans-Himalayan landscape to the dramatic village of Jharkot (3500m), with its large chörten, gompa and atmospheric animist totems. The trail continues to Khingar (3400m) and then follows the road down steeply to the medieval-looking village of Kagbeni (2840m).

DAY 12: KAGBENI TO JOMSOM
The Tibetan-influenced settlement of Kagbeni has a number of good lodges and is as close as you can get to Lo Manthang, the capital of the legendary kingdom of Mustang further to the north, without paying a US$500 permit fee.

From Kagbeni is a dusty, rocky but mostly flat stroll along the road to Jomsom (2760m). Jomsom is the major centre in the region and it has facilities such as a hospital, an ACAP visitor centre and a police checkpost (where you must register and get your ACAP permit stamped). This is the first of the Thakali villages of the Kali Gandaki River. Jomsom has regular morning flights to Pokhara and jeep service down to Ghasa, Beni and eventually Pokhara, and so this is where many travellers end their trek.

If you have some extra time it's worth continuing south to the traditional whitewashed stone village of Marpha (2680m), which has a gompa and several smaller shrines. The town boasts some of the most luxurious accommodation to be found along the trail, which makes it a good alternative to staying in Jomsom.

Try to be on the trail early in the morning in the Kali Gandaki Valley, as strong winds tend to pick up after 11am.

DAYS 13 TO 19: JOMSOM TO NAYA PUL
The Annapurna Circuit south of Jomsom follows the new road south through the Kali Gandaki Valley to Naya Pul. The trek is becoming less popular because of the road, although it's still a rewarding walk if you take the detours on the east bank that avoid the road as much as possible. ACAP is in the process of rebuilding trails and bridges on the east bank to enable trekkers to avoid the road completely. There are excellent lodges at Marpha, Tukuche, Larjung, Lete, Kalopani, Ghasa and Tatopani. Figure on three days to Tatopani or four to five days to Ghorepani.

South of Jomsom it's worth detouring down the east bank via Dhumba Lake to Katsaptcrenga Gompa, before returning to the road at Syang and continuing to Marpha.

Just south of Marpha another detour heads down the east bank from the Tibetan settlement around Chhairo Gompa to Chimang village, which offers superb views of Dhaulagiri, the world's sixth largest mountain.

Back on the west bank, Tukuche (2580m) is one of the valley's most important Thakali villages and once was a depot and customs spot for salt traders from Tibet. Several grand houses and gompas hark back to a more prosperous past.

The road continues to Khobang and Larjung (2560m) past good views of Dhaulagiri and Nilgiri North (7061m). This section of the Kali Gandaki Valley is claimed by some to be the deepest in the world, the rationale being that in the 38km between the peaks of Annapurna I and Dhaulagiri I (both above 8000m) the valley floor drops almost 4000m. Larjung is the base for a tough excursion up to the Dhaulagiri Icefall.

Another excursion branches off the road at Kokhethati, leading to Titi Lake (2670m) for views of the eastern flank of Dhaulagiri and then down to the villages of Konjo and Taglung, with their spectacular views of Nilgiri peak. The trails eventually rejoin the road just south of conjoined Lete (2480m) and Kalopani, both of which have fine accommodation and views.

The road continues south to Ghasa (2000m), the last Thakali village in the valley, and then a foot trail branches down the east side of the narrowing gorge, rejoining the road after a couple of hours at the waterfall of Rupse Chhahara (1560m). The road continues down to Dana and Tatopani (1190m), noted for its concrete hot springs.

From Tatopani you can hop on a jeep or bus to Beni and Pokhara or you can continue up the steep-side valley from Ghar Khola, gaining an epic 1600m past Sikha and Chitre to Ghorepani in the Annapurna foothills. This is one of the hardest days on the circuit.

An hour's climb from the ridge at upper Ghorepani (also known as Deorali) will take you to Poon Hill (3210m), one of the best Himalayan viewpoints in the lower hills. *Ghore* means 'horse' and *pani* 'water' and indeed, long caravans of pack horses were once a regular sight here.

From Ghorepani you can descend the long stone staircases to Nangathanti (2460m), Banthanti (2250m) and Ulleri, a large Magar village at 1960m, before continuing steeply to Tikedhunga, Birethanti (1000m) and the nearby roadhead at Naya Pul.

A two-day trail also runs from Ghorepani to Ghandruk, where you can join up with the Annapurna Sanctuary trek. This part of the trek is plagued by leeches during the monsoon.

NAYA PUL TO POKHARA

Buses to Pokhara stop in Naya Pul (Rs 100, two hours). Alternatively you can get back to Pokhara from Jomsom or Tatopani.

ANNAPURNA SANCTUARY TREK

Duration 10 to 14 days
Maximum elevation 4095m
Best season October to November
Start Phedi
Finish Naya Pul

AVALANCHES ON THE SANCTUARY TRAIL

There is significant danger of avalanches along the route to the Annapurna Sanctuary between Doban and Machhapuchhare Base Camp. Trekkers have died and trekking parties have been stranded in the sanctuary for days, the trail blocked by tonnes of ice and snow. Always check with the ACAP office in Chhomrong and lodges in Deorali for a report on current trail conditions, and do not proceed into the sanctuary if there has been recent heavy rain or snow.

This trek goes into the frozen heart of the Annapurna Range, a magnificent amphitheatre of rock and ice on a staggering scale. The trail starts in rice paddies and leads through a gorge of bamboo and forests to end among glaciers and soaring peaks – an unparalleled mountain experience. Other highlights include sublime views of fish-tailed Machhapuchhare and one of Nepal's largest and prettiest Gurung villages at Ghandruk, which is a short detour off the main trek.

The return trek can take as little as 10 days but 14 days will give you more time to soak up the scenery. You can tack a walk to the sanctuary onto the Annapurna Circuit for an epic 25- to 30-day walk.

There are several possible routes to the sanctuary, all meeting at Chhomrong. The diversion from the Annapurna Circuit Trek branches off from Ghorepani to reach Chhomrong via Tadapani.

Access: Pokhara to Phedi

Buses leave every 40 minutes or so from Pokhara's Baglung bus stand to Phedi (Rs 50, 1½ hours), a cluster of shacks, from where the trail starts up a series of stone steps.

The Trek
DAY ONE: PHEDI TO TOLKA

From Phedi the trail climbs steeply to Dhampus (1750m), which stretches for several kilometres along the ridge from 1580m to 1700m and has a number of hotels strung along the ridge. Theft is a problem in Dhampus, so take care.

The trail climbs to Pothana (1990m) and descends steeply through a forest towards Bichok. It finally emerges in the Modi Khola Valley and continues to drop to Tolka (1810m).

DAY TWO: TOLKA TO CHHOMRONG

From Tolka the trail descends a long stone staircase and then follows a ridge to the Gurung village of Landruk (1620m). Ten minutes from here the path splits – north takes you to Chhomrong and the sanctuary, or you can detour west downhill towards Ghandruk.

The sanctuary trail turns up the Modi Khola Valley to Himal Qu (also know as Naya Pul; 1340m). It then continues up to Jhinu Danda (1750m) and its nearby hot spring before a steep climb to Taglung (2190m), where it joins the Ghandruk to Chhomrong trail.

Chhomrong, at 2210m, is the last permanent settlement in the valley. This large and sprawling Gurung village has excellent lodges, fine views and an ACAP office where you can enquire about trail conditions in the sanctuary.

DAY THREE: CHHOMRONG TO BAMBOO

The trail drops down a set of stone steps to the Chhomrong Khola, and then climbs to Sinuwa and on through rhododendron forests to Kuldi (2470m). The trek now enters the upper Modi Khola Valley, where ACAP controls the location and number of lodges and limits their size. This section of the trail is a bottleneck and you may find lodges are full during the high season, in which case you may have to continue for an hour to the next accommodation in Doban or sleep in the dining room. In winter it is common to find snow from this point on. Continue on to Bamboo (2310m), which is a collection of three hotels. This stretch of the trail has leeches early and late in the trekking season.

DAY FOUR: BAMBOO TO HIMALAYAN HOTEL

The trail climbs through rhododendron forests to Doban (2540m) and on to Himalayan Hotel at 2840m. This stretch of the trail passes several avalanche chutes.

If you arrive early it's possible to continue on to Deorali to make the following day easier.

DAY FIVE: HIMALAYAN HOTEL TO MACHHAPUCHHARE BASE CAMP

From Himalayan Hotel it's on to Hinko (3100m) then to lodges at Deorali at the gateway to the sanctuary. The next stretch of trail is the most subject to avalanches and you detour temporarily to the east side of the valley to avoid a dangerous chute.

At Machhapuchhare Base Camp (which isn't really a base camp since climbing the mountain is not permitted), at 3700m, there is decent accommodation available. Be alert to signs of altitude sickness before heading off to Annapurna Base Camp.

DAY SIX: MACHHAPUCHHARE BASE CAMP TO ANNAPURNA BASE CAMP

The climb to the Annapurna Base Camp at 4130m takes about two hours and is best done early in the day before clouds roll in and make visibility a problem. If there is snow the trail may be difficult to follow. There are four lodges here, which can get very crowded at the height of the season. The frozen dawn is best observed from the glacial moraine a short stroll from your cosy lodge.

DAYS SEVEN TO 14: ANNAPURNA BASE CAMP TO NAYA PUL

On the return trip head south to Chhomrong (two days) and on to Ghandruk (one day) via the deep valley of the Khumnu Khola. From Ghandruk you can follow the valley directly down to Birethanti and Naya Pul in a day, or detour west to Ghorepani to visit Poon Hill, before descending to Birethanti (four days) and Naya Pul.

The two-day Ghorepani to Ghandruk walk is a popular way of linking the Annapurna Sanctuary trek with treks up the Kali Gandaki Valley. It's also used for shorter loop walks around Pokhara, including Ghorepani to Ghandruk (see p276).

NAYA PUL TO POKHARA

Buses to Pokhara stop in Naya Pul (Rs 100, two hours).

OTHER TREKS

The treks described earlier in this chapter are used by the vast majority of trekkers in Nepal. It's possible to head right off the beaten track to explore remote areas like Makalu and Kanchenjunga in the east or

Humla and Dolpo in the west, but you must be very self sufficient. In these relatively untouched areas there is little surplus food for sale and the practice of catering to Western trekkers has not yet developed. There are no lodges on these treks, so you will need to make camping arrangements through a trekking company and, for most regions, pay a trekking permit fee.

See Lonely Planet's *Trekking in the Nepal Himalaya* for the complete story on trekking in Nepal. It has comprehensive advice on equipment selection, a dedicated health and safety section, and comprehensive route descriptions for both the popular treks (covered briefly in this book) and interesting, less heavily used routes.

There are a number of short treks around the Pokhara area, these include the Phewa Tal Circuit, Ghachok trek and the Annapurna Skyline Trek (see p275 for more information). Other trekking options include the 18-day walk around Manaslu (Mountain of the Spirit), the world's eighth tallest mountain. The walk follows the Beri River past simple local teahouses into the Tibetan-influenced Nupri area, before crossing the 5100m Larkya La to join the Annapurna Circuit. Another trek that touches on the Annapurna Circuit is the seven-day Nar-Phu trek, which takes you to the spectacular villages of Nar and Phu near the Tibetan border.

Perhaps most popular of the restricted area treks is to the long-forbidden kingdom of Mustang, a remote and arid land of spectacular Tibetan monasteries, canyons and cave complexes that borders Tibet.

Nepal's far west is an up-and-coming area for trekking, especially the Dolpo region.

Treks here are relatively expensive because you have to figure in flights. One popular 12-day loop follows the Tarap Valley to the Tibetan-style villages and monasteries around Do Tarap, then crosses the breathtaking 5000m-plus passes of the Numa La and Baga La to arrive at turquoise Phoksumdo Lake, probably the most beautiful lake in Nepal. Another excellent trek is the 12-day traverse from Beni, northwest of Pokhara, to Tarakot in outer Dolpo, crossing six passes and a huge swathe of midwestern Nepal in the footsteps of the book *The Snow Leopard*.

Least visited of all is the far east, where two long routes lead right to the base of the world's third highest mountain, Kanchenjunga.

The Makalu Base Camp trek is another trek that gets you into the heart of the mountains, following the Barun Valley up to base camp at around 5000m, offering fine views of Everest and Lhotse. The trek starts at the Tumlingtar airstrip or trek in from Lukla in 11 days.

Treks in all of these remote areas are camping treks only. Treks in the following regions must be arranged by a trekking company in order to secure proper permits:

Area	Trekking fee
Kanchenjunga & lower Dolpo	US$10 per week for 1st 4 weeks, then US$20 per week after that
upper Mustang & upper Dolpo	US$500 for 10 days, then US$50 per day
Nar-Phu	US$90 for 1st week
Manaslu	US$75 per week low season, US$90 per week high season
Humla	US$90 for 7 days, then US$15 per day

Directory

CONTENTS

ACCOMMODATION

Accommodation options in this book are arranged according to budget and then subdivided by location. Budget travellers can expect to shell out from Rs 400 to Rs 1200 (US$5 to US$15) for a double room, which will normally have a private bathroom. Midrange rooms range from Rs 1200 to Rs 4000 (US$15 to US$50), with top-end groupings heading up from there. Most hotels have a wide range of rooms under one roof, including larger (often top-floor) deluxe rooms that are good for families and small groups.

In Kathmandu and Pokhara there is a wide variety of accommodation, from rock-bottom fleapits to five-star international hotels where a room costs US$150 a night. The intense competition between the many cheaper places keeps prices down and standards up – Kathmandu has many fine places with pleasant gardens and rooms for less than Rs 800 (US$10) a night including private bathroom and hot water. Some of Nepal's best deals are now to be found in its stylish midrange and top-end accommodation, discounted by up to 60% in places.

The main towns of the Terai have hotels of a reasonable standard, where rooms with fans and mosquito nets cost around Rs 400 (US$5), down to grimy, basic places catering to local demand from around Rs 50 (less than US$1). Some of the cheap places have tattered mosquito nets, if any at all. The cheaper places only have solar-heated hot-water showers, which won't be hot in the mornings or on cloudy days.

Elsewhere in the country the choice of hotels can be very limited, but you will find places to stay along most of the major trekking trails, making Nepal one of the few places in the world where you can trek for three weeks without needing a tent. On lesser-trekked trails places may be spartan – the accommodation may be dorm-style or simply an open room in which to unroll your sleeping bag – but the Annapurna and Everest treks have excellent lodges and guest houses every couple of hours.

All midrange and top-end hotels charge a value added tax (VAT) of 13% and often quote their prices in US dollars (though you can pay in rupees). Budget places quote prices in rupees and generally forget about the tax.

BOOK YOUR STAY ONLINE

For more accommodation reviews and recommendations by Lonely Planet authors, check out the online booking service at www.lonelyplanet.com/hotels. You'll find the true, insider low-down on the best places to stay. Reviews are thorough and independent. Best of all, you can book online.

DIRECTORY

Discounts

Nepal's hotel prices have always been highly seasonal, with peak season running from October to November and February to April and room rates fluctuating according to tourist demand. In this book we have generally given the hotel's advertised high-season room rates and, as a guide, also mentioned any discount we were offered during high-season research. You will find that rates drop even lower during the monsoon season (June to September).

The exact room rate you will be quoted depends on the season and tourist numbers. At many hotels the printed tariffs are pure fiction, published in the hope that you might be silly enough to pay them and to fulfil government star rating requirements. Some midrange hotels offer discounts for booking online (and a free airport transfer) but you'll get at least this much on the spot, if not more. If business is slow you can often negotiate a deluxe room for a standard-room rate. When business picks up (as is currently the case), you may just have to take what's on offer.

You can normally negotiate cheaper rates for longer stays. In the cool of autumn and spring you get a further discount on rooms that are air-conditioned simply by agreeing to turn off the air-con.

BUSINESS HOURS

Most government offices in Kathmandu are open from 10am to 5pm Sunday to Thursday during the summer and 10am to 4pm during the winter (roughly mid-November to mid-February). Offices close at 3pm on Friday and are generally closed for an hour during lunchtime. Saturday is deemed a holiday and almost all offices and some banks will be closed. Museums are generally closed on Tuesdays. See p369 for a list of public holidays.

Bars and clubs generally close quite early, around midnight, even in Kathmandu, where a government curfew is in place for bars in Thamel (note that the curfew was in place at the time of research and this situation could change).

CHILDREN

Few people travel with children in Nepal, yet with a bit of planning it is remarkably hassle-free. Check out Lonely Planet's *Travel With Children* for handy hints and advice about the pros and cons of travelling with kids.

In the main tourist centres (Kathmandu and Pokhara) most hotels have triple rooms and quite often a suite with four beds, which are ideal for families with young children. Finding a room with a bathtub can be a problem at the bottom end of the market. Many Kathmandu hotels have a garden or roof garden, which can be good play areas. Check them thoroughly, however, as some are definitely not safe for young children.

Walking the crowded and narrow streets of Kathmandu and other towns can be a hassle with young kids unless you can get them up off the ground – a backpack or sling is ideal. A pusher or stroller would be more trouble than it's worth unless you bring one with oversize wheels, suitable for rough pavements.

Eating out at restaurants with kids can be difficult. While the food is excellent, the service is usually quite slow. By the time the food arrives your kids will be bored stiff and ready to leave. It's less hassle if you eat breakfast at your hotel, have lunch at a place with a garden (there are plenty of these) where the

---

GOVERNMENT TRAVEL ADVICE

The following governments publish useful advice for travellers, highlighting entry requirements, medical facilities, areas with health and safety risks, civil unrest or other dangers, and are generally bang up to date.

Australian Department of Foreign Affairs and Trade (☎ 1300 139 281; www.smartraveller.gov.au)
Canadian Consular Affairs (☎ 1-800-267-6788; www.voyage.gc.ca)
New Zealand Ministry of Foreign Affairs and Trade (☎ 04-439 8000; www.safetravel.govt.nz)
UK Foreign and Commonwealth Office (☎ 020-7008 1500; www.fco.gov.uk/travel)
US Department of State (☎ 1-888-407-4747, 1-202-501-4444; http://travel.state.gov/travel)

children can let off steam, and in the evening go to the restaurant armed with colouring books, stories and other distractions to keep them busy.

Disposable nappies are available in Kathmandu and Pokhara, but for a price – better to bring them with you if possible. Cloth nappies can be a headache, but remember that disposable nappies are almost indestructible, and waste disposal in Nepal is already a major problem.

CLIMATE CHARTS

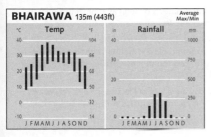

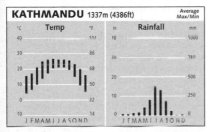

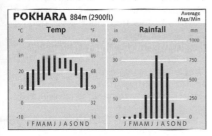

COURSES

Nepal offers travellers many opportunities to expand their skills and knowledge, with courses from language to traditional music on offer.

See p67 for details of cookery courses in Kathmandu and Pokhara.

Language

Nepali is not a difficult language to learn, and you will see notices around Kathmandu advertising language courses. Most schools offer courses or individual tuition. Expect to pay about US$50 for a two-week course or around US$3 per hour for private tuition.

Language centres in Kathmandu and Pokhara include the following:

Cosmic Brontosaurus Language School (Map p263; ☎ 9846069834; premk1979@yahoo.com; Pokhara; per hr Rs 200; ☺ noon-4pm) Offering individual or group lessons from beginner to advanced, the rather primitive classroom in a wooden shack along the lake is surrounded by banana plants and is the perfect spot to learn Nepali. With seven years' experience working with the UN as a translator, Prem, who runs the school, is a lovely guy.

Intercultural Training & Research Centre (ITC; Map p140; ☎ 01-4412793; www.itcnepal.com; Kathmandu) This well-respected language centre works with many NGOs, including the UK's Voluntary Service Overseas (VSO). It offers crash courses (three hours), 60-hour beginner courses and six-week intermediate courses. Tuition is one-on-one and costs around Rs 350 per hour. Contact Parbati Shrestha.

Kathmandu Environmental Education Project (KEEP; Map p140; ☎ 01-4216775; www.keepnepal .org; Thamel, Kathmandu; ☺ 10am-5pm Sun-Fri) Offers Nepali-language classes in the off-season between April and June. The 12-hour course costs US$40.

Kathmandu Institute of Nepali Language (Map p140; ☎ 01-4232652, 01 4437454; www.ktmnepali language.com; Bhagwan Bahal, Kathmandu) Offers a week's course (six hours) for Rs 1800.

There are often flyers around Bodhnath advertising Tibetan-language tuition and apartments to rent, as well as opportunities to volunteer-teach Tibetan refugees. The **Centre for Buddhist Studies** (☎ 01-4483575; www.cbs.edu .np; Kathmandu), based at the Rangjung Yeshe Institute (see p365), is part of Kathmandu University and offers a two-month Tibetan-language course (US$2180) from mid-June, with accommodation provided with local Tibetan families; it also offers longer university-accredited courses.

Music & the Arts

Gandharba Culture and Art Organisation (Map p140; http://gandharbas.nyima.org; Thamel, Kathmandu) Offers lessons in the *sarangi* (four-stringed instrument played with a bow) and it can probably find teachers for other instruments such as the *madal* (drum), *bansari* (flute) and *arbaj* (four-string guitar). Expect to pay around Rs 200 per hour.

PRACTICALITIES

■ Nepal's main English-language papers are the daily *Rising Nepal* (www.gorkhapatra.org.np), *Kathmandu Post* (www.kantipuronline.com) and *Himalayan Times* (www.thehimalayantimes .com), and the weekly *Nepali Times* (www.nepalitimes.com).

■ *ECS* (www.ecs.com.np; Rs 75) is a glossy expat-orientated monthly magazine with interesting articles on travel and culture, plus apartment listings.

■ The glossy *Nepal Traveller* (www.nepal-traveller.com) is a free monthly tourist magazine with information on sights, festivals and trekking, directories of airlines offices, embassies and so on.

■ In the Kathmandu Valley, tune into Kantipur FM (96.1FM), Hits FM (92.1FM) or HBC FM (104FM), or listen to the BBC World Service on 103FM.

■ Nepal TV (www.nepaltelevision.com.np) has an English news bulletin at 10pm. Most midrange and top-end hotels offer satellite channels, such as BBC World.

■ Electricity, when available, is 220V/50 cycles; 120V appliances from the US will need a transformer. Sockets usually take plugs with three round pins, sometimes the small variety, sometimes the large. Some sockets take plugs with two round pins. Local electrical shops sell cheap adapters.

■ Blackouts ('load shedding') for up to 16 hours a day are a fact of life across Nepal, especially in Kathmandu. Power surges are also likely, so bring a voltage guard with spike suppressor (automatic cut-off switch) for your laptop.

Trekkers Holiday Inn (☎ 01-4480334; trekkersholiday inn.com; Chuchepati) This Swiss-run centre midway between Kathmandu and Bodhnath offers courses on cookery, Ayurvedic medicine, singing bowl meditation and Nepali language (Rs 4500 for 15 hours). The hotel is hard to find; get yourself to Chuchepati Chowk, by the bust of Pasang Lhamo, head north, take the lane on the left and follow it as it curves.

Yoga, Buddhist Meditation & Massage

Nepal is a popular place for people to take up spiritual pursuits, particularly around the Kathmandu Valley, although Pokhara is becoming increasingly popular. Check the noticeboards in Thamel for up-to-date information about yoga and Buddhism courses and shop around before you commit yourself.

Ananda Yoga Center (☎ 01-4311048; www.ananda yogacenter.blogspot.com; Kathmandu Valley) On the edge of the valley at Satungal, overlooking Matatirtha Village, 8km west of Kathmandu, this is a nonprofit yoga retreat offering courses in reiki, hatha yoga and teacher training.

Ganden Yiga Chopen Meditation Centre (Pokhara Buddhist Meditation Centre; Map p263; www.pokhara buddhistcentre.com) Three-day Lamrin meditation and yoga courses (Rs 3300) as well as daily sessions at 10am (Rs 200) and 5pm (Rs 150).

Healing Hands Centre (www.ancientmassage.com; Maharajganj, Kathmandu) Various monthly courses in Thai massage. The five-day course (20 hours, US$200) teaches you how to give a full-body massage; there are also 10-day courses and one-month professional courses for US$900. Accommodation is available at the centre in the northeastern Kathmandu suburbs.

Himalayan Buddhist Meditation Centre (HBMC; Map p140; ☎ 01-4410402; www.fpmt-hbmc.org; ☽ 8am-9pm) This friendly place offers guided meditations and talks on Tibetan Buddhism, with free lectures Monday to Friday at 8.30am and 5.30pm and Saturday dharma lectures with teachers from Kopan Monastery (Rs 400 with lunch; register in advance). The centre also offers yoga and reiki classes, a vegetarian restaurant, a library and a film night every Friday.

Himalayan International Yoga Academy (HiYA; ☎ 01-2021259; www.yogainnepal.com) Located between Swayambhunath and Nagarjun hill. Offers yoga and meditation courses ranging from a couple of hours to a couple of weeks, with accommodation, vegetarian meals and alternative medicine treatments.

Kamma Healing Centre (Map p126; ☎ 01-4256618; kammacenter@gmail.com; Babar Mahal Revisited; ☽ closed Sat) Commercial classes in t'ai chi, yoga, transcendental meditation and anything else you can dream up. Yoga classes cost Rs 400 per hour; t'ai chi is Rs 4000 per month.

Kathmandu Center of Healing (☎ 9851070786; www.kathmanduhealing.org; Galfutar, Kathmandu) This place offers one-, two- and five-week professional courses in Thai massage. Other activities include yoga, dance, a monthly four-day reiki course and various 'healing seminars'. Contact Rabin.

Kopan Monastery (☎ 01-4821268; www.kopan -monastery.com) This monastery, north of Bodhnath, offers reasonably priced and popular seven-day (US$75) or 10-day (US$110) courses on Tibetan Buddhism, generally given by foreign teachers. There's also a popular annual one-month course (US$410) held in November, followed by an optional seven-day retreat. See p178 for more details.

Nepal Vipassana Centre Budhanilkantha (☎ 01-4371655); Kathmandu (Map p140; ☎ 01-4250581; nvc@ htp.com.np; Jyoti Bhawan Bldg, Kantipath, Kathmandu; ☺ 10am-5pm Sun-Fri) Ten-day retreats are held twice a month (starting on the 1st and 14th of the month) at its centre northeast of Kathmandu, just north of Budhanilkantha, and there are also occasional shorter courses. These are serious meditation courses that involve rising at 4am every morning, not talking or making eye contact with anyone over 10 days, and not eating after midday. The fee is donation only.

Nepali Yoga Center (☎ 061-532407; www.nepali yoga.com; Pokhara) Daily hatha yoga classes (1½ hours, Rs 400) at 7.30am and 4.30pm, plus one-/three-day courses (Rs 1000/3000).

Patanjali Yoga Center (Map pp114-15; ☎ 01-4278437; www.saptayoga.com) A recommended place for yoga, west of Kathmandu's city centre. Five- and 10-day courses involve attending the centre for three hours per day and include lunch. In theory there are drop-in classes daily at 7am and 4pm, but it's best to call to confirm in advance.

Rangjung Yeshe Institute (☎ 01-4483575; www .shedra.org) At Bodhnath's Ka-Nying Sheldrup Ling Gompa (see Map p174). The institute offers a fairly advanced 10-day course ('Vajrayana empowerment') on Tibetan Buddhist teachings, practice and meditation, led by the monastery's abbot Chokyi Nyima Rinpoche. The course is held in mid-November and costs US$100. The institute also offers a six-week summer course in Buddhist theory and meditation (US$1760) in June/July.

Sadhana Yoga (Map p273; ☎ 061-464601; www .sadhana-asanga-yoga.com; Pokhara) One to 21 days are offered at this yoga centre at the cost of around Rs 1800 per day, which includes accommodation, meals and steam and mud baths. It also offers a one-day Nepali cookery course.

CUSTOMS REGULATIONS

All baggage is X-rayed on arrival and departure, though it's a pretty haphazard process. In addition to the import and export of drugs, customs is concerned with the illegal export of antiques (see right). You may not import Nepali rupees, and only nationals of Nepal and India may import Indian currency. There are no other restrictions on bringing in either cash or travellers cheques, but the amount taken out at departure should not exceed the amount brought in. Officially you should declare cash or travellers cheques in excess of US$2000, or the equivalent, but no one seems to bother with this.

Antiques

Customs' main concern is preventing the export of antique works of art, with good reason, as Nepal has been a particular victim of international art theft over the last 20 years (see the boxed text, p61).

It is very unlikely that souvenirs sold to travellers will be antique (despite the claims of the vendors), but if there is any doubt, they should be cleared and a certificate obtained from the **Department of Archaeology** (Map p126; ☎ 01-4250683; Ramshah Path, Kathmandu) in the National Archives building. If you visit the department between 10am and 1pm you should be able to pick up a certificate by 5pm the same day. These controls also apply to the export of precious and semiprecious stones.

DANGERS & ANNOYANCES

Kathmandu is currently enjoying a much-needed period of political stability and public optimism. The strikes, demonstrations and turmoil that defined much of the last decade have reduced greatly in number and length. Don't count your chickens yet, though. The political situation remains somewhat tense in the Terai and political agitation could return to the capital at any moment.

HOW MANY FOUNTAIN PENS DO YOU HAVE, MADAM?

According to the customs sign in the Kathmandu airport arrivals hall, visitors are permitted to import the following articles for their personal use (and we quote): 'Cigarettes, 200 sticks; cigars, 50 sticks; alcoholic liquor, one bottle not exceeding 1.15L; one binocular; one movie camera films 12 rolls; one tape recorder with 15 tape reels or cassettes; one perambulator; 10 disk records; one tricycle; one stick; and one set of fountain pens.'

You can minimise the chances of bumping into trouble by heeding the following general advice:

- Register with your embassy in Kathmandu (see p368).
- Be flexible with your travel arrangements in case your transport is affected by a bandh (strike) or security situation.
- Don't trek alone. Lone women should avoid travelling alone with a male guide.
- Be familiar with the symptoms of altitude sickness when trekking and observe sensible acclimatisation; see p395.
- Avoid travelling on night buses.
- Keep photocopies of your passport, visa, air ticket and travellers cheques separate from the originals.

Demonstrations & Strikes

For the last decade Nepal has been wracked by frequent demonstrations and strikes – some called by politicians, some by students and some by Maoists, and some by all three! The political situation improved in 2008 but tensions remain and demonstrations still occur. Avoid large groups of slogan-chanting youths, in case you end up on the downstream side of a police *lathi* charge (a team of police wielding bamboo staves) or worse.

A normal procession or demonstration is a julus. If things escalate there may be a *chakka jam* (jam the wheels), when all vehicles stay off the street, or a bandh, when all shops, schools and offices are closed as well. When roads are closed the government generally runs buses with armed policemen from the airport to major hotels, returning to the airport from Tridevi Marg at the east end of Thamel.

For more information on the political situation and safety see p18.

If political instability returns, it pays to heed the following points:

- Keep an eye on the local press to find out about impending strikes, demonstrations and curfews – follow websites such as www.kantipuronline.com, www.nepalnews.com, www.thehimalayantimes.com, www.nepalitimes.com.np and www.nepalnews.net.
- Don't ever break curfews and don't travel during bandhs or blockades. Get very nervous if you notice that you are the only car on the streets of Kathmandu!
- Avoid marches, demonstrations or disturbances, as they can quickly turn violent.

Load Shedding

Electricity cuts ('load shedding') are a fact of life in Kathmandu and Pokhara, especially in winter when water and thus hydro power levels are at their lowest. Electricity is currently rationed across Kathmandu, shifting from district to district every eight hours or so. Most hotels post a schedule of planned electricity cuts, which can last up to 16 hours a day in both Kathmandu and Pokhara. Try to choose a hotel with a generator and make sure your room is far away from it.

Scams

Be wary of deals offered by gem dealers (especially in Thamel, Kathmandu) that involve you buying stones to sell for a 'vast profit' at home. The dealers' stories vary, but are usually along the lines of the dealer not being able to export the stones without paying heavy taxes, so you take them and meet another dealer when you get home, who will sell them to a local contact and you both share the profit. Falling for this ruse is not as unusual as you might expect.

Other scams include young kids asking for milk; you buy the milk at a designated store at an inflated price, the kid then returns the milk and pockets some of the mark-up.

Be wary of kids who seem to know the capital of any country you can think of; a request for money will arrive at some point. Then there are the 'holy men' who will do their best to plant a *tika* (a red paste denoting blessing) on your forehead, only to then demand significant payment.

Credit card scams are not unheard of; travellers have bought souvenirs and then found thousand of dollars worth of internet porn subscriptions chalked up on their bill.

Theft

While petty theft is not on the scale that exists in many countries, reports of theft from hotel rooms in tourist areas (including along trekking routes) do occasionally reach us, and theft with violence is not unheard of. Never store valuables or money in your hotel room.

One of the most common forms of theft is when backpacks are rifled through when left on the roof of a bus. Try to make your pack as theft-proof as possible – small padlocks and cover bags are a good deterrent.

There's little chance of ever retrieving your gear if it is stolen, and even getting a police report for an insurance claim can be difficult.

Try the tourist police, or, if there aren't any, the local police station. If you're not getting anywhere, go to **Interpol** (☎ 01-4412602) at the Police Headquarters in Naxal, Kathmandu. The documentation requires a passport photo and photocopies of your passport and visa; the process takes two days.

Traffic, Pollution & Touts

Traffic on Kathmandu's streets is a rumpus of pollution-belching vehicles with two, three and four wheels. The combination of ancient vehicles, low-quality fuel and lack of emission controls makes the streets of Kathmandu particularly dirty, noisy and unpleasant. Traffic rules exist, but are rarely enforced; be especially careful when crossing streets or riding a bicycle – traffic is supposed to travel on the left side of the road, but many drivers simply choose the most convenient side, which can make walking in Kathmandu a deeply stressful experience. Remember that pedestrians account for over 40% of all traffic fatalities in Nepal.

Consider bringing a face mask to filter out dust and emission particles, especially if you plan to ride a bicycle or motorcycle in Kathmandu. After a few days in the city you can definitely feel your throat burning.

A minor hassle in Thamel comes from the barrage of irritating flute sellers, tiger-balm hawkers, chess-set sellers, musical-instrument vendors, travel-agency touts, hashish suppliers, freelance trekking guides and rickshaw drivers. In Kathmandu's and Patan's Durbar Sq you'll also come across a string of would-be guides whose trade has been hit badly by the downturn in tourism. There's less hassle in Bhaktapur, though there are some persistent thangka (Tibetan paintings on cotton) touts.

Trekking & Hiking

Fired up by the gung-ho stories of adventurous travellers, it is also easy to forget that mountainous terrain carries an inherent risk. There are posters plastered around Kathmandu with the faces of missing trekkers and travellers. Several solo trekkers go missing every year from the Everest region and one foreign trekker was murdered in Langtang in 2002. In October 2005 two female hikers were murdered (in two separate cases) while hiking in the Nagarjun Forest Reserve, just 5km from Kathmandu. Several tourists have been robbed along the trails to the World Peace Pagoda and Sarangkot, outside Pokhara.

In rural areas of Nepal rescue services are limited and medical facilities are primitive or nonexistent. Helicopter evacuations are possible but the costs run into the thousands of US dollars.

Only a tiny minority of trekkers end up in trouble, but accidents can often be avoided or risks minimised if people have a realistic understanding of trekking requirements. At a minimum you should never trek alone. See p337 for more advice.

DISCOUNT CARDS

There aren't any noticeable discounts for holders of student or seniors cards. Those under 30 can get discounts on flights to India without a student card.

EMBASSIES & CONSULATES

Travellers continuing beyond Nepal may need visas for Bangladesh, China, India, Myanmar (Burma) or Thailand. The only visas dished out in Kathmandu for Tibet (actually a Chinese visa and a travel permit for Tibet) are for organised groups; individuals wishing to travel to China or Tibet may find it easier to get a visa before arriving in Nepal (Delhi is a good place to get one). See p384 for advice about travelling to Tibet.

To find Nepali embassies and consulates in other countries check out the websites of Nepal's **Ministry of Foreign Affairs** (www.mofa.gov .np) or **Department of Immigration** (www.immi.gov .np/location.php).

Foreign embassies and consulates located in Kathmandu include the following:
Australia (Map pp114-15; ☎ 01-4371678; www.nepal .embassy.gov.au; Bansbari) Beyond the Ring Rd.
Bangladesh (Map pp114-15; ☎ 01-4372843; fax 01-4373265; Maharajganj; 🕙 9am-1.15pm & 2-5pm Mon-Fri) Visa applications mornings only; tourist visas are not issued here, but are available on arrival in Dhaka, Bangladesh.
Canada (Map p126; ☎ 01-4415193; www.cconepal .org.np; Lazimpat)
China (Map p126; ☎ 01-4440286; www.chinaembassy .org.np; Hattisar; 🕙 9am-noon & 3-5pm Mon-Fri) Visa applications are accepted Monday, Wednesday and Friday 9.30am to 11.30am; passports are generally returned the next working day between 4pm and 4.30pm, though same-day express services are possible. If applying yourself you will need to have proof (such as an air ticket to Beijing

---

REGISTERING WITH YOUR EMBASSY

Officials of all embassies in Nepal stress the benefits of registering with them, telling them where you are trekking, and reporting in again when you return. The offices of the **Kathmandu Environmental Education Project** (KEEP; Map p140; ☎ 01-4216775; www.keepnepal.org; Thamel, Kathmandu; ☺ 10am-5pm Sun-Fri) and the **Himalayan Rescue Association** (HRA; Map p140; ☎ 01-4445505; www.himalayanrescue.org; Thamel, Kathmandu; ☺ 10am-1pm & 2-5pm Sun-Fri) stock registration forms from most embassies, so it's simple to provide the information.

You can also register online with the following countries. Include the contact details of your next of kin and your travel dates, itinerary, passport number and insurance details:

Australian Embassy (www.orao.dfat.gov.au)

British Embassy (www.britishembassy.gov.uk/nepal, https://www.locate.fco.gov.uk/locateportal)

New Zealand Embassy (www.kiwisoverseas.govt.nz)

US Embassy (https://travelregistration.state.gov)

---

or Shanghai) that you are not travelling via Tibet. The visa section is in Hattisar; the embassy is in Baluwatar (see Map pp114–15).

France (Map p126; ☎ 01-4412332; www.ambafrance-np.org; Lazimpat; ☺ 9am-12.30pm Mon, Tue, Thu & Fri)

Germany (Map pp114-15; ☎ 01-4412786; www.kathmandu.diplo.de; Gyaneshwar)

India (Map p126; ☎ 01-4410900; www.south-asia.com/embassy-india; Lainchhaur; ☺ 9.30am-noon & 1.30-5pm Mon-Fri) Visa applications 9.30am to noon, visa collections 4pm to 5pm. Allow a week for processing tourist visas, which cost around Rs 3050 depending on nationality (an extra Rs 1550 for US citizens), plus a Rs 330 telex fee (Rs 1000 telex fee for US citizens), and are valid for six months. Get to the embassy gates before 8am, take a token and wait to be called. After filling in the telex form (you need a black pen) you need to return three working days later to queue to pay for the visa and then queue again to pick it up. Agencies will do the queuing for you for a service fee of around Rs 1000 to Rs 2000 and will save you several days of grief. Transit visas (Rs 800; valid for 15 days from date of issue) are issued the same day, start from that date and are nonextendable. Two photos and a photocopy of your passport are required.

Israel (Map p126; ☎ 01-4411811; http://kathmandu.mfa.gov.il; Lazimpat; ☺ 9am-5pm Mon-Thu, to 3pm Fri)

Japan (Map pp114-15; ☎ 01-4426680; www.np.emb-japan.go.jp; Pani Pokhari)

Myanmar (Burma; Map p182; ☎ 01-5524788; fax 01-5523402; Chakupath, Patan) Located near Patan Dhoka (City Gate).

Netherlands (Map p182; ☎ 01-5523444; www.netherlandsconsulate.org.np; Bakhundol, Patan; ☺ 10am-noon Mon & Wed-Fri, to 11am Tue)

New Zealand (Map p126; ☎ 01-4412436; fax 01-4414750; Dilli Bazaar) Honorary consulate only, staffed by the famous expedition chronicler Elizabeth Hawley.

Pakistan (Map pp114-15; ☎ 01-4374024; fax 01-4374012; Narayan Gopal Chowk, Ring Rd, Maharajganj; ☺ 9am-5pm Mon-Fri)

Thailand (Map pp114-15; ☎ 01-4371410; www.thaiembassy.org/kathmandu; Bansbari; ☺ 8.30am-12.30pm & 1.30-4.30pm Mon-Fri) Most nationalities don't need a visa for stays of less than 30 days. Visa applications 9.30am to 12.30pm – two photos are required, there's a 24-hour turnaround and about a US$10 fee (you can only pay the visa fees into a local bank, which is a pain).

UK (Map p126; ☎ 01-4410583; www.ukinnepal.fco.gov.uk; Lainchhaur; ☺ 8.15am-12.30pm & 1.30-5pm Mon-Thu, 8.15am-1.15pm Fri) The British embassy and a separate consular section are housed in different buildings nearby each other.

US (Map pp114-15; ☎ 01- 4007200, after hours emergency 01-4007266; http://nepal.usembassy.gov; Maharaganj; US citizen services ☺ 1.30-4pm Mon-Fri)

GAY & LESBIAN TRAVELLERS

Nepal is the only country in South Asia that does not criminalise same-sex relations. A landmark Supreme Court hearing in December 2007 ordered the government to end discrimination against sexual minorities and to ensure equal rights. That said, there's not a big open gay scene in Nepal and gay Nepalis are vulnerable to police harassment and blackmail. Gay couples holding hands in public will experience no difficulties, as this is socially acceptable, but public displays of intimacy by anyone are frowned upon.

The **Blue Diamond Society** (☎ 01-4443350; www.bds.org.np) is the first gay organisation in Kathmandu. It provides education, support and advice to Nepal's gay and transgender community, and runs the country's only AIDS/HIV prevention program, partially thanks to a US$40,000 grant donated by Sir Elton John. Its founder recently became the country's first openly gay member of parliament. **Aashnepal Travel & Tours** (☎ 01-4228768; www .aashanepal.com.np) is a gay-friendly tour company in Kathmandu.

HOLIDAYS
Public Holidays
Many holidays and festivals affect the working hours of government offices and banks, which close for the following public holidays and some or all of the days of the festivals mentioned in the Events Calendar (p23). Note that this list is not exhaustive and the exact festival dates change annually.

Prithvi Narayan Shah's Birthday 10 January
Basanta Panchami January/February
Democracy Day 18 February
Maha Shivaratri February/March
Bisket Jatra (Nepali New Year) 14 April
Janai Purnima July/August
Teej August/September
Indra Jatra September
Dasain September/October
Tihar October/November
Constitution Day 9 November

INSURANCE
A travel-insurance policy to cover theft, loss and medical problems is an excellent idea in Nepal. There is a wide variety of policies available, so check the small print carefully. Some policies exclude 'dangerous activities', which may include riding a motorbike and trekking (and definitely bungee jumping and rafting). Choose a policy that covers medical and emergency repatriation, including helicopter evacuation for trekkers and general medical evacuation to Bangkok or Delhi, which alone can cost a cool US$40,000.

You may prefer a policy that pays doctors or hospitals directly rather than you having to pay on the spot and claim later. If you have to claim later make sure you keep all documentation. Some policies ask you to call back (reverse charges) to a centre in your home country where an immediate assessment of your problem is made.

Bear in mind that many insurance policies do not cover 'acts of terrorism', civil war or regions that your country's government advises against travel to, so double-check how your insurance company defines these notions and Nepal's political situation.

Worldwide cover to travellers from over 44 countries is available online at www.lonely planet.com/travel_services.

INTERNET ACCESS
Email and internet services are offered in dozens of places in Kathmandu and Pokhara and are generally cheap at around Rs 50 per hour. Internet access is also available in most other towns – you can even send email from Namche Bazaar on the Everest trek – but connections are usually slow and relatively expensive, as connection may involve a long-distance call to Kathmandu.

Most midrange and top-end hotels, restaurants and cafes in Kathmandu and Pokhara offer wi-fi if you have your own laptop. It is sometimes free but can cost anywhere from Rs 200 to Rs 700 for 24 hours access. Another option is to buy a WorldLink card (Rs 250), which gives you five hours of wi-fi access at several participating hotels and cafes in Kathmandu.

NEPALI CALENDARS
Nepali holidays and festivals are principally dated by the lunar calendar, falling on days relating to new or full moons. The lunar calendar is divided into bright and dark fortnights. The bright fortnight is the two weeks of the waxing moon, as it grows to become purnima (the full moon). The dark fortnight is the two weeks of the waning moon, as the full moon shrinks to become *aunsi* (the new moon).

The Nepali New Year starts on 14 April with the month of Baisakh. The Nepali calendar is 57 years ahead of the Gregorian calendar used in the West, thus the year 2010 in the West is 2067 in Nepal. You can convert between Nepali and Gregorian dates at www.umn.org.np/nepali.

The Newars, on the other hand, start their New Year from the day after Deepawali (the third day of Tihar), which falls on the night of the new moon in late October or early November. Their calendar is 880 years behind the Gregorian calendar, so 2010 in the West is 1130 to the Newars of the Kathmandu Valley.

DASAIN STOPPAGES

Dasain (15 days in September or October) is the most important of all Nepali celebrations. Tens of thousands of Nepalis hit the road to return home to celebrate with their families. This means that while villages are full of life if you are trekking, buses and planes are fully booked and overflowing, porters may be hard to find (or more expensive than usual) and cars are hard to hire. Many hotels and restaurants in regional towns close down completely, and doing business in Kathmandu (outside Thamel) becomes almost impossible.

The most important days, when everything comes to a total halt, are the ninth day (when thousands of animals are sacrificed) and the 10th day (when blessings are received from elder relatives and superiors). Banks and government offices are generally closed from the eighth day of the festival to the 12th day. For more information on the festival see p25.

LEGAL MATTERS

Hashish has been illegal since 1973, but it's still readily available in Nepal. Thamel is full of shifty, whispering dealers. Possession of a small amount involves little risk, although potential smokers should keep the less-than-salubrious condition of Nepali jails firmly in mind. Don't try taking any out of the country either – travellers have been arrested at the airport on departure.

If you get caught smuggling something serious – drugs or gold – chances are you'll end up in jail, without trial, and will remain there until someone pays for you to get out. Jail conditions in Nepal are reportedly horrific. Bribery may be an option to avoid jail in the first place but unless you can do it in a way which is deniable, you may just end up in deeper strife.

A handful of foreigners currently languish in jails in Kathmandu, mostly for drug offences. If you want to pay a humanitarian visit you can contact your embassy for a list of names and their locations. Take along items of practical use, such as reading matter, blankets and fresh fruit.

Killing a cow is illegal in Nepal and carries a punishment of two years in prison.

MAPS

The best maps of Nepal are those produced by Karto-Atelier, under the name Gecko Maps (www.geckomaps.com). These locally made maps are a result of German-Nepali collaboration and are very reliable. Maps of Nepal, Kathmandu and Chitwan are currently available.

There are many other locally produced and cheaper maps available in Nepal that prove quite adequate for trekkers. The main series are produced by Nepa Maps and Himalayan

Map House, though some good maps are produced by Shangri-La Maps (www.shangrilamaps.com). They are decent quality and reasonably priced at Rs 400 to Rs 800 each but they definitely aren't reliable enough to use for off-route trekking. These and other maps are sold at a string of glossy map shops throughout Thamel and elsewhere in Kathmandu.

For details of trekking maps and online map shops see p333.

MONEY

The Nepali rupee (Rs) is divided into 100 paisa (p). There are coins for denominations of one, two, five and 10 rupees, and bank notes in denominations of one, two, five, 10, 20, 25, 50, 100, 500 and 1000 rupees. This is a great contrast to a time not long ago, when outside the Kathmandu Valley it was rare to see any paper money. Mountaineering books from the 1950s often comment on the porters whose sole duty was to carry the expedition's money – in coins.

Away from major centres, changing a Rs 1000 note can be difficult, so it is always a good idea to keep a stash of small-denomination notes. Even in Kathmandu, many small businesses – especially rickshaw and taxi drivers – simply don't have sufficient spare money to allow them the luxury of carrying a wad of change.

ATMs

Standard Chartered Bank has ATMs in Kathmandu and Pokhara; you can get cash advances on both Visa and MasterCard 24 hours a day, though travellers have reported that these machines don't take cards that run on the Cirrus system. Other banks, such as the Himalaya Bank, also have ATMs but some only accept local cards. Frequent power outages can limit the machines' working hours, so use one when you see it's working. Using an ATM attached to a bank during business hours will minimise hassle in the rare event that the machine eats your card. It's not a bad idea to inform your bank that you'll be using your card abroad, otherwise they might suspect fraud and freeze your card (this applies to UK cards in particular).

Changing Money

Official exchange rates are set by the government's Nepal Rastra Bank and listed in the daily newspapers. Rates at the private banks vary, but are generally not far from the official rate.

There are exchange counters at the international terminal at Kathmandu's Tribhuvan Airport and banks and/or moneychangers at the various border crossings. Pokhara and the major border towns also have official moneychanging facilities, but changing travellers cheques can be time consuming elsewhere in the country, even in some quite large towns. If you are trekking, take enough cash in small-denomination rupees to last the whole trek.

The best private banks are Himalaya Bank, Nepal Bank Ltd and Standard Chartered Bank. Some hotels and resorts are licensed to change money but their rates are lower. Travellers cheques from the main companies are easily exchanged in banks in Kathmandu and Pokhara for a 2% surcharge.

When you change money officially, you are required to show your passport, and you are issued with a foreign exchange encashment receipt showing your identity and the amount of currency you have changed. Hang onto the receipts as you need them to change excess rupees back into foreign currency at banks. You can change rupees back into foreign currency at most moneychangers without a receipt.

If you leave Nepal via Kathmandu's Tribhuvan Airport, the downstairs exchange counter will change rupees back to foreign currency to the amount covered by your exchange receipts. Official re-exchange is not possible at any bank branches at the border crossings.

Many upmarket hotels and businesses are obliged by the government to demand payment in hard currency (euros or US dollars); they will also accept rupees, but only if you can show a foreign exchange encashment receipt that covers the amount you owe them. In practice this regulation seems to be widely disregarded. Airlines are also required to charge tourists in hard currency, either in cash US dollars, travellers cheques or credit cards, and this rule is generally followed.

MONEYCHANGERS

In addition to the banks there are licensed moneychangers in Kathmandu, Pokhara, Birganj, Kakarbhitta and Sunauli/Bhairawa. The rates are often marginally lower than the banks, but there are no commissions, they have much longer opening hours (typically from 9am to 7pm daily) and they are also much quicker, the whole process often taking no more than a few minutes.

Most licensed moneychangers will provide an exchange receipt; if they don't you may be able to negotiate better rates than those posted on their boards.

Credit Cards

Major credit cards are widely accepted at mid-range and better hotels, restaurants and fancy shops in the Kathmandu Valley and Pokhara only. Most places levy a 3% to 4% surcharge to counter the credit card company's fees to the vendor.

Branches of Standard Chartered Bank and some other banks such as Nabil Bank and Himalayan Bank give cash advances against Visa and MasterCard in Nepali rupees only (no commission), and will also sell you foreign-currency travellers cheques against the cards with a 2% commission.

The American Express (Amex) agent is Yeti Travels (p118) in Kathmandu. It advances travellers cheques to cardholders for a standard 1% commission.

International Transfers

In general it's easiest to send money through a private company such as Western Union (www.westernunion.com) or Moneygram (www.visitnepal.com/moneygram), which can arrange transfers within minutes. Western Union's agents in Nepal include Yeti Travels (p118), Sita World Travel (see p118) and Nabil Bank. Moneygram uses Easylink, with offices in Thamel, Bodhnath, Butwal and Pokhara. To pick up funds at a Western Union branch you'll need your passport and 10-digit transfer code.

Note that money can often only be received in Nepali rupees, rather than US dollars.

Tipping

Most tourist restaurants now incorporate a mandatory 10% service charge. Round up the fare for taxi drivers. Trekking guides and porter generally expect a tip of 15% to 20% for a job well done.

PHOTOGRAPHY & VIDEO

Bringing a video camera to Nepal poses no real problem and there are no video fees to worry about. The exception to this is in upper Mustang and Langtang border regions where an astonishing US$1000 fee is levied.

Airport Security

All luggage (including carry-on cabin baggage) is X-rayed at Kathmandu's Tribhuvan Airport on the way in and out of the country; signs on the X-ray equipment state that the machines are not safe for undeveloped film. Have exposed film inspected manually when leaving the country.

Film & Equipment

There are numerous camera and film shops in Kathmandu and Pokhara and good-quality film is readily available. Do check, however, that the packaging has not been tampered with and that the expiry date has not been exceeded. Out in the smaller cities and towns there is little choice and even greater chance of coming across expired film.

In Kathmandu there are numerous places offering a same-day service for print film (see p159). Typically, 100 ASA 36-exposure colour print film costs about Rs 150. Developing is typically around Rs 400 for 36 prints.

Slide film costs around Rs 450 for Sensia (100 ASA), Rs 650 for Provia and a bit less for Elitechrome (Rs 550). Slide processing is available in one or two places in Kathmandu at around Rs 500 for 36 mounted shots.

Almost all flavours of memory stick, flash card etc and batteries are available in Kathmandu. Note that travellers have reported buying cards in Kathmandu that do not have as much memory as the packet claims.

A panoramic camera can be very useful if you're trekking; it's the only way to do service to those jaw-dropping views. Some digital cameras have this feature built in.

Photographing People

Most Nepalis are content to have their photograph taken, but always ask permission first. Sherpa people are an exception and can be very camera-shy. Bear in mind that if someone poses for you (especially sadhus – holy men), they will probably insist on being given *baksheesh* (a tip).

For more advice and general rules for photographing people and events in Nepal see p75.

Restrictions

It is not uncommon for temple guardians to not allow photos of their temple and these wishes should be respected. Don't photograph army camps, checkpoints or bridges.

Technical Tips

Nepal is an exceptionally scenic country so bring plenty of film. To photograph Nepal's diverse attractions you need a variety of lenses, from a wide-angle lens if you're shooting in compact temple compounds to a long telephoto lens if you're after perfect mountain shots or close-ups of wildlife. A polarising filter is useful to increase contrast and bring out the blue of the sky.

Remember to allow for the intensity of mountain light when setting exposures at high altitude. At the other extreme it's surprising how often you find the light in Nepal is insufficient. Early in the morning, in the dense jungle of Chitwan National Park or in gloomy temples and narrow streets, you may find yourself wishing you had high-speed film. A flash is often necessary for shots inside temples or to 'fill in' shots of sculptures and reliefs.

Rechargeable batteries can be charged at most trekking lodges for a fee of Rs 100 to Rs 300 per hour. To charge batteries or an iPod on a trek, consider a solar charger like the iSun or Solio (www.solio.com).

POST

The postal service to and from Nepal is, at best, erratic but can occasionally be amazingly efficient. Most articles do arrive at their destination…eventually.

Couriers

For a 500g package of documents FedEx (www.fedex.com/np) and DHL (www.dhl .com) charge around US$40 and US$50 respectively to the US and UK, slightly less to Australia. FedEx offers a 25% discount if you drop documents directly to their office.

Packages other than documents cost up to 50% more for the same weight.

Parcel Post

Having stocked up on souvenirs and gifts in Nepal, many people send them home from Kathmandu. Parcel post is not cheap or quick, but the service is reliable. Sea mail is much cheaper than airmail, but it is also much slower (packages take about 3½ months) and less reliable. As an idea, a 2kg package to the UK/US/India costs Rs 1600/2000/600 via airmail, 25% less at 'book post' rate (a special rate for books only).

The contents of a parcel must be inspected by officials *before* it is wrapped. There are packers at the Kathmandu foreign post office who will wrap it for a small fee. The maximum weight for sea mail is 20kg; for airmail it's 10kg, or 5kg for book post.

Some specialised shipping companies, such as Diki Continental Exports in Kathmandu (p118), offer considerably cheaper rates than airmail and are not much more expensive than sea mail. It still goes by air; the catch is that it has to be picked up at an international airport and you'll have to deal with customs paperwork and fees there.

If an object is shipped out to you in Nepal, you may find that customs charges for clearance and collection at your end add up to more than the initial cost of sending it. Often it's worth paying extra to take it with you on the plane in the first place.

Rates

Airmail rates for a 20g letter/postcard are Rs 2/1 within Nepal, Rs 18/15 to India and surrounding countries, Rs 35/25 to Europe and UK and Rs 40/30 to the US and Australia. An aerogramme costs Rs 38 to the US and Australia and Rs 28 to Europe.

Registered mail costs an extra Rs 85 for international destinations.

SHOPPING

Nepal is a shopper's paradise, whether you are looking for a cheap souvenir or a real work of art. Although you can find almost anything in the tourist areas of Kathmandu, there are specialities in different parts of the Kathmandu Valley. Wherever you shop remember to bargain. You'll generally get the best prices in the morning, especially if you are the first customer of the day.

Prices are low for foreign products in Kathmandu and Pokhara, but you get what you pay for. Thamel's shops in particular are full of poor-quality Indian printed books, Pakistani pirated CDs and locally made clothes that don't quite fit properly.

Remember that antiques (over 100 years old) cannot be taken out of the country and baggage is inspected by Nepali customs thoroughly. It helps to get a receipt and a description of any major purchase from the shop where you bought it. See p365 for more information on taking antiques through customs.

Unless you are sure about their reliability, do not ask the shop where you made the purchase to send it for you. See left for details on posting goods home.

Clothing & Embroidery

Tibetan and Nepali clothes have always been a popular buy, but Western fashions made strictly for the tourist market have also become a big industry.

Embroidery is popular and there are lots of little tailor shops around Kathmandu where the sewing machines whir away late into the night adding logos and Tibetan symbols to jackets, hats and T-shirts. Mountaineers like to return from Nepal with jackets carrying the message that this was the Country X, Year Y expedition to Peak Z. You can also buy badges for your backpack saying that you walked to Everest Base Camp or completed the Annapurna Circuit.

A Nepali *topi* (cap) is part of Nepali formal wear for a man and they are traditionally made in Bhaktapur. There's a group of cap specialists between Indra Chowk and Asan Tole in the old part of Kathmandu.

BARGAINING

Haggling is regarded as an integral part of most commercial transactions in Nepal, especially when dealing with souvenir shops, hotels and guides. Ideally, it should be an enjoyable social exchange, rather than a conflict of egos. A good deal is reached when both parties are happy so keep things light; Nepalis do not appreciate aggressive behaviour. Remember that Rs 10 might make quite a difference to the seller, but in real terms it amounts to very little (less than US$0.15).

Jewellery

Kathmandu's many small jewellery manufacturers turn out a wide variety of designs with an equally wide range of standards. You can buy jewellery ready-made, ask them to create a design for you or bring in something you would like copied. There are several good shops around greater Thamel, particularly down towards Chhetrapati.

These outlets mainly cater to Western tastes but there are also shops for the local market as Nepali women, like Indian women, traditionally wear their wealth in jewellery. For a few rupees you can buy an armful of glass bangles or colourful beads by the handful.

If you are approached to buy gems it is likely to be a scam (see p366 for more information).

Masks & Puppets

Papier-mâché masks and colourful puppets are sold at shops in Kathmandu, Patan and Bhaktapur. Thimi is the manufacturing centre for masks, which are used in the traditional masked dances in September – it's interesting to see masks being made there. Ganesh, Bhairab and the Kumari are the most popular subjects for masks and they make good wall decorations.

Puppets make good gifts for children and are made in Bhaktapur as well as other centres. They're often of multiarmed deities clutching little wooden weapons in each hand. The puppet heads may be made of easily broken clay or more durable papier mâché. As usual, quality does vary and the more puppets you inspect the more you will begin to appreciate the differences.

Metalwork

Patan is the valley centre for bronze casting and the best variety of metalwork is found in the shops around Patan's Durbar Sq.

Paper Products

Locally produced paper from the *lokta* (daphne plant) is used to make picture frames, photo albums, cards and lanterns. The *lokta* bark is boiled and beaten with wooden mallets and the pulp is spread over a frame to dry. The finished product (often mistakenly called rice paper) folds without creasing and is used on all official Nepali documents.

There's a good selection in the shops of Thamel and Bhaktapur, where you can see the manufacturing process.

Pashmina

One of the most popular souvenirs is a shawl or scarf made from fine pashmina (the underhair of a mountain goat). The cost of a shawl depends on the percentage of pashmina in the mix and from which part of the goat's body the hair originated, starting from the cheapest back wool and rising through the belly and chest to neck hair, which is about five times more expensive than back hair.

There are literally dozens of shops in Thamel selling pashmina items. The cheapest shawls are a 70/30% cotton/pashmina blend, and these cost around Rs 1500 for a 78cm-by-2m shawl. Silk-pashmina blends cost around Rs 2500, while a pure pashmina shawl ranges from around Rs 3500 to US$275 for a pashmina ring shawl (named because they are fine enough to be pulled through a finger ring; also known as a water shawl).

Shahtoosh is a form of pashmina that comes from (and results in the death of) the endangered Tibetan antelope. *Shahtoosh* is illegal in Nepal.

Tea

Tea is grown in the east of Nepal, close to Darjeeling in India, where the finest Indian tea is grown. The Ilam, Ontu, Kanyan and Mai Valley teas are the best Nepali brands, but they are not cheap. Expect to pay anything from Rs 600 (in Ilam) to Rs 3000 (in Thamel) per kilogram for good Ilam tea, which is not much cheaper than Darjeeling tea. The excellently named 'super fine tipi golden flower orange pekoe' tea is about as good as it gets. Connoisseurs choose the first (March) or second (May) flush, rather than the substandard monsoon flush. Lemon tea flavoured with lemongrass is another favourite (Rs 150 per 100g).

Thangkas

Thangkas are Tibetan Buddhist paintings that depict fierce protector deities, aspects of the Buddha, various bodhisattvas (saints), historical figures, a mandala (geometric design) or the wheel of life.

Although there are some genuine antique thangkas to be found, it's highly unlikely that anything offered to the average visitor will date from much beyond last week. Judicious use of a smoky fire can add the odd century in no time. Thangkas do vary considerably in quality but buy one because you like it, not as a valuable investment.

Thangkas are available in Kathmandu's Thamel, Durbar Marg and Durbar Sq areas, as well as the Tibetan shops around Bodhnath. Like many other crafts, the more you see the more you will appreciate the different qualities available. Traditionally thangkas are framed in silk brocade.

Tibetan Carpets

Carpet weaving is a major trade in Nepal. The skill was brought by Tibetan refugees who have transplanted the craft with great success into their new home. Some of their output is now exported to Tibet, where the skills have largely been lost. A genuine Tibetan carpet purchased in Tibet is probably made by Tibetans, but in Nepal the Tamang people also make carpets.

Jawalakhel, on the southern outskirts of Patan, is the carpet-weaving centre in the valley. The traditional size for a Tibetan carpet is 1.8m by 90cm. Small square carpets are often used to make seat cushions.

Carpet quality depends on knots per inch and the price is worked out per square metre. A 60-knot carpet costs around Rs 1700 per sq metre, while a 100-knot carpet is Rs 4800 per sq metre.

Other Souvenirs

A khukuri (traditional knife of the Gurkhas) can cost from Rs 300 to Rs 2000. Most are made in eastern Nepal and come with a scabbard and a blade sharpener (*chakmak*). Notice the notch (*kaudi*) in the blade that allows blood to run off before hitting the hilt. You may well have trouble explaining the knife to customs officials in your country (always carry it in your check-in, rather than carry-on, baggage).

Bhaktapur is the centre for woodcarving, and you can find good objects in and around Tachupal Tole.

Cassettes and CDs of Nepali, Indian and Himalayan music are a fine souvenir of a visit to Nepal, though much of it is of the New Age variety. There are lots of music shops

in Kathmandu selling local music as well as pirated Western tapes and CDs (Rs 150 to Rs 250). The best-quality recordings are from Russia, though most come from Pakistan or Singapore. It's a good idea to test them out in the shop as there are a few rogues about. MP3 recordings are also available.

Tibetan crafts include a variety of religious items such as the dorje (thunderbolt symbol), prayer flags and the popular prayer wheels. Tibetans are keen traders, and prices at Bodhnath and Swayambhunath are often high. New Age Tibetophiles love Tibetan 'singing bowls', which have an alloy of seven metals that creates a ringing sound when you rotate a dowel around the rim, said to be conducive to meditative thought.

Dhoop (incense) is a popular buy, as are spices, ranging from single spices like *jeera* (cumin), *besar* (turmeric) and *methi* (fenugreek) to various kinds of masala mixes.

SOLO TRAVELLERS

Kathmandu, Pokhara and trekking lodges everywhere are supersociable places and it's not hard for solo travellers to hook up with other travellers.

Most hotels have different rates for single and double occupancy but the 'single room' may be much smaller than the double. The best deal is to get a double room for a single price.

Organised treks may charge you extra if you don't want to share a tent or room, though most other organised adventure activities don't do this.

TAX

Most hotel and restaurant bills come with a 13% value added tax (VAT), as well as a 10% service charge. The service charge is craftily calculated from the total after VAT, resulting in a whopping 24% surcharge to your bill.

It is possible to get the VAT refunded on consumer goods but it's an ordeal and is probably only relevant if you've made a major purchase. You need to have spent more than Rs 15,000 in stores that display refund stickers, have bought products less than 60 days before departure, have been in the country less than 183 days, and depart Kathmandu by air. Each individual receipt must be for more than Rs 1500. You must complete an application form at the store where you make the purchase and get two copies of the form stamped by customs officers before you check in for your flight. Take two copies of the form, along with photocopies of the photo and visa pages of your passport, to the Rastriya Banijya Bank desk after immigration. You should then get the 13% tax refunded, minus Rs 500 commission. Then you'll have to change those rupees into dollars, losing another commission.

TELEPHONE

The phone system works well (as long as the electricity is working) and making local, STD and international calls is easy. Reverse-charge (collect) calls can only be made to the UK, US, Canada and Japan.

The cheapest and most convenient way to make calls is through one of the hundreds of private call centres that have sprung up across the country. Look for signs advertising STD/ISD services. Many hotels offer international direct-dial facilities but always check their charges before making a call.

Private call centres charge around Rs 2 to Rs 40 per minute to most countries. Internet phone calls are cheaper, costing around Rs 10 per minute (calls to mobile phones are often more expensive), but these are only available in Kathmandu and Pokhara. There is some delay (echo) in the line when making internet calls, but it is generally fine for most purposes.

Most internet cafes offer internet phone calls through Skype (www.skype.com) for a couple of rupees per minute on top of their normal internet rates, so it's worth setting up an account and installing the software on your computer before you set off for Nepal.

Local phone calls cost around Rs 5 per minute, with long-distance domestic calls costing around Rs 10 per minute. Out in rural areas you may find yourself using someone's mobile phone at a public call centre.

Mobile Phones

Many Nepalis have a mobile phone but the mobile network in Nepal is not very reliable. The Nepali government cuts mobile service during times of political tension (activists coordinate their demonstrations by text messaging). Even when the network is up, connections are hit and miss. You will need an unlocked GSM 900 compatible mobile phone to use local networks.

Nepal Telecom (www.ntc.net.np) uses the GSM system with its Namaste Mobile network and has roaming agreements with companies such as Vodafone and BT Cellnet. Mero Mobile (www.spicenepal.com) offers prepaid SIM cards for Rs 500, which includes an activation fee and Rs 100 of calls, though coverage is not as good outside Kathmandu. Signing up for a SIM card is a laborious process that requires a photo, photocopy of your passport and visa, and sometimes even a fingerprint.

With a local SIM card you can make local and international calls and receive international texts but for some reason you can't send them. International calls to Europe or the US on a mobile cost between Rs 32 and Rs 47, though you can apparently get cheaper rates by routing the call through the prefix 1425 or 1424. Local calls cost between Rs 1 and Rs 4.

TIME

Nepal is five hours and 45 minutes ahead of GMT; this curious time differential is intended to make it very clear that Nepal is a separate place to India, where the time is five hours and 30 minutes ahead of GMT! There is no daylight-saving time in Nepal.

When it's noon in Nepal it's 1.15am in New York, 6.15am in London, 1.15pm in Bangkok, 2.15pm in Tibet, 4.15pm in Sydney and 10.15pm the previous day in Los Angeles, not allowing for daylight saving or other local variations.

TOILETS

Throughout the country, the 'squat toilet' is the norm, except in hotels and guest houses geared towards tourists. Next to the toilet (*charpi* in Nepali) is a bucket and/or tap, which has a two-fold function: flushing the toilet and cleaning the nether regions (with the left hand only) while still squatting over the toilet. More rustic toilets in rural areas may simply consist of a few planks precariously positioned over a pit in the ground.

TOURIST INFORMATION

The **Nepal Tourism Board** (☎ 01-4256909, 24hr tourism hotline 01-4225709; www.welcomenepal.com) operates an office in Kathmandu's Tribhuvan Airport and a more substantial office at the Tourist Service Centre in central Kathmandu (see p118), both of which have brochures and maps.

The other tourist offices in Pokhara, Bhairawa, Birganj, Janakpur and Kakarbhitta are virtually useless unless you have a specific inquiry.

TRAVELLERS WITH DISABILITIES

Wheelchair facilities, ramps and lifts (and even pavements!) are virtually nonexistent throughout Nepal and getting around the packed, twisting streets of traditional towns can be a real challenge if you are in a wheelchair. It is common for hotels to be multilevel, with most rooms on the upper floors, and many places – even midrange establishments – do not have lifts. Bathrooms equipped with grips and railings are not found anywhere, except perhaps in some of the top-end hotels.

There is no reason why a visit and even a trek could not be customised through a reliable agent for those with reasonable mobility. As an inspiration consider Eric Weihenmayer, who became the first blind climber to summit Everest in 2001 (and wrote a book called *Touch the Top of the World*), or Thomas Whittaker who summited in 1998 with an artificial leg, at the age of 50.

Also worth a read is the well-written and witty blog at http://disabledtraveler.blogspot .com from a disabled American lady who volunteered and even trekked in Nepal.

Accessible Journeys (☎ 800-846-4537; www.disability travel.com) is a US company that has experience in arranging private tours for disabled travellers. **Navyo Nepal** (☎ 01-4280056; www.navyonepal .com) in Nepal has some experience running cultural tours and treks for people with disabilities. A useful general website is Access-Able Travel Source (www.access-able.com).

VISAS

All foreigners, except Indians, must have a visa. Nepali embassies and consulates overseas issue visas with no fuss. You can also get one on the spot when you arrive in Nepal, either at Kathmandu's Tribhuvan Airport or at road borders: Nepalganj, Birganj/Raxaul Bazaar, Sunauli, Kakarbhitta, Mahendranagar, Dhangadhi and even the funky Kodari checkpoint on the road to Tibet.

A Nepali visa is valid for entry for three to six months from the date of issue. Children under 10 require a visa but are not charged a visa fee. Your passport must have at least six months validity. Citizens of South Asian countries and China need visas, but these are free.

You can download a visa application form from the websites of the Nepali embassy in Washington, DC (www.nepalembassyusa.org) or London (www.nepembassy.org.uk).

To obtain a visa upon arrival by air in Nepal you must fill in an application form and provide a passport photograph. Visa application forms are available on a table in the arrivals hall, though some airlines (like Thai) provide this form on the flight. To get a jump on the immigration queue, you can download the visa-on-arrival form from www.treks.com .np/visa. A single-entry visa valid for 15/30/90 days costs US$25/40/100. At Kathmandu's Tribhuvan Airport the fee is payable in any major currency but at land borders officials will probably require payment in cash US dollars; bring small bills.

Note that if you travel in 2011 the government is planning to offer a free visa to all those returning to Nepal for the second time as part of 'Visit Nepal Year'.

Multiple-entry visas are useful if you are planning a side trip to Tibet, Bhutan or India. You can change your single-entry visa to a multiple-entry visa at Kathmandu's Central Immigration Office (see p119) for US$20.

If you are just planning a lightning visit to Kathmandu it's possible to get a nonextendable one-day transit visa at Kathmandu airport for US$5, as long as you have an air ticket out of the country.

If you stay longer than the duration of your initial visa, you will require a visa extension (see below). Transit visas are nonextendable.

Don't overstay a visa. You can pay a fine of US$3 per day at the airport if you have overstayed less than 30 days (plus a US$2 per day visa extension fee). If you've overstayed more than a week get it all sorted out at Kathmandu's Central Immigration Office *before* you get to the airport, as a delay could cause you to miss your flight.

It's a good idea to keep a number of passport photos with your passport so they are immediately handy for trekking permits, visa applications and other official documents.

Visa Extensions

Visa extensions are available from immigration offices in Kathmandu and Pokhara only and cost a minimum US$30 (payable in rupees) for a 15-day extension, plus US$2 per day after that. For a multiple-entry visa add on US$20. If you'll be in Nepal for more than 60 days you are better off getting a 90-day visa on arrival, rather than a 60-day visa plus an extension.

Every visa extension requires your passport, money, one photo and an application form. Collect all these before you join the queue. Plenty of photo shops in Kathmandu and Pokhara will make a set of eight digital passport photos for you for around Rs 200.

Visa extensions are available the same day, sometimes within the hour. For a fee, trekking and travel agencies can assist with the visa extension process and save you the time and tedium of queuing.

You can extend your visa up to a total stay of 120 days without undue formality. You should be able to get a further 30 days extension but you may need to show an air ticket proving that you are leaving the country during that time period, since you are only allowed to stay in Nepal for a total of 150 days in a calendar year on a tourist visa.

You can get up-to-date visa information at the website of the Department of Immigration (www.immi.gov.np). See the Kathmandu (p119) and Pokhara (p256) sections for more details.

WOMEN TRAVELLERS

Generally speaking, Nepal is a safe country for women travellers. However, women should still be cautious. Nepali men may have peculiar ideas about the morality of Western women, given Nepali men's exposure to Western films portraying women wearing 'immodest' clothing. Dress modestly, which means wearing clothes that cover the shoulders and thighs – take your cue from the locals to gauge what's acceptable in the area. Several women have written to say that a long skirt is very useful for impromptu toilet trips, especially when trekking.

Sexual harassment is low-key but does exist. Trekking guides have been known to take advantage of their position of trust and responsibility and some lone women trekkers who hire a guide have had to put up with repeated sexual pestering. The best advice is to never hike or trek alone with a local male guide. **Chhetri Sisters Trekking** (☎ 061-462066; www.3sistersadventure.com) in Pokhara is run by women and specialises in providing female staff for treks.

The best chance of making contact with local women is to go trekking, as it is really only here that Nepali women have a role that brings them into contact with foreign tourists – often the man of the house is a trekking guide or porter, or is away working elsewhere, which leaves women running lodges and teahouses along the routes.

WORK

For Western visitors, finding work in Nepal is very difficult, though not impossible. The easiest work to find is teaching English, as there are many private schools and a great demand for English-language lessons. However, at less than US$100 a month the pay is very low. Other faint possibilities include work with airline offices, travel and trekking agencies, consultants or aid groups.

Officially you need a work (nontourist) visa if you intend to find employment (even unpaid) in Nepal and you should arrange this before you arrive in the country. Changing from a tourist visa once you are in the country is rarely permissible. The work permit has to be applied for by your employer and you are required to leave the country while the paperwork is negotiated. The process can take months and many people don't bother.

For information on volunteer opportunities in Nepal see p71.

Transport

CONTENTS

GETTING THERE & AWAY

ENTERING THE COUNTRY

Nepal makes things easy for foreign travellers. Visas are available on arrival at the international airport in Kathmandu and at all land border crossings that are open to foreigners, as long as you have passport photos to hand and can pay the visa fee in foreign currency (some crossings insist on payment in US dollars). For more information on visa regulations see p377.

Passport

To enter Nepal your passport must be valid for at least six months and you will need a whole free page for your visa.

AIR

Airports

Nepal has one international airport – **Tribhuvan International Airport** (☎ 01-4472256; www.tiairport.com.np), just east of Kathmandu. Little has changed here since the 1980s and dusty signboards still warn travellers not to import more than the prescribed number of tricycles, disk records and perambulators. There are no direct long-distance flights to Nepal – getting here from Europe, the Americas or Australasia will always involve a stop in the Middle East or Asia.

Facilities at the airport are limited – there are foreign exchange booths before and after immigration, and there is a small tourist information counter by the terminal exit. Fill out the forms for your visa on arrival before you go to the immigration counter. A small stand provides instant passport photos, but bring some from home to be safe.

On departure, you must pay the departure tax at the Nabil Bank counter inside the terminal before you check in – see the box, p381. It is possible to re-exchange Nepali rupees into US dollars here if you have your unused foreign-exchange encashment receipts (commission is Rs 50, or 2%). After immigration there's a VAT refund booth (see p375).

On departure, all baggage must go through the X-ray machine as you enter the terminal (insist that the security officers physically inspect any camera film). Make sure that custom officials stamp all the baggage labels for your carry-on luggage.

It pays to check in at least two hours before international flights. Always ask your hotel if there is a bandh (strike) planned for the day you intend to fly. Taxi drivers may refuse to carry passengers, but the government may run special bus services. Even on a bandh day, you should be safe if you arrange a taxi to the airport before 8am.

There are plans to transform Bhairawa airport into Lumbini International Airport, but this has been dragging on for years.

Airlines

Because Nepal does not lie on any major transit routes, flights to Kathmandu are expensive,

---

THINGS CHANGE...

The information in this chapter is particularly vulnerable to change. Check directly with the airline or a travel agent to make sure you understand how a fare (and ticket you may buy) works and be aware of the security requirements for international travel. Shop carefully. The details given in this chapter should be regarded as pointers and are not a substitute for your own careful, up-to-date research.

CLIMATE CHANGE & TRAVEL

Climate change is a serious threat to the ecosystems that humans rely upon, and air travel is the fastest-growing contributor to the problem. Lonely Planet regards travel, overall, as a global benefit, but believes we all have a responsibility to limit our personal impact on global warming.

Flying & Climate Change

Pretty much every form of motor travel generates CO_2 (the main cause of human-induced climate change) but planes are far and away the worst offenders, not just because of the sheer distances they allow us to travel, but because they release greenhouse gases high into the atmosphere. The statistics are frightening: two people taking a return flight between Europe and the US will contribute as much to climate change as an average household's gas and electricity consumption over a whole year.

Carbon Offset Schemes

Climatecare.org and other websites use 'carbon calculators' that allow jetsetters to offset the greenhouse gases they are responsible for with contributions to energy-saving projects and other climate-friendly initiatives in the developing world – including projects in India, Honduras, Kazakhstan and Uganda.

Lonely Planet, together with Rough Guides and other concerned partners in the travel industry, supports the carbon offset scheme run by climatecare.org. Lonely Planet offsets all of its staff and author travel.

For more information check out our website: lonelyplanet.com.

particularly during the peak trekking season (October to November). Savvy travellers fly to India first, and then pick up a cheap transfer to Kathmandu. All the airlines listed in this section have their offices in Kathmandu.

The flagship carrier of Nepal is **Nepal Jetlite** (NAC; code RA; Map p126; ☎ 01-4220757; www.royalnepal-air lines.com; Kantipath), formerly Royal Nepal Airlines (RNAC). As airlines go, this is a shoestring operation, and you may still see the old branding on tickets, office signboards and even the aircraft. It has only two aircraft for international flights and services are notoriously unreliable, though its safety record is comparable with other regional carriers. There are flights to Delhi, Dubai, Hong Kong, Bangkok and Kuala Lumpur.

At the time of writing **Cosmic Air** (code F5; Map p126; ☎ 01-4215525; www.cosmicair.com; Lal Durbar) had suspended its cheap flights to Delhi, but these are set to resume in 2009. Currently, the best connections to Delhi are with **Jet Airways** (code 9W; Map p126; ☎ 01-4446375; www.jetairways.com; Sundar Bhawan, Hattisar), and its subsidiary airline **Jetlite** (formerly Air Sahara; code S2; Map p126; ☎ 01-4446375; www.jetlite.com; Sundar Bhawan, Hattisar).

Following are other airlines serving Nepal:
Air Arabia (code G9; Map p126; ☎ 01-4233210; www .airarabia.com; near Yak & Yeti Hotel, Lal Durbar)
Air China (code CA; Map p126; ☎ 01-4440650; www .airchina.com; Dhobi Dhara)

Biman Bangladesh Airlines (code BG; Map p126; ☎ 01-4434869; www.biman-airlines.com; Nag Pokhari, Naxal)
China Southern Airlines (code CZ; Map p126; ☎ 01-4440761; www.flychinasouthern.com; Marcopolo Business Hotel, Kamal Pokhari)
Dragonair (code KA; Map p126; ☎ 01-4248944; www .dragonair.com; Kamaladi)
Druk Air (code KB; Map p126; ☎ 01-4239988; www .drukair.com.bt; Woodlands Complex, Durbar Marg)
Etihad (code EY; Map p126; ☎ 01-4233533; www .etihadairways.com; near Yak & Yeti Hotel, Lal Durbar)
GMG Airlines (code Z5; ☎ 01-4420252; www.gmgair lines.com)
Gulf Air (code GF; Map p126; ☎ 01-4435322; www .gulfair.com; Hattisar)
Indian Airlines (code IC; Map p126; ☎ 01-4410906; www.indian-airlines.in; Hattisar)
Korean Airlines (code KE; Map p126; ☎ 01-4252048; www.koreanair.com; Heritage Plaza I, Kamaladi)
Pakistan International Airways (PIA; code PK; Map p126; ☎ 01-4439234; www.piac.com.pk; Hattisar)
Qatar Airways (code QR; Map p126; ☎ 01-4440467; www.qatarairways.com; Sundar Bhawan, Hattisar)
Silk Air (code MI; Map p126; ☎ 01-4226582; www .silkair.com; Kamaladi)
Thai Airways (code TG; Map p126; ☎ 01-4223565; www.thaiair.com; Durbar Marg)

Tickets

During the autumn trekking season, from October to November, every flight into and out of Kathmandu can be booked solid, and travellers frequently have to resort to travelling overland to India to get a flight out of the region. To beat the rush, book well in advance and give yourself plenty of time between the end of your trek and your international flight home. If you are booking a flight in Kathmandu, book at the start of your trip, not at the end.

The other golden rule when flying out of Kathmandu is *reconfirm your booking*. Even if your airline does not require reconfirmation in other countries, they may insist on this in Kathmandu. Some hotels and travel agencies may be able to reconfirm your ticket on your behalf, but many airlines ask you to come into the office to reconfirm in person. Airline office queues can be shocking – unless you want to waste half of your day, be at the office before the doors open in the morning.

If you are connecting through Delhi, you may need to collect your luggage and check in separately for the connecting flight. Many travellers use this as an excuse for a stopover, but if you are just changing planes in Delhi, inform the ground staff on arrival so that an airline representative can collect and check in the bags on your behalf. Flying out of Kathmandu, bags are usually checked through to the final destination, but ask when you check in.

Asia

The most popular route between Asia and Kathmandu is the daily Thai Airways flight to/from Bangkok, though Nepal Airlines also covers this connection. There are also convenient flights to Hong Kong (Dragon Air), Kuala Lumpur (Nepal Airlines), Singapore (Silk Air), Seoul (Korean Airlines) and Guangzhou (China Southern Airlines). There are no direct flights to Japan; most people change in Bangkok, Singapore, Hong Kong or Seoul.

Air China flies to Chengdu and Lhasa, but you can only fly into Tibet as part of a tour group. You must also join an organised tour of Bhutan to fly to Paro on Druk Air. The once-popular Kathmandu–Dhaka–Yangon route is no longer running; the cheapest way to reach Myanmar is to fly

> **DEPARTURE TAX**
>
> When flying out of Kathmandu, you must pay an international departure tax of Rs 1695 in Nepali rupees at the Nabil Bank counter in the departures terminal. The tax is Rs 1356 if you are flying to South Asian Area Regional Cooperation (SAARC) countries (ie India, Pakistan, Bhutan or Bangladesh). There is no departure tax if you leave Nepal overland.

to Bangkok and change to an Air Asia flight (www.airasia.com).

STA Travel has useful branches in **Bangkok** (☎ 02-236 0262; www.statravel.co.th), **Malaysia** (☎ 2148 9800; www.statravel.com.my), **Singapore** (☎ 6737 7188; www.statravel.com.sg) and **Hong Kong** (☎ 2736 1618; www.statravel.com.hk).

Other recommended Asian agencies include **No 1 Travel** (☎ 03-3205 6073; www.no1-travel.com) in Japan and **Four Seas Tours** (☎ 2200 7760; www.fourseastravel.com), which is located in Hong Kong.

Australia & New Zealand

There are easy connections from Australia and New Zealand through Bangkok, Seoul, Singapore or Hong Kong.

Flight Centre has branches all over **Australia** (☎ 133 133; www.flightcentre.com.au) and **New Zealand** (☎ 0800 243 544; www.flightcentre.co.nz). There are also STA Travel branches in most large cities in **Australia** (☎ 134782; www.statravel.com.au) and **New Zealand** (☎ 0800 474 400; www.statravel.co.nz). For online bookings, try www.travel.com.au.

Canada

Flying from Canada, you can go east or west around the globe. Fares from Vancouver through Asia tend to be slightly cheaper than flights from Toronto via Europe or the Gulf. Jet Airways offers a convenient single-airline route from Toronto through Brussels to Delhi and on to Kathmandu.

Travel Cuts (☎ 1 866 246 9762; www.travelcuts.com) is Canada's national student travel agency. For online bookings try www.expedia.ca and www.travelocity.ca.

Continental Europe

Etihad, Qatar Airways and Gulf Air all offer smooth connections through the Gulf to

Paris, Frankfurt and other European cities. Jet Airways offers a useful connection from Brussels to Kathmandu via Delhi, or alternatively, you can take any flight to Delhi and change.

Flightbookers (www.ebookers.com) has regional flight-booking websites for countries across Europe including France, Germany, Spain, the Netherlands, Denmark, Finland, Norway and Sweden.

Other companies with branches around Europe include **STA Travel** (www.statravel.com) and **LastMinute** (www.lastminute.com). Just click on the country links at the bottom of their web pages.

Other recommended agencies include the following:

Airfair (☎ 0900 7717 717; www.airfair.nl) In the Netherlands.

Anyway (☎ 0892 302 301; www.anyway.fr) In France.

Barceló Viajes (☎ 902 200 400; www.barceloviajes .com) In Spain.

CTS Viaggi (☎ 06 441 1166; www.cts.it) In Italy.

Just Travel (☎ 089 747 3330; www.justtravel.de) In Germany.

Nouvelles Frontières (☎ 01 49 20 65 87; www .nouvelles-frontieres.fr) In France.

Voyageurs du Monde (☎ 0892 235 656; www.vdm .com) In France.

India, Pakistan and Bangladesh

Seats between Kathmandu and Delhi can be found for as little as US$120. Jet and Jetlite are the best carriers flying the Delhi–Kathmandu route, but you can also find cheap seats on Cosmic Air when the airline is flying. Indian Airlines flies to Delhi, Kolkata (Calcutta) and Varanasi (Benares); Nepal Airlines also flies between Kathmandu and Delhi twice a week. One reliable agent in India is **STIC Travels** (☎ 11- 237 37 135; www.stictravel.com).

You can get to Dhaka with Biman Bangladesh Airlines and GMG Airlines, and to Karachi with PIA.

UK & Ireland

There are easy connections to Kathmandu from London and Dublin with Etihad, Gulf Air and Qatar Airways, changing in the Gulf. All three airlines also fly from Manchester, Edinburgh and other regional UK airports. The fastest connection from London to Kathmandu is with Jet Airways, with one smooth change in Delhi.

Discount air travel is big business in London. Advertisements for many travel agencies appear in the travel pages of the weekend broadsheet newspapers, in *Time Out,* the *Evening Standard* and in the free magazine *TNT* (www.tntmagazine.com).

Recommended travel agencies include the following:

Flight Centre (☎ 0870 499 0040; www.flightcentre .co.uk)

Flightbookers (☎ 020-3320 3320; www.ebookers .com)

North-South Travel (☎ 01245-608291; www .northsouthtravel.co.uk)

STA Travel (☎ 0871 2 300 040; www.statravel.co.uk)

Trailfinders (☎ 0845 058 5858; www.trailfinders .co.uk)

Travel Bag (☎ 0800 804 8911; www.travelbag.co.uk)

USA

North America is halfway around the world from Nepal, so you can go east or west around the globe. Flying west involves a change in Asia – Korean Airlines offers easy connections through Seoul, but you could also change in Bangkok, Hong Kong or Singapore. Flying east normally involves a stop in Europe and again in the Gulf or in India. Jet Airways has a convenient route from New York with stops in Brussels and Delhi.

San Francisco is the discount ticket agent capital of America, although some good deals can be found in Los Angeles, New York and other big cities. The *New York Times, Chicago Tribune, LA Times* and *San Francisco Examiner* all produce weekly travel sections in which you'll find any number of travel agency ads.

For reasonably priced fares to Nepal, start with specialist travel agencies like **Third Eye Travel** (☎ 1-800 456 393; www.thirdeyetravel.com), **Angel Travel** (☎ 1-800 922 1092; www.angeltravel .com) and **USA Asia** (☎ 1-800 872 2742; www.usaasia travel.com). Younger travellers and students can find good fares through **STA Travel** (☎ 1-800 781 4040; www.statravel.com).

The following online agencies are also recommended:

- www.cheaptickets.com
- www.expedia.com
- www.itn.net
- www.lowestfare.com
- www.orbitz.com
- www.travelocity.com

LAND

Depending on the political situation and the condition of the roads, you may be able to enter Nepal overland at six border crossings – five from India and one from Tibet.

Bringing Your Own Vehicle

A steady trickle of people drive their own motorbikes or vehicles overland from Europe, for which an international carnet is required. If you want to abandon your transport in Nepal, you must either pay a prohibitive import duty or surrender it to customs. It is not possible to import cars more than five years old. Make sure you bring an international driving permit.

India

All of the land borders between India and Nepal are in the Terai. The most popular crossing point is Sunauli, near Bhairawa, which provides easy access to Delhi and Varanasi in India.

Border crossing (Nepal to India)	Page
Belahiya to Sunauli, for Varanasi, Agra & Delhi	p294
Mahendranagar to Banbassa, for Delhi & hill towns in Uttaranchal	p313
Kakarbhitta to Panitanki, for Darjeeling, Sikkim & Kolkata	p326
Birganj to Raxaul Bazaar, for Patna & Kolkata	p314
Nepalganj to Jamunaha, for Lucknow	p307

SUNAULI/BHAIRAWA

The crossing at Sunauli is by far the most popular route between India and Nepal. However, it is easy to get ripped off by dodgy travel agencies. Despite what anyone may claim, there are no through buses between Delhi and Kathmandu.

You can avoid being scammed, and have a more comfortable journey into the bargain, if you travel from Delhi to Gorakhpur by train (22 hours). You can then pick up a bus to Sunauli (Rs 60, three hours). There are also direct buses to Sunauli from Varanasi (Rs 150, 10 hours).

Once across the border, you can visit the Buddhist pilgrimage centre of Lumbini before you continue your journey. From Bhairawa buses run regularly to Kathmandu (Rs 425, eight hours) and Pokhara (Rs 300 to Rs 425, eight hours), usually passing through Narayangarh, where you can change for

Chitwan National Park. Buddha Air and Yeti Airlines fly daily to Kathmandu (35 minutes).

MAHENDRANAGAR

The western border crossing at Mahendranagar is also reasonably convenient for Delhi. There are daily buses from Delhi's Anand Vihar bus stand to Banbassa, the nearest Indian village to the border (INRs 160, 10 hours). Banbassa is also connected by bus with most towns in Uttaranchal.

From Mahendranagar there are slow overnight bus services to Kathmandu (Rs 1010, 15 hours) but it's better to do the trip in daylight and break the journey at Bardia National Park, Nepalganj or Narayangarh. Check that the road is open and make sure there are no security problems before you travel.

KAKARBHITTA

The eastern border crossing at Kakarbhitta offers easy onward connections to Darjeeling, Sikkim, Kolkata and India's Northeast States. Travel agencies in Kathmandu and Darjeeling offer 'through buses' across the border, but these all involve a change of vehicle at the border. It's just as easy to do the journey in stages.

At the time of writing, the Mahendra Hwy was blocked between Kakarbhitta and Kathmandu by the Sapt Kosi floods (for more information see p320). Efforts are underway to restore this important road link but, even if the road is blocked, you should be able to skirt around the blockage on local transport.

From Darjeeling, take a morning bus/jeep to Siliguri (INRs 60/80, two hours) then a bus (INRs 20, one hour) to Panitanki on the Indian side of the border. Jeeps also run to the border from Kalimpong (Rs 90, three hours) and Gangtok (Rs 160, 4½ hours) in Sikkim. Coming from Kolkata, you can take the overnight *Darjeeling Mail* from Sealdah Station to New Jalpaiguri (NJP) near Siliguri, then a bus to the border (INRs 243/659/901 in sleeper class/air-con 3-tier/air-con 2-tier).

From Kakarbhitta there are overnight buses to Kathmandu (Rs 1500, 17 hours) or Pokhara (Rs 1500, 17 hours) but it's more interesting to break the journey at Janakpur (Rs 350, five hours) or at Chitwan National Park (accessible from Sauraha Chowk on the Mahendra Hwy).

TICKET PACKAGES TO & FROM INDIA

Many travel agents claim to offer direct bus tickets between Kathmandu or Pokhara and cities in India. However, there are NO direct buses between India and Nepal – all of these tickets involve a change of bus, and of bus companies, at the border in Sunauli. Every year, Lonely Planet receives dozens of letters of complaint from travellers who have been scammed. Fortunately, there is so much transport on this route that you can easily do the trip in several stages without relying on travel agents who may or may not have your best interests at heart – see the Crossing the Border boxed text for details (p295).

Agents also offer bus and train packages via Gorakhpur, but again, it is easy to make the arrangements yourself, particularly now that Indian train tickets can be reserved online at www .irctc.co.in. See www.indianrail.gov.in for schedules and www.seat61.com/India.htm for advice about making a booking.

If you must go through an agent, one reliable company is **Wayfarers** (Map p140; ☎ 01-4266010; www.wayfarers.com.np; Thamel) in Kathmandu. It requires a minimum of a week to arrange tickets.

BIRGANJ/RAXAUL BAZAAR

The border crossing from Birganj to Raxaul Bazaar is handy for Patna and Kolkata. Buses run from the bus station in Patna straight to Raxaul Bazaar (INRs 100, eight hours). From Kolkata, take the daily *Mithila Express* – it leaves Kolkata's Howrah station at 3.45pm, arriving in Raxaul at 8.30am the next morning (INRs 256/723/1001 in sleeper class/air-con three-tier/air-con two-tier).

From Birganj, there are regular day/night buses to Kathmandu (Rs 350/400, eight hours) and Pokhara (Rs 350/425, seven hours), via Narayangarh (Rs 160, three hours). The are also regular services to most other towns around the Terai.

NEPALGANJ

Few people use the crossing at Nepalganj in western Nepal as it not particularly convenient for anywhere else. The nearest town in India is Lucknow, where you can pick up slow buses to Rupaidha Bazaar (INRs 160, seven hours), near the border post at Jamunaha. You might also consider taking a train to Nanpara, 17km from the border.

Over the border in Nepalganj, there are regular day/night buses to Kathmandu (Rs 540/857, 12 hours) and buses to Pokhara (Rs 825, 12 hours), passing through Narayangarh (Rs 584, eight hours). Yeti Airlines and Buddha Air have flights to Kathmandu (one hour) and Sita Air flies to Jumla (45 minutes).

Tibet

Officially, only organised 'groups' are allowed into Tibet from Nepal. The good news is that travel agencies in Kathmandu are experts in assembling overland groups to get around this restriction. In general, travellers face fewer restrictions entering Tibet through China, so it makes more sense to visit Nepal after a trip through Tibet, not before.

Travelling overland to Tibet from Nepal is not an easy option. Altitude sickness is a real danger: the maximum altitude along the road is 5140m and tours do not always allow sufficient time to acclimatise safely. The road is often closed by landslides during the monsoon months (May to August) and there are often additional restrictions on travel at times of political tension.

TRAVEL RESTRICTIONS

At the time of research, it was only possible to cross into Tibet with a Tibet Tourism Permit, which can only be arranged through a travel agency when you book a package tour to Lhasa. If you turn up at the border at Kodari with just a Chinese visa you'll be turned away, and Air China won't sell you an air ticket to Lhasa without this permit.

At the time of research, when people booked this tour they were put on a group visa and any existing Chinese visas in their passports were cancelled. Splitting from this group visa in Lhasa is almost impossible, but it is apparently possible to fly out of Tibet to Chengdu and then continue through China on a standard Chinese tourist visa.

TOUR OPTIONS

The quickest way to get into Tibet is to buy a fly-in package to Lhasa from Kathmandu. Depending on the political climate in Tibet, agencies can sometimes arrange a one-way flight (around US$273) with a visa and permits (around US$70) and airport transfers (around US$120). At times of political sensitivity you may have to book a pricier tour and a return flight, though you might be able to cancel the return leg in Lhasa.

The easiest way to visit Tibet from Nepal is to join a drive-in, fly-out overland jeep tour from Kathmandu to Lhasa, via Nyalam, Lhatse, Shigatse and Gyantse. Several agencies offer eight-day trips for around US$1000, including permit and visa fees, transport by cramped Land Cruiser, accommodation in dorms and shared twin rooms, sightseeing and a flight back to Kathmandu. Some agencies also offer pricey trips that include a detour to Mt Everest Base Camp (on the Tibetan side). There are also very expensive trekking trips from Simikot in far western Nepal to Purang in far western Tibet, and then on to Mt Kailash.

The agency will need one week to get your visa and permits. You will probably get between 12 and 15 days on your group visa so, theoretically, you can stay in Lhasa for up to a week after the tour. However, this is dependant on the goodwill of the authorities. Rates increase from July to September, and there are fewer tours from December to February.

Most of the companies advertising Tibet trips in Kathmandu are agencies for other companies – the following agencies run their own trips.

Ecotrek (Map p140; ☎ 01-4424112; www.ecotrek.com.np; Thamel)

Green Hill Tours (Map p140; ☎ 01-4700968; www.greenhill-tours.com; Thamel)

Royal Mount Trekking (Map p126; ☎ 01-4241452; www.royaltibet.com; Durbar Marg)

Tashi Delek Nepal Treks & Expeditions (☎ 01-4410746; tashidele@mail.com.np; Thamel)

Other travel companies in Thamel offering customised tours to Tibet include the following:
Adventure Silk Road (www.silkroadgroup.com)
Dharma Adventures (www.dharmaadventures.com)
Earthbound Expeditions (www.trektibet.com)
Explore Himalaya (www.explorehimalaya.com)

BUS

Nepal's state bus company Sajha Yatayat briefly operated a direct bus service between Kathmandu and Lhasa, but this was never open to foreigners and it has not been operating for years. However, there's always the chance that services could resume – ask locally.

GETTING AROUND

Getting around in Nepal can be a challenging business. Because of the terrain, the weather conditions and the condition of vehicles, few trips go exactly according to plan. Nepali ingenuity will usually get you to your destination in the end, but build plenty of time into your itinerary and treat the delays and mishaps as part of the rich tapestry that is Nepal. Oh, and bring snacks, lots of snacks.

Walking is still the most important method of getting from A to B in Nepal, particularly in the mountains where there are no roads and few airstrips. Elsewhere, people get around on buses, jeeps, motorcycles, trains and planes that seem to be held together more by faith than mechanical integrity.

The wise traveller avoids going anywhere during major festivals (for details see p23), when buses, flights and hotels are booked solid.

AIR

Considering the nature of the landscape, Nepal has an excellent network of domestic flights. Engineers have created runways deep in the jungle and high in the mountains, clinging to the sides of Himalayan peaks. However, pilots must still find their way to these airstrips using visual navigation and few years pass without some kind of air disaster in the mountains.

Air safety is something you should bear in mind when deciding to fly internally in Nepal, but this has to be weighed up against the risks of travelling by road and the time saved by flying. Given the choice between a 45-minute flight and a 17-hour bus ride on poorly maintained mountain roads, most people prefer to fly.

Because flights are dependant on clear weather, services rarely leave on time and many flights are cancelled at the last minute because of poor visibility. It is essential to build extra time into your itinerary. Even if you take off on time, you may not be able to land at your intended destination because of fog. It would be unwise to book a flight back to Kathmandu within three days of your international flight out of the country.

In the event of a cancellation, airlines will try to find you a seat on the next available flight (some airlines run extra flights to clear the backlog once the weather clears). If you decide not to wait, you should be able to cancel the ticket without penalty, though it can take a long time to arrange a refund.

Airlines in Nepal

The largest domestic airline is the notoriously unreliable **Nepal Airlines** (Map p126; ☎ 01-4220757; www.royalnepal-airlines.com; Kantipath), formerly Royal Nepal Airlines (RNAC). All things considered, Nepal Airlines has a comparable safety record to other domestic airlines, but if your destination is served by a private airline, this will almost always be the better option. Nepal Airlines currently has services to Biratnagar, Pokhara, Lukla, Phaplu, Bhojpur, Lamidanda, Tumlingtar, Suketar, Dolpo, Manang, Jumla and Simikot, among other airstrips.

Services are more reliable on Nepal's many private airlines, though fares are slightly higher. Most flights operate out of Kathmandu, but there are minor air hubs at Pokhara, Nepalganj in the southwest and Biratnagar in the southeast. Most airlines also offer scenic 'mountain flights' in the morning – if you're flying from Kathmandu you will probably have to wait until the airline finishes its morning quota of mountain flights before domestic services begin.

The following domestic airlines have offices in Kathmandu:

Agni Air (Map pp14-15; ☎ 01-4107812; www.agniair .com; Shantinagar) Serves Lukla, Pokhara, Tumlingtar and Jomsom.

Buddha Air (Map p126; ☎ 01-5542494; www .buddhaair.com; Hattisar) Destinations include Pokhara, Bhadrapur, Janakpur, Bharatpur, Bhairawa, Biratnagar and Nepalganj.

Cosmic Air (Map p126; ☎ 01-4215525; www.cosmicair .com; near Yak & Yeti Hotel, Lal Durbar) Serves Biratnagar – when flights are operating.

Sita Air (Map pp114-15; ☎ 01-4490103; www.sitaair .com.np; Sinamangal) Destinations include Lukla, Tumlingtar, Pokhara and Jomsom.

Yeti Airlines (Map p140; ☎ 01-4213002; www.yeti airlines.com; Thamel Chowk) The largest private airline; destinations include Pokhara, Biratnagar, Nepalganj, Lukla, Bhadrapur, Bhairawa, Jumla and Rara.

Tickets

Airlines come and go and schedules change, so it is best to make reservations through a travel agent, a trekking agency or your hotel. Foreign visitors must pay for airfares in hard currency, typically US dollars. Residents and Nepali citizens pay approximately 35% of the tourist price. There is a 10% to 15% penalty for cancellations before departure. If you fail to show up for the flight, you generally forfeit the ticket.

All travellers are charged an insurance surcharge of US$2 per leg, as well as a fuel surcharge of US$3 to US$24. Fares quoted in this book include all these surcharges. Tickets are

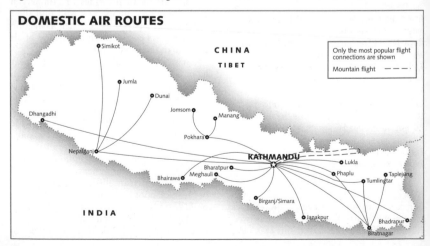

DOMESTIC AIR ROUTES

CHINA
TIBET

Only the most popular flight connections are shown
Mountain flight — — — ·

Simikot
Jumla
Dunai
Dhangadhi
Jomsom
Manang
Pokhara
Nepalganj
KATHMANDU
Lukla
Bharatpur
Phaplu
Taplejung
Bhairawa
Meghauli
Tumlingtar
Birganj/Simara
INDIA
Janakpur
Bhadrapur
Biratnagar

MOUNTAIN FLIGHTS

Every morning during the clear dry-season months (April to May), all the major private airlines offer mountain flights, with panoramic dawn views of the Himalaya and commentary on the passing peaks. Each passenger on the six- to 30-seat turbo props is guaranteed a window. The hour-long flight from Kathmandu costs US$163 (fuel charge included) but the quality of the views will depend on the prevailing weather conditions. If the flight is cancelled due to bad weather – not an uncommon occurrence – airlines offer a full-refund or a seat on a later flight.

---

not exchangeable between airlines. However, airlines have been known to swap passengers at the last minute! Always reconfirm your flight the day before you fly. If you 'drop off' the reservation list, it could be days before you get back on.

Kathmandu airport charges a domestic departure tax of Rs 169.5 (rounded up to Rs 170). Note that domestic airlines have a 15kg allowance for hold baggage – on some flights, you cannot even pay to carry excess baggage. Knives, cigarette lighters, gas cylinders and trekking poles are not permitted in carry-on luggage.

BICYCLE

There are plenty of bicycle-rental shops in Kathmandu and Pokhara, and this is a cheap and convenient way of getting around. Generic Indian and Chinese-made bicycles cost around Rs 150 per day to rent, but they can be real dogs to ride. Several cycling agencies in Kathmandu rent out imported mountain bikes for around Rs 700 per day. Children's bicycles can also be hired.

See p91 for detailed information on cycling in Nepal.

BUS

Buses are the main form of public transport in Nepal and they're incredibly cheap. Often they're also incredibly uncomfortable. Buses run pretty much everywhere and will stop for anyone, but you'll find it much easier to get a seat if you catch a bus at its source rather than mid-run. For longer-distance buses it's best to book a couple of days in advance.

Public Buses

Most towns in lowland Nepal are accessible by bus from Kathmandu or Pokhara, but Nepali buses are slow, noisy and uncomfortable, and breakdowns are almost guaranteed. Fortunately, services are frequent enough that you can always hop onto another bus if your first bus dies on a lonely stretch of highway.

On longer journeys, buses stop regularly for refreshments, but travel after dark is not recommended – drivers take advantage of the quiet roads to do some crazy speeding and accidents and fatalities are depressingly common. In fact, you are 30 times more likely to die in a road accident in Nepal than in any developed country. Some night buses stop for a few hours sleep, en route, but others keep blazing through the night with the music blaring at full volume.

The government bus company, known as Sajha Yatayat, has distinctive blue-and-white buses that service all the main routes except the far east and far west. Although marginally cheaper than private buses, these buses are generally very shabby, poorly maintained and rarely run to schedule.

Myriad private companies run 'ordinary buses' that are very similar to government buses, and faster, more expensive 'express buses' that offer seats with more padding and luxuries such as curtains to keep out the sun. Tickets can be purchased in advance at the relevant counter (ask locals where to go as signs are often in Nepali) or on board from the driver.

Large pieces of baggage go on the roof – the conductor will take your bag up for a tip or you can do it yourself. Theft from luggage is not uncommon so padlock your bags shut and tie the straps to the railings. Always keep an eye on your belongings at rest stops – backpacks are extremely easy for thieves to walk off with.

The fast, frequent and phenomenally crowded 'local buses' that run between smaller towns are handy for day trips, but you'll have your work cut out getting on board with a backpack. Prices for foreigners are often bumped up by unscrupulous conductors on these buses.

Note that road travel in the far east and west of Nepal can be impossible after the monsoon. Every year the rains lead to floods that destroy stretches of road and wash away bridges. At the time of the writing, repairs were ongoing

TRANSPORT

TRANSPORT

AIR-CONDITIONING OF THE GODS

With the cramped conditions inside Nepal's buses, many locals and foreigners prefer to ride up on the roof. For legal reasons, we are required to say this probably is not a good idea – but the truth is that it is probably not significantly more dangerous than riding inside. You'll also get the sense of being surrounded by the environment you are passing through, rather than viewing it through a murky window.

If you do ride on the roof, make sure you are well wedged in, so you don't catapult off when the bus swerves, brakes or lurches. It's also best to sit facing forwards – that way you can see low-hanging wires and branches before you get swatted. Make sure you have sunscreen and appropriate clothing too, as it can be surprisingly cold up there.

---

to the Mahendra Hwy between Mohanpur and Itahari following devastating floods on the Sapt Kosi in 2008 (for more information see p320). Where roads are blocked, it may be possible to get around the blockage on foot or by local transport – ask locals for advice.

Tourist Buses

Travel agencies run a number of useful bus services to popular tourist destinations, leaving from the Tourist Bus Park in Pokhara and the Thamel end of Kantipath in Kathmandu.

Greenline (Map p140; ☎ 4257544; www.greenline .com.np; Tridevi Marg) runs deluxe buses from Kathmandu to Pokhara (US$18, seven hours), Sauraha (for Chitwan National Park; US$15, six hours) and Lumbini (US$25, 10 hours). Buses booked through agencies cost Rs 400 to Rs 450 from Kathmandu to Pokhara or Sauraha.

CAR & MOTORCYCLE
Hire

There are no drive-yourself rental cars available in Nepal, but you can easily hire a car or jeep with a driver through a travel agency. Expect to pay between US$60 and US$100 per day, including fuel. Taxis are cheaper but you must negotiate a fare directly with the driver. Remember that you'll have to pay for the driver's return trip whether or not you return, as well as his food and accommodation for overnight trips.

Motorcycles can be rented in Kathmandu and Pokhara for around Rs 400 to 450 per day. You'll need an international driving permit or a licence from your own country that shows you are licensed to ride a motorcycle – a car drivers' licence won't cut it. You must also leave your passport as a deposit. See p162 and p272 for details.

Note that there are major fuel shortages in Nepal. Petrol stations can be dry for days

at a time and the only option for motorists is to queue for hours at the few stations that have fuel or to buy fuel in reused bottles from local shops.

Insurance

If you are planning to drive a motorbike in Nepal you should double-check to see if you are covered by your travel insurance. Rental companies rarely offer insurance and you will be fully liable for the vehicle and damage to other vehicles in the event of an accident.

Road Rules

If you do drive, be aware that you drive on the left-hand side of the road, left turns are allowed without stopping and that traffic entering a roundabout has priority over traffic already on the roundabout. Locals rarely signal and other vehicles will pull out regardless of whether or not anyone is coming – drive defensively. Try to avoid any dealings with traffic police; locals are routinely stung for bribes and foreigners are increasingly being targeted.

Finally, our best advice is to trust nothing and nobody. Expect kids, chickens, ducks, women, old men, babies, cows, dogs and almost anything else that can move to jump in front of you at any moment, without any kind of warning. Good luck.

Tours

The winding roads of Nepal are glorious for mountain riding and several companies run fully supported motorcycle tours. Contact the following companies for more information:

Asia-Bike-Tours (www.asiabiketours.com)
Ferris Wheels (www.ferriswheels.com.au)
Himalayan Offroad (☎ 01-4700770; www.himalayan offroad.com)
Himalayan Roadrunners (www.ridehigh.com)

HITCHING

It is possible to hitch rides on trucks and private vehicles but you will be expected to pay for your ride. The usual rules apply – never hitch alone and don't ride with drunken drivers.

LOCAL TRANSPORT

Autorickshaw & Cycle-Rickshaw

Cycle-rickshaws are common in the old part of Kathmandu and in towns in the Terai, and they provide an atmospheric way to explore the crowded and narrow streets. Prices are highly negotiable.

Nepal's noxious two-stroke, three-wheeled autorickshaws are being phased out everywhere, but a few are still hanging on in a couple of Terai towns.

Taxi

Metered taxis are found in larger towns such as Kathmandu and Pokhara, and these can be hired for local and long-distance journeys. Metered taxis have black licence plates; private cars that operate as taxis for long-distance routes have red plates. Taxis can be flagged down anywhere, and they loiter at official stops in tourist destinations such as Bhaktapur and Patan.

On some routes, taxi drivers may refuse to use the meter – this is often an attempt to scam a few extra rupees out of tourists, but it may also reflect the fact that traffic is so bad on some routes that the drivers will lose money from the fuel they burn getting you there on the meter. If a driver refuses to use the meter, try another taxi. If no taxis are willing to use the meter, haggle down to reach a reasonable price.

Tempo

Tempos are outsized autorickshaws that run on fixed routes in larger cities. The old, polluting diesel tempos have been replaced by electric and gas-powered *safa* (clean) tempos and petrol minibuses, dramatically reducing the smog in the Kathmandu Valley. Drivers pick up and drop off anywhere along the route; tap on the roof with a coin when you want to stop.

TOURS

Organised treks are the most common kind of tour in Nepal – see p328 for details – but there are also wildlife-spotting tours at many of Nepal's national parks (see p84) and some interesting sightseeing tours around the Kathmandu Valley (p170). Pretty much any travel agent in Nepal can organise a bespoke tour to match your interests, budget and timeframe.

For organised rafting and mountain-biking tours see p93 and p100.

TRAIN

Trains run from Janakpur to Jaynagar over the Indian border but only locals can cross here. Nevertheless, these narrow-gauge locos offer a slow but atmospheric method of seeing the countryside of the Terai. See p320 for more details.

TRANSPORT

Health

CONTENTS

Kathmandu has the best health facilities in the country but standards at clinics and hospitals decline the further you get from the capital. In mountainous areas, there may be no health facilities at all. Trekkers who become unwell in the mountains are generally evacuated to Kathmandu, or overseas in the event of something really serious. Always take out travel insurance to cover the costs of hospital treatment and emergency evacuations.

Many of the most popular areas for visitors are remote and inaccessible, so you should read up on the possible health risks. While trekking, it makes sense to carry an emergency medical kit so that you can treat any symptoms until you reach medical care.

BEFORE YOU GO

INSURANCE

If you become seriously injured or very sick while travelling in Nepal, you may need to be evacuated by air and this can be shockingly expensive. Considering the terrain and the potential health risks, it would be extremely unwise to travel to Nepal without adequate health insurance.

Prior to travel, read the small print of your insurance policy. Certain activities may be classified as 'adventure' or 'extreme' sports and these may require additional cover. Many policies will not cover you for activities above 4000m or for 'dangerous sports' such as paragliding or white-water rafting, and you may not be covered if you rent a motorcycle.

RECOMMENDED VACCINATIONS

Although many tropical diseases are present in Nepal, you do not officially require any immunisations to enter the country, unless you have come from an area where yellow fever is present – in which case, you must show proof of immunisation. However, if you plan to travel off the beaten track, you might want to take extra precautions, so discuss your requirements with your doctor. Remember to record any vaccinations you have on an International Health Certificate.

It is recommended that you seek medical advice at least six weeks before travelling because if you do need treatments some require multiple injections over a period of time. Note that some vaccinations should

---

EVERYDAY HEALTH

Measuring body temperature is the quickest way to check for fever. Normal body temperature is up to 37°C (98.6°F); more than 2°C (4°F) higher indicates a high fever. The normal adult pulse rate is 60 to 100 per minute (children 80 to 100, babies 100 to 140). As a general rule the pulse increases about 20 beats per minute for each 1°C (2°F) rise in fever.

Respiration (breathing) rate is also an indicator of illness. Count the number of breaths per minute: between 12 and 20 is normal for adults and older children (up to 30 for younger children, 40 for babies). People with a high fever or serious respiratory illness breathe more quickly than normal. More than 40 shallow breaths a minute may indicate pneumonia.

not be given during pregnancy or to people with allergies.

Vaccinations you might consider include:

Diphtheria & tetanus Vaccinations for these two diseases are usually combined and are recommended for everyone. After an initial course of three injections (usually given in childhood), boosters are necessary every 10 years.

Hepatitis A The vaccine for Hepatitis A (eg Avaxim, Havrix 1440 or VAQTA) provides long-term immunity (possibly lifelong) after an initial injection and a booster at six to 12 months.

Hepatitis B Vaccination involves three injections, the quickest course being over three weeks with a booster at 12 months.

Influenza 'Flu' is considered by many to be the most common vaccine-preventable illness in travellers. This vaccine is annual.

Japanese B encephalitis (JBE) This is a mosquito-borne viral encephalitis that occurs in the Terai and occasionally in the Kathmandu Valley, particularly during the monsoon. JBE vaccine is given as three injections over three to four weeks and boosted usually at three years. This vaccine is recommended for prolonged stays.

Meningococcal meningitis A single-dose vaccine boosted every three to five years is recommended for individuals at high risk and for extended stays.

Polio This serious, easily transmitted disease is still found in Nepal. Everyone should keep up to date with this vaccination, which is normally given in childhood. A booster every 10 years maintains immunity.

Rabies Vaccination should be strongly considered for long-term visitors, particularly if you plan to travel to remote areas. In Nepal, the disease is carried by street dogs and monkeys. Vaccination is strongly recommended for children, who may not report a bite. Pretravel rabies vaccination involves having three injections over 21 to 28 days. If someone who has been vaccinated is bitten or scratched by an animal they will require two vaccine booster injections, while those not vaccinated will require more. The booster for rabies vaccination is usually given after three years.

Tuberculosis (TB) This disease is highly endemic in Nepal, though cases are extremely rare among travellers. Most people in the West are vaccinated in childhood.

Typhoid Drug-resistant typhoid fever is a growing problem in Nepal, particularly in the Terai. If you are travelling in Nepal for long periods, you should consider vaccination. The vaccine is available as an injection or oral capsules – ask your doctor for advice.

Yellow fever This disease is not endemic in Nepal and a vaccine for yellow fever is required only if you are coming from an infected area. The record of this vaccine should be provided in a World Health Organization (WHO) Yellow Vaccination Booklet and is valid for 10 years.

MEDICAL CHECKLIST

Following is a list of items you should consider including in your medical kit – consult your pharmacist for brands available in your country.

- aspirin or paracetamol (acetaminophen in the USA) for pain or fever
- anti-inflammatory (ibuprofen) for muscle and joint pain, headache and fever
- antibiotics, particularly if travelling off the beaten track; in Nepal, antibiotics are sold without prescription, which has led to widespread resistance to some common antibiotics
- promethazine (Phenergan) for relief of severe nausea
- rehydration mixture to prevent dehydration during bouts of diarrhoea; particularly important when travelling with children
- antihistamine for allergies, eg hay fever. For skin conditions, carry hydrocortisone 1% cream
- cold and flu tablets, throat lozenges and nasal decongestant
- multivitamins for long trips, when dietary vitamin intake may be inadequate
- insect repellent, sunscreen, lip balm (with sunblock) and antibacterial eye drops
- calamine lotion, sting-relief spray or aloe vera to ease irritation from sunburn and insect bites or stings
- antifungal cream such as clotrimazole 1% for fungal skin infections and thrush
- antiseptic (such as povidone-iodine) for cuts and grazes
- bandages, crêpe wraps, Band-Aids (plasters) and other wound dressings
- water purification tablets or iodine
- scissors, tweezers and an electric thermometer (mercury thermometers are prohibited by airlines)
- sterile kit in case you need injections; discuss with your doctor
- motion sickness tablets, such as Dramamine, for long bus rides

OTHER PREPARATIONS

Visiting Nepal may take you to some very remote areas, so it makes sense to visit the doctor before you travel for a general checkup. If you have any pre-existing medical conditions bring any medication you need from home. Ask your physician to give you a written description of your condition and your medications with their generic names in case you have to visit a doctor in Nepal.

A thorough dental examination is highly recommended because reliable dental care is difficult to obtain outside Kathmandu. People who wear contact lenses should bring plenty of lens solution and take extra care with hygiene to avoid eye infections. Carry backup prescription glasses and sunglasses in case you can't wear your lenses at some point.

INTERNET RESOURCES

Medex (www.medex.org.uk) offers a free download of the useful booklet *Travel At High Altitude*, aimed at laypeople and full of good advice for staying healthy in the mountains. A Nepali translation of the booklet is also available on the website.

Other useful sites include the following:

Centers for Disease Control and Prevention (www.cdc.gov)

Fit for Travel (www.fitfortravel.scot.nhs.uk)

International Society for Mountain Medicine (www.ismmed.org)

Kathmandu CIWEC Clinic (www.ciwec-clinic.com)

MASTA (www.masta-travel-health.com)

Nepal International Clinic (www.nepalinternationalclinic.com)

EMERGENCY TREATMENTS FOR TREKKING

While trekking it may be impossible to reach medical treatment, so consider carrying the following drugs for emergencies (the concentrations in which these drugs are sold in Nepal are noted next to the drug):

■ azithromycin 250mg – a broad spectrum antibiotic, useful for traveller's diarrhoea; take the equivalent of 500mg per day for three consecutive days.

■ norfloxacin or ciprofloxacin 400mg – for traveller's diarrhoea, the usual treatment is two tablets daily for one week.

■ tinidazole 500mg – the recommended treatment for giardiasis is four pills all at once for two days; for amoebiasis, take four pills at once for three days, then diloxanide furoate 500mg three times a day for 10 days.

FURTHER READING

Lonely Planet's *Healthy Travel Asia & India* is packed with useful information including pretrip planning, emergency first aid, immunisation and disease information, and what to do if you get sick on the road. *Travel with Children* from Lonely Planet includes advice on travel health for younger children. A useful health-care overview for travel in remote areas is David Werner's *Where There Is No Doctor*.

Specific titles covering trekking and health include:

■ *Medicine for Mountaineering & Other Wilderness Activities* (James A Wilkerson) covers many medical problems typically encountered in Nepal.

■ *Mountain Medicine* (Michael Ward) is good background reading on the subject of cold and high-altitude problems.

■ *Altitude Illness: Prevention & Treatment* (Stephen Bezruchka) is essential reading for high-altitude trekking, written by an experienced Nepal trekker.

■ *Wilderness First Aid and Wilderness Medicine* (Dr Jim Duff and Peter Gormly) is an excellent portable companion, available in Nepal at KEEP (Rs 750) or published abroad by Cicerone.

IN TRANSIT

DEEP VEIN THROMBOSIS (DVT)

Deep vein thrombosis occurs when blood clots form in the legs during long plane flights, chiefly because of prolonged immobility, and it can cause serious complications. The chief symptom of DVT is swelling or pain in the foot, ankle or calf, usually but not always on just one side. To prevent DVT you should walk about the cabin, perform isometric compressions of the leg muscles (ie contract the leg muscles while sitting), drink plenty of fluids, and avoid alcohol and other dehydrating drinks.

MOTION SICKNESS

If you are prone to motion sickness, sit near the wing on aircraft or between the front and back wheels on buses to minimise movement. Fresh air usually helps; reading and cigarette smoke make things worse. Medication for motion sickness, which can cause drowsiness, has to be taken before the trip commences. Ginger and peppermint are natural preventatives.

IN NEPAL

AVAILABILITY & COST OF HEALTH CARE

Kathmandu has several excellent clinics, including the CIWEC Clinic Travel Medicine Center and Nepal International Clinic (see p117). While trekking, your only option may be small local health posts, and even these are few and far between. In remote areas, you should carry an appropriate medical kit and be prepared to treat yourself until you can reach a health professional. See p337 in the Trekking chapter for information on health and medical assistance on treks.

If you have to take antibiotics without medical supervision, take only the recommended dose at the prescribed intervals and use the whole course, even if the illness seems to be cured earlier. Stop immediately if there are any serious reactions. If you are allergic to any medicines, carry this information (eg on a bracelet) when travelling.

In Nepal, most medical treatment must be paid for at the point of delivery. If your insurance company does not provide upfront payment, be sure to obtain a receipt so you can reclaim later.

INFECTIOUS DISEASES
Conjunctivitis

Conjunctivitis is a bacterial or viral infection of the pink lining around the eye. Sufferers often awaken with a slightly swollen eye with increased redness in the pink and white. Antibiotic eye drops can clear up bacterial infections within a day or so. If the eye is severely painful, vision is impaired or the white part of the eye is very red, seek medical help from an eye specialist.

Hepatitis

There are several different viruses that cause hepatitis (inflammation of the liver) and they differ in the way that they are transmitted. The symptoms are similar in all forms of the illness and include fever, chills, headache, fatigue, feelings of weakness as well as aches and pains, followed by loss of appetite, nausea, vomiting, abdominal pain, dark urine, light-coloured faeces, jaundiced (yellow) skin and yellowing of the whites of the eyes.

Hepatitis A and E are transmitted by contaminated drinking water and food. Only consume food and water that you know has been prepared hygienically to avoid the viruses. Hepatitis A is virtually 100% prevented by using any of the current hepatitis A vaccines. Hepatitis E causes an illness very similar to hepatitis A and there is at present no way to immunise against this virus.

Hepatitis B is only spread by blood (unsterilised needles and blood transfusions) or sexual contact. Risky situations include having a shave, tattoo or body piercing with contaminated equipment.

HIV & AIDS

HIV and AIDS are growing problems in Nepal – these diseases can be spread by infected needles and blood transfusion, as well as through sexual contact with an infected person. Insist on brand-new disposable needles and syringes for injections. Blood used for transfusions is usually screened for HIV/AIDS but this cannot always be done in an emergency. Try to avoid a blood transfusion unless it seems certain you will die without it.

Malaria

Malaria is caused by the *Plasmodium* blood parasite and transmitted from person to person by mosquitoes. The disease can be fatal, but the risk to travellers in Nepal is very low. Antimalarial tablets are only recommended if you will be spending long periods in the Terai, particularly during the monsoon – ask your doctor for advice. There is no risk in Kathmandu or Pokhara, or on typical Himalayan trekking routes.

It makes sense to take measures to avoid being bitten by mosquitoes as dengue fever, another mosquito-borne illness, has been sporadically documented in the lowlands. Use insect repellent if travelling to the Terai, particularly if staying overnight in jungle

> **WARNING**
>
> Self-diagnosis and treatment can be risky, so you should seek medical help if you become ill. Although drug dosages appear in this text, they're for emergency treatment only. Correct diagnosis is vital.

areas or staying in cheap hotels. Plug-in mosquito killers are more effective than combustible mosquito coils, which can cause respiratory problems.

Rabies

The rabies virus causes a severe brain infection that is almost always fatal. Feral dogs and monkeys are the main carriers of the disease in Nepal. Rabies is different from other infectious diseases in that a person can be immunised after having been exposed. Human rabies immune globulin (HRIG) is stocked at the CIWEC clinic and the Nepal International Clinic in Kathmandu (see p117). In addition to the HRIG, five injections of rabies vaccine are needed over a one-month period. Travellers who have taken a preimmunisation series only need two rabies shots, three days apart, if they are bitten by a possibly rabid animal.

If you receive a bite or a scratch from an animal in Nepal, wash the wound with soap and water, then a disinfectant, such as povidone-iodine, then seek rabies immunisations. Considering the risk, it makes sense to keep your distance from animals in Nepal, particularly street dogs and monkeys.

Respiratory Infections

Upper respiratory tract infections (such as the common cold) are common ailments in Nepal. Respiratory infections are aggravated by high altitude, cold weather, pollution, smoking and overcrowded conditions, which increase the opportunities for infection.

Most upper respiratory tract infections go away without treatment, but any infection can lead to complications such as bronchitis, ear infections and pneumonia, which may need to be treated with antibiotics. Seek medical help in this situation.

No vaccine offers complete protection, but there are vaccines against influenza and pneumococcal pneumonia that might help. The influenza vaccine is good for no more than a year.

Sexually Transmitted Infections

As well as AIDS and Hepatitis B, sexually transmitted infections (STIs) such as gonorrhoea, herpes and syphilis are common in Nepal, but the risk to travellers is more likely to come from casual sexual relationships with other travellers. Seek medical help if you notice sores, blisters or rashes around the genitals and discharges or pain when urinating. Although abstinence from sexual contact is the only 100% effective prevention, using condoms helps.

FEVER

If you have a sustained fever (over 38°C) for more than two days while trekking and you cannot get to a doctor, an emergency treatment is a course of the broad-spectrum antibiotic azithromycin (500mg twice a day for seven days), but seek professional medical help as soon as possible.

TRAVELLER'S DIARRHOEA

Even veteran travellers to South Asia seem to come down with the trots in Nepal. It's just one of those things. The main cause of infection is contaminated water and food, due to low standards of hygiene. However, diarrhoea is usually self-limiting and most people recover within a few days.

Dehydration is the main danger with diarrhoea, particularly in children, pregnant women or the elderly. Soda water, weak black tea with a little sugar, or soft drinks allowed to go flat and half-diluted with clean water will help you replace lost liquids. In severe cases, take oral rehydration salts made up with boiled or purified water. In an emergency you can make up a solution of six teaspoons of sugar and half a teaspoon of salt to a litre of boiled or bottled water. If you are still passing small amounts of concentrated urine, you need to drink more. Stick to a bland diet as you recover.

Loperamide (Imodium) or diphenoxylate (Lomotil) can be used to bring temporary relief from the symptoms, but they do not cure the problem. Do not use these drugs if you have a high fever or are severely dehydrated. These drugs are never recommended for children under 12.

In the case of diarrhoea with blood or mucus (dysentery – see opposite), any diarrhoea with fever, profuse watery diarrhoea and persistent diarrhoea not improving after 48 hours, you should visit a doctor for a stool test. Antibiotics may be necessary. If you cannot reach a doctor, the recommended treatment is norfloxacin 400mg or ciprofloxacin 500mg twice daily for three days.

These drugs are not recommended for children or pregnant women. The preferred treatment for children is azithromycin in a dose of 10mg per kilogram of body weight per day (as a single dose each day for three days).

Two other common causes of persistent diarrhoea in travellers are giardiasis and amoebic dysentery.

Amoebic Dysentery

Caused by the protozoan *Entamoeba histolytica*, amoebic dysentery is characterised by a gradual onset of low-grade diarrhoea, often with blood and mucus. Infection persists until treated so you should seek medical advice if you think you have amoebic dysentery. Where this is not possible, tindazole or metronidazole are the recommended drugs. Treatment is a 2g single dose of tindazole daily or 250mg of metronidazole three times daily for five to 10 days. Alcohol should not be consumed while taking these medications. Side effects of these drugs include fatigue, nausea, abdominal discomfort and an unpleasant metallic taste that lingers in the mouth.

Cyclospora

This waterborne intestinal parasite infects the upper intestine, causing diarrhoea, fatigue and loss of appetite lasting up to 12 weeks. Fortunately, the illness is a risk in Nepal mainly during the monsoon, when few tourists visit. Iodine is not sufficient to kill the parasite but it can be removed by water filters and it is easily killed by boiling.

The treatment for *Cyclospora* diarrhoea is an antibiotic called trimethoprim and sulfamethoxazole (sold commonly as Bactrim) twice a day for seven days. This drug cannot be taken by people who are allergic to sulphur.

Giardiasis

Also known as giardia, giardiasis accounts for around 12% of the diarrhoea among travellers in Nepal. The disease is caused by a parasite, *Giardia Lamblia*, found in water that has been contaminated by waste from animals. Simply brushing your teeth using contaminated water is sufficient to get giardiasis, or any other gut bug.

Symptoms include stomach cramps, nausea, a bloated stomach, watery and foul-smelling diarrhoea, and frequent sulphurous burps and farts but no fever. Giardiasis can appear several weeks after exposure and symptoms may disappear and return for several months. The best treatment for giardiasis is four 500mg tablets of tinidazole taken as a single dose each day for two consecutive days. Side effects include mild nausea, fatigue and an unpleasant metallic taste in the mouth. Tinidazole cannot be taken with alcohol.

ENVIRONMENTAL HAZARDS
Acute Mountain Sickness

Above 2500m, the concentration of oxygen in the air you breathe starts to drop off markedly, reducing the amount of oxygen that reaches your brain and other organs. Decreasing air pressure at altitude has the additional effect of causing liquid to leak from the capillaries into the lungs and brain, which can be fatal. Fortunately, the human body has the ability to adjust to the changes in pressure and oxygen concentration as you gain altitude, but this is a gradual process.

The health conditions caused by the effects of altitude are known collectively as altitude sickness or acute mountain sickness (AMS). If allowed to develop unchecked, AMS can lead to coma and death. However, you can avoid this potentially deadly condition by limiting your rate of ascent, which will allow your body to adjust to the altitude. There is also a 100% effective treatment if you do experience serious symptoms – descend immediately.

If you go trekking, it is important to read up on the causes, effects and treatment of altitude sickness before you start walking. Attend one of the free lectures on altitude sickness given by the Himalayan Rescue Association in Kathmandu (p337). The onset of symptoms of AMS is usually gradual, so there is time to adjust your trekking schedule or retreat off the mountain if you start to feel unwell. Most people who suffer severe effects of AMS have ignored obvious warning signs.

ACCLIMATISATION

If you were flown to the summit of Mt Everest, you would have a few minutes of consciousness before you passed out and died. However, climbers have made it to the summit safely by ascending slowly and allowing their bodies to gradually adjust to the increasing altitude.

The process of acclimatisation is still not fully understood, but it is known to involve modifications in breathing patterns and heart rate and an increase in the oxygen-carrying capacity of the blood. Some people have a faster

HEALTH

rate of acclimatisation than others, but almost anyone can trek to high altitudes as long as the rate of ascent does not exceed the rate at which their body can adjust. If you develop altitude sickness, it doesn't mean you can never go to high altitude again, but it does mean you will have to climb more slowly in future.

SYMPTOMS

On treks above 4000m, almost everyone experiences some symptoms of mild altitude sickness – breathlessness and fatigue linked to reduced oxygen in the blood being the most common.

Mild symptoms usually pass if you stop ascending and give your body time to 'catch up' with the increase in altitude. Once you have acclimatised at the altitude where you first developed symptoms, you should be able to slowly continue your ascent. Serious symptoms are a different matter – if you develop any of the serious symptoms described below, you should descend immediately.

AMS is a notoriously fickle affliction and it can affect trekkers and walkers who are accustomed to walking at high altitudes as well as people who have never been to altitude before. AMS has been fatal at 3000m, although 3500m to 4500m is the usual range.

Mild Symptoms

Mild symptoms of AMS are experienced by many travellers above 2800m. Symptoms tend to be worse at night and include headache, dizziness, lethargy, loss of appetite, nausea, breathlessness, irritability and difficulty sleeping. Be alert for these symptoms – experiencing mild symptoms of AMS does not mean you have to end your trek, but you should take these symptoms as a warning sign that you are not sufficiently acclimatised.

Never ignore mild symptoms of AMS – this is your body giving you an alarm call. You may develop more serious symptoms if you continue to ascend without giving your body time to adjust.

Serious Symptoms

AMS can become more serious without warning and it can be fatal. Serious symptoms are caused by the accumulation of fluid in the lungs and brain, and include breathlessness at rest, a dry, irritative cough (which may progress to the production of pink, frothy sputum), severe headache, lack of coordination (typically leading to a 'drunken walk'),

confusion, irrational behaviour, vomiting and eventually unconsciousness and death.

PREVENTION

If you fly or travel by road into an area above 2500m, take it easy for at least three days. Within a week you should be ready for something a bit more adventurous, but do not push yourself to do anything that you are not comfortable with.

If you trek above 2500m, observe the following rules:

- Ascend slowly – where possible, do not sleep more than 300m higher than the elevation where you spent the previous night. If any stage on a trek exceeds this increase in elevation, take at least one rest day to acclimatise before you start the ascent. If you or anyone else in your party seems to be struggling, take a rest day as a precaution.
- Climb high, sleep low – it is always wise to sleep at a lower altitude than the greatest height reached during the day. If you need to cross a high pass, take an extra acclimatisation day before you cross. Be aware that descending to the altitude where you slept the previous night may not be enough to compensate for a very large increase in altitude during the day.
- Trek healthy – you are more likely to develop AMS if you are tired, dehydrated or malnourished. Drink extra fluids while trekking. Avoid alcohol and limit your intake of caffeine to reduce the risk of dehydration. Eat light, high-carbohydrate meals for more energy. Avoid sedatives or sleeping pills and don't smoke – this will further reduce the amount of oxygen reaching your lungs.
- If you feel unwell, stop – if you start to display mild symptoms of AMS, stop climbing. Take an acclimatisation day and see if things improve. If your symptoms stay the same or get worse, descend immediately.
- If you show serious symptoms, descend – if you show any serious symptoms of AMS, descend immediately to a lower altitude. Ideally this should be below the altitude where you slept the night before you first developed symptoms. Most lodges can arrange an emergency porter to help you descend quickly to a safe altitude.

TREATMENT

Treat mild symptoms by resting at the same altitude until recovery. Take paracetamol or aspirin for headaches. Diamox (acetazolamide) can be used to reduce mild symptoms of AMS. However, it is not a cure and it will not stop you from developing serious symptoms. The usual dosage of Diamox is 125mg to 250mg twice daily. The medication is a diuretic so you should drink extra liquid to avoid dehydration. Diamox may also cause disturbances to vision and the sense of taste and it can cause a harmless tingling sensation in the fingers.

If symptoms persist or become worse, descend immediately – even 500m can help. If the victim cannot walk without support, they may need to be carried down. Any delay could be fatal; if you have to descend in the dark, seek local assistance.

In the event of severe symptoms, the victim may need to be flown to a lower altitude by helicopter. Getting the victim to a lower altitude is the priority – get someone else from the group to call for helicopter rescue and start the descent to the pick-up point. Note that a helicopter rescue can cost you US$2500 to US$10,000.

Emergency treatments for serious symptoms of AMS include supplementary oxygen, nifedipine, dexamethasone and repressurisation using a device known as a Gamow bag (this should only be administered by health professionals), but these only reduce the symptoms and they are not a 'cure'.

The only effective treatment for sufferers of severe AMS is to descend rapidly to a lower altitude. These treatments should never be used to avoid descent or to enable further ascent.

Cuts, Bites & Stings

Wash any cut well and treat it with an antiseptic such as povidone-iodine or antibiotic ointment and sterile gauze dressing. Where possible avoid bandages and Band-Aids, which can keep wounds wet.

Bee and wasp stings are usually painful rather than dangerous. Calamine lotion or a sting-relief spray will give relief and ice packs will reduce the pain and swelling. However, people who are allergic to bees or wasps can go into anaphylactic shock and require immediate medical care.

BEDBUGS, LICE & SCABIES

Bedbugs love dirty mattresses and bedding in cheap hotels. If you notice drops of blood on bedclothes or on the wall, sleep somewhere else. Bedbugs leave itchy bites in neat rows – calamine lotion or a sting-relief spray can help.

All lice cause itching and discomfort. They make themselves at home in your hair (head lice), your clothing (body lice) or in your pubic hair (crabs) and spread through contact with an infected person or their belongings. Powder or shampoo treatment will kill the lice. Infected clothing should then be washed in very hot, soapy water and left in the sun to dry.

Also caused by a tiny parasite, scabies is spread by person-to-person contact and is relatively common in some schools and orphanages. Scabies is treated by specific medicated creams.

LEECHES

These blood suckers haunt Nepal every monsoon season. Leeches are insidious predators and they often attach themselves to the legs and feet of trekkers, even squeezing in through the eyelets of trekking boots. Their saliva contains an anaesthetic so you may not notice you have been bitten until you remove your shoes. Salt or a lighted match end will make them fall off, after which you can apply antiseptic cream. Do not pull them off, as the bite is more likely to become infected. An insect repellent may help keep them away.

Food

There is an old colonial adage that says 'if you can cook it, boil it or peel it you can eat it…otherwise forget it'. Vegetables and fruit should be washed with purified or boiled water or peeled where possible. Beware of ice cream that is sold anywhere it might have melted and refrozen. Undercooked meat should be avoided and be wary of fish in areas where there is no refrigeration.

If a place looks clean and well run and the vendor also looks clean and healthy, then the food is probably safe. In general, places that are packed with travellers or locals will be fine, while empty restaurants are questionable.

Frostbite

In extreme cold, extremities such as the fingers, toes and nose can freeze. Symptoms include a whitish or waxy cast to the skin, plus itching, numbness and pain. The effects of severe frostbite are not reversible and treatment can involve amputation, so take steps to protect your extremities from the cold.

In the event of frostbite, warm the affected areas in warm (not hot) water or cover with blankets until the skin becomes flushed. Protect affected areas from further damage with bulky gauze dressings. Pain and swelling are inevitable but blisters should not be broken. Seek medical attention immediately.

Heat Exhaustion

Dehydration and salt deficiency can cause heat exhaustion. Give your body time to adjust to high temperatures, drink sufficient liquids and do not do anything too physically demanding.

Salt deficiency is characterised by fatigue, lethargy, headaches, giddiness and muscle cramps; salt tablets may help, but adding extra salt to your food is better.

Hypothermia

Hypothermia occurs when the body loses heat faster than it can produce it and the core temperature of the body falls; it can be fatal. It is surprisingly easy to progress from very cold to dangerously cold through a combination of wind, wet clothing, fatigue and hunger, even if the air temperature is above freezing.

Symptoms of hypothermia include exhaustion, numb skin (particularly toes and fingers), shivering, slurred speech, lethargy, lack of coordination, dizziness and muscle cramps. To treat mild hypothermia, the victim should be taken somewhere out of the wind and rain and given dry clothing, hot liquids and easy-to-digest food.

When trekking or travelling through cold or wet areas, it is best to dress in layers; silk, wool and fleece are all good insulating materials. A hat and gloves will protect parts of the body that are prone to heat loss. Wear an outer layer that is windproof, and preferably waterproof as well.

If you will be trekking away from human habitation, bring a 'space' blanket to keep you warm if you are forced to camp out; and carry food that contains simple sugars to generate heat quickly, and fluid to drink.

Sunburn

It is very easy to get sunburnt in Nepal, particularly at altitude. As well as causing immediate irritation and discomfort, sunburn can lead to premature skin ageing and skin cancer in later years. Use a sunscreen with a high sun protection factor (SPF), sunglasses with UV protection, a lip balm containing sunblock and wear a wide-brimmed hat to protect the face and the back of the neck.

Those with fair complexions should bring reflective sunscreen (containing zinc oxide or titanium oxide) with them. Apply the sunscreen to your nose and lips (and especially the tops of your ears if you are not wearing a hat).

Water

Water in Nepal can be contaminated with all sorts of nasties. If you don't know for certain that the water is safe you should assume the worst. Ice should be avoided except in up-market tourist-oriented restaurants. While trekking, purify your own water, rather than buying purified water in polluting plastic bottles. Soft drinks, beer and tea and coffee are normally fine, but avoid other products made from milk or water unless you are sure they are safe.

WATER PURIFICATION

The easiest way to purify water is to boil it thoroughly. However, at higher altitudes, water boils at a lower temperature and germs are less likely to be killed. Most trekkers prefer to purify water using iodine drops or tablets. Chlorine tablets (eg Puritabs or Steritabs) kill many pathogens but are not effective against giardia and amoebic cysts. Follow the directions carefully – filter water through a cloth before adding the chemicals and be sure to wet the thread on the lid to your water bottle. Once the water is purified, vitamin C can be added to remove the unpleasant iodine taste.

Trekking filters take out all parasites, bacteria and viruses, and make water safe to drink. However, it is very important to read the specifications so that you know exactly what the filter removes from the water. If a filter does not remove all the bugs present in Nepal, you are probably better off with iodine drops.

WOMEN'S HEALTH
Gynaecological Problems

Antibiotic use, synthetic underwear, sweating and contraceptive pills can lead to fungal vaginal infections, especially when travelling in hot climates. Fungal infections are characterised by a rash, itch and discharge. Nystatin, miconazole or clotrimazole pessaries, or vaginal cream are the usual treatments, but some people use vinegar or lemon-juice douches, or yoghurt. Maintaining good personal hygiene and wearing loose-fitting clothes and cotton underwear may help prevent these infections.

Sexually transmitted infections are a major cause of gynaecological problems. Symptoms include a smelly discharge, painful intercourse and sometimes a burning sensation when urinating. Medical attention should be sought and sexual partners must also be treated. Besides abstinence, the best thing is to practise safe sex using condoms.

Pregnancy

You should think carefully about travelling to Nepal while pregnant. Some vaccinations are not advisable during pregnancy, and many of the health problems commonly encountered in Nepal can have serious complications for the developing child. Dehydration from diarrhoea is especially dangerous and prompt fluid intake is often important for pregnant women. Pregnant women should avoid all unnecessary medication, although vaccinations should still be taken where needed.

If you must travel while pregnant, avoid the first three months and the last three months before delivery. Airlines often restrict travel for women who are more than 32 weeks into gestation.

HEALTH

Language

CONTENTS

Nepali is closely related to Hindi, and both languages belong to the Indo-European family. It's quite easy to get by with English in Nepal; most of the people visitors will have to deal with in the Kathmandu Valley and in Pokhara will speak some English. Along the main trekking trails, particularly the Annapurna Circuit, English is also widely understood.

Nonetheless, it's interesting to learn at least a little Nepali and it's quite an easy language to pick up. For a more comprehensive language guide, get a copy of Lonely Planet's *Nepali Phrasebook*, which includes Nepali script throughout.

Although Nepali is the national language and is used as a lingua franca (linking language) between all the country's ethnic groups, there are many other languages spoken in Nepal. The Newars of the Kathmandu Valley, for example, speak Newari; other languages are spoken by the Tamangs, Sherpas, Rais, Limbus, Magars, Gurungs and other groups. In the Terai (bordering India), Hindi and Maithili, another Indian language of this region, are often spoken (see the table on this page for a breakdown of languages spoken in Nepal).

Even if you learn no other Nepali, there is one word every visitor soon picks up – *namaste* (pronounced na·ma·*ste*). Strictly translated it means 'I salute the god in you', but it's used as an everyday greeting that encompasses everything from 'Hello' to 'How are you?' and even 'See you again soon'. It should be accompanied with the hands held in a prayerlike position, the Nepali gesture equivalent to Westerners shaking hands.

STUDYING NEPALI

Peace Corps and other aid workers pick up a working knowledge of the language very quickly and there are language courses available that will enable you to get by with just four to eight weeks of intensive study. See Courses (p363) for details. In books, one of the best sources for the serious language student is *Teach Yourself Nepali* by Michael Hutt and Abhi Subedi, which covers both written and spoken Nepali.

PRONUNCIATION
Vowels

a	as the 'u' in 'hut'
ā	as the 'ar' in 'garden' (no 'r' sound)
e	as the 'e' in 'best' but longer
i	as the 'i' in 'sister' but longer
o	as the 'o' in 'sold'
u	as the 'u' in 'put'
ai	as the 'i' in 'mine'
au	as the 'ow' in 'cow'

Consonants

Most Nepali consonants are quite similar to their English counterparts. The exceptions

LANGUAGES OF NEPAL	
Language	**% of Total Population**
Nepali	47.8
Maithili	12.1
Bhojpuri	7.4
Tharu	5.8
Tamang	5.1
Newari	3.6
Magar	3.3
Rai	2.7
Awadhi	2.4
Limbu	1.4
Gurung	1.2
Sherpa	0.7
Other	6.5

are the so-called retroflex consonants and the aspirated consonants. Retroflex sounds are made by curling the tongue tip back to touch the roof of the mouth as you make the sound; they are indicated in this guide by an underdot, eg ṭ or ḍ as in *Kaṭhmaṇḍu*.

Aspirated consonants are sounded more forcefully than they would be in English and are made with a short puff of air; they are indicated in this guide by h after the consonant, eg *kh* as in *khānuhos* (please). You should ensure that you don't confuse the Nepali aspirated combinations *ph* and *th* with their English counterparts in words such as 'phone', 'this' and 'thin'. In Nepali, *ph* is pronounced as the 'p' in 'pit', and *th* is pronounced as the 't' in 'time'.

Both retroflex and aspirated consonants are best learned by having a native speaker demonstrate them for you. You could start with *Kaṭhmaṇḍu*, which contains both retroflex and aspirated consonants.

ACCOMMODATION

Where is a ...?	... *ka*·hã chha
campsite	*shi*·vir
guest house	*pā*·hu·na ghar
hotel	*ho*·ṭel
lodge	laj

What is the address?
the·*gā*·nã ke ho
Please write down the address.
the·*gā*·nã *lekh*·nu·hos
Can I get a place to stay here?
ya·hã bãs *paun*·chha
May I look at the room?
ko·thã her·na sak·chhu
How much is it per night?
ek *rāt*·ko *ka*·ti *pai*·sā ho
Does it include breakfast?
bi·*hā*·na·ko *khā*·na *sa*·met ho

clean	*sa*·*fā*
dirty	*mai*·lo
fan	*pan*·khā
hot water	*tā*·to *pā*·ni
room	*ko*·thã

CONVERSATION & ESSENTIALS

Hello/Goodbye.	na·ma·*ste*
How are you?	ta·*pāi*·lai *kas*·to chha
Excuse me.	ha·*jur*
Please (give me).	*di*·nu·hos

Please (you have).	*khā*·nu·hos
Thank you.	*dhan*·ya·bad

Unlike in the many other countries, verbal expressions of thanks are not the cultural norm in Nepal. Although neglecting to say 'Thank you' may make you feel a little uncomfortable, it is rarely necessary in a simple commercial transaction; foreigners going round saying *dhanyabad* all the time sound distinctly odd to Nepalis.

I	ma
Yes. (I have)	chã
No. (I don't have)	*chhai*·na
OK.	*theek*·cha
Where?	*ka*·hã
here	*ya*·hã
there	*tya*·hã
good/pretty	*ram*·ro
I don't need it.	*ma*·lai cha·*hi*·na
I don't have it.	ma *san*·ga *chhai*·na
Wait a minute.	ek chhin *par*·kha·nos

EMERGENCIES

Help!	*gu*·*hār*
It's an emergency!	*ā*·paṭ par·yo
There's been an accident!	dur·*gha*·ṭa·nã *bha*·yo
Please call a doctor.	*dāk*·ṭar·lai bo·*lāu*·nu·hos
Where is the (public) toilet?	shau·*chā*·la·ya *ka*·hã chha
I'm lost.	ma ha·*rā*·ye

HEALTH

Where can I find a good doctor?	*ram*·ro *dak*·ṭar *ka*·hã *pāin*·cha
Where is the nearest hospital?	*ya*·hã *na*·ja·*rai ka*·hã chha
I don't feel well.	*ma*·lāi *san*·cho *chhai*·na
I have diarrhoea.	di·*shā lãg*·yo
I have altitude sickness.	lekh *lāg*·yo
I have a fever.	*jo*·ro *ā*·yo
I'm having trouble breathing.	sãs pher·na sak·*di*·na
medicine	*au*·sa·dhi
pharmacy	*au*·sa·dhi pa·sal

I have ...	*ma*·lāi ... *lāg*·yo
asthma	*dam*·ko bya·thā
diabetes	ma·dhu·*me*·ha
epilepsy	*chā*·re rog

LANGUAGE DIFFICULTIES

Do you speak English?	ta·*pāi* an·*gre*·ji *bol*·na *sak*·nu *hun*·chha
I only speak a little Nepali.	ma *a*·li *a*·li ne·*pā*·li *bol*·chhu
I understand.	ma *bujh*·chu
I don't understand.	*mai*·le bu·*jhi*·na
Please say it again.	*phe*·ri *bha*·ṇu·hos
Please speak more slowly.	ta·*pāi* bi·*stā*·rai *bol*·nu·hos

NUMBERS

0	*sun*·ya	शून्य
1	ek	एक
2	*du*·i	दुइ
3	tin	तीन
4	chār	चार
5	panch	पाँच
6	chha	छ
7	sāt	सात
8	āth	आठ
9	nau	नौ
10	das	दस
11	e·*ghār*·a	एघार
12	*bā*·hra	बाह्र
13	*te*·hra	तेह्र
14	*chau*·dha	चौध
15	*pan*·dhra	पन्ध्र
16	*so*·hra	सोह्र
17	*sa*·tra	सत्र
18	a·*thā*·ra	अठार
19	un·*nais*	उन्नाईस
20	bis	बीस
21	ek kais	एककाईस
22	bais	बाईस
23	teis	तेईस
24	*chau*·bis	चौबीस
25	*pach*·chis	पच्चीस
26	*chhab*·bis	छब्बीस
27	sat·*tais*	सत्ताईस
28	at·*thais*	अट्ठाईस
29	u·*nan*·tis	उनन्तीस
30	tis	तीस
40	*chā*·lis	चालीस
50	pa·*chās*	पचास
60	*sā*·thi	साठी
70	sat·ta·ri	सत्तरी
80	*a*·si	असी
90	*nab*·be	नब्बे
100	ek say	एक सय
1000	ek ha·*jār*	एक हजार
10,000	das ha·*jār*	दस हजार
100,000	ek lākh	एक लाख
200,000	*du*·i lākh	दुइ लाख
1,000,000	das lākh	दस लाख

SHOPPING & SERVICES

Where is the market?	ba·*zār ka*·hā chha
What is it made of?	*ke*·le *ba*·ne·ko
How much?	*ka*·ti
That's enough.	*pugyo*
I like this.	*ma*·le yo *ram*·ro *lag*·yo
I don't like this.	*ma*·lai yo *ram*·ro lag·*en*·a

money	*pai*·sa
cheap	*sas*·to
expensive	ma·*han*·go
less	kam
more	*ba*·dhi
little bit	a·li·*ka*·ti

bank	baink
... embassy	... *rāj*·du·tā·vas
museum	sam·grā·*hā*·la·ya
police	pra·*ha*·ri
post office	post *a*·fis
stamp	*ti*·ka
envelope	kham
tourist office	*tu*·rist *a*·fis

What time does it open/close?
 ka·ti *ba*·je *khol*·chha/*ban*·da *gar*·chha
I want to change some money.
 pai·sā *sāt*·nu man·*lāg*·chha

SIGNS

खुला	Open
बन्द	Closed
प्रवेश	Entrance
निकास	Exit
प्रवेश निषेध	No Entry
धूम्रपान मनाही छ	No Smoking
मनाही/निषेध	Prohibited
शाचालय	Toilets
तातो	Hot
चिसो	Cold
खतरा	Danger
रोक्नुहोस	Stop
बाटो बन्द	Road Closed

Internet

Is there a local internet cafe?
 ya·hā in·*tar*·neṭ *kyah*·phe chha
I'd like to get internet access.
 ma·lai in·*tar*·neṭ *cha*·hi·yo
I'd like to check my email.
 i·mel chek *gar*·nu·par·yo
I'd like to send an email.
 i·mel pa·*ṭhau*·nu·par·yo

TIME & DATES

What time is it?	*ka·*ti *ba·*jyo
It's one o'clock.	ek *ba·*jyo
minute	*mi·*nat
hour	*ghan·*tā
day	din
today	*ā·*ja
yesterday	*hi·*jo
tomorrow	*bho·*li
now	*a·*hi·le
week	*hap·*tā
month	*ma·*hi·nā

What day is it today?	*ā·*ja ke bār
Today is ...	*ā·*ja ... ho

Monday	*som·*bār
Tuesday	*man·*gal bār
Wednesday	*budh·*bar
Thursday	*bi·*hi·bār
Friday	*su·*kra·bār
Saturday	*sa·*ni·bār
Sunday	*āi·*ta·bār

TRANSPORT

bus	bus
taxi	*tyakh·*si
boat	nāu
ticket	*ti·*kaṭ

How can I get to ...?
... *ko·*lā·gi *ka·*ti *pai·*sā *lāg·*chha
Is it far from here?
yo hā ba ta ko tā dhā chha
Can I walk there?
hi·*ḍe·*ra *ja·*na *sa·*kin·chhu

I want to go to ...
ma ... *·*mā *jān·*chhu
Where does this bus go?
yo bus *ka·*hā *jān·*chha
How much is it to go to ...?
... *jā·*na *ka·*ti *par·*chha
I want a one-way/return ticket.
*jā·*ne/*jā·*ne·*āu·*ne *ti·*kaṭ *di·*nu·hos
Does your taxi have a meter?
ta·*pāi* ko *tyakh·*si mā *me·*ter chha

TREKKING

Which way is ...?
... *jā·*ne *ba·*to *ka·*ta *par·*chha
Is there a village nearby?
na·ji·kai gaun *par·*chha
How many hours/days to ...?
... *ka·*ti *ghan·*ṭā/din
Where is the porter?
bha·ri·ya *ka·*ta *ga·*yo
I want to sleep.
*ma·*lai *sut·*na man *lag·*yo
I'm cold.
*ma·*lai *jā·*ḍo *lag·*yo
Please give me (water).
*ma·*lai *(pa·*ni) *di·*nu·hos

way/trail	*sā·*no *ba·*ṭo
bridge	pul
downhill	o·*rā·*lo
uphill	u·*kā·*lo
left	*bā·*yā
right	*dā·*yā
cold	*jā·*do
teahouse	*bhat·*ti

Glossary

Beware of the different methods of transliterating Nepali and the other languages spoken in Nepal. There are many and varied ways of spelling Nepali words. In particular the letters 'b' and 'v' are often interchanged. See p67 for useful food and drink words and p400 for other words and phrases.

ACAP – Annapurna Conservation Area Project

Aditya – ancient *Vedic* sun god, also known as Suriya

Agni – ancient *Vedic* god of the hearth and fire

Agnipura – Buddhist symbol for fire

AMS – acute mountain sickness, also known as altitude sickness

Annapurna – the goddess of abundance and an incarnation of *Mahadevi*

Ashoka – Indian Buddhist emperor who spread Buddhism throughout the subcontinent

Ashta Matrikas – the eight multi-armed mother goddesses

Avalokiteshvara – as *Gautama Buddha* is the *Buddha* of our era, so Avalokiteshvara is the *bodhisattva* of our era

bagh chal – traditional Nepali game

bahal – Buddhist monastery courtyard

ban – forest or jungle

bandh – strike; see also *julus* and *chakka jam*

betel – mildly intoxicating concoction of areca nut and lime, which is wrapped in betel leaf and chewed

Bhadrakali – Tantric goddess who is also a consort of *Bhairab*

Bhagwati – a form of *Durga,* and thus a form of the goddess *Parvati*

Bhairab – the 'terrific' or fearsome Tantric form of *Shiva* with 64 manifestations

bhanjyang – mountain pass

Bhimsen – one of the Pandava brothers, from the *Mahabharata,* seen as a god of tradesmen

bhojanalaya – basic Nepali restaurant or canteen

Bhote – Nepali term for a Tibetan, used in the names of rivers flowing from Tibet

Bodhi tree – a pipal tree under which the *Buddha* was sitting when he attained enlightenment, also known as 'bo tree'

bodhisattva – a near-*Buddha* who renounces the opportunity to attain *nirvana* in order to aid humankind

Bön – the pre-Buddhist animist religion of Tibet

Brahma – the creator god in the Hindu triad, which also includes *Vishnu* and *Shiva*

Brahmin – the highest Hindu caste, said to originate from *Brahma's* head

Buddha – the 'Awakened One'; the originator of Buddhism

chaitya – small *stupa,* which usually contains a *mantra* rather than a Buddhist relic

chakka jam – literally 'jam the wheels', in which all vehicles stay off the street during a strike; see also *bandh* and *julus*

chakra – *Vishnu's* dislike weapon; one of the four symbols he holds

Chandra – moon god

chautara – stone platforms around trees, which serve as shady places for porters to rest

Chhetri – the second caste of Nepali Hindus, said to originate from *Brahma's* arms

Chomolangma – Tibetan name for Mt Everest; literally 'Mother Goddess of the World' (also spelt Qomolangma)

chörten – Tibetan Buddhist *stupa*

chowk – historically a courtyard or marketplace; these days used more to refer to an intersection or crossroads

daal – lentil soup; the main source of protein in the Nepali diet

Dalai Lama – spiritual leader of Tibetan Buddhist people

danda – hill

deval – temple

Devi – the short form of *Mahadevi,* the *shakti* to *Shiva*

dhaka – hand-woven cotton cloth

dharma – Buddhist teachings

dhoka – door or gate

Dhyani Buddha – the original Adi *Buddha* created five Dhyani Buddhas, who in turn create the universe of each human era

doko – basket carried by porters

dorje – Tibetan word for the 'thunderbolt' symbol of Buddhist power; *vajra* in Nepali

durbar – palace

Durga – fearsome manifestation of *Parvati, Shiva's* consort

gaida – rhinoceros

Ganesh – son of *Shiva* and *Parvati,* instantly recognisable by his elephant head

Ganga – goddess of the Ganges

Garuda – the man-bird *vehicle* of *Vishnu*

Gautama Buddha – the *Buddha* of our era

Gelugpa – one of the four major schools of Tibetan Buddhism

ghat – steps beside a river; a 'burning ghat' Is used for cremations
gompa – Tibetan Buddhist monastery
gopi – milkmaids; companions of *Krishna*
gufa – cave
Gurkhas – Nepali soldiers who have long formed a part of the British army; the name comes from the region of Gorkha
Gurung – western hill people from around Gorkha and Pokhara

Hanuman – monkey god
harmika – square base on top of a *stupa's* dome, upon which the eyes of the *Buddha* are painted
hathi – elephant
himal – range or massif with permanent snow
hiti – water conduit or tank with waterspouts
hookah – water pipe for smoking
howdah – riding platform for passengers on an elephant

Indra – king of the *Vedic* gods; god of rain

Jagannath – *Krishna* as Lord of the Universe
janai – sacred thread, which high-caste Hindu men wear looped over their left shoulder
jatra – festival
jayanti – birthday
jhankri – faith healers who perform in a trance while beating drums
Jogini – mystical goddesses and counterparts to the 64 manifestations of *Bhairab*
julus – a procession or demonstration; see also *bandh* and *chakka jam*

Kali – the most terrifying manifestation of *Parvati*
Kalki – *Vishnu's* tenth and as yet unseen incarnation during which he will come riding a white horse and wielding a sword to destroy the world
Kam Dev – *Shiva's* companion
karma – Buddhist and Hindu law of cause and effect, which continues from one life to another
KEEP – Kathmandu Environmental Education Project
Khas – Hindu hill people
khat – see *palanquin*
khata – Tibetan prayer scarf, presented to honoured guest or Buddhist *lama*
khola – stream or tributary
khukuri – traditional curved knife of the *Gurkhas*
kosi – river
kot – fort
Krishna – fun-loving eighth incarnation of *Vishnu*
Kumari – living goddess; a peaceful incarnation of *Kali*
kunda – water tank fed by springs

la – mountain pass
lama – Tibetan Buddhist monk or priest
lingam – phallic symbol signifying *Shiva's* creative powers

Machhendranath – patron god of the Kathmandu Valley and an incarnation of *Avalokiteshvara*
Mahabharata – one of the major Hindu epics
Mahadeva – literally 'Great God'; Shiva
Mahadevi – literally 'Great Goddess', sometimes known as *Devi;* the *shakti* to *Shiva*
Mahayana – the 'greater vehicle' of Buddhism; a later adaptation of the teaching which lays emphasis on the *bodhisattva* ideal
makara – mythical crocodilelike beast
Malla – royal dynasty of the Kathmandu Valley responsible for most of the important temples and palaces of the valley towns
mandala – geometrical and astrological representation of the path to enlightenment
mandir – temple
mani – stone carved with the Tibetan Buddhist chant *om mani padme hum*
Manjushri – Buddhist *bodhisattva*
mantra – prayer formula or chant
Mara – Buddhist god of death; has three eyes and holds the *wheel of life*
math – Hindu priest's house
mela – country fair
misthan bhandar – Indian-style sweet house and snack bar

naga – serpent deity
Nagpura – Buddhist symbol for water
nak – female *yak*
namaste – traditional Hindu greeting (hello or goodbye), with the hands brought together at chest or head level, as a sign of respect
Nandi – *Shiva's vehicle, the bull*
Narayan – *Vishnu* as the sleeping figure on the cosmic ocean; from his navel *Brahma* appeared and went on to create the universe
Narsingha – man-lion incarnation of *Vishnu*
Newari – people of the Kathmandu Valley
nirvana – ultimate peace and cessation of rebirth (Buddhism)

om mani padme hum – sacred Buddhist *mantra,* which means 'hail to the jewel in the lotus'

padma – lotus flower
pagoda – multistoreyed Nepali temple, whose design was exported across Asia
palanquin – portable covered bed usually shouldered by four men; also called a *khat*

Parvati – *Shiva's* consort
pashmina – goat-wool blanket or shawl
Pashupati – *Shiva* as Lord of the Animals
path – small raised platform to shelter pilgrims
phanta – grass plains
pipal tree – see *Bodhi tree*
pokhari – large water tank, or small lake
prasad – food offering
prayer flag – square of cloth printed with a *mantra* and hung in a string as a prayer offering
prayer wheel – cylindrical wheel inscribed with a Buddhist prayer or *mantra* that is 'said' when the wheel spins
Prithvi – *Vedic* earth goddess
puja – religious offering or prayer
pujari – priest
purnima – full moon

rajpath – road or highway, literally 'king's road'
Ramayana – Hindu epic
Rana – a hereditary line of prime ministers who ruled Nepal from 1846 to 1951
rath – temple chariot in which the idol is conveyed in processions
rudraksha – dried seeds worn in necklaces by *sadhu*s

SAARC – South Asian Association for Regional Cooperation; includes India, Nepal, Pakistan, Bangladesh and Sri Lanka
sadhu – wandering Hindu holy man
Sagarmatha – Nepali name for Mt Everest
sal – tree of the lower Himalayan foothills
saligram – a black ammonite fossil of a Jurassic-period sea creature that is also a symbol of *Shiva*
sankha – conch shell, one of *Vishnu's* four symbols
Saraswati – goddess of learning and creative arts, and consort of *Brahma*; carries a lutelike instrument
seto – white
Shaivite – follower of *Shiva*
shakti – dynamic female element in male/female relationships; also a goddess
Sherpa – Buddhist hill people of Tibetan ancestry famed for work with mountaineering expeditions; with a lower-case 's' means trek leader
shikhara – Indian-style temple with tall corn cob–like spire
Shitala Mai – ogress who became a protector of children
Shiva – the most powerful Hindu god, the creator and destroyer; part of the Hindu triad with *Vishnu* and *Brahma*
sindur – red vermilion dust and mustard oil mixture used for offerings
sirdar – leader/organiser of a trekking party
stupa – bell-shaped Buddhist religious structure, originally designed to hold the relics of the *Buddha*
Sudra – the lowest Nepali caste, said to originate from *Brahma's* feet
sundhara – fountain with golden spout

tabla – hand drum
tahr – wild mountain goat
tal – lake
Taleju Bhawani – Nepali goddess, an aspect of *Mahadevi* and the family deity of the *Malla* kings of the Kathmandu Valley
Tantric Buddhism – form of Buddhism that evolved in Tibet during the 10th to 15th centuries
tappu – island
Tara – White Tara is the consort of the *Dhyani Buddha* Vairocana; Green Tara is associated with Amoghasiddhi
teahouse trek – independent trekking between village inns (ie no camping)
tempo – three-wheeled, automated minivan commonly used in Nepal
Thakali – people of the Kali Gandaki Valley who specialise in running hotels
thali – literally a plate with compartments for different dishes; an all-you-can-eat set meal
thangka – Tibetan religious painting
third eye – symbolic eye on *Buddha* figures, used to indicate the *Buddha's* all-seeing wisdom and perception
thukpa – noodle soup
tika – red sandalwood-paste spot marked on the forehead, particularly for religious occasions
tole – street or quarter of a town; sometimes used to refer to a square
tonga – horse carriage
topi – traditional Nepali cap
torana – carved pediment above temple doors
Tribhuvan – the king who in 1951 ended the *Rana* period and Nepal's long seclusion
trisul – trident weapon that is a symbol of *Shiva*
tumpline – leather or cloth strip worn across the forehead or chest of a porter to support a load carried on the back
tunala – carved temple struts
tundikhel – parade ground

Uma Maheshwar – *Shiva* and *Parvati* in a pose where *Shiva* sits cross-legged and *Parvati* sits on his thigh and leans against him
Upanishads – ancient *Vedic* scripts, the last part of the *Vedas*

vahana – a god's animal mount or *vehicle*
Vaishnavite – follower of *Vishnu*
Vaisya – caste of merchants and farmers, said to originate from *Brahma's* thighs
vajra – the 'thunderbolt' symbol of Buddhist power in Nepal; *dorje* in Tibetan
Vajra Jogini – a Tantric goddess, *shakti* to a *Bhairab*
Vedas – ancient orthodox Hindu scriptures
Vedic gods – ancient Hindu gods described in the *Vedas*

vehicle – the animal with which a Hindu god is associated

vihara – Buddhist religious buildings and pilgrim accommodation

Vishnu – the preserver; one of the three main Hindu gods along with *Brahma* and *Shiva*

wheel of life – Buddhist representation of how humans are chained by desire to a life of suffering

yak – cowlike Nepali beast of burden (only pureblood animals of the genus *Bos grunniens* can properly be called yaks; crossbreeds have other names)

yaksha – attendant deity or nymph

Yama – *Vedic* god of death; his messenger is the crow

Yellow Hats – name sometimes given to adherents of the *Gelugpa* school of Tibetan Buddhism

yeti – abominable snowman; mythical hairy mountain man of the Himalaya

yogi – yoga master

yoni – female sexual symbol, equivalent of a *lingam*

zamindar – absentee landlord and/or moneylender

The Authors

JOE BINDLOSS
Coordinating author, Around the Kathmandu Valley, Kathmandu to Pokhara

Joe made his first trip to Nepal as a fresh-faced backpacker in the early 1990s and something clicked. Since then, he's been back numerous times to walk the trekking trails of the Khumbu and explore the Kathmandu Valley by rented motorcycle. His favourite moment while researching this book was climbing the 5420m Cho La pass on a blanket of freshly fallen snow. The lowlight was having emergency root canal surgery after cracking a tooth on a tough piece of buffalo jerky. When not researching guidebooks for Lonely Planet, Joe lives in London with a growing collection of Buddhist paraphernalia picked up on his travels.

TRENT HOLDEN
Pokhara, the Terai & Mahabharat Range

In all the countries he's travelled, Trent has found that nowhere compares to the craziness and serendipity of the subcontinent. Hence it's to Trent's great pleasure that *Nepal 8* is his first assignment for Lonely Planet. He first visited Nepal in 2001, during the tragedy of the royal massacre, and (despite this shock) it is a country he has felt passionate about ever since. Working as an editor at Melbourne's Lonely Planet office for the past five years, he figured it was about time to escape the nine-to-five grind for the more exciting adventures of authoring. Trent lives in Melbourne, and loves the Ramones and reading Charles Bukowski.

BRADLEY MAYHEW
Kathmandu, Trekking

A self-professed mountain junkie, Bradley has been travelling to Nepal and the Himalaya for over 15 years, including several months each in north Pakistan, Ladakh, Tibet and Bhutan. Never happier than when he's above 4000m, British-born Bradley currently lives under the big skies of Yellowstone County, Montana.

He coordinated the last two editions of this Nepal guide and is the coauthor of Lonely Planet's *Tibet, Bhutan* and *Trekking in the Nepal Himalaya,* as well as a dozen other titles. Bradley is currently filming a five-part documentary retracing the route of Marco Polo.

LONELY PLANET AUTHORS

Why is our travel information the best in the world? It's simple: our authors are passionate, dedicated travellers. They don't take freebies in exchange for positive coverage so you can be sure the advice you're given is impartial. They travel widely to all the popular spots, and off the beaten track. They don't research using just the internet or phone. They discover new places not included in any other guidebook. They personally visit thousands of hotels, restaurants, palaces, trails, galleries, temples and more. They speak with dozens of locals every day to make sure you get the kind of insider knowledge only a local could tell you. They take pride in getting all the details right, and in telling it how it is. Think you can do it? Find out how at **lonelyplanet.com**.

Behind the Scenes

THIS BOOK

This 8th edition of *Nepal* was written by Joe Bindloss (coordinating author), Trent Holden and Bradley Mayhew. Bradley also worked with Joe on the previous edition with Stan Armington, and the 6th edition with Lindsay Brown and Wanda Vivequin. The 5th edition was written by Hugh Finlay. This guidebook was commissioned in Lonely Planet's Melbourne office, and produced by the following:

Commissioning Editors Will Gourlay, Suzannah Shwer, Sam Trafford

Coordinating Editor Anna Metcalfe

Coordinating Cartographer Owen Eszeki

Coordinating Layout Designer Pablo Gastar

Managing Editor Bruce Evans

Managing Cartographer Shahara Ahmed

Managing Layout Designer Indra Kilfoyle

Assisting Editors Kate Daly, Andrea Dobbin, Michala Green, Anne Mulvaney

Assisting Cartographers Enes Basic, Ross Butler, Dennis Capparelli, Joshua Geoghegan, Eve Kelly, Khanh Luu, Marc Milinkovic, Simon Tillema

Cover Designer Marika Mercer

Project Manager Fabrice Rocher

Language Content Coordinator Laura Crawford

Thanks to Lucy Birchley, Yvonne Bischofberger, Sally Darmody, Diana Duggan, Huw Fowles, Chris Girdler, Martin Heng, Craig Kilburn, Lisa Knights, Chris Lee Ack, Wayne Murphy, Amanda Sierp, Lyahna Spencer

THANKS
JOE BINDLOSS

I'd like to dedicate my work on this book to my partner Linda and Tyler, the new arrival in the Bindloss household. In Kathmandu, thanks to Niraj Shreshtra, Tony Jones, Dil, Rajesh, Balaram and Santosh at Himalayan Encounters for tips and good company. A big thank you is also due to Mandy Gaskin, Rob Workman and Danielle and Max. On a personal note, thanks to Dr Neil Pande at Healthy Smiles for services in dentistry above and beyond the call of duty. Thanks also to Gar Powell Evans for lightening the load in Helambu, and to Julie, Harry and Jacques for letting him come. Credit finally to all the travellers who wrote in with advice and recommendations.

TRENT HOLDEN

Biggest thanks goes to Melissa Adams, my parents (Tim and Larysa), my brothers and their partners Luke and Jacqui, Chris and Cindy, nephew Tom and nieces Kate and Sasha. For their assistance, thanks to

---

THE LONELY PLANET STORY

Fresh from an epic journey across Europe, Asia and Australia in 1972, Tony and Maureen Wheeler sat at their kitchen table stapling together notes. The first Lonely Planet guidebook, *Across Asia on the Cheap*, was born.

Travellers snapped up the guides. Inspired by their success, the Wheelers began publishing books to Southeast Asia, India and beyond. Demand was prodigious, and the Wheelers expanded the business rapidly to keep up. Over the years, Lonely Planet extended its coverage to every country and into the virtual world via lonelyplanet.com and the Thorn Tree message board.

As Lonely Planet became a globally loved brand, Tony and Maureen received several offers for the company. But it wasn't until 2007 that they found a partner whom they trusted to remain true to the company's principles of travelling widely, treading lightly and giving sustainably. In October of that year, BBC Worldwide acquired a 75% share in the company, pledging to uphold Lonely Planet's commitment to independent travel, trustworthy advice and editorial independence.

Today, Lonely Planet has offices in Melbourne, London and Oakland, with over 500 staff members and 300 authors. Tony and Maureen are still actively involved with Lonely Planet. They're travelling more often than ever, and they're devoting their spare time to charitable projects. And the company is still driven by the philosophy of *Across Asia on the Cheap*: 'All you've got to do is decide to go and the hardest part is over. So go!'

Basudev Tripathi, Carol Hummer, Rob from Bardia, Suresh, Gisella McGuiness, Dhurba Giri, Jack from Pokhara, Mohan, Raelee Chapman and Jane Ormond. A special thanks to my fellow authors Joe and Bradley, as well as Sam Trafford, Will Gourlay, Tasmin McNaughtan and Emma Gilmour. Finally, I'd like to thank the production team working on Nepal – Anna Metcalfe, Owen Eszeki and Pablo Gastar.

BRADLEY MAYHEW

Thanks to David Allardice who generously helped update the rafting and kayaking section, which he originally wrote several editions ago. Thanks to Peter Knowles for putting us in touch and to Tony Jones for his comments on the text. *Namaste* as always to Rajan Simkhada and Mukhiya Gurung, both of whom have helped out in numerous ways throughout my times in Kathmandu. Cheers to Niraj, Lalit and the boys at Encounter. Thanks to Bidur Dangol at Vajra Books in Kathmandu for several useful leads. Cheers to Andre who joined me on the epic trek out to Dolpo. Thanks also to Trent and Joe for their input into my chapters and of course to Kelli for her love and support.

OUR READERS

Many thanks to the travellers who used the last edition and wrote to us with helpful hints, useful advice and interesting anecdotes:

A Hans Abbink, Karenza Adhikari, Vera Aeiou, Caroline Alle, Matthieu Allereau, Anca Ansink, Natascha Arens, Sergi Argemi, Lein Ausems **B** Gary B, Sher Bahadur, Linda Bakkum, Caroline Ballou, Cool Baral, Ian Bedford, Kathie Bell, Lucjan Berezowski, Edo and Simone Berger-Bleumink, Malou Besselink, Lee Birch, Orçun Birol, Mohamed Biskri, Cath Bowdler, Patricia Brown, Julie Burke, Leonid Butov, Julia Byatte **C** Sami Calado, Marta Cañizares, Kathryn Carmichael,

James Caudwell, Heather Chapman, Audrey Chatfield, Joanne Chatfield, Nelson Chen, Bouchoux Christophe, Paul Claes, Tony Clarey, A Corks, Jocelyn Corniche, Henry Coulter **D** Diana Davies, Theo De Bray, Virginia De Santis, Roos De Vlugt, Dan Demianiw, Ine Deviaene, Laura Dijkerman, Esther Dobson, Elizabeth Doel, Ian Duckling, Craig Durkee **E** Kristjan Edwards, Susan Eggleton, Cecilia Ekelöf, Iris Ennenbach, Amy Errmann, Roz Evans **F** Chip Faircloth, Paul Fauset, Viviana Fernandez, Johnny Fletcher, Marc Forster, Kelli Fraser, Ivette Fred, Michael Fritz, Marian Fry **G** Mark Gleeson, Wieslaw Goraczko, Scott Greenlees, Aubrey Groves, Amy Groves, Silvia Gruber, Bob Guglielmino **H** Stephanie Haase, Patrick Hackett, Martin Rune Hansen, Deborah Heijboer, Celine Heinbecker, Boaz Hetsroni, Tim Holliday, Ameila Holt, Jonathan and Marysia Holubecki-France, Klara Holubova, Ashley Howard, Rishi Høynes, Gemma Humphrey **I** Imke Imke, Sindy Irmscher **J** Sherelyn Jackson, S Jane, Birgit Jänen, Tej Bahadur Jarga, Cecilia Jensen, Peter Jensen, Kent Johnson, Leigh Jones, Jipen Joske **K** Mike Kalvoda, Sabine Karkó, Sheila Kay, Hans-Jürgen Keller, Glynis Kingston, Heinz Kintzl, Kathryn Kirk, Michael Kiworr, Melissa Kok, Kristina Krutskikh, Karel Kunc, Elizabeth Kuo **L** Hanneke La Riviere, Emilie Labetoulle, Jenny Lama, Terry Landau, Nathalie Le Blanc, Heidi Leisinger, Elizabeth Lemert, Nienke Lesuis, Frederic Levesque, Neville Lewis, Charlie Litteck, Ken Lonsdale, John Lucas, Francisco Chong Luna, Sam Lunney **M** GV Macca, Sunny Mall, Henry Maryke, Scott Mason, Hannah Matthews, Steve Thompson, Mike McCarty, Heather McKenny, Nicolas Merky, Melita Miletic, Mahdi Shariati Moghaddam, Dounia Mondet, Anthony Moore, Susan Moore, Frances and Hugh Morley, Heidi Müller **N** Adrien Namos, Augustus Nasmith Jr, David Nisbetnz **O** Siobhan O'Brien **P** Mahesh Pahari, Felieke Pak, Palavra, Jessica Passero, Ian Peachey, Laurence Peharpre, Natalie Peselev, Louise Pianta, Tim Pickering, Neil Pike, Neil Pitt, Pedro Piza, Jane Popiolek, Philip Price **R** Ali Raad, Rajendra Rai, Dillimanson Rajnath, Cornelia Reiwald, Paul Roberts, Vanessa Rogers, Patrick Roman **S** Nick Sankey, Parasuram Sapkota, Peter Saraber, Ingrid Schabel, Heiner Schenk, Christoph Schwab, David Sears, Nilkantha Sharma, J Sheard, William Siemens, Veronika Simon, Neil Smith, Pablo Soledad, SJ Srinivas, Samantha Staddon, Theo Steinert, Sjoerd Stoffels, Alan Sussman, Gabi Szlatki **T** Pam Taak, Chad Taylor, Wim Ter Keurs, Ritesh Thapa, Tron Thibault, Graham Tillotson, Dorothee Tuecks

---

SEND US YOUR FEEDBACK

We love to hear from travellers – your comments keep us on our toes and help make our books better. Our well-travelled team reads every word on what you loved or loathed about this book. Although we cannot reply individually to postal submissions, we always guarantee that your feedback goes straight to the appropriate authors, in time for the next edition. Each person who sends us information is thanked in the next edition – and the most useful submissions are rewarded with a free book.

To send us your updates – and find out about Lonely Planet events, newsletters and travel news – visit our award-winning website: **lonelyplanet.com/contact**.

Note: we may edit, reproduce and incorporate your comments in Lonely Planet products such as guidebooks, websites and digital products, so let us know if you don't want your comments reproduced or your name acknowledged. For a copy of our privacy policy visit lonelyplanet.com/privacy.

V Janneke Van De Wijgert, Marcel Van Hak, Linda Van Hal, Claudia Vialkowitsch, Dan Von Seggern **W** Lesley Wall, Erlend Walseth, Ariel Weber, Alex Whittam, Ulli Wigelmann, Nan Williamson, Walter Willium, Mandy Wisse **Z** Elsa Ziemann, Paul Zwartjes.

ACKNOWLEDGMENTS
Many thanks to the following for the use of their content:

Globe on title page ©Mountain High Maps 1993 Digital Wisdom, Inc.

Internal photographs: by Lonely Planet Images and by Richard I'Anson p245, p247 (#3, 4), p252 (#1, 2); Scott Darsney p246 (#1); Jane Sweeney p246 (#2); Chris Klep p247 (#5); Anders Blomqvist p248 (#1), p249 (#3), p250 (#2); Christian Aslund p248 (#2); Lindsay Brown p250 (#1); Ryan Fox p251 (#3); Andrew Peacock p251 (#4).

All images are the copyright of the photographers unless otherwise indicated. Many of the images in this guide are available for licensing from Lonely Planet Images: www.lonelyplanetimages.com.

Index

GREENDEX

Thanks to the campaigning work of nongovernmental organisations, former mountaineers and Nepali activists, Nepal has caught the green bug. However, for every tour company offering environmentally friendly treks, there are a dozen more who use the word 'eco' as a sales ploy only. The following options have been selected because they meet our criteria for sustainable tourism. If you have any recommendations, email us at talk2us@lonelyplanet.com.au. For more on the environmental issues affecting Nepal see the Environment chapter (p77).

MAP LEGEND
ROUTES

Primary	Mall/Steps
Secondary	Tunnel
Tertiary	Walking Tour
Lane	Walking Tour Detour
Under Construction	Walking Trail
Unsealed Road	Walking Path
One-Way Street	Track

TRANSPORT

Ferry	Rail
Bus Route	Cable Car, Funicular

HYDROGRAPHY

River, Creek	Glacier
Intermittent River	Water

BOUNDARIES

International	Ancient Wall
State, Provincial	Cliff
Disputed	

AREA FEATURES

Airport	Forest
Area of Interest	Land
Building	Market
Campus	Park
Cemetery, Christian	Sports
Cemetery, Other	Urban

POPULATION

⊛ CAPITAL (NATIONAL)	⊚ CAPITAL (STATE)
● Large City	⊙ Medium City
○ Small City	○ Town, Village

SYMBOLS

Sights/Activities
- Buddhist
- Castle, Fortress
- Christian
- Golf
- Hindu
- Islamic
- Kayaking, Rafting
- Monument
- Museum, Gallery
- Point of Interest
- Pool
- Ruin
- Trekking
- Zoo, Bird Sanctuary

Eating
- Eating

Drinking
- Drinking
- Café

Entertainment
- Entertainment

Shopping
- Shopping

Sleeping
- Sleeping
- Camping

Transport
- Airport, Airfield
- Border Crossing
- Bus Station
- Cycling, Bicycle Path
- General Transport
- Taxi Rank

Information
- Bank, ATM
- Embassy/Consulate
- Hospital, Medical
- Information
- Internet Facilities
- Police Station
- Post Office, GPO
- Telephone
- Toilets

Geographic
- Lookout
- Mountain, Volcano
- National Park
- Pass, Canyon
- Shelter, Hut
- Waterfall

LONELY PLANET OFFICES

Australia
Head Office
Locked Bag 1, Footscray, Victoria 3011
☎ 03 8379 8000, fax 03 8379 8111
talk2us@lonelyplanet.com.au

USA
150 Linden St, Oakland, CA 94607
☎ 510 250 6400, toll free 800 275 8555
fax 510 893 8572
info@lonelyplanet.com

UK
2nd fl, 186 City Rd,
London EC1V 2NT
☎ 020 7106 2100, fax 020 7106 2101
go@lonelyplanet.co.uk

Published by Lonely Planet Publications Pty Ltd
ABN 36 005 607 983

MIX
Paper from
responsible sources
FSC™ C021741